EDUCATIONAL ADMINISTRATION

THEORY,
RESEARCH,
AND
PRACTICE

♦♦♦

EDUCATIONAL ADMINISTRATION

THEORY, RESEARCH, AND PRACTICE

◆◆◆

Fifth Edition

Wayne K. Hoy
The Ohio State University

Cecil G. Miskel
University of Michigan

McGraw-Hill, Inc.

New York   St. Louis   San Francisco   Auckland   Bogotá
Caracas   Lisbon   London   Madrid
Mexico City   Milan   Montreal   New Delhi   San Juan
Singapore   Sydney   Tokyo   Toronto

This book was developed by Lane Akers, Inc.

Educational Administration
Theory, Research, and Practice

This book is printed on acid-free paper.

3 4 5 6 7 8 9 0   DOC   DOC   9 0 9 8 7

ISBN   0-07-030645-1

This book was set in ITC Garamond and Gill Sans by The Clarinda Company.
The editors were Lane Akers and Sheila H. Gillams;
the design was done by Paradigm Design;
the production supervisor was Richard A. Ausburn.
R. R. Donnelley & Sons Company was printer and binder.

Library of Congress Cataloging-in-Publication Data

Hoy, Wayne K.
    Educational administration: theory, research, and practice /
Wayne K. Hoy, Cecil G. Miskel. —5th ed.
        p.   cm.
    Includes bibliographical references (p.   ) and index.
    ISBN 0-07-030645-1
    1. School management and organization—United States.   I. Miskel,
Cecil G.   II. Title.
LB2805.H715   1996
371.2′00973—dc20   95-21457

About the Authors

◆◆◆

Wayne K. Hoy received his B.S. from Lock Haven State College in 1959 and his D.Ed. from The Pennsylvania State University in 1965. After teaching at Oklahoma State University for several years, he joined the Rutgers University Graduate School of Education faculty in 1968, where he was a distinguished professor, departmental chair, and Associate Dean for Academic Affairs. In 1994, he was appointed the Novice G. Fawcett Chair in Educational Administration at The Ohio State University. His primary professional interests are theory and research in administration, the sociology of organizations, and the social psychology of administration.

In 1973, he received the Lindback Foundation Award for Distinguished Teaching; in 1987, he was given the Graduate School of Education Alumni Award for Professional Research; in 1991, he was honored by The Pennsylvania State University with their Excellence in Education Award; and in 1992, he received the Meritorious Research Award from the Eastern Education Research Association. He is past secretary-treasurer of the National Conference of Professors of Educational Administration (NCPEA) and is past president of the University Council for Educational Administration (UCEA).

Professor Hoy is coauthor with Professors D. J. Willower and T. L. Eidell of *The School and Pupil Control Ideology* (1967); and with Patrick Forsyth, *Effective Supervision: Theory into Practice* (1986); with C. J. Tartar and R. Kottkamp, *Open Schools/Healthy Schools* (1991); and with C. J. Tartar, *Administrators Solving the Problems of Practice* (1995). He is also on the editorial boards of the *Journal of Educational Administration, Journal of Research and Development in Education,* and *McGill Journal of Education* and serves as editor of the McGraw-Hill Primis Knowledge Base Project and the Allyn & Bacon Case Series in Educational Administration.

Cecil G. Miskel has been dean of and a professor in the School of Education at the University of Michigan since October 1988. He served the University of Utah as a professor and chairperson of the Department of Educational Administration from 1982 to 1983 and dean of the Graduate School of Education from 1983 to 1988. He also spent twelve years at the University of Kansas, where he held positions as assistant, associate, and full professor of educational administration as well as associate dean for research administration and associate vice-chancellor for research, graduate studies, and public service. His public school experience includes being a science teacher and principal in the secondary schools of Oklahoma.

Professor Miskel holds an undergraduate degree in science education from the University of Oklahoma, and master of science and doctor of education degrees from Oklahoma State University. In addition to his administrative responsibilities, he continues to teach graduate classes and guides scholarly inquiry in school organization and administration. He served as editor of the *Educational Administration Quarterly* for the 1987 and 1988 volumes and is currently a member of its editorial board. In addition to being a coauthor of the five editions of *Education Administration: Theory, Research, and Practice,* Professor Miskel has published widely in a variety of scholarly journals.

Dedicated to the women who share my life—
Elsie, Anita, and Kelly Hoy

◆◆◆

Dedicated to Sue—
My true love and best friend—Cecil

Contents in Brief

◆◆◆

Preface		xxvii
1	**Theoretical and Historical Foundations**	1
2	**The School as a Social System**	26
3	**Structure in Schools**	46
4	**Individuals in Schools**	90
5	**Culture and Climate of Schools**	126
6	**Power and Politics in Schools**	170
7	**External Environments of Schools**	202
8	**Effectiveness and Quality of Schools**	236
9	**Deciding**	266
10	**Motivating**	308
11	**Communicating**	340
12	**Leading**	372
13	**A Final Look at the School as a Social System**	406
Bibliography		421
Indexes		473

Contents

◆◆◆

Preface   xxvii

1 Theoretical and Historical Foundations   1

Preview   1

Theory: A Scientific Concept   1

   Theory and Science Defined   1

   Components of Theory   3

      Concepts   3

      Assumptions and Generalizations   4

   Research and Theory   5

      Hypotheses   6

   Theory and Practice   7

Classical Organizational Thought   9

Human Relations Approach   12

Social Science Approach   15

Emergent Nontraditional Perspectives   17

   The Post-Modernism and Poststructural Approaches   18

   Critical Theory   19

   Feminist Theory   19

Theoretical Developments in Educational Administration   20

Summary and Suggested Readings   23

How to Use This Book   24

Key Concepts and Ideas   25

2 The School as a Social System   26

Preview   26

A Systems Perspective   27

     Rational Systems   27
     Natural Systems   29
     Open Systems   30

Key Properties of Open Systems   30

     Inputs, Transformation, and Outputs   31
     Feedback   32
     Boundaries   32
     Environment   32
     Homeostasis   33
     Entropy   33
     Equifinality   33

Social-Systems Models: Basic Assumptions   33

Elements of a Social System   35

     Structure   35
     Individual   37
     Culture   38
     Politics   39
     Environment   40
     Outcomes   41
     Internal Feedback Loops   42
     External Feedback Loops   43

Summary and Suggested Readings   43

Notes   44

Key Concepts and Ideas   44

◆3 Structure in Schools   46

Preview   46

Weberian Model of Bureaucracy   47

Division of Labor and Specialization   47
Impersonal Orientation   48
Hierarchy of Authority   48
Rules and Regulations   48
Career Orientation   48
Efficiency   49
Ideal Type   49

Criticisms of the Weberian Bureaucratic Model   49

Functions and Dysfunctions of the Model   49
Functions and Dysfunctions of Rules   50
Neglect of the Informal Organization   53

The Development of Informal Organization   53
A Hypothetical Illustration in Schools   54

Dual Structure of the Bureaucratic Model   57
A Feminist Critique of Bureaucracy   58

Formal Structure in Schools   59

Hall on Bureaucratic Structure   60

Organizational Types   60
Changing School Structures   62

Bolman and Deal on Structure   64

Mintzberg on Structure   66

Coordinating Mechanisms   66
Key Parts   67
Mintzberg's Perspective Applied to Schools   69

Loose Coupling Perspective   76

Professional and Bureaucratic Conflict   79

Organizational Accommodations to
Professional-Bureaucratic Conflict   80
Individual Accommodations to
Professional-Bureaucratic Conflict   81

Local and Cosmopolitan Orientations   82
Different Kinds of Locals   82
A Dual Orientation   83

Professional and Bureaucratic Orientations in Schools   83

Summary and Suggested Readings   85

Notes   86

Key Concepts and Ideas   87

4 Individuals in Schools   90

Preview   90

Information Processing   92

Cognitive Architecture: Structures and Processes   92

Schemas   93
Metacognitive Processes   94

Models of Information Processing   95

Rational Model: An Optimizing Approach   95
Limited-Capacity Model: A Satisficing Approach   95
Expert Model: A Chunking Approach   96
Cybernetic Model: An Interacting Approach   97

Cognition and Organizational Analysis   97

Motivation   98

A Framework for Motivational Theories   99
Need and Value Theories   100

*Need Hierarchy Theory: Maslow's Hierarchical
Model   100*
Research and Evaluation of Maslow's Theory   103

Values Theory: McClelland's Theory
of Achievement **104**

Cognitive-Choice Theories **106**

Expectancy Theory **107**
Research and Evaluation of
Expectancy Theory **110**
Attribution Theory **111**

Metacognition Approaches **113**

Self-Efficacy Theory **113**
Development of Self-Efficacy **114**
Research and Evaluation of
Self-Efficacy Theory **115**
Goal-Setting Theory **116**
Research and Evaluation of Goal Theory **120**

Synthesis: A Motivation Sequence **121**

Summary and Suggested Readings **122**

Notes **124**

Key Concepts and Ideas **124**

5 Culture and Climate of Schools **126**

Preview **126**

Organizational Culture **127**

Definition of Organizational Culture **128**
Levels of Organizational Culture **129**

Culture as Shared Norms **129**
Culture as Shared Values **130**
Culture as Tacit Assumptions **132**
Level of Analysis **135**

Different Types of Culture **135**
School Culture **136**

Organizational Climate   140

Definition of Organizational Climate   140
Teacher-Principal Behavior: Open to Closed   141

The Open Climate   142
The Closed Climate   142
Criticisms of the OCDQ   143

The Revised Organizational Climate Descriptive
Questionnaire for Elementary Schools (OCDQ-RE)   143

Open Climate   146
Engaged Climate   146
Disengaged Climate   147
Closed Climate   147

The Revised Organizational Climate Descriptive
Questionnaire for Secondary Schools (OCDQ-RS)   148
The Revised Organizational Climate Descriptive
Questionnaire for Middle Schools (OCDQ-RM)   149
OCDQ: Some Research Findings   149

Organizational Dynamics: Healthy to Unhealthy   150

Organizational Health Inventory (OHI)   152

Healthy School   154
Unhealthy School   154

The Organizational Health Inventories for Middle and
Elementary Schools   155

OHI: Some Research Findings   156

Pupil-Control Orientation: Custodial to Humanistic   157

The Custodial School   158
The Humanistic School   158
The Pupil-Control Ideology (PCI) Form   158

PCI: Some Research Findings   159

Contrast and Comparison   161

Changing the Culture and Climate of Schools 162

The Clinical Strategy 162
The Growth-Centered Strategy 163
Changing Norms 164

Summary and Suggested Readings 166

Notes 167

Key Concepts and Ideas 168

 Power and Politics in School 170

Preview 170

Sources of Authority: Legitimate Power 171

Authority and Administrative Behavior in Schools 173

Sources of Power 176

Administrative Uses of Power 178

Etzioni's Typology of Power 180

Mintzberg's Typology of Power 183

A Comparison 186

Organizational Power and Politics 187

The External Coalition 187
The Internal Coalition 188
Coalitions, Politics, and Structure 189

The Power Game 190

Political Tactics 191
Political Games 193
Conflict Management 198

Summary and Suggested Readings 200

Note 201

Key Concepts and Ideas 201

7 **External Environments of Schools** 202

Preview 202

External Environments: Definition and Examples 203

Information Perspective 206

A Typology of Information Environments 206
Environmental Uncertainty 207
Research and Evaluation of the
    Information Perspective 208

Resource-Dependence Perspective 209

Research and Evaluation of the Resource-
    Dependency Perspective 211
Toward a Synthesis of the Information and
    Resource-Dependence Perspectives 212
Administering Information and Resource
    Environments 213

Internal Coping Strategies 213
Interorganizational Coping Strategies 217

Institutional Perspective 220

Key Concepts 220
Conceptual Foundations 221

Conformity and Institutional Environments 222
*Educational Diversity and Multiple
    Institutional Environments* 224
Stability and Institutional Environments 224

Research and Evaluation of Institutional Perspective 225
Administering Institutional Environments 227

Buffering Strategies 228
Boundary-Spanning Strategies 229

Changing Institutional Environments for Education 230

Summary and Suggested Readings 232

Notes 233

Key Concepts and Ideas 233

8 Effectiveness and Quality of Schools   236

Preview   236

Organizational Effectiveness of Schools   238

Goal Model of Organizational Effectiveness   239

Types of Goals   239
Assumptions and Generalizations   239
Criticisms of the Goal Approach   240

System-Resource Model of
Organizational Effectiveness   240

Assumptions and Generalizations   241
Criticisms of the System-Resource Approach   241

An Integrated Goal and System-Resource Model
of Effectiveness   242

Time   242
Multiple Constituencies   243
Multiple Criteria   244
*Integrating Time, Multiple Constituencies,
and Multiple Criteria: A Goal and
System-Resource Model*   245

Three Outcome Criteria   246

Academic Achievement   247

Input-Output Research   247
Input-Throughput-Output Research   249

Job Satisfaction   251

Definition   252
Discrepancy Model of Job Satisfaction   252
Situational Model of Job Satisfaction   253
*A Brief Overview of the
Job-Satisfaction Research*   254

Perceived Organizational Effectiveness   255

Quality of Schools   256

Deming on Quality   257

Deming's Principles of Management   257
Research, Theory, and Practice:
Some Observations   262

Summary and Suggested Readings   263

Notes   264

Key Concepts and Ideas   265

 Deciding   266

Preview   266

The Classical Model: An Optimizing Strategy   267

The Administrative Model: A Satisficing Strategy   267

Some Basic Assumptions   268
Decision-Making Process: An Action Cycle   271

Step 1. Recognize and Define the Problem or Issue   271
Step 2. Analyze the Difficulties in
the Existing Situation   273
Step 3. Establish Criteria for a Satisfactory
Solution   274
Step 4. Develop a Plan or Strategy for Action   274
Step 5. Initiate the Plan of Action   278

**The Incremental Model: A Strategy of Successive
Limited Comparisons**   279

The Mixed-Scanning Model: An Adaptive Strategy   281

The Right Strategy for the Situation   284

**The Garbage-Can Model: Nonrational
Decision Making**   284

**Janis-Mann Conflict Theory: Stress and Irrationality
in Decision Making**   287

Participation in Decision Making   289

Hoy-Tartar Model of Shared Decision Making   290

The Propositions 290

Putting It Together 294

A Caution on Group Decision Making: Groupthink 297

Conditions That Foster Groupthink 297

Avoiding Groupthink 298

The Case of the Anonymous Letter 299

Discussing the Case 302

Summary and Suggested Readings 303

Notes 304

Key Concepts and Ideas 305

 Motivating 308

Preview 308

**General Principles Underlying Motivational
Enhancement Programs** 310

Goal Setting 311

Management by Objectives 311

Definition and Application 311

Research and Evaluation of MBO 312

Individual Goal Setting 314

Incentive Systems 315

Intrinsic and Extrinsic Incentives 316

Money 317

Merit Pay 318

Redesign of Work 319

Herzberg's Approach to Motivation and
Job Enrichment 320

Herzberg's Theory of Motivation 320

Herzberg's Approach to Job Enrichment 322

Work Design and the Job-Characteristics Model   323

*Research and Evaluation of the
Job-Characteristics Model*   325

Application   326

Work Design in Schools   326

Professionalization in Schools   327

Characteristics of a Professional   328

Career Ladders for Teachers   330

*Research and Evaluation of
Career-Ladder Programs*   332

Career Paths in Educational Administration   333

School Leaders as Motivators   335

Summary and Suggested Readings   337

Notes   338

Key Concepts and Ideas   338

◆ **11 Communicating**   340

Preview   340

Theoretical Approaches to Communication   342

Components of a General Model of the Communication
Process   344

One-Way Communication   344
Two-Way Communication   345
*Channels of Communication: Methods
of Exchanging Symbols*   348
*Sources in the Communication Process:
Senders and Receivers*   352
Feedback   353
Communicating in Context   353

Organizational Perspectives of Communication 355

Organizational Communication and Networks 356

Purposes of Communication in
   School Organizations 358

Formal Communication Networks in Schools 358

Informal Communication Networks in Schools 361

Complementary Networks: Formal and
   Informal Communication 362

   Substance 362

   Direction 363

External Environment and Organizational
   Communication 365

Research on Organization Communication 365

Improving Communication Processes 366

Summary and Suggested Readings 369

Notes 370

Key Concepts and Ideas 371

 Leading   372

Preview 372

Definitions of Leadership 373

The Nature of Leaders' Work 375

A Contingency Schema for Understanding Leadership 376

Traits and Leadership 376

   Early Trait Research 377
   Current Perspectives on Leadership Traits 377

Situations and Leadership 380
Behaviors and Leadership 382

The Ohio State Leadership Studies **382**
Related LBDQ Research **383**
A Recent Perspective on Leader Behavior **384**

Leadership Effectiveness **385**
An Elaborated Contingency Schema for Understanding
   Leadership **386**

Fiedler's Contingency Model of Leadership **387**

Leadership Style **387**
Situational Control **388**
Leader Effectiveness **390**
The Match: Style and Situation **390**
Research and Evaluation of Fiedler's Theory **391**

Transformational Leadership **392**

Multifactor Leadership Questionnaire **395**
Research and Evaluation **396**

Improving Leadership in Schools **397**

Educating Future Leaders **397**
Selecting New Administrators through Assessment Centers **398**
Assuming a New Position: Succession **399**

Selection Process **399**
Reason for the Succession **400**
Source of the New Leader **400**
Mandate for Action **400**

Engineering the Situation **401**
Transforming Schools and Strengthening Their Cultures **401**

Summary and Suggested Readings **402**

Notes **403**

Key Concepts and Ideas **404**

◈13 A Final Look at the School as a Social System 406

A Model of Synthesis 406

Structure in Schools 407
Individual in the School 408
Culture and Climate of Schools 409
Power and Politics in Schools 410
External Environments of Schools 411
Effectiveness and Quality 412

Feedback Loops 412

Deciding 413
Motivating 413
Communicating 414
Leading 414
Administrator Behavior, Interdependent Elements,
and Equifinality 415

Continuing Dilemmas 417

Coordination and Communication 417
Bureaucratic Discipline and Professional Expertise 418
Administrative Planning and Individual Initiative 419

Conclusion 420

Bibliography 421

Indexes

Author Index 473
Subject Index 485

Preface

◆◆◆

Our first four editions reflected the current state of knowledge in educational administration. The books grew from our strongly held beliefs that a substantive body of knowledge about educational organizations was available but neglected by both professors and practitioners in educational administration. We continue to believe that administrative practice can become more systematic, reflective, and guided by sound theory and research. To those ends we used an open social systems perspective to explain the structure and processes of educational organizations.

Our social systems model of schools continues its evolution. In this edition we specify four critical elements of organizational life—the structural, individual, cultural, and political—as well as four administrative processes—deciding, motivating, communicating, and leading. The latest version of the open-systems model is both powerful and easy for students, professors, and practitioners to use. We not only describe the relevant new developments in the field, both new models and recent research, but we have eliminated those works that are less useful. Our elaboration of contemporary concepts and empirical applications should help administrators deal more effectively with day-to-day operations of schools. Politics, organizational culture, and structure remain important topics in this edition. However, new theories of information processing, motivation, quality, and leadership have been incorporated into our discussion of administration. Moreover, where appropriate, we have explored critical ideas from such emergent perspectives as critical theory, postmodernist theory, and feminist theory. Finally, the new perspectives are compared and contrasted with those frameworks that have stood the test of time.

Our colleagues and students continue to be important sources of ideas and constructive criticism. We would like to thank Michale Arnold; Terry Astuto, New York University; Jim Bliss, Rutgers University; Nicholas Burbules, University of Illinois; Paul Cordeiro, University of Connecticut; William Firestone, Rutgers University; Patrick Forsyth, Penn State University; Richard V. Hatley, University of Missouri; William C. Heeney, Stephen F. Austin State University; Robert Kottkam, Hofstra University; Muriel Mackett, Northern Illinois

University; Betty Malen, University of Washington; Samuel Moore, Michigan State University; Rodney Ogawa, Syracuse University; Karen Osterman, Hofstra University; Paul Pintrich, University of Michigan; Brian Rowan, University of Michigan; Gail Schneider, University of Wisconsin at Milwaukee; Mark R. Shibles, University of Connecticut; Paula Short, Penn State University; Mark Smylie; Christopher Sny, Ohio University; Joan D. Stipetic, University of New Hampshire; C. J. Tarter, St. Johns University; Donald J. Willower, Penn State University; and Anita Woolfolk, Ohio State University. We also want to express our appreciation to Lisa Lavey, who made extensive contributions to the preparation of the manuscript.

Finally, we continue to owe a special thanks to all our students who have helped enrich the explanations and ground the theories with their experiences.

Wayne K. Hoy
Cecil G. Miskel

Theoretical and Historical Foundations

Although we set out primarily to study reality, it does not follow that we do not wish to improve it; we should judge our researches to have no worth at all if they were to have only a speculative interest. If we separate carefully the theoretical from the practical problems, it is not to the neglect of the latter; but, on the contrary, to be in a better position to solve them.

—Emile Durkheim
The Division of Labor in Society

PREVIEW

1. The purpose of organizational science is to understand the world of organizations.

2. Organizational theory is a set of interrelated concepts, definitions, and generalizations that systematically describes and explains patterns of regularities in organizational life.

3. The functions of theory are to explain, to guide research, to generate new knowledge, and to guide practice.

4. Theory informs practice in three important ways: it forms a frame of reference; it provides a general model for analysis; and it guides reflective decision making.

5. The evolution of organizational thought and theory can be viewed from four vantage points: classical, human relations, social science, and emerging, nontraditional perspectives.

6. Classical theory emphasizes the formal organization as the key to understanding behavior.

7. Human relations theory sees informal and individual relations as most important in organizational activities.

8. The social science perspective balances recognition of both the formal and the informal organization in explaining human action.

9. Emergent nontraditional perspectives challenge the assumptions of mainline theory and provide alternative explanations of organizational life.

10. Post-modernism, critical theory, and feminist theory are three important emergent perspectives.

The science of educational administration is as new as the modern school; the one-room schoolhouse of rural America did not need specialized administrators. Systematic study of administration and development of theories of organization and administration are twentieth-century phenomena. Before exploring the theoretical and historical foundations of educational administration, however, we need a basic understanding of what theory is in the scientific sense. Consequently, we begin the chapter by defining theory and science, delineating the major components of theory, and discussing the interrelationships among theory, research, and practice.

THEORY: A SCIENTIFIC CONCEPT

Much of the skepticism about theory is based on the assumption that educational administration is incapable of becoming a science. This is a skepticism that has plagued all social sciences. Theory in the natural sciences, on the other hand, has attained respectability not only because it necessarily involves precise description but also because it describes ideal phenomena that "work" in practical applications.

Most people think that scientists deal with facts while philosophers delve into theory. Indeed, to many individuals, including educational administrators, facts and theories are antonyms; that is, facts are real and their meanings self-evident, while theories are speculations or dreams. Theory in educational administration, however, has the same role as theory in physics, chemistry, biology, or psychology—that is, providing general explanations and guiding research.

THEORY AND SCIENCE DEFINED

The purpose of all science is understanding the world in which we live and work. Scientists describe what they see, discover regularities, and formulate theories (Babbie, 1990). Organizational science attempts to describe and explain regularities in the behavior of individuals and groups within organizations. Organizational scientists seek basic principles that provide a general understanding of the structure and dynamics of organizational life, a relatively recent goal in educational administration (Roberts, Hulin, and Rousseau, 1978).

Some researchers view science as a static, interconnected set of principles that explains the universe in which we live. We view **science** as a dynamic process of developing, through experimentation and observation, an interconnected set of principles that in turn produces further experimentation and observation (Conant, 1951). In this view the basic aim of science is to find general explanations, called *theories*. Scientific theories are created by thoughtful individuals trying to understand how things work; however, no theory is ever taken as final because a better one may be devised at any time. Indeed, one of the basic strengths of science is that it is self-critical and self-corrective (Willower, 1994). The norms of science are oriented toward open-mindedness, public communication of results, and an impersonal criteria of assessment (Zuckerman, 1987).

As the ultimate aim of science, theory has acquired a variety of definitions. Some early agreement emerged in the field of educational administration that the definition of theory produced by Herbert Feigl (1951) was an adequate starting point. Feigl defines theory as a set of assumptions from which a larger set of empirical laws can be derived by purely logicomathematical procedures. Both Andrew Halpin (1958) and Daniel E. Griffiths (1959) supported this definition. Donald J. Willower (1975) later cautioned, however, that Feigl's definition is so rigorous as to exclude most theory in educational administration. A more general and useful definition for the social sciences was provided by Fred N. Kerlinger (1986: 9): "A theory is a set of interrelated constructs (concepts), definitions, and propositions that present a systematic view of phenomena by specifying relations among variables, with the purpose of explaining and predicting phenomena." Willower's (1975: 78) definition is more parsimonious: "a body of interrelated, consistent generalizations that serves to explain."

In the study of educational administration, the following definition of theory seems most useful: **Theory** is a set of interrelated concepts, assumptions, and generalizations that systematically describes and explains regularities in behavior in educational organizations. Moreover, hypotheses may be derived from the theory to predict additional relationships among the concepts.

This definition suggests three things. First, theory logically comprises concepts, assumptions, and generalizations. Second, its major function is to describe, explain, and predict regularities in behavior. Third, theory is heuristic; that is, it stimulates and guides the further development of knowledge.

Theories are by nature general and abstract; they are not strictly true or false but rather useful or not. Theories are useful to the extent that they generate accurate predictions about events and help us more easily to understand and influence behavior. Albert Einstein, one of the greatest theorists of all times, and Leopold Infeld (Einstein and Infeld, 1938) capture the essence of theorizing in the following quotation:

> In our endeavor to understand reality we are somewhat like a man trying to understand the mechanism of a closed watch. He sees the face and the moving hands, even hears its ticking, but he has no way of opening the case. If he is ingenious he may form some picture of a mechanism which could be responsible for all the things he observes, but he may never be quite sure his picture is the only one which could explain his observations. He will never be able to compare his picture with the real mechanism, and he cannot even imagine the possibility of the meaning of such a comparison. (p. 31)

Reality exists, but our knowledge of it always remains elusive and uncertain. It should not be surprising that different individuals often draw different conclusions from the same perceptual experiences because they hold different theories that affect their interpretation of events (Cary and Smith, 1993). Our knowledge consists of our theories. The form of the theory, however, is less important than the degree to which it generates useful understanding. Ultimately, research and theory are judged by their utility (Griffiths, 1988).

The use of theory in organizational analysis seems indispensable to reflective practice. The beginning student of educational administration may ask, "Do these theories and models really exist?" Our position is the same as Mintzberg's (1989). The models, theories, and configurations used to describe organizations in this book are mere words and pictures on pages, not reality itself. Actual organizations are much more complex than any of these representations; in fact, our conceptual frameworks are simplifications of organizations that underscore some features and neglect others. Hence, they distort reality. The problem is that in many areas we cannot get by without theoretical guidance (implicit, if not explicit theories), much as a traveler cannot effectively navigate unknown territory without a map.

Our choice is not usually between reality and theory but rather between alternative theories. Mintzberg (1989) captures the dilemma nicely:

> No one carries reality around in his or her head, no head is that big. Instead we carry around impressions of reality, which amount to implicit theories. Sometimes these are supplemented with explicit frameworks for identifying the concepts and interrelating them—in other words, with formal theories, built on systematic investigation known as research, or at least on systematic consideration of experience. In fact, some phenomena cannot be comprehended without such formal aid—how is one to develop an implicit theory of nuclear fission, for example? (p. 259)

We all use theories to guide our actions. Some are implicit and others are explicit; in fact, many of our personal implicit theories are formal ones that have been internalized. To paraphrase John Maynard Keynes, practical administrators who believe themselves to be exempt from any theoretical influences are usually the slaves of some defunct theory. Good theories and models exist, and if we do our job well in this book, they will exist where all useful knowledge must exist—in our minds.

COMPONENTS OF THEORY

The nature of theory can be better understood by looking at the meanings of each of the components of theory and how they are related to one another.

Concepts

A **concept** is a term that has been given an abstract, generalized meaning. A few examples of concepts in administration are centralization, formalization, leadership, morale, and informal organization. Scientists invent concepts that help them study and analyze a given phenomenon systematically. In other words, they invent a language to describe behavior in the real world. Two important advantages are derived from defining theoretical concepts (Reynolds, 1971). First, theorists, researchers, and practitioners can agree on the meaning of such terms. Second, their abstractness and generality ensure that the concepts are independent of any spatial or temporal setting.

Although concepts are by definition abstract, different levels of abstraction are used (Willower, 1963). Examples of terms arranged along a concrete to abstract continuum are Jefferson Elementary School, school, service organization, organization, social system, and system. Each succeeding term is more general and abstract. Generally speaking, terms that are specific to a particular time or place are concrete and are less useful in developing theories. Most concepts, generalizations, and theories discussed in this book are in the middle range—that is, they are somewhat limited in scope rather than all-embracing. They are not attempts to summarize all we know about organizations; rather, they explain some of the consistencies found in organizations, particularly schools.

A concept can be defined in at least two ways. First, it may be defined in terms of other words or concepts. For instance, we might define permissiveness as the degree to which a teacher employs a relaxed mode of pupil control—that is, permissiveness is defined in terms of "relaxedness." Although this kind of definition often provides one with a better understanding of the term, it is inadequate from a scientific point of view. The researcher must be able to define the concept in measurable terms. A set of operations or behaviors that has been used to measure a concept is its **operational definition.** For example, an operational definition of permissiveness might be the number of hall passes a teacher issues per day. This definition is limited, clear, and concise. The concept is the specific set of operations measured. IQ is the standard operational definition of intelligence, and leadership can be operationalized using Bass's Multi-factor Leadership Questionnaire (Bass, 1985a). Operationalism mandates that the procedures involved in the relation between the observer and the measures for observing be explicitly stated so that they can be duplicated by any other equally trained researcher (Dubin, 1969).

A concept that has an operational definition is often referred to as a variable. In fact, many researchers and scientists loosely use the terms *concept* and *variable* interchangeably. Technically, however, a **variable** is a property of a concept to which numerical values are assigned. The number can represent a category (e.g., gender: male or female), the magnitude of the property (e.g., age in years), or the presence or absence of the property (e.g., participation: yes or no). Variables are thus concepts that have operational measures and take on values.

Assumptions and Generalizations

An **assumption** is a statement that is taken for granted or accepted as true. Assumptions, accepted without proof, are not necessarily self-evident. For example, Jay Galbraith (1973) offers the following two assumptions concerning organizational design:

1. There is no one best way to organize.

2. Any way of organizing is not equally effective.

The first assumption challenges the conventional idea that there are universal design principles for effective organizations, regardless of time or place. The second assumption challenges the notion that complexity and diversity in organizations make it futile to seek guiding principles. W. Richard Scott (1987a) adds a third assumption:

> **3.** The best way to organize depends on the nature of the environment to which the organization relates.

We offer a rival assumption:

> **4.** The best way to organize depends on the complexity of the organizational task to be completed.

The first three assumptions are the foundation of a contingency theory of organizational design that explains how the internal features of an organization must match the demands of the environment if the organization is to adapt and produce effectively (see Chapter 7).

A **generalization** is a statement or proposition that indicates the mutual relationship of two or more concepts. In other words, a generalization links concepts in a meaningful fashion. Many kinds of generalizations are found in theoretical formulations: (1) assumptions are generalizations if they specify the relationship among two or more concepts; (2) hypotheses are generalizations with limited empirical support (see below); (3) **principles** are generalizations with substantial empirical support; and (4) **laws** are generalizations with an overwhelming degree of empirical support (more than principles). Depending on the level of empirical support, the same generalization, at different stages of theory and research development, can be a hypothesis, a principle, or a law.

RESEARCH AND THEORY

Research is inextricably related to theory; therefore, many of the misconceptions and ambiguities surrounding theory are reflected in the interpretation of the meaning and purpose of research. Kerlinger (1986:10) provides us with the following clear definition: "Scientific research is systematic, controlled, empirical, and critical investigation of hypothetical propositions about the presumed relations among natural phenomena." This definition suggests that research is guided by hypotheses that are empirically checked against observations about reality in a systematic and controlled way. Furthermore, the results of such tests are then open to critical analyses by other researchers.

Haphazard observations followed by the conclusion that the facts speak for themselves do not qualify as scientific research; in fact, such unrefined empiricism can distort reality and does not lead to the systematic development of knowledge. Well-conceived surveys and ethnographic studies for the express purpose of developing hypotheses are at times useful starting points in terms of hypothesis and theory development. Ultimately, however, knowledge in any discipline is expanded by research that is guided by hypotheses that are derived from theory. In brief, facts from research are not as important as the general patterns and explanations that they provide.

Hypotheses

A **hypothesis** is a conjectural statement that indicates a relationship between at least two variables. Several examples of different kinds of hypotheses illustrate this point.

H-1: Academic emphasis of secondary schools is positively related to student achievement.

H-2: The greater the degree of centralization in a school, the greater the extent of teacher alienation.

H-3: The greater the degree of collective teacher efficacy in a school, the higher the level of academic achievement.

H-4: Schools with open organizational climates have higher levels of shared teacher decision making than those with closed climates.

H-5: The greater the community participation in the activities of school, the higher the level of academic achievement.

Several observations can be made about these hypotheses. First, each hypothesis specifies the relationship between at least two variables. Second, each clearly and concisely describes that relationship. Third, the variables of each hypothesis are such that each could be empirically tested. For example, H-1 expresses the relationship between two variables—academic emphasis and student achievement. Schools that have high academic emphases are predicted to have higher student achievement levels. Academic emphasis is measured by the extent to which high but achievable academic goals are set for students in an orderly, serious, and supportive learning environment (Hoy and Feldman, 1987). Student achievement can be measured by a battery of standardized tests.

Hypotheses bridge the gaps between theory and research and provide a means to test theory against observed reality. Hypotheses developed to test theory are deduced directly from theory. For example, hypothesis H-2 can be derived from bureaucratic theory discussed in Chapter 3. H-3 is based on motivation theory discussed in Chapter 4. H-5 can be derived from the conceptual perspectives on organizational climate provided in Chapter 5.

The hypothesis is the researcher's bias. If it is deduced from a theory, the investigator expects that it will be supported by data. Hypothesis testing as a part of the theory-research process is essential to the development of knowledge in any field of study. Support of the hypothesis in empirical research demonstrates the usefulness of the theory as an explanation. The fact that knowledge depends in part upon unsupported theories and assumptions should not cause discouragement. The goal of organizational researchers is to test our assumptions and theories, refining explanations and reformulating the theories as more data are gathered and analyzed.

FIGURE 1.1

Theoretical System

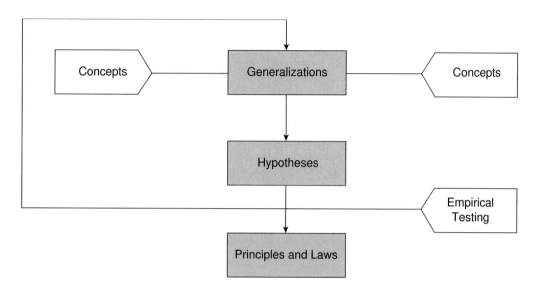

The basic form of knowledge in all disciplines is similar; it consists of concepts, generalizations, and theories, each dependent on the one preceding it (Willower, 1963). Figure 1.1 summarizes the basic components of theory that are necessary to the development of knowledge. It shows that concepts are eventually linked together into generalizations that in turn form a logically consistent set of propositions providing a general explanation of a phenomenon (a theory). The theory is empirically checked by the development and testing of hypotheses deduced from the theory. The results of the research provide the data for accepting, rejecting, reformulating, or refining and clarifying the basic generalizations of the theory. Over time, with continued empirical support and evidence, the generalizations develop into principles that explain the phenomenon. In the case of organizational theory, principles are developed to explain the structure and dynamics of organizations and the role of the individual in organizations. Theory is both the beginning and the end of scientific research. On the one hand, it serves as the basis for generating hypotheses to test verifiable propositions that describe and predict observable empirical phenomena. On the other hand, the ultimate objective of all scientific endeavor is to develop a body of substantive theory.

THEORY AND PRACTICE

Theory is directly related to practice in at least three ways. First, theory forms a frame of reference for the practitioner. Second, the process of theorizing provides a general mode of analysis of practical events. And third, theory guides decision making.

Theory gives practitioners the analytic tools needed to sharpen and focus their analysis of the problems they face (Dewey, 1933). The administrator so armed can develop alternative solutions to pragmatic problems. Administrators themselves maintain that the most important qualification for their jobs is the ability to use concepts. It is a mistake, however, to assume that the ability to label aspects of a problem by using theoretical constructs from sociology or psychology automatically provides a solution to a problem. Designating a problem as one of role conflict, goal displacement, or cognitive processing, for instance, does not in itself solve the problem; it may, however, organize the issues so that a reasonable plan of action can emerge.

The theory-practice relationship goes beyond using the concepts of theorists to label the important aspects of a problem. The scientific approach provides a way of thinking about events for both theorists and practitioners alike. Indeed, the scientific approach is the very embodiment of rational inquiry, whether the focus is theoretical analysis and development, a research investigation, organizational decision making, or problem solving at the personal level. A good general description of this approach is found in John Dewey's (1933) analysis, *How We Think*. The process involves identifying a problem, conceptualizing it, proposing generalizations in the form of hypotheses that provide answers to the problems, deducing the consequences and implications of the hypotheses, and testing the hypotheses.

Some differences do exist in the specific ways that theorists, researchers, and practitioners implement and use the scientific approach, but the differences are a matter of degree of rigor and level of abstraction rather than approach. Theorists operate on a higher level of abstraction and generality than researchers, who test hypotheses. Practitioners, in turn, operate on an even lower level of abstraction than researchers because they are primarily concerned with specific problems and events in their organizations.

Similarly, theorists and researchers typically use the scientific approach more rigorously than practitioners, and for good reason. Theorists usually preface their propositions with the phrase "other things being equal," and researchers attempt to control all other variables except those under study. In contrast, practitioners function in a world where other things typically are not equal and all variables are not controllable. Practitioners are constrained by their position, responsibilities, authority, and the immediacy of their problems. Although they do not abandon a reflective approach, practitioners are forced to be more flexible in applying the scientific method. For example, educational administrators are probably less concerned than theorists or researchers with generalizability—that is, the extent to which their solutions work for other administrators in other districts. Nonetheless, the approach of theorists, researchers, and thoughtful practitioners is basically the same; it is a systematic and reflective one.

One final relationship between theory and practice needs to be mentioned. We can define administration as both the art and the science of applying knowledge to administrative and organizational problems. Arthur Blumberg (1984, 1989) calls it a craft. Such definitions imply that administrators have access to knowledge needed for making decisions. Without theory, however, there is virtually no foundation for knowledge, for the meaningful research that provides information presupposes a theory. Unfortunately, theory and research in educational administration continue to make only modest gains at best.

Administrative theory does influence practice. Over the last ninety years, the evolution of organizational thought can be divided into four general phases: classical organizational thought, human relations, social science approach, and emerging nontraditional perspectives. Since the 1950s, organizational thought has continued to change and develop as the field of organizational studies becomes increasingly controversial and complex.

CLASSICAL ORGANIZATIONAL THOUGHT

Frederick Taylor, the father of the scientific management movement, sought ways to use people effectively in industrial organizations. Taylor's background and experience as laborer, clerk, machinist, foreman, chief draftsman, and finally, chief engineer reinforced his belief that individuals could be programmed to be efficient machines. The key to the **scientific management** approach is the machine metaphor.

Taylor and his associates thought that workers, motivated by economics and limited by physiology, needed constant direction. In 1911 Taylor (1947) formalized his ideas in *Principles of Scientific Management.* A sampling of his ideas reveals the flavor of his managerial theory.

- *A large daily task:* Each person in the establishment, high or low, should have a clearly defined daily task. The carefully circumscribed task should require a full day's effort to complete.

- *Standard conditions:* The worker should be given standardized conditions and appliances to accomplish the task with certainty.

- *High pay for success:* High pay should be tied to successful completion.

- *Loss in case of failure:* Failure should be personally costly.

- *Expertise in large organizations:* As organizations become increasingly sophisticated, tasks should be made so difficult as to be accomplished only by a first-rate worker.

Taylor and his followers—the human engineers—focused on physical production, and their **time and motion studies** sought workers' physical limits and described the fastest method for performing a given task (Barnes, 1949: 556–67).

- The two hands should begin and end motions simultaneously.

- Arm movements should be simultaneous and made in opposite and symmetrical directions.

- Smooth, continuous hand motions are preferable to zigzag or straight-line motions involving sudden or sharp changes in direction.

- Tools, materials, and controls should be close to and in front of the operator.
- Tools should be combined whenever possible.

Although Taylor's work had a narrow physiological focus and ignored psychological and sociological variables, he demonstrated that many jobs could be performed more efficiently. He also helped the unskilled worker by improving productivity enough to raise the pay of unskilled nearly to that of skilled labor (Drucker, 1968).

In a similar vein, traditional or classical organizational thought, often called *administrative management theory,* concentrates on the broad problems of departmental division of work and coordination. While Taylor's human engineers worked from the individual worker upward, the administrative managers worked from the managing director downward. Their focuses were different, but their contributions complemented one another.

Henri Fayol, like Taylor, took a scientific approach to administration. Fayol was a French mining engineer and successful executive who later taught administration. According to Fayol (Urwick, 1937: 119), administrative behavior consists of five functions, which he defined as follows.

- To plan means to study the future and arrange the plan of operations.
- To organize means to build up material and human organization of the business, organizing both people and materials.
- To command means to make the staff do their work.
- To coordinate means to unite and correlate all activities.
- To control means to see that everything is done in accordance with the rules which have been laid down and the instructions which have been given.

Luther Gulick (1937) later amplified these functions in answer to the question, "What is the work of the chief executive?" He responded, "POSDCoRB," an acronym for his seven administrative procedures: planning, organizing, staffing, directing, coordinating, reporting, and budgeting.

To the administrative managers, **division of labor** was essential. Accordingly, the more a task could be broken down into its components, the more specialized and, therefore, the more effective the worker would be in performing the task. To complement the division of labor, tasks were grouped into jobs, and these jobs were then integrated into departments. Although the criteria for division could pose conflicting demands, division of labor and the departmentalization it entailed were necessary aspects of management.

Span of control, or the number of workers supervised, was a second principle. In subdividing from the top downward, each work unit had to be supervised and coordinated with other units, and the span of control considered to be most effective was five to ten subordinates. This rule of thumb is still widely used in building administrative organizations. The pyramid-shaped structures stemming from this second principle are headed by a single executive, with power and authority flowing uniformly from the top to the bottom.

A third operating tenet of the administrative manager was the **principle of homogeneity** of positions. According to Gulick, a single department could be formed of positions grouped in any of four different ways: major purpose, major process, clientele, or location. *Major purpose* joined those who shared a common goal. *Major process* combined those with a similar skill or technology. *Clientele* or material grouped those who dealt with similar clients or materials. Organization based on *location* or geographic area brought together those who worked together regardless of function (Urwick, 1937).

Organizing departments in these four ways presents obvious problems. For example, should a school health activity be placed in a department of education or of health? How one answers the question will alter the nature of the service. Homogenizing departments in one of the four ways does not homogenize them in all ways. "The question is not which criterion to use for grouping," James D. Thompson (1967: 57) has observed, "but rather in which priority are the several criteria to be exercised."

Both the human engineers and the scientific managers emphasized formal or bureaucratic organization. They were concerned with the division of labor, the allocation of power, and the specifications for each position; they conspicuously neglected individual idiosyncrasies and the social dynamics of people at work. This perspective, aptly termed a "machine model," implies that an organization can be constructed according to a blueprint, as one would build a bridge or an engine (Worthy, 1950). In summary, the basic features of the traditional or classical administrative models are contained in the following list:

- *Time and motion studies:* The task is carried out in a way that minimizes time and effort.

- *Division of labor and specialization:* Efficiency can be attained by subdividing any operation into its basic components to ensure workers' performance.

- *Standardization of tasks:* Breaking tasks into component parts allows for routinized performance.

- *Unity of command:* To coordinate the organization, decision making is centralized, with responsibility flowing from top to bottom.

- *Span of control:* Unity of command and coordination are possible only if each superior at any level has a limited number of subordinates (five to ten) to direct.

- *Uniqueness of function:* One department of an organization should not duplicate the functions performed by another.

- *Formal organization:* The focus of analysis is on the official organizational blueprint; semiformal and informal structures created by the dynamic interaction of people within the formal organization are not analyzed.

The greatest shortcoming of machine theory was its rigid conception of organization. As James G. March and Herbert Simon (1958) have observed, the structure and functioning of an organization may be greatly affected both by events outside the organization and by events imperfectly coordinated within it, and neither of these occurrences can be fixed in advance.

HUMAN RELATIONS APPROACH

The human relations movement developed in reaction to the formal tradition of the classic models of administration. Mary Parker Follett (1941), who wrote a series of brilliant papers dealing with the human side of administration, believed that the fundamental problem in all organizations was developing and maintaining dynamic and harmonious relationships. In addition, Follett (1924: 300) thought that conflict was "not necessarily a wasteful outbreak of incompatibilities, but normal process by which socially valuable differences register themselves for enrichment of all concerned." Despite Follett's work, the development of the human relations approach is usually traced to studies done in the Hawthorne plant of the Western Electric Company in Chicago. These studies are basic to the literature describing informal groups, and the study of informal groups is basic to an analysis of schools.

The **Hawthorne studies** (see Roethlisberger and Dickson, 1939) began with three experiments conducted to study the relation of quality and quantity of illumination to efficiency in industry. The first illumination experiment was made in three departments. The level of illumination intensity in each department was increased at stated intervals. The results were puzzling. Increased production rates did not correspond with increased lighting, nor did production decline with reduced illumination.

In a second experiment, a test group in which illumination intensities were varied was compared to a control group with illumination held constant. Both groups showed increases in production rates that were not only substantial but also nearly identical.

Finally, in a third experiment, when the lighting for the test group was decreased and that for the control group held constant, the efficiency of both groups increased. Furthermore, the production rates increased in the test group until the light became so poor that the workers complained they could no longer see what they were doing.

The results were neither as simple nor as clear-cut as the experimenters had originally anticipated. Two conclusions seemed justified: employee output was not primarily related to lighting conditions; and too many variables had not been controlled in the experiments. The startling nature of the findings stimulated more research.

Two Harvard professors—Elton Mayo, an industrial psychologist, and Fritz Roethlisberger, a social psychologist—were retained to continue studying the relationship between physical conditions of work and productivity. The company suspected that psychological as well as physiological factors were involved. From 1927 through 1932 the two researchers conducted a series of experiments that have since become research classics in the social sciences—the Hawthorne studies. The investigators formulated six questions related to the problems of fatigue (Roethlisberger and Dickson, 1939: 28).

- Do employees actually get tired out?
- Are rest pauses desirable?
- Is a shorter working day desirable?
- What are the attitudes of employees toward their work and toward the company?
- What is the effect of changing the type of working equipment?
- Why does production fall off in the afternoon?

To control intervening variables, six female workers were placed in separate room for observation. All six performed the standardized task of assembling telephone relays. During the initial phase of work in the Relay Assembly Test Room, physical conditions were held constant and then changed periodically. The frequency and duration of rest pauses, for instance, were systematically manipulated, while both the workday and workweek were varied. During one period, two 5-minute rest periods were established, one in the morning and another in the afternoon. These rest pauses were later lengthened to 10 minutes. In another period, six 5-minute rest breaks replaced two. Change in experimental conditions continued for more than a year. The investigators had not anticipated the findings. Output increased, but the increase was independent of any change in rest pauses or working hours. Production was not related to any specific experimental change.

After a host of experimental manipulations, the researchers reestablished the original conditions of work with no rest periods, no special lunch periods, and the original long workday and workweek. Both the daily and weekly production level rose to a point much higher than under the nearly identical conditions of the preexperimental setting. The investigators were further perplexed by the improvement of the workers' attitudes and morale during the long series of experiments. Simple, mechanistic manipulation of working conditions could explain neither the Relay Assembly Test Room experiments nor the similar results of the illumination studies. Obviously, something was happening, but what?

One hypothesis advanced was that the increased output and morale were due to relief from fatigue afforded by rest periods. Subsequent data analysis did not support this explanation. An alternative hypothesis suggested that improved wage incentives were responsible for heightened production and morale. Although the women's pay had been based on group piecework in their regular department, the wage incentive had been slight because the group was so large. In the small experimental group, the women were given an opportunity to earn in more direct proportion to the individual effort expended; hence, production increased. Two separate studies—the Second Relay Assembly Group and the Mica Splitting Test Group—were undertaken to test the wage incentive hypothesis. The studies indicated that the wage incentive factors alone could not have produced the continuous increase in output. Moreover, the power of wage incentives depended on other factors.

Only after further analysis did the researchers examine the experimental situation itself, which had altered the self-images and interpersonal relations of those in the work group. The nature of the supervision also had changed. To maintain cooperative subjects, supervision became informal, nondirective, and personal. Workers were permitted to talk freely in a more relaxed atmosphere, and because they had become objects of considerable attention, they saw their involvement in the experiment as a source of pride. In essence, social relations had been restructured to foster a friendly and cohesive work group. The impact of social conditions became a highly significant finding, and, as the Hawthorne studies continued, increased attention was focused on the social relations within work groups.

The research program's final phase, known as the Bank Wiring Study, analyzed the work group's social structure. Fourteen men—nine wiremen, three soldermen, and two inspectors—assembling terminal banks for use in telephone exchanges, were placed in a Bank Wiring Observation Room. The only other change in working conditions was the presence of a single investigator in the room to observe the workers' behavior. An interviewer remained outside the room and periodically interviewed the men. This phase of the Hawthorne studies lasted seven months and concluded in May 1932.

One generalization became clear almost immediately. The workers' behavior did not conform to the official job specifications. An informal organization emerged that affected performance. **Informal organization** is an unofficial social structure that emerges within the organization that has informal leaders as well as informal norms, values, sentiments, and communication patterns.

Patterns of interactions developed as soon as the men were thrown together in the observation room. Friendships formed and two well-defined groups emerged. The informal cliques were evident in interaction patterns both on and off the job. For example, one clique, rather than another, engaged in certain games during off hours. Even more important than the different interaction patterns were the informal norms that emerged to govern behavior and unify the group. Too much work, and one was a rate buster. Too little work constituted the equally serious, informal offense of chiseling. A no-squealing norm also emerged; no group member should say anything that might injure a fellow member. Other norms included not acting officiously or self-assertively; one was expected to be a "regular guy" and not to be noisy and anxious for attention and leadership.

The work group enforced respect for informal norms through ostracism, sarcasm, and invective to pressure deviant members. One mechanism to enlist compliance was binging—a quick, stiff punch on the upper arm. The bing was not physically damaging, nor was it meant to be; it was a symbolic gesture of group displeasure.

Much activity in the group countered formal role prescriptions. Wiremen and soldermen did not stick to their jobs as prescribed but frequently traded jobs and helped each other. The group also restricted production. Group norms defined a fair day's work below management's expectations, although not so far below so as to be unacceptable. Most work was done in the morning. Faster workers simply slowed their pace earlier or reported less work than they had accomplished to save production for slow days. The informal production levels were consistently maintained, even though higher production was possible. Because the group was on a piece rate, higher output would have meant higher wages. Thus, behavior was a function of group norms, not economic incentives.

The experiments at the Hawthorne plant were the first to question many of the basic assumptions made by human engineers and scientific managers. The following propositions summarize the conclusions of the Hawthorne studies.

- Economic incentive is not the only significant motivator. In fact, noneconomic social sanctions limit the effectiveness of economic incentives.
- Workers respond to management as members of an informal group, not as individuals.
- Production levels are limited more by the social norms of the informal organization than by physiological capacities.
- Specialization does not necessarily create the most efficient organization of the work group.
- Workers use informal organization to protect themselves against arbitrary management decisions.
- Informal social organizations interact with management.
- A narrow span of control is not a prerequisite to effective supervision.
- Informal leaders are often as important as formal supervisors.
- Individuals are active human beings, not passive cogs in a machine.

Although these findings date from the 1920s and 1930s, they remain important. The human relations approach, however, is not without its detractors. Amitai Etzioni (1964) suggests that the human relations approach grossly oversimplifies the complexities of organizational life by glossing over the realities of work. Organizations have conflicting values and interests as well as shared ones; they are a source of alienation as well as human satisfaction. Worker dissatisfaction is just as likely to be symptomatic of real underlying conflicts of interests as indicative of a lack of understanding of the situation. Put simply, organizations are often not one big "happy family." Contemporary critics of the human relations movement (Clark et al., 1994) also argue that the concern for workers was not authentic, but rather it was used by management as a tool or strategy to manipulate subordinates. Nevertheless, one conclusion is clear: the human relations approach tempered the scientific managers' concentration on organizational structure with an emphasis on employee motivation and satisfaction and group morale.

SOCIAL SCIENCE APPROACH

Because the classical human relations approaches ignored the impact of social relations and formal structure, respectively, the social science approach used both perspectives and added propositions drawn from psychology, sociology, political science, and economics. The approach differs from other social sciences only in its subject matter: work behavior in formal organization (Simon, 1968).

Chester I. Barnard (1938) was one of the first to apply a social science approach with his analysis of organizational life in *Functions of the Executive*. The product of Barnard's years as president of Bell Telephone Company of New Jersey, this book offers a comprehensive theory of cooperative behavior in formal organizations.

Barnard provided the original definitions of formal and informal organizations and cogently demonstrated the inevitable interaction between them. Barnard (1940) himself summarized the contributions of his work in terms of structural and dynamic concepts. The structural concepts he considered important were the individual, the cooperative system, the formal organization, the complex formal organization, and the informal organization. His important dynamic concepts were free will, cooperation, communication, authority, the decision process, and dynamic equilibrium.

Herbert Simon (1947), in *Administrative Behavior,* extended Barnard's work and used the concept of organizational equilibrium as a focal point for a formal theory of work motivation. The organization was seen as an exchange system in which inducements are exchanged for work. Employees remain in the organization as long as they perceive the inducements as larger than their work contributions. By integrating economics, psychology, and sociology, the inducements-contributions schema illustrates the interdisciplinary nature of the theory.

Simon criticized classical organization theory because, he maintained, it was based on simple untested proverbs. He saw administration as a process of rational decision making that influenced the behavior of members of the organization. Simon (1947) succinctly characterized his perspective as follows:

> What is a scientifically relevant description of an organization? It is a description that, so far as possible, designates for each person in the organization what decisions that person makes, and the influence to which he is subject in making each of these decisions. (p. 36)

The organization, although providing the framework, information, and values for rational decisions, is limited in its ability to collect and process information, search for alternatives, and predict consequences. Therefore, questions are resolved through satisficing rather than through optimizing. In Simon's view, no best solution exists to any given problem, but some solutions are more satisfactory than others.

Other theoretical formulations in social science (see Chapter 3) evolved from the writings of Max Weber (1947). Although many of Weber's views are closer to those espoused by the scientific managers than by the social scientists, Weber's discussions of bureaucracy and authority have provided present-day theorists with a starting point in their conceptions of organizations as social systems that interact with and are dependent upon their environments.

It remained to Talcott Parsons (1960), however, to stress the importance of the environment on the organization and anticipate a conception of the organization as an open system—a social system dependent on and influenced by its environment. Open-systems theory is the general framework for exploring the conceptual foundations of educational administration in this text. Although many theories and conceptual frameworks are discussed in our analyses, the open-system perspective is the overarching framework.

EMERGENT NONTRADITIONAL PERSPECTIVES

Thus far our treatment of organizational thought has been conventional and orthodox; in fact, much of the remainder of this book emphasizes mainline theory and research, which is anchored in the traditions and scientific methods of the social sciences. There are emerging, however, a number of critical alternative approaches to scrutinizing organizations. These perspectives should not be neglected because, taken together, they present a major intellectual challenge to the established knowledge about organizational behavior, and they force discussion of important, but often ignored, organizational problems.

Emergent nontraditional perspectives question both the assumptions and the methods of science. More specifically, they often repudiate the claims of objectivity, causality, rationality, materialistic reality, and the universal rules of inquiry used by the scientific social sciences and substitute subjectivity, indeterminacy, irrationality, illusion, and personal interpretation. Confidence in emotion replaces impartial observation. Relativism is sought rather than objectivity. Fragmentation is preferred to unity, the unique to the regular (Rosenau, 1991). Moreover, as David Clark and his colleagues (1994) note, the alternative views have often been inspired by neo-Marxist approaches that maintain:

- People are active agents in constructing their worlds.
- Knowledge and power are inextricably related.
- Facts are embedded in a social context; hence, they are interpreted through a social, value-laden process.
- Social structures and formal hierarchies conceal as much as they reveal.

These challenges and counterassertions have recently become a part of the study of organizations. The perspectives supply a countervailing set of forces to traditional organizational science and theory. These alternative views focus attention on important contemporary organization issues—the irrational, the unique, the repressed, the borderline, the rejected, the marginal, the silenced, the decentered, and the powerless. Three alternative perspectives—post-modernism, critical theory, and feminist theory—are used to illustrate some of the challenges to the conclusions of mainline organizational theory. The three have much in common: they overlap in their assumptions; they question contemporary organizational thought; and, to be sure, they are all critical of scientific social analysis.

THE POST-MODERNISM
AND POSTSTRUCTURAL APPROACHES

Post-modern approaches dispute the basic assumptions of modern social sciences and reject the knowledge of standard organizational science and theory. Although the two are not identical, we use **post-modernism** as a broad term to include post-structuralism because the small differences between the two approaches (ones of emphasis rather than substance) seem inconsequential (Huyssen, 1984, Sarup, 1989; Rosenau, 1992). Post-modernism (Derrida, 1978, 1981; Foucault, 1983, 1984) is oriented toward a cultural critique, is uncompromisingly against logical empiricism, and holds to a highly personal individual, nongeneralized, emotional form of knowledge (Vaillancourt, 1986).

Deconstruction and interpretation are the post-modernists' tools. Their aim is to undo all constructions. **Deconstruction** shreds the text by revealing its contradictions and inconsistencies; however, the intent is not to revise, improve, or offer a better vision (Rosenau, 1992). No interpretation is correct, but rather there are multiple interpretations. For post-modernists, the world consists of plural constructions and diverse realities. Post-modernists are antifoundational; that is, they contend that questions of fact, correctness, validity, and clarity can neither be posed nor answered by science (Fish, 1989). Thus, a major goal of post-modernists is to deconstruct modern social science knowledge. In organizational science the attack is on the foundations of the knowledge, contemporary organizational theory itself.

Although deconstruction may at first blush seem abstract, complex, and haphazard, it is not nearly as complicated once its basic principles and strategies are distilled. Pauline Rosenau (1992) captures the heart of the deconstructive method with the following set of guidelines:

- Find an exception to a generalization in the text and push it until the generalization becomes absurd; use the exception to destroy the generalization.
- Interpret the contentions in the text being deconstructed in their most extreme form.
- Avoid absolutes in deconstructing a text, but cultivate a sense of intellectual excitement by making startling and radical claims.
- Deny the legitimacy of all dichotomies because a few exceptions can always be found to undermine them.
- Accept nothing; reject nothing. It is difficult to criticize a deconstructive argument if no clear views are articulated.
- Write to permit the greatest number of interpretations; ambiguity and obfuscation are to be cultivated not avoided. The key is "to create a text without finality or completion, one with which the reader can never be finished." (Wellberg 1985: 243)
- Use new and unorthodox terminology to obscure familiar positions.
- Never agree to a change of terminology and "always insist that the working of the deconstructive argument is sacrosanct." (Ellis 1989: 145)

CRITICAL THEORY

The task critical theorists set for themselves is to demystify through critique. The approach is antiorganizational theory; it is a Marxist attack on the status quo, which emphasizes the alienated state of humanity in general and workers in particular. A **critical theory** of organization tries to deconstruct social reality to demonstrate how modern organizations serve the dominant economic and political interests. It is assumed that those in control seek to legitimate their power through the creation and perpetuation of a belief system that stresses the need for order, authority, and discipline (Burrell and Morgan, 1979). The critique attempts not only to highlight the alienated state of workers but to change it by illuminating "false consciousness." Jack Culbertson (1981) succinctly summarizes the perspective of critical theory as follows:

> It seeks fundamental and major change through direct links with and impact on practice. It seeks to do this through penetrating critiques of the status quo and through the foreshadowing of new and compelling human possibilities for development. (p. 5)

Thus like the post-modernists, critical theorists use the method of deconstruction to attack modern organizational thought, but they are not content simply to demonstrate inconsistencies and contradictions in current knowledge and practice. Rather, they want to change basic societal and organizational structures that are responsible for alienation, repression, and inequality. Theirs is a normative mission of human emancipation, one that is critical of contemporary American society. For example, with regard to schools, critical theorists attempt to reframe the dominant perspectives on schooling by raising such questions as: Whose voices in the educational process have been silenced and why? Whose interests are served by current structures of authority, curriculum, and pedagogy? What is the relationship among what is taught, how it is taught, and the dominant economic and political coalitions in society? (Clark et al., 1994).

FEMINIST THEORY

The feminist movement is also influencing contemporary organizational thought and theory. Feminism is viewed as incompatible with modern organizations (Ferguson, 1984). Feminists argue that organizations are dominated by a male culture that emphasizes conformity, deference to authority, loyalty, competition, aggressiveness, and efficiency. Individuals are treated as commodities that are valued only for their contribution to organizational success. The "feminist side" of relations is devalued in bureaucratic organizations. Those individual and group characteristics that are traditionally associated with the female role (supportive, nonassertive, emotional, dependent, attentive to others, and expressive) are subordinated to conventional male characteristics (analytic, aggressive, rational, independent, impersonal, and instrumental). In fact, some feminists (Calas and Smirich, 1992) charge that organizational research and theory are male baised—that is, oriented to male ways of knowing. They question the very nature of theory and research on organizations. For example, Kathy Ferguson (1984: xii) charges that mainstream social science research serves as apologia for contemporary organizational society by "justifying it, defending it, or regretfully arguing that things must be as they are."

The **feminist critique** takes two divergent forms: liberal feminists who take the existing organizational society as a given and seek to integrate women into that society, and radical feminists who wish to change society by replacing bureaucratic structures (Ferguson, 1984). Both groups maintain that women are oppressed by organizations, but the liberal feminists advocate adopting strategies that work within bureaucratic structures while the radical feminists advocate the elimination of such structures rather than their amelioration. It is the radical feminists who want to create a feminist discourse to resist modern organizations and in their place create a new form of organization that is antibureaucratic—one in which "the groups are decentralized; they rely on personal, face-to-face relations rather than formal skills; they are egalitarian rather than hierarchical; and they see resources to be shared, not hoarded" (Ferguson, 1984: 189–90).

THEORETICAL DEVELOPMENTS IN EDUCATIONAL ADMINISTRATION

As detailed by Roald Campbell and his colleagues (1987), developments in educational administration parallel those in the broad field of administration. Similar to Taylor's scientific managers, although lacking the rigor of the human engineers, early students of educational administration such as Franklin Bobbit (1913) looked at organizational behavior from the vantage point of job analyses. They observed administrators at work, specifying the component tasks to be performed, determining more effective ways to perform each task, and suggesting an organization to maximize efficiency. Raymond E. Callahan's (1962) analysis of schools and of the "cult of efficiency," concentrating on the period from 1910 through 1030, clearly indicates the influence of the scientific managers.

By 1940, however, the impact of the Hawthorne studies was evident in writing and exhortation on democratic administration. The ill-defined watchword of the period was "democratic"—democratic administration, democratic supervision, democratic decision making, democratic teaching. As Roald Campbell (1971) noted, this emphasis on human relations and democratic practices often meant a series of prescriptions as to how conditions ought to be and how persons in an organization ought to behave. Sometimes these prescriptions took the form of principles.

Supposed principles abounded, but they were usually no more than the observations of successful administrators or the democratic ideologies of college professors. In the 1940s and early 1950s, educational administration, as a democratic approach, was long on rhetoric and woefully short on research and practice (Campbell, 1971). In the 1950s, however, the social science approach started to make inroads, and by the 1960s a full-scale theory movement emerged to guide the study and teaching of educational administration. Democratic prescription was replaced by analysis, field orientation and raw observation by theoretical research. In addition, concepts from many disciplines were incorporated into educational administration research.

The theory movement in educational administration was limited, however, by a closed-system perspective. Like its parent, the general field of organizational theory, the focus of the analyses was on attempts to explain the internal workings of schools without reference to elements in the environment. Thus, it is not surprising that progress toward relevant theory and research in educational administration slowed in the 1970s. The social and political unrest of the late 1960s and the financial and political exigencies of the 1970s—civil rights demonstrations and riots, Vietnam and Watergate, oil crises and other resource shortages—all impinged on the study and practice of educational administration by raising questions about inequality, accountability, and the management of decline. Clearly, environmental factors are important forces affecting life in schools. The tenor of the 1970s not only inspired a renewed press in the field for practice, action, and immediate results but underscored the limitations of closed-system models. To be sure, research and theory in educational administration advanced during these two decades, but progress was modest. Moreover, criticisms of the social science approach in general and organizational theory in particular were forthcoming from reflective scholars as the extravagant expectations of the theory movement gave way to disillusionment.

By 1979, Griffiths described educational administration as a field in intellectual turmoil. Organizational theory and traditional research were under attack on a number of fronts. The logic of mainstream theory that described organizations as rational instruments of purpose, the focus on the internal operation of organizations with little regard for the influence of the environment, and the universality of organizational theories—all provided bases for criticism. Moreover, Marxist sociologists turned to critiques of traditional organizational theory by interpreting institutional life in terms of power, conflict, contradictions, crisis, and class struggle. For example, Heydebrand (1977) maintains that organizational theory has been dominated by strong ideological forces, which have successfully reproduced and legitimized the structure of capitalist society. Finally, contemporary organizational theory was criticized on epistemological grounds. The positivist model of the natural sciences was questioned as the appropriate one for the social and behavioral sciences (Culbertson, 1988).

The social science approach faces increased challenges from practitioners, professors, and the public who demand relevance and utility in theory and research (Greenfield, 1975; Willower, 1979). The feminist critique by Charol Shakeshaft (1986) and Flora Ida Ortiz and Catherine Marshall (1988) of educational administration also demonstrates the neglect of gender issues in administrative theory and research.

One danger of applying theoretical knowledge from the social sciences is the tendency to overgeneralize it to all situations. Too many behavioral scientists and practitioners assume that their theories apply universally; instead of asking under what conditions ideas and propositions are appropriate, they assume such ideas are always correct. They may think, for example, that participative management is always effective. The quest for universals and simple popular solutions has often led to disillusionment with the social sciences (Lorsch, 1979).

If contemporary organizational theory and research are to remain productive and useful, they should be driven by the problems of practice. Thus, our theories and research will have to be more situationally oriented, address emerging gender and political issues, and be diverse. The complexity of organizations and human behavior demands theoretical and research pluralism. Many theoretical approaches, both mainstream and nontraditional, are needed to understand organizational behavior. Similarly, research methods should be appropriate to the problem at hand; that is, divergent research procedures are essential. In brief, contemporary organizational theory and research can and should offer administrators a set of conceptual guidelines that help them solve the complex problems of practice.

Griffiths (1994), building on the work of Astley (1992), Lawrence (1992), and Weick (1992), proposes the following set of criteria to select appropriate theories for research problems:

- *Feasibility:* Is the theory usable? Is there a good fit between the theory and the problem?
- *Excitement:* Will the theory promote new insights or merely reinforce old ones?
- *Context:* Is the theory appropriate in the context of the current problem?
- *Cost:* Can the individual afford to use the theory, especially in terms of time and effort?
- *User friendly:* Is the language of the theory understandable and enlightening to users?
- *Fruitful:* Does the theory lead to problem solutions?

The same criteria can be used to determine which theories are likely to be most useful to practitioners; most of the theoretical perspectives in this book score reasonably high on these criteria.

Although problems in the development of theory in educational administration remain, that does not mean that the effort should be abandoned. Willower (1987) concludes his review of twenty-five years of inquiry into educational administration with the observation that theoretical explanation linked to careful empirical work is central to the whole enterprise of educational administration. We concur.

The perspective of this text is open-ended and pragmatic. Knowledge is seen as the product of systematic inquiry, which is guided by theory and subjected to public procedures that are replicable. The fact that our knowledge may be flawed or incomplete should not cause discouragement; it simply underscores the tentative nature of knowledge. New evidence will render many contemporary theories less useful. In this regard, we are like sailors who must repair a rotting ship at sea. We trust all but the weakest timber, which we must replace (Roberts, Hulin, and Rosseau, 1978). The knowledge that the timbers we trust today will be replaced tomorrow because they are also rotten in no way suggests that our trust has been misplaced.

When systematic methods of inquiry are brought to bear on a range of facts, we are better able to understand and to control them more intelligently and less haphazardly (Dewey, 1929). Consequently, in this book we draw upon whatever research and theories seem useful to help administrators solve the problems of practice. Our goal is to provide tentative explanations of social affairs, explanations that help administrators to understand the order and regularities of social behavior in organizations. Administrators who have at their disposal sets of concepts and basic principles of organizational life have powerful tools for observing, interpreting, and changing educational practice.

SUMMARY AND SUGGESTED READINGS

Theory is not simply idealistic speculation, nor is it "common sense." Because facts do not speak for themselves, a framework is needed to give facts meaning. Organizational theory provides that framework and functions in the same way theory does in the natural sciences and in the other social sciences: it provides an explanatory system connecting otherwise unrelated information. In addition, theory gives direction to empirical research; it may generate new knowledge, and it serves as a rational guide to action as well. Theory is refined through research, and when theory, in the light of research findings, is applied to individual action, it is transformed into practice.

We can speak of four periods in the evolution of administrative science. First, classical organizational thought, starting with Taylor's scientific analysis of work, focused on the formal organizational structure. The Hawthorne studies placed the informal organization at the heart of a new philosophy of management, the human relations approach. While scientific management has been criticized for mechanizing employees, human relations often became an oversimplified solution for all problems. A third and contemporary phase, the social science approach, balances recognition of both formal and informal organizations, and in part, it is a synthesis of the preceding two, using modern social science methods in its analyses. Finally, such emergent nontraditional perspectives as post-modernism, critical theory, and feminist theory are challenging many of the assumptions of mainstream social science theory.

The challenge of the twenty-first century is clear. Social science theory must become more refined, useful, and situationally oriented. Organizational theory must explain rational, nonrational, and irrational elements of behavior as well as environmental constraints on organizational life. There is a growing body of organizational theory and research that provides a reasonably coherent set of conceptual capital that can substitute for the stereotypes, superstitions, and dubious beliefs that administrators often use to ground their decisions. Our approach in this text is pragmatic, pluralistic, and empirical: we try to select the best theories, frameworks, and research that will help administrators understand and explain the complex nature of order and change in organizations.

We recommend several other insightful discussions of the utility of organizational theory for practice and research (Bacharach, 1989; Van de Ven, 1989; Weick, 1989; Whetten, 1989; Handy, 1993). The evolution of organizational thought has been treated comprehensively by a number of other scholars (Burrell and Morgan, 1980; Gross and Etzioni, 1985; Scott, 1992; Handy, 1993; Clark et al. 1994). Gareth Morgan (1986) provides a useful alternative and novel way of viewing organizations. He uses metaphors to develop images of organizations that represent important partial truths about them. Contemporary organizational theory, however, is not without its critics (Greenfield and Ribbins, 1993; English, 1994; Foster, 1986). Finally, for two recent attempts to map the domain of knowledge in educational administration, see Hoy, Astuto, and Forsyth (1994) and Donmoyer, Schurich, and Imber (1994).

There are many journals containing research relevant to educational administration. Two journals in education that link administrative theory and research are the *Educational Administration Quarterly* and the *Journal of Educational Administration. Planning and Changing, The Journal of School Leadership,* and *The Canadian Administrator* are examples of research journals that focus on the application of research and theory to practice in educational administration. Finally, a great many administrative journals publish important papers from all areas of administration; they include such journals as the *Academy of Management Journal, Academy of Management Review, Administrative Science Quarterly, Journal of Management Inquiry, Organizational Behavior and Human Decision Processes, Organizational Science,* and *Personnel Psychology.*

HOW TO USE THIS BOOK

Obviously, you will make the final judgment on how best to study this book. We suggest, however, that you seriously consider the following strategy. Each chapter begins with a short summary called the "Preview." You may have a tendency to skip over the preview to get right to the meat of the text. Don't. Take time to study the preview, which is deliberately short and terse. Research on information processing (Reder and Anderson, 1980; Anderson, 1990) suggests that memory for a text is facilitated by the initial study of the key points of the exposition. Hence, the previews are the most important points covered in the book. Each chapter also reinforces the preview with a concluding summary. Check yourself. Make sure that you have mastered the points in the preview and final summary. If you have not, there has been a serious shortcoming in learning. Of course, we hope you will learn more than the general ideas in the summary, but what you learn beyond that will depend on you—your purposes, your interest, and your perseverance.

John R. Anderson (1990), a cognitive psychologist interested in learning theory, elaborates the role of preview summaries in learning. Such summaries have three functions. First, they reflect the general structure of each chapter. If you have mastered the summary, you will know how the major themes and ideas of the chapter relate to each other. Second, preview summaries outline the most important new concepts and ideas. You fix in memory the key points and prepare yourself for how the text will relate, expand, and clarify the ideas. Third, the previews provide criteria against which you can test your mastery of the chapter.

Anderson suggests that to use these previews to greatest advantage, you make up a list of questions, based on the preview, to keep in mind as you read the text. When you finish the chapter, you should be able to answer the questions and elaborate on each issue. The question-generation process should guide your reading and encourage you to think more deeply about the text. The process also encourages you to do some spacing in your study. You might proceed by first studying the main points in the preview and developing your questions. Then skim the entire chapter. Next read each section carefully and then review that section. Finally, review the whole chapter, making sure that you can answer your guiding questions and that you know the key concepts and ideas introduced in the text.

KEY CONCEPTS AND IDEAS

Assumption	Operational definition
Concept	Post-modernism
Critical theory	Principle
Deconstruction	Principle of homogeneity
Division of labor	Science
Feminist critique	Scientific management
Formal organization	Span of control
Generalization	Standardization
Hawthorne studies	Theory
Hypothesis	Time and motion studies
Informal organization	Unity of command
Law	Variable

The School as a Social System

There is little point in general models if they do not give rise to specific conceptual derivations and empirical applications which illuminate, in however modest a degree, significant day-to-day practices.

—Jacob W. Getzels and James M. Lipham
Educational Administration as a Social Process

PREVIEW

1. Three competing systems perspectives exist: rational, natural, and open. These views of organizations are relatively distinct, partially complementary, and partially conflicting. Nevertheless, an open-systems perspective has the potential to combine rational and natural elements in the same framework.

2. An open system is a set of interacting elements that acquires inputs from the outside, transforms them, and produces outputs for the environment. Schools are such social systems; they are open to their environments.

3. Social systems have four important elements or subsystems: the structural, the individual, the cultural, and the political. Organizational behavior is a function of the interaction of these elements. Other things equal, the greater the degree of congruence among the elements of the system, the more effective it is.

4. The environment is also a critical aspect of organizational life; it not only provides resources for the system but also provides additional constraints and opportunities.

5. Formal organizations as social systems seek to achieve their goals if they are to survive and prosper.

6. We posit a congruence postulate: Other things being equal, the greater the degree of congruence among the elements of the system, the more effective the system.

7. Our open-systems model of schools provides a conceptual basis for organizational analysis and administrative problem solving.

26

The system concept has a rich history in the physical as well as the social sciences. Indeed, as both Alfred N. Whitehead (1925) and George C. Homans (1950) have observed, the idea of an organized whole, or system, occurring in an environment is fundamental and essential to science.

A SYSTEMS PERSPECTIVE

A significant development in the analysis of organizational behavior is the distinction between open and closed systems. Early system analyses of the school (Getzels and Guba, 1957) viewed organizations as closed systems—that is, sealed off from the outside world. Explanations were given in terms of the internal workings of the organization with little or no attention to external constraints in the environment. Today, however, few contemporary organizational theorists accept the premise that organizations can be understood in isolation of events occurring externally; in fact, Marshall Meyer (1978: 18) argues "the issue of open versus closed systems is closed, on the side of openness."

Although contemporary organizational thought is anchored in modern social science, three competing systems perspectives have emerged and continue, each with its share of advocates. W. Richard Scott (1987, 1992) calls them the rational-systems, natural-systems, and open-systems perspectives. These three popular views of organizations are relatively distinct, yet they are partly overlapping, partly complementary, as well as partly conflicting; and each has its antecedents in earlier organizational thought. Drawing heavily from Scott's (1992) work, each will be discussed in some detail.

RATIONAL SYSTEMS

The **rational-systems perspective** views organizations as formal instruments designed to achieve specific organizational goals. Rationality is the extent to which a set of actions is organized and implemented to achieve predetermined goals with maximum efficiency (Scott, 1992). The rational approach has its early roots in the classical organizational thought of the scientific managers. Thus, the behavior in organizations is seen as purposeful, disciplined, and rational. The concerns and concepts of rational-systems theorists are conveyed by such terms as "information," "efficiency," "effectiveness," "optimization," "implementation," "rationality," and "design." Furthermore, emphasis is placed upon the limitations of individual decision makers in the context of organizations; hence, the notions of opportunities, constraints, formal authority, rules and regulations, compliance, jurisdiction, objectives, mission, and coordination represent key elements of rationality.

Goal specificity stands out as one of the two critical elements in producing rationality in organizations (Scott, 1992). Goals are the desired ends that guide organizational behavior. Specific goals direct decision making, influence the formal structure, specify the tasks, guide the allocation of resources, and govern design decisions. Ambiguous goals hinder rationality because without clear goals, ordering alternatives and making rational choices are not possible; hence, even when the general organi-

27

zational goals are vague (as they often are in education), the actual daily operations are guided by specific objectives. Educators may argue endlessly about the merits of progressive and traditional education, but within each school considerable agreement develops around issues such as graduation requirements, discipline policies, and school regulations.

Formalization, or the level of rules and job codification, is another feature that makes organizations rational; formalization produces standardization and regulation of work performance. Rules are developed that precisely and explicitly govern behavior; jobs are carefully defined in terms of acceptable behaviors; role relations are defined independently of personal attributes of incumbents; and sometimes the work flow itself is clearly specified. Formalization is the organization's means to make behavior predictable by standardizing and regulating it. As Simon (1947: 100) cogently states, "Organizations and institutions permit stable expectations to be formed by each member of the group as to the behavior of the other members under specific conditions. Such stable expectations are an essential precondition to a rational consideration of the consequences of action in a social group."

Formalization also contributes to the rational functioning of the organization in a number of other important ways (Scott, 1992). It makes visible the structure of the organizational relationships; thus, formal structures can be modified by managers to improve performance. Management by objectives (MBO), planning, programming, and budgeting systems (PPBS), strategic planning, and performance evaluation and review techniques (PERT) are examples of technical tools used by managers to facilitate rational decision making. Formal structure also promotes discipline and decision making based on facts rather than emotional ties and feelings; in fact, formalization reduces to some extent both positive and negative feelings that members have toward each other. As Merton (1957: 100) observes, "Formality facilitates the interaction of the occupants of offices despite their (possibly hostile) private attitudes toward one another." Moreover, formalization renders the organization less dependent on particular individuals. The replacement of individuals is routinized so that appropriately trained individuals can be replaced with minimal disturbance. Even leadership and innovation needs are addressed by formalization. As Seldon Wolin (1960: 383) notes, "Organization, by simplifying and routinizing procedures, eliminates the need for surpassing talent. It is predicated on average human beings."

Advocates of the rational-systems perspective focus on the importance of goals and formal structure in determining organizational behavior. Taylor, Fayol, Gulick, and Urwick were early proponents of this perspective. Although Weber and Simon also emphasize the significance of formal structure and rationality in organizations, both were also concerned with the interplay between formal structure and the satisfaction of participants. Simon (1947: 148) claims, "No formal organization will operate effectively without an accompanying informal." And Weber's contribution to organizational analyses is noted aptly by Scott (1987: 72), "Although it is clearly possible to criticize and improve upon many specific aspects of Weber's formulation, he remains the acknowledged master of organization theory: the intellectual giant whose conceptions continue to shape definitions of the central elements of administrative systems, and whose historical and comparative vision continues to challenge and inform our more limited views of organizational forms." These ideas will be explored further in Chapter 3.

NATURAL SYSTEMS

The **natural-systems perspective** provides another view of organization that stands in contrast to the rational-systems perspective. The natural-systems perspective had its early roots in the human relations approach of the 1930s; it developed in large part as a reaction to the scientific managers and perceived inadequacies of the rational-systems model. While rational-systems proponents conceive of organizations as structural arrangements deliberately devised to achieve specific goals, natural–systems advocates view organizations as primarily social groups trying to adapt and survive in their particular situation. Natural-systems analysts generally agree that goal specificity and formalization are characteristics of organizations, but they argue that other attributes are of much greater significance; in fact, some maintain that formal goals and structure have little to do with what is actually happening in organizations (Scott, 1992; also see Etzioni, 1961; Perrow, 1978).

The natural-systems view focuses on similarities among social groups. Thus, organizations, like all social groups, are driven primarily by the basic goal of survival—not by specifically devised goals of particular institutions. Gouldner (1959: 405) captures the essence of the natural-systems approach when he states, "The organization, according to this model, strives to survive and to maintain its equilibrium, and this striving may persist even after its explicitly held goals have been successfully attained. This strain toward survival may even on occasion lead to the neglect or distortion of the organization's goals." Survival, then, is the overriding goal. Formal organizations are viewed not primarily as means for achieving specific ends but as ends in themselves.

Just as the natural-systems analysts generally disregard goals as important attributes of organizations, they also view as unimportant the formal structures constructed to achieve goals. While they acknowledge that formal structures do exist, behavior in organizations is regulated primarily by informal structures that emerge to transform the formal system. In this regard, Scott (1987) noted:

> Individual participants are never merely hired hands but bring along their heads and hearts: they enter into the organization with individually shaped ideas, expectations, and agendas, and they bring them differing values, interests, and abilities. . . . Participants within formal organizations generate informal norms and behavior patterns: status and power systems, communication networks, sociometric structures, and working arrangements. (p. 55)

In sum, goals and structure do not make organizations distinctive; in fact, formal features of organization are overshadowed by more generic attributes such as the desire for the system to survive and the characteristics of the individuals. While the rational-systems perspective stresses the importance of structure over individuals, the natural-systems approach emphasizes individuals over structure. In the stark terms of Warren G. Bennis (1959), the rational-systems focus is on "structure without people," while the clear reversal of priorities in the natural-systems model produces an orientation of "people without organization."

OPEN SYSTEMS

The **open-systems perspective** was a reaction to the unrealistic assumption that organizational behavior could be isolated from external forces. Competition, resources, and political pressures from the environment affect the internal workings of organizations. The open-systems model views organizations as not only influenced by environments but also dependent on them. At a general level, organizations are easily pictured as open systems. Organizations take inputs from the environment, transform them, and produce outputs (see Figure 2.1). For example, schools are social systems that take resources such as labor, students, and money from the environment and subject these inputs to an educational transformation process to produce literate and educated students and graduates.

The open-systems model has the potential to provide a synthesis (Etzioni, 1964)—a way of combining the rational and natural perspectives. Organizations are complex and dynamic. They have formal structures to achieve specified goals, but are composed of people who have their own idiosyncratic needs, interests, and beliefs that often conflict with organizational expectations. Thus, organizations have planned and unplanned features, rational and irrational characteristics, and formal and informal structures. In some organizations rational concerns dominate the relationships while natural, social relationships predominate in others; in fact, over time the relative emphasis on rational and natural concerns changes and these shifts in structure are associated with environmental conditions. In all organizations, however, both rational and natural elements coexist within a system that is open to its environment.

Some scholars argue that contemporary organizations are either open, natural systems or open, rational systems, which are adaptations to different kinds of environments (Lawrence and Lorsch, 1967). Our view is that schools are open systems confronted with both rational and natural constraints that change as the environmental forces change; to neglect either the rational or the natural elements is shortsighted. Open-systems theory is our general framework for exploring the conceptual foundations of educational administration in this text. Although many theories are discussed in our analyses, the open-systems perspective is the overarching framework that underscores four internal subsystems that interact to influence organizational behavior: the structural, cultural, individual, and political systems.

KEY PROPERTIES OF OPEN SYSTEMS

An open system is concerned with both structure and process; it is a dynamic system with both stability and flexibility, with both tight and loose structural relation-

FIGURE **2.1**

Open System with Feedback Loop

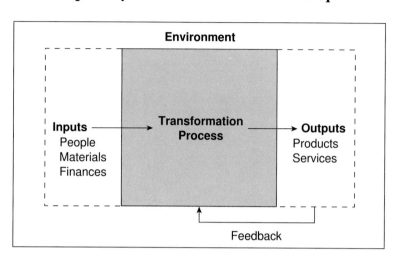

ships. The organization as an arrangement of roles and relationships is not static. To survive, the organization must adapt and to adapt, it must change. The interdependence of the organization and its environment is critical. Instead of neglecting the environment, as the rational-systems perspective does, or seeing it as hostile, as is the case with the natural-systems perspective, "the open-systems model stresses the reciprocal ties that bind and interrelate the organization with those elements that surround and penetrate it. Indeed, the environment is even seen to be the source of order itself" (Scott, 1987: 91).

There is some agreement about the key properties and processes that characterize most social systems. We begin by presenting, defining, and discussing nine central concepts.

INPUTS, TRANSFORMATION, AND OUTPUTS

An open system is a set of interacting elements that acquires **inputs** from the outside, transform them, and produce outputs for the environment. People, raw materials, information, and money are the typical inputs for organizations. In the **transformational process,** these inputs are changed into something of value called **outputs,** which are then exported back into the environment. Outputs are usually products and services, but they may also include employee satisfaction and other byproducts of the transformation process. Classrooms, books, computers, instructional materials, teachers, and students are critical inputs for schools. Ideally, students are transformed by the school system into educated graduates, who then contribute to the broader environment, or society. These three elements of an open system are illustrated in Figure 2.1.

FEEDBACK

The system's capacity for feedback facilitates the repetitive and cyclic pattern of "input-transformation-output." **Feedback** is information about the system that enables it to correct itself. Formal communication structures—PTA and various advisory councils—and informal political contacts are established inside and outside the school building to provide feedback to the school. Unlike mechanical systems, however, social systems do not always use the information to change. The superintendent of a school system who receives information about falling SAT scores and increased difficulties of graduates to get jobs and enter the colleges of their choice, can use this information to identify factors within the system that are contributing to the problem and take corrective action. Yet not all superintendents choose to act. Hence, although feedback provides self-correcting opportunities, the potential is not always realized.

BOUNDARIES

Systems have **boundaries**—that is, they are differentiated from their environments. The boundaries are less clear for open than for closed systems, but they do exist. Are parents part of the school system? It depends. In some schools they are considered part of the schools and in others they are not. Regardless of whether parents are considered to be inside the boundaries, schools expend substantial energy in boundary-spanning activities such as parent-teacher meetings, community service projects, and adult education programs.

ENVIRONMENT

The **environment** is anything outside the boundaries of the system that either affects the attributes of the internal components or is changed by the social system itself (see Chapter 7 for a detailed consideration of external environment). For a specific school, district policies, central administrators, other school buildings, and the community are important features of the school's environment. Although organizational environment is typically understood to refer to conditions external to the organization, the clear separation of the organization from its environment is virtually impossible when applied to open systems such as schools. Schools incorporate aspects of environment. Most of the techniques, skills, and knowledge are not invented by the school; they are brought within its boundaries and become part of the system. Likewise, beliefs, norms, rules, and understandings are not only "out there" but also are part of the organization. As Scott (1983: 16) cogently concludes, "Participants, clients, constituents all participate in and are carriers of culture. Thus institutional environments are notoriously invasive." In practice, however, some administrators attempt to control the openness of the school. For example, only appropriate clientele are allowed into the school building, people from the street are locked out, and visitors are required to sign in at the principal's office.

HOMEOSTASIS

The process by which a group of regulators acts to maintain a steady state among the system components is called **homeostasis.** A biological analogy illustrates the concept: when an organism moves from a warm environment to a cold one, homeostatic mechanisms trigger reactions to maintain body temperature. Similarly, in a school building, crucial elements and activities are protected so that overall stability is maintained. Systems that survive tend to move toward a steady state—equilibrium. This steady state, however, is not static. Energy from and to the environment is continuously imported and exported. Although any force that threatens to disrupt the system is countered by forces that seek to maintain the system, systems do exhibit a growth dynamic. Events that throw the system out of balance are addressed by actions that are calculated to move the system toward a new state of balance, or equilibrium. As administrators are well aware, disruptive stresses upset this equilibrium and create temporary periods of disequilibrium. A community group may demand that a course such as sex education be deleted. This causes disequilibrium, but the system either changes itself or neutralizes the disruptive forces impinging on it; that is, it restores equilibrium.

ENTROPY

The tendency for any system to run down—to cease to exist—is called **entropy.** Open systems can overcome entropy by importing energy from their environment. Organizations, for example, seek to maintain a favorable position with respect to their environments by adapting to changing environmental demands. A press from a state department of education for new programs typically results in accommodation to those demands, albeit with more taxes and resources for the system.

EQUIFINALITY

The principle of **equifinality** suggests that systems can reach the same end from different initial positions and through different paths. Thus, no one best way exists to organize and, likewise, there is no one best way to reach the same end. For instance, schools may select a variety of means (e.g., discovery learning, independent projects, interactive technologies) to achieve improvements in critical thinking skills of students.

SOCIAL SYSTEMS MODELS: BASIC ASSUMPTIONS

The notion of a **social system** is a general one. It can be applied to social organizations that are carefully and deliberately planned or to those that emerge spontaneously. The school is a system of social interaction; it is an organized whole comprising interacting personalities bound together in an organic relationship (Waller, 1932). As a social system, the school is characterized by an interdependence of parts, a clearly defined population, differentiation from its environment, a complex network of social relationships, and its own unique culture. As with all formal organizations, analysis of the school as a social system calls attention to both the planned and unplanned—the formal and informal—aspects of organizational life.

Thus far in our discussion of systems we have made several implicit assumptions. Let us now make these and others explicit as we examine the school as a social system. We have gleaned these assumptions from the literature, but the primary sources are Jacob W. Getzels and Egon G. Guba (1957); Getzels, James Lipham, and Ronald F. Campbell (1968); Charles E. Bidwell (1965), and W. Richard Scott (1992).

- Social systems are open systems. Schools are affected by the values of the community, by politics, and by history. In brief, they are affected by outside forces.

- Social systems are peopled. People act on the basis of their needs as well as their roles and statuses. In schools, people perform the roles of administrator, teacher, student, custodian, and so forth.

- Social systems consist of interdependent parts, characteristics, and activities that contribute to and receive from the whole. When one part is affected, a ripple goes through the social system. For example, when the principal is confronted by parental demands for new courses, not only is the principal affected directly but so are the teachers and students.

- Social systems are goal oriented. Indeed they often have multiple goals. In a school, student learning and control are just two of many goals. The central goal of any school system is the preparation of its students for adult roles.

- Social systems are structural. Different components are needed to perform specific functions and allocate resources. School systems are to some degree bureaucratic; they have division of labor, specialization, and hierarchy.

- Social systems are normative. Formal rules and regulations as well as informal norms prescribe appropriate behavior. Expectations are well known by all participants.

- Social systems are sanction bearing. The norms for behavior are enforced with reward and punishment. Formal mechanisms include expulsion, suspension, termination, tenure, and promotion. Informal sanctions include the use of sarcasm, ostracism, and ridicule.

- Social systems are political. Power relations inevitably enter into social relations in groups.

- Social systems are conceptual and relative. The social systems construct is a general one that applies to social organizations regardless of size. For one purpose, a classroom can be considered a social system. For other purposes, the school or school district may be taken as a social system.

- All formal organizations are social systems. But all social systems are not formal organizations.

These assumptions suggest that a school consists of a number of important elements or subsystems that affect organizational behavior.

ELEMENTS OF A SOCIAL SYSTEM

All social systems have some activities and functions that are accomplished in a fairly stable fashion. For example, if we conceive of society itself as a social system, then the routine and imperative functions of educating, protecting, and governing are performed by educational, legal, and governmental institutions. Regardless of the nature of the social system, patterns of behavior become regular and routine.

When the accomplishment of an objective requires collective effort, individuals often set up organizations specifically designed to coordinate the activities and to furnish incentives for others to join them in this purpose. Such an organization—explicitly established to achieve certain goals—is a **formal organization.** Our concern is with the school social system as a formal organization.

Figure 2.2 pictures the major elements, or subsystems, of a social system. Behavior in formal organizations is influenced not only by structural and individual elements but also by cultural and political elements. *Structure* is defined in terms of formal bureaucratic expectations, which are designed and organized to fulfill the goals of the organization. The *individual* is viewed in terms of the personal needs and cognitive understandings of work roles; the individual provides the energy and capacity to achieve the goals. *Culture* is the shared work orientations of participants; it gives the organization special identity. *Politics* is the system of informal power relations that emerge to resist other systems of control. Further, all the elements and interactions within the system are constrained by important forces from the *environment;* that is, the system is open. Finally, formal organizations as social systems must solve the basic problems of adaptation, goal achievement, integration, and latency if they are to survive and prosper.[1]

The model of formal organization that we are proposing takes all of these factors into consideration. We begin by examining internal elements of the system and then discuss the impact of the environment on the school and its outcomes.

STRUCTURE

Bureaucratic expectations are formal demands and obligations set by the organization; they are the key building blocks of organizational structure. **Bureaucratic roles** are defined by sets of expectations, which are combined into positions and offices in the organization. In schools, the positions of principal, teacher, and student are critical ones and each is defined in terms of a set of expectations. The bureaucratic expectations specify the appropriate behavior for a specific role or position. A teacher, for instance, has the obligation to plan learning experiences for students and has the duty to engage students in a pedagogically effective manner. Bureaucratic

FIGURE **2.2**

Internal Elements of the System

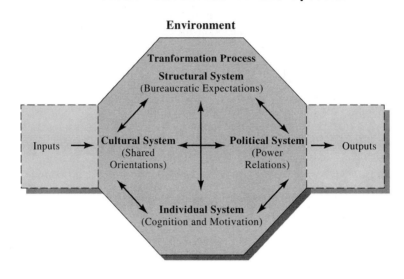

roles and expectations are the official blueprints for action, the organizational givens of the office.

Some formal expectations are critical and mandatory; others are more flexible. Many roles are not precisely prescribed; that is, the expectations associated with most positions are wide ranging. This range of freedom makes it feasible for teachers with quite different personalities to perform the same roles without undue tension or conflict (Parsons and Shils, 1951). Roles derive their meaning from other roles in the system and in this sense are complementary. For example, it is difficult, if not impossible, to define either the role of student or that of teacher in a school without specifying the relationship of teacher to student. Likewise, the role of principal is dependent on its relationship to the roles of teacher and student.

From a vast array of vague and contradictory expectations, formal organizations select a few general bureaucratic expectations that are reasonably consistent with the organization's goals. These expectations often are formalized, codified, and adopted as official rules and regulations of the organization; they may delineate such things as arrival times, building assignments, and job descriptions. Specialization— the expectation that employee behavior will be guided by expertise—complements the rules and regulations. Thus, a teacher is expected to behave in appropriate ways based on the school's rules and the expertise demanded by the instructional job.

Put simply, formal organizations such as schools have structures composed of bureaucratic expectations and roles, a hierarchy of offices and positions, rules and regulations, and specialization. Bureaucratic expectations define organizational roles;

roles are combined into positions and offices; and positions and offices are arranged into a formal hierarchy of authority according to their relative power and status. Rules and regulations are provided to guide decision making and enhance organizational rationality, and labor is divided as individuals specialize in tasks. Behavior in an organization is determined in part by this structural arrangement.

INDIVIDUAL

The fact that a social unit has been formally established does not mean that all activities and interactions of its members conform strictly to structural requirements— the official blueprint. Regardless of official positions and elaborate bureaucratic expectations, members have their own individual needs and cognitive understandings of their jobs.

Just as not all expectations are relevant for the analysis of organizational behavior, not all individual needs are relevant to organizational performance. What are those facets of the individual that are most instrumental in determining an individual's organizational behavior? We postulate two important cognitive aspects of the individual: motivational work needs and cognition. Work motivation constitutes the single most relevant set of needs for employees in formal organizations. We will elaborate extensively later, but for now **work needs** are defined as basic forces that motivate work behavior.

Cognition is the individual's use of mental representations to understand the job in terms of perception, knowledge, and expected behavior. Workers seek to create meaningful, coherent representations of their work regardless of its complexity. They learn what their job is about by monitoring and checking their own behavior. Their needs, personal beliefs, and previous experiences become the bases for constructing organizational reality and interpreting their work. Their motivation and cognition are influenced by such factors as beliefs about personal control and competence, individual goals, personal expectations for failure and success, and work motives. In brief, the salient aspects of the individual system are work needs and cognitive orientations to work; organizational behavior is in part a function of both.

Although we have examined the influence of structural *(S)* and individual *(I)* elements separately, behavior is a function *(f)* of the interaction of bureaucratic role expectations and the relevant work orientations of the organizational member [$B = f(S \times I)$]. For example, the evaluation of the teaching staff is affected by district policy as well as by the principal's own needs. The rules and regulations state that the principal is expected to evaluate each teacher at given intervals with a specified evaluation instrument. The principal acts as a result of this policy. Each principal's behavior differs in the evaluation meetings, perhaps because of individual cognition and motivational needs. One building administrator who has a great personal desire for social acceptance from the teachers may treat these sessions as an opportunity for friendly socializing rather than for evaluating. But another principal, lacking such a need for social acceptance, may follow the book and remain analytical in the evaluation. The two principals are affected by both elements, but the first is more influenced by individual needs and the second by bureaucratic role expectations.

FIGURE **2.3**

Interaction of Bureaucratic and Individual Elements Affecting Behavior

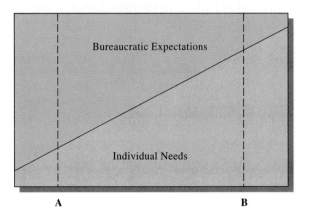

The ratio of bureaucratic expectations to individual work needs, which at least partly determines behavior, will vary with the specific type of organization, the specific job, and the specific person involved. Figure 2.3 presents pictorially the general nature of this interaction. Vertical line *A* represents a hypothetical situation in which the proportion of behavior controlled by the bureaucratic structure is relatively large, while line *B* (at the right) represents the situation in which behavior is primarily controlled by individual needs.

Military organizations commonly are considered to be represented by line *A*— more bureaucratic control—whereas research and development organizations are better represented by line *B*. Most schools probably fall between these two extremes. Free, open-concept, or Montessori schools would be close to line *B*. Church-related schools are typically thought to be closer to line *A*. Where do administrators and students fall in this regard? Individuals differ; some tend toward line *B*—free spirits—and some toward line *A*—bureaucrats. In our example of the two principals in evaluation sessions, the first with a high need for social acceptance would be near line *B* and the second closer to line *A*.

CULTURE

There is a dynamic relationship between bureaucratic role demands and individual work needs as people are brought together in the workplace. Organizations develop their own distinctive cultures. As organizational members interact, shared values, norms, beliefs, and ways of thinking emerge. These **shared orientations** form the culture of the organization. Culture distinguishes one organization from another and provides members with a sense of organizational identity (Hellriegel, Slocum, and Woodman, 1992; Daft, 1994). In a school, shared beliefs and informal norms among teachers have a significant impact on behavior. Culture provides members with a commitment to beliefs and values that go beyond themselves; they belong to a group that is larger than themselves. When the culture is strong, so is their identification with the group and the influence of the group.

Culture represents the unwritten, feeling part of the organization (Daft, 1994). Communication of feelings is easy among peers, especially friends. Shared orientations help maintain cohesiveness and feelings of personal integrity, self-respect, and belonging. Because many interactions in organizations are informal, they are personal and not dominated by authority. They furnish opportunities for the individual to maintain his or her personality against the attempts of the bureaucratic organization to submerge, if not destroy, it (Barnard, 1938). Members receive important rewards from the group and group norms are significant in guiding their behavior. For example, accepted informal procedures, not formal rules, may develop among the teachers for disciplining students; in fact, the custodial informal norms for controlling students become the criteria for judging "effective" teaching in many schools. Good control is equated with good teaching.

Behavior in formal organizations is influenced not only by structural and individual elements but also by emergent values and shared orientations of the work group. Organizational culture, with its important group norms, values, and beliefs, is another powerful force that affects organizational behavior.

POLITICS

Structure represents the formal dimension of the school social system while the personal aspect of the system is represented in the individual. Culture is the collective dimension of the system that blends the formal with the personal to create a system of shared beliefs. But it is the political dimension that spawns the informal power relations that emerge often to resist other systems of legitimate control. Members who work within the confines of the structure, culture, and individual systems usually contribute directly to the needs of the organization at large. Structure provides formal authority; culture generates informal authority; and the individual brings the authority of expertise to the organization. Politics, in contrast, is typically informal, often clandestine, and frequently illegitimate. It is illegitimate because it is behavior usually designed to benefit the individual or group at the expense of the organization. Consequently, politics is divisive and conflictual, pitting individuals and groups against each other and against the organization at large (Mintzberg, 1983a).

Politics, however, is an inevitable part of organizational life. There are always those who want to seize power for their own personal ends. In its extreme, one can conceive of an organization "as a mass of competing power groups, each seeking to influence policy in terms of its own interest, or, in terms of its own distorted image of the [organization's] interest" (Strauss, 1964: 164). **Power relations** get played out in a variety of ways: political tactics and games, bargaining, and conflict resolution. Members are invariably forced to play the power game of politics. Allison (1971: 168) puts it succinctly, "Power . . . is an elusive blend . . . of bargaining advantages, skill, and will in using bargaining advantages. . . . "Although politics is informal, divisive, and typically illegitimate, there is little doubt that it is an important force influencing organizational behavior.

To understand organizational life one must look at both formal and informal as well as legitimate and illegitimate forms of power. Hence, structure, individual, culture, and politics are critical elements of the social systems of all organizations. Behavior in a formal organization is a function of the interaction of these elements.

ENVIRONMENT

As a general definition, environment is everything that is outside the organization. But unlike physical systems, social systems are open; hence, the boundaries are much more ambiguous and the environment more intrusive. There is no doubt that environment is critical to the organizational functioning of schools. It is the system's source of energy. It provides resources, values, technology, demands, and history—all of which place constraints and opportunities on organizational action.

Which features of the environment are most salient for constraining behavior in schools? There is no quick or simple answer. Both broad and specific environmental factors influence the structure and activities of schools. Larger social, legal, economic, political, demographic, and technological trends have a potentially powerful impact on schools, but the effects of such general environmental forces are by no means clear. In contrast, interested constituencies and stakeholders, such as parents, taxpayers, unions, regulatory agencies, colleges and universities, state legislatures, accrediting agencies, and educational associations, have more immediate and direct effects on schools. But again the results are not certain.

The response of the school to environmental factors is conditioned by the degree of uncertainty, the degree of structure or organization, and the degree of scarcity in the environment. School decision makers monitor the environment for information, and their perceptions determine to a large degree the future directions of the organization. Schools, like all organizations, attempt to reduce uncertainty and control their environments; therefore, administrators often resort to strategies to minimize external effects. Moreover, if the groups and organizations of the environment are highly organized, then the school is faced with a potent set of demands and constraints, and the result will likely be compliance. Finally, schools compete in an environment made up of various resource pools. If resources of a particular kind are scarce, then the internal structure and activities will develop in ways that will facilitate their acquisition.

In brief, schools are open systems that are affected by external forces. Although there is basic agreement on the importance of the environment, its complexity makes analysis difficult. Nonetheless, we need to consider what factors individually and in relation to others create the basic external demands, constraints, and opportunities to which schools respond. We will return to a detailed analysis of the environment in Chapter 7.

OUTCOMES

A school, then, can be thought of as a set of elements—individual, structural, cultural, and political. However, behavior in organizations is not simply a function of its elements and environmental forces; it is a function of the interaction of the elements. Thus, organizational behavior is the result of the dynamic relationship among its elements. More specifically, behavior is a function of the interaction of structure, individual, culture, and politics as constrained by environment forces. To understand and predict the behavior in schools, it is useful to examine the six pairs of interactions among the elements in terms of their harmony. We posit a **congruence postulate:** other things being equal, the greater the degree of congruence among the elements of the system, the more effective the system.[2] For example, the more consistent the informal norms and the formal expectations, the more likely the organization will be to achieve its formal goals. Likewise, the better the fit between individual motivation and bureaucratic expectations, the more effective the performance. In Table 2.1, examples of critical questions concerning the congruence of each pair of key elements are outlined.

Performance outcomes are indicators of goal accomplishment. Performance outcomes include such indicators as achievement, job satisfaction, absenteeism, and overall performance quality. In any case, the critical aspects of behavior are defined by the outputs of the system. The model assumes that the effective achievement of these behavioral outcomes is a function of the degree of congruence among the system elements. Hence, **organizational effectiveness** is the degree to which actual outcomes are consistent with expected outcomes. The key elements, their interactions, the demands and constraints of the environment, and the behavioral outcomes are summarized in Figure 2.4.

TABLE **2.1** Congruence between Pairs of Key Elements			
Congruence Relationships			**Crucial Questions**
Individual	←→	Structural	To what extent do individual work needs enhance bureaucratic expectations?
Individual	←→	Culture	To what extent are shared orientations of organizational culture consistent with individual work needs?
Individual	←→	Politics	To what extent do power relations conflict with individual work needs?
Structural	←→	Cultural	To what extent do the bureaucratic expectations reinforce the shared orientations of the cultural system?
Structural	←→	Political	To what extent do the power relations undermine bureaucratic expectations?
Political	←→	Culture	To what extent do the power relations conflict with and undermine the shared orientations of the culture?

FIGURE **2.4**

Social System Model for Schools

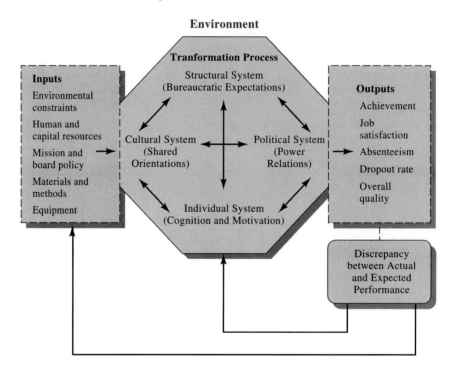

INTERNAL FEEDBACK LOOPS

The social-systems model pictured in Figure 2.4 also has both internal and external feedback mechanisms. For example, the formal school structure and the informal groups both attempt to influence individual behavior (Abbott, 1965b). Feedback informs individuals how the bureaucratic structure and the informal organization view their behavior. Although the bureaucracy has formal mechanisms and the work group informal ones, both have internal feedback loops.

The formal school organization provides an official definition of the position, its rank in the hierarchy, and a set of expected behaviors that go with it. In fact, the bureaucratic structure has an established incentive pattern for ensuring appropriate behavior. If the school bureaucracy approves of an individual's performance, positive rewards reinforce his or her behavior. If that person's behavior is evaluated as inferior, positive incentives are reduced and negative incentives are increased.

Informal groups similarly influence behavior. As our discussion of the Hawthorne studies in Chapter 1 explained, group norms control behavior. In the school building, norms exist within and among all informal peer groups. For example, teachers expect their peers to act appropriately to control students. If a teacher fails to maintain discipline in the classroom, the other teachers apply sanctions: sarcasm and ostracism in the teachers' lounge can have devastating effects on an individual.

EXTERNAL FEEDBACK LOOPS

Behavior in schools also is monitored through external feedback loops. The culture of the community provides environmental constraints that directly influence bureaucratic expectations, group norms, organizational goals, and indirectly influence individual needs. In spite of attempts by a school to isolate itself, it remains open to community, state, and national forces. The introduction of AIDS education into the school curriculum, for example, rarely goes unnoticed by the public. In fact, organized community groups provide important inputs about what they consider the goals and outcomes of an acceptable AIDS education program.

Social behavior in a school is thus affected directly by at least four internal elements, or subsystems—structure, individual, culture, and politics. Moreover, as Figure 2.4 illustrates, internal and external feedback reinforce appropriate organizational behavior. When there is a discrepancy between expected and actual outcomes, the feedback loops inform individuals and groups inside and outside the system.

The social-systems model gives a dynamic view of the school, with the feedback mechanisms and elements providing the action components. Good, bad, and neutral events occur constantly, and the dynamic nature of the system becomes even more evident when we consider the ways that students, teachers, and administrators affect one another's behavior. Systems analysis focuses on how the totality—elements and activities—produces a given result. The dynamic result is not predictable with complete accuracy because of the infinite variations that can occur as bureaucracy, subgroups, and individuals modify goals, express values, and exert power through leadership, decision making, and communication.

SUMMARY AND SUGGESTED READINGS

Social systems consist of bounded, purposeful, and mutually interacting elements. Regulated by feedback, such systems continuously attempt to maintain equilibrium. We have drawn upon the work of a number of organizational theorists to develop a model of the school as a social system. According to our model for schools, organizational behavior is determined by the interaction of at least four key elements—bureaucratic expectations, shared orientations, cognition and work needs, and power relations. Moreover, all the elements and interactions within the system are constrained by important demands from the environment as the organization seeks to achieve its goals. In addition, internal and external feedback mechanisms reinforce appropriate organizational behavior.

We believe a systems framework is useful for integrating theory, research, and practice in educational organizations. All behavior is part of an interconnected and complex social system. We need to stop seeing ourselves and our actions as separate; they are not. A systems perspective not only helps us organize our knowledge, it also emphasizes a way of thinking about interrelationships and connectedness. Peter Senge (1990) asserts that a systems perspective is a theoretical framework composed of a body of knowledge that has been developed over the past fifty years. Systems thinking makes the full patterns clearer and helps us see how to change them. We agree.

Our social-systems model calls attention to a number of important organizational concepts and processes. Contemporary theory and research are used to elaborate the components of the model: organizational structure, individual cognition and work motivation, internal climate and culture, politics, external environment, and effectiveness. In addition, key administrative processes are used to influence the interaction among these social system elements. Significant bodies of knowledge inform attempts to motivate, decide, communicate, and lead in school organizations. Each of the following chapters considers in substantial detail the major theoretical and research underpinnings of the social-systems model and its administrative processes.

All students should read two classic analyses of social systems: Getzels and Guba's (1957) treatment of the school as a social system and Katz and Kahn's (1966) pioneering development of open-systems theory. Senge's contemporary work, *The Fifth Dimension* (1990), is a popular and perceptive attempt to use systems thinking to build "learning organizations." A number of other organizational theorists have provided open-systems models of organizations that differ in detail from the model presented here (e.g., Nadler and Tushman, 1983, 1989; Harrison, 1987; Hanson, 1991). Scott's (1992) comprehensive treatment of systems perspectives is difficult, but worth the effort. Finally, Thomas Greenfield and Peter Ribbins (1993) provide a critical analysis of organizational theory in general and social-systems theory in particular.

NOTES

1. Our model is primarily a synthesis and extension of the work of Getzels and Guba (1957); Abbott (1965b); Leavitt, Dill, and Eyring (1973); Scott (1981, 1987); Mintzberg, (1983a); Nadler and Tushman (1983, 1989); Lipham (1988).

2. Many theoretical formulations have proposed such an assumption. For example, see Getzels and Guba (1957); Etzioni (1975); and Nadler and Tushman (1989).

KEY CONCEPTS AND IDEAS

Boundaries	Environment
Bureaucratic roles	Equifinality
Cognition	Feedback
Congruence postulate	Formal organization
Entropy	Formalization

Goal specificity

Homeostasis

Inputs

Natural-systems perspective

Open-systems perspective

Organizational effectiveness

Outputs

Power relations

Rational-systems perspective

Shared orientations (of culture)

Social system

Transformational process

Work needs

Structure in Schools

The educational system of a given society reflects that social system,
and at the same time it is the main force perpetuating it. It may be
perceived as the most powerful means of social control to which
individuals must submit, and as one of the most universal models
of social relationships to which they will refer later.

—Michael Crozier
The Bureaucratic Phenomenon

1. Five key organizational features define the classic Weberian bureaucracy: division of labor, impersonal orientation, hierarchy of authority, rules and regulations, and career orientation.

2. The Weberian model is criticized because of its dysfunctional consequences, neglect of the informal organization, internal inconsistencies, and gender bias.

3. Rules have both positive and negative consequences for organizational participants; administrators must consider both.

4. Bureaucratic and professional dimensions of organization combine to define four structural arrangements for schools: Weberian, authoritarian, professional, and chaotic.

5. There is no one best way to organize. Building effective structures demands matching the structure with its goals, environment, technology, people, and strategy.

6. Designing an effective organizational structure also involves balancing a host of countervailing forces created by the basic organizational dilemma of needing both order and freedom.

7. Organizations monitor and control work by mutual adjustment, direct supervision, standardization of work, standardization of outputs, and standardization of skills.

8. The key elements of structure are the strategic apex, middle line, operating core, support staff, and technostructure.

9. School structures vary widely. Some are simple structures; others are machine bureaucracies; a few are professional bureaucracies; most are hybrids, but for some, structure is irrelevant—they are politicized.

10. Structural elements can be tightly and loosely coupled; both arrangements have positive and negative consequences and both exist in schools.

11. A fundamental source of conflict for professionals working in organizations comes from the systems of social control used by bureaucracies and the professions.

12. Organizations accommodate to this conflict by establishing loose structures, developing dual authority structures, or engaging in socialization.

13. Individuals accommodate to this conflict by adopting a local orientation, a cosmopolitan orientation, or occasionally, a dual orientation.

The structural element of the school as social system is found in its formal organization. Max Weber's (1947) classic analysis of bureaucracy is a good beginning point for our discussion of the organizational structure in schools because it is the theoretical basis of most contemporary treatments (e.g., Blau and Scott, 1962; Hall, 1962; 1991; Perrow, 1986; Bolman and Deal, 1991; Scott, 1992).

WEBERIAN MODEL OF BUREAUCRACY

Almost all modern organizations, including schools, have the characteristics enumerated by Weber: a division of labor and specialization, an impersonal orientation, a hierarchy of authority, rules and regulations, and a career orientation.

DIVISION OF LABOR AND SPECIALIZATION

According to Weber, **division of labor** and **specialization** mean that "the regular activities required for the purposes of the bureaucratically governed structure are distributed in a fixed way as official duties" (Gerth and Mills, 1946: 196). Because the tasks in most organizations are too complex to be performed by a single individual, division of labor among positions improves efficiency. In schools, for example, division of labor is primarily for instructional purposes. Within that division, subspecialties are based on level—elementary and secondary—and subject—math, science, and so forth.

Efficiency increases because division of labor produces specialization, which in turn leads to employees who become knowledgeable and expert at performing their prescribed duties. Such division enables the organization to employ personnel on

47

the basis of technical qualifications. Hence, division of labor and specialization produce more expertise in school personnel.

IMPERSONAL ORIENTATION

Weber (1947: 331) argued that the working atmosphere of a bureaucracy should provide an **impersonal orientation,** "the dominance of a spirit of formalistic impersonality, 'sine ira et studio,' without hatred or passion, and hence without affection or enthusiasm." The bureaucratic employee is expected to make decisions based on facts, not feelings. Impersonality on the part of administrators and teachers assures equality of treatment and facilitates rationality.

HIERARCHY OF AUTHORITY

Offices are arranged vertically in bureaucracies; that is, "each lower office is under the control and supervision of a higher one (Weber, 1947: 330)," which produces a **hierarchy of authority.** This bureaucratic trait is made manifest in the organizational chart, with the superintendent at the top and assistants, directors, principals, teachers, and students at successively lower levels.

Hierarchy is perhaps the most pervasive characteristic in modern organizations. Almost without exception, large organizations develop a well-established system of superordination and subordination, which attempts to guarantee the disciplined compliance to directives from superiors that is necessary for implementing the various tasks and functions of an organization.

RULES AND REGULATIONS

Weber (1947: 330) asserts that every bureaucracy has a system of **rules and regulations,** a "consistent system of abstract rules which have normally been intentionally established. Furthermore, administration of law is held to consist in the application of these rules to particular cases." The system of rules covers the rights and duties inherent in each position and helps to coordinate activities in the hierarchy. It also provides continuity of operations when there are changes in personnel. Rules and regulations thus ensure uniformity and stability of employee action.

CAREER ORIENTATION

Since employment in a bureaucratic organization is based on technical qualifications, employees think of their work as a career. Whenever there is such a **career orientation,** Weber (1947: 334) maintains, "there is a system of promotion according to seniority, achievement, or both. Promotion is dependent on the judgment of superiors." To foster loyalty to the organization, individuals with special skills must be protected from arbitrary dismissal or denial of promotion. Employees are protected in the sense that superiors are encouraged to make dispassionate decisions. Bureaucracies also institutionalize protection through such deeds.

EFFICIENCY

To Weber (1947: 337), bureaucracy maximizes rational decision making and administrative efficiency: "Experience tends to universally show that the purely bureaucratic type of administrative organization . . . is, from a purely technical point of view, capable of attaining the highest degree of efficiency." Division of labor and specialization produce experts, and experts with an impersonal orientation make technically correct, rational decisions based on the facts. Once rational decisions have been made, the hierarchy of authority ensures disciplined compliance to directives and, along with rules and regulations, a well-coordinated system of implementation and uniformity and stability in the operation of the organization. Finally, a career orientation provides the incentive for employees to be loyal to the organization and to produce extra effort. These characteristics function to maximize administrative efficiency because committed experts make rational decisions that are executed and coordinated in a disciplined way.

IDEAL TYPE

Although Weber's conception of bureaucracy is an **ideal type** that may or may not be found in the real world, it does highlight or emphasize basic tendencies of actual organizations. Hence, as an ideal type, it is quite useful for analytic purposes. As Alvin Gouldner (1950) explains, the ideal type may serve as a guide to help us determine how a formal organization is bureaucratized. Some organizations will be more bureaucratically structured than others. A given organization can be more bureaucratized on one characteristic and less on another. The model, as a conceptual scheme, raises important questions about organizing different kinds of formal bureaucracies. For example, under what conditions are the dimensions of bureaucracy related in order to maximize efficiency? Under what conditions does such an arrangement hinder efficiency?

CRITICISMS OF THE WEBERIAN BUREAUCRATIC MODEL

The Weberian model of bureaucracy has been attacked on a number of fronts. First, Weber is criticized for not being attentive to the dysfunctional features of his formulation. Second, the model has been criticized for its neglect of the informal organization. Third, Weber does not deal with the potential internal contradictions among the elements in the model. Finally, feminists denounce the model as gender biased. We turn to an analysis of each of these criticisms.

FUNCTIONS AND DYSFUNCTIONS OF THE MODEL

Weber's model of bureaucracy is functional in that application of the principles can promote efficiency and goal attainment. There is, however, the possibility of dysfunctional, or negative consequences—a possibility to which Weber pays limited attention. Let us consider each of the above bureaucratic characteristics or principles in terms of both possible functions and dysfunctions.

Although division of labor and specialization can produce expertise, they also can produce boredom. The literature is replete with instances where such boredom leads to lower levels of productivity or to a search on the part of employees for ways to make their work life more interesting. The Hawthorne studies discussed in Chapter 1, particularly the Bank Wiring Observation Room studies, provide one example. Indeed, many highly bureaucratized organizations that have experienced the negative consequences of extreme division of labor are enlarging employee responsibility to alleviate boredom.

Impersonality may improve rationally in decision making, but it also may produce a rather sterile atmosphere in which people interact as "nonpersons," resulting in low morale. Low morale, in turn, frequently impairs organizational efficiency.

Hierarchy of authority does enhance coordination, but frequently at the expense of communication. Two of the major dysfunctions of hierarchy are distortion and blockage in communication. Every level in the hierarchy produces a potential communication block because subordinates are reluctant to communicate anything that might make them look bad in the eyes of their superiors; in fact, there is probably a tendency to communicate only those things that make them look good or those things that they think their superiors want to hear (Blau and Scott, 1962).

Rules and regulations, on the one hand, do provide for continuity, coordination, stability, and uniformity. On the other hand, they often produce organizational rigidity and goal displacement. Employees may become so rule oriented that they forget that the rules and regulations are means to achieve goals, not *ends* in themselves. Disciplined compliance with the hierarchy, and particularly with the regulations, frequently produces rigidity and an inability to adjust. Such formalism may be exaggerated until conformity interferes with goal achievement. In such a case, the infamous characteristic of bureaucratic red tape is vividly apparent (Merton, 1957).

Career orientation is healthy insofar as it produces a sense of employee loyalty and motivates employees to maximize effort. Promotion, however, is based on seniority and achievement, which are not necessarily compatible. For example, rapid promotion of high achievers often produces discontent among the loyal, hard-working, senior employees who are not as creative.

The potential dysfunctional consequences of each bureaucratic characteristic are not adequately addressed in Weber's ideal type. Table 3.1 summarizes some of the dysfunctions as well as the functions of the Weberian model. The question now becomes: Under what conditions does each characteristic lead to functional but not dysfunctional consequences? Whatever the answer to this question, the model remains quite useful as both an analytical tool and a guide to scientific research.

FUNCTIONS AND DYSFUNCTIONS OF RULES

To illustrate the analytic and research usefulness of the model, we focus on Gouldner's (1954) discussion of organizational rules. Almost without exception, large, formal organizations have systems of rules and regulations that guide organizational

TABLE **3.1** Functions and Dysfunctions of the Weberian Model		
Bureaucratic Characteristic	**Dysfunction**	**Function**
Division of Labor	Boredom	Expertise
Impersonal Orientation	Lack of morale	Rationality
Hierarchy of Authority	Communication blocks	Disciplined compliance and coordination
Rules and Regulations	Rigidity and goal displacement	Continuity and uniformity
Career Orientation	Conflict between achievement and seniority	Incentive

behavior. For example, most school districts have elaborate policy manuals. Rules are so universally present because they serve important functions.

Organizational rules have an explication function—that is, they explain in rather concise and explicit terms the specific obligations of subordinates. Rules make it unnecessary to repeat a routine order; moreover, they are less ambiguous and more carefully thought out than the hasty verbal command. Rules act as a system of communication to direct role performance.

A second function of rules is to screen—that is, to act as a buffer between the administrator and his or her subordinates. Rules carry a sense of egalitarianism because they can be applied equally to everyone. An administrator's denial of a request from a subordinate can be on the grounds that the rules apply to everyone, superior and subordinate alike, and cannot be broken. Subordinate anger is therefore redirected to the impersonal rules and regulations. As Gouldner (1954) explains, rules impersonally support a claim to authority without forcing the leader to legitimize personal superiority; conversely, they permit a subordinate to accept directives without betraying his or her sense of being any person's equal.

Organizational rules may also legitimize punishment. When subordinates are given explicit prior warning about what behavior will provoke sanctions and about the nature of those sanctions, punishment is legitimate. As Gouldner (1954) indicates, there is a deep-rooted feeling in our culture that punishment is permissible only when the offender knows in advance that certain behaviors are forbidden; ex post facto judgments are not permissible. In effect, rules not only legitimize but impersonalize the administration of punishment.

Rules also serve a bargaining, or "leeway," function. Using formal rules as a bargaining tool, superiors can secure informal cooperation from subordinates. By *not* enforcing certain rules and regulations, one's sphere of authority can be expanded through the development of goodwill among subordinates. Rules are serviceable because they create something that can be given up as well as given use.

For each functional consequence of rules discussed thus far, a corresponding dysfunctional outcome results. Rules reinforce and preserve apathy by explicating the minimum level of acceptable behavior. Some employees remain apathetic because they know how little is required for them to remain secure. When apathy is fused with hostility, the scene is set for "organizational sabotage," which occurs when conforming to the letter of the rule violates the express purpose of the rule (Gouldner, 1954).

Although rules screen the superior from subordinates, that protection may become dysfunctional. **Goal displacement** develops; the means, in this case rules, become ends in themselves. By using rules to make important decisions, administrators may focus attention on the importance of a rule orientation, often at the expense of more important goals.

Another dysfunctional consequence that emerges from the screening and punishment functions of rules is legalism. When rules and punishments are pervasive, subordinates can adopt an extremely legalistic stance. In effect, they become "Philadelphia lawyers," willing and potentially able to win their case on a technicality. In its extreme form, employees may use legalism as an excuse for inactivity in any area not covered by a rule. When an individual is asked why he or she is not performing a reasonable task, the pat answer is "no rule says I have to." To say the least, such extreme legalism creates an unhealthy climate in schools.

The leeway function of rules—not enforcing them in exchange for informal cooperation—involves the ever-present danger of being too lenient. The classic example of this kind of permissiveness is seen in the indulgency pattern described in Gouldner's study of a factory in which few, if any, rules were enforced; although superior-subordinate relations were friendly, productivity suffered. The functions and dysfunctions of rules are summarized in Table 3.2.

School administrators who are aware can avoid the dysfunctional consequences of rules, but the path is not easy. For example, by taking advantage of the screening function of bureaucratic rules, administrators can gain and maintain some control over organizational activities. They anticipate that general and impersonal rules will be "good" because they provide direction without creating status distinctions. Control is thus maintained by using bureaucratic rules. Use of bureaucratic rules, however, may produce unanticipated consequences. Because bureaucratic rules provide knowledge about minimum acceptable standards (explication function), an unanticipated consequence may be that minimums become maximums (apathy-preserving and goal-displacement dysfunctions), and the difference between actual behavior and

TABLE **3.2** **The Double-Edged Nature of Bureaucratic Rules**

Functions		Dysfunctions
Explication	⟵———————————⟶	Apathy reinforcement
Screening	⟵———————————⟶	Goal displacement
Punishment-legitimizing	⟵———————————⟶	Legalism
Leeway	⟵———————————⟶	Indulgency

expected behavior for goal achievement becomes visible and unacceptable, thereby prompting close supervision. In brief, because the equilibrium originally sought by instituting the bureaucratic rules is upset, the demand for more control is created.

Thus, although rules are used to mitigate some tensions, they may create others. As a matter of fact, rules may actually perpetuate the tensions that they were meant to dispel. For example, close supervision can produce high visibility of power relations and a high degree of interpersonal tension; yet the use of rules to reduce tension may unintentionally perpetuate the need for additional close supervision; hence, the cycle begins again. The major problems of low motivation and minimal role performance simply are not solved by more rules.[1]

Educational administrators must learn how to anticipate and avoid the negative consequences of bureaucratic rules. They must ask: How can the functional consequences of rules be maximized and the dysfunctional consequences minimized? Gouldner's (1954) research provides some guidelines. He maintains that rules having a punishment-centered pattern are most likely to evoke negative consequences. **Punishment-centered rules** are initiated by either workers or administrators, but not jointly, to coerce the other group to comply; and they result in punishment of one group by the other when the rules are violated, producing tension and conflict.

On the other hand, **representative rules** are initiated and supported by both workers and administrators; they are enforced by the administration and obeyed by the workers; and they result in educational programs where rules are violated because violation is interpreted as a lack of information. Representative rules are least likely to evoke dysfunctional consequences because they have been jointly initiated and are generally supported by the parties concerned. Therefore, representative rules, as contrasted with punishment-centered rules, are more likely to have the desired functional consequences without many of the unintended dysfunctional consequences.

NEGLECT OF THE INFORMAL ORGANIZATION

The Weberian model of organization also has been criticized for its omission of the informal structure. **Informal organization** is a system of interpersonal relations that forms spontaneously within all formal organizations. It is a system that is not included in the organizational chart or official blueprint. It is the natural ordering and structuring that evolves from the needs of participants as they interact in their workplace. It contains structural, normative, and behavioral dimensions; that is, it includes informal structure, informal norms, and informal patterns of leadership (Scott, 1992). Teachers, administrators, and students within schools inevitably generate their own informal systems of status and power networks, communication, and working arrangements and structures.

The Development of Informal Organization

As people interact in organizations, networks of informal relations emerge that have important effects on behavior. Official as well as unofficial roles, norms, values, and leaders all shape individual behavior. Informal relations comprise patterns of such social interactions as communicating, cooperating, and competing. When individuals find themselves together in formal organizations, informal interaction inevitably occurs. People talk to each other about personal and social issues. As a consequence, some individuals are liked, others disliked. Typically, people seek continued interactions with those they like and avoid interactions with those they dislike. These informal social exchanges produce differences in social relations among group members and, importantly, define the informal status structure of the group.

A member's status in the group, therefore, depends upon the frequency, duration, and character of interaction patterns with others, and the extent to which the individual is respected by others in the group. Consequently, some group members are actively sought out while others are avoided; some are admired, others are not; some are leaders, others are followers; and most are integrated as members of a group, although a few are isolated.

The informal interactions produce subgroups; cliques develop within the group structure, some of which have more status, power, and significance than others. Clique membership provides status in the larger group through the prestige of the subgroup. In brief, the differential patterns of interactions among individuals and groups, and the status structure defined by them, define the social structure of the informal organization.

In addition to the social structure, a normative orientation emerges that serves a guide for behavior. As individuals engage in social interaction, common conceptions of desirable and acceptable behavior occur. Common values arise to define ideal states of affairs, and social norms develop that prescribe what individuals should do under different situations and the consequences of deviations from those expectations. Norms contain two important features: a general agreement about appropriate behavior and mechanisms to enforce expectations. The distinction between norms and values is sometimes a fuzzy one, but generally values define the ends of human behavior, and social norms provide the legitimate and explicit means for pursuing those ends (Blau and Scott, 1962). Finally, and in addition to the general values and norms which are shared and expected to integrate the group, sets of expectations are differentiated according to the role or status position of the individual in the group. The role of "task master" is quite different from the role of "group comedian"; the role of leader is quite different from the role of follower. In brief, the main components of informal organization are the social structure and normative orientation of the group.

A Hypothetical Illustration in Schools

Imagine the situation of a new school, where the superintendent hires a new principal who in turn hires an entire new staff of teachers, none of whom know each other. At the beginning of the year, we simply have a collection of individuals bound together by the formal requirements of the school and their jobs. The professional staff, however, will quickly become more than the sum of the individuals composing it. Behavior will not only be determined by the formal expectations of the school but also by the informal organization that spontaneously emerges as the participants interact.

As school begins, faculty and staff begin to work together, attend meetings, eat together, socialize in the faculty lounge, and plan school activities. Teacher relations will, in part, be determined by the physical features of the school, such as a faculty lounge, a faculty lunch room, the library, and the arrangement of the classrooms; the technical aspects of the job—for example, department structure, team teaching, and extracurricular responsibilities; and social factors such as the leadership styles of the superintendent and principals. The initial relations of teachers in a school can be examined in terms of formal activities and interactions. Teachers have a need to keep their jobs, and a formal system has been established to achieve school objectives. This formal organization comprises a hierarchy of authority, division of labor, formal rules and regulations, impersonality, and a formal communication structure, developed and implemented to achieve school goals.

A number of consequences follow from the establishment of the initial, formal relations. New sentiments develop that are different from the work-motivated ones that brought teachers together in the first place. The new sentiments are ones of liking and disliking other teachers and groups within the school. Some of the teachers will become well liked and respected; their colleagues will frequently ask them for advice and seek them out. Such sentiments and behavior serve as the basis for an informal ranking of individuals and groups. Moreover, new informal activities will develop, some of which are a direct reaction to the formal organization. For example, the inability of faculty to influence policy through the formal structure may result in informal activities, conversations, and initiatives. New patterns of interaction will elaborate themselves in the school—for example, association in cliques, informal webs of communication, discipline networks centering on informal leadership, and a status structure among groups of teachers. Some informal groups will become more prestigious and powerful than others.

In addition to the informal social structure that develops, a system of informal shared values and beliefs will emerge—the normative orientation. The faculty will define ideal and appropriate behavior. Their ideal, for example, may be a school characterized by hard work, mastery of the basics, an academic orientation, and positive student-teacher relations. To this end, norms emerge to guide teacher behavior: few hall passes will be issued; substantial and meaningful homework assignments will be made; orderly and industrious classrooms will be maintained; and extra help for students will be readily available. If teachers violate these norms, they lose the respect of their colleagues, and social sanctions will be applied. They may find themselves disparaged and isolated by their colleagues. Teachers will also assume specific informal roles; an unofficial teacher spokesperson may serve as a powerful liaison with the principal; another teacher may provide a strong critical voice of school policy in faculty meetings; still another teacher may organize social activities for the faculty; and there may be the teacher who always offers comic relief, especially when events are tense.

The informal organization, then, arises from the formal organization and then reacts to it. The development of group norms, the division into cliques, and the ranking of individuals and subgroups are conditioned directly by the formal structure and indirectly by the school environment. Hence, we can begin with the formal system of the school and argue that the informal is continually emerging from the formal and continually influencing the formal. The formal and informal systems go

FIGURE **3.1**

Elements of the Formal and Informal Organization

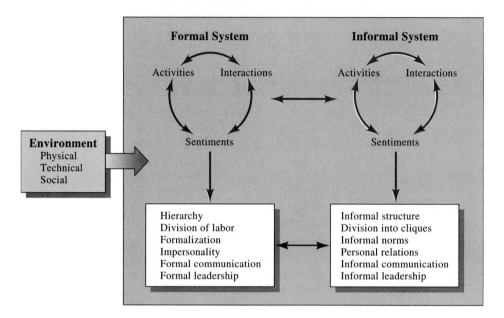

together; after all, there is only one organization. Yet the distinction is useful because it calls attention to the dynamic nature of organizational life in schools and to the continuous processes of elaboration, differentiation, and feedback in schools. The dynamic character of the informal organization as well as its interplay with the formal organization are summarized in Figure 3.1.

The impact of the informal on the formal organization can be constructive or destructive. For example, the Bank Wiring Room Study (see Chapter 1) showed that the informal organization restricted production. Evidence also exists, however, that the informal organization can be a constructive force in efficient operation of bureaucratic organizations as well as a mechanism for change. In Chester Barnard's (1938) classic theoretic analysis of organizations, he argued that informal organizations have at least three crucial functions: as effective vehicles of communication, as a means of developing cohesion, and as devices for protecting the integrity of the individual.

Formal communications systems in organizations such as schools are typically insufficient and are inevitably supplemented by informal ones; in fact, informal communication systems, so-called grapevines, exist in all organizations regardless of how elaborate the formal communications system (Iannaconne, 1962; Hoy and Forsyth, 1986; Robbins, 1991) and are used constructively in effective organizations (Peters and Waterman, 1982). The informal structure provides a channel for circumventing formally prescribed rules and procedures. Many pressing problems emerge for which efficient solutions or communications are not possible within the formal framework; hence, the informal structure assumes added importance. Official communications must be routed through the "chain of command," which often is a long-drawn-out process. Frequently, circumventing the official communication channel through the grapevine appears to be precisely what is necessary for solving crucial problems (Page, 1946; Peters and Waterman, 1982). The knowledgeable and flexible administrator uses the grapevine, thus avoiding the bureaucratic frustration of those who only play it by the book. As a communication vehicle, the grapevine often provides efficient machinery. Indeed, generally speaking, the informal organization is an important device for implementing many important organizational objectives.

Informal organization also can promote cohesion. Patterns of social relationships usually emphasize friendliness, cooperation, and preservation of the group. Informal groups emerge spontaneously and are built on shared interests and friendships. They arise from such simple events as common classroom areas, liking certain colleagues, shared lunch hours, car pools, same planning periods, and other fortuitous activities. Such situations and the accompanying social relationships can provide the social cement that binds faculty by promoting an atmosphere of cordiality and friendliness that is potent enough to cause members to feel that they belong to the group; cohesion and solidarity are the by-products of informal groups (Boyan, 1951; Robbins, 1991).

The informal organization functions to maintain a sense of personal integrity, self-respect, and independence for individuals (Barnard, 1938). Unlike the formal, the informal is not dominated by hierarchy, impersonality, and formal authority. Rather, the informal is an outgrowth of the individual and personal needs of members. It is a means by which teachers can maintain their individual personalities in spite of organizational demands that invariably attempt to depersonalize individuals (Hoy and Forsyth, 1986).

The informal organization exists. It is not an enemy to be eliminated or suppressed; on the contrary, it can be a useful vehicle for improving efficiency. It is irrational to administer a formal organization, such as a school, according to the purely technical criteria of rationality and formality because that ignores the nonrational aspects of informal organization (Blau, 1956). From a theoretical perspective, our position is that administrative practice is enhanced by using both the formal (rational) and the informal (nonrational) components of schools.

DUAL STRUCTURE OF THE BUREAUCRATIC MODEL

Another frequent criticism of the Weberian model is the internal contradictions among certain bureaucratic principles of organization. According to Weber, all characteristics of his ideal type are logically consistent and interact for maximum organizational efficiency; however, both theoretical and empirical analyses indicate that things are not so smooth and integrated in the real world of organizational functioning.

Talcott Parsons (1947) and Gouldner (1954) question whether the guiding principle of bureaucracy is authority based on technical competence and knowledge or authority based on legal powers and discipline. Weber (1947: 339) maintains that "bureaucratic administration means fundamentally the exercise of control on the basis of knowledge." On the other hand, he writes, "The content of discipline is the consistently rationalized, methodically trained and exact execution of the received order, in which all personal criticism is unconditionally suspended and the actor is unswervingly and exclusively set for carrying out the command" (Gerth and Mills, 1946: 196). Hence, Weber is proposing the central importance of discipline as well as expertise. Is bureaucratic administration based primarily on expertise, or is it based on disciplined compliance with directives? Unless one assumes that there will be no conflict between authority based on "technical competence and expertise" and that based on "incumbency in a hierarchical position," the seed of contradiction and conflict rests within these two authority bases that are integral to the Weberian model. In fact, Gouldner (1954) and Constas (1958) suggest that Weber may have been implicitly describing not one but two types of bureaucracy, a conclusion supported by a number of empirical studies (Stinchcombe, 1959; Udy, 1959).

Similarly, Blau and Scott's (1962) analysis of the dual nature of the Weberian model also led them to conclude that Weber failed to distinguish bureaucratic from professional principles. They similarly maintain that bureaucratic discipline and professional expertise are alternative methods for coping with uncertainty. Discipline reduces the scope of uncertainty, while expertise provides the knowledge to handle uncertainty. The crux of the problem seems to be that professionals are often employees of bureaucratic organizations; hence, these alternative modes of rationality are frequently mixed, producing strain and conflict. A typical example is the school principal. Does his or her authority reside in the bureaucratic office or in professional expertise? Obviously, a mixture is present and seems to result in some degree of strife.

A FEMINIST CRITIQUE OF BUREAUCRACY

Feminists are often critical of bureaucratic organizations in fundamental ways that go far beyond the common accusation that qualified women in modern organizations do not receive equal treatment or compensation (Scott, 1992). Joanne Martin (1990b), for example, argues that in spite of Weber's analysis of the central features of bureaucracy being gender neutral and universal in his description of administration based on expertise, women are disadvantaged. The emphasis on full-time commitment and extensive training as qualifications for job holding hinders women who routinely confront the conflicting demands of job and family responsibilities. Not only do women often lack equal access to training programs but discussions of bureaucracy frequently overlook the interdependence of job and family responsibilities, treating work as public and masculine and family as private and feminine (Bose, Feldberg, and Sokoloff, 1987; Martin, 1990a). Hence, bureaucracies are gender biased not only in their *application* of appointment and promotion criteria but also in their *selection* of the criteria (Scott, 1992).

Feminists also argue that bureaucratic structures perpetuate systems of male domination. Ferguson (1984), for one, argues that bureaucracy with its patent emphasis on authority, rules, regulations, and rationality, recreates paternalistic domination. Bureaucratic structures give priority to masculine virtues and values. Scott (1992: 325) explains, "The principles by which organizations are structured—inequality, hierarchy, impersonality—devalue alternative modes of organizing that are alleged to be more characteristic of women's values: equalitarian and personalized associations." In the same vein, Ferguson (1984) argues that bureaucratic control invades social life by "feminizing" participants—that is, by making them nonassertive and dependent; in fact, women are bound to supportive roles by structures that see feminine characteristics as subordinate and masculine ones as dominate. Male characteristics of independence, rationality, and competitiveness are dominant instrumental features of bureaucracy while the more feminine features of dependence, emotionality, and cooperation are subordinate properties of organizations. The hallmarks of achievement—competition and independence—are quite different from the nurturant expressive behaviors of the feminine style (Gilligan, 1982; Ferguson, 1984). In fact, the feminine side is often repressed and devalued by bureaucracies creating an oppression of women. Bureaucracies are not caring institutions, but reproducers of patriarchy and reinforcers of patterns of domination (Clark et al., 1994).

Feminist critics also challenge the bureaucratic notion that superior domination though hierarchical patterns of authority is essential to achievement of important goals; in fact, they argue that hierarchy is typically restrictive of the growth of the group and individual members (Denhardt and Perkins, 1976). Moreover, the usual defense of the hierarchical division of labor as a structural device to develop expertise and improve efficiency is seen largely as a guise to conceal the control function of hierarchy. Invariably all workers, but especially women, are isolated, alienated, and depersonalized as communications are mystified and the dominance of bureaucratic control is disguised. Radical feminists make it clear that they are committed to an **antibureaucratic structure:** groups are decentralized; personal, face-to-face relations are substituted for impersonal rules and regulations; relationships are egalitarian not hierarchical; and skills and information are to be shared, not hoarded (Ferguson, 1984).

FORMAL STRUCTURE IN SCHOOLS

Schools are formal organizations with many of the same characteristics as bureaucratic organizations. Max Abbott (1965a: 45), for example, using the characteristics of the Weberian model developed earlier in this chapter, has concluded: "The school organization as we know it today . . . can accurately be described as a highly developed bureaucracy. As such, it exhibits many of the characteristics and employs many of the strategies of the military, industrial, and governmental agencies with which it might be compared." The bureaucratic model is the one that many school administrators adopt, and this may explain why the model can be used to analyze behavior in schools (Abbott, 1965a; Miles, 1965; Firestone and Herriott, 1981; Abbott and Caracheo, 1988; Corwin and Borman, 1988).

A basic assumption of bureaucracies is that every subordinate has less technical expertise than his or her superior. This assumption certainly does not apply in schools, nor does it apply in other professional organizations. On the contrary, professionals often have more competence and technical expertise than the administrators who occupy a higher level in the organization. Consequently, to find strain and tension in schools between teachers and administrators should not be surprising.

Rather than thinking of schools as bureaucratic or nonbureaucratic, a more useful approach is to examine the degree of bureaucratization with respect to the important components of the Weberian model. Such an approach differentiates types of organizational structures and also provides a tool to test empirically the extent to which the theoretical components of the model are consistent. Richard H. Hall (1962, 1987, 1991), Lee Bolman and Terrence Deal (1991), and Henry Mintzberg (1979, 1989) are among the theorists and researchers who have systematically examined structure.

HALL ON BUREAUCRATIC STRUCTURE

One of the earliest systematic attempts to measure bureaucratization is Hall's (1962) development of an organizational inventory to measure six central characteristics of bureaucratic structure: (1) hierarchy of authority, (2) specialization, (3) rules for incumbents (i.e., those assuming an organizational role), (4) procedure specifications, (5) impersonality, and (6) technical competence. D. A. MacKay (1964) subsequently adapted and modified the organizational inventory in his study of the bureaucratization of schools. He measured bureaucratic patterns in schools using the school organizational inventory (SOI), a questionnaire that operationalizes the same six dimensions of structure.

The interrelationships of these bureaucratic characteristics of schools also have been explored empirically (Kolesar, 1967; Isherwood and Hoy, 1973; Abbott and Caracheo, 1988). Studies indicate that there are two relatively distinct patterns of rational organization rather than one completely integrated bureaucratic pattern. Hierarchy of authority, rules for incumbents, procedural specifications, and impersonality tend to vary together, and specialization and technical competence similarly vary together; however, the two groups are found to be independent of or inversely related to each other.

Organizational Types

In the school, as in other kinds of organizations, the components of Weber's ideal type do not necessarily form an inherently connected set of variables; instead, there are likely to be distinct types of rational organization. These results are summarized in Table 3.3.

In Table 3.3 we have labeled the first set of characteristics "bureaucratic" and the second set "professional." The distinction once again calls attention both to the potential conflict between authority based on technical competence and expertise and that based on holding an office in a hierarchy and to the potential incompati-

TABLE **3.3**	Two Types of Rational Organization in the School Setting
Organizational Characteristics	**Organizational Patterns**
Hierarchy of authority	Bureaucratic
Rules for incumbents	
Procedural specifications	
Impersonality	
Technical competence	Professional
Specialization	

bility between professionalization and bureaucratization. To lump together the bureaucratic and professional patterns in a single model of bureaucracy seems to obscure important differences among schools. Indeed, separating two patterns of rational organization and administration makes it possible to explore combinations of the two patterns. For example, if each pattern is dichotomized, as shown in Figure 3.2, then four types of organizations are possible.

A Weberian school structure is one in which professionalization and bureaucratization are complementary; both are high. This pattern is similar to the ideal type described by Weber, hence we call it a **Weberian structure.**

An **authoritarian structure** emphasizes bureaucratic authority at the expense of professional consideration. Authority is based on position and hierarchy. Disciplined compliance to the rules, regulations, and directives is the basic principle of operation. Power is concentrated and flows from top to bottom. Rules and procedures are impersonally applied. The superior always has the last say. Furthermore, promotions to administrative positions typically go to those who have been loyal to the organization and to their superiors. In many respects, this authoritarian structure is similar to the one Gouldner (1954) described as a punishment-centered bureaucracy.

FIGURE **3.2**

Typology of School Organizational Structure

		Professional Pattern	
		High	Low
Bureaucratic Pattern	High	Weberian	Authoritarian
	Low	Professional	Chaotic

A **professional structure** is one in which substantial decision making is delegated to the professional staff. Members of the staff are viewed as professionals who have the expertise and competence to make important organizational decisions. Rules and procedures serve as guides rather than as strict formats to be applied uniformly. Special cases are likely to be the rule rather than the exception. Teachers have much power in the organizational decision-making process. In brief, decisions are made by those who have the knowledge and expertise to make them. We refer to this type of school structure as professional.

Finally, a **chaotic structure** has a low degree of bureaucratization and professionalization, therefore confusion and conflict typify day-to-day operations. Inconsistency, contradiction, and ineffectiveness are likely to pervade the chaotic structure. Invariably, strong pressures will arise to move toward one of the other structural types.

This typology presents four potential school structures that are quite different and probably have different consequences for teachers and students alike. Henry Kolesar (1967), for example, found that a sense of student powerlessness was significantly higher in authoritarian than in professional school structures. Geoffrey Isherwood and Wayne K. Hoy (1973) uncovered the same finding for teachers in the two types of schools. Overall, the sense of powerlessness among teachers was much greater in authoritarian than in professional structures. But organizationally and socially oriented teachers (those who identify themselves with the values and goals of the organization and of family and friends, respectively) had less of a sense of powerlessness in the authoritarian structure than professionally oriented teachers. Apparently, individual work orientation mediates the relationship between organizational structure and alienation. Teachers with an organizational orientation may not be alienated by authoritarian structures and procedures and indeed may be quite content. Gerald H. Moellar and W. W. Charters' (1966) finding that teachers in highly bureaucratic systems had more sense of power than those in less bureaucratic systems lends support to this speculation.

It is also true that the type of school organizational structure may influence student achievement. Research (MacKay, 1964; B. Anderson, 1971; MacKinnon and Brown, 1994) suggests the possibility that highly bureaucratic structures may have negative effects on student achievement and innovation. Finally, the evidence continues to mount that specialization (professional pattern) and centralization (bureaucratic pattern) are mildly, but negatively related (Hage, 1980; Corwin and Herriott, 1988; Hall, 1991).[2]

Changing School Structures

The classification of school structures into these four structural types seems useful; in fact, the typology can serve as a basis for a theory of school development. Chaotic structures are ineffective and candidates for swift action. Boards of education will be under great pressure from both within and without to bring order to the existing chaos. The typical response is to get "new leadership." The new leadership invariably turns to starkly bureaucratic and authoritarian procedures to gain order. That is, it seems likely that chaotic structures will move to authoritarian ones.

Authoritarian structures are mechanistic. Power and authority rest almost exclusively in a tightly coupled organizational structure; administrators engage in unilateral decision making and teachers are expected to comply with their directives without question. Relations are typically formal, impersonal, and vertical. A single set of clear, formal goals buttressed by bureaucratic authority guide organizational behavior. Instruction is coordinated by administrative enforcement of schedules, rules, and procedures. Expected conflict is moderate—lower than that found in chaotic structures, but higher than that found in Weberian and professional structures. School effectiveness is predicted to be moderate, provided the environment is supportive, stable, and simple.

The next logical step in an evolutionary development of school structure is toward a Weberian configuration. Here the forces of centralization and specialization are balanced. The bureaucratic attributes of hierarchy, rules, procedures, and impersonality complement the technical competence and specialization of teachers. Administrators and teachers share in decision making, with both groups focused on common interests and with both committed to a single set of shared goals. Conflict between teachers and administrators is limited, yet the couplings between organizational parts are moderately tight. In brief, there is an integration of formal and informal properties. School effectiveness is predicted to be high, and such a structure should function most effectively in a simple and stable environment.

Most individuals prefer order to chaos; hence, movement from a chaotic structure to an authoritarian one is relatively straightforward. The challenge, however, of moving an authoritarian school structure to a Weberian one is much more difficult. Our own experience and research (Isherwood and Hoy, 1973; Firestone and Herriott, 1982; Hoy, Blazovsky, and Newland, 1983; Abbott and Carecheo, 1988) suggest that many schools remain basically authoritarian; they do not readily evolve into Weberian structures. Nonetheless, we expect to see pressures for movement toward Weberian and professional structures as the reform in education presses for teacher empowerment (Casner-Lotto, 1988; Maeroff, 1988; Sickler, 1988; Goldring and Chen, 1992), school-based management (Sirotnik and Clark, 1988; Malen, Ogawa, and Kranz, 1990; Malen and Ogawa, 1992), decentralization (Brown, 1990; Hill and Bonan, 1991; Bimber, 1993), and a general restructuring of schools (Cohen, 1987; Elmore, 1988; David, Purkey, and White, 1989; Clune and White, 1990).

As the occupation of teaching becomes more fully professionalized, a few school structures may evolve from Weberian to professional structures. The professional structure is loose, fluid, and informal. Teacher professionals control decision making; indeed, teacher groups are the dominant source of power. Administrators are subordinate to teachers in the sense that their primary role is to serve teachers and facilitate the teaching-learning process. The burden for integrating the activities of the school rests with the teacher professionals. Professional structures are complex organizations with a highly professional staff, multiple sets of goals, high teacher autonomy, and horizontal rather than vertical relations. Ultimately, the effectiveness of such organizations depends almost exclusively on the expertise, commitment, and service of the teachers. Professional organizations have the potential for high effectiveness in a stable and complex environment.

TABLE 3.4	Types of School Structures and Their Properties			
Organizational Property	Chaotic Structure	Authoritarian Structure	Weberian Structure	Professional Structure
Integrating Principle	None	Formal goals and bureaucratic authority	Bureaucratic authority and professional authority	Professional authority
Goals	Irrelevant	A single set of clear, formal goals	A single set of clear, shared goals	Multiple sets of goals
Dominant Source of Power	Political	Bureaucratic	Bureaucratic and professional	Professional
Decision-making Process	Nonrational and individualistic	Top-down and rational	Shared and rational problem solving	Horizontal-rational and incremental
Coordination of Instruction	None	Administrative enforcement of rules and schedule	Professional standardization of instruction	Standardization of training
Expected Level of Conflict	High	Moderate	Limited	Low
Coupling	Loose	Tight	Moderately tight	Loose
Predicted Effectiveness	Low	Moderate	High	High
Expected Environment	Dynamic and hostile	Simple and stable	Simple and stable	Complex and stable

We have proposed a model of school development in which schools move progressively from chaotic to authoritarian to Weberian to professional structures. There is nothing inevitable about the evolution; in fact, we suspect it will be difficult for schools to become professional structures or even Weberian structures in the near future. Moreover, it is likely that many school structures will slip back to chaos as the environment becomes turbulent. Remember also that the four types of structures are ideal types; most schools are variations on these four themes. Nonetheless, the framework should be useful to administrators and students of school organizations as they analyze and attempt to change their own school structures and empower teachers. In Table 3.4 we have summarized the characteristics of each of these school structures and predicted some the likely outcomes.

BOLMAN AND DEAL ON STRUCTURE

Bolman and Deal (1991) develop a structural perspective based on the following set of assumptions:

- Organizations are established primarily to achieve specific goals.

- Organizational structure can be designed to fit its special set of circumstances—that is, to match its goals, environment, technology, people, and strategy.

- Organizations are most effective when environmental turbulence and personal preferences are constrained by the forces of rationality; structure focuses individuals on their jobs rather than their individual preferences.

- Specialization promotes individual expertise and consequently better performance.

- Coordination and control are necessary for effectiveness. Depending on the task, coordination can be achieved through informal communication, formalization of work, standardization of outcomes, direct control, or standardization of training.

- Organizational problems frequently occur because of inappropriate structures and systems; such problems can be overcome through restructuring and developing more responsive systems.

These assumptions assume that organizations can control their environment as they rationally pursue their explicit goals. But rationality requires a high degree of certainty, predictability, and efficiency. Consequently, organizations spend a significant amount of time and energy trying to control their environments. In fact, Galbraith (1973) argues that uncertainty is the prime force in determining the structure of an organization. To cope with uncertainty, organizations either reduce their need for information or increase their capacity to process information.

Organizations divide work by creating specialized roles, positions, and units. They combine these elements into a unified whole by linking together vertical and horizontal elements of the organization. The right structure—one that is adaptable, efficient, and effective—is constrained in large part by the organization's goals, strategies, technology, and environment. In general, organizations operating in relatively simple and stable environments are most likely to employ simple and centralized structures. But as the environment becomes turbulent and unpredictable, structures are likely to become more complex and flexible.

Creating a good structure in organizations is a persistent dilemma; indeed, there is no one best way to organize. Bolman and Deal (1991) summarize a set of critical issues and dilemmas that all organizations struggle with as they try to find the right structure:

- *Differentiation versus integration:* The classic problem of the need to divide the work and the need to coordinate it

- *Gaps versus overlaps:* Ensuring that critical functions are built into the structure while limiting needless redundancies and wasted effort

- *Underuse versus overload:* Distributing load so that individuals have neither too little nor too much work

- *Clarity versus creativity:* Making role expectations clear without promoting rigidity and undermining creativity
- *Autonomy versus interdependence:* Providing workers with independence while fostering collaboration and teamwork
- *Loose versus tight coupling:* Creating a system of rules and coordinating procedures that bind the organization together without holding it back
- *Centralization versus decentralization:* The problem of distributing power and delegating authority
- *Goalless versus goal-bound:* Clearly communicating current goals while avoiding old, irrelevant ones
- *Irresponsible versus unresponsive:* The problem of responding to clients' needs in a responsible fashion
- *Conformity versus overconformity:* Ensuring that workers conform to their roles without creating overconcern for strict adherence to rules and regulations

All organizations must grapple with these structural dilemmas if they are to become efficient and effective. We turn to Mintzberg's general analysis of structural configurations and then to configurations most likely found in schools.

MINTZBERG ON STRUCTURE

Henry Mintzberg (1979; 1980; 1981; 1983 a, b; 1989) provides another, more comprehensive conceptual framework for examining organizational structure. He describes structure simply as the ways in which an organization divides its labor into tasks and then achieves coordination among them. Five basic **coordinating mechanisms** are the fundamental means organizations use to monitor and control work: mutual adjustment, direct supervision, standardization of work processes, standardization of outputs, and standardization of worker skills. These mechanisms glue the organization together.

Coordinating Mechanisms

Mutual adjustment is coordination through the simple process of informal communication. Workers coordinate their efforts by informal discussion and adjustment. Mutual adjustment is direct and basic; it is necessary not only in the simplest organization but also in the most complicated.

Direct supervision is coordination through personal command. One individual has the responsibility for monitoring and controlling the work of others. As the size of an organization increases, the more likely it is that mutual adjustment will become less effective and direct supervision more necessary. As work activities become more and more complicated, however, neither mutual adjustment nor direct supervision is sufficient. Hence, the work is standardized; coordination of parts is achieved by incorporating them in a carefully planned program for the work. There are three basic ways to obtain standardization in organizations: standardize the work processes, the outputs, or the skills.

Standardization of work is achieved by specifying or programming the contents of the work. The written directions to develop a lesson plan are an example. The process of developing the plan is described carefully in step-by-step directions.

Standardization of output is attained by specifying the results of the work; the fundamental dimensions of the product or of the performance are enumerated. Taxicab drivers, for example, are not usually given a route; they are merely told the destination. Similarly, teachers may simply be told that the student should be able to perform at a basic level in a given area; the means to achieve that level may be left to the teacher. The outcomes of the work are described carefully and employees are expected to achieve the standard.

Standardization of skills is a coordination mechanism that provides indirect control of work. Here skills and knowledge are standardized by specifying the kind of training required to do the work. Training supplies workers with patterns of work to be performed as well as the bases of coordination. Mintzberg observes that when an anesthesiologist and a surgeon meet in the operating room, typically little communication occurs; by virtue of their respective training, each knows precisely what to expect. Their standardized skills provide most of the coordination.

Key Parts

Although most organizations of any size use all five means of coordination, each organization specializes in one, a fact that has important consequences for the basic structure of the organization. Mintzberg also identifies five key parts of the organization (see Figure 3.3). These are the significant aspects of the structure, each with a critical function to perform.

The **operating core** comprises those who perform the basic work—activities directly related to the production of products and services. The core is the heart of the organization; it produces the essential output. In schools, teachers are the operating core and teaching and learning are the outcomes.

The administrative component of the organization has three parts. First, the **strategic apex** consists of the top administrators (superintendent and assistants) who are charged with the responsibility of ensuring that the organization effectively serves its mission. Those administrators below, who connect the apex with the operating core through the formal authority structure, constitute the **middle line.** In school systems, principals are the middle managers. Any organization that relies primarily on direct supervision for control and coordination is bound to have a large middle line. The **technostructure** is the administrative component charged with the responsibility of planning. It is composed of analysts who standardize the work of others and apply their analytic techniques to help the organization adapt to its environment. These analysts design, plan, and train, but they do not directly manage. Curriculum coordinators and instructional supervisors are often members of the school technostructure; their role is to help teachers design and plan instruction and to provide in-service opportunities for professional growth and development.

FIGURE **3.3**

The Five Basic Parts of Organizations

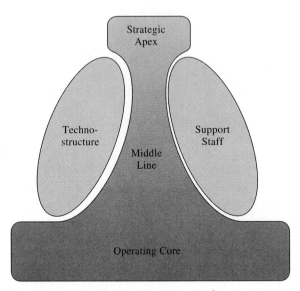

Source: Henry Mintzberg, The Structuring of Organizations
(Englewood Cliffs, NJ: Prentice-Hall, 1979), p. 20.

Finally, a fifth component—the **support staff**—is composed of specialized units that exist to provide support for the organizations outside the operating work flow. In schools, for example, we find a building and grounds department, a maintenance department, a cafeteria, and a payroll department. None of these units is part of the operating core, but each exists to provide indirect support for the school.

These five key parts of the organization and the five coordination mechanisms that hold them together serve as the basis for five configurations.

- *Simple structure:* The strategic apex is the key part and direct supervision is the central coordinating device.

- *Machine bureaucracy:* The technostructure is the key part and standardization of work processes is the central coordinating device.

- *Professional bureaucracy:* The operating core is the key part and standardization of skills is the central coordinating device.

- *Divisionalized form:* The middle line is the key part and standardization of outputs is the central coordinating device.

- *Adhocracy:* The support staff is the key part and mutual adjustment is the central coordinating device.[3]

Our discussion will focus on the forms most likely to be found in schools.

FIGURE **3.4**

Configurations of School Structure

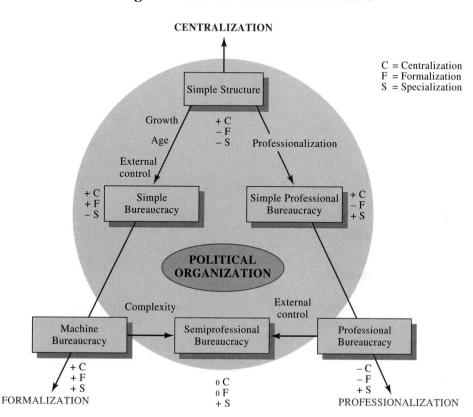

CENTRALIZATION

C = Centralization
F = Formalization
S = Specialization

Simple Structure

Growth

Age

+ C
– F
– S

External
control

Professionalization

+ C
+ F
– S

Simple
Bureaucracy

Simple Professional
Bureaucracy

+ C
– F
+ S

**POLITICAL
ORGANIZATION**

Complexity

External
control

Machine
Bureaucracy

Semiprofessional
Bureaucracy

Professional
Bureaucracy

+ C
+ F
+ S

FORMALIZATION

0 C
0 F
+ S

– C
– F
+ S

PROFESSIONALIZATION

Mintzberg's Perspective Applied to Schools

The configurations that Mintzberg describes are abstract ideals, yet these simplifications of more complex structures do come to life in the analysis of schools.
Schools experience the basic forces that underlay these configurations: the pull to
centralize by top management, the pull to formalize by the technostructure, and the
pull to professionalize by teachers.[4] Where one pull dominates, then the school will
likely be organized close to one of the configurations we have discussed (see Figure
3.4). One pull, however, does not always dominate and the basic processes may have
to coexist in balance. Highly professional teachers may have their efforts tightly
directed by a dynamic administrator as in a simple professional bureaucracy.
Although such an arrangement may work well over the short run, it leads to conflict
between the administration and teachers. We turn to structural configurations
expected in most schools.

SIMPLE STRUCTURE An organization that is coordinated by a high degree of direct supervision, that has a small strategic apex with virtually no middle line, and that is highly centralized is a **simple structure.** In such an organization there is little elaboration—little technostructure, little support staff, little division of labor and specialization, and a small administrative hierarchy.

Since power over important decisions tends to be centralized in the hands of the top administrator, the strategic apex is the key part of the organization. Standardization in a simple structure is unnecessary because things are worked out as they arise; there are loose, informal working relations among participants. Thus, communication flows informally, but most of it is between the top administrator and everyone else. The name tells it all—the structure is simple.

New organizations usually begin simply and elaborate their administrative structures as they grow. Many small organizations, however, retain a simple structure. Informal communications remain effective and coordination is attended to by a one-person strategic apex. There are variants of the simple structure. For example, the *autocratic organization* is a simple structure where the top administrator hoards power and rules by fiat; and the *charismatic organization* is a variant where the leader has the same power not because it is hoarded but because the followers lavish it upon the leader. The major strength of the simple structure is its flexibility; only one person must act.

The simple structure is of interest because many schools, particularly small elementary school districts, have such a structure. They are administered by autocratic and sometimes charismatic principals who rule with an iron hand. Although some teachers enjoy working in a small, intimate school, where its charismatic principal leads the way, others perceive the simple structure as highly restrictive and autocratic. Such structures are highly dependent upon the expertise, imagination, and energy of the chief executive. As the executive goes, so goes the organization. These are highly centralized structures with the top administrator making all major decisions and formal authority flows in one direction—top down. Schools with simple structures face especially difficult problems in executive succession and as growth renders direct supervision inadequate. A simple structure can be relatively enduring or only a phase in the development and maturing of an organization. Organizational structures that rely on any form of standardization for coordination are defined by Mintzberg (1979, 1989) as bureaucratic. Of the common school configurations derived from Mintzberg's formulation, the simple structure is the only one that is nonbureaucratic; its structure is organic.

MACHINE BUREAUCRACY An organization that is fine-tuned and standardized to run as an integrated, regulated machine is called a **machine bureaucracy.** The work processes in this kind of structure are routine and standard. Indeed, standardization of work is the prime coordinating mechanism and the technostructure is the key part of the structure because it contains the analysts who do the standardizing. In these organizations, a high degree of centralization is supported by considerable formalization: rules and regulations permeate the structure; formal communication *predominates* at all levels; and decision making follows the hierarchical chain of authority.

This is the Weberian structure of bureaucracy—standardized responsibilities, technical qualifications, formal communication channels, rules and regulations, and hierarchy of authority. It is a structure geared for precision, speed, unambiguity, continuity, unity, subordination, and efficiency. Machine bureaucracy is obsessed with control; a control mentality develops from top to bottom. As Mintzberg (1979: 321) cogently notes, "The problem in the Machine Bureaucracy is not to develop an open atmosphere where people can talk the conflicts out, but to enforce a closed, tightly controlled one where the work can get done despite them."

Considerable power rests with the administrators of the strategic apex; in fact, the only others to share much power with the top administrators are the analysts of the technostructure because their role is standardizing the work processes of the organization. Machine structures work best when the work is routine—that is, when an integrated set of simple, repetitive, tasks must be performed precisely and consistently by people (Mintzberg, 1979).

A few schools or school districts are machine bureaucracies; they are usually large districts where an elaborate technostructure attempts to standardize the work or in states with elaborate statewide technostructures. Behavior is formalized by an extensive set of rules, procedures, and job descriptions. Moreover, power tends to be highly centralized in the apex of the structure; authority flows downward. Although many schools have the trappings, most are not machine bureaucracies in the pure sense because typically they lack an elaborate administrative structure, a large middle line, and an elaborate technostructure. In fact, the structure of many public schools is a cross between the simple structure and the machine bureaucracy—what Mintzberg calls a simple bureaucracy.

PROFESSIONAL BUREAUCRACY Bureaucratic structure can be defined in terms of "the extent to which behavior is predetermined or predictable, in effect, standardized" (Mintzberg, 1979: 86). Thus, organizations can be bureaucratic without being centralized. A **professional bureaucracy** is a structure that permits both decentralization and standardization at the same time. These organizations use standardization of skills as the prime coordinating mechanism; the operating core is the key organizational part; and professionalization is the crucial process. All such structures rely on the skills and knowledge of their operating professionals to function effectively.

The professional bureaucracy receives its coordination indirectly by relying on the standardization of skills that professionals have acquired in their training; hence, it is not surprising to find relationships in these organizations to be much more loosely coupled than in machine or simple bureaucracies. Professionals are hired and given considerable control over their own work. Many professionals work relatively independently of their colleagues, but closely with their clients. For example, teacher autonomy seems undeniable in some schools. Teachers work alone in their classrooms, are relatively unobserved by colleagues and superiors, and possess broad discretionary authority over their students (Bidwell, 1965). This structural looseness of the school supports a professional basis of organization; however, the demand for uniformity in product, the need for movement of students from grade to grade and school to school in an orderly process, and the long period over which students are schooled require a standardization of activities and hence, a bureaucratic basis of school organization (Mintzberg, 1979).

The administrative structure of the professional bureaucracy is relatively flat. It does not need an elaborate hierarchy to control and coordinate or a technostructure to design work standards. Professionals control themselves and, in a sense, develop their own work standards. The standards of the professional bureaucracy originate largely from outside its structure, in self-governing associations to which the professionals belong. These associations set general standards that are taught by the universities and used by all organizations of the profession. As we have noted before, two sources generate organizational authority. Machine and simple bureaucracies rely on the authority of the position or office, and professional bureaucracies are built on the authority of knowledge and expertise.

Professional bureaucracy is decentralized; a great deal of power rests with the professionals in the operating core. The work is too complex to be supervised directly by managers or standardized by analysts; hence, professionals have a great deal to say about what they do and how they do it. Professionals have close working relations with clients and loose ones with colleagues. It makes more sense to think in terms of a personal strategy for each professional rather than an integrated organizational strategy. Some schools have the characteristics of the professional bureaucracy—a skilled operating core, standardized work skills, professional norms and autonomy, professional associations, structural looseness, and a flat administrative structure. Such schools are staffed by highly competent and well-trained teachers who control their own work and who seek collective control over decisions that affect them.

We have suggested that some small elementary schools are simple structures; they are centralized, but informal structures. The chief administrator provides strong (often autocratic) direction in an informal atmosphere unfettered with rules and regulations. A few schools are machine bureaucracies; they are usually found in large districts where an elaborate technostructure attempts to standardize the work or in states with elaborate statewide technostructures. Behavior is formalized by an extensive set of rules, procedures, and job descriptions. Moreover, power tends to be highly centralized in the apex of the structure; authority flows downward. A few schools are also professional bureaucracies. They are staffed by highly competent and well-trained teachers who control their own work. The structure is decentralized and democratic among the professionals. Although some schools fit into one of these three configurations, most schools are hybrid variants of the three "ideal types" that have been described.

SIMPLE BUREAUCRACY The **simple bureaucracy** has the basic characteristics of both a simple structure and a machine bureaucracy: it is highly centralized and highly bureaucratic, but it has a relatively flat administrative structure. Nonetheless, control remains a major obsession, hence such organizations are confronted by most of the dysfunctional characteristics of bureaucracy already discussed in our analysis of the Weberian model. As long as control, accountability, standardized educational outcomes, and inexpensive services are demanded by society for schools, simple bureaucratic structures will be a common configuration for schools.

Although there is high centralization and formalization in simple bureaucracies, there is limited specialization. Firestone and Herriott (1981, 1982) refer to such school structures as rational bureaucracies, and their research suggests that a large number of elementary schools, perhaps most, are simple bureaucracies in which a single set of agreed-upon goals guides internal behavior. The power and authority of the principal is dominant. Instruction and curriculum are standardized and teachers are supervised directly by the principal. Teachers' activities are for the most part controlled by the principal and coordinated by an elaborate system of fixed rules, standard procedures, and administrative schedules.

SIMPLE PROFESSIONAL BUREAUCRACY Another hybrid variant, the **simple professional bureaucracy,** is more common in secondary than elementary schools. This variant is a combination of the simple structure and the professional bureaucracy. Centralization is high, but so is specialization. Here highly trained teacher-professionals practicing standard teaching skills often take the lead from a strong principal. The formal authority of the principal, however, is complemented by the professional authority of teachers; in fact, principals maintain their effective use of power only as long as the teachers perceive their interests and the interests of their students effectively being served. Teachers and administrator share goals, and the goodwill and cooperation of teachers is essential, as the principal provides strong direction and leadership. In this configuration the school is like a symphony orchestra; it is staffed with skilled teachers who teach a standardized curriculum under the watchful eye of a strong professional and sometimes dictatorial principal. The principal is the person with recognized ability to guide the professional enterprise.

SEMIPROFESSIONAL BUREAUCRACY Another variation of organizational structure sometimes found in schools is a blend of the machine and the professional bureaucracy. The structure of a **semiprofessional bureaucracy** is not as centralized or formalized as the machine bureaucracy nor is it as loose as the professional bureaucracy. Although some aspects of the curriculum and instruction are standardized, teacher professionals go about the business of teaching in a reasonably autonomous fashion. Within broad constraints, teachers have the freedom to set their own instructional goals, and although principals have substantial authority in these structures, it is shared with teachers. Delegation and shared decision making are not uncommon. The complexity of learning and teaching and the demands of the school public for accountability are countervailing forces that promote this configuration. This structure promotes professionalism within a context of moderate structure and is sometimes the configuration found in secondary schools staffed with a highly competent faculty and administrators who are committed to the professional development of their school.

POLITICAL ORGANIZATION The **political organization** has to do with power, not structure. Politics is usually overlaid on all conventional organizations, but at times it becomes so powerful that it creates its own configuration. In effect, it captures the organization and becomes its dominating process. In such situations, power is exercised in illegitimate ways. There is no primary method of coordination, no single dominant part of the organization, no clear form of decentralization; everything depends on informal power and politics, marshaled to win individual issues (Mintzberg, 1989).

When power becomes so pervasive that it dominates, coordination as well as the formal structure become irrelevant; in fact, politics acts to the detriment of coordination by producing disorder. Negotiation, coalition formation, and political games are the keys to understanding life in such structures. Indeed, political activity is a substitute for the legitimate systems of influence found in conventional configurations. Power and politics will be discussed in detail in Chapter 6.

Conflict is usually high in the political organization; thus, there is pressure for negotiation and alliance formation. The political organization, however, is a dysfunctional configuration for schools because it hinders learning and teaching. Too much energy and activity are diverted to game playing, negotiations, and political machinations. Teaching and learning become secondary considerations. Schools are politicized from time to time and occasionally develop into political organizations, but such structures in schools are usually short-lived because of their ineffectiveness.

The six conventional configurations and their key properties are summarized in Table 3.5. Together they provide another theoretical perspective for examining organizational structure of schools and for planning change. Our own long-term predilection for schools is for the professional model, but the evidence (Firestone and Herriott, 1981, 1982; Hoy, Blazovsky, and Newland, 1983) suggests that most schools are not professional organizations. Moreover, it is unlikely that schools will move dramatically to the configuration that Mintzberg calls a professional bureaucracy; however, movement toward simple professional and semiprofessional organizations not only seems possible but highly desirable, especially if schools and teaching are to become more fully professional.

A number of elements in the situation influence the particular configuration of schools. For instance, the age and size of a school are likely to influence its structure. As schools age and grow, informal relations and direct supervision are likely to be replaced by formalization and bureaucratic control. When the technical system is defined as complex (that is, teaching viewed as a complex process requiring individualization and multiple and changing strategies), then a highly professional workforce is needed and decentralization of decision making is required. When, on the other hand, the technical system is defined as routine (that is, teaching is viewed as a routine process of providing standard and simple minimum skills), then the technical system can be regulated through bureaucratic procedures. Moreover, the more organizations are controlled externally, the more centralized and bureaucratic they tend to become. Mintzberg argues that the two most effective means to control an organization from the outside are to hold its most powerful decision maker responsible and to impose specific standards, usually in the form of rules and regulations.

As school districts are increasingly faced with demands for accountability, minimum basic skills, tests for graduation, and myriad other performance targets from state departments of education, the pulls are for more formalization, more centralization, less professionalization, and a more well-developed state technostructure to regulate and control schools. On the other hand, school reformers continue to

TABLE 3.5 School Structures and Their Properties

Organizational Property	Simple Structure	Simple Bureaucracy	Machine Bureaucracy	Simple-Professional Bureaucracy	Semiprofessional Bureaucracy	Professional Bureaucracy	Political Organization
Structure							
Centralization	High	High	High	High	Moderate	Low	Irrelevant
Formalization	Low	High	High	Low	Moderate	Low	Irrelevant
Specialization	Low	Low	High	High	High	High	Irrelevant
Key Part	Apex	Apex and technostructure	Technostructure	Apex and core	Technostructure and core	Operating core	None
Integrating Principle	Formal authority	Formal goals and formal authority	Formal goals	Formal authority and professional authority	Professional authority	Professional authority	Informal power and exchange
Goals	Leader's goal	A single set of clear, formal goals	A single set of clear, formal goals	A single set of clear, shared goals	Multiple sets of goals	Multiple sets of goals	Competing goals among groups and alliances
Dominant Source of Power	Chief administrator	Administrators	Administrators	Administrators and teachers	Teachers and administrators	Teachers	Informal coalitions and alliances among teachers and administrators
Coordination of Instruction	Direct supervision	Direct supervision and standardization of instruction	Standardization of instruction	Direct supervision and standardization of skills	Standardization of skills; standardization of instruction	Standardization of skills	None
Expected Conflict	Low	Limited	Moderate	Moderate	Limited	Low	High
Coupling	Loose	Tight	Tight	Moderately tight	Moderately loose	Loose	Loose
Possible Example	Elementary school	Elementary school	Large urban district	Secondary school	Secondary school	University	Uncommon

lament the negative impact of bureaucratic control and call for redesigning school structures to make them more hospitable to competent and skilled teachers (Darling-Hammond, 1985; Darling-Hammond and Wise, 1985; McNeil, 1986, 1988a, 1988b; Elmore, 1988; Wise, 1988; Prestine, 1991); here the pull is for less formalization, more decentralization, and increased professionalization.

LOOSE COUPLING PERSPECTIVE

A body of theory and research challenges some of the notions of the school as a bureaucratic structure. Investigators are questioning rationalistic assumptions about the relationship of structure and process to organizational goals. Terrence E. Deal and Lynn E. Celotti (1980) argue that the formal organization and the administration of the school do not significantly affect methods of classroom instruction. In similar fashion, James G. March and Johan P. Olsen (1976) refer to educational organizations as "organized anarchies." Karl E. Weick (1976) and Howard E. Aldrich (1979) propose that elements or subsystems in organizations are often tied together loosely and argue that educational institutions are good examples of loosely coupled systems. Finally, John Meyer and associates (Meyer and Rowan, 1977, 1978; Meyer et al., 1978; Rowan, 1982; Meyer and Scott, 1983) propose an institutional explanation to describe loose coupling in schools as they assert that bureaucratic structure and instruction are disconnected (see Chapter 7). In brief, schools are seen as organizations with ambiguous goals, unclear technologies, fluid participation, uncoordinated activities, loosely connected structural elements, and a structure that has little effect on outcomes. Analyses such as these are of the **loose coupling perspective** and are useful additions to standard bureaucratic theory.

More than three decades ago Charles Bidwell (1965) analyzed structural looseness in school organizations. He noted that in order to deal with the problem of variability in student abilities on a day-to-day basis, teachers need to have freedom to make professional judgments. Professional autonomy seems undeniable in schools. Teachers work alone in their classrooms, are relatively unobserved by colleagues and administrators, and possess broad discretionary authority over their students. The result is a structural looseness *within* the school. Similarly, structural looseness exists *among* the school units in the system. Administrators and teachers of each school enjoy broad discretionary powers with respect to curriculum, teaching methods, and teacher selection. For example, even though the system recruits teachers, they typically are not assigned to a particular school without the principal's approval.

The structural looseness of the school supports a professional basis of organization; however, the demand for uniformity in product, the need for movement of students from grade to grade and school to school in an orderly process, and the long period of time over which students are schooled require a routinization of activities and, hence, a bureaucratic basis of school organization. Bidwell (1965), therefore, depicts the school as a distinctive combination of bureaucracy and structural looseness.

Loose coupling theorists (Weick, 1976; Aldrich, 1979) and institutional theorists (Meyer, 1978; Meyer and Rowan, 1977, 1978; Rowan, 1982) focus on the disconnectedness of behavior and outcomes in organizations. Weick (1976) develops probably the most thorough analysis of the concept of loose coupling. By **loose coupling,** he conveys "the image that coupled events are responsive, but that each event also preserves its own identity and some evidence of its physical or logical separateness" (Weick, 1976: 5). Loose coupling connotes weak or infrequent ties between elements that are minimally interdependent; hence, the phrase is invoked to refer to a variety of situations.

Most organizations are concerned with who does the work and how well it is performed. Weick (1976) suggests that in schools there is loose control over how well the work is done. Inspection of the instructional activities is infrequent, and even when evaluation of teaching does occur, it is usually perfunctory. Under these conditions, tight organizational controls over who does the work—through such activities as hiring, certifying, and scheduling—is exerted.

The Weick thesis is expanded by Meyer and Rowan (1977, 1978). They claim that educators typically "decouple" their organizational structure from instructional activities and outcomes and resort to a **logic of confidence.** Their argument is that schools are basically personnel-certifying agencies of society. Standardized curricula and certified teachers produce standardized types of graduates, who are then given their appropriate place in the economic and stratification system on the basis of their certified educational backgrounds. Ritual classifications such as elementary teacher, English teacher, principal, fourth-grader, or college prep student provide the basis for tightly structured educational organizations. Schools gain community support and legitimacy by conforming to the legal and normative standards of the wider society. Much less control is exerted over teaching activities because close supervision and rigorous evaluation might uncover basic flaws in the instructional program and produce uncertainties. It is much easier to demonstrate conformity to abstract ritual classifications than to evaluate the effectiveness of the teaching-learning process. Therefore, schools decouple their ritual structure from instructional activities and buttress the decoupling by embracing an assumption of good faith (Okeafor and Teddlie, 1989). The community has confidence in members of the board of education, who in turn have confidence in the teachers. These multiple exchanges of confidences are supported by an abiding faith in the process by which school officials have been certified as professionals.

Empirical evidence to support the existence, extent, and patterns of loose couplings in schools is mixed. On the one hand, a number of studies depict the school as a highly centralized and formalized organization; in fact, one of the most salient features of secondary schools in New Jersey is the apparent rigid hierarchy of authority (Hoy, Newland, and Blazovsky, 1977; Hoy, Blazovsky, and Newland, 1980, 1983). High school teachers maintain that they must ask permission and get approval before they do "almost anything"; even small matters have to be referred to a superior for a final answer (Hoy, Newland, and Blazovsky, 1977).

On the other hand, the picture of schools presented by Meyer and Rowan (1978), and others (Abramowitz and Tenenbaum, 1978; Deal and Celotti, 1980; Meyer, 1978) is quite different. These investigators paint schools as loosely coupled systems where instructional work is basically removed from the control of the organizational structure. Perhaps when teachers claim that they must ask permission and get approval before they do almost anything they are excluding instructional activity. Although it seems hard to believe that teachers make such a distinction, professional discretion of teachers may be so broad and their autonomy so great concerning classroom instruction that questions of supervision are considered by teachers only within a framework of routine school and classroom management practices.

Several studies on the images of school organizations by William Firestone and his colleagues (Firestone and Herriott, 1981, 1982; Firestone and Wilson, 1985; Herriott and Firestone, 1984) specifically examine contrasting school structures. Their work suggests that schools can be grouped into two clusters: rational bureaucracy, and anarchy or loosely coupled system. Elementary schools were much more likely to be rational bureaucracies characterized by goal consensus, hierarchy of authority, centralization, formalization, and limited teacher autonomy. Secondary schools, in contrast, were more loosely coupled systems with more teacher autonomy but with little goal consensus and much less centralization.

The crude distinction between bureaucracy and loosely coupled systems can be misleading (Corwin and Borman, 1988) and counterproductive. Most elementary schools are more tightly structured than secondary schools, but it is a matter of degree. Routine tasks and functions are bureaucratically organized in secondary schools. In fact, a comparative analysis of public secondary schools and social welfare agencies by Hoy and his colleagues (Hoy, Blazovsky, and Newland, 1983) found schools to be dramatically more formalized and centralized than the welfare agencies. Not one welfare agency had as much hierarchical control or rule enforcement as the *least* centralized or least formalized high school. Finally, in a comprehensive review of the loose coupling literature, R. M. Ingersoll (1993: 108) concludes "that the loose coupling perspective has offered an incomplete and faulty view of the organization of schools."

Are public schools, then, rigid bureaucracies that need to be loosened or organizational anarchies that need to be tightened? Our analysis leads us to the conclusion that there are probably at least two basic organizational domains: a bureaucratic one consisting of the institutional and managerial functions of mediating between the school and community, implementing the law, administering internal affairs, procuring and allocating necessary resources, and mediating between students and teachers; and a professional one involved with the actual technical processes of teaching and learning.[5] The bureaucratic domain is typically a tightly linked and cohesive structure, at times too rigid, preventing adaptation and producing alienation among teachers. The professional sphere is much more loosely structured; teachers have broad discretion to make professional judgments about the teaching-learning process; at times, too much independence produces conflict, confusion, and coordination problems—reducing productivity and hindering efficiency.[6] Schools are affected by their environment; they are open systems. As forces in society change, pressures to tighten and loosen organization linkages also vary. Clearly, administrators need to know the organization and be aware of and sensitive to the negative consequences of *both* tight and loose coupling. In general, the public school is a distinctive combination of bureaucratic and professional elements, a theme which we will now explore in more detail.

PROFESSIONAL AND BUREAUCRATIC CONFLICT

Professionals and semiprofessionals employed in formal organizations bring into focus a basic conflict between professional values and bureaucratic expectations. Although many similarities exist between professional and bureaucratic principles, the potential for conflict remains because differences do exist. The major similarities and differences are summarized in Table 3.6.

Both bureaucrats and professionals are expected to have technical expertise in specialized areas, to maintain an objective perspective, and to act impersonally and impartially. Professionals, however, are expected to act in the best interests of their clients, while bureaucrats are expected to act in the best interests of the organization. This apparent conflict between the interests of clients and the organization poses a problem for many formal organizations, but for service organizations such as schools, social work agencies, and hospitals it may not be a major dilemma. Unlike business concerns, the prime beneficiary of service organizations is the client. For service organizations, then, the prime objective of both the bureaucrat and the professional is the same—service to clients.

A fundamental source of **professional-bureaucratic conflict** does emerge from the system of social control used by bureaucracies and the professions. Professionals attempt to control work decisions. They have been taught to internalize a code of ethics that guides their activities, and this code of behavior is supported by colleagues. Professionals are basically responsible to their profession, and at times they may be censured by their colleagues. On the other hand, control in bureaucratic organizations is not in the hands of the colleague group; discipline stems from one major line of authority. As Blau and Scott (1962: 63) explain, "Performance is controlled by directives received from one's superiors rather than by self-imposed standards and peer-group surveillance, as is the case among professionals." Considerable

TABLE **3.6** Basic Characteristics of Professional and Bureaucratic Orientations: Similarities and Differences	
Professional Orientation	**Bureaucratic Orientation**
Technical expertise	Technical expertise
Objective perspective	Objective perspective
Impersonal and impartial approach	Impersonal and impartial approach
Service to clients	Service to clients
Major Sources of Conflict	
Colleague-oriented reference group	Hierarchical orientation
Autonomy in decision making	Disciplined compliance
Self-imposed standards of control	Subordinated to the organization

variation exists, however, among various professional groups and in the scope of their professional domains. For example, elementary and secondary school teachers may have a relatively narrow scope, while physicians and scientists typically have broad authority (Scott, 1981). The ultimate basis for a professional act is professional knowledge; however, the ultimate justification of a bureaucratic act is its consistency with the organizational rules and regulations and approval by a superior. Therein lies the major source of conflict between the organization and the profession—conflict between "professional expertise and autonomy" and "bureaucratic discipline and control."

Nevertheless, Scott (1981, 1987, 1992) argues that, while some conflict exists between professional and bureaucratic principles, the two arrangements are not incompatible in all respects. Both represent alternative paths to the rationalization of a field of action—and at a general level, the two orientations are compatible. But the interaction between bureaucrats and professionals can be strained. Teachers resent interference and directives from the administration and call for shared governance in schools. Of course, different ways are used to resolve the conflicts. In some organizations major structural changes have been made. In others, many professionals have developed orientations that are compatible with the demands of their bureaucratic organizations.

ORGANIZATIONAL ACCOMMODATIONS TO PROFESSIONAL-BUREAUCRATIC CONFLICT

One method of accommodation is the development of professional organizations, which are established specifically to produce, apply, preserve, or communicate knowledge. Professional organizations are characterized by the goals they pursue, by the high proportion of professionals (at least 50 percent), and by the authority relations where the professionals have superior authority over the major goal activities. Examples of professional organizations include universities, colleges, many schools, research organizations, therapeutic mental hospitals, larger general hospitals, and social-work agencies. However, full-fledged professional organizations employ professionals whose educational preparation is usually five or more years; semiprofessional organizations—for example, many elementary and secondary schools— employ individuals whose professional education is less than five years (Gross and Etzioni, 1985).

Gross and Etzioni (1985) further observe that differences in education produce differences in goals and privileges. Full-fledged professional organizations are primarily devoted to the creation and application of knowledge; their professionals are typically protected by the guarantee of privileged communication. Semiprofessional organizations are primarily concerned with the communication of knowledge rather than its creation; their professionals generally do not have the guarantee of privileged communication. Elementary schools constitute the most common example of the semiprofessional organization. The differences in training, the type and amount of knowledge, privileged communication, and the use of knowledge apparently are associated with differences in administrative authority. In semiprofessional organizations, professional work has less autonomy, and semiprofessionals often have personality traits and skills more compatible with administrators than in professional organizations. Hence, semiprofessional organizations are managed more frequently by semiprofessionals themselves than by others. For example, almost all principals and superintendents are former teachers.

Similarly, Mintzberg (1979) noted that professional bureaucracies rely on standard skills and knowledge, training, and socialization for the coordination of organizational activities. Trained and indoctrinated specialists—that is, professionals—are hired to do the basic work in professional bureaucracies, and they are granted considerable control over their own work. This control means that professionals work in relative independence of their colleagues, but closely with their clients. Bidwell (1965) observes that structural looseness in the school organization produces considerable autonomy for teachers. Teachers tend to work alone in their classrooms in relative isolation from colleagues and administrators. Consequently, schools tend to be structured loosely to allow teachers broad discretionary autonomy within their classrooms.

Another method of structural accommodation used to alleviate the bureaucratic-professional conflict is exhibited by hospital organizations. Two authority lines—one administrative and one professional—coexist in many hospitals. The hospital administrator is in charge of the business side of the enterprise, but the professional side is governed by a hierarchy of doctors, which stands completely outside the administrative structure (Hall, 1954). Nevertheless, strains remain, especially where professional considerations conflict with bureaucratic ones. Likewise, bifurcation of the professional and bureaucratic domains in some schools reduces the conflict between professional and bureaucratic authority, yet tensions between them persist. At best, a dual authority structure seems a partial solution.

INDIVIDUAL ACCOMMODATIONS TO PROFESSIONAL-BUREAUCRATIC CONFLICT

Even if no changes occur in the organizational structure, professionals may develop role orientations or attitudes that facilitate adjustment to the bureaucratic role demands. Some professionals retain a high commitment to professional skills and develop a strong orientation to reference groups outside the organization; they thus maintain a strong professional orientation. These individuals are dedicated to the profession in general, not to any particular organization. Other professionals may become less committed to professional skills and develop an orientation to a particular organization. They are more interested in approval from administrative superiors within the organization than from professional colleagues outside; a bureaucratic orientation therefore develops. Either of these orientations may be functional: if future personal goals involve securing an administrative position, a bureaucratic orientation may lead to promotions in the organization; if advancement within the profession is desired, a professional orientation may produce the desired outcomes.

Local and Cosmopolitan Orientations

A number of studies have systematically identified and explored individual accommodations to the conflict between professional and organizational commitment. Alvin Gouldner's (1954) classic study of a small liberal arts college is a good example. He identifies two latent organizational types-cosmopolitans and locals—and distinguishes the bases for their accommodation to such conflict. **Cosmopolitans** are those low on loyalty to the employing organization, high on commitment to specialized role skills, and likely to use an outer reference group. **Locals** are those high on loyalty to the employing organization, low on commitment to specialized role skills, and likely to use an inner reference group.

Gouldner's study indicates that the tension and conflict created by an organization's bureaucratic needs for expertise and its social system latency needs for loyalty can be met by adopting either a local or a cosmopolitan orientation. Studies of intellectuals in labor unions (Lensky, 1959), nurses in hospitals (Corwin, 1961), scientists in industrial organizations (Pelz and Andrews, 1966), and workers in social-welfare agencies (Blau and Scott, 1962) tend to support Gouldner's findings. However, a longitudinal study by Jeffery R. Cornwall and Andrew J. Grimes (1987) suggested that professional behaviors influenced professional role orientation over time. In other words, the assumption that cosmopolitan-local orientations were stable and set during training was not supported. Rather, socialization forces—for example, the reward structure and peer influences—can and do change the cosmopolitan-local orientations.

Different Kinds of Locals

Robert V. Presthus (1958, 1962, 1978) provides another conceptual perspective for examining individual accommodations to bureaucratic pressures. His analysis is concerned primarily with locals who tend to adjust successfully in bureaucratic organizations. Presthus postulates that bureaucratic organizations, with their patent status structures and power apparatuses, tend to generate anxiety in organizational members. To most, anxiety is an unpleasant and annoying tension that produces actions to reduce anxiety. Therefore, tension reduction becomes a powerful motivator and reinforcer of organizational behavior. Individuals accommodate themselves to tension by becoming upward mobiles, indifferents, or ambivalents.

Upward mobiles are identified as individuals who embrace the goals of the organization. The organization's values are their values; therefore, in any situation, but especially in conflict situations, organizational values are decisive. Upward mobiles believe in hierarchical authority and accept its demands. Furthermore, upward mobiles are oriented toward ascending the status structure, and they have a genuine, deep, and abiding respect for authority.

Indifferents adopt the most common mode of accommodation. They reject the organizational values of success and power. Their orientation essentially is extravocational and outside the organization. Indifferents separate work from the more meaningful aspects of their lives. To indifferents, work simply is a job that provides economic capital; the job is not a central interest in life.

Ambivalents usually are a small minority who cannot resist the appeals of the organization but still often fail to gain organizational power and success. Ambivalents need security, yet they cannot make the accommodations necessary to achieve it. Ambivalents have an aggressive sense of individuality that frequently does not fit into the bureaucracy's structured way of operating. Moreover, ambivalents are typically unable to accept organizational premises; instead, they make decisions on a particularistic point of view, rejecting authority, adopting permissive views of dissent, and accepting their own impulses rather than their organization's standards. Unlike upward mobiles and indifferents, who represent successful local patterns of accommodation, ambivalents exemplify inappropriate adjustments that typically result in resignation, aggression, or withdrawal.

A Dual Orientation

Thus far, our analysis has dealt with organizational accommodations to the professional-bureaucratic conflict and with individual accommodations in which the employee has chosen either commitment to the profession or commitment to the organization, not to both. A few studies do suggest that under certain conditions professionals may be committed to both their professions and their organizations. Barney Glaser (1965) refers to this as a **dual orientation,** both local and cosmopolitan. Similarly, William Kornhauser (1962) labels individuals who hold this dual perspective as a mixed type. Whatever the label, it appears that in some organizational contexts, an integration of bureaucratic and professional cultures is reflected in an orientation to both the organization and the profession.

Glaser (1965) identifies two conditions that tend to generate a dual orientation among scientists working in organizations. A dual orientation is possible when (1) the organizational goals and the institutional goals (of science) are compatible and (2) the scientists are highly motivated. Russell Thornton's (1970) study of junior college teachers also tends to support the development of a dual orientation when organizational practices are consistent with professional objectives. In particular, the more professional the criteria of performance, the more professional the authority relationship and the more professional the supervision. Under this condition the organizational and professional commitments among junior college teachers become compatible. When a high degree of professionalism in organizational involvement exists, individuals can be committed both to the profession and to the organization. Such a dual orientation is especially desirable in service organizations such as schools.

PROFESSIONAL AND BUREAUCRATIC ORIENTATIONS IN SCHOOLS

Whether or not teaching is a full-fledged profession is debatable. However, few would argue either that teachers are closer to the professional end of an occupational continuum than blue-collar and white-collar workers, or that they are further from the professional pole than physicians or lawyers. Nonetheless, the growth of theory and knowledge in teaching, the increased requirements for teacher education, teachers' sense of responsibility for student welfare, strong professional associations, and increased claims for teacher autonomy provide the basis for considering teaching a profession. Behind the drive to professionalize teaching is the desire for increased status and more control over work—in order to gain not only more responsibility but also more authority or power. For many years, teachers believed that they had professional obligations, such as staying after school to help students with their work; now they are demanding professional rights as well, such as selecting their own colleagues.

As we have already discussed, the characteristics of bureaucratic organizations are not totally compatible with a professional work group. Findings that many conflicts in schools derive from more general conflict between bureaucratic and professional principles should not be surprising. For example, Ronald G. Corwin (1965) studied teacher conflict in schools and found that almost half of the conflict incidents involved teachers in opposition to administrators. The higher the level of professional orientation, the greater the number of conflicts. Similarly, DiPaola and Hoy (1994) in a recent study of teachers found that professional orientation was related to teacher militancy.

Few teachers escape the oral or written exhortations on "professionalism." Some administrators use the term "professionalism" as a cry to rally support for the school or for a given decision. For example, a decision to initiate a merit salary program in one school subsequently resulted in a confidential note to all teachers notifying them of their salaries plus the following addendum: "Salary is a confidential and personal matter. It is your professional obligation not to discuss your salary with other teachers." A safe prediction is that many educational administrators have a conception of a "professional" teacher as one who is loyal to the administration and the organization—that is, one who has a bureaucratic orientation.

Given the bureaucratization of schools and the growing professionalization of teachers, continued conflict seems likely. In teaching, the immediate issues of conflict revolve around the amount of control teachers should have over the selection of textbooks, teaching procedures and methods, and curriculum reform and development; however, the underlying issue is neither peculiar to teaching nor to school organizations. The conflict is between professional expertise and autonomy and bureaucratic discipline and control.

As long as the basic bureaucratic structure of the school tends to be authoritarian, teacher authority will continue to be a major source of tension. If the organizational structure of the school becomes more professional, then the chances for ameliorating the conflict and tension will be greatly improved. In fact, a dual orientation (local-cosmopolitan) of teachers might be the rule rather than the exception. In professional organizational structures, teachers might increasingly have high commitments both to the organization and to the profession. Some research supports the notion that bureaucratic orientation and professional attitudes of teachers need not be in conflict if schools increase the professional autonomy of teachers (Marjoribanks, 1977; DiPaoli and Hoy, 1994).

Several other studies of teacher orientations are relevant. Edward Kuhlman and Wayne K. Hoy (1974) studied the bureaucratic socialization of new school teachers.

They were interested in the extent to which the professional and bureaucratic orientations of beginning teachers were changed as a result of initial socialization attempts by the school organization. They theorized that a dual-role orientation might emerge among new teachers as they were socialized. New teachers, however, did not become both more professional and more bureaucratic in orientation during the first year of teaching. On the contrary, secondary teachers became significantly more bureaucratic and less professional during the first year. The orientations of beginning elementary teachers remained relatively constant, although as a group they were significantly more bureaucratic than secondary teachers. The hypothesis was not supported that a dual orientation would evolve during the initial experience of teaching and would enhance the effectiveness of both the professional and the organization. Furthermore, Harold Wilensky's (1964) contention regarding an interpenetration of bureaucratic and professional cultures in many organizations was not supported by the findings in secondary schools.

The forces of bureaucratic socialization in a majority of secondary schools seem strong. Most schools begin almost immediately to mold neophytes into roles devised to maintain stability, to encourage subordination, and to promote loyalty to the organization; in fact, the socialization process begins with the student-teaching experience. Student teachers, as a result of their practice teaching experience, appear to become significantly more bureaucratic in orientation (Hoy and Rees, 1977). Similar socialization forces and outcomes have been reported for other aspiring professions, especially for social work (Enoch, 1989).

In sum, research portrays the school as a service organization staffed predominantly with professionals and semiprofessionals. The structure of the school organization is basically bureaucratic, with authoritarian trappings. Teachers as a group are becoming somewhat more professional and more militant; yet the bureaucratic structure, especially at the secondary level, seems quite effective at socializing new members to the appropriate bureaucratic stance, often at the expense of professional considerations. Hence, the school milieu comprises a number of countervailing forces. One hopes that administrators and teachers alike will strive to make school organizations more professional and less authoritarian. In such organizations a dual orientation seems likely to become increasingly prevalent, with teachers who are highly committed to both the profession and the school.[7]

SUMMARY AND SUGGESTED READINGS

Virtually all organizations have the distinctive characteristics of bureaucracy—division of labor, specialization, impersonality, hierarchy of authority, rules and regulations, and career orientation—described by Max Weber in his theory of bureaucracy. Weber's model has been criticized because it pays insufficient attention to possible dysfunctional consequences of each component, neglects the significance of the informal organization, ignores the conflict between disciplined compliance and expertise, and is gender biased. Nevertheless, the Weberian perspective provides a strong conceptual basis for examining school structures; indeed, most schools have many of the features of bureaucracy.

Three contemporary views of organizational structure are examined. First, Hall's approach is used to develop four types of school organizational structures—Weberian, authoritarian, professional, and chaotic—that are quite different and seem to have different consequences for students and teachers. This typology is then used to outline a theory of structural development in schools. Bolman and Deal remind us that there is no one best way to organize; designing an effective organizational structure involves balancing many contradicting forces created by the organization's need for both order and freedom. Another analysis of the structure of organizations is provided by Mintzberg. He describes structure simply as the ways in which an organization divides its labor into tasks and achieves coordination among them. His analysis and framework when applied to schools yield six conventional configurations of school structure as well as a political model of schools. Indeed, the framework provides a basis for synthesizing much of the literature on school structure.

A loose coupling perspective offers a useful addition to bureaucratic and structural theories. The framework challenges many of the assumptions of bureaucratic theory and depicts the school as a distinctive combination of bureaucracy and structural looseness, one in which the institutional structure is decoupled from instructional activities. The natural tendency for bureaucratic and professional elements in school to conflict provides both the school structure and the individual teacher with a challenge to accommodate and change.

We recommend that all students read March and Simon's classic analysis, *Organizations* (1958, 1993). This book is about hierarchical structures and rational decision making. The introduction to the second edition is an intriguing reflection on the world of organizations during the past thirty-five years by two of the most distinguished organizational theorists of this century. For those students enthralled with the construct of bureaucracy, start with Weber (1947). Mintzberg supplies a readable and extensive contemporary treatment of organizational structure in *Mintzberg on Management* (1989). No one who is a student of organization should miss Ferguson's *The Feminist Case Against Bureaucracy* (1984). Finally, the research on Catholic Schools (Coleman, 1990; Bryk, Lee, and Holland, 1993) is beginning to provide some strong evidence of how organizational structures influence a school's ability to achieve its goals.

NOTES

1. The intended and unintended results of using rules to gain control has been described as Gouldner's model, and it is discussed in more detail in March and Simon (1993).

2. The Aston studies done by D. S. Pugh and his associates (1968, 1969, 1976) at the University of Aston in Birmingham, England, is a comprehensive set of studies of bureaucracy using interview inventories to assess the structure of work organizations rather than questionnaires. The technique has been used by

Canadian researchers (Newberry, 1971; Kelsey, 1973; Holdaway, et al., 1975; Sackney, 1976) at the University of Alberta and by U.S. researchers (Sousa and Hoy, 1981; Guidette, 1982; Haymond, 1982) at Rutgers University to study educational organizations. Regardless of research strategy, the results of the study of bureaucratic structures in schools are quite consistent.

3. To these five original configurations, Mintzberg (1989) recently has added two additional ones—the missionary organization and the political organization. Sometimes either ideology or politics becomes so pervasive that it overrides the standard configurations and creates its own configuration. If the organization's ideology (culture) becomes so strong that its entire structure is built around it, Mintzberg labels the configuration a missionary organization. If the politics becomes so strong that it captures the organization, the configuration is labeled a political organization. But typically, politics (Chapter 6) and ideology (Chapter 5) are components of the standard forms; they are overlays on the five conventional configurations.

4. Mintzberg (1979) also identifies the pull to Balkanize by managers of the middle line and the pull to collaborate by the support staff, which are less pronounced in schools and found predominately in divisional structures and adhocracies.

5. The institutional, managerial, and technical functions in schools are discussed in detail by Parsons (1967).

6. For an insightful discussion of the separate zones of control of principals and teachers, see Lortie (1969).

7. Carlson (1962) provides an intriguing research analysis of local-cosmopolitan orientations for superintendents as they affect administrator behavior, and Hoy and Aho (1973) and Ganz and Hoy (1977) do the same thing for secondary and elementary principals, respectively.

KEY CONCEPTS AND IDEAS

Ambivalents	Hierarchy of authority
Antibureaucratic structure	Ideal type
Authoritarian structure	Impersonal orientation
Career orientation	Indifferents
Chaotic structure	Informal organization
Coordinating mechanisms	Locals
Cosmopolitans	Logic of confidence
Direct supervision	Loose coupling
Division of labor	Loose coupling perspective
Dual orientation	Machine bureaucracy
Goal displacement	Middle line

Mutual adjustment

Operating core

Political organization

Professional bureaucracy

Professional-bureaucratic conflict

Professional structure

Punishment-centered rules

Representative rules

Rules and regulations

Semiprofessional bureaucracy

Simple bureaucracy

Simple structure

Specialization

Standardization of output

Standardization of skills

Standardization of work

Strategic apex

Support staff

Technostructure

Upward mobiles

Weberian structure

Individuals in Schools

Ultimately the behaviorist paradigm was largely abandoned because
psychologists belatedly recognized that it was impossible to explain
human action without reference to consciousness, that is without
reference to what people believe, think, expect, desire, remember,
anticipate, imagine, plan, and intend.

—Edwin A. Locke
Organizational Behavior and Human Decision Processes

PREVIEW

1. Cognitive theories of information processing and motivation provide useful insights about managing and working with individuals in schools.

2. Cognitive architecture is a set of structures and mechanisms (e.g., schemas and metacognitive processes) that underlie and produce cognitive activity.

3. There are four types of information processing: rational, limited capacity, expert, and cybernetic.

4. Work motivation is a set of energetic forces that originate both within as well as beyond an individual's being, which initiate work-related behavior and determine its form, direction, intensity, and duration.

5. Motivation theories can be organized into three related paradigms. *Need and value theories* view the motivating force as coming from some type of internal tension or arousal; *cognitive-choice theories* focus on processes involved in individual decision making and selection; *metacognition theories* center on self-regulation and motivational processes that govern the effect of goals on behaviors.

6. Values are enduring beliefs about preferable outcomes; they give expression to human needs and guide actions.

7. Expectancy-choice theory is supported empirically; individuals work hard when they think that working hard is likely to result in valued rewards.

8. When individuals make causal attributions, they are essentially seeking and creating knowledge, which they use to better manage themselves and their environments.

9. Self-efficacy contributes to motivation by determining what goals individuals set for themselves, how much effort they expend, how long they persevere in the face of difficulties, and their resilience to failures.

10. Within organizational science, goal-setting theory is widely supported. Goal-setting effects generalize across tasks, settings, subjects, countries, performance criteria, time spans, individuals, groups, and different methods of goal setting.

11. A motivation sequence—needs, values, expectancy choice, goal setting—integrates motivational models by showing the complementary linkages among them.

When administrators analyze their organizations, impersonal concepts of school structure many times overshadow a consideration of such individual and personal concepts as knowledge, motivation, and emotion. When this happens, a distorted picture develops because schools are places teaming with people. When visiting a school as students arrive in the morning or observing students and teachers work on classroom activities, one is struck by the number and diversity of individuals who are learning and growing. As indicated earlier (see Chapter 2), students, teachers, and administrators bring with them and develop their own individual orientations to their jobs in schools. What facets of the individual are most instrumental in determining work and other behaviors in schools? Conversely, what characteristics of the individual are most likely to be influenced by other dimensions of the school? Responses to these questions can be framed in many ways because individuals are so complex and because insights regarding human behavior are rooted in many perspectives and disciplines. We believe that a powerful way to gain insights about students, teachers, and administrators as individuals in school contexts is through the study of human cognition.

Cognition is the use of mental representations to understanding human perception, thoughts, knowledge, motivation, and behavior. During the past twenty years or so, the words "cognitive revolution" have commonly been heard. Prior to 1970, strictly behavioral approaches dominated psychology and the study of the individual. The founding and best-known scholars of behaviorism include Ian Pavlov, John B. Watts, E. L. Thorndike, and B. F. Skinner. The behaviorist paradigm puts forth two related propositions. First, researchers should restrict themselves to public methods of observation, which any scientist could apply and quantify. Subjective ruminations and private introspection are strictly forbidden. Second, the focus should be exclusively on behavior. Topics such as mind, thinking, or imagination and concepts such as plans, desires, or intentions should absolutely be avoided. According to the behaviorists, all psychological activity can be explained adequately without resorting to mysterious mentalistic images (Gardner, 1987). While these positions seem extreme to us, they have had tremendous influence in education, particularly in special education where practice has been dominated by the various technologies of behavioral psychology.

Howard Gardner (1987) concludes that an initial and critical break with behaviorism occurred at a 1948 conference on "Cerebral Mechanisms in Behavior." In this defining moment, Karl Lashley effectively challenged the doctrine of behaviorism and legitimated the scientific study of the mind. Since the early 1950s, the cognitive approach has become the central paradigm in psychology. It addresses fundamental questions about the human mind, its functioning, and its influence on individual behavior. These questions have dealt with critical and basic issues for schools— learning, language and literacy, planning, thinking, problem solving and decision making, imagination, and to a lesser extent, motivation.

Hence, we believe that educational administrators can gain significant insights into managing and working with students and teachers by understanding contemporary approaches to cognition. Two formulations—information processing and motivation—are the bases of a number of cognitive approaches. While we do not attempt to build a grand theory, we note likely linkages among the different approaches to understanding individuals.

INFORMATION PROCESSING

A popular approach to understanding the human mind has been and is information processing. The founding metaphor in information processing is the computer. Gardner (1991) observes that early information-processing approaches took the digital computer as the preeminent model of cognition. In this view an individual's mind resembles a computer; hence, we speak of such mechanical parts as storage buffers, memory stores, internal processing mechanisms, and output. Much as computers have changed, rapid shifts have occurred with the tenets of information-processing theory. Proponents, however, remain interested in specifying mechanisms of problem solving, especially with a stress on logical and numerical relations. According to Gardner (1987), a defining feature of cognitive activities is mental representations at a level of analysis entirely separate from both biological and sociological or cultural levels. **Information processing** is a system of representation that bridges the gap between the brain and nervous system and behavior; its representations take the forms of cognitive structures and processes for accessing and using the information (Hunt, 1991). As a caution, Robert G. Lord and Karen J. Maher (1991a) observe that cognitive science may be in the midst of a paradigm shift. As in the traditional approach, information-processing theory is symbolically oriented and concerned with a variety of conscious processes.[1]

COGNITIVE ARCHITECTURE: STRUCTURES AND PROCESSES

Cognitive architecture is a set of mechanisms and structures that underlie and produce cognitive activity. This architecture (1) specifies the nature and organization of memory, (2) defines basic or easily performed cognitive processes, and (3) sequences these processes to produce intelligent behavior. Information processing is conceptualized as occurring within the cognitive architecture of an individual (Lord and Maher, 1991a). The basic idea is that individuals have internal mental models or symbol systems of the external world that guide processing of many tasks such as decision making and interacting with others.

Schemas

A fundamental notion is that information is organized into interconnected units. These packages of information can be thought of as data structures used to represent concepts stored in memory (Lord and Maher, 1991a). The basic memory unit of cognitive architecture has been given a variety of labels such as "schema," "schemata," "scripts," "cognitive representations," "cognitive maps," "mental maps," "production systems," "propositional networks," "knowledge structures," and "habits of mind." While modest variations in meaning exist among these labels, they are all assumed to be internal, cognitive representations of knowledge. For consistency and simplicity, we will use schema(s) in our discussion.

A **schema** represents organized knowledge about given concepts or types of experience in an individual's memory. It contains not only the characteristics of the concept but the relationships among the characteristics (Hunt, 1991). In Karl Weick's (1979) view, schemas are abridged, generalized, and changeable mental representations that serve as initial frames of reference for action and perception. The key point is that schemas are internal mental models of the outside world. People use schemas to understand environments, deal with job problems, and achieve goals (Wofford, 1994). For example, the schema that most people hold of a school is a building with classrooms, teachers, students, and principal.

Schemas order the features associated with recurrent events (Gardner, 1987). For example, the schema of most school days is similar for all of us. It begins with the students and school personnel getting ready for school, then making it to school using a variety of forms of transportation. As told in elaborate stories by our parents and grandparents who attended rural schools before 1950, the schema called for students walking great distances to school. Upon arrival, the halls echo with the noisy chatter of the students coming together; the principal tours the building; and teachers ready for class. As the bell rings for the first period, students (for the most part) scurry to class. After changing classes several times, the day ends with the final chaos of the students leaving school. In other words, schemas provide individuals with mental pictures that help them understand present and future situations; reliance on their use is largely effortless or automatic, and frees the individual's attention for other tasks (Louis and Sutton, 1991).

Schemas arise from a variety of sources. They can reflect the content and structure of information presented in a school class or of a field of study such as chemistry or history. They can arise from actual or vicarious experiences of everyday life. Individuals can also create their own schemas as they learn and integrate new information with prior knowledge. That is, schemas reflect the active construction of reality. Individuals create meaning and refine the meanings with the raw data of the objective world. Hence, schemas are part of the cognitive architecture that enables people to store, organize, remember, and elaborate new information; it guides future perceptions and learning (Pintrich, 1988).

Individuals, especially experts, have extensive stores of task-relevant knowledge in a highly organized long-term memory. In fact, one way to define expertise is as rich, elaborated schemas. Herbert A. Simon (1987) estimates that experts may have as many as 200,000 patterns stored in long-term memory. Under conditions of "business as usual," schemas are efficient and effective guides in perceiving, interpreting, and responding to familiar social situations. Experienced assistant principals, for example, can handle routine discipline problems easily and quickly. They have heard "all" the reasons for the disruptive behavior before, know the school policies, and have a repertoire of disciplinary actions that work. In other words, the stories or excuses, policy, and disciplinary practices can be conceived of as linked schemas in the minds of expert assistant principals. Sometimes, however, reliance on habits of the mind is not sufficient. Novel, discrepant, and new situations call for active thinking, for individuals to engage in more conscious activity. For example, a routine fist fight in the cafeteria produces a bloody nose and the later discovery that the bleeder is HIV positive. The HIV finding underscores the shortcomings of existing schema and calls for the creation of new ones that will allow the assistant principal to handle this new problem effectively.

Schemas also serve as criteria against which newly encountered events are judged (Gardner, 1987). Schemas can be powerful screens; they aid memory and action, but they also can cause individuals to misperceive events or to misremember them. Throughout life, mental models play an important role. They help an individual assimilate new experiences. Experienced individuals are a virtual repository of schemas, which can be called upon to help deal with situations that may be unfamiliar to less experienced citizens or people not knowledgeable about the current culture. Yet, entrenched schemas may prevent people from making fresh and uncontaminated judgments about people, situations, and events. In the example of the experienced assistant principals, the existing mental models of students sent to their offices may preclude them from hearing unique or different extenuating reasons put forth by the students. Some assistant principals may view African-American students as troublemakers. They find it exceedingly difficult to break through their stereotypical schemas regardless of the circumstances.

Metacognitive Processes

Gardner (1987) observes that human beings differ from lower organisms in two critical respects—cognitive processes and intelligence. First, humans have the capacity to join together two or more independent schemas to perform a new task. Second, humans become aware of the contents of their schema and use the knowledge productively and in new ways. In other words, we can gain access to and control of our information-processing systems. Individuals are not simply at the mercy of their senses; they engage in self-monitoring to understand and control their thinking—that is, **metacognitive processing,** or metacognition.

Similarly, Bandura (1986) believes that, if there is any characteristic that is distinctively human, it is the capability for reflective self-consciousness. This enables people to analyze their experiences and to think about their own thought processes.

By reflecting on their varied experiences and on what they know, individuals can derive generic knowledge about themselves and the world around them. This metacognitive activity allows individuals to monitor their ideas, act on them, predict occurrences of them, judge the adequacy of their thoughts, and change them accordingly. Bandura (1986) further asserts that metacognitive processing depends upon accessibility of schema and flexibility of thinking. People channel and monitor their attention, and draw on their knowledge of cognitive strategies, personal capabilities, and task demands, in considering courses of action. Then they evaluate and revise their thinking when initial efforts fail to produce desired results. Metacognition refers to both the knowledge and its regulation. Metacognitive skills include planning, monitoring, and goal setting as well as the connection between task demands of the situation and the individual's capabilities.

MODELS OF INFORMATION PROCESSING

Lord and Maher (1990, 1991b) propose four models of information processing—rational, limited capacity, expert, and cybernetic. Each depicts a qualitatively different perspective on how individuals process information. They differ primarily in their emphasis on automatic (schema) or controlled (conscious) processing and the amount of memory required.

Rational Model: An Optimizing Approach

The optimal use of extensive information in a deliberate, thoughtful manner epitomizes the **rational model.** The key assumption in this model is that individuals have unlimited capacity to identify alternatives, to evaluate them, and to combine information in an objectively optimal fashion. Moreover, these models assume that people can simultaneously access information and optimally combine it to select the most desirable alternative. In other words, rational models assume extensive use of information and optimizing procedures prior to behavior. Many prescriptive models of decision making, planning, and problem solving are based on this approach to information processing. When it comes to describing actual behavior of individuals in decision-making, planning, and problem-solving situations, however, rational models of information processing are limited (see Chapter 9). Memory constraints, for example, usually make exhaustive processing impossible. Even though rational models generally are not descriptively accurate, they are prescriptively useful in specifying how optimal decisions may be reached. In addition, such processing is relatively slow, can be sidetracked by other problems that divert attention, and can be thwarted by the lack of information (Lord and Maher, 1991b; Lord and Hall, 1992).

Limited-Capacity Model: A Satisficing Approach

In contrast to rational models, limited-capacity models focus on how people simplify information processing while still generating adequate behaviors (Lord and Maher, 1990). The **limited-capacity model** acknowledges that people rely on existing cognitive structures such as schemas in part because their memory capacity is limited. People function effectively in familiar situations using less information and relying on general schemas. One of the simplest and most influential limited-capacity models is the satisficing model first proposed by Simon (1947). Rather than assuming exhaustive processing, satisficing predicts that processing stops when an acceptable alternative is found (see Chapter 9). Limited-capacity models assume that individuals work with a very limited conception of the problem and consider only a few of all possible alternatives. Though useful, limited-capacity processing can result in biases and systematic errors, especially in novel or discrepant situations. However, limited-capacity models are often descriptively accurate but prescriptively weak. In other words, they do describe how people many times make judgments, but they do not specify the best ways to make them. For example, when teachers and principal are confronted with the problem of adopting a new textbook, they will likely only consider the five or six on the approved adoption list and neglect the others.

Expert Model: A Chunking Approach

The expert is a person of any age who has mastered the concepts and skills of a discipline or domain and can apply the knowledge in new settings (Glaser and Chi, 1989; Gardner, 1991). Performance and understanding occur when individuals are able to take information and skills they have learned in schools or other settings and apply them flexibly and appropriately in new situations. For example, when expert teachers change schools or school districts, they are able to teach in their new classrooms.

A key assumption of the expert model is that people rely on well-organized and highly developed knowledge structures in their specific content areas of expertise (Lord and Maher, 1991b). Although rational models assume an exhaustive collection of information, which is combined using logical and conscious processes, expert models depend more on intuitive, schema-based processes. In general, experts substitute preexisting knowledge or schema for effortful, analytic processing, thus minimizing the search required to solve problems. Experienced professionals such as teachers and administrators often rely on such nonrational (not irrational), intuitive processes to solve problems and make decisions. The **expert model** depends on experts' capacities to recognize immediately key aspects of situations—chunks—and to use their knowledge and understanding to move efficiently to solution formulation and implementation (Lord and Hall, 1992). Experts perceive large meaningful patterns or "chunks of information" in their domain (Glaser and Chi, 1989).

Experts can recognize and move more quickly than novices because they differ in the way they structure, acquire, and process information (Lord and Maher, 1991b; Kraiger, Ford, and Salas, 1993). First, mental models of novices and experts vary in the type and complexity of stored elements. Novices create separate mental models for problem definition and solution strategies; experts form more complex knowledge structures that contain both problem definition and solutions (Glaser and Chi, 1989). Second, the mental models of experts and novices have different organizations. The knowledge of experts is organized, integrated, and structured with the critical elements strongly connected; the knowledge of novices is less organized, less integrated, and loosely linked. Third, experts have superior short-term and long-term memories. Given their well-developed and organized schemas, experts are better able to recall information about recent and distant events related to a current problem. Finally, the metacognitive or self-monitoring skills of experts are superior to those of novices. Experts know when they do not understand and they have the capability to evaluate alternatives that will lead to recovery (Yekovich, 1993). The overall result is that experts can process information or perform tasks more efficiently and in a qualitatively different manner from the way novices do.

To summarize, experts can be highly efficient processors of information but only in specific social or task-related areas. In this sense, Lord and Maher (1991b) find the expert model to be descriptively limited. Experts are not superior information processors in general, only in the domains for which they have richly elaborated knowledge structures. In these specific domains, experts can perform tasks effortlessly and effectively; novices must devote much more time and effort to attain only mediocre levels of performance. When experts' knowledge structures are congruent with task demands, expert processing may be the preferred manner of information processing. In such situations, Lord and Maher (1991b) believe that expert models are prescriptively appropriate. For instance, a principal with substantial experience in curriculum design may formulate strategies for creating new instructional materials intuitively through the use of expert processes, whereas principals who lack such experience may have to depend on the advice of others who have substantial experience or on extensive research.

Cybernetic Model: An Interacting Approach

Cybernetic models are much more dynamic than the other models, make limited demands on memory, and emphasize processing information and feedback while performing actions. These models conceptualize information processing and actions as being spread over time. A **cybernetic model** is similar to a limited-capacity model in its use of schemas and to an expert model in its use of situation-specific knowledge structures; however, it intermixes the interpretation of past social information with planning future activities and executing current behaviors. Cybernetic models rely heavily on feedback from the task or social environment. Thus, while cybernetic processing may be simple, it works well only when feedback is available and initial mistakes are not too costly. Under these conditions, cybernetic processing is often nearly optimal and is both descriptively and prescriptively accurate within a fairly narrow domain (Lord and Maher, 1991b).

COGNITION AND ORGANIZATIONAL ANALYSIS

While cognition is primarily focused on internal structures and processes of individuals, the information-processing metaphor has also been applied to organizational theory. For example, organizations have been described as information processing systems, interpretive systems, and as minds (Schneider and Angelmar, 1993). Likewise, Weick (1979) speculates that cognitive descriptions of organizations are built on dual images of organizations as bodies of thought and organizations as sets of thinking practices.

Using cognitive models to study organizations is based on the following logic (Schneider and Angelmar, 1993): Individuals think (cognition) and administrators are people (organizational behavior). Therefore, administrators must think (administrator cognition); and administrators happen to think in organizations while engaged in various tasks such as decision making and problem solving (cognition in organizations).

Therefore, **organizational cognition** is the organization's counterpart to individual cognition; it is the way that problems are solved and decisions are made in organizations. As a caution one must remember that only people think; organizations do not think. However, many organizational conceptions are based on metaphors of individual cognition—for example, shared values and visions, group think, shared understandings, and images. Hence, a school's culture could be seen as the total of individuals' shared beliefs or cognitive schemas (Walsh and Ungson, 1991).

Alternatively, mental models represent abstractions of the world that are symbolic rather than literal translations. Thus, individuals with different mental models—for example, teachers compared to students, teachers in different subject areas, or people of different genders or cultures—may not experience the "same" organizational world. One function of a common school culture is to create fairly similar mental models for organization members (Lord and Maher, 1991a).

In sum, information-processing models of individual cognition offer educational administrators significant insights into managing and working with individuals and school organizations. Information-processing approaches are particularly appropriate because of their focus on learning, problem solving, and decision making. However, there has been little research or theory development that attempts to link motivation and human information processing. Martin E. Ford (1992) excludes information processing from the motivation domain, but hypothesizes that information processing carries out the directions crafted by the motivational processes. Similarly, Paul Pintrich, Ronald W. Marx, and Robert A. Boyle (1993) suggest that it seems reasonable to assume that cognitive information processing is influenced by cognitive motivational processes.

MOTIVATION

Albert Bandura (1990) observes that for years the attention of cognitive scholars has been focused on how the mind works in representing, processing, organizing, and retrieving knowledge. More recent efforts, however, have been made to infuse this austere cognitivism with some affect and passion. Current work on individual motivation is cognitively based and adds a sense of emotion to understanding human functioning and behavior.

As a basic postulate, most contemporary theories of motivation hold that the major determinants of human behavior are concepts such as beliefs, needs, perceived efficacy, attributions, expectations, goals, and anticipations that individuals have about future events. In other words, individuals have thoughts about events that have happened to them and expectations about what might happen in the future if they pursue a given course of action, and, if asked, will probably indicate what they intend to do about some goal (Campbell and Pritchard, 1976). Hence, people think in ways that affect motivation.

Formulations that view behavior as purposeful, goal directed, and based on conscious or subconscious intentions are labeled *cognitive theories of motivation.* Cognitively based theories of motivation generally assume that individuals engage in some form of conscious behavior relating to the performance of tasks. People are seen as being reasoning, thinking individuals who often consider the anticipated consequences of their actions at work. Therefore, cognitive theories of motivation try to formulate models about the thought processes people go through as they decide to participate and perform in the workplace (Steers and Porter, 1991). At all levels of explanation, cognitive motivational factors play a role in explaining both the choice of action and its degree of success (Locke and Latham, 1990).

The many different components of motivation as well as the diverse philosophical positions regarding the nature of human beings make it virtually impossible to gain consensus on a single definition of motivation (Pinder, 1984). In fact, the word "motivation" is used in a variety of ways. At the most general level, motivation refers to a process governing individual choices among different forms of voluntary activities (Vroom, 1964). Ruth Kanfer (1990) elaborates the definition by arguing that because motivation is not directly observable, we must infer motivational processes from the analysis of individual behavior. Hence, motivation involves the initiation or start of behavior, direction of behavior, intensity of action (cognitive and physical effort), and persistence of the behavior over time. Because the current focus is on work behavior (as opposed to all behavior) in schools, a definition for work motivation is needed. Craig C. Pinder (1984: 8) offers the following definition: "**Work motivation** is a set of energetic forces that originate both within as well as beyond an individual's being, to initiate work-related behavior, and to determine its form, direction, intensity, and duration." The challenge for administrators is to develop highly motivated teachers who are actively engaged in teaching and learning, open to new ideas and approaches, and committed to students and change over the lifetime of their teaching careers.

A FRAMEWORK FOR MOTIVATIONAL THEORIES

Over the past four decades, a plethora of cognitive motivation theories have been created. No one theory is currently able to explain all of the elements of work behavior. The result is a complex and sometimes confusing array, even web, of models, each emphasizing different structures, concepts, and processes. Kanfer (1990) provides a useful organizing scheme by grouping theories into three related paradigms. First, *need and value theories* hypothesize that the energizing force for action stems from some type of internal tension or arousal. Needs in Maslow's theory and learned dispositions or motives in McClelland's model fall into this category. Second, *cognitive-choice theories* focus on cognitive processes involved in decision making and choice. Vroom's expectancy theory and Weiner's attribution theory are the cognitive choice models discussed in this chapter. Third, *metacognition theories* center on self-regulation and motivational processes that form the foundation of goal-directed behaviors. Bandura's concept of self-efficacy and Locke's work on goal setting are widely recognized in this area.

In the remainder of this chapter, we will examine theories within each of the three categories. We have selected theories that seem most useful in explaining individual work behavior in school organizations.

NEED AND VALUE THEORIES

Historically, the so-called need and value theories have been among the most important models of work motivation. Indeed, one of the most pervasive concepts in the area of work motivation is that of human needs. We continually hear discussions about certain students, teachers, and administrators who have high needs for affiliation, achievement, power, self-actualization, or recognition. Although several need-value theories can be identified in the literature, we will focus on two theories—need hierarchy (Maslow, 1965, 1970) and learned needs or values (McClelland, 1961, 1965). These theories advance the basic argument that human needs and values constitute fundamental forces behind behavior in organizational work settings.

Need Theory: Maslow's Hierarchical Model

Edwin A. Locke (1991b) observes that needs are used loosely in everyday conversation, but in their biological context, needs are requirements for an organism's survival and well-being. More formally, **needs** are internal states of disequilibrium that cause individuals to pursue certain courses of action in order to regain internal equilibrium (Steers and Porter, 1991). Or as Christopher Hodgkinson (1991: 94) states, "The idea behind need is that of a discrepancy or undesirable imbalance in a state of affairs. Needs imply tension and disequilibrium and provide a dynamic for rectifying action." Consequently, the ultimate objective of goal-directed action is need fulfillment or the reduction of disequilibrium. The concept of need explains at a most basic level why living organisms behave and is the standard to judge whether a specific action is healthy or not. Locke (1991b) provides the following observations about the nature and operation of needs:

- Needs do not account for individual differences because people have the same basic needs; for example, everyone needs food, water, self-esteem.

- Needs operate cyclically and are never permanently satisfied.

- Needs exist even if the individual is not aware of them (e.g., need for certain nutrients).

- Needs can lead to many different actions (e.g., individuals attempt many things to be accepted by peers).

- A particular behavior can stem from more than one need (e.g., earning money can link into many different needs).
- Needs confront people with a requirement for action, if they choose to live.

Maslow's *need hierarchy theory* has become a widely discussed perspective in the study of human motivation. The model was derived primarily from Maslow's experience as a clinical psychologist and not from systematic research (Campbell and Pritchard, 1976; Steers and Porter, 1983). His theory posits a **need hierarchy**— a basic innate or inborn set of human needs arranged in a hierarchical order (Kanfer, 1991).

Five basic categories of needs, arranged in hierarchical levels (identified and described in Figure 4.1) constitute the foundation of Maslow's (1970) model. At the first level of the hierarchy are physiological needs, which consist of such fundamental biological functions as hunger and thirst. Safety and security needs, the second level, derive from the desire for a peaceful, smoothly running, stable society. On the third level, belonging, love, and social needs are extremely important in modern society. Maslow contends that maladjustment stems from frustration of these needs. He believes that some proportion of youth rebellion, for example, is motivated by the profound need to belong to a group. Esteem needs, at the fourth level, reflect the desire to be highly regarded by others. Achievement, competence, status, and recognition satisfy esteem needs. Finally, Maslow maintains that discontent and restlessness develop unless individuals do what they are best suited to do—that is, unless they meet their need for self-actualization, the fifth level. The meaning of self-actualization is a subject of much discussion. A succinct and simple definition of self-actualization is that it is the need to be what an individual wants to be, to achieve fulfillment of life goals, and to realize the potential of his or her personality (Campbell and Pritchard, 1976). Maslow viewed self-actualization as a process, not an end state. Individuals are continually in the process of becoming more and more of what they are uniquely capable of becoming (Cherrington, 1991).

Maslow's needs are related to one another and are arranged in a hierarchy of prepotency, or urgency for survival, of the individual. The more prepotent a need is, the more it precedes other needs in human consciousness and demands to be satisfied. This observation leads to the fundamental postulate of Maslow's theory: higher-level needs become activated as lower-level needs become satisfied. Thus, Maslow points out that a person lives by bread alone—when there is no bread. But when there is plenty of bread, other and higher needs emerge. They, in turn, dominate the person, and, as they become satisfied, are displaced by new needs. The sequence—increased satisfaction, decreased importance, increased importance of next higher need level—repeats itself until the highest level of the hierarchy is reached. Therefore, individual behavior is motivated by an attempt to satisfy the need that is most important at that point in time (Lawler, 1973).

The successive emergence of higher needs is limited because lower-level needs are never completely satisfied; moreover, if an individual cannot satisfy needs at a given level for any period of time, those needs again become potent motivators. A completely satisfied need is not an effective motivator. Hence, the concept of

FIGURE **4.1**

Maslow's Need Hierarchy Theory

Level 5:
Self-
actualization or
Self-fulfillment
Achievement
of potential
Maximum
self-development,
creativity, and self-expression

Level 4:
Esteem
Self-respect—achievement,
competence, and confidence
Deserved respect of others—status,
recognition, dignity, and appreciation

Level 3: Belonging, Love, and Social Activities
Satisfactory associations with others
Belonging to groups
Giving and receiving friendship and affection

Level 2: Safety and Security
Protection against danger and threat
Freedom from fear, anxiety, and chaos
Need for structure, order, law, limits, and stability

Level 1: Physiological Needs

| Hunger | Sex | Smell | Sleep |
| Thirst | Taste | Touch | |

gratification is as important as that of deprivation. Maslow reasons that gratification releases the person from the domination of one need, allowing for the emergence of a higher-level need. Conversely, if a lower-order need is left unsatisfied, it reemerges and dominates behavior.

A common misconception about Maslow's theory is that one need must be entirely satisfied before the next level of needs emerges. Maslow asserts that normal individuals are usually only partially satisfied in all their basic needs. A more realistic description of the need structure is that the percentage of satisfaction decreases as one goes up the hierarchy of prepotency. Maslow argues that for the majority of people, needs at the first three levels are regularly satisfied and no longer have much motivational effect; however, satisfaction of esteem and self-actualization needs is rarely complete. The higher-level needs continually motivate. In other words, most behavior is motivated by needs from more than one level of the hierarchy and new need states do not emerge in a crisp, all or nothing lockstep fashion (Pinder, 1984).

Several observations about work in educational organizations can be made using Maslow's theory. First, although physiological needs seem reasonably well met for educators, some students are deprived of even the most basic needs and therefore present a potent motivational problem. Moreover, the needs for safety and security, the second hierarchical level, certainly can become motivating factors for school employees and students alike. Violence, to and from school and within the school, has increasingly become a way of life for many students. It is difficult to concentrate on studying or teaching when you are frightened. Administrative actions that arouse uncertainty with respect to continued employment, or discrimination, can affect every individual from custodian to superintendent. Furthermore, Maslow theorizes that broader aspects of the attempt to seek safety and security are seen in the preference many people have for familiar rather than unfamiliar things, for the known rather than the unknown. In schools, those people who have high safety needs may resist change and desire job security, injury-compensation plans, and retirement programs to satisfy those needs.

The need to belong causes an individual to seek relationships with co-workers, peers, superiors, and subordinates. For educators, friendship ties, informal work groups, professional memberships, and school memberships satisfy this need. The need for esteem and status, the fourth hierarchical level, causes an educator to seek control, autonomy, respect from and for others, and professional competence. Finally, the need for self-actualization motivates educators to be the best people they are capable of being. This need is less frequently apparent than others, however, because many individuals are still concerned with lower-level needs. Nevertheless, Maslow (1965) clearly advocates that organizations such as schools should provide the highest level of need satisfaction that is possible because self-actualizing students, teachers, and administrators are the best performers.

Maslow's need hierarchy theory, then, is based on three fundamental postulates (Cherrington, 1991).

- Individual needs are universal and arranged in a hierarchy.

- Unfilled needs lead individuals to focus exclusively on those needs.

- Lower-level needs must be largely satisfied before higher-level needs can be felt and pursued.

Research and Evaluation of Maslow's Theory

Maslow's need hierarchy theory presents an interesting paradox: the theory is highly familiar and popularly accepted, but its validity is dubious (Locke, 1991b). Little research evidence exists to support it (Wahba and Bridwell, 1976; Pinder, 1984). There is no clear evidence showing that human needs are classified into five distinct categories, or that these categories are structured in any special hierarchy. In fact, the findings of a number of studies do not support the fundamental assumption of a hierarchy of prepotency; other studies have found modest support (Miner, 1980; Steers and Porter, 1983; Landy and Becker, 1987; Cherrington, 1991). Of three studies published since 1980, one strongly challenges the theory (Rauschenberger, Schmitt, and Hunter, 1980); and two show only modest support (Betz, 1984; Lefkowitz, Somers, and Weinberg, 1984).

Porter's (1963) investigations of business managers indicate that the need for self-actualization is generally the least satisfied. Esteem and security needs were more often satisfied for middle-level managers than for lower-level managers. Similarly, higher-ranking officers in the military reported greater need fulfillment and relative satisfaction than did lower-ranking officers. The results were interpreted to support Maslow's theory because higher-level managers tend to have more challenging, autonomous jobs where it is possible to pursue growth needs, while lower-level managers tend to have more routine jobs, making it more difficult to satisfy these needs (Steers and Porter, 1991). In contrast, other studies of business managers typically do not support these findings (Miner, 1980).

In educational settings, an early study by Frances M. Trusty and Thomas J. Sergiovanni (1966) reports that the largest deficiencies for professional educators were satisfying esteem and self-actualization needs. In a more recent investigation, Mary Beth G. Anderson and Edward F. Iwanicki's (1984) findings are supportive of Trusty and Sergiovanni. However, the later study indicated a relatively large increase in the deficiency for security needs. Trusty and Sergiovanni also found that administrators, when compared to teachers, have fewer esteem need deficiencies and more self-actualization need deficiencies. The authors conclude that teachers' lack of self-esteem represents the largest source of need deficiency for them. Similarly, a study by Grace B. Chisolm and her colleagues (1980) shows that administrators exhibit fewer need deficiencies than teachers on all five subscales—security, social, esteem, autonomy, and self-actualization. The greatest area of deficiency for both administrators and teachers is satisfaction of autonomy needs. Given continuing speculations about schools being loosely coupled systems (see Chapter 3), this finding is somewhat surprising.

Although Maslow's formulation was popular during the 1960s, it currently receives little empirical attention (Kanfer, 1990). To gain a significant place in contemporary work, the need hierarchy framework requires substantial revision and new empirical support. The theory might be strengthened by reexamining the needs using more contemporary ideas from the cognitive perspective (Landy and Becker, 1987). For example, human needs may well be useful as a starting point in conceptualizing motivation as a sequence of cognitive processes (Locke, 1991b).

Values Theory: McClelland's Theory of Achievement

In contrast to needs, **values** are what people consider or believe beneficial to their welfare. They are enduring beliefs about which code of conduct or end state is individually preferable (Rokeach, 1973). Values give expression to human needs and guide actions. Examples of end state or terminal values include wisdom, self-respect, pleasure, and equality; modes of conduct or instrumental values include ambitious, competent, logical, and responsible (Rokeach, 1973; Weber, 1993). Needs are sources of values (Hodgkinson, 1991).[2] While people may not be aware of their needs, values are in the consciousness and they are acquired or learned. Hence, the concept of values is the cognitive representation of needs and implies that people have a conscious awareness of their motives (Erez and Earley, 1993). Values can also be viewed as one link between needs and behavior. They bridge the gap between what is required and what the person actually does (Locke, 1991b). As such, they assist individuals to organize their behavior. For example, the value of achievement may lead one to become an educator. That is, the individual is motivated toward some worthwhile "ought" state (Cropanzano, James, and Citera, 1992).

David C. McClelland's (1961, 1965, 1985) theory of achievement is commonly called need achievement or *n*-achievement theory.[3] However, Locke (1991b) concludes that rather than a theory of innate needs, McClelland's theory is based on a complex of values. These values are learned in formal instructional settings or acquired through the events and activities people experience in their culture (Cherrington, 1991). Hence, McClelland's theory of achievement is appropriately classified as a value-based approach to motivation. Specifically, it identifies a complex of values that were first associated with successful entrepreneurship in business settings. McClelland believed that it is the prospect of achievement satisfaction, not money, that motivates the successful entrepreneur.

This theory is also closely associated with the information-processing theory of learning (Cherrington, 1991). As such, it can be partially explained by schema in information-processing theory. For example, values or motives can be represented as learned behavioral predispositions that influence the way individuals perceive situations and motivate them to pursue particular goals.

In contrast to Maslow's fixed hierarchy and innate needs, McClelland's framework asserts that all motives are learned; they become arranged in a hierarchy of potential for influencing behavior; and they vary from person to person. As people develop, they learn to associate positive and negative feelings with certain things that happen to and around them. Accordingly, the achievement value is learned when opportunities for competing with standards of excellence become associated with positive outcomes (Pinder, 1984). For an individual, achievement is directed toward the top of the motive or value hierarchy and it takes only minimal achievement cues to activate the expectation of pleasure. Thus, the likelihood of achievement striving is increased. Under such circumstances weaker motives will probably give way to the achievement motive and assume a distinct secondary role in influencing behavior (Miner, 1980).

McClelland (1961, 1985) hypothesized that individuals who place a high value on achievement have three key characteristics. First, they have a strong desire to assume personal responsibility for performing a task or solving a problem. Consequently, they tend to work alone rather than with others. If the job requires others, they tend to choose co-workers based upon their competence rather than their friendship.

This type of person will prefer situations that allow an individual to take personal responsibility and get personal credit for the outcomes (Miner, 1980). For example, compared to those with low achievement values, individuals with high achievement values are more attracted to reward for performance systems (Turban and Keon, 1993). Second, individuals who place a high value on achievement tend to set moderately difficult goals and take intermediate levels of risk. Where tasks are too hard, the chance of succeeding and probability of motive satisfaction are low. Easy tasks represent things that anyone can do, thus little satisfaction will be gained in accomplishing them. Achievement-motivated individuals tend to calculate the risks and select situations in which they anticipate feeling slightly overextended by the challenges, but not too overextended (Miner, 1980). Third, individuals who place a high value on achievement have a strong desire for performance feedback. These individuals want to know how well they have done, and are anxious to receive knowledge of the results, regardless of whether they have succeeded or failed (Cherrington, 1991). There is little opportunity for achievement satisfaction when a person cannot tell success from failure.

High-value achievers are characterized by their single-minded absorption with task accomplishment (Cherrington, 1991). Consequently, the achievement value is an important motive in schools because when students, teachers, and administrators have a single-minded preoccupation, they are frequently successful. McClelland concluded from his research that the achievement value, like other cognitive structures, is apparently learned at an early age and largely influenced by child-rearing practices and other influences of parents. McClelland (1965) also has demonstrated that training programs that focus on developing achievement values can produce entrepreneurial behavior among adults where it previously did not exist. Consequently, a broad strategy for changing motives is through education and training (Katzell and Thompson, 1990). The idea is that motives and values pertinent to achievement and work behavior are subject to education. Achievement motivation can be strengthened in schools and other settings through training, with favorable consequences for future success. As a caveat, however, most of McClelland's research evidence pertains to boys and men, so his theory is currently limited to males. Attempts to generalize it to females have not been particularly successful (Pinder, 1984).

Charol Shakeshaft (1986), for instance, cites a number of studies that suggest the lack of success by women in obtaining administrative positions is due to lowered aspirations or lack of motivation. Shakeshaft challenges this conclusion and asserts that aspiration and motivation typically are defined only using male perspectives and experience. Her criticism certainly seems applicable to the research on McClelland's model of achievement motivation. Shakeshaft offers two explanations of how aspiration should be interpreted for women. Women aspire to be leaders but the traditional definition of aspiration fails to fit female experience and therefore, if measured by this definition, it appears that women do not aspire to leadership. Alternatively, women aspire to be leaders but organizational and societal barriers prevent women from acknowledging or acting upon their aspirations, and consequently, it appears again that women lack aspiration for leadership. Our position is that aspiration or achievement values are important concepts in understanding individual motivation and probably manifest themselves differently for females and males in schools.

COGNITIVE-CHOICE THEORIES

Choice theories have enjoyed tremendous popularity during the past two decades (Kanfer, 1990). Decisional-choice models are part of a larger family of Expectancy × Value ($E \times V$) theories that have their roots in cognitive theories dating from the 1930s—for example, the work of Edward C. Tolman (1932) and Kurt Lewin (1938). In these models expectancy reflects the individual's belief that he or she can accomplish the task, and values reflect the individual's interest and commitment to achieving the task. The model assumes that most people engage in behavior to the extent that they believe they can accomplish a task that is important to them. All $E \times V$ formulations hold that individuals behave somewhat hedonistically when choosing between tasks and levels of effort. That is, individuals tend to seek pleasure and avoid pain (Steers and Porter, 1991). Two of the best-known examples of cognitive-choice theories are expectancy motivation (Vroom, 1964) and attribution (Weiner, 1986). Both will be described in the following sections.

Expectancy Theory

While expectancy models have a long history in psychology, the approach was popularized and modified specifically for work settings during the 1960s by Victor Vroom (1964) and others (Graen, 1963; Galbraith and Cummings, 1967; Porter and Lawler, 1968). In fact, Vroom (1964) sparked an explosion of research with his formulation of expectancy theory. His model was developed to predict choices among jobs, tasks, and effort levels that yield the highest perceived benefits (Kanfer, 1990). During the late 1960s through the early 1980s, the prevalence of expectancy theory in the literature clearly indicates its centrality to the research on motivation in organizations. Although the frequency of publication has declined, its use has continued (Miller and Grush, 1988). Expectancy theory presents a complex view of individuals in organizations. The basic assumptions, concepts, and generalizations of expectancy theory, however, are easily identified and portrayed.

ASSUMPTIONS Expectancy theory rests on two fundamental premises. First, individuals make decisions about their own behavior in organizations using their abilities to think, reason, and anticipate future events. Motivation is a conscious or cognitive process governed by laws. People subjectively evaluate the expected value of outcomes or personal payoffs resulting from their actions, and then they choose how to behave.

The second assumption is not unique to expectancy theory, and in fact, it was posed in Chapter 2 as a generalization from social systems theory; forces in the individual and the environment combine to determine behavior. Individual values and attitudes, for instance, interact with environmental components, such as role expectations and school culture, to influence behavior.

CONCEPTS Expectancy theory builds on these assumptions with three fundamental concepts—expectancy, instrumentality, and valence. **Expectancy** is the subjective probability or degree of certainty that a given effort will yield a specified performance level. Stated differently, it is the extent to which an individual believes that a given level of activity will result in a specified level of goal accomplishment. The expectancy question is: If I work hard, will I be successful? For example, if teachers think that a high probability exists of improving student achievement by increasing their own efforts, then educators have a high expectancy level. If students strongly believe that they can design and implement a project in science, then the students have high expectancy levels.

Instrumentality is the perceived probability that an incentive will be forthcoming after a given level of performance or achievement. Instrumentality is high when individuals perceive a strong association between performance and being rewarded. The instrumentality question is: If I succeed, what will I receive in return? If teachers think that high student achievement in their classrooms is likely to result in public recognition of their teaching ability, then instrumentality is high. Similarly, if the students perceive that successfully designing and implementing a science project will increase their knowledge about science, then their instrumentalities are high.

Valence is the perceived positive or negative value, worth, or attractiveness that an individual ascribes to potential goals, outcomes, rewards, or incentives for working in an organization. The concept of valence is similar to the concept of values—that is, what people consider or believe beneficial to their welfare or important in their own right. It is the strength of a person's desire for a particular reward. In other words, valences refer to the level of satisfaction the person expects to receive from them, not from the real value that the person actually derives from them (Pinder, 1984). The valence question is: How do I feel about the consequences of my efforts? Feelings of competence, autonomy, recognition, accomplishment, and creativity, for example, represent valued work outcomes for educators and produce high levels of satisfaction.

In general, motivation to behave in a certain way is greatest when the individual believes that:

- He or she has the ability to perform at the desired level (high expectancy).
- The behavior will lead to anticipated outcomes (high instrumentality)
- These outcomes have positive personal values (high valence).

When faced with choices about behavior, the individual goes through a process of considering three questions:

- The expectancy question: Can I perform the task if I work hard?
- The instrumentality question: If I perform at the desired level, what are the outcomes?
- The valence question: How do I like these outcomes?

The individual then decides to behave in the way that appears to have the best chance of producing the desired outcomes (Nadler and Lawler, 1977). In other words, individuals consider alternatives, weigh costs and benefits, and select a course of action of maximum utility (Landy and Becker, 1987).

AN EXPECTANCY MODEL A synthesis of the foregoing assumptions, concepts, and statements produces a general expectancy model of motivation. The model is presented with an illustration for the educational setting in Figure 4.2. Moving across the top from left to right, the force of motivation (FM) leads to an observed level of effort by the individual. Effort combines with a number of factors (i.e., ability, task difficulty, favorableness of the situation) to yield a certain level of performance. The probability that a given effort will yield a certain level of performance (expectancy) serves as feedback to modify the force of motivation. The instrumentality of the performance level is assessed by the individual. The probabilities of receiving certain

FIGURE **4.2**

Expectancy Theory and an Illustration
for the Educational Setting

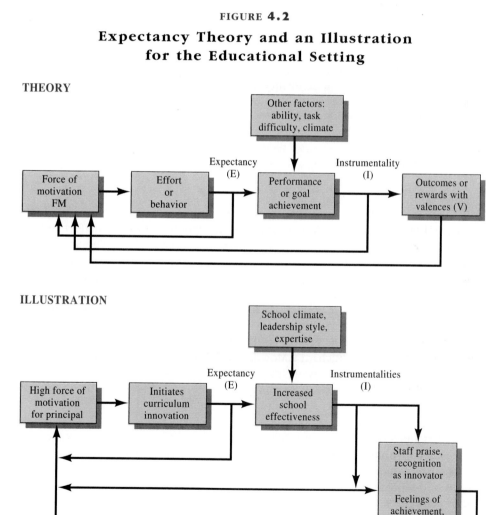

outcomes are assessed and again act as information to change the force of motivation. The outcomes are evaluated for their desirability. In turn, their subjective values become feedback affecting the force of motivation. The overall formulation of **expectancy theory** is that the force of motivation is a function of the interaction of expectancy, instrumentality, and valence.

The lower portion of Figure 4.2 depicts the expectancy model in a school setting. Essentially, the school principal exhibits a high force of motivation. He or she initiates a new curriculum innovation and perceives the effort as having a good chance of improving the school effectiveness levels (expectancy). Student achievement or attitudes are likely to improve as a result of the new program (instrumentality). No doubt, the principal perceives the improvement of academic performance as a strong positive outcome (valence). Thus, expectancy, instrumentality, and valence combine to produce a strong motivational force to implement the program. Of course, the supportiveness and expertise of the staff, the principal's leadership style, and the school climate will also have an impact on the effectiveness levels as well as the innovation. Rewards will be forthcoming.

Research and Evaluation of Expectancy Theory

Several authors (Heneman and Schwab, 1972; Mitchell, 1974; Campbell and Pritchard, 1976) have systematically reviewed the literature reporting research based on expectancy motivation theory and their conclusions are similar. The force of motivation in an expectancy model has been demonstrated to be positively correlated with job satisfaction, effort, and performance in a variety of settings. While the relationships between force of motivation and independent ratings of effort and performance have been significant statistically on a consistent basis, the associations have not been as strong as originally anticipated. In other words, expectancy motivation is an important factor in effort and performance, but other factors in the environment also are important contributors. In fact, stronger support for expectancy theory has been shown for predictions of job choice than for task effort or job performance (Kanfer, 1990).

Investigations conducted in educational organizations based on expectancy theory show similar results. Richard T. Mowday (1978) found that school principals with higher expectancy motivation are more active in attempting to influence district decisions than those with low expectancy motivation. In a study examining the relationship between school structure and teacher motivation, H. Scott Herrick (1973) found strong negative correlations between expectancy motivational force and centralization and stratification. Thus, schools that were highly centralized and stratified were staffed with teachers having low forces of expectancy motivation.

In a study of secondary schools teachers, Cecil Miskel, JoAnn DeFrain, and Kay Wilcox (1980) related the force of motivation to job satisfaction and perceived job performance. The force of motivation was significantly related to job satisfaction and perceived performance for both groups. Similarly, Miskel and his colleagues David McDonald and Susan Bloom (1983) found that expectancy motivation of teachers was consistently related to teacher job satisfaction, student attitudes toward school, and perceived school effectiveness. Robert Kottkamp and John A. Mulhern (1987) found that expectancy is positively related to both the openness of school climate and humanism in pupil control ideology. Linda L. Graham (1980) found that expectancy theory predicted the satisfaction, participation in activities, and achievement of college students.

One criticism is that expectancy theory overemphasizes linearity. For example, if any component—expectancy, valence, instrumentality—increases, then motivation force becomes greater. The role of rationality is also overemphasized. Obviously, individuals neither have the information-processing capacity to consider all of the relevant information nor do they always select the best alternative when deciding how to act.

In sum, expectancy theory has generated a large number of investigations in educational as well as business settings. The results are generally supportive. Pinder (1984) concludes that there are grounds for optimism that the theory is a reasonably valid model of the causes of work behavior. The following conclusions are warranted from the literature:

- Expectancy theory is an excellent predictor of job satisfaction.
- Expectancy theory predicts performance but not as well as it predicts satisfaction.
- Expectancy theory demonstrates that people work hard when they think that working hard is likely to lead to desirable outcomes.

Attribution Theory

As individuals see events happen to themselves and others, they ask why. They then make inferences or attributions about causes. Students may ask: Why did I fail the final examination? Was it because of a lack of effort? Or am I not smart enough to understand the material? Based on such observations and questions, Bernard Weiner (1972, 1985, 1986) uses the attribution concept to create a cognitive choice model of motivation. In essence, **attribution theory** focuses on causal explanations that individuals make about past behaviors, especially in regard to achievement efforts, and how attributions influence behavior through their effects on expectancies. Attribution theorists assume that individuals naturally search for understanding about why events happen, especially when the outcome is important or unexpected (Stipek, 1993). When people make causal attributions, they are essentially seeking or creating knowledge. Once the knowledge is available, they can use it to better manage themselves and their environments.

Causal attributions are perceptions of the cause of achievement outcomes (Stipek, 1993). The most common attributions made in achievement situations such as schools are ability and effort. For example, in terms of ability, I passed the test because I am smart or, conversely, I failed because I am dumb; in terms of effort, I did or did not study. Other attributions are made about task difficulty (how hard the test was) and luck (guessing the answers). These specific causal attributions—ability, effort, task difficulty, luck—become more important determinants of achievement behavior as they are considered in conjunction with three structural dimensions.

Weiner (1985, 1986) posits that information gained from performance feedback and rewards is assessed through three structural dimensions of causal attributions—locus, stability, and controllability. **Locus** defines the location of the cause as internal or external. Ability and effort are the most common internal factors on the locus dimension. Task difficulty and luck are common external determinants of outcomes. The **stability** dimension designates causes as constant or varying over time. Ability is stable because an individual's aptitude for a task is thought to be relatively fixed, whereas effort is unstable because people can vary their labor from one situation to another. **Controllability** refers to personal responsibility, or whether a cause is subject to one's own choice. Effort is controllable because individuals are thought to be responsible for how hard they try. In contrast, ability and luck are generally believed to be beyond personal control (Weiner, 1986; Kanfer, 1990; Graham, 1991).

Attribution theory also offers an explanation of the emotional reactions that individuals have toward success and failure (Weiner, 1985). According to Sandra Graham (1991), emotions are hypothesized to be associated with each causal dimension. The locus dimension is primarily linked to pride and other esteem-related affects. We feel pride when we succeed because of our abilities and efforts, whereas low self-esteem is the consequence of attributing failure to internal factors. The stability dimension is linked to emotions that implicate future expectations. For instance, stable causes for failure produce hopelessness, apathy, and resignation. The controllability dimension is linked to a set of social emotions that includes guilt, shame, pity, and anger. One feels guilty when the causes of personal failure are due to controllable factors. This includes both the lack of effort and deciding not to take responsibility for action. Shame is more likely to be experienced when personal failures are due to uncontrollable factors such as ability.

By attaching emotional reactions to the three attributional dimensions, outcomes may be perceived to have internal and unstable causes yet fall within an individual's responsibility and choice (Kanfer, 1990). For example, if new teachers perceive their failure to engage students in a class project as being caused by a lack of preparation, then they will suffer low self-esteem and guilt for their poor performance. Their perception of the cause as being internal, unstable, and controllable—that is, within their power to change—enables them to be optimistic for future success. However, highly experienced teachers who have repeatedly failed to engage students in classroom projects are likely to attribute the cause of their failure to a lack of ability—that is, the cause is internal, stable, and uncontrollable. These teachers expect repeated failures, hopelessness, low self-esteem, and shame. They have low motivation to perform in the classroom.

Some criticize attribution theory as no more than naive psychology that is just common sense (Graham, 1991). For example, we pity the handicapped but feel anger toward the lazy who are unwilling to work, or we expect to repeat our successes when we have high ability. Some might contend that such causal attributions are part of our shared ways of thinking about our social world and not scientific knowledge. Attribution theorists believe, however, that an important goal is to systematize what we know to be common sense and place it in a conceptual framework that accounts for a wide array of social phenomena. The research shows consistent support for the attribution mechanisms and effects of expectancy for future performance (Miner, 1980; Weiner, 1986; Kanfer, 1990).

The central ingredients of attribution theory can be summarized with a series of questions:

- The causal question: What are the causes of the outcome?
- The locus question: Is the cause internal (ability, effort) or external (task difficulty, luck)?
- The stability question: Are causes fixed or changing?
- The controllability question: Can I control the causes?

Students, teachers, and administrators will be highly motivated when they know the causes of the outcomes; the causes are internal; the causes are amenable to change; and the causes are under their control.

Overall, expectancy and attribution models of choice theory provide important perspectives about how cognitive processes are involved in individual work motivation in schools. Choice theories continue to enjoy popularity, with a significant amount of scholarly activity surrounding each formulation. However, the area with the greatest scholarly activity involves theories dealing with self-regulation, commonly called metacognition approaches.

METACOGNITION APPROACHES

In contrast to need-value and cognitive-choice paradigms, metacognition theories concentrate on processes that govern the impact of goals on behavior. The goal construct is central. Descriptions of motivation in these perspectives focus on self-governing mechanisms that determine how motivational force is transformed into behavior and performance. A distinct advantage of such models is that they link intentions, goals, behavior, and performance (Kanfer, 1990). We focus on two metacognition approaches—self-efficacy and goal-setting theory.

Self-Efficacy Theory

Among all the aspects of self-knowledge and self-regulation, personal efficacy is probably the most influential in everyday life. **Self-efficacy** is a person's judgment about his or her capability to organize and execute a course of action that is required to attain a certain level of performance (Bandura, 1986, 1991). In other words, it is an individual's overall judgment of his or her perceived capacity for performing a task. For example, the belief of a mathematics teacher that he or she can successfully teach calculus to a class of twelfth-grade students is an efficacy judgment. Similarly, principals with high self-efficacy might believe that they could have a positive effect on student achievement or increase the emphasis on academic learning in schools. Note that, in contrast to causal attributions where the focus is on the past, perceptions of self-efficacy represent future expectations of being able to attain certain levels of performance.

Self-efficacy beliefs contribute to motivation by determining the goals that individuals set for themselves, how much effort they expend, how long they persevere in the face of difficulties, and their resilience to failures (Wood and Bandura, 1989; Bandura, 1993). The stronger people believe in their capabilities, the greater and more persistent are their efforts. People tend to avoid tasks and situations that exceed their capacity; they seek activities they judge themselves capable of handling. The consequences of high self-efficacy—willingness to approach and persist on tasks, selection of task and situation, a focus on problem-solving strategies, reduced fear and anxiety, positive emotional experiences—affect achievement outcomes (Stipek, 1993). Hence, people who have the same skills but different levels of personal efficacy may perform at different levels because of the way they use, combine, and sequence their skills in a changing context (Gist and Mitchell, 1992).

Development of Self-Efficacy

Self-efficacy expectations develop from a variety of sources, including performance feedback, previous history, and social influence. However, self-efficacy is postulated to develop from four primary sources of experience—mastery experiences, modeling, verbal persuasion, and physiological arousal.

The most important source is mastery experiences. Performance successes and failures (i.e., actual experiences) in completing tasks have strong effects on self-efficacy. Recurrent successes raise efficacy perceptions; regular failures raise self-doubts and reduce self-efficacy, especially if failure occurs early in a task sequence and does not reflect a lack of effort or opposing external influences. Efficacy is facilitated as gradual accomplishments build skills, coping abilities, and exposure needed for task performance.

Modeling affects self-perceptions of efficacy through two processes. First, it provides knowledge. Watching an expert complete a task conveys effective strategies for managing similar tasks in different situations. Second, people partly judge their capabilities using social comparisons. Seeing or visualizing people similar to oneself successfully perform a task can raise one's own beliefs about self-efficacy. By observing people modeling certain behaviors, individuals convince themselves that if others can do it, they can at least achieve some improvement in their performance. Modeling experiences are most influential for individuals in situations in which they have limited personal experience with the task.

Verbal persuasion is widely used to try to talk people into believing that they have the capacity to achieve what they want to accomplish. Social persuasion alone has limited power to create lasting increases in self-efficacy, but it can contribute to successful performance if the heightened appraisal is within realistic bounds. To the extent that self-efficacy is boosted through verbal persuasion and people try hard to succeed, verbal persuasion can promote the development of skills and a sense of self-efficacy (Bandura, 1986; Gist, 1987; Wood and Bandura, 1989).

People also rely partly on information from their physiological state to judge their capability. Individuals make judgments about anticipated performance based on pos-

FIGURE **4.3**

A Schematic for Self-Efficacy

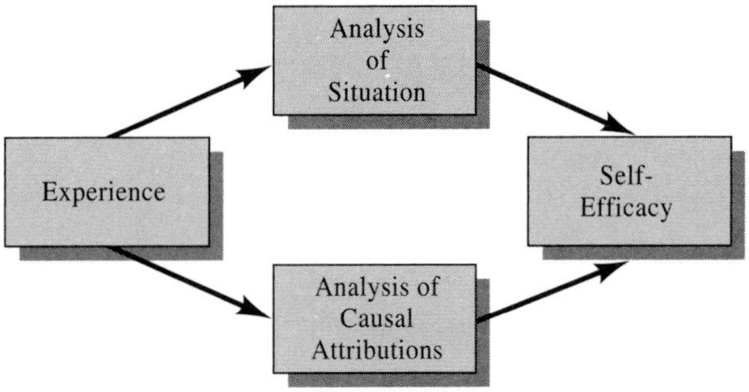

itive arousal such as excitement and enthusiasm and on negative factors such as fear, fatigue, stress, and anxiety. General physical condition, personality factors (Type A), and mood can all induce arousal (Gist, 1987). Hence, another way to modify beliefs of self-efficacy is for individuals to enhance their physical well-being and to reduce their stress (Wood and Bandura, 1989).

Gist and Mitchell (1992) propose that the relationships between the four types of experience and self-efficacy are mediated by analyses of the task situation and causal attributions. This set of relationships is shown in Figure 4.3. Based on experience, several situational factors might be considered. An analysis of the situation in terms of task requirements, human resources, and the school organization produces inferences about what it will take to perform successfully. In preparing to teach calculus to twelfth graders, for example, a teacher would determine the mathematical ability and motivational levels of the students; availability of instructional resources such as books, outside tutors, and computer support; and the environmental emphasis on student achievement. An analysis of causal attributions from previous experience in similar situations is likely to affect efficacy judgments. What produced earlier success? In the example of teaching calculus to twelfth graders, the actual experiences of the teacher in previous years, new modeling experiences, persuasion by the principal and colleagues, and his or her physical state will be filtered through the dimensions of locus, stability, and controllability. Gist and Mitchell believe that these analysis processes of the situation and attributions yield summary-level judgments that define self-efficacy.

Research and Evaluation of Self-Efficacy Theory

In the general organization and management literature, empirical studies of self-efficacy have produced consistent results. Self-efficacy is associated with such work-related performance as productivity, coping with difficult tasks, career choice, learning and achievement, and adaptability to new technology (Gist and Mitchell, 1992). Similar results are evident in educational settings. Self-efficacy research in schools tends to focus on one of two areas or approaches. The first group of studies tests for the effects of student and teacher self-efficacy on various motivational and achievement indicators. The general finding is that self-efficacy is positively related to student achievement (Armor et al., 1976), course grades (Pintrich and Garcia, 1991), student motivation (Midgley, Feldlaufer, and Eccles, 1989), teacher adoption of innovations (Berman et al., 1977; Smylie, 1988), superintendents' rating of teachers' competence (Trentham, Silvern, and Brogdon, 1985), and classroom management strategies of teachers (Ashton and Webb, 1986). Moreover, experimental studies have consistently found that changing self-efficacy beliefs can lead to better use of cognitive strategies and higher levels of academic achievement for mathematics, reading, and writing tasks (Schunk, 1991).

The second area or approach explores the personal and situational factors in schools that influence the self-efficacy of students and teachers. Anita E. Woolfolk and Wayne K. Hoy (Hoy and Woolfolk, 1990; Woolfolk and Hoy, 1990; Woolfolk, Rosoff, and Hoy, 1990; Hoy and Woolfolk, 1993) have found the following: personal efficacy is related to bureaucratic orientation of prospective teachers, increases during student teaching, is positively related to organizational health variables of principal influence and academic emphasis in the school, and is related to a humanistic approach to controlling students.

To recapitulate, self-efficacy is an important motivational factor that influences a number of behavioral and performance outcomes. To a substantial extent, self-efficacy is learned through a variety of experiences. Hence, self-efficacy is dynamic; it can change over time as new information and experiences are acquired. Issues that remain unresolved include the extent to which self-efficacy and performance can be raised and the overall elasticity of self-efficacy (Gist and Mitchell, 1992). Therefore, four conclusions are warranted:

- Individuals who have stronger beliefs about their capabilities are more successful and persistent in their efforts.
- Individuals tend to avoid tasks and situations that exceed their capacity.
- Individuals seek activities they judge themselves capable of handling.
- Individuals develop self-efficacy through mastery experiences, modeling, persuasion, and physiological arousal.

These conclusions are generated by four key questions:

- *The self-efficacy question:* Do I believe in myself to accomplish a task?
- *The difficulty question:* How hard is the task?
- *The capacity question:* Do I have the ability to accomplish the task?
- *The source question:* How do I develop a positive sense of self-efficacy?

Goal-Setting Theory

Although its historical origins date to the early twentieth century, Edwin A. Locke and his associate Gary P. Latham (Locke 1968; Locke and Latham, 1984, 1990) are generally recognized for the development and renewed interest in goal-setting theory. As a cognitive approach of work motivation, goal-setting theory gained popularity during the 1970s and is now arguably the leading approach. The basic postulate of the theory is that intentions to achieve a goal constitute the primary motivating force behind work behavior. Goals direct both mental and physical actions of individuals. Based on the work of Locke and Latham (1990), we developed the schematic illustration of goal-setting theory shown in Figure 4.4.

DETERMINANTS OF GOAL CHOICE The goal-setting process begins with the assumption that the individual has certain motivational dispositions and knows something about the nature and properties of organization—for example, possible incentives that exist in the work environment (see Figure 4.4). This knowledge is gained through experience in the organization and the exercise of reason. Because action or behavior is required to fulfill personal needs, the individual necessarily must judge the elements in the environment to determine which actions will enhance the individual's well-being. Values are thus the basis for choosing among alternative courses of action. Using a code of personal values or set of standards, the individual judges which behaviors are good or bad, right or wrong, for or against personal interests. This evaluation is made by estimating the relationship between perceptions of the outcomes available in the environment and assessments of personal expectancies, self-efficacy, and attributions. Based on the selected alternative, the individual anticipates new conditions in the work environment and projects outcomes for the anticipated performance and satisfaction. Based on these personal (and other) determinants, the individual formulates the goals or set of intentions and is ready to act.

FIGURE **4.4**

A Schematic of Goal Theory

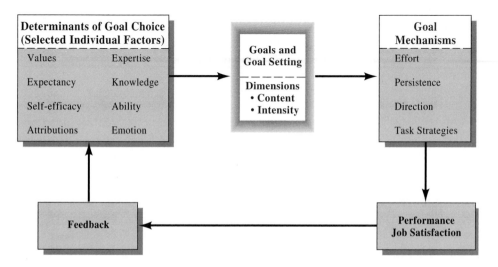

INDIVIDUAL GOALS Defined simply, a **goal** is what an individual is consciously and intentionally trying to do. Goals are aims or outcomes that an individual would like to achieve. They define for the individual an acceptable level of performance or direction of action. In terms of individual motivation, goals are always within the person, although they are often constructed from context information (Ford, 1992). For example, teachers will commonly adopt goals shared by other teachers or developed by the school.

Locke and Latham (1990) observe that goals like other mental processes have two main dimensions—content and intensity (see Figure 4.4). **Goal content** is the object or result being sought. Typically, goal content involves some aspect of the external world, although it is possible for people to have psychological goals such as high self-respect, happiness, and less anxiety. Examples of concrete or specific goal content might include useful pieces of information, a good grade, a new curriculum, or an improved set of teaching skills. Examples of more abstract content might include achievement, self-esteem, and cognitive activities. Attempts to specify the content of people's goals apparently have received little attention (Ford, 1992). One likely source to define goal content would be need and value theories. Goal content directs and influences behavior because different goals require varying amounts of effort. In fact, goal content varies for individuals in several ways—time perspective (short term or long term), difficulty (easy or hard), number (few or many), and specificity (concrete or abstract).

Goal intensity is the effort required to form the goal, the importance that a person assigns the goal, and the commitment to the goal. The research on goal intensity has dealt primarily with the determinants and effects of commitment. Commitment is the degree to which the individual is attached to the goal, considers it important, is determined to reach it, and keeps it in the face of setbacks and obstacles. Factors that enhance commitment are those that convince people that achieving the goal is possible and important or appropriate (Latham and Locke, 1991). Commitment influences and regulates energy expenditure because important goals are more likely to be accepted, to elicit intense involvement, and thus to foster persistent actions (Miner, 1980). It is virtually axiomatic that if there is no commitment to goals, then goal setting does not work (Locke, Latham, and Erez, 1988). Hence, goal setting is consciously conceiving a desired future state in terms of goal content and intensity.

GOAL MECHANISMS Locke and Latham (1990) postulate four **goal mechanisms,** three direct (effort, persistence, direction) and one indirect (task strategies), to explain the effect of goals on action (see Figure 4.4). They believe that the three direct goal mechanisms correspond to the three attributes of motivated action— arousal (initiation), choice (direction), and duration (maintenance). Goals affect arousal by creating intensity of effort that the individual expends on a task. They affect choice by leading people to direct attention to and take action with respect to goal-relevant activities while ignoring other activities. They affect duration by leading people to persist in their actions until the goal is reached.

Once an individual has a goal and decides to act on it, these three mechanisms are brought into play automatically. We learn at an early age that, to achieve a goal, we must exert effort, persist over time, and pay attention to the goal and our progress. In some instances, however, these direct mechanisms are not sufficient to achieve the goal. In such cases the individual also has to engage in a process of problem solving in order to discover how the goal can be reached. Problem solving involves discovering or creating suitable task strategies. Similar to the schema concept in information processing, task strategies are conscious or deliberate action plans motivated by goals. In terms of information processing, using task strategies would include recalling existing schemas and probably constructing new ones. Thus, task strategies can be thought of as cognitive structures and processes that also constitute an indirect goal mechanism.

PERFORMANCE AND JOB SATISFACTION As shown in Figure 4.4, two basic outcomes of goal-setting actions are performance and satisfaction. Level of performance is the degree of goal attainment. Performance falling short of the goal is unsatisfactory. Conversely, performance achieving or exceeding the goal is positive. Similarly, job satisfaction is an affective or emotional consequence of effectively completing a personally engaging and significant task or goal. If the rewards associated with goal attainment provide the individual with what he or she wants and values, the individual experiences satisfaction with the job. Hence, both performance and satisfaction form the basis of feedback to individuals about their goals and goal-setting process (Ford, 1992).

FEEDBACK Feedback provides individuals with knowledge of results about job performance and satisfaction levels. This knowledge of results allows individuals to appraise outcomes in two different fashions. A cognitive appraisal can be made about performance. Through this process an individual uses the knowledge of results to gain a conceptual understanding of why the performance was at a particular level and how it might be improved. The reasons, for example, might include the nature of the task, the person's ability, and the effort expended. Almost simultaneous with the cognitive appraisal, a value appraisal is made. As an emotional response to the knowledge of results, the outcomes are evaluated against the individual's value standards. Value appraisal might affect other cognitive motivation factors such as expectancies, efficacy, attributions, and emotions. These cognitive and value appraisals can include not only previous performance and satisfaction but projections about the future. Hence, cognitive and value appraisals of feedback information are hypothesized to lead to adjustments in the determinants of goal choice and subsequently future goals and actions (Locke and Latham, 1990).

In sum, goal-setting theory maintains that most human action is purposive; behavior is regulated and maintained by goals and intentions. The most fundamental effect of goals on mental or physical actions is to direct thoughts and overt behavior to one end rather than another. Because pursuit of some goals requires greater mental concentration and physical effort than others, goals, in the process of directing action, also regulate energy expenditure. For example, if a teacher decides (sets a goal) to develop a new set of lesson plans rather than to use existing guides, this action necessarily requires more directed, sustained effort than using the available plans.

Research and Evaluation of Goal Theory

Early support for Locke's ideas came primarily from a series of well-controlled laboratory experiments. Most of these studies used college students who performed relatively simple tasks for short periods of time. Since the theory originally relied only on evidence from sheltered and contrived situations, the theory's proponents next attempted to respond to the following question: Can a practice so deceptively simple as setting specific, difficult goals increase the performance of employees in natural organizational settings where experimental effects are absent and goal acceptance is not easily obtained? The evidence from field studies does indicate that goal theory is valid for describing employee behavior in organizations such as schools (Latham and Yukl, 1975; Locke and Latham, 1990).

In particular, two generalizations drawn from goal theory continue to enjoy substantial support from findings produced by both laboratory and field research methods (Locke and Latham, 1990). First, difficult goals, if accepted, result in higher levels of performance than easy ones. An explanation of the goal-difficulty effect is that hard goals lead to greater effort and persistence than do easy goals, assuming they are accepted. Similarly, hard goals make self-satisfaction contingent on a higher level of performance than do easy goals. Second, specific and difficult goals produce higher levels of performance than vague, nonquantitative goals, such as do your best, work at a moderate rate, or no goals at all. An explanation for this finding is that vague or general goals are inherently ambiguous and people give themselves the benefit of the doubt in evaluating their performance. With ambiguous standards, individuals assume that they have met the "do your best" criterion. From the standpoint of goal-setting theory, however, a specific hard goal clarifies for the person what constitutes effective performance, and the person is no longer able to interpret a wide range of performance levels as indicative of excellent performance (Latham and Locke, 1991).

A third and controversial generalization deals with the source of goals, commitment, and performance. Goals can be set in three ways: individuals can choose their own goals; they can be set jointly or participatively; or they can be assigned by others. Because of the contradictory research findings, Locke and Latham (1990) helped design an elaborate set of research projects to test the effects of participation in goal settings on commitment and performance. The results indicated that the motivational effects of assigned goals are as powerful as participatively set goals in generating high goal commitment and subsequent performance. Likewise, self-set goals are not consistently more effective in bringing about goal commitment or an increase in performance than other methods of goal setting. On the whole, therefore, all three methods of setting goals are equally effective.

In sum, Locke and Latham (1990) conclude that the supporting evidence for goal theory is overwhelming:

- Difficult goals, if accepted, result in higher levels of performance than do easy ones.

- Specific and difficult goals produce higher levels of performance than do vague, nonquantitative goals.
- Goals are strong motivators regardless of whether they are self-selected, jointly chosen, or assigned by others.

Moreover, goal-setting effects generalize across a wide range of tasks, situations, subjects, countries, performance criteria, and time spans. The results hold at both the individual and at group levels and across different methods of goal setting. Few other theories in organizational science can claim such wide-ranging support.

SYNTHESIS: A MOTIVATION SEQUENCE

The plethora of motivational models that we have just reviewed creates great difficulty in gaining an overall understanding of individual motivation. Locke (1991b) opines that a primary reason for the difficulty in integrating most theories is that they pertain to different phases of a motivational sequence. To alleviate this problem and to advance the field's understanding of individual motivation, Locke proposes a **motivation sequence** to integrate the various components that we have reviewed. An adaptation of the motivation sequence proposed by Locke is shown in Figure 4.5.

Each component of the sequence has been discussed in some detail and will not be repeated. Locke notes that the sequence begins with needs. Thus needs, such as

FIGURE **4.5**

A Motivation Sequence

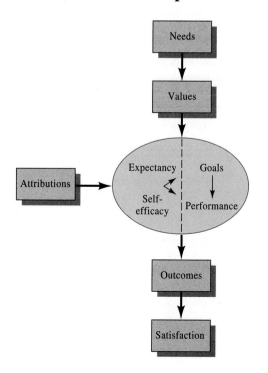

described in Maslow's model, constitute the foundation of motivation. Needs confront individuals with the requirement for action, if they choose to live. However, needs cannot be translated into goals until they have a cognitive representation in the form of values (Erez and Earley, 1993). Thus, values play a necessary role in ascribing cognitive meanings to needs and in transforming needs into goals and intentions for action. Values from achievement motivation and from the valence concept in expectancy theory fall into this step of the sequence. Next, Locke (1991b) describes the relation of values to goals as from general to specific. Goals can be viewed as applications of values to specific situations. Goals reflect an individual's values as they are applied in a given situation. As shown in Figure 4.5, expectancy and self-efficacy not only affect the goals individuals choose but also have powerful effects on performance. Locke believes, however, that goals and self-efficacy are the most direct and immediate motivational determinants of performance. In addition, attributions individuals make about their performance impact subsequent emotions and actions. As a consequence of their performance or actions, people experience rewards (see Chapter 10) and punishments. The final step in the sequence consists of the satisfaction individuals derive from the rewards they receive.

Within the sequence, Locke (1991b) also designates a motivation core and motivation hub. Individual values constitute the **motivation core,** or the essence of motivation. It is at this stage that individuals become unique by using values to guide choices and actions. He believes that values are key to personal identity. As the values of individuals become more developed, intense, and integrated, the stronger is the sense of identity. The **motivation hub** comprises the linkages among the goal, performance, and self-efficacy components. The hub is the center of activity and Locke asserts that the motivational hub is where the action is. He thinks that the linkages in the hub constitute a theoretical convergence where fundamental motivational truths have been discovered—what people do is powerfully influenced by their goals and by their perceived confidence in being able to take action.

While the motivation sequence is not a grand theory of human motivation, it does help provide a useful and integrative perspective. It shows how various theories deal with different phases of the motivation sequence as well as possible linkages among the many theories of individual motivation.

SUMMARY AND SUGGESTED READINGS

By focusing on cognition, it is easy to overemphasize the individual and neglect the social and organizational contexts. Healthy individuals do not live within themselves; they live within many contexts (e.g., schools, classrooms, families, gangs, and social clubs). As cognitive approaches have become popularized, new models of information processing and motivation have emerged. They provide useful insights into how people think and interact with their environments.

Information-processing models describe the nature and organization of memory, define basic cognitive processes, and sequence these processes to produce intelligent behavior. The basic idea is that individuals have internal mental models (symbol systems) of the external world that guide such tasks as decision making, problem solving, and interacting. Four models of information processing are rational, limited capacity, expert, and cybernetic.

Early theories of motivation portrayed humans as reactive organisms compelled by internal and external forces (e.g., instincts, needs, incentives, reinforcers) that were essentially beyond their control (Ford, 1992). It was assumed that if one could "punch" the correct buttons, motivation would result. This highly mechanistic view still guides the way many people think about human motivation in education, in educational reform, and in designing jobs for students and educators—topics we will turn to in Chapter 10, "Motivating." Contemporary theories of motivation assume that the individual is highly complex and to a considerable extent, able to decide on appropriate courses of action. In other words, individuals are capable of controlling and influencing their own behavior. The major cognitive determinants of individual behavior are beliefs, needs, values, self-efficacy, causal attributions, expectations, and goals. Several cognitive theories use various combinations of these concepts to explain how and why the individual initiates, directs, and maintains work behavior.

The multitude of concepts and different models make it difficult to gain an overall understanding or grand model of individual motivation. However, a broad perspective is created by synthesizing the models into a motivational sequence (see Figure 4.5).

Although information processing and motivation as cognitive processes can be separated conceptually for study, in reality they are virtually never independent. All cognitive knowledge is appraised (e.g., "Is this fact good, bad, or irrelevant to me?"). This motivational appraisal is one way knowledge is put into action. Similarly, all motivation is based on information processing (e.g., "I want to teach with an active project method because it is good for my students."). Hence, most action is guided by both information processing and by individual motivation (Locke and Latham, 1990).

Cognition, information processing, and motivation all have extensive bodies of literature. A good point of access to cognitive approaches is through the books of Howard Gardner (1987, 1991). They explore a wide range of historical, philosophical, and educational issues and provide excellent foundations for further reading. Lord and Maher (1991b) supply a comprehensive treatment of information processing in leadership and management contexts. Efficient access to the literature dealing with motivation in organizations can be gained through Kanfer's (1990) integrative review in which she gives extensive consideration to a wide range of motivation theories. The collection of readings by Steers and Porter (1991) discusses a variety of models. A classic work, of course, is Maslow's (1970), *Motivation and Personality.* Locke and Latham's (1990) book on goal-setting theory is a must for all students of organizations. It not only details the theory and all of the components, but the book contains an extensive review of the research literature. Journals that frequently publish articles on information processing and work motivation include *Journal of Applied Psychology, Organization Behavior and Human Decision Processes,* and *Academy of Management Review.* Finally, for a metacritical perspective, you should consult the article by Sievers (1986).

NOTES

1. In contrast to the traditional approach, connectionist theory, as an emerging and complementary perspective, relies more on biological metaphors of the brain and neurological processes than on information processing. For an excellent presentation of the tenets of connectionist theory, see Lord and Maher (1991a).

2. Christopher Hodgkinson (1978, 1991) offers a powerful analytic model of the value concept and its many applications in educational leadership.

3. According to Campbell et al. (1970), McClelland sought to refine and investigate a subset of motives from a longer list developed by H. A. Murray. Three motives received the most attention—need for achievement, need for power, and need for affiliation. Achievement motivation has received the most attention and was formalized into a theory of expectancy achievement motivation. For present purposes, we limit our discussion to the value portion of the theory.

KEY CONCEPTS AND IDEAS

Attribution theory

Causal attributions

Cognition

Cognitive architecture

Controllability

Cybernetic model

Expectancy

Expectancy theory

Expert model

Feedback

Goal

Goal content

Goal intensity

Goal mechanisms

Information processing

Instrumentality

Limited-capacity model

Locus

Metacognitive processing

Motivation core

Motivation hub

Motivation sequence

Need hierarchy

Needs

Organizational cognition

Rational model

Schema

Self-efficacy

Stability

Valence

Values

Work motivation

Culture and Climate of Schools

The behavior of a group cannot be predicted solely from an understanding of the personality of each of its member. Various social processes intervene . . . the group develops a "mood," an "atmosphere." In the context of the organization, we talk about a "style," a "culture," a "character."

—Henry Mintzberg
Power In and Around Organizations

PREVIEW

1. Organizational culture and organizational climate are two contemporary perspectives for examining the distinctive characters of schools; they are partly competing, partly complementary.

2. Organizational culture is manifest in norms, shared values, and basic assumptions, each occurring at a different level of abstraction.

3. Strong organizational cultures can improve or hinder the effectiveness of an organization; different cultures are effective depending on environmental constraints.

4. School cultures can be interpreted by analyzing their symbols, artifacts, rites, ceremonies, icons, heroes, myths, rituals, and legends.

5. Often the most important thing about events in organizations is not what happened but what the events mean.

6. Organizational climate is a relatively enduring quality of a school that is manifest in teachers' collective perceptions of organizational behavior.

7. The climate of schools can be viewed from a variety of vantage points; three useful perspectives are the openness of behavior, the health of interpersonal relations, and the humanism of pupil-control ideologies.

8. Each of these climate perspectives can be reliably measured using the appropriate survey instrument.

9. The openness and health of a school are related to a number of important organizational outcomes including perceptions of school effectiveness and student achievement.

10. Humanism in pupil-control ideology is related to teacher efficacy as well as to such student outcomes as higher self-actualization, less alienation, and a better quality of school life.

11. There is no quick and simple way to change the culture or climate of schools, but long-term planning is more likely to produce change than will short-term fads.

12. Three complementary strategies for organizational change are a clinical view, a growth-centered approach, and a norm-changing plan.

Behavior in organizations is not simply a function of formal expectations and individual cognition and motivation. The relationships among these elements are dynamic. Participants bring with them to the workplace a host of unique attributes, sentiments, values, needs, motives, and cognitions. These individual characteristics mediate the rational and planned aspects of organizational life. Moreover, a collective sense of identity emerges that transforms a simple aggregate of individuals into a distinctive workplace "personality" or culture.

This indigenous feel of the workplace has been analyzed and studied under a variety of labels, including "organizational character," "milieu," "atmosphere," "ideology," "climate," "culture," "emergent system," and "informal organization." Our analysis of the internal workplace environment will focus on two related concepts—organizational culture and organizational climate. Each of these notions suggests a natural, spontaneous, and human side to the organization; each suggests that the organizational whole is greater than the sum of its parts; and each attempts to uncover the shared meanings and unwritten rules that guide organizational behavior.[1]

ORGANIZATIONAL CULTURE

Concern for the culture of the work group is not new. As we have seen, in the 1930s and 1940s, both Elton Mayo (1945) and Chester Barnard (1938) were stressing the importance of work-group norms, sentiments, values, and emergent interactions in the workplace as they described the nature and functions of informal organization. Philip Selznick (1957) extended the analysis of organizational life by viewing organizations as institutions rather than merely rational organizations. Institutions, according to Selznick (1957: 14), are "infused with value beyond the technical requirements at hand." This infusion of value produces a *distinctive identity* for the organization; it defines organizational character. Selznick (1957) continues:

> Whenever individuals become attached to an organization or a way of doing things as persons rather than technicians, the result is apprising of the device for its own sake. From the standpoint of the committed person, the organization is changed from an expendable tool into a valued source

of personal satisfaction. . . . Where institutionalization is well advanced, distinctive outlooks, habits, and other commitments are unified, coloring all aspects of organizational life and lending it a social integration that goes well beyond formal co-ordination and command. (p. 14)

Indeed, it is Selznick's formulation of organizations as institutions, each with distinctive competence and organizational character, that provides a basis for contemporary analyses of organizations as cultures (Peters and Waterman, 1982).

Organizational culture is an attempt to get at the feel, sense, atmosphere, character, or image of an organization. It encompasses many of the earlier notions of informal organization, norms, values, ideologies, and emergent systems. What distinguishes the contemporary formulation—as culture—is its anthropological basis. Meryl Reis Louis (1985) explains:

The question is not for strictly psychological or sociological components of the phenomenon, as was the case in the past. Rather, the uniquely integrative and phenomenological core of the subject, in which the interweaving of individuals into a community takes place, has finally become the subject of investigation among social scientists. (p. 27)

The popularity of the term "organizational culture" is in part a function of a number of popular books on successful business corporations. The basic theme of all these analyses is that effective organizations have strong and distinctive corporate cultures and that a basic function of executive leadership is to shape the culture of the organization.

DEFINITION OF ORGANIZATIONAL CULTURE

The notion of culture brings with it conceptual complexity and confusion. No intact definition for culture from anthropology exists; instead, we find numerous, diverse definitions. It should not be surprising, therefore, that there are many definitions of organizational culture. For example, William Ouchi (1981: 41) defines organizational culture as "symbols, ceremonies, and myths that communicate the underlying values and beliefs of that organization to its employees." Jay Lorsch (1985: 84), on the other hand, uses culture to mean "the beliefs top managers in a company share about how they should manage themselves and other employees and how they should conduct their business." Henry Mintzberg (1989: 98) refers to culture as organization ideology, or "the traditions and beliefs of an organization that distinguish it from other organizations and infuse a certain life into the skeleton of its structure." Alan Wilkins and Kerry Patterson (1985: 265) maintain that, "an organization's culture consists largely of what people believe about what works and what does not," while Joanne Martin (1985: 95) argues that "culture is an expression of people's deepest needs, a means of endowing their experiences with meaning." Stephen Robbins (1991: 572) defines organization culture as "a common perception held by the organization's members; a system of shared meaning." Howard Schwartz and Stanley Davis (1981: 33) regard culture as "a pattern of beliefs and expectations shared by the organization's members 'that produces' norms that powerfully shape the behavior of individuals and groups in organization." But Edgar Schein (1985:6) argues that the culture should be reserved for "the deeper level of basic assumptions and beliefs that are shared by members of an organization, that operate unconsciously, and that define in a basic 'taken-for-granted' fashion an organization's view of itself and its environment."

Organizational culture, then, is typically defined in terms of *shared orientations that hold the unit together and give it a distinctive identity.* But substantial disagreement arises about what is shared—norms, values, philosophies, perspectives, beliefs, expectations, attitudes, myths, or ceremonies. Another problem is determining the intensity of shared orientations of organizational members. Do organizations have a basic culture or many cultures? Moreover, there is disagreement on the extent to which organizational culture is conscious and overt or unconscious and covert.

LEVELS OF ORGANIZATIONAL CULTURE

One way to begin to untangle some of the problems of definition is to view culture at different levels. As illustrated in Figure 5.1, culture is manifest in norms, shared values, and basic assumptions, each occurring at different levels of depth and abstraction.

Culture as Shared Norms

A fairly concrete, some would say superficial, perspective on culture emerges when behavioral norms are used as the basic elements of culture (see Figure 5.1). **Norms** are usually unwritten and informal expectations that occur just below the surface of experience. Norms directly influence behavior. They are much more visible than either values or tacit assumptions; consequently, they provide a clear means for helping people understand the cultural aspects of organizational life. Moreover, if we are concerned with changing organizational behavior, then it is important to know and understand the norms of that culture. As Allen and Kraft (1982) cogently note:

> Norms are a universal phenomena. They are necessary, tenacious, but also extremely malleable. Because they can change so quickly and easily, they present a tremendous opportunity to people interested in change. Any group, no matter its size, once it understands itself as a cultural entity, can plan its own norms, creating positive ones that will help it reach its goals and modifying or discarding the negative ones. (pp. 7–8)

Norms are also communicated to participants by stories and ceremonies that provide visible and potent examples of what the organization stands for. Sometimes stories about people are created to reinforce the basic norms of the organization. The principal who stood by the teacher despite overwhelming pressure from parents and superiors becomes a symbol of the cohesiveness and loyalty in a school's cul-

FIGURE **5.1**

Levels of Culture

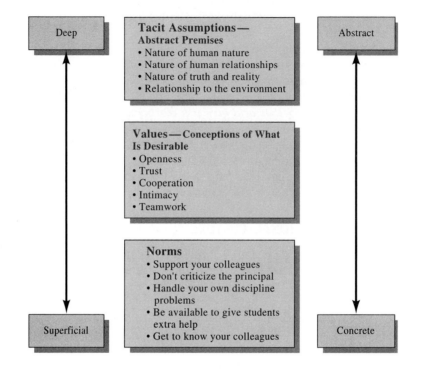

ture; it is a story that is retold many times to new teachers. Teachers quickly learn the norms, "don't tell tales out of school," "support your colleagues," and "support your principal." Norms determine the way people dress and talk; the way participants respond to authority, conflict, and pressure; and the way people balance self-interests with organizational interests. Examples of norms include the following: don't rock the boat; don't criticize fellow teachers to students or parents; all men wear neckties; handle your own discipline problems; don't let students out of class before the bell rings; and change the bulletin boards frequently. As noted in Chapter 2, norms are enforced by sanctions; people are rewarded and encouraged when they conform to norms and are confronted, ostracized, or punished when they violate the cultural norms of the group. In brief, the norms of the work group define a major slice of the culture of the organization.

Culture as Shared Values

At a middle level of abstraction, culture is defined as shared values. **Values** are conceptions of what is desirable. They are reflections of the underlying assumptions of culture, and lie at the next level of analysis. Values often define what members should do to be successful in the organization. When we ask people to explain why they behave the way they do, we may begin to discover the central values of the organization. Shared values define the basic character of the organization and give the organization a sense of identity. If members know what their organization stands for, if they know what standards they should uphold, then they are more likely to make decisions that will support those standards. They are also more likely to feel part of the organization and that organizational life has important meaning.

William Ouchi's (1981) book on the success of Japanese corporations was one of the first contemporary analyses of corporate culture. Ouchi argued that the success of effective corporations in both Japan and America was a function of a distinctive corporate culture, one that was internally consistent and characterized by the shared values of intimacy, trust, cooperation, teamwork, and egalitarianism. Success of these organizations was not as much a matter of technology as it was of managing people. He labeled the American organizations with these values Theory Z cultures.

Theory Z organizations have a number of properties that promote this distinctive culture (see Table 5.1). Long-term employment opportunities create in employees a sense of security and commitment to the organization; participants become invested in the organization. The process of slower rates of promotion creates more opportunities for broadening experiences and diverse career paths as employees perform different functions and occupy different roles. This effectively produces company-specific skills and promotes career development. Participative and consensual decision making demands cooperation and teamwork, values that are openly communicated and reinforced. Individual responsibility for collective decision making demands an atmosphere of trust and mutual support. Finally, concern for the total person is a natural part of the working relationship, which tends to be informal and emphasizes the whole person and not just the individual's work role. This holistic perspective promotes a strong egalitarian atmosphere, a community of equals who work cooperatively on common goals rather than relying on the formal hierarchy. Thus, Theory Z organizations are structured and operate to promote the basic values of intimacy, trust, cooperation, and egalitarianism. These **core values** of the culture are the dominant values that are accepted and shared by most of the organizational members; they influence virtually every aspect of organizational life.

TABLE 5.1 Theory Z Organization and Culture	
Organizational Characteristic	**Core Value**
1. Long-term employment ⟶	Organizational commitment
2. Slower promotion rates ⟶	Career orientation
3. Participative decision making ⟶	Cooperation and teamwork
4. Individual responsibility for group decisions ⟶	Trust and group loyalty
5. Holistic orientation ⟶	Egalitarianism

Several other studies (Deal and Kennedy, 1982; Peters and Waterman, 1982) of successful corporations also suggest the pivotal importance of strong organizational cultures in fostering effectiveness. Deal and Kennedy (1982) suggest that successful organizations share some common cultural characteristics. They argue that such organizations have:

- A widely shared organizational philosophy
- A concern for individuals that is more important than formal rules and policies
- Rituals and ceremonies that build a common identity
- A well-understood sense of the informal rules and exceptions
- A belief that what employees do is important to others

Therefore, sharing information and ideas is encouraged.

Thomas J. Peters and Robert H. Waterman (1982: 15) found that excellent companies were brilliant on the basics: "Tools didn't substitute for thinking. Intellect didn't overpower wisdom. Analysis didn't impeded action. Rather these companies worked hard to keep things simple in a complex world." Effective companies persisted and thrived because they had strong cultures. The shared values of those cultures included the following:

- *A bias for action:* Planning is not a substitute for action.
- *A client orientation:* Serve your customers.
- *An innovative orientation:* Respect autonomy and entrepreneurship.
- *A people orientation:* Productivity comes through people.
- *An achievement orientation:* High-quality products are essential.

In **strong cultures,** beliefs and values are held intensely, shared widely, and guide organizational behavior. It might be tempting to jump to the conclusion that a specific set of values define excellence in organizations, but that would be unjustified. What promotes excellence yesterday does not necessarily promote it today or tomorrow (Aupperle, Acar, and Booth, 1986; Hitt and Ireland, 1987). In fact, a strong culture can be a liability in times of rapid change because the organization's culture may be so ingrained that it prevents adaptation to new constraints. Hanson (1991) observes that in many ways the link between culture and effectiveness is same as that between structure and effectiveness. Both culture and structure can undermine outcomes by either stagnating or disrupting the system through rigidities, conflicts, and hidden agendas.

Culture as Tacit Assumptions

At its deepest level, culture is the collective manifestation of tacit assumptions. When members of an organization share a view of the world around them and their place in that world, culture exists. That is, a pattern of basic assumptions has been invented, discovered, or developed by the organization as it learned to cope with its problems of external adaptation and internal integration. This pattern has worked well enough to be considered valid and it is taught to new members as the correct way to perceive, think, and feel in relation to those problems. Since the assumptions have worked repeatedly, they have become so basic that they are taken for granted, tend to be nonconfrontable and nondebatable, and thus are highly resistant to change. From this perspective, the key to understanding organizational culture is to decipher the tacit assumptions shared by members and to discover how these assumptions fit together into a cultural pattern or paradigm.

Tacit assumptions, as shown in Figure 5.1, are abstract premises about the nature of human relationships, human nature, truth, reality, and environment. For example, is human nature basically good, evil, or neutral? How is truth ultimately determined—is it revealed or discovered? What are the assumed relationships among members of the group—primarily hierarchical, collateral, or individualistic? Five categories of cultural assumptions have emerged from the research and provide a framework for analysis. See Table 5.2.[2] The categories are helpful because it has been demonstrated that they can be used to build coherent patterns of core organizational beliefs. When organizations develop consistent and articulate patterns of basic assumptions, they have strong cultures.

Schein (1985) gives examples of two strong, but contrasting cultures. Company A has a strong, distinctive culture based on the following assumptions:

- Truth ultimately comes from individuals.
- Individuals are responsible, motivated, and capable of governing themselves.
- Truth is ultimately determined through debate, which necessitates much conflict and testing of ideas in group meetings.
- Members of an organization are a family; they accept, respect, and take care of each other.

These core assumptions give rise to such shared values as individualism, autonomy, openness, and authority of knowledge.

TABLE 5.2   Categories of Cultural Assumptions

The Nature of Relationships	Are relationships between members of the organization assumed to be primarily lineal (i.e., hierarchical)? Or are they group oriented? Or do the relationships focus on individuals?
Human Nature	Are human beings considered to be basically good, basically evil, or neither good nor evil?
The Nature of Truth	Is "truth" (i.e., correct decisions) revealed by external authority figures? Or is truth determined by a process of personal investigation and testing?
The Environment	Is there a basic belief that human beings can master the environment? Or that they must be subjugated by the environment? Or that they should attempt to harmonize with the environment?
Universalism/ Particularism	Should all members of the organization be evaluated by the same standards? Or should certain individuals be given preferential treatment?

In contrast, company B is guided by the following assumptions.

- Truth ultimately comes from older, wiser, better-educated, and more experienced participants.
- Participants are capable and willing to give commitment and loyalty to the organization (to be good "soldiers").
- Relationships are basically hierarchical.
- Each member has a niche that is his or her territory that cannot be invaded.
- Members of the organization are a family who take care of each other.

Here the core assumptions produce such values as respect for authority, respect for territory, and conflict avoidance.

Using this broad perspective of culture, each of the five categories of assumptions described in Table 5.2 should be examined to determine whether there is a consistent pattern of consensus. Then a judgment can be made on whether there is a strong or weak culture, or culture conflict among several groups.

There is no simple way to uncover the basic patterns of assumptions that underlie what people value and do. Schein (1985, 1990) develops an elaborate set of procedures to decipher the culture of an organization. It is an approach that combines anthropological and clinical techniques and involves a series of encounters and joint explorations between the investigator and various motivated informants who live in the organization and embody its culture. Joint effort usually involves extensive data-gathering activities that explore the history of the organization, critical events, organizational structure, myths, legends, stories, and ceremonies. Questionnaires are eschewed as devices to identify tacit assumptions; at best, it is argued, such instruments produce only some of the espoused values of group members. A few researchers (Rousseau, 1990; O'Reilly, Chatman, and Caldman, 1991; Chatman and Jehn, 1994), however, have attempted to assess the shared values of culture using quantitative instruments.

Level of Analysis

The most penetrating definitions of culture emphasize the deepest level of human nature or at least refer to shared ideologies, beliefs, and values (Kilmann, Saxton, and Serpa, 1985). Such definitions are advocated by theorists interested in understanding culture rather than managing it. Organizational participants, however, have difficulty openly identifying their tacit assumptions or discussing their basic assumptions; in fact, they describe such exercises as merely academic. At the other extreme, those definitions of culture that focus on behavioral norms are more useful to consultants and practitioners who are interested in assessing and changing organizational cultures. According to Kilmann and his associates (1985), organizational members seem more willing and able to identify the prevailing norms of the culture and to discuss them with minimal levels of threat and discomfort. Although the more abstract approaches to defining culture initially seem to be more penetrating, in practice they are less useful; and although the more superficial approaches seem to ignore the more fundamental bases of culture, in practice they offer some specific ways to manage culture, albeit in a very narrow way. Clearly we have much to learn about culture. Therefore, at this point in the development of the concept of organizational culture it is valuable to view and study culture at *all* three levels—that is, in terms of shared norms, core values, and tacit underlying assumptions.

DIFFERENT TYPES OF CULTURE

Although there may be no one best culture, strong cultures promote cohesiveness, loyalty, and commitment, which in turn reduce the propensity for members to leave the organization (Mowday, Porter, and Steers, 1982). Moreover, Robbins (1991) summarizes a number of important functions performed by the organization's culture:

- Culture has a boundary-defining function; it creates distinctions among organizations.
- Culture provides the organization with a sense of identity.
- Culture facilitates the development of commitment to the group.
- Culture enhances stability in the social system.
- Culture is the social glue that binds the organization together; it provides the appropriate standards for behavior.
- Culture serves to guide and shape the attitudes and behavior of organizational members.

It is important to remember, however, that a strong culture can be either functional or dysfunctional—that is, it can promote or impede effectiveness.

There are different types of organizational cultures. Dan Dennison's (1990) study of corporate culture and effectiveness suggests that effective organizations are ones in which there is a fit among strategy, environment, and culture. Dennison proposed categories of culture based on the relationship between the organization's strategic emphasis and the needs of the environment; that is, (1) the extent to which the strategic emphasis is internal or external, and (2) the extent to which the environment requires change or stability. Thus, four kinds of cultures are identified: the adaptability culture, the mission culture, the involvement culture, and the consistency culture.

The *adaptability culture* is defined by a strategic emphasis on the external environment and a focus on change and flexibility. The culture nurtures values, norms, and beliefs that support the capacity of the organization to monitor the environment and respond quickly to the needs of customers or clients. Put simply, if the external environment requires flexibility, the culture should encourage adaptability if it is to be effective.

The *mission culture* is also concerned with serving the external environment, but here the needs of stability and direction are important. Shared vision is critical in the mission culture. The vision supplies workers with meaning that goes beyond the routine accomplishment of their work. Members share a vision that gives them clarity and purpose in their work. Leaders shape behavior by emphasizing the mission and vision of the organization. If the external environment requires stability and direction, then a culture that provides mission and vision should be effective.

TABLE **5.3** Culture, Strategy, and Environment: A Culture Typology		
Type of Culture	**Strategic Emphasis**	**Environmental Needs**
Adaptability Culture	External	Change and flexibility
Mission Culture	External	Stability and direction
Involvement Culture	Internal	Change and flexibility
Consistency Culture	Internal	Stability and direction

The *involvement culture* has as its primary purpose the involvement and participation of members as it deals with a rapidly changing environment. The key to success in this culture is creating a sense of responsibility and commitment to the organization. If the external environment is changing rapidly and the strategic emphasis is internal, then member involvement is critical.

The *consistency culture* has an internal focus and a stable external environment. This culture is imbued with logical and methodical ways of doing business. Dependability and reliability are the trademarks of this culture. The symbols, ceremonies, and leaders support cooperation, tradition, and standard routines and policies for achieving goals. In a stable environment, an integrated, reliable, and efficient organization can be highly effective. The four cultures are summarized in Table 5.3.

SCHOOL CULTURE

Although organizational culture has become a fashionable construct for analysis in education, much of the recent discussion of school culture remains analytical, philosophical, and rhetorical rather than empirical (see Cusick, 1987). It is not difficult, for example, to use the research results on corporate cultures (Ouchi, 1981; Deal and Kennedy, 1982; Peters and Waterman, 1982) and the effective schools research (Brookover et al., 1978; Rutter et al., 1979; Clark, Lotto, and Astuto, 1984) to develop an ideal description of an effective school culture. For instance, Terrence Deal (1985) proposes that effective schools have strong cultures with the following elements: (1) shared values and a consensus on "how we get things done around here," (2) the principal as a hero or heroine who embodies core values, (3) distinctive rituals that embody widely shared beliefs, (4) employees as situational heroes or heroines, (5) rituals of acculturation and cultural renewal, (6) significant rituals to celebrate and transform core values, (7) balance between innovation and tradition and between autonomy and control, and (8) widespread participation in cultural rituals.

What are the core values that transform a school into an effective institution? Schools are for students; experiment with your teaching; teaching and learning are cooperative processes; stay close to your students; strive for academic excellence;

demand high, but realistic performance; be open in behavior and communication; trust your colleagues; and be professional. Are these core values or empty slogans? If these beliefs are strongly shared and widely enacted, then these sloganlike themes can define a strong school culture. Unfortunately, there is little systematic research that directly examines the institutional cultures of effective schools.

Anthropological and sociological studies of school cultures are needed. The thick descriptions of qualitative studies are necessary to map the basic assumptions and common values of the cultures of schools. Educational researchers must consider the school as a whole and analyze how its practices, beliefs, and other cultural elements relate to the social structure as well as give meaning to social life. To understand culture one must be immersed in the complex clustering of symbols people use to give meaning to their world. In this vein, Geertz (1973) asserts:

> Believing with Max Weber that man is an animal suspended in webs of significance he himself has spun, I take culture to be those webs, and the analysis of it to be therefore not an experimental science in search of law but an interpretive one in search of meaning. It is explication I am after, construing social expressions on their surface enigmatical. (p. 5)

William Firestone and Bruce Wilson (1985) provide a useful framework for beginning to study the organizational cultures of schools. They suggest that the analysis of school culture can be addressed by studying its content, the expressions of culture, and primary communication patterns.

The symbols through which culture is expressed often help identify important cultural themes. Three symbol systems communicate the contents of a school's culture: stories, icons, and rituals. **Stories** are narratives that are based on true events, but they often combine truth and fiction. Some stories are **myths;** that is, they communicate an unquestioned belief that cannot be demonstrated by the facts. Other stories are **legends** that are retold and elaborated with fictional details. For example, the principal, who stood by her teachers despite overwhelming pressure from parents and superiors, becomes a symbol of the cohesiveness and loyalty in the school's culture. It is a story that is retold many times to new teachers, one that takes on special meaning as it is interpreted and embellished. Stories are often about organizational heroes or heroines who epitomize the organization; they provide insight into the core values of the organization.

Icons and rituals are also important. **Icons** are physical artifacts that are used to communicate culture (logos, mottoes, and trophies), and **rituals** are the routine ceremonies and rites that provide visible examples of what is important in the organization. Janice Beyer and Harrison Trice (1987) identify rites of passage, degradation, enhancement, and integration as examples of routine ceremonies used to develop and sustain organizational culture. Table 5.4 contains some school examples of these four rites and their likely consequences. Much of the culture of a school can be constructed from artifacts, rites, rituals, and ceremonies related to assemblies, faculty meetings, athletic contests, community activities, cafeteria, report cards, awards and trophies, lesson plans, and the general decor of the school.

TABLE 5.4	Examples of School Rites, Ceremonies, and Consequences	
Type	**Examples**	**Possible Consequences**
Rites of Passage	Student teaching Tough class for neophytes Lunch duty Retirement	Facilitate transition to new role; socialization
Rites of Degradation	Negative evaluation Public rebuke	Reduce power; reaffirm appropriate behavior

Rites of Enhancement	Assembly recognition:
	    Teacher of the year
	    Debate team champions
	    Football champions
		Enhance power;
		reinforce appropriate behavior

Rites of Integration	Holiday party Coffee group Teacher's lounge	Encourage common experiences that bind the group together

The examination of the informal communication system is also important in the cultural analysis of the school. The communication system is a cultural network itself (Bantz, 1993; Mohan, 1993). As Deal and Kennedy (1982) have observed, storytellers, spies, priests, cabals, and whisperers form a hidden hierarchy of power within the school that communicates the basic values of the organization. Myth makers are storytellers who are so effective in informal communication that they create organizational myths. The identification of not only the myths but the process of their creation are important to a full understanding of culture.

Studies of organizational culture often try to capture the essence of culture by using metaphors. For example, Steinoff and Owens (1989) use the following four metaphors to describe school cultures:

- *The family:* The school is seen as a home or team and the principal is the parent or coach.
- *The machine:* The school is described as a smoothly running or rusty machine and the principal is a workaholic or slug.
- *The cabaret:* The school is a circus or Broadway show with the principal as the ringmaster or master of ceremonies.
- *The little shop of horrors:* The school is unpredictable and a nightmare reminiscent of the French Revolution and the principal is a self-cleaning statue or a Jekyll and Hyde.

Similarly, Deal and Wise (1983) use the metaphors of factories, jungles, and temples to describe schools with principals as CEOs, lion tamers, and gurus.

Good contemporary research on school culture, however, is sparse. Although there have been numerous analyses of corporate cultures and extrapolations of those findings to public schools, few educational researchers have tested those findings directly in schools. There are several important theoretical and practical issues that must be addressed in the study of school culture. We have suggested that the conceptual frameworks developed by Firestone and Wilson (1985) and Deal (1985) are useful in the analysis of school cultures. Bates (1987), however, argues that such formulations treat organizational culture as synonymous with managerial culture and are much too narrow to capture the essence of culture. This observation leads to a more general issue of whether most schools have a culture or a variety of subcultures. To expect schools to bear unique and unitary cultures may be more hope than fact, but the issue is ultimately an empirical one.

Whether culture can or should be intentionally managed will be hotly contested. Much of the early literature on school cultures is directed toward change and school improvement and assumes that understanding culture is a prerequisite to making schools more effective (Deal, 1985; Metz, 1986; Rossman, Corbett, and Firestone, 1988; Deal and Peterson, 1990). The success of cultural change and its influence on effectiveness are worthy topics for inquiry. One argument suggests that the process of changing culture is influenced by the level and number of cultures in the organization. A change of norms, for example, is more likely than a change in shared values or tacit assumptions. Others contend that any change is difficult and fraught with ethical dilemmas. For example, Schein (1985) strongly argues that a large part of an organization's culture represents the ways its members have learned to cope with anxiety; therefore, attempts to change culture can be tantamount to asking people to surrender their social defenses. To Schein, the issue of cultural change becomes an ethical question. In a somewhat similar vein, Bates (1987) maintains that advocates of strong organizational cultures are conducting cultural analyses on behalf of managers. What is good for management is not necessarily good for the workers (Hoy, 1990).

Although frameworks for examining school culture in terms of the shared values, beliefs, and ideologies are available, the determination of culture at this level of analysis is not easy. The core values of a group or school may be easier to determine than the tacit assumptions, but the analysis remains difficult and time-consuming. Anthropological studies of schools using ethnographic techniques and linguistic analysis are imperative if we are to begin to assess the culture of schools.

The analysis of schools in terms of culture calls attention to the symbolic nature of social interactions in schools (Bolman and Deal, 1991; Cunningham and Gresso, 1993). Often what is done or said is not nearly as important as its symbolic significance. Examining the culture of schools provides a less rational, more uncertain, and less linear view of organizational life than the standard perspectives on structure, rationality, and efficiency.

Lee Bolman and Terrence Deal (1991) refer to the culture perspective as the "symbolic frame" for viewing organizations. They argue that the frame is based on the following unconventional assumptions about the nature of organizations and behavior:

- What is most important about events in organizations is *not* what happened, but *what they mean.*
- Events and meanings, however, are often unclear because events have different meanings for different people. Individuals use different schemas to interpret their experiences.
- Because events are typically ambiguous or uncertain, it is difficult to know what happened, why it happened, and what will happen next.
- The greater the ambiguity and uncertainty in events, the more difficult it is to use rational approaches in organizational analysis.
- Confronted with ambiguity and uncertainty, people create symbols and stories to resolve confusion and provide understanding.
- Thus, for many organizational events, their importance rests with what they express rather than what is produced; secular myths, rituals ceremonies, and sagas give people the meanings they seek.

One conclusion from the literature on organizational culture is clear: much of what occurs in school organizations must be interpreted in the context of the school's culture.

ORGANIZATIONAL CLIMATE

Although the term "organizational culture" is currently in vogue, the concept of organizational climate has generated much more research and until recently was used by most organizational theorists to capture the general feel or atmosphere of schools. Unlike culture, from the beginning, organizational climate has been tied to the process of developing measuring instruments (Pace and Stern, 1958; Halpin and Croft, 1963). Climate has its historical roots in the disciplines of social psychology and industrial psychology rather than in anthropology or sociology.

DEFINITION OF ORGANIZATIONAL CLIMATE

Climate was initially conceived as a general concept to express the enduring quality of organizational life. Renato Taguiri (1968: 23) notes that "a particular configuration of enduring characteristics of the ecology, milieu, social system, and culture would constitute a climate, as much as a particular configuration of personal characteristics constitute a personality."

B.H. Gilmer (1966: 57) defines organizational climate as "those characteristics that distinguish the organization from other organizations and that influence the behavior of people in the organizations." George Litwin and Robert Stringer (1968: 1) introduce perception into their definition of climate—"a set of measurable properties of the work environment, based on the collective perceptions of the people who live and work in the environment and demonstrated to influence their behavior." Over the years, there has been some consensus on the basic properties of organizational climate. Marshall Poole (1985) summarizes the agreement as follows:

- Organizational climate is concerned with large units; it characterizes properties of an entire organization or major subunits.
- Organizational climate describes a unit of organization rather than evaluates it or indicates emotional reactions to it.
- Organizational climate arises from routine organizational practices that are important to the organization and its members.
- Organizational climate influences members' behaviors and attitudes.

School climate is a broad term that refers to teachers' perceptions of the general work environment of the school; it is influenced by the formal organization, informal organization, personalities of participants, and organizational leadership. Put simply, the set of internal characteristics that distinguish one school from another and influence the behavior of each's members is the **organizational climate** of the school. More specifically, **school climate** is a relatively enduring quality of the school environment that is experienced by participants, affects their behavior, and is based on their collective perceptions of behavior in schools. The definition of organizational climate as a set of internal characteristics is similar in some respects to early descriptions of personality. Indeed, the climate of a school may roughly be conceived as the personality of a school—that is, personality is to individual as climate is to organization.

Although the definitions of climate and culture are blurred and overlapping, one suggested difference is that culture consists of shared assumptions, values, or norms while climate is defined by shared perceptions of behavior (Ashforth, 1985). To be sure, there is not a large conceptual step from shared assumptions (culture) to shared perceptions (climate), but the difference is real and may be meaningful.

Since the atmosphere of a school has a major impact on the organizational behavior, and since administrators can have a significant, positive influence on the development of the "personality" of the school, it is important to describe and analyze school climates. Climate can be conceived from a variety of vantage points (see Anderson, 1982; Miskel and Ogawa, 1988), but only three perspectives are described in this chapter. Each provides the student and practitioner of administration with a valuable set of conceptual capital and measurement tools to analyze, understand, map, and change the work environment of schools.

TEACHER-PRINCIPAL BEHAVIOR: OPEN TO CLOSED

Probably the most well-known conceptualization and measurement of the organizational climate in schools is the pioneering study of elementary schools by Andrew W. Halpin and Don B. Croft (1962). They began mapping the organizational climate of schools when they observed that (1) schools differ markedly in their feel, (2) the concept of morale did not provide an index of this feel, (3) "ideal" principals who are assigned to schools where improvement is needed are immobilized by the faculty, and (4) the topic of organizational climate was generating interest.

The approach they used involved developing a descriptive questionnaire to identify important aspects of teacher-teacher and teacher-principal interactions. Nearly

1,000 items were composed, each of which was designed to answer the basic question: To what extent is this true of your school? From this original bank of items they developed a final set of 64 items called the Organizational Climate Description Questionnaire (OCDQ). The OCDQ is usually administered to the entire professional staff of each school, with each respondent asked to describe the extent to which each statement characterizes his or her school. The responses to each item are scaled along a four-point continuum: rarely occurs, sometimes occurs, often occurs, and very frequently occurs.

Halpin and Croft not only mapped climate profiles for each of the seventy-one elementary schools in their original sample but also identified, through factor analysis, six basic clusters of profiles—that is, six basic school climates that are arrayed along a rough continuum from open to closed. These climates are: open, autonomous, controlled, familiar, paternal, and closed. A behavioral picture of each climate can be sketched. To illustrate, we will briefly develop composites for the two extremes—the open and closed climates.

The Open Climate

The distinctive feature of the open climate is its high degree of thrust and esprit and its low disengagement. This combination suggests a climate in which both the principal and faculty are genuine in their behavior. The principal leads through example by providing the proper blend of structure and direction as well as support and consideration—the mix dependent upon the situation. Teachers work well together and are committed to the task at hand. Given the "reality-centered" leadership of the principal and a committed faculty, there is no need for burdensome paperwork (hindrance), close supervision (production emphasis), or impersonality or a plethora of rules and regulations (aloofness). Acts of leadership emerge easily and appropriately as they are needed. The open school is not preoccupied exclusively with either task achievement or social needs satisfaction, but both emerge freely. In brief, the behavior of both the principal and faculty is authentic.

The Closed Climate

The closed climate is virtually the antithesis of the open climate. Thrust and esprit are low and disengagement is high. The principal and teachers simply appear to go through the motions, with the principal stressing routine trivia and unnecessary busywork (hindrance), and the teachers responding at minimal levels and exhibiting little satisfaction. The principal's ineffective leadership is further seen in close supervision (production emphasis), formal declarations and impersonality (aloofness), as well as a lack of consideration for the faculty and an inability or unwillingness to provide a dynamic personal example. These misguided tactics, which are not taken seriously, produce teacher frustration and apathy. The behavior of both principal and teachers in the closed climate is least genuine; in fact, inauthenticity pervades the atmosphere of the school.

As defined by the OCDQ, the climate is clearly a description of the perceptions of the faculty. Some may raise the question of whether the climate is really open. We agree with Halpin and Croft that the climate is open (or closed) if the faculty describes it as such. Whether or not it really is cannot be answered and is probably irrelevant. Perceptions of what is "out there" motivate behavior.

Criticisms of the OCDQ

Although the OCDQ has been a widely used measure of school climate, it has a number of limitations. The instrument has been criticized because it may not be well suited to study large, urban, or secondary schools (Carver and Sergiovanni, 1969). At least part of the problem stems from attempting to designate discrete climates based on Halpin and Croft's "prototypic profile method" of determining climate. The norms used to classify the schools using the prototypic profile method are based on the seventy-one elementary schools in the original study. Not surprisingly, urban and large secondary schools invariably have closed climates.

Paula Silver (1983) is critical of the conceptual underpinnings of the OCDQ; she argues that the framework lacks a clear underlying logic, is cumbersome, and lacks parsimony. For example, she notes that although the hindrance subtest is defined by Halpin and Croft as one dimension of teacher behavior, the concept refers to administrative demands rather than interpersonal behavior of teachers. Other conceptual problems also arise. Halpin and Croft (1962) themselves question the adequacy of their concept of consideration by suspecting that two or more facets of considerate behavior have been confounded within a single measure. Moreover, the concept measured by the production-emphasis subtest seems mislabeled. The measure clearly taps close administration and autocratic behavior, not an emphasis on high production standards. Directive behavior is a more apt description of this aspect of principal behavior.

In a comprehensive empirical attempt to appraise the OCDQ, Andrew Hayes (1973) urged revision of the instrument. His analyses strongly suggested that many of the items on the OCDQ were no longer measuring what they were intended to measure, that some of the subtests were no longer valid (e.g., aloofness), that the reliabilities of some of the subtests were low, and that the instrument needed a major revision. Recent revisions of the OCDQ developed at Rutgers University address many of the criticisms of the original instrument (see Hoy and Clover, 1986; Kottkamp, Mulhern, and Hoy, 1987; Hoy, Tarter, and Kottkamp, 1991; Hoy et al., 1994); in fact, three new and simplified versions of the OCDQ were formulated for elementary, middle, and secondary schools—the OCDQ-RE, OCDQ-RM, and the OCDQ-RS.

THE REVISED ORGANIZATIONAL CLIMATE DESCRIPTIVE QUESTIONNAIRE FOR ELEMENTARY SCHOOLS (OCDQ-RE)

The revised climate instrument (Hoy and Clover, 1986; Hoy, Tarter, and Kottkamp, 1991) is a 42-item measure with six subtests that describe the behavior of elemen-

TABLE **5.5**	The Six Dimensions of the OCDQ-RE	
	Description	**Sample Items**
	Principal's Behavior	
1. Supportive Behavior	Reflects a basic concern for teachers. The principal listens and is open to teacher suggestions. Praise is given genuinely and frequently, and criticism is handled constructively. Supportive principals respect the professional competence of their staffs and exhibit both a personal and a professional interest in each teacher.	The principal uses constructive criticism. The principal compliments teachers. The principal listens to and accepts teachers' suggestions.
2. Directive Behavior	Requires rigid, close supervision. Principals maintain close and constant control over all teacher and school activities, down to the smallest details.	The principal monitors everything teachers do. The principal rules with an iron fist. The principal checks lesson plans.
3. Restrictive Behavior	Hinders rather than facilitates teacher work. The principal burdens teachers with paperwork, committee requirements, routine duties, and other demands that interfere with their teaching responsibilities.	Teachers are burdened with busywork. Routine duties interfere with the job of teaching. Teachers have too many committee requirements.
	Teachers' Behavior	
4. Collegial Behavior	Supports open and professional interactions among teachers. Teachers are proud of their school, enjoy working with their colleagues, and are enthusiastic, accepting, and mutually respectful of the professional competence of their colleagues.	Teachers help and support each other. Teachers respect the professional competence of their colleagues. Teachers accomplish their work with vim, vigor, and pleasure.
5. Intimate Behavior	Reflects a cohesive and strong network of social support among the faculty. Teachers know each other well, are close personal friends, socialize together regularly, and provide strong support for each other.	Teachers socialize with each other. Teachers' closest friends are other faculty members at this school. Teachers have parties for each other.
6. Disengaged Behavior	Refers to a lack of meaning and focus to professional activities. Teachers are simply putting in time and are nonproductive in group efforts or team building; they have no common goal orientation. Their behavior is often negative and critical of their colleagues and the organization.	Faculty meetings are useless. There is a minority group of teachers who always oppose the majority. Teachers ramble when they talk at faculty meetings.

tary teachers and principals. Three dimensions of principal behavior—supportive, directive, and restrictive—are identified. Supportive principal behavior is reflected by genuine concern and support of teachers. In contrast, directive principal behavior is starkly task oriented with little consideration for the personal needs of the teachers, and restrictive behavior produces impediments for teachers as they try to do their work. Likewise, three critical aspects of teacher behavior are identified—collegial, intimate, and disengaged behavior. Collegial behavior is supportive and professional interaction among teacher colleagues, while intimate behavior involves close personal relations among teachers not only in but also outside of school. On the other hand, disengaged behavior depicts a general sense of alienation and separation among teachers in school. It is also interesting to note that the Australian version of the OCDQ for primary schools has only four dimensions, factors similar to the dimensions of supportive, directive, disengaged, and intimate (Thomas and Slater, 1972; Brady, 1985).

In the tradition of the original OCDQ, the six dimensions of organizational climate are measured by having teachers describe the interactions between and among teachers and the principal. The six dimensions of the OCDQ-RE are defined and sample items for each are provided in Table 5.5.

A factor analysis of the subtests of the OCDQ-RE revealed that the conceptualization and measure of climate rested on two underlying general factors. Disengaged, intimate, and collegial teacher behavior formed the first factor, while restrictive, directive, and supportive behavior defined the second factor. Specifically, the first factor was characterized by teachers' interactions that are meaningful and tolerant (low disengagement); that are friendly, close, and supportive (high intimacy); and that are enthusiastic, accepting, and mutually respectful (high collegial relations). In general, this factor denotes an openness and functional flexibility in teacher relationships. Accordingly, it was labeled **openness in faculty relations** and an openness index can be created by combining the collegial, intimacy, and disengagement scores.

The second factor is defined by principal behavior that is characterized by the assignment of meaningless routines and burdensome duties to teachers (high restrictiveness); by rigid, close, and constant control over teachers (high directiveness); and by a lack of concern and openness for teachers and their ideas (low supportive). In general, the second factor depicts principal behavior along an open-to-closed continuum, with functional flexibility and openness at one pole and functional rigidity and closedness at the other; hence, the second general factor is the degree of **openness** (or closedness) **in principal behavior** and an openness index for principal behavior can be created by combining the supportiveness, restrictiveness, and directiveness scores.[3]

The conceptual underpinnings of the OCDQ-RE are consistent and clear. The instrument has two general factors—one a measure of openness of teacher interactions and the other a measure of openness (or closedness) of teacher-principal relations. Moreover, these two openness factors are independent. That is, it is quite possible to have open faculty interactions and closed principal ones or vice versa. Thus, theoretically, four contrasting types of school climate are possible. First, both factors can be open, producing a congruence between the principal's and teachers' behavior. Second, both factors can be closed, producing a congruence of closedness. Moreover, there are two incongruent patterns. The principal's behavior can be open with the faculty, but teachers may be closed with each other; or the principal may be closed with teachers, while the teachers are open with each other (see Figure 5.2). Table 5.6 provides a summary of the patterns of four climate prototypes. Using this information, a behavioral picture of each climate can be sketched.

Open Climate

The distinctive features of the **open climate** are the cooperation and respect that exist within the faculty and between the faculty and principal. This combination suggests a climate in which the principal listens and is open to teacher suggestions, gives genuine and frequent praise, and respects the professional competence of the faculty (high supportiveness). Principals also give their teachers freedom to perform without close scrutiny (low directiveness) and provide facilitating leadership behavior devoid of bureaucratic trivia (low restrictiveness). Similarly, teacher behavior supports open and professional interactions (high collegial relations) among the faculty. Teachers know each other well and are close personal friends (high intimacy). They cooperate and are committed to their work (low disengagement). In brief, the behavior of both the principal and the faculty is open and authentic.

Engaged Climate

The **engaged climate** is marked, on the one hand, by ineffective attempts by the principal to control, and on the other, by high professional performance of the teachers. The principal is rigid and autocratic (high directiveness) and respects neither the professional competence nor the personal needs of the faculty (low supportiveness). Moreover, the principal hinders the teachers with burdensome activities and busywork (high restrictiveness). The teachers, however, ignore the principal's behav-

FIGURE **5.2**

Typology of School Climates

		Principal Behavior	
		Open	Closed
Teacher Behavior	Open	Open Climate	Engaged Climate
	Closed	Disengaged Climate	Closed Climate

TABLE **5.6**	Prototypic Profiles of Climate Types			
Climate Dimension	**Climate Type**			
	Open	**Engaged**	**Disengaged**	**Closed**
Supportive	High	Low	High	Low
Directive	Low	High	Low	High
Restrictive	Low	High	Low	High
Collegial	High	High	Low	Low
Intimate	High	High	Low	Low
Disengaged	Low	Low	High	High

ior and conduct themselves as professionals. They respect and support each other, are proud of their colleagues, and enjoy their work (highly collegial). Moreover, the teachers not only respect each other's competence but they like each other as people (high intimacy), and they cooperate with each other as they engage in the task at hand (high engagement). In short, the teachers are productive professionals in spite of weak principal leadership; the faculty is cohesive, committed, supportive, and open.

Disengaged Climate

The **disengaged climate** stands in stark contrast to the engaged climate. The principal's behavior is open, concerned, and supportive. The principal listens and is open to teachers (high supportiveness), gives the faculty freedom to act on their professional knowledge (low directiveness), and relieves teachers of most of the burdens of paperwork and committee assignments (low restrictiveness). Nonetheless, the faculty is unwilling to accept the principal. At worst, the faculty actively works to immobilize and sabotage the principal's leadership attempts; at best, the faculty simply ignores the principal. Teachers not only do not like the principal but they neither like nor respect each other as friends (low intimacy) or as professionals (low collegial relations). The faculty is simply disengaged from the task. In sum, although the principal is supportive, concerned, flexible, facilitating, and noncontrolling (i.e., open), the faculty is divisive, intolerant, and uncommitted (i.e., closed).

Closed Climate

The **closed climate** is virtually the antithesis of the open climate. The principal and teachers simply appear to go through the motions, with the principal stressing routine trivia and unnecessary busywork (high restrictiveness) and the teacher responding minimally and exhibiting little commitment (high disengagement). The principal's ineffective leadership is further seen as controlling and rigid (high directiveness) as well as unsympathetic, unconcerned, and unresponsive (low supportiveness). These misguided tactics are accompanied not only by frustration and apathy but also by a general suspicion and lack of respect of teachers for each other as either friends or professionals (low intimacy and noncollegial relations). Closed climates have principals who are nonsupportive, inflexible, hindering, and controlling and a faculty that is divisive, intolerant, apathetic, and uncommitted.

THE REVISED ORGANIZATIONAL CLIMATE DESCRIPTIVE QUESTIONNAIRE FOR SECONDARY SCHOOLS (OCDQ-RS)

Although the original OCDQ emerged from a sample of elementary schools, the framework also is appropriate for the analysis of secondary schools. Accordingly, a 34-item climate instrument was constructed to describe the behavior of secondary teachers and principals (Kottkamp, Mulhern, and Hoy, 1987; Hoy, Tarter, and Kottkamp, 1991). The instrument is composed of five dimensions—two of the dimensions describe principal behavior and the other three focus on teacher behavior. The dimensions are summarized as follows:

- Supportive behavior is characterized by genuine concern for the personal and professional welfare of the teachers.
- Directive behavior is rigid, domineering management.
- Engaged behavior reflects a faculty that is not only committed to each other but also committed to their students and school.
- Frustrated teacher behavior describes a general pattern of interference in the school that distracts from the basic task of teaching.
- Intimate behavior depicts a close network of social relations among the faculty.

Although most of these aspects of secondary school climate are conceptually similar to those at the elementary levels, their measures are not identical. A factor analysis of the subtests of the OCDQ-RS yielded two underlying general factors. Supportive, directive, engaged, and frustrated behaviors defined a major first factor, while intimate teacher behavior formed an independent minor factor. The first factor identifies schools that have energetic principals who lead by example, are helpful and supportive, and work toward both the satisfaction of social needs and task achievement of faculty. Teachers find the work environment facilitating, not frustrating, and they energetically engage in their teaching task optimistic about both their colleagues and their students. This first factor is remarkably similar to Halpin and Croft's conception of openness; hence, it was named openness and conceptualized along a continuum from open to closed. At the secondary school level, however, intimacy was not part of the openness cluster. That is, schools could be either open or closed and still demonstrate a high or low degree of intimacy among the faculty; thus, intimacy stood alone as a second general factor.

Open secondary principal behavior is reflected in genuine relationships with teachers where the principal creates an environment that is supportive and helpful (high supportiveness), encourages teacher initiative (low directiveness), and frees teachers from administrative trivia (low frustration) so they can concentrate on the task of teaching. In contrast, closed principal behavior is rigid, closed, and nonsupportive. Open teacher behavior is characterized by sincere, positive, and supportive relationships with students, administrators, and colleagues (high engagement); teachers are committed to their school and the success of their students (high engagement); and the work environment is facilitating rather than frustrating (low frustration). In brief, openness in secondary schools refers to climates where both the teachers' and principal's behaviors are authentic, energetic, goal directed, and supportive, and in which satisfaction is derived from both task accomplishment and need gratification.

Because the four subtests of the OCDQ-RS all load strongly on the openness factor, it is possible to create an index of the degree of openness of the climate of secondary schools. An openness index for each school can be created by combining the supportive, engaged, directive, and frustrated scores.[4]

THE REVISED ORGANIZATIONAL CLIMATE DESCRIPTIVE QUESTIONNAIRE FOR MIDDLE SCHOOLS (OCDQ-RM)

Not all schools are elementary or high schools; in fact, middle schools have all but replaced traditional junior high schools. Which is the appropriate instrument to measure the climates of middle schools—the OCDQ-RE or the OCDQ-RS? Such a choice is not necessary. A special climate instrument, the OCDQ-RM, has been designed expressly for middle schools (Hoy et al., 1994; Hoffman et al., 1994). Unlike elementary and secondary schools, teacher intimacy is not an important aspect of middle schools. Instead, teacher commitment to students emerges as a unique dimension of the climate of middle schools. Open middle school climates have teachers who are committed to the achievement of their students. The conceptual underpinnings of the middle school climate, however, are quite similar to elementary schools; the same four major climate types are found—open, engaged, disengaged, or closed climates.

OCDQ: SOME RESEARCH FINDINGS

The revised versions of the OCDQ are relatively recent developments, however a consistent body of research is beginning to emerge. We do know, for example, that the openness index from the original OCDQ is highly correlated with the new and refined subtests that measure openness. Moreover, openness in climate is positively related to open and authentic teacher and principal behavior (Hoy et al., 1994). Thus, it is expected that results from earlier studies will be in large part replicated and refined with the new measures.

Those earlier OCDQ studies demonstrated that the openness of a school's climate was related to the emotional tone of the school in predictable ways. Schools with open climates have less sense of student alienation toward the school and its personnel than those with closed climates (Hartley and Hoy, 1972). As one might also suspect, studies that examine relationships between characteristics of the principal and the climate of the school often indicate that, in comparison to closed schools, open schools have stronger principals who are more confident, self-secure, cheerful, sociable, and resourceful (Anderson, 1964). Moreover, the teachers who work under principals in open schools express greater confidence in their own and the school's effectiveness (Andrews, 1965). Such principals have more loyal and satisfied teachers (Kanner, 1974).

More recent research (Tarter and Hoy, 1988; Reiss, 1994) with the new climate instruments also shows that open school climates are characterized by higher levels of loyalty and trust, both faculty trust in the principal and in colleagues, than closed climates. Principals in open schools also generate more organizational commitment to school—that is, identification and involvement in school—than those in closed climates (Tarter, Hoy, and Kottkamp, 1990). Further, openness of the climate is positively related to teacher participation in decision making (Barnes, 1994) as well as to ratings of school effectiveness (Hoy, Tarter, and Kottkamp, 1991) and, in middle schools, to student achievement in mathematics, reading, and writing (Hannum, 1994).

In conclusion, the three climate measures are useful devices for general charting of school climate in terms of teacher-teacher and teacher-principal relationships. The subtests of each instrument seem to be valid and reliable measures of important aspects of school climate; they can provide climate profiles that can be used for research, evaluation, in-service, or self-analysis. In addition, the openness indices provide means of examining schools along an open-closed continuum. Halpin and Croft suggest that openness might be a better criterion of a school's effectiveness than many that have entered the field of educational administration and masquerade as criteria. Openness is likely an important condition in fostering effective organizational change. Similarly, principals who want to improve instructional effectiveness are more likely to be successful if they first develop an open and trusting climate (Hoy and Forsyth, 1987). Although there is much argument about what constitutes school effectiveness (see Chapter 8), there is less doubt that the OCDQ measures provide a useful battery of scales for diagnostic as well as prescriptive purposes.

ORGANIZATIONAL DYNAMICS: HEALTHY TO UNHEALTHY

The **organizational health** of a school is another framework for conceptualizing the general atmosphere of a school (Hoy and Forsyth, 1986; Hoy and Feldman, 1987; Hoy, Tarter, and Kottkamp, 1991). The idea of positive health in an organization is not new and calls attention to conditions that facilitate growth and development as well as to those that impede healthy organizational dynamics.

Matthew Miles (1969: 378) defines a healthy organization as one that "not only survives in its environment, but continues to cope adequately over the long haul, and continuously develops and extends its surviving and coping abilities." Implicit in this definition is the notion that healthy organizations deal successfully with disruptive outside forces while effectively directing their energies toward the major goals and objectives of the organization. Operations on a given day may be effective or ineffective, but the long-term prognosis is favorable in healthy organizations.

All social systems, if they are to grow and develop, must satisfy the four basic problems of adaptation, goal attainment, integration, and latency (Parsons, Bales, and Shils, 1953). In other words, organizations must successfully solve (1) the problem of acquiring sufficient resources and accommodating to their environments, (2) the problem of setting and attaining goals, (3) the problem of maintaining solidarity within the system, and (4) the problem of creating and preserving the unique values of the system. Thus, the organization must be concerned with the instrumental needs of adaptation and goal achievement as well as the expressive needs of social and normative integration; in fact, it is postulated that healthy organizations effectively meet both sets of needs. Talcott Parsons (1967) also suggests that formal organizations such as schools exhibit three distinct levels of responsibility and control over these needs—the technical, managerial, and institutional levels.

The technical level produces the product. In schools, the technical function is the teaching-learning process, and teachers are directly responsible. Educated students are the product of schools, and the entire technical subsystem revolves around the problems associated with effective learning and teaching.

The managerial level mediates and controls the internal efforts of the organization. The administrative process is the managerial function, a process that is qualitatively different from teaching. Principals are the prime administrative officers in schools. They must find ways to develop teacher loyalty and trust, motivate teacher effort, and coordinate the work. The administration controls and services the technical subsystem in two important ways: first, it mediates between the teachers and those receiving the services, students and parents; and second, it procures the necessary resources for effective teaching. Thus, teacher needs are a basic concern of the administration.

The institutional level connects the organization with its environment. It is important for schools to have legitimacy and backing in the community. Administrators and teachers need support to perform their respective functions in a harmonious fashion without undue pressure and interference from individuals and groups outside the school.

This Parsonian framework provides an integrative scheme for conceptualizing and measuring the organizational health of a school. Specifically, a **healthy organization** is one in which the technical, managerial, and institutional levels are in harmony. The organization is meeting both its instrumental and its expressive needs and is successfully coping with disruptive outside forces as it directs its energies toward its mission.

ORGANIZATIONAL HEALTH INVENTORY (OHI)

The organizational health of secondary schools is defined by seven specific interaction patterns in schools (Hoy and Feldman, 1987). These critical components meet both the instrumental and the expressive needs of the social system as well as represent the three levels of responsibility and control within the school.

The institutional level is examined in terms of the school's integrity. That is, institutional integrity is the school's ability to adapt to its environment and cope in ways that maintain the soundness of its educational programs. Schools with integrity are protected from unreasonable community and parental demands.

Four key aspects of the managerial level are considered—principal influence, consideration, initiating structure, and resource support. Influence is the ability of the principal to affect the decisions of superiors. Consideration is principal behavior that is open, friendly, and supportive, while initiating structure is behavior in which the principal clearly defines the work expectations, standards of performance, and procedures. Finally, resource support is the extent to which the principal provides teachers with all materials and supplies that are needed and requested.

Morale and academic emphasis are the two key elements of the technical level. Morale is the trust, enthusiasm, confidence, and sense of accomplishment that pervade the faculty. Academic emphasis, on the other hand, is the school's press for student achievement. These seven dimensions of organizational health are summarized by level of responsibility and functional need in Table 5.7. The Organizational Health Inventory, or OHI, is a 44-item descriptive questionnaire composed of seven subtests to measure each of the basic dimensions of organizational health. Like the OCDQ, the OHI is administered to the professional staff of the school. Teachers are asked to describe the extent to which each item characterizes their school along a four-point scale: rarely occurs, sometimes occurs, often occurs, and very frequently occurs. Sample items of the OHI, grouped by subtest, also are listed in Table 5.7.

Health profiles for three schools are graphed in Figure 5.3. School A represents a school with a relatively healthy climate; all dimensions of health are substantially above the mean. School C, in contrast, is below the mean in all aspects of health, and school B is a typical school—about average on all dimensions.

The subtests of the OHI are modestly correlated with each other; that is, if a school scores high on one subtest, there is some tendency to score higher on some of the other subtests. Furthermore, factor analysis of the subtests have demonstrated that one general factor, called school health, explains most of the variation among the subtests. The seventy-eight secondary schools in the sample arrayed themselves along a continuum with a few schools having profiles of very healthy organizations, a few with very unhealthy profiles, and most schools with somewhat mixed profiles in between the extremes. An index of health can be developed simply by combining the scores of the seven subtests; the higher the sum, the healthier the school dynamics (Hoy, Tartar, and Kottkamp, 1991). It is possible to sketch the behavioral picture

	Description	**Sample Items**

TABLE 5.7   Dimensions of Organizational Health

	Description	**Sample Items**
	Instructional Level	
1. Institutional Integrity	Describes a school that has integrity in its education program. The school is not vulnerable to narrow, vested interests from community and parental demands. The school is able to cope successfully with destructive outside forces (instrumental need).	Teachers are protected from unreasonable community and parental demands. The school is vulnerable to outside pressures.* Select citizen groups are influential with the board.*
	Managerial Level	
2. Principal Influence	Refers to the principal's ability to affect the action of superiors. The influential principal is persuasive, works effectively with the superintendent, but simultaneously demonstrates independence in thought and action (instrumental need).	The principal gets what he or she asks for from superiors. The principal is able to work well with the superintendent. The principal is impeded by superiors.*
3. Consideration	Behavior by the principal that is friendly, supportive, open, and collegial (expressive need).	The principal is friendly and approachable. The principal puts suggestions made by the faculty into operation. The principal looks out for the personal welfare of faculty members.
4. Initiating Structure	Behavior by the principal that is task and achievement oriented. The principal makes his or her attitudes and expectations clear to the faculty and maintains definite standards of performance (instrumental need).	The principal lets faculty members know what is expected of them. The principal maintains definite standards of performance. The principal schedules the work to be done.
5. Resource Support	Refers to provisions at a school where adequate classroom supplies and instructional materials are available, and extra materials are easily obtained (instrumental need).	Extra materials are available when requested. Teachers are provided with adequate materials for their classrooms. Teachers have access to needed instructional materials.
	Technical Level	
6. Morale	Refers to a sense of trust, confidence, enthusiasm, and friendliness that is exhibited among teachers. Teachers feel good about each other and, at the same time, feel a sense of accomplishment from their jobs (expressive need).	Teachers in this school like each other. Teachers accomplish their jobs with enthusiasm. The morale of teachers is high.
7. Academic Emphasis	Refers to the school's press for achievement. High but achievable academic goals are set for students; the learning environment is orderly and serious; teachers believe in their students' ability to achieve; and students work hard and respect those who do well academically (instrumental need).	The school sets high standards for academic performance. Students respect others who get good grades. Students try hard to improve on previous work.

*Score is reversed.

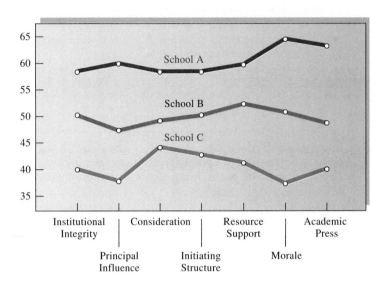

FIGURE **5.3**

Health Profiles of Three Schools

for each of the poles of the continuum—that is, the prototypes for very healthy and unhealthy school climates.

Healthy School

The healthy school is protected from unreasonable community and parental pressures. The board successfully resists all narrow efforts of vested interest groups to influence policy. The principal of a healthy school provides dynamic leadership—leadership that is both task oriented and relations oriented. Such behavior is supportive of teachers and yet provides direction and maintains high standards of performance. Moreover, the principal has influence with his or her superiors as well as the ability to exercise independent thought and action. Teachers in a healthy school are committed to teaching and learning. They set high, but achievable goals for students; they maintain high standards of performance; and the learning environment is orderly and serious. Furthermore, students work hard on academic matters, are highly motivated, and respect other students who achieve academically. Classroom supplies and instructional materials are accessible. Finally, in a healthy school teachers like each other, trust each other, are enthusiastic about the work, and are proud of their school.

Unhealthy School

The unhealthy school is vulnerable to destructive outside forces. Teachers and administrators are bombarded with unreasonable demands from parental and community groups. The school is buffeted by the whims of the public. The principal does not provide leadership: there is little direction, limited consideration and support for teachers, and virtually no influence with superiors. Morale of teachers is low. Teachers feel good neither about each other nor about their jobs. They act aloof, suspicious, and defensive. Finally, the press for academic excellence is limited. Everyone is simply "putting in time."

THE ORGANIZATIONAL HEALTH INVENTORIES FOR MIDDLE AND ELEMENTARY SCHOOLS

Given the differences among elementary, middle, and high schools, it should not be surprising that there are different versions of the health inventory. The conceptual foundations are the same for all versions, but the items and dimensions used to measure school health are slightly different depending on the school level (Hoy, Tarter, and Kottkamp, 1991; Barnes, 1994).

The Organizational Health Inventory for elementary schools (OHI-E) (Podgurski, 1990; Hoy, Tarter, and Kottkamp, 1991) and for middle schools (OHI-RM) (Barnes, 1994) have the same strong psychometric properties as the original OHI for high schools. All the measures are reliable and have strong validity. In general, the differences in the measures are ones of differentiation of elements.

Compared to high schools, elementary schools have relatively simple structures. Consequently, as one moves from the elementary to the middle to the high school, the dimensions of climate become increasingly differentiated as structure becomes more complex. All three school levels are concerned with institutional integrity and with academic emphasis and teacher morale or affiliation, but the leadership of the principal becomes more differentiated as one moves from elementary to middle to high schools. At the elementary level there are only two dimensions of leadership, but these two divide into four by high school. Resource influence divides into principal influence and resource support as one moves from elementary to middle school, and collegial leadership behavior separates into initiation of structure and consideration as one moves from the middle to the high school (see Table 5.8). Thus, at the high

TABLE **5.8** Comparison of the Elements of Health at School Levels

Elementary	Middle	High School
Institutional integrity	Institutional integrity	Institutional integrity
Collegial leadership	Collegial leadership	Initiating structure
		Consideration
Resource influence	Resource Support	Resource support
	Principal influence	Principal influence
Teacher affiliation	Teacher affiliation	Morale
Academic emphasis	Academic emphasis	Academic emphasis

school level, initiation of structure, consideration, principal influence, and resource support are all relatively separate dimensions of principal behavior.

In other words, elementary and middle school principals typically have more integrated leadership approaches. At the middle level, principal influence and resource support are integrated into one role, and at the elementary level, further integration of roles occurs as initiation of structure and consideration combine to form a unified collegial approach to leading teachers. The results suggest that, in general, the leadership of secondary schools is more complex and likely more difficult than that of elementary schools.

OHI: Some Research Findings

The OHI is a new instrument, and research using it is limited. Yet the OHI is a useful tool, with three versions—one each for elementary, middle, and high schools. The instruments measure key dimensions of organizational health of schools. Moreover, the conceptual underpinnings are consistent with many of the characteristics of effective schools. In addition, a study of high schools in Taiwan demonstrated stability in the factor structure of the OHI across cultures (Liao, 1994).

Research findings using the OHI are also encouraging. As one would expect, the healthier the organizational dynamics, the greater the degree of faculty trust in the principal, trust in colleagues, and trust in the organization itself (Tarter and Hoy, 1988; Hoy, Tarter, and Wiskoskie, 1992). Not surprisingly too, there is a correlation between the openness and the health of schools; healthy schools have high thrust, high esprit, and low disengagement (Hoy and Tarter, 1990). In brief, open schools tend to be healthy and healthy schools tend to be open. Health is also related to the organizational commitment of teachers to their schools; healthy schools have more committed teachers (Tarter, Hoy, and Bliss 1989; Tarter, Hoy, and Kottkamp 1990). Research findings also show that organizational health is positively related to student performance; the healthier the school climate, the higher the achievement levels on math and reading achievement test scores of high school students (Hoy and Tarter, 1990); and the healthier the climate of middle schools, the higher the student achievement levels on standardized math, reading, and writing tests (Hannum, 1994). A study of elementary teachers also demonstrated that a healthy school climate was conducive to the development of teacher efficacy, the belief that they could positively influence student learning (Hoy and Woolfolk, 1993). Our own research continues to demonstrate that school health is related to a host of other important school variables. For example, it is positively related to humanism, teacher participation in decision making, a strong school culture, and a variety of measures of school effectiveness. Finally, it seems likely that a school's health will be significantly related to less student alienation, lower dropout rates, and higher student commitment.

In conclusion, the health of a school can be reliably determined by use of the appropriate OHI instrument. Moreover, sound interpersonal dynamics in school life are not only important as ends in themselves but are predictive of school effectiveness, student achievement, organizational commitment, humanism in teacher attitudes, and faculty trust in colleagues and trust in the principal. Healthy schools are likely to have committed teachers who trust each other, who trust the principal, who hold high academic standards, who are open, and who have students who achieve at high levels. In such schools, the improvement of instruction and the continued professional development of teachers and administrators are achievable goals.

PUPIL-CONTROL ORIENTATION: CUSTODIAL TO HUMANISTIC

Another way to conceptualize the social climate of the school is in terms of dominant control patterns that teachers and principals use to control students. Willard Waller (1932), in one of the first systematic studies of the school as a social system, called attention to the importance of pupil control with regard to both structural and normative aspects of the school culture. In fact, most studies that have focused on the school as a social system have described antagonistic student subcultures and attendant conflict and pupil problems (Gordon, 1957; Coleman, 1961; Willower and Jones, 1967). Donald J. Willower and Ronald G. Jones (1967) have described pupil control as the "dominant motif" within the school social system, the integrative theme that gives meaning to patterns of teacher-teacher and teacher-principal relations.

Control is a problem that all organizations face. Richard O. Carlson's (1964) analysis of the relationship of a client to a service organization indicates that public schools are the type of service organization in which control is likely to be the most acute problem. Public schools, along with prisons and public mental hospitals, are service organizations that have no choice in the selection of clients, and the clients must (in the legal sense) participate in the organization. These organizations are confronted with clients who may have little or no desire for the services of the organization, a factor that accentuates the problem of client control. As a strong cautionary note, there are important distinctions to be made when comparing public schools with prisons and public mental hospitals. For example, prisons and public mental hospitals are "total institutions" (Goffman, 1957); schools are not. Moreover, schools normally use much less intense coercive practices. The point is that, although control is probably an essential ingredient of all group life, it is especially important in service organizations in which clients are unselected and participation is mandatory.

Both empirical and conceptual considerations lead to the same conclusion: pupil control is a central aspect of school life. Given its saliency, the concept can be used to distinguish among school climates. The conceptualization of pupil control and research initiated by Donald J. Willower, Terry I. Eidell, and Hoy (1967) at the Pennsylvania State University provide the basis for such a perspective.[5]

The Penn State researchers postulated a pupil-control continuum from custodial to humanistic. These terms refer to contrasting types of individual ideology and the corresponding types of school organizations that they seek to rationalize and justify. The concern here is primarily with the social-beliefs component of climate. Thus, pupil-control ideology is how school officials view the students. Prototypes or composite descriptions of schools with humanistic and custodial pupil-control orientations will now be briefly presented.

THE CUSTODIAL SCHOOL

The model for the **custodial orientation** is the traditional school, which provides a rigid and highly controlled setting in which maintenance of order is primary. Students are stereotyped in terms of their appearance, behavior, and parents' social status. Teachers who hold a custodial orientation conceive of the school as an autocratic organization with a rigid pupil-teacher status hierarchy. The flow of power and communication is unilateral and downward; students must accept the decisions of their teachers without question. Teachers do not attempt to understand student behavior but instead view misbehavior as a personal affront. They perceive students as irresponsible and undisciplined persons who must be controlled through punitive sanctions. Impersonality, cynicism, and watchful mistrust pervade the atmosphere of the custodial school.

THE HUMANISTIC SCHOOL

The model for the **humanistic orientation** is the school conceived of as an educational community in which students learn through cooperative interaction and experience. Learning and behavior are viewed in psychological and sociological terms. Self-discipline is substituted for strict teacher control. A humanistic orientation leads to a democratic atmosphere with two-way communication between pupils and teachers and increased self-determination. The term "humanistic orientation" is used in the sociopsychological sense suggested by Erich Fromm (1948); it stresses both the importance of the individual and the creation of an atmosphere that meets student needs.

THE PUPIL-CONTROL IDEOLOGY (PCI) FORM

In order to operationalize the concept the pupil-control orientation along the custodial-humanistic continuum, the Pupil-Control Ideology (PCI) form was developed by Willower, Eidell, and Hoy (1967: 47–48). The PCI is a 20-item scale with five response categories for each item, ranging from strongly agree to strongly disagree. A sample of specific items follow:

- It is desirable to require pupils to sit in assigned seats during assemblies.
- Directing sarcastic remarks toward a defiant pupil is a good disciplinary technique.
- Pupils should not be permitted to contradict the statements of a teacher in class.
- Too much pupil time is spent on guidance and activities and too little on academic preparation.

Reliability coefficients of the PCI instrument have been consistently high (Packard and Willower, 1972; Packard, 1988). Likewise, construct validity has been supported in numerous studies (Hoy, 1967, 1968; Willower, Eidell, and Hoy, 1967; Appleberry and Hoy, 1969; Hoy and Woolfolk, 1989). A critical discussion of the validity of the PCI is provided by John Packard (1988). The pupil-control orientation can be measured by pooling the individual orientations of the professional staff of the school; this represents an estimate of the modal orientation of the school and provides an index of the degree of custodialism (or humanism) in pupil-control orientation of the school.

PCI: Some Research Findings

The PCI instrument does not provide the complex measure of either the OCDQ or the OHI. Yet the concept of pupil control and its measurement allows another view of the school climate, one that focuses on teacher-student relations rather than principal-teacher relations. Perhaps the PCI is a better measure of culture than climate because it deals directly with shared ideologies rather than shared perceptions of behavior. At any rate, the concept of pupil-control ideology has proved to be a powerful predictor of the tone or feeling of the school. Appleberry and Hoy (1969) found that humanism in the pupil-control orientation of schools and the openness of the organizational climate of schools are strongly correlated.

Furthermore, in order to test the usefulness of the custodial-humanistic framework as an index of school tone or climate, Hoy and Appleberry (1970) used the OCDQ variables to compare the most humanistic schools and the most custodial schools in terms of their climate profiles. Schools with a custodial, pupil-control orientation had significantly greater disengagement, less esprit, more aloofness, and less thrust than those with a humanistic, pupil-control orientation. In other words, humanistic schools seem more likely than custodial schools to have the following:

- Teachers who work well together with respect to the teaching-learning task
- Teachers who have high morale and are satisfied because of their sense of task accomplishment and fulfillment of social needs
- Principals who deal with teachers in an informal, face-to-face situation rather than "go by the book"
- Principals who do not supervise closely but instead motivate through personal example
- A climate marked by openness, acceptance, and authenticity.

Humanism in pupil-control orientation and openness of norms, although different elements of school climate, seem to be highly compatible.

In brief, pupil-control orientation not only provides important information about pupil-teacher relations but also suggests a great deal about the nature of teacher-teacher and teacher-principal relations. For example, a recent study of prospective teachers demonstrated the importance of pupil control in developing a sense of efficacy in neophytes (Woolfolk and Hoy, 1990). Given the importance of pupil control, the custodial-humanistic framework provides a general picture of the school's character, one that can yield a number of general predictions about the nature of the school in a host of important areas. The custodial-humanistic framework also can be used to generate several hypotheses:

- Custodial schools will have more alienated students than will humanistic schools.
- Custodial schools will have more goal displacement than will humanistic schools.
- Custodial schools will have less open communication both horizontally and vertically than will humanistic schools.
- Formal leadership patterns will be accepted more readily in humanistic than in custodial schools.
- Humanistic schools will produce a greater sense of self-efficacy among teachers than will custodial schools.

Although these propositions are meant to be only illustrations of the usefulness of the framework, the first hypothesis has actually been the basis of a comprehensive study of alienation of 8,600 high school students in forty-five schools. Using the PCI, Hoy (1972) examined the relationship between custodial schools and student sense of alienation. The results of the study provided qualified support for the general hypothesis guiding the investigation—namely, the more custodial and closed the school climate, the greater the student sense of alienation. Custodial schools had students who had a greater sense of powerlessness and normlessness than students from humanistic schools; however, such was not the case with student sense of meaninglessness. Meaninglessness is the sensed inability of students to predict future outcomes. Apparently, custodial schools provide structure and direction. The fact that events are predictable, even if they are alienating in other terms, may mitigate against a sense of meaninglessness developing in schools. Alternatively, one might speculate that in response to the threat and general alienation produced by custodialism, the strength and significance of the student subculture may be enhanced, thereby providing social support and cohesion among students and facilitating meaningful activity in the student subculture.

Self-actualization is the other side of the alienation coin. Students are engaged in the ongoing process of growing to their full potential in terms of creative expression, interpersonal effectiveness, and self-fulfillment. Does the school climate influence such development? John Deibert and Hoy (1977) explored this question in a comprehensive study involving more than 4,000 students in forty high schools. As predicted, the humanistic school, not the custodial, provided a healthy social climate for the development of a mature self-image for students; the more humanistic the pupil-control orientation of the school, the greater the chance that high school seniors were moving toward self-actualization. Moreover, Frederick Lunnenburg (1983) found that student perceptions of a humanistic school climate were positively related to their motivation, task orientation, problem solving, and seriousness to learn, and in a later study, Lunnenburg and Linda J. Schmidt (1989) showed a consistent negative relationship between a custodial orientation and students' perceptions of the quality of school life.

Several other studies also have underscored the atmosphere of the school and the student's sense of involvement and identification with the school as important factors in the student's educational growth and development (Coleman et al., 1966;

Heath, 1970). That evidence suggests a need for public high schools that are less custodial, more humanistic, and more open in climate. Changes in that direction are more easily described than made, and inevitably, they are slow in coming and often unsuccessful; nevertheless, the effort should be made.

CONTRAST AND COMPARISON

We have developed two perspectives—organizational culture and organizational climate—to describe the nature of the workplace. Both frameworks attempt to capture the intangible feel of organizational life. Individual schools may serve the same mission, but their traditions and organizational ideologies will invariably differ.

Culture is the fashionable term. Scholars of organizational culture use the qualitative and ethnographic techniques of anthropology and sociology to study the character of organizations. They are interested in "thick descriptions" that help students understand the symbols that are used to give meaning to the social world of organizations. They emphasize the organization as a whole, as a natural system, and how its practices, beliefs, and cultural elements function to maintain a social structure (Ouchi and Wilkins, 1985). Thus, the culture is defined in terms of symbolic systems, and its analysis becomes an abstract and interpretative one in search of meaning.

In some contrast, scholars of climate typically use quantitative techniques and multivariate analyses to identify patterns of perceived behavior in organizations. Climate researchers usually assume that organizations are rational instruments to accomplish purpose; hence, they search for critical patterns of behavior. The historical roots for the study of climate are in social and industrial psychology rather than in anthropology or sociology. Survey techniques and multivariate statistics are used to map patterns of behavior that are significant in influencing organizational outcomes. Emphasis is placed on more concrete attributes of organizational life. The basic similarities and differences of the perspectives are summarized in Table 5.9.

It is premature to define culture as an aspect of climate (Anderson, 1982; Miskel and Ogawa, 1988) or to define climate as an outcome of culture (Ouchi and Wilkins,

TABLE **5.9** Contrasting Characteristics of Organizational Culture and Organizational Climate		
	Organizational Culture	**Organizational Climate**
Discipline	Anthropology and sociology	Psychology and social psychology
Method	Ethnographic techniques	Survey research
	Linguistic analysis	Multivariate statistics
Level of Abstraction	Abstract	More concrete
Shared Orientations	Assumptions and ideology	Perceptions of behavior

1985; Schein, 1985: Moran and Volkwein, 1992). Moreover, confusion becomes chaos when the "school effectiveness" research masquerades as studies of climate or culture (Hoy, 1990). The distinction between the two frameworks is useful; it provides practitioners and students with competing conceptual schemes for understanding the dynamics of school life. The contrasting perspectives bring with them a natural tension, one that can breath vitality and life into the study of schools.

CHANGING THE CULTURE AND CLIMATE OF SCHOOLS

We have little information on, let alone answers to, the complex problem of changing the school workplace. Two things are clear, however. There is no quick and simple way to change the culture or climate of schools. Long-term systemic effort is more likely to produce change than short-term fads.

Three general strategies for change are presented. Alan Brown (1965) has developed a clinical strategy as well as a growth-centered approach; and Ralph Kilmann (1984) has successfully implemented a procedure for changing the normative culture of organizations. The three strategies are not alternatives to each other; they can be used simultaneously and, indeed, all seem necessary for effective change. The clinical strategy focuses on the nature of the relationships among the school's subgroups; the growth-centered strategy is concerned with the nature of individual development within the school; and the normative procedure is used to change organizational norms. Each of these change strategies offers potential guidelines for the practicing administrator and will be reviewed briefly.

THE CLINICAL STRATEGY

The manipulation of intergroup and interpersonal interactions can foster change. Such a **clinical strategy** for change can proceed through the following steps.

1. *Gaining knowledge of the organization:* The approach begins with a thorough knowledge of the dynamics of the school organization. Such knowledge, of course, comes through careful observation, analysis, and study. The perceptive principal may have acquired much of this knowledge through experience, but typically, a more systematic analysis is enlightening and valuable. As a prelude to such a study, he or she must understand the salient aspects of organizational life including the basic norms and values of the faculty. The conceptual perspectives provided by such measures as the OCDQ, OHI, and PCI can substantially aid this learning about the school organization.

2. *Diagnosis:* The second step in the process is diagnostic. Here again conceptual capital, from a variety of perspectives, can provide labels for diagnosing potential trouble areas. Poor esprit, high disengagement, custodialism, distorted communication, unilateral decision making, weak motivation,

and low academic expectations are examples of such conceptual labels. The extent to which these concepts are clearly defined in the mind of the practitioner and fit together in a broader perspective probably mediates the effectiveness of the diagnosis.

3. *Prognosis:* In the third step, the "clinician" judges the seriousness of the situation and develops a set of operational priorities to improve the situation.

4. *Prescription:* The appropriate course of action is often hidden. Suppose we decided that the school's atmosphere is too custodial in pupil-control orientation. How can the situation be remedied? We might replace a number of "custodial" teachers with younger "humanistic" teachers. Research suggests, however, that the pupil-control ideology of beginning teachers becomes significantly more custodial as they become socialized by the teacher subculture (Hoy, 1967, 1968, 1969; Hoy and Woolfolk, 1989), which in this case tends to equate tight control with good teaching. Merely replacing a number of custodial teachers without altering basic teacher norms about pupil control will probably have little or no impact. Altering basic teacher norms calls for a more sophisticated strategy (see below). A first step in such a strategy is to eliminate teacher and administrator ignorance about the PCI—that is, to erase the shared misperceptions of educators with respect to pupil-control ideology. Teachers generally think that principals are much more custodial in pupil-control ideology than they themselves are, and conversely, principals typically believe that teachers are more custodial in pupil-control orientation than they report themselves to be (Packard and Willower, 1972). These common misperceptions need to be swept away if a more humanistic perspective is to be achieved. In other words, developing prescriptions at first seems easy enough, but experience shows that solutions to various school problems are usually oversimplified and often irrelevant. If administrators are going to be successful in changing the school climate and culture, then they must change the norms and values of the teacher subculture as well as the basic, shared assumptions of the faculty and administration.

5. *Evaluation:* The last step in the clinical strategy is to evaluate the extent to which prescriptions have been implemented and are successful. Because planned change in social systems is often slow, continuous monitoring and evaluation are required.

THE GROWTH-CENTERED STRATEGY

A **growth-centered strategy** simply involves the acceptance of a set of assumptions about the development of school personnel and the use of these assumptions as the basis for administrative decision making. The assumptions are the following.

1. *Change is a property of healthy school organizations.* The principal should see organizations, and hence organizational climate, in a constant state of flux.

2. *Change has direction.* Change can be positive or negative, progressive or regressive.

3. *Change should imply progress.* Change should provide movement of the organization toward its goals. Of course not all change represents progress; yet the principal's stance is progress oriented.

4. *Teachers have high potential for the development and implementation of change.* Principals are always ready to provide teachers with more freedom and responsibility in the operation of the school.

These basic assumptions, if acted upon, would allow for a growth policy, which in turn leads to increased opportunities for professional development. From this perspective, administrators would remove obstacles from the path of professional growth and not manipulate people. Finally, the approach should help facilitate a climate of mutual trust and respect among teachers and administrators.

The clinical and growth-centered approaches do not conflict in their assumptions, although they have different focuses—organizational and individual. The astute administrator draws on both strategies to change the climate of the school.

CHANGING NORMS

Most organizational members can list the norms that operate in their work group and even suggest new norms that would be more effective for improving productivity or morale (Kilmann, Saxton, and Serpa, 1985). A number of ways can be used to surface actual norms, but participants are usually reluctant to specify norms *unless* they are confident that the information will not be used against them or the organization. Thus, anonymity and confidentiality of respondents are crucial in identifying the salient norms in an organization.

Kilmann and his associates (1985) have successfully used small groups in workshop settings to elicit norms. He suggests that with just a little prodding and a few illustrations to get the group started, members quickly begin to enumerate many norms; in fact, they revel in being able to articulate what beforehand was not formally stated and rarely discussed.

Prevailing norms map the "way things are" around the organization. Indeed, norm statements often begin with "around here." For example, "Around here, it is all right to admit mistakes, as long as you don't make them again." The key norms of an organization are usually related to such important areas as control, support, innovation, social relations, rewards, conflicts, and standards of excellence. To begin to identify the norms of a school, teachers might be asked to list their views of the school in terms of "around here" statements. For example, they are ask to complete the following statements:

1. At the end of a typical faculty meeting, everyone _____.

2. Around here, the real basis for reward _____.

3. Around here, control of students _____.

4. Around here, decisions are reached through _____.

5. Around here, risk taking _____.

6. Around here, differences in opinion are handled by _____.

7. Around here, achievement standards _____.

8. Around here, we handle problems by _____.

Unlike tacit assumptions, norms often can be revealed by carefully constructed survey instruments. The Kilmann-Saxton Culture-Gap Survey (Kilmann and Saxton, 1983), for example, has been used to determine not only the actual norms but also the desired norms of organizations. The instrument consists of 28 norm pairs in the areas of task support, task innovation, social relationships, and personal freedom. An example of a norm pair from the survey is the following: "(a) Share information only when it benefits your own work group, versus (b) share information to help the organization make better decisions." Members are asked to describe both the actual norms and the desired ones. The current normative culture is then determined as well as the gap between the desired and actual norms.

Kilmann (1984) recommends the following five step procedure as a **norm-changing strategy:**

- *Surface new norms.* Teachers, usually in a workshop setting, identify the norms that guide their attitudes and behaviors.

- *Articulate new directions.* Teachers discuss where the school is headed and identify new directions that are necessary for progress.

- *Establish new norms.* Teachers identify a set of new norms that they believe will lead to improvement and organizational success.

- *Identify culture gaps.* Examine the discrepancy between actual norms (step 1) and desired norms (step 3). This discrepancy is a culture gap; the larger the gap, the more probable that the existing norms are dysfunctional.

- *Close the culture gaps.* The act of listing new norms often results in many group members actually adopting the new and desired norms (Kilmann, 1984). But the teachers as a group must also agree that the desired norms will replace the old norms and that the changes will be monitored and enforced. Subsequent teacher meetings can then be used to reinforce the new norms and prevent regression to old norms and practices.

John Miner (1988) notes that this process is especially useful in identifying and changing negative aspects of an organization's culture. For example, negative norms surfaced in step 1 can be replaced by more desirable norms identified in step 3, as follows:

- *From:* Don't rock the boat; don't volunteer to do anything extra; don't share information; don't tell your colleagues or superiors what they don't want to hear.

- *To:* Experiment with new ideas; help others when they need help; communicate openly with your colleagues; persist in identifying problems.

Miner (1988) argues that this group approach to cultural change may be more useful for identifying dysfunctional aspects of the culture than for bringing about real change, and Schein (1985) charges that this process deals at best with the superficial aspects of culture. Nonetheless, Kilmann's five-step process seems a useful vehicle for helping groups of teachers get specific information about the nature of their workplace and for developing a plan for change. The process, together with the clinical and growth-centered approaches, provides teachers and administrators with specific techniques and procedures to change the character of the workplace.

SUMMARY AND SUGGESTED READINGS

Two related and overlapping perspectives are used to analyze the character of the workplace. Organizational culture and organizational climate both go beyond the formal and individual aspects of organizational life. Each concept deals with the natural, spontaneous, and human side of the organization as attempts are made to uncover shared meanings and unwritten rules that influence behavior.

Organizational culture is the set of shared orientations that holds a unit together and gives it a distinctive identity. Although climate tends to focus on shared perceptions, culture is defined in terms of shared assumptions, values, and norms. These three levels of culture—shared assumptions, values, and norms—are explored as alternative ways of describing and analyzing the school cultures. The recent popularity of culture is an outgrowth of the business literature, which suggests that effective organizations have strong corporate cultures.

Organizational climate is a broad concept that denotes members' shared perceptions of tone or character of the workplace; it is a set of internal characteristics that distinguishes one school from another and influences the behavior of people in schools. Three important conceptualizations of school climate were considered. The climate of interaction among teachers can be described along an open to closed continuum, and can be measured by organizational climates–description questionnaires, the OCDQ-RE, OCDQ-RM, and OCDQ-RS. Another conceptualization of climate examines the organizational health of schools—that is, the extent to which the school is meeting both its instrumental and its expressive needs while simultaneously coping with disruptive outside forces as it directs its energies toward its mission. The health of the school can be mapped using the appropriate Organizational Health Inventory (OHI); separate and reliable versions of the OHI exist for elementary, middle, and high schools.

Finally, still another perspective views school climate in terms of a continuum of control over students, from humanistic to custodial, and is measured by the Pupil-Control Ideology (PCI) form.

The chapter concludes with three strategies that practitioners can use to change the nature of the school workplace. A clinical strategy deals with the nature of the relationships among the school's subgroups; a growth-centered strategy emphasizes the nature of individual development within the school; and a group procedure offers a strategy to change organizational norms.

Edgar Schein's (1985) book, *Organizational Culture and Leadership,* remains one of the most comprehensive analyses of organizational culture. Students should not overlook this incisive treatment. For a diverse look at culture, a recent collection of readings, *Reframing Organizational Culture,* provides readers with exemplars of culture research as well as critiques, commentaries, and expositions (Frost et al., 1991). For those interested in corporate cultures, the early works of Peters and Waterman (1982) and Ouchi (1981) are worthwhile and provide a nice backdrop for Dennison's (1990) study of *Corporate Culture and Organizational Effectiveness.*

Students should begin their study of school climate with Andrew Halpin and Don Croft's (1963) pioneering study *The Organizational Climate of Schools.* Hoy, Tarter, and Kottkamp (1991) provide the results of ten years of research and development in *Open Schools/Healthy Schools: Measuring Organizational Climate.* This book gives researchers four valid and reliable instruments to study schools and provides practitioners with the tools to diagnose problems and analyze the climate of their schools. The instruments, norms, scoring instructions, and interpretations of results are all carefully illustrated. If you are going to study school climate, don't miss this work. Finally, *The School and Pupil Control Ideology* (Willower, Eidell, and Hoy, 1967) is a seminal work on control in schools.

NOTES

1. Informal organization is another concept that describes the nature of the workplace in terms of the social structure and culture of the work group. You might find it useful to review the discussion of informal organization in Chapter 3.

2. Table 5.2 adapted from the work of W. Gibb Dyer, "The Cycle of Cultural Evolution in Organizations," in R. H. Kilmann, M. J. Saxton, R. Serpa, et al. *Gaining Control of the Corporate Culture* (San Francisco: Jossey-Bass, 1985) pp. 206–209.

3. The specifics for calculating the openness indices are found in Hoy, Tarter, and Kottkamp, 1991.

4. The specifics for calculating the openness index are found in Hoy, Tarter, and Kottkamp, 1991. Norms were developed on a large sample of New Jersey elementary and secondary schools. Step-by-step directions for scoring and interpreting results are provided.

5. Most of this large body of the research can be found in the Pupil Control Studies Archives, The Pennsylvania State University, Pattee Library, University Park, PA 16802.

KEY CONCEPTS AND IDEAS

Clinical strategy	Norms
Closed climate	Open climate
Core values	Openness in faculty relations
Custodial orientation	Openness in principal behavior
Disengaged climate	Organizational climate
Engaged climate	Organizational culture
Growth-centered strategy	Organizational health
Healthy organization	Rituals
Humanistic orientation	School climate
Icons	Stories
Legends	Strong cultures
Myths	Tacit assumptions
Norm-changing strategy	Values

Power and Politics in Schools

Political realists see the world as it is: an arena of power politics moved primarily by perceived immediate self-interests, where morality is rhetorical rationale for expedient action and self-interest. It is a world not of angels but of angles, where men speak of moral principles but act on power principles. . . .

—Saul Alinsky
Rules for Radicals

PREVIEW

1. Power is a broad construct that includes both legitimate and illegitimate methods of ensuring compliance.

2. Power can be classified not only as legitimate or illegitimate but also as formal or informal; hence, four basic kinds of organizational power exist: two forms of legitimate power—formal and informal authority—and two kinds of illegitimate power—coercive and political.

3. Legitimate power is more likely to promote commitment and compliance, while illegitimate power produces conflict and alienation.

4. Organizations are political arenas in which power and politics are central.

5. Coalitions of individuals and groups bargain to determine the distribution of power in organizations.

6. The external coalition can be dominated, divided, or passive; and affects the internal coalition.

7. The internal coalition can be personalized, bureaucratic, ideologic, professional, or politicized; and affects the distribution of power.

8. Power and politics are realities of organizational life.

9. Although the means of politics are illegitimate, the ends need not be; politics can be cruel and destructive or considerate and constructive.

10. Ingratiation, networking, and information and impression management are common political tactics used by organizational members to gain advantage.

11. Political games are played to resist authority, to counter the resistance to authority, to build power bases, to defeat rivals, and to produce organizational change.

12. Conflict can be successfully managed by competing, collaborating, accommodating, compromising, or avoiding—depending on the situation.

All social organizations control their participants, but the problem of control is especially important in formal organizations. Formal organizations are planned and deliberately structured to achieve goals, but often they cannot rely on their members to perform their obligations without additional incentives (Kotter, 1985). Thus organizations establish formally structured distributions of rewards and sanctions to support organizational expectations, regulations, and orders. This control structure encourages behavior consistent with organizational norms by making such behavior more desirable (Gross and Etzioni, 1985).

The essence of organizational control is power. The classic definition of **power** is the ability to get others to do what you want them to do, or as Weber (1947: 152) defines it, "the probability that one actor within a social relationship will be in a position to carry out his own will despite resistance." Power for our purposes is a general and comprehensive term. It includes control that is starkly coercive as well as control that is based on nonthreatening persuasion and suggestion. Authority has a narrower scope than power. Weber (1947: 324) defines authority as "the probability that certain specific commands (or all commands) from a given source will be obeyed by a given group of persons." Weber is quick to indicate that authority does not include every mode of exercising power or influence over other persons. He suggests that a certain degree of voluntary compliance is associated with legitimate commands.

In brief, organizations are created and controlled by legitimate authorities, who set goals, design structure, hire and manage employees, and monitor activities to ensure behavior is consistent with the goals and objectives of the organization. These official authorities control the legitimate power of the office or positions, but they are only one of many contenders for other forms of power in organizations (Bolman and Deal, 1991).

SOURCES OF AUTHORITY: LEGITIMATE POWER

Authority relationships are an integral part of life in schools. The basis of many student-teacher, teacher-administrator, or subordinate-superior relations is authority. Unfortunately, many individuals view authority and authoritarianism as synonymous. Because this is not the case, authority as a theoretical concept must be clearly defined.

Contrary to some popular beliefs, the exercise of authority in a school typically does not involve coercion. Herbert A. Simon (1957a: 126–127) proposed that **authority** is distinguished from other kinds of influence or power in that the subordinate "holds in abeyance his own critical faculties for choosing between alternatives and uses the formal criterion of the receipt of a command or signal as his basis of choice." Therefore, two criteria of authority in schools are crucial in superior-subordinate relationships: (1) voluntary compliance to legitimate commands; and (2) suspension of one's own criteria for decision making and acceptance of the organizational command.

Peter Blau and W. Richard Scott (1962) argue that a third criterion must be added to distinguish authority from other forms of social control. They maintain that a value orientation arises that defines the use of social control as legitimate, and this orientation arises only in a group context. Authority is legitimized by a value that is held in common by the group. Blau and Scott conclude that a basic characteristic of the authority relation is the subordinates' willingness to suspend their own criteria for making decisions and comply with directives from the superior. This willingness results largely from social constraints exerted by norms of the social collectivity (teachers and students) and not primarily from the power the superior (administrator) brings to bear. Such social constraints are not typical of coercive power and other types of social influence. Authority relations in schools, then, have three primary characteristics: (1) a willingness of subordinates to comply; (2) a suspension of the subordinates' criteria for making a decision prior to a directive; and (3) a power relationship legitimized by the norms of a group.

Authority exists when a common set of beliefs (norms) in a school legitimizes the use of power as "right and proper." Weber (1947) distinguishes three types of authority—charismatic, traditional, and legal—according to the kind of legitimacy typically claimed by each.

Charismatic authority rests on devotion to an extraordinary individual who is leader by virtue of personal trust or exemplary qualities. Charismatic authority tends to be nonrational, affective, or emotional and rests heavily on the leader's personal qualities and characteristics. The authority of the charismatic leader results primarily from the leader's overwhelming personal appeal, and typically a common value orientation emerges within the group to produce an intense normative commitment to and identification with the person. Thus students may obey classroom directives because of a teacher's personal "mystique."

Traditional authority is anchored in an established belief in the sanctity of the status of those exercising authority in the past. Obedience is owed to the traditional sanctioned *position* of authority, and the person who occupies the position inherits the authority established by custom. In a school, for example, students may accept the authority of the position and the teacher because their parents and grandparents did so before them.

Legal authority is based on enacted laws that can be changed by formally correct procedures. Obedience is not owed to a person or position per se but to the *laws* that specify to whom and to what extent people owe compliance. Legal authority thus extends only within the scope of the authority vested in the office by law.

In schools, obedience is owed to the impersonal principles that govern the operation of the organizations. Other scholars and organizational theorists have extended these basic concepts of authority. Robert Peabody (1962) distinguishes the bases of formal authority—legitimacy and position—from the bases of functional authority—competence and personal or human relations skills, while Blau and Scott (1962) simply describe the authority relation as formal or informal dependent on the source of legitimacy for the power.

Formal authority is vested in the organization and is legally established in positions, rules, and regulations. In joining the organization, employees accept the authority relation because they agree, within certain limits, to accept the directives of their supervisors; the organization has the right to command and the employees have the duty to obey (March and Simon, 1958). The basis of formal authority, then, rests with the legally established agreement between the organization and the employees.

Functional authority has a variety of sources, including authority of competence and authority of person. Although Weber treats authority of competence as part of the legal-rational pattern of bureaucracies, competence is not always limited to position. Technical competence can provide the source for legitimate control and directives in a formal organization regardless of the specific position held. This fact poses a dilemma and conflict for professionals.

Informal authority is still another source of legitimate control stemming from personal behavior and attributes of individuals. Regardless of formal position, some organizational members develop norms of allegiance and support from their colleagues. These informal norms buttress and legitimize their power and provide informal authority.

AUTHORITY AND ADMINISTRATIVE BEHAVIOR IN SCHOOLS

Authority is a basic feature of life in schools because it provides the basis for legitimate control of administrators, teachers, and students. A primary source of control is formal authority that is vested in the office or position and not in the particular person who performs the official role (Merton, 1957). When administrators, teachers, and students join a school organization, they accept the formal authority relation. They agree within certain limits to follow directives that officials issue for the school. In short, school members enter into contractual agreements in which they sell their promises to obey commands (Commons, 1924).

Formal authority, anchored and buttressed by formal sanctions, has a somewhat limited scope. The existence of what Chester Barnard (1938) refers to as a bureaucratic "zone of indifference"—in which subordinates, including administrator and teacher professionals, accept orders without question—may be satisfactory for eliciting certain minimum performance levels, but it seems likely that this does not lead to an efficient operation. Formal authority promotes minimal compliance with directives and discipline, but it does not encourage employees to exert effort, to accept responsibility, or to exercise initiative (Blau and Scott, 1962; Kotter, 1985). Therefore,

FIGURE **6.1**

Types of Authority Positions

		Formal Authority	
		Yes	No
Informal Authority	Yes	Formal Leader	Informal Leader
	No	Officer	Follower

a basic challenge facing all administrators, and one especially significant for first-level line supervisors such as school principals, is to find methods to extend their influence over their professional staff beyond the narrow limits of formal positional authority.

Wayne Hoy and his colleagues (1971, 1974) have elaborated and empirically examined these ideas. They reasoned that many school administrators have the power and authority of their offices alone. In a sense, they are sterile bureaucrats, not leaders. Barnard (1938) suggests that only when the authority of leadership is combined with the authority of position will superiors be effective in inducing subordinates to comply with directives outside the bureaucratic zone of indifference. Indeed, the possession of both formal and informal authority distinguishes formal leaders from officers and informal leaders. Figure 6.1 illustrates these relationships.

How can school administrators broaden the bases of their authority and enhance their leadership position? The informal organization is an important source of authority that frequently remains untapped. Where formal authority is legitimized by legal contracts and position, informal authority is legitimized by the common values and sentiments that emerge in the work group. In particular, informal authority arises from the loyalty that the superior commands from group members (Blau and Scott, 1962). The significance of subordinate loyalty to superiors is clear. Administrators who command subordinate loyalty seems to have a distinct advantage in enlarging their authority base.

Although authoritarian principal behavior and teacher loyalty to principals are probably incompatible, one strategy some administrators use for extending the scope of formal authority over subordinates is domination (Blau and Scott, 1962). Authoritarian administrators, for example, attempt to increase control by resorting to formal sanctions or to threats of using those sanctions; however, their prolonged use probably tends to undermine their authority. Subordinates, particularly professionals, resent constant reminders of their dependence on the superior, especially in an egalitarian culture. Given a strategy of domination and close supervision, authoritarian administrators are *unlikely* to command loyalty and support from professionals easily. Blau (1955) neatly called this the *dilemma of bureaucratic authority.* The dilemma depends on the power of sanction, but it is weakened by frequent resort to sanctions. In fact, nonauthoritarian and supportive supervisors seem likely to engage in a contrasting strategy—one of leadership in which services and assistance are furnished to subordinates. Using formal authority to perform special favors, services, and support can create social obligations and build goodwill among subordinates. The result should be enhanced development of subordinate loyalty and informal authority.

The nature of supervision in schools should focus on helping, not directing, teachers to improve their teaching for a number of reasons. Teachers work in closed rooms and are not easily observed. Moreover, teachers frequently make strong claims for professional autonomy, and close supervision seems likely to be seen as an infringement on that autonomy. Finally, teachers attach great importance to authority based on professional competence—much more so than similar professional groups such as social workers (Peabody, 1962). Therefore, it should not be surprising that consistently the research demonstrates that authoritarian principals in schools are not successful at generating trust and teacher loyalty while supportive ones are highly successful (Hoy and Rees, 1974, Isaacson, 1983; Mullins, 1983; Hoffman et al., 1994; Reiss, 1994). Close, authoritarian control of teachers does not generate informal authority; supportive and helpful supervision does.

Emotional detachment and hierarchical independence are two other important characteristics of principal-teacher relationships. Emotional detachment is the ability of administrators to remain calm, cool, and collected in difficult situations; and hierarchical independence is the extent to which administrators demonstrate their autonomy from superiors as they interact with teachers. Principals stand in the middle—with the higher administration on one side and professional teaching faculty on the other. Their effectiveness depends on the support they receive from both, yet they are likely to be the objects of conflicting pressures from both groups. Consequently, emotional detachment from subordinates and independence from superiors are important in establishing social support from teachers for principals. Indeed, the research has demonstrated the significance of both, but especially emotional detachment, in generating teacher loyalty to principals (Hoy and Williams, 1971; Hoy and Rees, 1974; Isaacson, 1983; Mullins, 1983).

Similarly, hierarchical influence is another attribute of administrators who are likely to tap into the informal teacher groups for authority to lead. Administrators who are able and willing to exert their influences with their superiors on teachers' behalf are respected and valued by teachers, and they earn the confidence, support, and loyalty of their teachers (Isaacson, 1983; Mullins, 1983).

Finally, the authenticity of the principal in dealing with teachers is a critical factor in the administrative process, enabling principals to generate teacher loyalty and informal authority. Leader authenticity is a slippery concept. People glibly talk about genuine, real, and authentic behavior, yet clear definition is another matter. Based on the work of James Henderson and Hoy (1983) and Hoy and Henderson (1983), principal authenticity is defined as the extent to which teachers describe their principals as accepting responsibility for their own actions, as being nonmanipulating, and as demonstrating a salience of self over role. In contrast, inauthentic principals are viewed as those who pass the buck, blame others and circumstances for not being successful, manipulate teachers, and hide behind their formal position. As one would expect, leader authenticity is strongly related to commanding trust and teacher loyalty (Hoffman, 1993).

The implications of these empirical studies seem clear. If educational administrators are to be successful in developing informal authority, then they need to behave in ways that foster teacher loyalty. In this regard, authoritarian behavior is doomed to failure. Instead, administrators need to be supportive, be independent, and use their influence to help teachers. Furthermore, even in difficult situations, administrative behavior needs to be emotionally tempered, calm, and considerate. Perhaps most important, principals should be authentic in their behavior; they need to show a willingness to share in the blame, to be nonmanipulative of teachers, and to be unfettered by bureaucratic role demands (Blau and Scott, 1962; Hoffman, 1993; Reiss, 1994).

SOURCES OF POWER

Although authority implies legitimacy, not all power is legitimate. Power can be used by individuals, groups, or organizations. For example, a department or group can have power, which suggests that it has the ability to influence the behavior of other individuals or groups, perhaps in personnel or budgeting decisions. Likewise, an individual can have power, which indicates success in getting others to comply with directives or suggestions. Leaders have power; they get others to comply with their directives. As we have seen, whether a leader or not, most administrators have power simply because as representatives of the organization, they have the power of the organization. But administrators can derive power from personal as well as organizational sources; those who have power influence the behavior of others. One of the first attempts to analyze sources of power was the pioneering work of John R. P. French and Bertram H. Raven (1968). Their focus was on the bases of interpersonal power and led them to the identification of five kinds of power—reward, coercive, legitimate, referent, and expert. Their typology of interpersonal power has been extended to the organizational level.

Reward power is the administrator's ability to influence subordinates by rewarding their desirable behavior. The strength of this kind of power depends on the attractiveness of the rewards and the extent of certainty that a person can control the rewards. For example, the principal who controls the allocation of teaching assignments or developmental grants for teaching innovations, or who can release teachers from routine housekeeping duties, has reward power over teachers in that school. Teachers may comply with the principal's requests because they expect to be rewarded for compliance. It is important, however, that the rewards be linked to compliance and that the influence attempts are proper and ethical. Philip Cusick (1981) describes one principal's attempt to use reward power by administering the schedule, additional assignments, and unallocated resources. The principal controlled just the things that many teachers desired. The principal could award a department chairperson with a free period, a favorite class, a double lunch period, an honors section, or support for a new activity.

Coercive power is an administrator's ability to influence subordinates by punishing them for undesirable behavior. The strength of coercive power depends on the severity of the punishment and on the likelihood that the punishment cannot be avoided. Punishment can take many forms—official reprimands, undesirable work assignments, closer supervision, stricter enforcement of the rules and regulations, denial of salary increments, or termination. Punishment is not without its negative effects. An official reprimand to a teacher for consistently leaving school early may result in frequent absenteeism, refusing to provide extra help to students unless specified in the contract, and a general tendency to avoid all but the essential aspects of the job. Interestingly, the same relationship can be viewed as one of reward power in one situation but as coercive power in another. For example, if a teacher obeys a principal through fear of punishment, it is coercive power; but if another teacher obeys in anticipation of a future reward, it is reward power.

Legitimate power is the administrator's ability to influence the behavior of subordinates simply because of formal position. Subordinates acknowledge that the administrator has a right to issue directives and they have an obligation to comply. Every administrator is empowered by the organization to make decisions within a specific area of responsibility. This area of responsibility defines the activities over which the administrator has legitimate power. The further removed a directive is from the administrator's area of responsibility, the weaker his or her legitimate power. When directives from an administrator are accepted without question, they fall within the subordinate's "zone of indifference." Such an order lies within an area that was anticipated at the time the employee contracted with the organization and is seen by the employee as a legitimate obligation. For example, teachers expect to compute and turn in grades on time for each marking period. Outside the zone, however, legitimate power fades quickly. It is one thing for the principal to insist that grades be promptly computed and turned in to the office; it is quite another to order teachers to change a grade. The legitimacy of the first request is clear, but not so for the second; hence, compliance with the second request is questionable.

Referent power is an administrator's ability to influence behavior based on subordinates' liking and identification with the administrator. The individual with referent power is admired, is respected, and serves as a model to be emulated. The source of referent power rests with the extraordinary personality and interpersonal skills of the individual. For example, young teachers may identify with the principal and seek to imitate the personal demeanor and perhaps the leadership style of the more experienced and well-liked principal. Not only individuals but groups can have referent power. Members of a positive reference group can also provide a source of referent power. Referent power does not rest simply with the official power holders of an organization. Teachers as well as principals can have referent power; in fact, any highly attractive individual who develops respect, trust, and loyalty among colleagues is likely to develop such power.

Expert power is the administrator's ability to influence subordinates' behavior based on specialized knowledge and skill. Subordinates are influenced because they believe that the information and expertise held by the administrator are relevant, are helpful, and are things they themselves do not have. Like referent power, expert power is a personal characteristic and does not depend on occupying a formal position of power. Expert power is, however, much narrower in scope than referent power. The useful knowledge defines the limits of expert power. New administrators are likely to have a time lag in the acquisition of expert power because it takes time for expertise to become known and accepted by subordinates. New principals have to demonstrate that they know how to perform their administrative functions with skill before teachers become accepting of their attempts to implement new practices and procedures.

These five types of power can be grouped into two broad categories—organizational and personal. Reward, coercive, and legitimate power are bound to the organizational position. The higher the position, the greater the potential for power. In contrast, referent and expert power depend much more on the personal attributes of the administrator, such as personality, leadership style, knowledge, and interpersonal skill. In brief, some sources of power are more amenable to organizational control, while others are more dependent on personal characteristics.

ADMINISTRATIVE USES OF POWER

A large portion of any administrator's time is directed at "power-oriented" behavior—that is, "behavior directed primarily at developing or using relationships in which other people are to some degree willing to defer to one's wishes" (Kotter, 1978: 27). Administrators possess varying degrees and combinations of the types of power that have just been discussed. Moreover, the way administrators use one type of power can hinder or facilitate the effectiveness of other kinds.

Reward power is likely to produce positive feelings and facilitate the development of referent power, but coercive power has the opposite effect (Huber, 1981). Moreover, subordinates may view administrators who demonstrate expertise as having more legitimate power. In fact, expert power may be the most stable form of power. In one study, changes in the reward structure of an organization increased the perceived use of coercive power and reduced the perceived use of reward, legitimate, and referent power of the administrator, but expert power remained stable (Green and Podsakoff, 1981).

Gary Yukl (1981) offers some guidelines to administrators for building and using each of the five kinds of power. The likely consequences of the uses of power are important considerations for administrators. Table 6.1 summarizes the probable outcomes of each form of power in terms of commitment, simple compliance, or resistance. For example, the use of referent power is most likely to promote commitment, next most likely to result in simple compliance, and least likely to create resistance and develop alienation. Commitment is most likely with the use of referent and expert power; legitimate and reward power are most likely to promote a

| TABLE **6.1** | Probable Subordinate Responses to Power |

Probable Subordinate Responses to Power

Type of Power	Commitment	Simple Compliance	Resistance
Referent	XXX	XX	X
Expert	XXX	XX	X
Legitimate	XX	XXX	X
Reward	XX	XXX	X
Coercive	X	XX	XXX

XXX	Most likely
XX	Less likely
X	Least likely

simple compliance; and coercive power will probably produce resistance and eventually alienation. Amitai Etzioni (1975) draws similar conclusions in his analysis of the consequences of using power in organizations.

Referent power depends on personal loyalty to the administrator that grows over a relatively long period of time. The development of loyalty to one's superior is a social exchange process, which is improved when administrators demonstrate concern, trust, and affection for their subordinates. Such acceptance and confidence promote goodwill and identification with superiors, which in turn create strong loyalty and commitment. Referent power is most effective if administrators select subordinates who are most likely to identify with them, make frequent use of personal appeals, and set examples of appropriate role behavior—that is, lead by example.

Expertise itself is usually not enough to guarantee commitment of subordinates. Successful use of expert power requires that subordinates recognize the administrator's knowledge and perceive the exercise of that expertise to be useful. Thus, administrators must demonstrate their knowledge convincingly by maintaining credibility, keeping informed, acting decisively, recognizing subordinate concerns, and avoiding threats to the self-esteem of subordinates. In short, administrators must promote an image of expertise and then use their knowledge to demonstrate its utility.

Authority is exercised through legitimate power. Legitimate requests may be expressed as orders, commands, directives, or instructions. The outcome of the administrator's request may be committed compliance, simple compliance, resistance, or alienation depending of the nature and manner of the request. There is less likelihood of resistance and alienation if the administrator makes the request politely and clearly, explains the reasons for the request, is responsive to the concerns of subordinates, and routinely uses legitimate authority (Yukl, 1981, 1994).

The use of reward power is a common administrative tactic to achieve compliance with organizational rules or specific leader requests. The rewards may be either explicit or implicit, but it is important that they are contingent on compliance with administrative directives. Compliance is most likely when the request is feasible, the incentive is attractive, the administrator is a credible source of the reward, the request is proper and ethical, and the compliance to the request can be verified. There are some dangers in the use of rewards. Reward power can be perceived by subordinates as manipulative, a common cause of subordinate resistance and hostility. Moreover, the frequent use of reward power can define the administrative relationship in purely economic terms; thus, subordinate response becomes calculated on the basis of tangible benefits. When rewards are given to express an administrator's personal appreciation for a job well done, however, it can become a source of increased referent power. People who repeatedly provide incentives in an acceptable manner gradually become more well liked by the recipients of the rewards (French and Raven, 1968).

Most effective administrators try to avoid the use of coercive power because it typically erodes the use of referent power and creates hostility, alienation, and aggression among subordinates. Absenteeism, sabotage, theft, job actions, and strikes are common responses to excessive coercion. The use of coercion is usually considered when the problem is one of discipline and is most appropriate when used to deter behavior detrimental to the organization—for example, stealing, sabotage, violation of rules, fighting, and direct disobedience to legitimate directives (Yukl, 1981, 1994). To be most effective subordinates need to be informed about the rules and penalties for violations. Coercion is never without the potential to alienate; thus, discipline must be administered promptly, consistently, and fairly. The administrator must maintain credibility, stay calm, avoid appearing hostile, and use measured and appropriate punishments. The alienating effects of coercive power make it a measure of last resort.

Power need not be thought of as a constraining force on subordinates. **Empowerment** is the process by which administrators share power and help others use it in constructive ways to make decisions affecting themselves and their work (Schermerhorn, Hunt, and Osborn, 1994). More than ever before, administrators and reformers are trying to empower teachers (Conley and Bacharach, 1990; Midgley and Wood, 1993). Empowerment gets translated into shared decision making, delegation of authority, teamwork, and site-based management (see Chapter 9). Rather than viewing power as the domain of administrators, it is increasingly seen as something to be shared by everyone in more collegial organizations (Lugg and Boyd, 1993).

ETZIONI'S TYPOLOGY OF POWER

Etzioni (1975) has used the concept of power and subordinates' response to power, which he calls compliance, as the basis of a theory of organization. Here the focus is on organizational power—how the organization directs the behavior of its members. Etzioni's typology of power is based upon the *means* used to make individuals comply with organizational directives; he identifies three types of power: coercive, remunerative, and normative.

Coercive power depends on either the actual application or the threatened application of physical sanctions. In-school detention, suspension, expulsion, and corporal punishment represent typical coercive methods that can be used to gain student compliance.

Remunerative power rests upon the management of material resources and rewards. Salaries, wages, bonuses, and fringe benefits are common applications of remunerative power used to control the behavior of employees.

Normative power derives from the allocation and manipulation of symbolic rewards and sanctions. It can be exercised by influencing esteem, status, or prestige through the manipulation of positive symbols such as honors, grades, and recommendations.

Corresponding to each type of power are three reactions to power that Etzioni characterizes in terms of the intensity and direction of subordinate involvement. Involvement ranges along a continuum from positive through neutral to negative. Intense positive involvement is called *commitment;* intense, negative involvement is termed *alienation;* and mild involvement is referred to as *calculation.* The continuum is illustrated in Figure 6.2.

Compliance is the relationship between the kinds of power applied to subordinates and their resulting involvement in the organization. The classifications of power and involvement apply to all individuals in a social system; however, the focus is on lower participants, the subordinates at the lowest level of an organization's hierarchy. Students in schools are at the bottom of the structure and are the lower-level participants.

FIGURE **6.2**

Etzioni's Compliance Types

Power		Involvement		
		Alienation	Calculation	Commitment
	Coercive	Coercive		
	Renumerative		Utilitarian	
	Normative			Normative

FIGURE **6.3**

Zones of Involvement

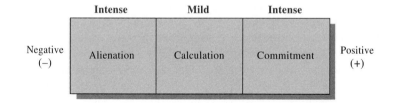

The type of power applied by the organization to the lower participants and the kind of involvement or response they develop form the basis for Etzioni's compliance typology. Although the three kinds of power and the three kinds of involvement yield a compliance topology with nine categories, three main organizational types are derived (see Figure 6.3). The three diagonal cases shown in the figure, which Etzioni calls "congruent types," are found most frequently (Hall, Hass, and Johnson, 1967; Etzioni, 1975). The compliance relationship is said to be congruent when the nature of participants' involvement in an organization is consistent with the kind of power it applies to them. For instance, coercive power tends to generate alienation; hence, when the match is found, the relationship is congruent.

Each organizational level has its own compliance relationships; however, the predominant compliance pattern of lower-level subordinates is used to classify organizations, for two reasons. Compliance is more problematic at that level than at others, and organizations can be more easily distinguished from each other at the lower level. Although the three patterns of compliance exist in virtually all organizations, most organizations rely much more on one pattern than on the others; hence, organizations are classified according to their predominant compliance patterns as coercive, utilitarian, or normative. Further, within each type, organizations can be ordered in terms of their relative emphasis on the predominant pattern (Etzioni, 1975).

Coercive organizations use force or the threat of force as the primary means to control the activities of lower-level subordinates, and the collective response to such power is a high degree of alienation. The two most typical kinds of coercive organizations in contemporary American society are prisons and custodial mental hospitals. Force is the major means of control, and alienation is typical of inmates and patients.

Utilitarian organizations rely mostly on remuneration to gain power over lower-level subordinates, and the response is calculative involvement. Blue-collar industries are typical utilitarian organizations. There are other organizations in this category, however, that may be arranged according to the degree of utilitarianism they exhibit. Following blue-collar industries, which are most strongly utilitarian, are white-collar industries, business unions, farmers' organizations, and peacetime military organizations, each succeedingly less utilitarian.

Normative organizations primarily use normative power to maintain control over lower participants, who generally are highly committed to the organization. Typical examples of normative organizations are religious organizations including churches, orders, and monasteries; general hospitals; colleges and universities; and social unions. Religious organizations are most "purely" normative because they use normative power more exclusively and receive greater commitment from the rank-and-file participants than others. Public schools, therapeutic mental hospitals and professional organizations, law firms, and newspapers are less purely normative than are religious organizations. Although the major means of inducing compliance is still normative in such organizations, secondary means of gaining compliance play important roles. For example, in therapeutic mental hospitals, coercion is a significant means of exercising control and in professional firms, remuneration is important.

Public schools characteristically employ normative power to control students. Typical normative techniques to achieve student compliance include manipulation of grades and honors, sarcasm, reprimands, demerits, teachers' appeals for good behavior, and modification of peer pressure. Coercion remains a secondary form of control in schools. Although corporal punishment has nearly disappeared in schools, in-school detention, suspension, and expulsion continue to be used as a last resort. Furthermore, the compulsory nature of public schools virtually guarantees the existence of many uninterested students who resist school. This underlying coercion sets the stage for the development of alienated students and the use of some coercion in schools. Nevertheless, public schools primarily use normative measures to gain student compliance.

Schools can be ordered in terms of their relative emphases on normative and coercive control of students. In those schools where coercion plays a more significant role, students are more alienated (Hoy, 1972). Interestingly, most elementary schools emphasize normative compliance to a greater extent than secondary schools do (Willower, Eidell, and Hoy, 1967). But even where student alienation is greatest—for example, in schools where disciplinary cases are concentrated—coercive actions play less important roles than normative means (Etzioni, 1975).

MINTZBERG'S TYPOLOGY OF POWER

Henry Mintzberg (1983a) proposes another way to analyze power in and around organizations. In his view, power in organizations stems from control over a *resource,* a *technical skill,* or a *body of knowledge.* In all cases, however, to serve as a basis for power the resource, skill, or knowledge has to be important to the functioning of the organization; it must be in short supply; and it must not be readily replaceable. In other words, the organization must need something that only a few people can supply. For example, the principal who has primary responsibility for determining tenure for teachers has resource power. The assistant principal who has the interpersonal skills to deal effectively with irate parents, students, and teachers has power, as does the teacher who is alone in the school, in understanding the elements of a new curriculum thrust.

A fourth general basis of power derives from *legal prerogatives,* which gives some individuals the exclusive right to impose choices. School boards have the legal right to hire and fire administrators and teachers; they are vested with such power through state statute. School administrators in turn are often required by state law to evaluate the competence of nontenured teachers. Moreover, they are delegated the right to issue orders to employees, which are tempered by other legal prerogatives that grant power to teachers and their associations.

Finally, power often comes to those who have *access* to power holders. Many principals' secretaries have power because of their access to and influence with those who wield power. Similarly, friends of the board president or superintendent or principal often change the course of organizational decision making.

Mintzberg also proposes a set of four internal power systems that are the basic sources for controlling organizational life: the system of authority, the system of ideology, the system of expertise, and the system of politics. The system of authority contributes to attainment of the formal goals as defined by the organization; the system of ideology contributes to the achievement of informal objectives that emerge as the organization develops its culture; and the system of expertise controls the behavior of professionals as they subject themselves to the standards of their professional training. These three systems of control typically contribute to the needs of the organization; that is, they are legitimate. But those with power also have personal needs. In the process of striving to accomplish the broader organizational needs, individuals find they have discretion, and discretion opens the way to political power. Thus a system of political power emerges that is not sanctioned by the formal authority, ideology, or certified expertise; in fact, it is typically divisive, parochial, and illegitimate.

The **system of authority** is the formal flow of power through legitimate channels. There are two subsystems of control here, personal and bureaucratic. *Personal control* is wielded by giving orders, setting decision premises, reviewing decisions, and allocating resources. Together these four personal means of controlling give administrators considerable power to orient the decisions and actions of their faculties. *Bureaucratic control,* on the other hand, rests with the imposition of impersonal standards that are established to guide the general behavior of teachers across a whole range of areas—for example, the time when they are expected to be at school each day, cafeteria duty, and grading and homework requirements.

The **system of ideology** is the informal agreements among teachers about the school and its relationships to other groups. The character of the work group in terms of climate and culture are the terms we use in this text (see Chapter 5) to capture the essence of the system of ideology. The openness of the climate and the basic values of the school culture provide powerful sources of power and control.

The **system of expertise** is the interplay among experts or professionals to solve critical contingencies that the organization confronts. Faced with the complex tasks of teaching and learning, schools hire specialists (e.g., teachers, counselors, psychologists, and administrators) to achieve their basic goals. The need for autonomy to make professional decisions often conflicts with the system of formal authority, perhaps an inevitable consequence of professionals working in bureaucratic structures (see Chapter 3). As teachers continue to become increasingly professional, the demand for greater autonomy and power seems likely, and the granting of such power will likely be at the expense of the formal authority system.

The **system of politics** is the network of organizational politics, which lacks the legitimacy of the other three systems of power. It is a system that also lacks the consensus and order found in the other systems. There is no sense of unity or pulling together for a common good. This system can be described as a set of political games that power holders play. The games can coexist with the legitimate systems, be antagonistic to the systems, or substitute for the legitimate systems of control.

School administrators must not only recognize these systems of influence, they must know how to tap into and use them. Clearly the system of authority is the beginning point for school administrators. Their positions are vested with power, but the personal and bureaucratic control of the position is not usually sufficient to motivate teachers to expend extra effort or to be creative in their service to the school and students. The danger to the school administrator is exclusive reliance on the system of authority. To do so is to limit commitment to the school and to risk producing resistance and alienation among teachers.

What Mintzberg calls the system of ideology is akin to what others refer to as the culture or climate of the school (see Chapter 5). Organizational ideology can produce a sense of mission among members. First-level administrators, such as principals, are key actors in the development of ideology. The goal is to create a belief among teachers and students that there is something special about their school, that it has a distinctive identity or unique culture. We have already discussed some of the ways that principals can tap into the informal organization, develop loyalty and trust, and enlarge the scope of their authority. Informal authority, however, is another beginning, not an end. Ultimately, the principal must go beyond commanding personal loyalty and generate an organizational commitment in which teachers give loyalty to the school and take pride and identity from it. Of course, the consequence of a strong ideology is to redistribute power; that is, power becomes more evenly distributed among educators.

Although the systems of authority and ideology promote coordination and compliance, they are rarely sufficient. When work is complex, experts or professionals are required, and with them come demands for autonomy to make decisions on the basis of professional considerations, not on the basis of authority or ideology. The power of the administrators needs to be shared with professionals. As teaching becomes more fully professionalized as an occupation, teacher empowerment will likely become a reality rather than merely a slogan, and many more schools will move toward organizational structures that are professional bureaucracies (see Chapter 3).

Our discussion of Mintzberg's systems of power makes one thing clear for school administrators: they must be ready to share power. Those who hoard power are likely to become victims of teacher and student dissatisfaction, alienation, and hostility. Moreover, the inadequacy of their systems of control is likely to open the way in schools for the play of informal power of a more clandestine nature—that is, political power, a topic to which we will return later in this chapter.

A COMPARISON

Our analysis of authority and power has covered a number of conceptual views (see Table 6.2). The perspectives can be compared in terms of the extent to which the power is legitimate or illegitimate and formal or informal. By definition, the three formulations of authority consider only legitimate power. In contrast, the three perspectives on power all deal with both legitimate and illegitimate control as well as formal and informal power, but none of the frameworks is so comprehensive as to consider all four combinations of power; hence, we propose a synthesis. The French and Raven typology provides a classic analysis of interpersonal power, while Etzioni and Mintzberg focus their analyses on organizational power. Etzioni uses power to develop a comprehensive theory of organizational compliance, and Mintzberg develops four systems of influence to explore the power configurations in and around organizations. It is only Mintzberg's formulation, however, that considers power that is both illegitimate and informal—the system of internal politics. We propose a synthesis of power relations to include formal and informal authority (legitimate power), and coercive and political power (illegitimate).

TABLE **6.2**	Comparison of Sources of Power and Authority					
	Peabody	Blau and Scott	Weber	Etzioni	French and Raven	Mintzberg
Legitimate Formal Power	Formal authority	Formal authority	Bureaucratic authority	Remunerative power	Reward power and legitimate power	System of authority
Legitimate Informal Power	Functional authority	Informal authority	Charismatic authority and traditional authority	Normative power	Referent power and expert power	System of ideology and system of expertise
Illegitimate Formal Power				Coercive* power	Coercive* power	
Illegitimate Informal Power						Systems of politics*

*The power can be legitimate, but it is typically not.

In analyzing power, a structural perspective calls attention to authority—the legitimate, formal power of the office or position (see Chapter 3). A cultural perspective underscores the legitimate, informal power of the organizational culture (see Chapter 5). An individual perspective emphasizes the legitimate, informal role of expertise and knowledge in generating power (see Chapter 4). But it is the political perspective that calls attention to the illegitimate, informal power that is inherent in organizations.

ORGANIZATIONAL POWER AND POLITICS[1]

Politics is "individual or group behavior that is informal, ostensibly parochial, typically divisive, and above all, in the technical sense, illegitimate—sanctioned neither by formal authority, accepted ideology, nor certified expertise" (Mintzberg, 1983a: 172). Although there are powerful individuals, the political arenas of organizations are composed of **coalitions** of individuals—groups who bargain among themselves to determine the distribution of power (Cyert and March, 1963). Despite all attempts to integrate individual needs in the service of the organization's goals, individuals have their needs to fulfill. Inevitably, they get caught up in attempts to satisfy their own more parochial needs, and in the process, they form coalitions with others who have similar aspirations. These major interest groups are varied and diverse; for example, they represent departmental, professional, gender, and ethnic groups as well as internal and external interests. Moreover, there are enduring differences in values, beliefs, knowledge, and perceptions among the coalitions. These differences are stable, change slowly, and are sources of much tension and conflict. Many of the most important organizational decisions concern allocating scarce resources. Thus a critical question becomes: How does each coalition articulate its preferences and mobilize its power to obtain resources (Bolman and Deal, 1991)?

THE EXTERNAL COALITION

Significant outside influencers of schools include a myriad of groups such as teacher associations, unions, parent-teacher associations, taxpayer groups, state departments of education, consortia of colleges and universities, professional organizations, the media, and other organized special interest groups (see Chapter 7). Most of these outside-influence groups are trying to bring their own interests and external power to bear on the activities of the school. Their problem, of course, is figuring out how to achieve the outcomes they desire when they are functioning outside the official decision-making structure of the school. Mintzberg (1983) notes that the impact of the external coalition on the organization varies dramatically, and he proposes a continuum of three external coalitions—dominated, divided, and passive.

A **dominated external coalition** is composed of one sole, powerful influencer or a set of external influencers acting in concert. In such cases the external coalition is so powerful that it dominates not only the internal coalition but also the board of education and the superintendent. Indeed, the board and superintendent are simply tools for the external coalition. For example, on occasion, a community issue such "back to basics" can become so popular that a concerted effort by an organized group of external influencers can come to dominate not only curriculum change but, if left unchallenged, the basic policy and activities of the school.

Dominant coalitions do not remain unchallenged; in fact, it seems only a matter of time until other groups and individuals will coalesce and act. Without a dominant external power coalition, the power system of an organization changes in fundamental ways. When the external coalition is divided among independent and competing external individuals and groups of influencers, the organization is pushed in different directions as it attempts to respond to conflicting pressures.

A **divided external coalition** exists when a few, usually two or three, different sets of influencers emerge such that there is a rough balance of influence among the conflicting groups. For example, in school communities the balance can be between two external coalitions, one conservative and the other progressive. The curriculum and instructional programs often are battlegrounds for control as the coalitions compete. Their power struggles are reflected on the board of education and inevitably spill over into the internal coalitions within the school. In fact, Mintzberg (1983) claims a divided external coalition often has the effect of politicizing the board as well as the internal coalition.

A **passive external coalition** is reached when the number of outside groups of external influencers continues to increase to the point where the power of each is diffuse and limited. The external coalition becomes passive and power is concentrated within the organization. Apathy becomes the natural strategy for the large, dispersed group (Olsen, 1965, 1968b). The external environment is relatively stable and calm as influencers remain dispersed and passive.

THE INTERNAL COALITION

Just as the organization can be influenced by the external coalition, it is also affected by internal groups of influencers—the internal coalition. The external coalition shapes the kind of internal coalition that emerges. A dominated external coalition tends to weaken the internal coalition; a divided external coalition tends to politicize it; and a passive external coalition tends to strengthen it, often at the level of the central administration. But regardless of the kind of external coalition, it is through the efforts of the internal coalition that the organization functions. Five types of internal coalitions can develop—personalized, bureaucratic, ideologic, professional, and politicized (Mintzberg, 1983).

Two kinds are dominated by the system of authority. The **personalized internal coalition** is one in which power is concentrated in the hierarchy of authority in the person of the chief executive officer, who rules the internal coalition. The superintendent, for example, controls the critical decisions and functions of the school in such a situation. There is little political game playing by insiders here.

In a **bureaucratic internal coalition,** power is also concentrated in the formal system of authority, but here its focus is on bureaucratic controls—rules, regulations, and procedures. Although bureaucratic controls tend to limit politics, political games arise—for example, between line and staff or among principals as they try to build empires and enlarge their own school budgets, usually at the expense of other schools in the district.

Sometimes the system of ideology is so pervasive as to dominate; then an **ideologic internal coalition** controls the organization. For example, if the culture of a school is so strong and unified, teaches do not simply accept the goals and objectives, they share them as their very own. The administrator may seem to have great power because he or she embodies the culture, but the fact is that in sharing beliefs everyone shares power. Collegiality and egalitarianism prevail (Sergiovanni, 1992), and internal politics is very limited because of the strong sharing of beliefs.

In a **professional internal coalition,** the system of expertise dominates the organization. Highly trained experts—professionals—surrender a great deal of power to their organizations and the institutions that train them (Mintzberg, 1983). Here politics is usually substantial because of the conflict between the systems of authority and expertise—what we have discussed as professional-bureaucratic conflict in Chapter 3. The professional internal coalition then is a playing field for a wide assortment of political games, yet politics is held in check by expertise.

Finally, in some organizations, dominant power rests not on authority, not on culture or ideology, and not on expertise. In a **politicized internal coalition** power rests on politics. Here antagonistic, political games dominate the organization and either substitute for or drive out legitimate power.

COALITIONS, POLITICS, AND STRUCTURE

The external coalition does have an effect on the internal coalition. When the external is dominated, the likely consequence is a strong bureaucratic internal coalition. One only has to think of the company town to envision an organization controlled by the owners of the company, who may or may not live in the town. Organizations simply become instruments for those who control the company; the chief executive officer is merely a manager for the owners. In like fashion, schools in such communities are controlled by the same external group. The board, superintendent, teachers—indeed, virtually everyone knows who is in control. Organizational politics is hazardous and almost nonexistent. A few public schools are confronted with a dominated external coalition. In fact, any community in which a power elite controls the major activities is likely to face this constraint (Hunter, 1953; Dahl, 1961; Kimbrough, 1964). School structures in these situations will tend toward simple and authoritarian ones.

When the external environment is divided, a politicized internal coalition is most likely. The conflict and disagreement outside the school spills over into the school. The issues that divide the public at large will divide the board, teachers, and administrators. For instance, communities are becoming increasingly polarized into conservative and liberal factions. Conservatives favor the teaching of basics, Eurocentric culture, tradition, and stability, while liberals are for teaching higher-order thinking, emergent values, multiculturalism, and reform. Such conflicting perspectives and values are the basis of division and politics not only in the community but in the

| TABLE **6.3** | Internal and External Coalitions and Likely Structure |

Systems of Influence/Control

Internal Coalition	Personal	Bureaucratic	Ideology	Expertise	Political	External Coalition	Likely Structure
Personalized	Dominant	Limited	Some	Limited	Limited	Dominated Passive	Simple or Authoritarian
Bureaucratic	Some	Dominant	Limited	Limited	Limited	Passive	Bureaucratic
Ideologic	Limited	Limited	Dominant	Limited	Limited	Passive	Egalitarian (Missionary)
Professional	Limited	Limited	Limited	Dominant	Some	Passive	Professional
Political	Limited	Limited	Limited	Limited	Dominant	Divided	Political or Chaotic

schools as well. Indeed, the political activities of a divided external coalition may dominate the internal operations of the school in ways that are antagonistic to legitimate means of control. Vicious politics and chaos can become the rule rather than the exception.

When the external environment is passive, the internal coalition will likely be personalized, bureaucratic, ideologic, or professional. In other words, the leadership within the organization will control the dominant internal coalition; hence, it may be controlled by the administration, the bureaucracy (formal procedures), the culture, or the professionals themselves. Internal politics will exist, but politics will not substitute for legitimate control. The school structure will be simple, bureaucratic, egalitarian, or professional depending on the dominant internal coalition. These relationships are summarized in Table 6.3.

THE POWER GAME

Power matters; it is an important aspect of what an organization does and it affects what its members do. Hirschman (1970), in his classic book, *Exit, Voice, and Loyalty,* observes that participants in any system have three basic options:

- Leave; find another place—exit.
- Stay and play; try to change the system—voice.
- Stay and contribute as expected; be a loyal member—loyalty.

Those members who leave the organization cease to be influencers; those who are loyal choose not to participate as active influencers; but those who choose to stay and speak out become players in the power game. Access to power itself, however, is not sufficient. Power players must also have the *will* to play, which means they must be willing to expend the energy to be successful as well as the *skill* to act strategically and tactically when necessary. Power is an elusive blend of negotiating advantages and then willingly and skillfully exploiting those bargaining advantages (Allison, 1971).

Politics is a fact of organization life. Mintzberg (1983) argues that internal politics is typically clandestine and illegitimate because it is designed to benefit the individual or group, usually at the expense of the organization; therefore, the most common consequences of politics are divisiveness and conflict. Conflict is not necessarily bad; in fact, it sometimes calls attention to problems in the legitimate systems of control. Remember, however, that politics is not typically sanctioned by formal authority, ideology, or certified expertise; in fact, it arises because of default, weakness in the other systems of influence, or by design, to resist or exploit others in control. Notwithstanding its lack of legitimacy, politics, like all forms of power, can solve important organizational problems (Mintzberg, 1983):

- Politics ensures that the strongest members of the organization are brought into positions of leadership.
- Politics ensures that all sides of an issue are debated; the systems of authority, ideology, and sometimes even expertise tend to promote only one.
- Politics are often needed to promote change blocked by the formal organization.
- Politics can ease the execution of decisions; administrators play political games to get their decisions implemented.

There is no guarantee that those who gain power will use it rationally or justly, but power and politics are not always demeaning and destructive. Politics can be a vehicle for achieving noble purposes (Bolman and Deal, 1991).

Where the formal system is usually a highly organized structure, George Strauss (1964) observes that the political system is a mass of competing power groups, each seeking to influence organizational policy for its own interests, or at least, in terms of its own distorted image of the organization's interest. Successful politics requires organizational members to bargain, negotiate, jockey for position, and engage in a myriad of politic games, strategies, and tactics to influence the goals and decisions of their organization. As we have already noted, these politics can coexist with other more legitimate forms of power, array themselves in opposition to the legitimate power, or become substitutes for weak legitimate systems of control. With this view in mind, we turn to three important topics—political tactics, political games, and conflict management.

POLITICAL TACTICS

All members of an organization can engage in organizational politics. In fact, it seems likely that, regardless of level or position, everyone is a player in the game of politics. Thus, we turn to a set of political tactics that are commonly used by employees at all levels (Vecchio, 1988).

Ingratiation is a tactic used to gain the goodwill of another through doing favors, being attentive, and giving favors. It is based on what sociologists call the "norm of reciprocity," a pervasive norm in American society. Help a colleague or superior and the person feels obliged to return the favor or repay the positive action. Teachers often attempt to gain the goodwill and obligation of their colleagues and principals by going beyond their duty in helping others. Daniel Griffiths and his colleagues (1965), in a study of teacher mobility in New York City, described how this tactic was used by teachers to become administrators. A sizable number of teachers volunteered for jobs that were perceived to be irritants by most teachers: teacher in charge of the lunchroom, administrator of the annual field day, school coordinator for student teachers, or trainer of the school track team. None of these jobs was paid, but they earned the teachers the goodwill and attention of superiors and frequently gained them more important positions such as assistant principal or acting chair.

Networking is the process of forming relationships with influential people. Such people may or may not be in important positions, but they often have access to useful information. Teachers who have close, friendly relations with the teachers' union representative or principal usually have access to important information. Likewise, teachers who have contacts with the spouse of the board president or who have an indirect link to the superintendent or who know the union head are also likely to gain valuable inside information.

Information management is a tactic used by individuals who want to control others or build their own status. Although having critical information is useful in itself, the techniques used to spread the information can enhance one's position in both the formal and informal organizations. Releasing information when it has full impact can promote self-interest and defeat the ambitions of others. The key to information management is first to get crucial information (networking) and then to use it skillfully, making things known to others in ways that increase their dependence and build your reputation as one who "really knows" what is happening. Teachers who have networks that garner them important information are typically major actors in the political life of the school, and their careful nurturing and managing of that knowledge usually enhances their roles as important players in the political games of the school.

Impression management is a simple tactic that most everyone uses from time to time to create a favorable image. The tactic includes dressing and behaving appropriately, underscoring one's accomplishments, claiming credit whenever possible, and creating the impression of being important, if not indispensable. The key is to build an image such that others see you as knowledgeable, articulate, sensible, sensitive, and socially adept.

Some tactics are natural and legitimate; others are devious and illegitimate. When the tactics are based on dishonesty, deceit, and misinformation, they are hard to justify on moral grounds. Robert Vecchio (1988) argues that on the grounds of self-defense, one should be familiar with such devious political tactics as scapegoating, nurturing conflict by spreading false rumors, excluding rivals from important meetings, and making false promises. Although political tactics are a fact of organizational life, not all are viewed as legitimate (Cox, 1982). Moreover, there are a number of common blunders that are costly political mistakes: violating the chain of command, losing your temper in public, saying no too often to superiors, and challenging cherished beliefs (Vecchio, 1988). Such tactics, as we have discussed, are the bases of organizational politics.

POLITICAL GAMES

One way to describe more fully organizational politics is to conceive of it as a set of political games that are played by organizational participants. The games are complex, with intricate and subtle tactics played according to the rules. Some rules are explicit, others implicit. Some rules are quite clear, others fuzzy. Some are very stable, others ever-changing. But the collection of rules, in effect, defines the game. First, rules establish position, the paths by which people gain access to positions, the power of each position, and the action channels. Second, rules constrict the range of decisions and action that are acceptable. Third, rules sanction moves of some kinds—bargaining, coalitions, persuasion, deceit, bluff, and threat—while making other moves illegal, immoral, or inappropriate (Allison, 1971).

Mintzberg (1983) identifies five general kinds of games that organizational members play: games to resist authority, games to counter that resistance, games to build power bases, games to defeat opponents, and games to change the organization. Relying heavily on Mintzberg's work, each will be discussed.

Insurgency games usually are played to resist formal authority. They range from resistance to sabotage to mutiny. When an order is issued, there is typically some discretion in executing the order. Since there is no guarantee that the order will be carried out to the letter, the individual served the order can manipulate the action to serve his or her ends. For decisions supported, one can go beyond the spirit, if not the letter. For those not supported, Graham Allison (1971: 173) notes that one can "maneuver, to delay implementation, to limit implementation to the letter but not the spirit, and even to have the decision disobeyed."

Participants at the bottom of the structure have little power over the organization; hence, they sometimes attempt control by circumventing, sabotaging, and manipulating the formal structure (Mechanic, 1962). Teacher professionals can and do resist formal actions of the administration. A rule requiring teachers to stay 15 minutes after school each day to help students with their work can easily be undermined by all teachers staying exactly 15 minutes—that is, by meeting the letter but not the spirit of the rule. If the climate of the school (see Chapter 5) is not healthy, then most likely the insurgency is symptomatic of more endemic problems rather than the particular issue itself. Administrators, however, often use more authority to fight resistance to authority. For example, when rules are ignored or undermined, a typical administrative response is to develop further rules and buttress their enforcement with close supervision and punishment for those who do not comply. The attempted solution usually fails because it does not deal with the cause of the problem, only the symptom. Thus, if administrators are to successfully counter insurgency, they must expend a great deal of their own political skill together with the power and authority of their position "to persuade, cajole, and bargain with operators to get what they want" (Mintzberg 1983: 193). They end up bargaining and making informal deals with key actors in the system.

Power-building games are used by participants to build a power base. Superiors, peers, or subordinates can be used in the process. The *sponsorship game* is a simple one in which a subordinate attaches himself or herself to a superior and then professes absolute loyalty in return for a piece of the action. For example, the young teacher who would be principal sometimes tries to enlist the sponsorship of an influential vice-principal or principal. Rosabeth M. Kanter (1977) notes that such sponsors provide three important services for their protégés. They fight for them and stand up for them in meetings; they enable them to get information and bypass formal channels; and they provide a signal to others, a kind of reflective power. Of course, there are costs in the sponsorship game. When the sponsor falls, the protégé is also in danger, and there is great danger if the young teacher goes against the sponsor or does not show proper deference. Sponsorship is a vulnerable means of power, yet it is a frequent power game played by many at virtually all levels in the organization. Principals, assistant principals, teachers, and secretaries all can play if they can find a sponsor and are willing to provide a service in return for a share of the power.

The power-base game is also played among colleagues; here it becomes an *alliance-building game.* Mintzberg (1983) describes the process in the following way: Either an individual develops a concern and seeks supporters, or a group of individuals concerned about an issue seek out an informal leader who can effectively represent their position and around whom they can coalesce. Thus the nucleus of an interest group is formed. Some interest groups disappear as the issue is resolved, but others persist because the players have a number of common issues; they become factions. Interest groups and factions often lack the power to win an issue on their own. Consequently, they enlist the aid of other interest groups or factions to enlarge their power base. Thus alliances are formed. Groups are enticed, threatened, and cajoled to join the alliance. Kanter (1977: 185) notes, "Peer alliances often worked through direct exchange of favors. On lower levels information was traded; on higher levels bargaining and trade often took place around good performers and job openings." The alliance continues to grow until no more players are willing to join, or until it dominates, or until it runs into a rival alliance. Over time issues are won and lost and there is a gradual shifting of membership, but there is a basic stability in the membership of an alliance.

The *empire-building game* is the attempt of an individual, usually in middle management, to enhance his or her power base by collecting subordinates and groups. Empire building is fought over territory. In most school systems, empire building takes place as a budgeting game. Principals want a disproportionate share of the total budget. There is rivalry and feuding among principals as they compete for scarce resources; they want more teachers, more support staff, more computers, more space, more of everything than their competitors have. The goal of the game is simple: get the largest possible allocation for your school. The strategies are fairly clear: always request more than you need because the request will be cut; highlight all rational arguments that support a large budget and suppress those that do not; and always use all the budget for the year, even if some is wasted. In fact, some administrators like to go a "little in the red" to demonstrate that their allocations were inadequate, a risky strategy that may cause scrutiny of expenditures.

Expertise is another base upon which to build power. The *expertise game* is usually played by professionals who really have developed skills and expertise needed by the organization. They play the power game aggressively by exploiting their knowledge to the limit. They emphasize the uniqueness and importance of their talents as well as the inability of the organization to replace them. At the same time, they strive to keep their skills and talents unique by discouraging any attempts to rationalize them. Occasionally a master teacher will develop a reputation in a district as a truly outstanding teacher. Such a teacher has an edge in developing a power base not only based of expertise but also in terms of playing the alliance and sponsorship games. Moreover, principals who demonstrate rare administrative and leadership skills can use that power as a base to engage in alliance and empire building as well as in sponsorship. Indeed, principals who are successful in building a strong power base become formidable candidates for the superintendency.

The last of the power-building games is *lording,* in which those who have legitimate power "lord it over" those who are their subordinates, thus exploiting them in illegitimate ways. Individuals with limited power are tempted to play the lording game. Kanter (1977: 189) asserts, "When a person's exercise of power is thwarted or blocked, when people are rendered powerless in the larger arena, they tend to concentrate their power needs on those over whom they have even a modicum of authority." Teachers who are frustrated by the full weight of strong bureaucratic control and an authoritarian principal may displace control downward to students, demonstrating that they too can flex their power as they boss their students around. In like fashion, the principal who is ruled with an iron fist by the superintendent may be tempted to lord it over the teachers. Although such behavior may give the players a sense of power over someone, it is no way to build a substantial power base.

Rival games are those to defeat competitors. The *line and staff game* is a classic confrontation between middle line managers with formal authority and staff advisors with specialized expertise. In schools it often is a conflict between the principal of a school and a district-wide curriculum coordinator. The curriculum coordinator reports directly to the superintendent and so does the principal. In a sense the players are peers. The object of the game is to control behavior in the school. The curriculum coordinator is the expert, but the principal is the formal authority. The game becomes one of the formal authority of the line against the informal authority of expertise. The battles arise over issues of change. Staff are concerned with change and improvement. The curriculum coordinator wants changes in the curriculum. But change often produces conflict and turmoil. Principals as line administrators are responsible for smoothly running organizations; principals have a vested interest in relative stability. The battle lines are drawn. The superintendent will likely get involved, but there is usually no simple solution as each party in the game develops its respective case and mobilizes political allies.

The *rival-camps game* occurs when there are two and only two major alliances facing each other. These are generally vicious games in which all the stops are pulled, and in which there are winners and losers. The game can be between two personalities, between two units, or between forces for stability and change. Proposed changes, for example, can split the organization into two factions—the old guard and the new guard. Normally, the battle is resolved with one group winning and the organization moving ahead with its work. But occasionally no group can win decisively. Schools often have to balance the traditional goals of teaching basic skills with the progressive goals of social and emotional development. So while the balance sometimes shifts one way or the other, the battles continue.

Change games are designed to alter the organization or its practices. The *strategic-candidates game* can be played by anyone in the organization. All it takes is an individual or group to seek a strategic change by using the legitimate system of authority to promote a proposal or project—its "strategic candidate." Those who are successful in initiating an important change gain a large amount of power in the organization. Since many strategic decisions get made in ways that are fundamentally unstructured, they invite political gamesmanship, as different alliances and factions champion their cause—that is, their candidates for change (Mintzberg, Raisinghani, and Theoret, 1976). The strategic-candidates game combines the elements of most of the other games. Mintzberg (1983) describes the process as follows:

> Strategic candidates are often promoted in order to build empires, and they often require alliances; rivalries frequently erupt between line and staff or between rival camps during the game; expertise is exploited in this game and authority is lorded over those without it; insurgencies sometimes occur as byproducts and are countered; capital budgets often become the vehicles by which strategic candidates are promoted; and sponsorship is often a key to success in this game. (p. 206)

The *whistle-blowing game* has become increasingly more common in all organizations. It is designed to use inside information on particular behavior that an individual believes violates an important norm or perhaps the law. The player blows the whistle by informing an external authority of the foul play. Since the informer is circumventing the legitimate channels of control and is subject to reprisal, the player typically attempts to keep the contact a secret. For example, the story may be published in the newspaper and attributed to an unidentified source. Whistle-blowing is often a dramatic affair that does cause change in the organization, but it is a high-risk game. Whistle-blowers are typically not admired.

Perhaps the most intense of all the games is the *Young Turks game*. The stakes are high; the goal is not simple change or change to counter authority, but rather "to effect a change so fundamental that it throws the legitimate power into question" (Mintzberg, 1983: 210). The Young Turks challenge the basic thrust of the organization by seeking to overturn its mission, displace a major segment of its expertise, replace its basic ideology, or overthrow its leadership. This is major rebellion and the consequences are severe. Curriculum reform is one area in schools where the Young Turks game is played. Alliances develop and the showdown comes in an intense struggle in which teachers, staff, and administrators find themselves in one of two rival camps, either "for" or "against" the change. If the existing legitimate power yields to the Young Turks, the old guard will never have the same authority; indeed, the organization will never be the same because it is quite likely that the Young Turks will take over leadership. If the Young Turks lose, on the other hand, they are permanently weakened. They frequently leave the organization, and sometimes a schism is created within the organization. This is often an all-or-nothing game—win it all or lose it all.

Mintzberg's system of political games is summarized in Table 6.4. There is virtually no research literature that examines the relationships among political games, but there are a number of studies of noneducational organizations that probe into specific political games commonly played (Kanter, 1977; Zald and Berger, 1978). There is little doubt that much game playing occurs in school organizations; however, usually the system of politics coexists with the legitimate means of authority without dominating it. In Mintzberg's (1983: 217) words, "Here the System of Politics seems to consist of a number of mild political games, some of which exploit the more legitimate systems of influence, and in the process actually strengthen them,

TABLE **6.4**   Summary of Political Games

Game	Purpose	Primary Players
Insurgency	Resist authority	Administrators/teachers/staff
Counterinsurgency	Counter resistance to authority	Administrators
Sponsorship	Build power base	Upwardly mobile administrators/teachers
Alliance Building	Build power base	Administrators/teachers
Empire Building	Build power base	Administrators
Budgeting	Build power base	Administrators
Expertise	Build power base	Administrators/teachers
Lording	Build power base	Administrators/teachers
Line versus Staff	Defeat rivals	Administrators/staff
Rival Camps	Defeat rivals	Administrators/teachers
Strategic Candidates	Produce change	Administrators/teachers
Whistle-blowing	Produce change	Administrators/teachers/staff
Young Turks	Produce change	Administrators/teachers

others which weaken them, but only to a point, so that politics remains a secondary force."

CONFLICT MANAGEMENT

Since power and organizational politics inevitably produce conflict, we conclude our analysis of power with a brief discussion of conflict management. Administrators are faced with the classic confrontation between individual needs and organizational expectations; consequently, they spend a substantial amount of time attempting to mediate conflict. Kenneth Thomas (1976) provides a useful typology for examining five **conflict-management styles.** He identifies two basic dimensions of behavior that can produce conflict: attempting to satisfy one's concerns (organizational demands in the case of administrators), and attempting to satisfy others' concerns (individual needs of the members). Attempting to satisfy organizational demands can be viewed along an assertive-unassertive continuum, while attempting to satisfy individual needs can be conceptualized from uncooperative to cooperative. Figure 6.4 shows the five conflict management styles that are generated.

An *avoiding style* is both unassertive and uncooperative. Here the administrator ignores conflicts hoping that they will remedy themselves. Problems are simply put on hold. When they are considered, drawn-out procedures are used to stifle the conflict and secrecy is used as a tool to avoid confrontation. Often the administrator will turn to bureaucratic rules to resolve the conflict.

A *compromising style* is a balance between the needs of the organization and those of the individual. The focus of this style is on negotiating, looking for the middle ground, trade-offs, and searching for solutions that are satisfactory or acceptable to both parties.

FIGURE **6.4**

Conflict-Management Styles

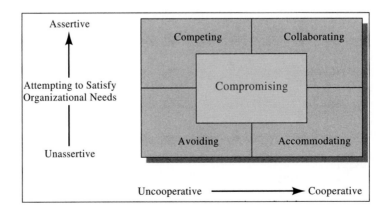

The use of a *competitive style* creates win-lose situations. The administrator is assertive and uncooperative in attempts to resolve conflict. Invariably, competition produces rivalry, with the objective being to achieve the goals at the expense of others. Power is used to achieve submission—to win.

The *accommodating style* is unassertive and cooperative. The administrator gives in to the demands of the subordinates; it is a submissive and compliant approach.

The *collaborating style* is assertive and cooperative. This is a problem-solving approach. Problems and conflicts are seen as challenges. Difference are confronted and ideas and information are shared. There is a concerted effort to find integrative solutions, those in which everyone wins.

Thomas (1977) proposes that each of the five styles may be effective depending on the situation; in fact, using data collected from a set of chief executives, he matches the five conflict-management styles with the appropriate situations:

Competing

- When quick, decisive action is essential—e.g., emergencies
- When critical issues require unpopular action—e.g., cost cutting
- When issues are vital to the welfare of the organization
- Against individuals who take unfair advantage of others

Collaborating

- When both sets of concerns are so important that only an integrative solution is acceptable; compromise is unsatisfactory
- When the goal is to learn
- To integrate insights from individuals with different perspectives
- When consensus and commitment are important
- To break through ill feelings that have hindered relationships

Compromising

- When the objectives are important, but not worth the potential disruption
- When there is a "standoff"
- To gain temporary settlements to complex problems
- To expedite action when time is important
- When collaboration or competition fails

Avoiding

- When the issue is trivial
- When the costs outweigh the benefits of resolution
- To let the situation cool down
- When getting more information is imperative
- When others can solve the problem more effectively
- When the problem is a symptom rather than a cause

Accommodating

- When you find you have made a mistake
- When the issues are more important to others
- To build goodwill for more important matters
- To minimize losses when defeat is inevitable
- When harmony and stability are particularly important
- To allow subordinates a chance to learn from their mistakes

As with so many things, there is no one best way to manage conflict. Rather, successful conflict management is likely by carefully matching the style with the situation, a topic to which we will return in our discussion of leadership (see Chapter 12).

SUMMARY AND SUGGESTED READINGS

Power is a basic element of organizational life. It can be legitimate and willingly accepted by subordinates or it can be coercive, illegitimate, and resisted. Our analysis begins by examining legitimate power—authority. Weber identifies three types of authority based upon the source of legitimacy: charisma, tradition, or the law. Peabody extends the notion by distinguishing the bases of formal authority—legitimacy and position—from the bases of functional authority—competence and personal or human relations skills. Finally, Blau and Scott simplify the foundations of legitimate power in organizations by classifying authority as formal or informal.

Next, a general analysis of power is undertaken using French and Raven's bases of interpersonal power—reward, coercion, legitimacy, reference, and expertise—and extending their framework to the organizational level. In another formulation of power, Etzioni examines the relationship between power and compliance and concludes that the more normative the power, the greater the degree of subordinate commitment. Mintzberg provides still another perspective on power; he describes four systems of power: authority, ideology, expertise, and politics. His framework makes explicit the importance of organizational politics. In brief, four basic kinds of organizational power exist: two forms of legitimate power—formal and informal authority—and two kinds of illegitimate power—coercive and political.

Politics is a fact of organizational life. Although there are powerful individuals, the political arenas of organizations are composed of coalitions of individuals and groups, which bargain among themselves to determine the distribution of resources. External as well as internal coalitions influence organizational politics. Political tactics are the bases of a system of political games played to resist authority, to counter resistance, to build power bases, to defeat opponents, and to change the organization. The system of politics typically coexists with the more legitimate systems of influence without dominating them, but power and politics generate conflict. Thus, our analysis concludes with a model of conflict management.

All students of administration should read Niccolo Machiavelli's classic, *The Prince*. Lee Bolman and Terry Deal (1991) present a nice overview of the political frame of organizations in their book, *Reframing Organizations*. Two comprehensive analyses of power in organizations are Amitai Etzioni's (1975) *A Comparative Analysis of Complex Organizations* and Henry Mintzberg's (1983a) *Power In and Around Organizations*. Etzioni uses the concept of power to create a comprehensive theory of organizations. Mintzberg develops a theory of power and politics in organizations. In our view, Mintzberg's treatment of power and politics is the most comprehensive of its kind. No one interested in organizations should miss it. Finally, Rosabeth Moss Kanter (1977) examines organizational politics in her insightful analysis of *Men and Women of the Corporation*.

NOTE

1. This section draws heavily on the power analysis of Mintzberg (1983).

KEY CONCEPTS AND IDEAS

Authority

Bureaucratic internal coalition

Change games

Charismatic authority

Coalitions

Coercive power

Conflict-management styles

Divided external coalition

Dominated external coalition

Empowerment

Expert power

Formal authority

Functional authority

Ideologic internal coalition

Impression management

Informal authority

Information management

Ingratiation

Insurgency games

Legal authority

Legitimate power

Networking

Normative power

Passive external coalition

Personalized internal coalition

Politicized internal coalition

Politics

Power

Power-building games

Professional internal coalition

Referent power

Remunerative power

Reward power

Rival games

Strategic candidates game

System of authority

System of expertise

System of ideology

System of politics

Traditional authority

External Environments of Schools

> It becomes evident that the choices of expanding organizations about what units to add are not random but are, rather, partially determined by conditions in the institutional environment.
>
> —Brian Rowan
> *"Organizational Structure and the Institutional Environment: The Case of Public Schools"*

PREVIEW

1. Schools are open systems and depend on exchanges with elements in the environment to survive.

2. Multiple and complex environmental influences come from different levels of society and affect what happens in schools.

3. Two general perspectives of environment are analyzed—task and institutional.

4. The task perspective includes both the information and the resource-dependency theories, which define task environment as all aspects of the external setting that are potentially relevant for goal setting, goal achievement, effectiveness, and survival.

5. The information perspective treats the external environment as a source of information for decision makers. Complexity, stability, and uncertainty are the major concepts of the model.

6. The resource-dependence perspective views the environment as a place to gain scarce resources (e.g., fiscal, personnel, information and knowledge, and products and services) for support of the technical processes of the school.

7. In contrast to the task perspectives, institutional theory assumes that the environment encourages schools to conform to powerful sets of rules and requirements that are imposed by the legal, social, professional, and political contexts of organizations.

8. Institutional theory asserts that school structures and processes mirror the norms, values, and ideologies institutionalized in society. The essence of the theory is that the environment of schools presses more for form than for substance.

9. School organizations do not have to be passive instruments of the external environment; both internal and external coping strategies can be used to manage the environment.

10. Environments for schools may be shifting their emphasis from primarily institutional to more task concerns. If a shift is occurring, it represents fundamental change in the environments of schools that will have profound effects.

The open-systems concept (see Chapter 2) highlights the vulnerability and interdependence of organizations and their environments. External environments are important because they affect the internal structures and processes of organizations; hence, one is forced to look both inside and outside the organization to explain behavior within school organizations. Indeed, the larger social, cultural, economic, demographic, political, and technological trends all influence the internal operations of schools and districts. Because school organizations are conceptualized as part of a larger universe or environment, an argument can be made that anything that happens in the larger environment may affect the school and vice versa. For example, one needs only to observe the race by school districts to purchase personal computers and other information technologies to see the effects that recent technology has had on the internal processes of schools.

The emphasis on the external environments of organizations is not new. However, the extent to which organizations are connected to and affected by the larger environment has been underestimated (Scott and Meyer, 1991). In fact, W. Richard Scott (1992) asserts that the central understanding emerging from open-systems theory is that all organizations are incomplete and depend on exchanges with other organizations in the environment as a condition of their survival.

Environment, like a number of other terms in organizational theory, is not a firmly defined concept. Consensus exists about neither what constitutes an organization's environment nor the essential issues to be considered in discussions of it (Bowditch and Buono, 1985). Nevertheless, similar definitions and three theoretical perspectives—that is, information, resource dependence, and institutional—provide useful descriptions and explanations of environments and their effects on schools.

EXTERNAL ENVIRONMENTS: DEFINITION AND EXAMPLES

Numerous definitions of organizational environment occur in the literature.

- "Environment is typically seen as everything outside the boundaries of an organization, even though the boundaries are often nebulous and poorly drawn." Lee G. Bolman and Terrence Deal (1984: 44)

- "Organizational environment is defined as all elements that exist outside the boundary of the organization and have the potential to affect all or part of the organization." Richard L. Daft (1989: 45)

- "The external environment consists of those relevant physical and social factors outside the boundaries of the organization . . . that are taken into consideration in the decision-making behavior of individuals in that system." Gerald Zaltman, Robert Duncan, and Jonny Holbek (1973: 114)

A common theme of these definitions is that environment is treated as a residual category of potential and real effects. Defining environment as a residual component of school organizations may be sufficient when the focus of attention is on the internal processes of the school itself, but not when treating the environment as a causal force that is influencing the structure and activities of schools (Zaltman, Duncan, and Holbek, 1973). Similarly, Scott (1992) observes that to subscribe to the idea of organizations as open systems is to recognize that organizations such as schools are penetrated by their environments in ways that obscure and confound any simple criterion for distinguishing the environment from the organization. The two most common sets of conceptual formulations of organizational environments are task (technical) and institutional. As each theoretical perspective is discussed, specific definitions of the two environments will be provided.

As shown in Figure 7.1, multiple environmental influences come from different levels of society and affect what happens in schools. Technological and informational developments, political structures and patterns of legal norms, social conditions and cultural values, economic and market factors, and population and demographic characteristics influence school structures and processes. Within a specific locality, myriad groups play key roles in affecting educational practices—for example, individual parents, taxpayer associations, business groups, legislatures, and accrediting agencies influence school policy.

Administrators tend to focus monitoring and planning processes on local environmental elements and often fail to recognize that environmental factors in the larger society also have the potential to influence not only the organization itself but local environments as well. Changing demographics—for example, age, sex, race, and ethnicity distributions in the population—will likely bring tremendous pressures for change in virtually all American schools. For example, the increasing percentage of educationally disadvantaged children entering and remaining in the schools during the 1990s and beyond has significant implications for educational attainment (Pallas, Natriello, and McDill, 1989). These are the students whose schools have traditionally been unable to serve in highly effective ways. That is, low achievement levels and high absenteeism and dropout rates have characterized the academic careers of the educationally disadvantaged. Without fundamental changes in the ways schools and other organizations educate children, the problems of school effectiveness and the pressures on schools will increase. Thus, demographic trends suggest that external environments of schools are characterized by growing uncertainty and importance.

William R. Dill (1958) proposed task environment as a useful concept in understanding external influences on organizations. **Task environment** is all aspects of

FIGURE **7.1**

Selected External Constituencies for School Districts

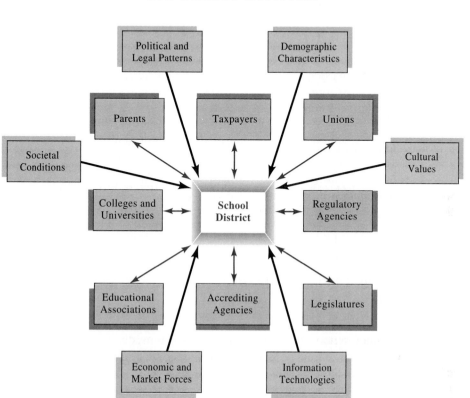

the external environment that are potentially relevant to goal setting, goal achievement, effectiveness, and survival. This conception emphasizes that most organizations are created to perform some type of work and to achieve goals. Moreover, organizations are not self-sufficient and must enter into exchanges with the external environment to gain the needed information and resources for survival. Information and resource-dependency perspectives are the best-known examples of task-environment theories. These perspectives emphasize the ways that organizations succeed by developing effective structures to coordinate and control work processes and to regulate environmental demands (Scott, 1992; Meyer, Scott, and Deal, 1992). A second approach to understanding external environments is the institutional perspective. In this formulation, little emphasis is placed on task goals, effectiveness, and efficiency. Instead, the basic premise is that the chances of organizational survival are highest when school structures and processes mirror the norms, values, and ideologies institutionalized in society (Rowan, 1993). The information, resource-dependence, and institutional perspectives will be reviewed, evaluated, and applied for school settings.

INFORMATION PERSPECTIVE

The external environment in the **information perspective** is a source of information that decision makers use in maintaining or changing the internal structures and processes of their organizations. In this framework, the **external environment** is defined as information about external factors as perceived by organizational participants. Perceptions of information by decision makers link the external environment to actions taken by participants in the organization (Aldrich and Mindlin, 1978). Stated as a hypothesis, organizational changes are explained by variations in perceived information, as filtered by the information-processing schema, of decision makers about the external environment (Koberg and Ungson, 1987).

While it is true that actions are based on administrator and teacher perceptions of the environment, such perceptions are not likely to be completely idiosyncratic to a particular person or school setting (Aldrich and Pfeffer, 1976). A variety of social processes combine to create similar perceptions. For instance, hiring educators with similar backgrounds, imitating programs from other schools, and following professional norms and governmental regulations promote the development of a common frame of reference for perceiving environmental information.

A TYPOLOGY OF INFORMATION ENVIRONMENTS

Specific formulations of the information perspective have typically been based on typologies using a variety of seemingly similar dimensions, concepts, or continuums of complexity, stability, and uncertainty. Examples include typologies constructed by Fred E. Emery and Eric L. Trist (1965), James D. Thompson (1967), Paul R. Lawrence and Jay W. Lorsch (1967), Robert B. Duncan (1972), and Ray Jurkovich (1974). To increase the clarity and ease in dealing with their ideas, we have grouped the concepts under two continuums: environmental complexity (simple to complex) and environmental stability (stable to unstable).

Environmental complexity, ranging from simple to complex, is the number, similarity, and linkage among the elements to which an organization must relate. Simple environments have relatively small numbers of homogeneous, unlinked elements that exercise comparatively little influence on the organization; complex environments have large numbers of diverse, linked entities that exert significant influence on the organization. As the complexity of the environment increases, so does the number of positions and units within the organization, which increases internal complexity (Daft, 1989). In schools, for example, the number and types of at-risk children is an indicator of environmental complexity. As schools have adapted to educate an increasingly diverse array of children, several categories of special teachers, school psychologists and counselors, and social workers have evolved.

Environmental stability, ranging from stable to unstable, is the extent to which elements in the environment are shifting or dynamic. Stable environments experience little and slow change; unstable environments experience abrupt and rapid

FIGURE **7.2**

Integrated Typology of Organizational Environments and Uncertainty

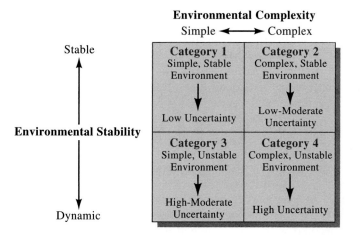

change. Stability occurs in situations where the set of relationships among elements remain constant and in situations that are either unchanging or changing slowly. Instability arises in situations that are loose and erratic. In unstable conditions, both the value and kinds of environmental elements are changing unpredictably (Jurkovich, 1974). For administrators in schools, creating a sense of stability is critical for maintaining an image of effective leadership and is an ongoing social pressure (McCabe and Dutton, 1993).

Different theorists have used slightly different terms to designate each dimension. Examples include:

- *Simple to complex axis:* Homogeneous to diverse, unlinked to linked, random to clustered, and few to many elements
- *Stable to unstable axis:* Static to shifting, placid to unstable, not dynamic to dynamic, calm to turbulent, predictable to unpredictable, and unchanging/changing

Combining the two dimensions—complexity and stability—produces the four-category typology shown in Figure 7.2. Each category also depicts the degree of uncertainty expected in the environment.

ENVIRONMENTAL UNCERTAINTY

A primary concern of the information perspective is uncertainty. **Environmental uncertainty** is the inability of decision makers in an organization to make accurate predictions because existing conditions in the external environment prevent them from having adequate information (Milliken, 1987; McCabe and Dutton, 1993). Uncertainty is a fundamental problem for organizations, and dealing with it is the essence of the administrative process (Thompson, 1967). As shown in Figure 7.2, Duncan (1972) hypothesized that as environments are classified from category 1 (simple, stable) to category 4 (complex, unstable), the degree of uncertainty increases. Information generated by unstable and complex environments, for example, is likely to be in the form of questionable, suspicious, and ambiguous communications. Hence, the more complex and unstable the environment, the greater the environmental uncertainty for the organization.

The level of uncertainty is determined by the kind, clarity, and amount of information that organizational decision makers have about trends and changes in environmental conditions. Uncertainty produces problematic situations. Thus, when uncertainty is high, additional or new information categories or cognitive schema are required for administrators to process and make sense of the information from the environment; preferences regarding possible outcomes become less clear; alternative courses of action and their outcomes become increasingly unpredictable and risky; strategies and tactics become relatively difficult to communicate and implement; and potential outcomes from a decision are not known.

When confronted with environmental uncertainty, educators and schools often attempt to cope by creating special units or programs specifically to deal with the problem (Thompson, 1967). The idea is that schools adapt to produce environmental fit—that is, school organizations match their structures and processes to their perceived external environments (Miller, 1992; Pennings, 1992). As more and diverse groups become interested in education, for example, special units, such as offices of public information, government relations, community involvement, and business partnerships are created to monitor their activities, report perceived information about their goals and behaviors to key administrators, and engage the groups in information exchanges in an effort to gain their support.

RESEARCH AND EVALUATION OF THE INFORMATION PERSPECTIVE

Jane H. Karper and William Lowe Boyd (1988) studied state educational policy making during a period of increasing environmental instability. Specifically, they examined policy making that resulted from the statewide movement to increase educational quality that was sparked by the *Nation at Risk* report (National Commission on Excellence in Education, 1983). Karper and Boyd observe that many governors seized the initiative on educational reform. Hence, environmental uncertainty for schools and educational agencies increased dramatically. The researchers found that, by the mid-1980s, an extraordinary shift had taken place in the relationships among the key educational special-interest groups. These groups had moved from conflict and competition to collaboration and cooperation, forming a broad new coalition to advance and protect funding levels. As the environment became turbulent (category 4), the organizations adjusted to the new conditions by making the transition from competitive operations to multilateral agreements.

To study different conditions of environmental stability, Lawrence and Lorsch (1967) investigated the perceptions of organizational decision makers about the environment in three different industries. The researchers were interested in perceived environmental complexity and effectiveness. Their findings and conclusions supported the earlier findings of William R. Dill (1958). When organizations are confronted with complex and dynamic environments, they are able to maintain or increase their effectiveness through additional flexibility in their structural configurations. Similarly, decentralization is an appropriate response to increased uncertainty because, as the environment becomes more uncertain, more information is needed (Govindarajan, 1988). An effective way to deal with the situation is to move the level of decision making to where the information exists rather than to move it upward in the hierarchy.

Robert B. Duncan (1972) elaborated and empirically tested the typologies of Thompson and Lawrence and Lorsch. He found support for the general hypothesis that the levels of uncertainty for organizations increase significantly across each category from 1 to 2 to 3 to 4 (see Figure 7.2). The simple, stable environment creates the most certainty for organizations, and the complex, unstable, the most uncertainty. Moreover, low stability in the environment was a more important contributor to uncertainty than was high complexity. Both dimensions, however, interact to produce enhanced environmental uncertainty. Similarly, a consistent finding is that organizational innovation is positively related to environmental uncertainty. Explanations for this finding are that higher levels of uncertainty generate more innovation through opportunity seeking and adaptation to change, and increased levels of innovation create the perception of uncertainty among administrators (Russell and Russell, 1992).

In sum, the central characteristics of the information perspective are threefold:

- The focus is on the decision makers' perceptions of their environments rather than on the actual characteristics. As a result, the internal structures and processes will be influenced but not totally determined by the external environment.

- Perceived environmental uncertainty affects the degree of flexibility and bureaucratic nature of organizations. As the environment becomes more uncertain, the organization becomes more flexible and organic—that is, less formalized and less centralized.

- Empirical studies based on the information perspective typically measure environmental factors using subjective perceptions of organizational members. The research findings have been generally supportive of the information perspective.

RESOURCE-DEPENDENCE PERSPECTIVE

In contrast to the information perspective, the **resource dependence perspective** views the environment as a place to gain scarce resources for the task and technical processes of the organization. Four general types of environmental resources are typically identified—fiscal, personnel (e.g., students, teachers, administrators, school volunteers, and board members), information and knowledge (e.g., outcomes from research, development and evaluation projects), and products and services (e.g., instructional materials and test scoring services) (Aldrich, 1972; Benson, 1975). Organizations both compete for and share the environmental resources.

Environmental resources are commonly conceptualized on a continuum of **scarcity** to **munificence**—that is, the extent or capacity of the environment to provide resources that support stability and sustained growth of the organization. The relative abundance of resources in the environment is the ultimate determinant of sufficient input for any organization. When resources are munificent, survival is relatively easy and the pursuit of wide-ranging task goals becomes possible (Castrogiovanni, 1991). For example, school districts in wealthy environments might have high property evaluations that produce relatively large tax revenues with small tax levies. With an abundant capacity, the school district would likely offer a wide range of curricular and extracurricular programs. Under conditions of limited capacity or scarcity, competition for resources among subgroups can take the form of a zero-sum game with each subgroup caring more about its share of finite resources than for the overall welfare of the organization. For example, school districts in impoverished environments would be limited to a basic academic curriculum with extracurricular programs competing for what might be left over.

Dependence is defined both by the extent of need for or importance of a resource and its availability (i.e., scarcity/munificence) in the environment. For educational settings, dependence is directly related to the school organization's need for resources controlled by a second organization, and inversely related to the resource availability from other organizations. That is, if the school organization cannot accomplish its goals without the resources controlled by another organization and is unable to secure them elsewhere, the school organization becomes dependent on the second organization. Conversely, as resources are provided, the supplier gains power over the school. A major consequence of competition for resources is the development of dependencies among organizations in the environment. Notice that dependence is an attribute of the relationship between the organizations and not an attribute of an individual organization in isolation (Aldrich and Mindlin, 1978; Sutcliffe, 1994). It follows that the greater the resource dependence, the more the organizations communicate with each other (Van de Ven and Ferry, 1980).

Recent events in school finance illustrate the dependence concept. As fiscal resources from local property taxes and federal grants decline, school districts have an increased need to secure additional appropriations from state legislatures. Since greater percentages of their budgets were supplied by the state, the dependence of school districts on state governments grew dramatically. In a parallel fashion, the power of the state over local school districts expanded and state legislatures and offices of education were able to dictate educational reforms to school districts—for example, curriculum framework and testing programs.

The fundamental proposition of resource-dependence theory is that if organizations are unable internally to generate all the resources or functions to maintain themselves, then they must enter into exchanges with elements in the environment that can supply the required resources.[1] In exchange for resources, the external groups or organizations may not only consume the organization's outputs but demand certain actions or changes from the organization. For example, individuals who have been educated and trained in the schools contribute their efforts to society, and society demands that schools offer particular types of training. Hence, a basic hypothesis is that organizational changes are explained by the abilities of competing organizations to acquire and control critical resources (Koberg and Ungson, 1987).

Because all organizations are dependent on their environments, external control of organizational behavior is possible and constraint inevitable. If they are not responsive to the demands of their environments, organizations cannot thrive and may not survive. But demands often conflict; thus, organizations cannot thrive or even survive by simply responding to every environmental demand. The challenge for school decision makers is to determine the extent to which the school organization can and must respond to various environmental demands and the implications of those responses for the school.

While organizations must depend on their environments, they strive to gain control over resources, to avoid becoming dependent on others, and to make others dependent on them. Therefore, the resource-dependence model also portrays organizations as active and capable of changing as well as responding to their environments. Administrators manage their environments as well as their organizations; in fact, Pfeffer (1976) maintains that managing the environment may be more important than managing the organization. Members of the organization make active, planned, and conscious responses to environmental contingencies. Organizations attempt to absorb uncertainty and interdependence either completely, as through merger or consolidation, or partially, as through cooptation or the movement of personnel among organizations. Attempts are made to stabilize relations with other organizations, using tactics ranging from tacit collusion to legal contracts. Educational organizations, for example, establish external advisory groups composed of leading individuals from related organizations or publics to stabilize their relationships with other important parties.

RESEARCH AND EVALUATION OF THE RESOURCE-DEPENDENCY PERSPECTIVE

In a study based on resource-dependency theory, Michael Aiken and Jerald Hage (1968) hypothesized that, as interdependence is established between organizations, problems of internal coordination and control increase. Their findings indicate that organizations with more joint programs, and thus a higher degree of dependence on the environment, are more complex themselves, have somewhat less centralized decision-making processes, are more innovative, have greater frequency of internal communication, and tend to be less formalized than organizations with fewer joint programs. Support for the work of Aiken and Hage is provided by the findings of Mindlin and Aldrich (1975) that the higher the dependence on other organizations, the lower the formalization and standardization of organizational structure.

Hall (1987) believes that the impact of resource changes on decision making is demonstrated in a study by John H. Freeman (1979). When enrollments or budgets plunge, rational decisions should be made about which programs and personnel are to be trimmed or eliminated. Freeman found, however, that rationality was not the prime decision-making criterion. Categorical programs from the federal government and programs of importance to special-interest groups, even those with limited demand, could not be cut. The decisions in the local school districts reflected external pressures, rather than the rational decisions that school officials might have made themselves.

In sum, three generalizations capture the essence of resource-dependency theory (Aldrich and Mindlin, 1978):

- As organizations become increasingly dependent on their environments for securing resources, they require and tend to exhibit more flexible and adaptive structures that are more informal, less standardized, and decentralized.

- Dependence on external elements for resources often leads to interorganizational relationships such as joint programs and cooptation.

- Research based on this perspective uses archival, observational, and other "objective" methods to gather data.

TOWARD A SYNTHESIS OF THE INFORMATION AND RESOURCE-DEPENDENCE PERSPECTIVES

Although research studies have indicated support for the information and resource-dependence perspectives, results are far from conclusive (Koberg and Ungson, 1987). Conceptually, the explanatory power of environmental effects is enhanced by the synthesis of the two perspectives. An attempt to integrate the information and resource-dependency perspectives has been made by Aldrich and Mindlin (1978). They note that discussions of uncertainty and dependence imply that the concepts vary independently of each other. For example, the information perspective maintains that coping with uncertainty forces the organization to employ less formal and more decentralized decision-making processes. In contrast, the resource-dependency perspective holds that similar structural arrangements are necessary when, in the process of obtaining valuable resources, organizations become dependent on other organizations. "Thus, a higher degree of environmental coordination is expected simultaneously to decrease the organization's uncertainty but to increase its dependence" (Scott, 1992: 135). Similarly, an organization's resource dependencies may be significant determinants of how environmental changes are interpreted, but they do not have significant effects on administrators' certainty about environment or about how to respond to a changing environment (Milliken, 1990).

The perspectives can be joined in at least two ways. First, the probable joint impact of uncertainty and dependence can be considered. An interactive effect probably exists for securing scarce resources. That is, the effects of either dependence or uncertainty will be felt most strongly when the other factor is also present.

Second, the perspectives can be integrated through the study of decision makers' perceptions of the environment. While the information perspective immediately directs attention to the role of perception, perceptions of resource dependence by decision makers also clearly play a large part in determining their reactions to the environment (Aldrich and Mindlin, 1978). The essential question for administrators is: "How can environmental uncertainty be reduced without increasing dependence?" (Wood and Gray, 1991: 141).

ADMINISTERING INFORMATION AND RESOURCE ENVIRONMENTS

Because environmental factors can threaten or constrain school autonomy and effectiveness, administrators often try to minimize external effects on internal school operations. Such attempts raise questions about the extent to which school organizations control, or even create, their own environments (Bowditch and Buono, 1985). Do organizations react to their environments, coping as best they can? Or, instead, do they control their environments, imposing structure on disorder, achieving dominance and predictability? The answers to these questions are not simple. While it is tempting to say yes to both, situations are so dynamic that once control is achieved, it is easily lost (Gross and Etzioni, 1985). In line with the questions, attempts to reduce environmental influence from the information and resource-dependence perspectives can be grouped as internal or interorganizational coping strategies. Both sets of strategies are designed to protect key processes from environmental influences by increasing certainty and gaining additional resources.

Internal Coping Strategies

Environments seek to impose task or technical constraints on organizations such as schools. By adapting to task-environmental pressures, organizations reap rewards for effective control and coordination of work processes (Fennell and Alexander, 1987). In addition, organizations try to isolate their technical cores—for example, instructional activities in schools—from external influences. For educational organizations, buffering, planning and forecasting, spanning organizational boundaries, and adjusting internal operations are coping strategies widely applicable to schools.

BUFFERING The strategy of isolation is based on the assumption that efficiency can be maximized only when the technical core is not disturbed by external uncertainties. **Buffering** uses structures and processes to insulate or surround internal activities and absorb environmental disturbances. Buffering creates a protective layer between the organization and its environment (Miner, Amburgey, and Stearns, 1990; Pennings, 1992). Therefore, specific departments, roles, and processes are created in schools to deal with uncertainty and dependence from a variety of environmental elements. Purchasing, planning, human resource, curriculum, and facilities departments are created to buffer teachers from factors in the school's environment. These departments transfer materials, services, information, money, and other resources between the environment and school. In addition, a primary role of the principal consists of dealing with parental complaints about teachers. The goal of buffering is to make the technical core as nearly as closed system as possible and, thereby, enhance efficiency (Daft, 1989).

PLANNING AND FORECASTING In unstable environments and at high levels of dependence, buffering strategies probably cannot provide adequate protection for the instructional program. Under the conditions of high uncertainty and dependence, school organizations can attempt to control environmental fluctuations by planning and forecasting strategies. **Planning and forecasting** strategies anticipate environmental changes and take actions to soften their adverse effects. Under these circumstances, a separate planning department is frequently established. In uncertain and dependent situations, planners must identify the important environmental elements, and analyze potential actions and counteractions by other organizations. Planning must be extensive and forecast a variety of scenarios. As conditions continue to change, the plans must be updated. To the extent that educators can accurately forecast environmental fluctuations, they have an opportunity to reduce uncertainty (Robbins, 1983).

SPANNING ORGANIZATIONAL BOUNDARIES **Boundary spanning** is creating internal roles that cross organizational boundaries and link the school with elements in the external environment. This is also an important strategy for coping with environmental uncertainty and dependence. Two classes of functions are typically performed by boundary spanning roles: detecting information about changes in the external environment and representing the organization to the environment (Aldrich and Herker, 1977).

For the detection function, boundary roles concentrate on the transfer of information between the environment and the school. Boundary personnel scan and monitor events in the environment that can create abrupt changes and long-term trends, and communicate the information to decision makers (Daft, 1989). By identifying new technological developments, curricular innovations, regulations, and funding patterns, boundary personnel provide data that enable the school to make plans and adjust programs. In contrast to buffering personnel, boundary spanners act to keep the school organization an open system in harmony with the environment. A number of individuals in schools—for example, superintendents and principals—play both buffering and boundary-spanning roles. Other school boundary-spanning roles include administrators in public information, government relations, and research and development departments.

For the representation function, boundary-spanning personnel send information into the environment from the organization. The idea is to influence other people's perceptions of the organization. Schools often have offices of public information whose expressed purpose is to communicate information to significant stakeholders. Other district offices also can serve this function. For example, community and adult education programs, which primarily attract taxpaying patrons, can exemplify the quality of instruction that is available to the district's students. Business and legal departments can inform legislators about the school district's needs or views on political matters. Similarly, the boards of education and school advisory committees link the school organization to important constituencies in the environment in a highly visible way to create the impression, if not always the opportunity, for interests to be expressed. Thus, women, minority group members, and students are appointed in increasing numbers to a variety of advisory committees (Aldrich and Herker, 1977). Promoting a positive image of the school can reduce uncertainty and dependence on the various elements in the environment. Hence, boundary spanners play key roles in interorganizational relations (Friedman and Podolny, 1992) and can be highly influential with key decision makers in the organization (At-Twaijri and Montanari, 1987).

ADJUSTING INTERNAL OPERATIONS Work based on the information and resource-dependence perspectives and on innovation and change suggest a structural contingency approach to organizational design (Aldrich and Mindlin, 1978; Pennings, 1992). The way an organization should be designed depends in part on its environment. In other words, no one best way exists to organize schools. Rather, the most effective school structure is one that adjusts to its important environmental elements.

The first researchers to indicate that different types of organizational structure might be effective in different environments were Tom Burns and G. M. Stalker (1961). They found that the type of structure that existed in dynamic environments was different from the type that existed in stable environments. When the external environment was stable, the internal organization was "mechanistic" or highly bureaucratic—that is, characterized by formal rules and regulations, standard operating procedures, and centralized decision making; interpersonal relationships were formal, impersonal, rigid, and clear-cut. Relying heavily on programmed behaviors, mechanistic organizations performed routine tasks effectively and efficiently, but responded relatively slowly to unfamiliar events.

In highly unstable environments, the internal organization was "organic" or informal—that is, it exhibited few rules, informal agreements about operating procedures, and decentralized decision making; interpersonal relations were informal, personal, flexible, and somewhat ambiguous. Burns and Stalker did not conclude that the mechanistic model was inferior to the organic model, but rather, that the most effective structure is one that adjusts to the requirements of the environment—a mechanistic design in a stable environment and an organic form in an unstable environment. Recently, Danny Miller (1992) found considerable support for the contingency or environmental fit model. Organizations that achieve the best fit with external uncertainty exhibit the least number of interdependencies among internal structures and processes. In contrast, organizations showing the poorest fit with uncertainty have the strongest associations among structures and processes.

Organizational arrangements to fit each environmental condition of the typology based on uncertainty have also been proposed. A synthesis of the proposed configurations is summarized in Figure 7.3. Similar recommendations have been made by Duncan (1979), Mintzberg (1979), and Daft (1983).

Taken separately, the two dimensions suggest different organizational configurations. When the environment is simple, internal structures and processes are also

FIGURE **7.3**

Contingency Model for Environmental Uncertainty and School Structure

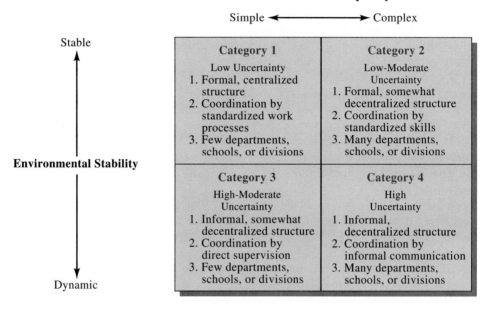

Environmental Complexity

Simple ←————————→ Complex

Stable

Environmental Stability

Dynamic

Category 1	Category 2
Low Uncertainty	Low-Moderate Uncertainty
1. Formal, centralized structure	1. Formal, somewhat decentralized structure
2. Coordination by standardized work processes	2. Coordination by standardized skills
3. Few departments, schools, or divisions	3. Many departments, schools, or divisions
Category 3	**Category 4**
High-Moderate Uncertainty	High Uncertainty
1. Informal, somewhat decentralized structure	1. Informal, decentralized structure
2. Coordination by direct supervision	2. Coordination by informal communication
3. Few departments, schools, or divisions	3. Many departments, schools, or divisions

simple. As complexity increases, however, an organization needs more departments to analyze and relate to the increased elements and information in its environment. When the environment is stable, internal arrangements tend to be routine, formal, and centralized—that is, more mechanistic. As instability increases, the structures and processes tend to become less formal and more decentralized—that is, more organic. Moreover, planning assumes added importance because the organization reduces uncertainty by anticipating future changes.

Simple, stable environments yield centralized bureaucratic structures that rely on standardized work processes. In simple, stable environments, for example, school districts would have extensive curricular plans and all teachers would be expected to follow the guides using the same teaching behaviors. By contrast, complex, stable environments lead to somewhat decentralized structures. School districts in complex, stable environments try to coordinate the instructional program through standard skills of teachers. These schools become bureaucratic because of the standard knowledge and procedures learned in formal training programs and imposed on the organization by certification and accrediting agencies (Mintzberg, 1979).

Simple, unstable environments also produce some flexibility in the bureaucratic structure, but decisions tend to remain centralized. Schools in this type of environment use direct supervision to coordinate the instructional program—that is, administrators emphasize classroom observation and evaluation procedures. Complex, unstable environments lead to flexible, informal, and decentralized structures. In complex, unstable environments, school organizations must decentralize decisions to administrators, specialists, and teachers who can comprehend the issues. The school must be responsive to unpredictable changes. Informal communication becomes the prime coordinating mechanism as individuals and groups cope with the uncertain environment. Therefore, the basic postulate is that as complexity and instability increase, so does the number of positions and departments within the school organization. As suggested by open-systems theory, each major element in the environment requires an employee or department to deal with it (Daft, 1989). From the environment, the personnel department hires people who want to work in the district; government relations employees negotiate with state legislators and education officials; and finance people deal with bankers.

Just as the information perspective suggests a structural contingency approach, so does the resource-dependence model. According to resource-dependence theory, the environment does not impose strict requirements for survival. Therefore, a wide range of possible actions and organizational structures are possible; hence, criteria guiding decisions and determining structures become both important and problematic. Internal power differences are important because no single optimal structure or set of actions aligns the organization with its environment. Instead, a range of choices or strategies of alignment are available. The influence of a variety of internal stakeholders may determine, in interaction with the demands of external constituencies, the response of the organization. Resource-dependence theory highlights the importance of environmental factors in promoting and restraining organizational decisions and actions, yet at the same time leaves room for the operation of strategic choice on the part of organizational members as they maneuver through known and unknown contexts. In other words, the resource-dependence model posits that although environmental influences are important, environmental constraints do not reduce the feasible set of structures to only one form. Rather, a variety of internal structures and actions are consistent with the survival of the organization, which means that although the organization may have the goal of survival, survival does not imply only a single or very limited set of structural forms (Aldrich and Pfeffer, 1976).

As a note of caution in applying the findings from contingency research, structural and process variations occur across schools as a result of active alternative generation and search procedures to adapt and change the environment. In fact, Boyd (1976) argues that schools are neither "mirror images" of the communities they serve nor are they completely insulated bastions dominated by unresponsive and self-serving professional educators. To a considerable extent, school organizations can shape their environments to fit their capabilities.

Interorganizational Coping Strategies

Thus far we have described ways in which school organizations can adapt internally to the external environment. Schools also reach out and change their environments.

James G. March (1981) even asserts that, in part, organizations create their environments. Two types of strategies are used to manage the external environment—establishing favorable linkages and shaping environmental elements. A point to be remembered about attempts to control the environment is that it, too, has some organized character and the ability to fight back (Katz and Kahn, 1978).

ESTABLISHING FAVORABLE LINKAGES One way organizations seek to control their environments is by establishing linkages with other organizations (Gross and Etzioni, 1985). Interorganizational linkages are important because they increase organizational power, reduce uncertainty, increase performance by ensuring a stable flow of critical resources, and protect the organizations from adverse effects of environmental uncertainty and scarcity (Stearns, Hoffman, and Heide, 1987). The connections are often in complex networks that try to regularize the flow of information and reduce uncertainty. The primary social process is believed to be some form of social exchange. Organizations create links by exchanging information, personnel, funds, equipment, and other needed items. In short, resources are exchanged in an effort to control the environment.

In business organizations a favorite mechanism to reduce competition and dependence is the merger. If a source of raw material is uncertain, buying the supplier removes the dependence on the external element. Although educational organizations cannot rely on mergers, they do enter into joint ventures with other organizations. School districts form *partnerships* with private foundations, universities, and federal and state governments to share the risks and costs associated with large-scale innovations and research projects. Current examples of joint ventures include Headstart, Follow Through, Individually Guided Education, special education programs, and vocational education. The number of joint ventures may be the best predictor of organizational influence on the environment (Boje and Whetten, 1981).

Cooptation represents another strategy of developing favorable linkages. Coopting means bringing leaders from important elements in the environment or the elements themselves into the policy structure of the school organization. Cooptation occurs when influential citizens are appointed to boards of education or to advisory committees. The evidence is mixed, however, for increasing the influence of organizations through advisory councils. Some research is supportive (Pfeffer, 1972); others are not (Boje and Whetten, 1981).

Another typical example of cooptation is the hiring of militant teachers or other activists to administrative positions. In these roles the coopted individuals have an interest in the school and are introduced to the needs of the district. As a result they are more likely to include the district's interests in their decision making and less likely to be critical of the decision in which they participated.

SHAPING ENVIRONMENTAL ELEMENTS Politicking is a primary method of shaping environmental elements for school districts. Political activity includes techniques to influence government legislation and regulation. School district officials and paid lobbyists express their views to members of state and federal legislators and other governmental officials. Political strategy can be used to erect barriers against unwanted influences and to establish rules favorable to existing schools and their policies. For example, public schools have engaged in extensive efforts to block state and federal support to private schools. Intense lobbying campaigns have been leveled against proposals concerning such initiatives as tuition tax credits, schools of choice, and educational vouchers.

Pooling resources is a related strategy to shape the external environment by forming educational associations that usually have both professional and political missions. A significant portion of the work to influence the environment for education is accomplished jointly with other organizations that have similar interests—for example, Parent-Teacher Association, National Education Association, American Federation of Teachers, American Association of School Administrators, Council for American Private Education, and National Federation of Urban-Suburban School Districts. The list is long. By pooling resources, individual educators or educational organizations can afford to pay people to carry out activities such as lobbying legislators, influencing new regulations, promoting educational programs, and presenting public relations campaigns. These associations attempt to use state certification boards to restrict entry, regulate competition, and maintain stability in the profession.

Karper and Boyd (1988) describe how the formation of coalitions and lobbying activities increases during periods of increasing uncertainty. Education interest groups in Pennsylvania responded to challenging circumstances during the mid-1980s by increasing the number, specialization, and sophistication of their lobbyists, and by forming a grand coalition to maximize their strength. As would be suggested by the information perspective, the findings indicate that the groups believed that they had to increase the amount of information they had and could share. In turn, the need for information fostered increasing specialization and sophistication within the lobbying groups. The groups increased their research capacity, engaged in policy analysis, and employed higher levels of technology.

A successful attempt to shape educational policy has been detailed by Tim L. Mazzoni and Betty Malen (1985). They analyzed a series of case studies dealing with constituency mobilization to impact state educational policy. In essence, an alliance consisting of the Minnesota Catholic Conference and the Citizens for Educational Freedom wanted the legislature to provide tax concessions for private school parents. Using both electoral and lobbying tactics, the alliance was able to persuade the legislature to endorse a tax concession package. The alliance kept the issue continuously on the legislative agenda, energized sympathetic lawmakers to carry its bills, and, most important, mobilized grassroots constituency pressure to sway votes among legislators. Mazzoni and Malen concluded that the political strategy of constituency mobilization had a significant impact on this policy issue.

The overall implication for practice is that school organizations do not have to be simple, passive instruments of the external environment. Both internal and external coping strategies can be used to buffer environmental influences and actually to change the demands. Structures, programs, and processes can be developed by educational administrators to manage the environments of their school organizations.

INSTITUTIONAL PERSPECTIVE

The **institutional perspective** is becoming a dominant approach to understanding organizations and their environments. Brian Rowan (1993) characterizes it as one of the most vital formulations in organizational theory today. The roots of institutional theory are found in the works of Philip Selznick (1949, 1957). His ideas were revitalized and elaborated by Meyer and Rowan (1977) to create a "new" institutional theory. Since the late 1970s institutional theory has generated widespread interest among scholars and provides valuable conceptual and practical insights about schools.[2] As a general theoretical approach in sociology, the formulation tends to be somewhat abstract; hence, it is essential to define the key terms—institution, institutionalization, and institutional environment.

KEY CONCEPTS

All social systems have some activities and functions that are accomplished in a stable and recurring fashion. For example, if we conceive of society itself as a social system, then the routine functions of educating, protecting, and governing are performed by the educational, legal, and governmental institutions. Regardless of the nature of the social system, as patterns of behavior become regular and routine, they are said to be institutionalized, and the social properties or structures established to perform these institutionalized functions are called institutions (Hoy and Miskel, 1991).

Ronald L. Jepperson (1991) tightens the definition. He defines **institution** as a social order or pattern that has attained a state or property. *Order,* or *pattern,* refers to standard interaction sequences. Institutions are then social patterns that reproduce themselves. An institution can be a formal organization, but it does not have to be. For example, objects that are commonly thought of as institutions include marriage, family, voting, the handshake, formal organizations, schools, attending school, teaching, teaching profession, academic tenure, the school principal, labor unions, and schooling. When violations of the social order or pattern are counteracted in a regulated way by rewards and sanctions, the pattern is said to be institutionalized. In other words, institutions are social patterns that, when chronically reproduced, owe their survival to relatively self-activating social processes. **Institutionalization,** then, is simply the process of attaining the status of an institution—that is, the ways by which social processes, obligations, or actualities assume a rulelike status in social thought and action (Meyer and Rowan, 1977).

In elaborating the ideas, Jepperson (1991) asserts that all institutions simultaneously empower and control; they are vehicles for activity within constraints. All institutions are frameworks of programs and rules establishing identities and activity schema for such identities. For instance, a school organization considered as an institution is a packaged social technology, with accompanying rules and instructions for its incorporation and employment in a social setting. Institutions, then, embody common actions or standardized activities in situations that become taken for granted.

Institutions such as schools are taken for granted in the sense that they are treated as fixtures in a social environment and are explained as performing a function in that environment.

The **institutional environment,** therefore, is characterized by the elaboration of rules and requirements to which individual organizations must conform if they are to receive support and legitimacy. In modern societies, the environmental requirements (e.g., rules, norms, values, and ideologies) are rational in form, with the chief sources of rationalization being governments and professions. State or federal education agencies like to create bureaucratic arrangements that centralize discretion and allow limited autonomy to local practitioners. Professionals and their associations prefer weaker and more decentralized structures that locate maximum discretion in the hands of local educators. Whatever the source, however, organizations are rewarded for conforming to these institutional rules, beliefs, and ideologies (Meyer and Rowan, 1977; DiMaggio and Powell, 1991; Scott, 1991; Scott and Meyer, 1991).

In fact, rationalized myth is commonly used in discussions of institutions and their environments. Myths are widely held beliefs that cannot be or typically are not objectively tested. They are true because they are believed. Myths become rationalized when they take the form of bureaucratic or professional rules specifying procedures necessary to accomplish a given end (Scott, 1992). **Rationalized myths,** then, are rules specifying procedures to accomplish an outcome that are based on beliefs that are assumed to be true or are just taken for granted. For example, a rationalized myth is the use of psychological tests and classification systems to place students in special education classes. These diagnostic approaches are rational because they provide procedures for assessing intellectual and emotional processes. They are myths because their use depends heavily on endorsements by professional associations, accrediting bodies, and funding agencies (D'Aunno, Sutton, and Price, 1991).

CONCEPTUAL FOUNDATIONS

Institutional theory is similar to the task-environmental theories, information and resource dependence. Both institutional and task-environment theories focus on organization-environment relations rather than on internal influences. The task-environment theories, however, concentrate on task or technical environments to gain information and resources from the external environment. In contrast, institutional environments encourage conformity to powerful sets of rules and requirements that are imposed by the legal, social, professional, and political contexts of organizations (Fennell and Alexander, 1987). Both task-environment and institutional theories promote "rational" organizational forms.

Technical environments emphasize a rationality that incorporates a set of prescriptions for matching means and ends in ways that produce desirable and predictable outcomes. Meyer, Scott, and Deal (1992) conclude that from the technical perspective, schools are peculiarly ineffective organizations. Schools neither have clear, efficacious technologies nor do they control their work processes adequately, particularly those involved in teaching and learning. By comparison, institutional environments press "rationales" as rationality. That is, institutional rationality provides an explanation that makes past actions understandable, acceptable, and seemingly accountable. Task and institutional environments should not be viewed as mutually exclusive factors, however; they can and do coexist. In other words, technical and institutional factors are not dichotomous, but instead are separate dimensions along which environments can vary. Schools and churches, for example, operate in relatively strong institutional but weak technical environments (Powell, 1991; Scott, 1991; Scott and Meyer, 1991). Important ideas in institutional theory include conformity, diversity, and stability.

Conformity and Institutional Environments

Institutional theory emphasizes that organizations are open systems, which are strongly influenced by their environments. Moreover, many of the most decisive forces are not rational pressures for more effective performance but social pressures to conform to conventional beliefs (Scott, 1992). Hence, a basic premise of institutional theory is that organizational structures and processes mirror the norms, values, and ideologies institutionalized in society. Accordingly, organizations conform with institutionalized rules and procedures to gain legitimacy—that is, cultural support for the organization. In other words, institutional conformity promotes the apparent success and long-term survival of the organization, independent of any effects that conformity might have on technical productivity. By designing a formal structure that conforms to the prescriptions of the institutional environment, an organization demonstrates that it is acting on collectively valued purposes in a proper and adequate fashion (Meyer and Rowan, 1977; Rowan, 1993). This thesis is particularly salient to educators because organizations lacking clear technologies and not operating in competitive markets—that is, public school systems—are especially likely to adopt institutionalized elements and conform to the institutional environment (DiMaggio, 1988).

Similarly, Paul J. DiMaggio and Walter W. Powell (1983, 1991) contend that organizational change in institutional environments makes organizations more alike without making them more efficient. Organizations within the same institutional environments tend to become homogenized. Public schools within a given country, for example, resemble each other. Their buildings and pedagogies are similar, with classrooms designed for a teacher, a set of students, and similar ways of engaging in teaching and learning processes. DiMaggio and Powell identify three mechanisms that promote institutional conformity.

Coercive conformity stems from political influence and problems of legitimacy. Conformity results from both informal and formal pressures exerted by other organizations and by cultural expectations in the society. A common and visible coercive pressure for school change is government mandate. Based on both federal and state regulations, for example, schools now hire special education teachers to serve special-needs children, develop curriculum materials for core and special subjects, and give students achievement tests that conform to government standards.

Moreover, informal mechanisms—for example, the beliefs in our society's culture about serving children—support these government mandates for special education services.

Imitative conformity results from adopting standard responses from other sources to reduce uncertainty. When organizations such as schools have weak technologies and ambiguous goals, they may model themselves on other organizations that they perceive to be more legitimate and successful. Rodney T. Ogawa (1992) offers the following example of an imitative process: A school adopts a new structure to enhance efficiency. If the new structure is perceived to improve performance, others may copy it. Over time, schools may adopt the new structure, not for the technical purpose of improving efficiency but for the institutional purpose of gaining legitimacy with constituents by mimicking a successful organization. A specific instance is the adoption of school-based management arrangements by a few urban school districts, an idea designed to deal with a multitude of problems, such as low academic achievement and tight budgets. As word spread of the successes enjoyed by these "innovative" districts, other districts uncritically implemented the innovation, even though they did not share the problems encountered by the original adopters. Betty Malen (1993) similarly concludes that school-based management is tied to a belief that attaches virtue to innovation and helps school districts retain their reputations as progressive systems.

Normative conformity comes primarily from professionalization. As we show in Chapter 10, professionalization of educators has developed rapidly. Two aspects of professionalization are particularly important in producing conformity in school organizations. The first rests on formal education and cognitive knowledge. Professionals learn standard methods of practice and normative rules about appropriate behavior. The second comes from the growth and elaboration of professional networks and associations that span organizations and allow new models to diffuse rapidly. Associations or labor unions of teachers and administrators, for example, facilitate the exchange of information among professionals and provide policies and practices that can be copied throughout education.

Through these conformity forces, schools produce similar structures and services and begin to resemble each other. Schools tend to look very much alike (Ogawa, 1992). In fact, pressures for conformity probably produce a surprising level of homogeneity within the American public school system. Meyer, Scott, and Deal (1992) found that schools go to great lengths to maintain their legitimate status as schools. They seek accreditation by conforming to a set of rules that are professionally specified or legally mandated. They hire licensed teachers who are assigned carefully defined students. The students are classified in grades that are given standardized meanings throughout the country. Finally, the teachers and students engage a curriculum that in turn is organized in fairly standardized categories of science, English, and mathematics. In other words individual schools conform to and are constrained by institutional rules of what society defines a school to be. Or as Samuel Bacharach and Bryan Mundell (1993) conclude, schools are expected to reflect the goals, values, and culture of broader society.

Educational Diversity and Multiple Institutional Environments

While there are strong environmental pressures for conformity, considerable diversity is also evident within the larger K-12 educational sector. In contrast to highly centralized national systems in many countries, the institutional environments of American schools are complex and have many layers. American schools operate amid pressures from parents, community groups, and local governments, many agencies of the federal and state governments, and a wide array of professional and special interest groups at all levels of society (Meyer, Scott, and Strang, 1987).

Many policy makers, citizens, parents, scholars, and educators probably have not recognized and taken seriously the diversity of the K-12 educational sector. When considering K-12 education in the United States, they see primarily the pervasive public school system. Yet well-developed subsectors of private, vocational, day-care, and alternative approaches also coexist with or within the public subsector of K-12 education. In fact, the persistence and increasing frequency of calls for market approaches to education (e.g., public and private choice, alternative schools, and voucher plans) may signal an increasing interest in private and alternative forms of education. An important point of speculation about this diversity and moves to strengthen the various subsectors is that different institutional environments may not only exist for each subsector of the K-12 system but produce different educational structures and processes.

Rowan (1993) asserts that a strong case can be made that each subsector has a relatively unique institutional environment. He also proposes that by virtue of their institutional location, public schools have had to define a broad mission and are heavily penetrated by rationalizing forces. Conversely, private schools have been able to define narrow missions and are not subject to the kinds of pressures faced by the public schools. Therefore, a reasonable hypothesis is that in comparison to public schools, private schools have different institutional environments and reflect different structures and processes—for example, smaller size, less bureaucratization, little or no vocational education, fewer curriculum offerings, a communal learning and support environment, and different governance arrangements. Empirical support for this hypothesis is provided by the work of Anthony S. Bryk, Valerie E. Lee, and Peter B. Holland (1993).

Stability and Institutional Environments

In contrast to the common belief that uncertainty is increasing, Meyer and Rowan (1977) theorize that institutional environments tend to stabilize both internal and external relationships. They reason that centralized governments, professional associations, and coalitions among organizations provide for standardized operating procedures and stability. Environmental demands, characteristics of inputs and outputs of schools, and technical processes are brought under the jurisdiction of institutional meanings and control. Support is guaranteed by agreements instead of depending on performance. Regardless of whether schools educate students, for instance, people remain committed to schools and continued funding almost becomes automatic. Moreover, Meyer and Rowan argue that institutional environments buffer organizations from turbulence and allow for conformance relationships to remain stable. Changes occur more slowly as the number of agreements increases. In fact, pervasive collective agreements among organizations grant near monopolies and ensure clienteles for organizations such as schools and professional associations. Thus, American school districts are near monopolies and have experienced high stability. The price for this legitimacy has been to conform to ever-widening rules about classifications and credentials of students and teachers, and the official content of the curriculum. In return, school districts are protected by rules that make education as defined by the institutional classifications compulsory. As a point of speculation, the institutional environment may be changing. The increased calls by citizens, policy makers, and business representatives for alternative schools and heightened technical performance suggest that previous institutional agreements are being questioned. We will return to this possibility later in this chapter.

In sum, institutional theory offers a substantially different perspective on the school organization–environment relationships rather than information and resource-dependence theories. Schools maintain conformity with institutionalized rules and ideologies and expend little effort in controlling and coordinating instructional processes and outcomes. The image conveyed is form over substance (Ingersoll, 1993). Since the reemergence of institutional theory in the mid-1970s, a substantial body of research in educational settings has developed.

RESEARCH AND EVALUATION OF INSTITUTIONAL PERSPECTIVE

Bacharach and Mundell (1993) believe that the research literature on the politics of educational policy can be reinterpreted using institutional theory. Many of the studies dealing with local, state, and federal interest groups can be explained by their desire to impose a particular set of rules and ideologies on schools, and in turn how the schools adopted or buffered themselves from the rationalized myths. In addition to research on political processes, a number of studies that explicitly use institutional theory have been conducted in educational settings.

Meyer (1992) observes that American education is distinctive in the decentralization of its funding and control to state and local levels. The federal government has little constitutional authority to regulate education and attempts to build such authority have largely been unsuccessful. Although the federal role has expanded, the role is largely restricted to funding and authority in various special educational programs spread across multiple federal agencies. Consequently, the institutional environment of public education at the federal level involves the centralization of funding without substantive authority; and the linkages at local, state, and national levels tend to be loose, circuitous, and indirect. Meyer calls this pattern *fragmented centralization.* Extending this reasoning, Meyer, Scott, and Strang (1987) assert that school districts have an obvious interest in gaining funds by meeting the federal legal requirements for participation. One response is to develop an administrative system with competence to search out funding prospects, learn how to conform to program and reporting requirements, and smooth the whole process. Support was found for the hypothesis that increments in federal funding produced larger additions to the administrative staffs of school districts than did increments in state or local revenues, a finding consistent with underlying institutional theory.

Institutional theory also offers an explanation of school district consolidation (i.e., merging of two or more districts into one). David Strang (1987) studied school district consolidation from 1938 through 1980. During this period over 100,000 school districts failed to survive. To a substantial extent, these deaths were affected by changes in the institutional environment—that is, the ideology about the appropriate size and structure of schools changed. Consolidation does preserve local control, albeit in larger, more bureaucratic districts. At the same time, however, local school administrators in consolidated districts now must attend to state and national policies to a greater extent than before they were merged. Strang found, for instance, that the more centralized the state's control was over education, the more extensive the consolidation. The new consolidated districts were larger and more complex organizations that were more susceptible to central initiatives across a range of state and national policy issues.

Based on the assumption that structural elements are first legitimated in the environment and then adopted by local organizations, Rowan (1982) traced the incorporation of three occupations into California school district structures. He charted how health, psychological, and curriculum services and occupations were created and institutionalized by the rules and ideologies of state agencies, legislatures, and professional groups, and then incorporated into the structure of local school districts. As early as 1909, the legislature passed legislation permitting school personnel to make medical inspections of children. The original purpose of the inspections was to combat the spread of infectious diseases. After the legislation passed, crusaders engaged in institution building. The result was that by 1935, yearly medical inspections were mandated by the *School Code*. Moreover, larger school districts were always more likely than small districts to incorporate occupations, but that independent of size, districts added and subtracted occupations as support for an occupation ebbed and flowed in the institutional environment. In addition, the most successful adoption was health services and the least successful was curriculum services. This is interesting because health services are the most removed from the technical core of instruction and curriculum is the closest.

Ogawa (1994) recently asserted that the United States is awash in a second wave of reform. The aim is not to renew and enhance existing structures, but to make fundamental changes in them. Using institutional theory, he studied a widely popular reform called school-based management. The basic idea in this reform is to delegate important decisions from the district to the school level. His findings suggest that the movement to school-based management was institutionalized. The primary proponents—National Governors' Association, Carnegie Forum on Education and the Economy, American Federation of Teachers, and various academics—basically represented the interests of the education profession. The groups articulated two overarching goals: first, to improve the effectiveness of public schools; and second, to enhance the professional status of teachers. Ogawa observes that the goals seek to shift greater control to teachers and emphasize the importance of public education, which has been compared unfavorably with private education by proponents of school choice. At face value, these goals could be taken as a move to promote a task or technical effectiveness. However, when asked to explain their advocacy for school-based management, the groups invoked broad societal interests and ignored more parochial or personal goals. Hence, Ogawa concludes that the findings are consistent with institutional theory. The proponents justified their preferred structural elements by linking them to widely shared cultural beliefs or institutions.

A criticism of institutional theory is that its broad emphasis on processes of conformity has led to a downplay of the role of active agency and resistance in organization-environment relations (Goodstein, 1994). A narrow focus on conformity processes deflects theoretical interest away from explaining the circumstances in which institutionalization is contested or incomplete. Organizations such as schools can exercise some choice in responding to institutional pressures. This criticism does suggest an important area needing additional conceptual development and empirical testing.

Clearly, the interest in and development of institutional theory is growing rapidly. The literature already reflects "old" and "new" versions of the general approach. Rowan (1993) concludes that research supports the basic premise of institutional theory that organizational structures respond to trends in the institutional environment. Perhaps the most important contribution of institutional theory, however, has been the reconceptualization of organizational environments. Meyer and Rowan's (1977) article called attention to a neglected facet of environments: institutionalized or symbolic elements such as beliefs, rules, and roles are capable of affecting organizational forms independent of resource flows and technical requirements. After a period of rapid growth, institutional theory has entered a phase of more deliberate development and consolidation (Scott, 1987, 1991).

ADMINISTERING INSTITUTIONAL ENVIRONMENTS

Scott (1992) indicates that there are clear differences in the way organizations respond to technical (i.e., information and resource) and institutional aspects of the environment. Most links with technical environments involve exchanges of information and resources. While some ties to institutional environments involve exchanges, especially information, the institutional perspective postulates that organizations are constituted by elements drawn from their environments. Because institutional environments are different from technical and resource-dependence environments, and because of the recent development of institutional theory, less is known about how organizations relate to their institutional environments (Scott, 1992). The basic and ubiquitous notion in administering institutional environments is that school organizations will be rewarded for having a legitimate reputation (Elsbach and Sutton, 1992). As with information and resource-dependence models, variations of buffering and boundary-spanning strategies also appear useful in managing institutional environments.

Buffering Strategies

Recall from our earlier discussion that buffers are structures and processes that insulate or surround internal activities and absorb environmental disturbances. Buffering essentially creates a protective layer between the organization and its environment. A major problem to resolve by buffering mechanisms is conflicts between pressures for technical efficiency and institutional rules. From an institutional perspective, decoupling and managing the image are two ways to buffer school organizations from their environments.

DECOUPLING Meyer and Rowan (1977) say that organizations designed for efficiency ideally attempt to maintain a close alignment between their structures and their technical activities. Close alignment in institutionalized organizations makes public a record of inefficiency and inconsistency. As a consequence, organizations functioning in institutionalized environments attempt to decouple their institutional structures from their technical structures and activities. **Decoupling** is intentionally neglecting to provide adequate control of work processes (Ingersoll, 1993). Decoupling divides organizations into two parts: one primarily links to the institutional environment and one produces the technical activities. Thus, the technical portion faces inward to its technical core and turns its back on the environment, while the institutional part turns its back on the technical core in order to focus on conforming to its institutional environment (Meyer, Scott, and Deal, 1992).

Decoupled school organizations exhibit a number of characteristics. For example, activities are performed beyond the purview of administrators and professionalism is actively encouraged. Goals are made ambiguous and categorical ends are substituted for technical ends—that is, schools produce students, not academic learning (Meyer and Rowan, 1977). Organizations decouple for several reasons. Decoupling masks or buffers inconsistencies, irrationalities, and poor task performance that might undermine public faith in the organization. Moreover, decoupled organizations can incorporate and display structural elements that conform to institutionalized conventions and yet preserve some autonomy of action. In inconsistent or conflicting environments, decoupling represents a particularly useful strategy (Scott, 1992).

MANAGING THE IMAGE This strategy involves impression management to portray structures and actions in ways to garner endorsement (Elsbach and Sutton, 1992). Impression management makes extensive use of symbolic categories and coding rules. Similar to cognitive schema (see Chapter 4), symbolic categories are created to select, identify, classify, and label the things or people being processed by the organization. Coding rules are the essence of institutional frameworks; they provide the distinctions among things and people that allow standard operating or taken-for-granted procedures to be employed (Scott, 1992). Meyer and Rowan (1977), for instance, state that using cost analysis to justify school projects in an institutional norm can provide a rationale if a project fails. Administrators whose plans have failed can demonstrate to other administrators, teachers, the board of education, and the public that the procedures were prudent and that decisions were made rationally. Hence, institutionalized practices and impression management help justify their actions and portray a positive image to constituents. Such symbolic activities can produce shared meanings and value that in turn result in commitments, support, and legitimacy of the school organization (Ogawa, 1992).

Boundary-Spanning Strategies

Earlier in this chapter, boundary spanning, or bridging, was defined as activities that create internal roles to cross organizational boundaries and link the school organization with elements in the external environment. Meyer and Rowan (1977), DiMaggio and Powell (1991), and Scott (1992) propose conformity as the central boundary-spanning strategy in institutional environments. By incorporating institutional rules, beliefs, and ideologies into their own structures, organizations become more homogeneous and gain legitimacy. Scott proposes three types of bridging strategies that can be used to manage institutional environments.

CATEGORICAL CONFORMITY According to Scott (1992), this is a broad and general strategy. It basically is a process whereby institutional rules become taken-for-granted distinctions and provide organizations with a basis to pattern their structures. These distinctions are examples of widely shared cognitive schema. The cognitive structures become built into our language and become widely believed. Meyer and Rowan (1978) refer to this as a system of ritual categories. There are elaborate rules for classifying teachers—for example, elementary or secondary—and each category has its own specifications and credentials. Students, similarly, are categorized by grade level, ability level, and courses completed. Standard categories and ritual classification procedures involve not only educators and students but curriculum topics and schools (e.g., alternative and traditional) as well. Schools that incorporate these shared cognitive belief systems—that is, exhibit categorical conformity—enhance their legitimacy and increase their resource capacities.

STRUCTURAL CONFORMITY Sometimes institutional environments impose very specific structural requirements on schools as a condition of acceptance and support (Scott, 1992). External mandates cause schools to implement new programs. In the past three decades, many special education programs—for example, mildly learning disabled to severely and profoundly retarded and hearing, visual, and other impairments—have been incorporated in educational organizations to meet various legislative laws, administrative rules, and parental beliefs. Using various arrangements, schools have developed structures to conform to the special need categories designated in the institutional environments. Administrators know the score—success comes with meeting the demands for institutional conformity rather than with instructional efficiency (Rowan, 1981). As mentioned earlier, schools often borrow or imitate successful structural forms when they confront uncertainty. Thus, by choice and coercion, schools frequently use structural conformity as a mechanism for adapting to the environment (Scott, 1992).

PROCEDURAL CONFORMITY Meyer and Rowan (1977) observe that despite the lack of coordination and control of the technical activities, schools are not anarchies. Day-to-day activities occur in an orderly fashion. In fact, institutional environments pressure schools to carry out activities in specified ways. School organizations can respond with rational myths that detail the steps to be followed in carrying our certain types of procedures. For example, schools tightly control such processes as hiring teachers with proper credentials, assigning students to classes, and scheduling events (Meyer and Rowan, 1978). Adherence to procedural specifications is a method by which stable school forms can be created and legitimated to work in institutional environments. By using socially acceptable procedures to execute controversial activities, schools can maintain the impression that they are rational and legitimate (Scott, 1992).

In sum, practical methods for administering the institutional environments of schools remain somewhat undeveloped. The foregoing sets of buffering and bridging strategies appear to offer substantial insights for developing specific tactics to manage the institutional environments of schools.

CHANGING INSTITUTIONAL ENVIRONMENTS FOR EDUCATION

The web of multiple levels of government rules, norms of professional associations, and ideological consensus of the public about what schools look like and do has produced a relatively stable institutional environment for public K-12 education. Current activities may indicate that the institutional environment for education is changing in the United States. That is, existing institutional explanations are being questioned. Worried about economic competitiveness in world markets, American businesspeople and policy makers are challenging the decoupling and rationalized myths about teaching and instruction. The longevity, intensity, and diversity of calls for educational reform may indicate that the public consensus is declining and destablization of the institutional environment is occurring. For example, Susan H. Fuhrman, Richard F. Elmore, and Diane Massell (1993) assert that pressure for increased and more consistent results from schools will continue to mount. In particular, calls for systemic reform and competitive markets in K-12 education may reflect a shift in school environments from primarily institutional to task or technical.

Since the early 1980s, the reform movement in the United States has been characterized by a wave metaphor—first, second, and now the third wave, called systemic reform. **Systemic reform** is a comprehensive change program designed to modify schools in an integrated, coordinated, and coherent fashion to achieve clearly stated educational outcomes (Fuhrman, Elmore, and Massell, 1993). A powerful coalition of business, policy, and governmental groups are backing systemic reform. The recent enactment of the Goals 2000 program by the federal government gives powerful impetus to a systemic-reform movement in the United States. The basic priority of systemic reform is to define ambitious curriculum content and achievement standards in core academic subjects and to tightly couple the goals with an assessment program. The alignment of curriculum content and achievement standards with assessment procedures creates an accountability system for monitoring the efficiency and effectiveness of K-12 schools. Systemic-reform proponents plan to augment the accountability system with changes in educator preparation and practices, instructional materials, governance, and finance. From the perspective of environmental theory, we hypothesize that a goal of systemic reform of K-12 education is to increase the influence of technical and decrease the influence of institutional environments.

As Ogawa's (1994) work indicates, a crucial point in systemic reform is whether the current initiatives promote technical efficiency and effectiveness or societal arguments, further governmental standardization, and professional control. If the goals of systemic reformers are to be achieved, technical environments must become the dominant form for schools and tight linkages must develop for accountability, efficiency, and effectiveness. If the switch to technical environments does not occur, the systemic-reform efforts may produce a new, thicker web of rationalized myths and further institutionalize the environments of public K-12 education. Alternatively, further reliance on rationalized myths in the face of intense public calls for reform might force a break in the near monopoly of public education and produce a competitive market for K-12 education.

Paul E. Peterson (1989) maintains that the quasi-monopoly of K-12 public education is so pervasive a fact in the United States that its existence is pretty much taken for granted. During the last century public education has captured a powerful set of legitimating symbols—social democracy, equal opportunity, and a common homogenizing experience in a pluralistic society. In other words, the schools have been institutionalized and have assumed a near monopoly position.

Intense criticism of the academic performance of American public schools and popular presentations of the positive achievements of private and foreign schools (Stevenson and Stigler, 1992; Bryk, Lee, and Holland, 1993) have led many to question the monopolistic position of public K-12 schools. John E. Chubb and Terry M. Moe (1990) have been particularly articulate in arguing that the best way to improve American schools is to set them free in a competitive marketplace. **Competitive market** means that people choose the school and type of education that they think best meet their educational needs. Free-market proponents believe that competitive forces produce better educational services than do monopolized responses and unleash strong incentives for school reform. In a competitive market, it is reasoned that parents and students will opt for the public or private schools, which they think are most efficient and effective. If consumers are not satisfied with the outcomes, they can just walk away and thereby send clear signals to educators about the level of school performance. Without such feedback, stimuli for improvement remain weak and monopolistic indifference reigns (Boyd and Walberg, 1990). Methods commonly proposed to produce a competitive educational market include establishing parental choice and alternative schools in both public and private settings, and offering state-issued tuition vouchers or scholarships that can be used to pay for the students' cost of schooling.

As is the case with systemic reformers, advocates of competitive-market strategies are attempting to place technical environments ahead of institutional environments. Competitive-market supporters are hypothesizing that parents and students will choose schools with ambitious academic goals, excellent teachers and administrators, motivating instructional materials, high efficiency and effectiveness, and strong accountability systems. Even if market-driven schools are established on a relatively widespread basis, forces in the institutional environment, however, will likely counter the drive to enhance their technical environments. For example, market-driven schools will likely develop their own rationalized myths, will operate in environments institutionalized by government agencies and professional associations, and will be strongly resisted by the current holders of the K-12 education monopoly.

Because public school systems employ ambiguous technologies and operate in a near-monopolized market, they have been particularly likely to adopt institutionalized elements and conform to the institutional environment (DiMaggio, 1988). Hence, shifting the environment from primarily institutional to technical represents fundamental change and would have profound effects on how schools operate.

SUMMARY AND SUGGESTED READINGS

Open-systems theory highlights the vulnerability and interdependence of school organizations and their environments. External environment is important because it affects the internal structures and processes of organizations. In this chapter, three perspectives of the environment have been presented. The first two—information and resource-dependence theory—are primarily concerned with task or technical elements of the external environment that are potentially relevant to goal setting, goal achievement, effectiveness, and survival. These models emphasize that schools are created to perform some type of work and to achieve goals. The information perspective assumes that the environment is a source of information to be used by organizational decision makers. The resource-dependence approach assumes that organizations cannot generate internally the needed resources and that resources must come from the environment. In contrast, the third perspective—institutional theory—assumes that environments encourage schools to conform to powerful sets of rules and requirements that are imposed by the legal, social, professional, and political contexts of organizations. The essence of institutional theory is that the environment of schools presses more for form than substance. Nevertheless, technical and institutional environments do coexist; schools now function in relatively strong institutional but weak technical environments. Current drives for systemic reform and competitive markets suggest that worried businesspeople and policy makers may be seeking to place a heightened emphasis on task environments. A shift from primarily institutional to technical environments would shatter the rationalized myths and lead to fundamental changes in schools, a shift that will be bitterly fought by current institutional forces.

Because external environments can threaten organizational autonomy and effectiveness, administrators often try to minimize external effects on internal school operations. Their responses can be classified as either internal or interorganizational coping strategies. Internal coping strategies include buffering the technical core, planning and forecasting, adjusting internal processes, conforming to environmental expectations, and spanning organizational boundaries. Interorganization coping strategies include establishing favorable linkages with important external constituencies and shaping environmental elements through political action. By using the coping strategies, administrators can, to some degree, manage the environments of their schools.

To explore the information perspective in greater depth, a number of classic sources should be consulted—for example, Emery and Trist (1965), Thompson (1967), Lawrence and Lorsch (1967), and Terreberry (1968). To understand resource-dependence theory, one must read the work of Pfeffer (1972, 1981, 1982). Probably the most widely cited source for this perspective is by Pfeffer and Salancik (1978). Excellent sources for institutional theory are anthologies by Meyer and Scott (1983) and Powell and DiMaggio (1991). The latter collection includes the classic article by Meyer and Rowan (1977) and an updated version of a classic by DiMaggio and Powell (1983). In education, works by Rowan (1981, 1982, 1993), Ogawa (1994), and Malen (1993) are particularly useful. While scholarly work is evident for all three models, theoretical development and research seem most active for institutional theory.

NOTES

1. The primary proponent of resource-dependence theory probably has been Jeffrey Pfeffer. References to his work include the following: Pfeffer (1972, 1981, 1982); Pfeffer and Salancik (1978); Pfeffer and Leblebici (1973); and Aldrich and Pfeffer (1976). The present discussion of resource-dependence theory draws heavily from these sources.

2. The old and new approaches to institutional theory share many similarities and exhibit several substantial differences. A detailed comparison of the older and more recent formulations is made by Powell and DiMaggio (1991).

KEY CONCEPTS AND IDEAS

Boundary spanning	Decoupling
Buffer	Dependence
Buffering	Environmental complexity
Coercive conformity	Environmental stability
Competitive market	Environmental uncertainty

External environment

Imitative conformity

Information perspective

Institution

Institutional environment

Institutionalization

Institutional perspective

Munificence

Normative conformity

Planning and forecasting

Rationalized myths

Resource-dependence perspective

Scarcity

Systemic reform

Task environment

Effectiveness and Quality of Schools

> Whether quality is a fad or a substitute for effectiveness is, in our opinion, less important than that we learn from the contributions of both constructs in future work.

> —Kim S. Cameron and David A. Whetten
> *Higher Education: Handbook of Theory Research*

PREVIEW

1. Organizational effectiveness and quality are key concepts in open-systems theory.

2. The goal model and the system resource model are two theoretical bases for making judgments and for taking the action necessary to work toward school effectiveness.

3. Within a goal model, schools are effective if the outcomes of their activities meet or exceed their organizational goals.

4. Within a system resource model, schools are effective when they secure an advantageous bargaining position and acquire a disproportionate share of scarce and valued resources.

5. An integrated goal-system resource model of organizational effectiveness emphasizes both the effectiveness and the quality of all aspects of the system. Time and multiple constituencies are also important dimensions of the model.

6. Three important performance outcome indicators of schools are academic achievement, job satisfaction, and perceived organizational effectiveness.

7. Pragmatic discussions of quality have begun to replace theoretical analyses of organizational effectiveness, but the constructs are complementary, not opposites.

8. The most popular approach to quality is Deming's philosophy of total quality management.

9. Total quality management is a set of fourteen interrelated principles of management.

10. Quality schools have as their purpose the continual improvement of learning and teaching.

11. Quality school administrators lead their schools by transforming their culture into one that emphasizes cooperation, trust, openness, and continuous improvement.

12. The elements of a system including the transformational process are integrated by four major administrative functions—deciding, motivating, communicating, and leading.

Issues of organizational effectiveness and quality represent fundamental challenges to practice in school administration. When educators, school patrons, or policy makers gather, school quality and effectiveness frequently drive the conversation. Terms such as "accountability," "academic achievement," "test scores," "teaching performance," "student dropout rates," "job satisfaction," and "productive learning culture" infuse these conversations. Education is certainly not devoid of effectiveness indicators and quality assessments. Educators and the public acknowledge that different schools achieve different levels of success, even with similar student populations. Based on real or imagined information, parents decide, for example, to locate in a given area because they know that James Madison Elementary maintains high academic expectations and standards while John Dewey Elementary uses high-quality motivational and innovative teaching methods. Moreover, schools report results to the public that educators believe represent their accomplishments and innovative practices. Patrons are invited to art shows, music performances, science fairs, and athletic events because these activities illustrate school quality and productivity. At the level of practice, effectiveness and quality indicators are known and used.

The practical interest in school effectiveness and quality issues intensified significantly during the 1980s. The *Nation at Risk* report in 1983 crystallized the performance problems of schools in the minds of Americans, especially business officials and policy makers. The public came to the clear recognition that the world economy had become intensely competitive and interdependent, that academic achievement in America's schools was not competitive internationally, and that societal demographics for the United States were changing in fundamental ways—for example, an aging population and an emerging multicultural citizenry. As a consequence the focus on school performance intensified and the concern no doubt will continue through this decade.

Issues of organizational effectiveness and quality also constitute key concepts in open-systems theory. In Chapter 2 (see Figures 2.1 and 2.4), we proposed an open social-systems framework of school organization using input, process, and output components. In Chapters 3 through 7, we made detailed analyses of four internal process elements—individual, structural, cultural, and political—and the external environment of schools. As an overall generalization of open-systems theory, we stated that outputs of schools are a function of the interaction of structure, individual, culture, and politics as constrained by environmental forces. Moreover, school outputs constitute the performance outcomes of students, teachers, and administrators that can be used as indicators of organizational effectiveness and can be assessed for their quality.

During the past twenty years, organizational effectiveness has been a premier concept in organizational theory. Kim S. Cameron and David A. Whetten (1995) recently observed, however, that the dominance of effectiveness in the organizational sciences is being challenged by the construct of quality. As a fashionable, perhaps faddish, organizational performance concept, Cameron and Whetten document a fundamental shift away from effectiveness to quality. This shift can be seen in such popular books as *Theory Z* (Ouchi, 1981), *Out of Crisis* (Deming, 1986) and *In Search of Excellence* (Peters and Waterman, 1982). These books emphasize words such as "quality," "excellence," "continuous improvement," and "transformation" rather than organizational effectiveness. According to Cameron and Whetten, this shift in emphasis can be partly explained by a basic change of focus from abstract theoretical formulations of effectiveness to practical applications of quality in organizational studies. For example, concerns about a loss of economic competitiveness and unsatisfactory academic achievement in schools fueled the drive to find best practices and ways to improve the quality of schools.

However, it is only the phrase "organizational effectiveness" that is disappearing from contemporary scholarship and not the need to assess outcomes and to make appraisals about admirable practices. While "effectiveness" and "quality" are not synonyms, they both are ways to describe and explain organizational performance. Therefore, we believe the concepts are complementary perspectives on school performance. Hence, we will use an open social-systems framework to present the major theoretical formulations and associated research for the concepts of both organizational effectiveness and quality.

ORGANIZATIONAL EFFECTIVENESS OF SCHOOLS

The concept of effectiveness is both the apex and the abyss in organizational analysis. It is the apex because all theories of organizational and administrative practices are ultimately aimed at identifying and producing effective performance. It is an abyss because the theories of organizational effectiveness and lists of criteria are neither necessary nor sufficient to evaluate the concept (Cameron, 1984). Both the importance and the confusion surrounding organizational effectiveness are apparent for schools. For example, when specific questions about effectiveness are raised, the controversy intensifies: What criteria? How are the criteria to be defined? Who determines the criteria? How are the indicators to be measured? Is effectiveness a short-term or a long-term phenomenon?

To ask global questions about whether a school is effective or ineffective, however, is of limited value. Effectiveness is not one thing; hence, a one-dimensional definition is not adequate. Rather, a school or any other organization can be effective and ineffective. Without a theoretical guide, it is meaningless to claim that one school is more effective than another, to say that a given indicator is a measure of effectiveness, or to design ways to enhance school effectiveness. The goal model and the system-resource model are two theoretical guides for making these judgments and for taking the action necessary to work toward school effectiveness.[1]

GOAL MODEL OF ORGANIZATIONAL EFFECTIVENESS

Traditionally organizational effectiveness has been defined in terms of the degree of goal attainment. Similar to the definition of individual goals in Chapter 4, organizational goals are simply the desired states that the organization is trying to attain. Within a goal model, goals and their relative accomplishment are essential in defining organizational effectiveness. Goals provide direction and reduce uncertainty for participants and represent standards for assessment of the organization. In a **goal model,** a school is effective if the outcomes of its activities meet or exceed its goals.

Types of Goals

In a goal model of organizational effectiveness, a distinction must be made between official and operative goals (Steers, 1977). **Official goals** are formal declarations of purpose by the board of education concerning the nature of the school's mission. These statements usually appear in board of education publications and faculty and staff handbooks. Official goals typically are abstract and aspirational in nature (e.g., all students will achieve their full potential). They are usually timeless, and serve the purpose of securing support and legitimacy from the public for schools rather than for guiding the behavior of professional educators.

In contrast, **operative goals** reflect the true intentions of a school organization. That is, operative goals mirror the actual tasks and activities performed in the school irrespective of its claims. Hence, official goals in schools may be operative or inoperative depending on the extent to which they accurately represent actual educational practices. Some operative goals are widely published (e.g., efforts to place students with handicaps in regular classrooms), while others are not (e.g., efforts to provide custodial care of students for six to eight hours per day). In fact, attractive official goals in some districts act as expedient covers to less attractive operative goals such as racism and sexism.

Assumptions and Generalizations

Assumptions of the goal model of organizational effectiveness include the following.

- A rational group of decision makers sets the goals.
- The number of goals are few enough to be administered.
- The goals are clearly defined and understood by participants.

- The goals supply the criteria for evaluating effectiveness (Campbell, 1977; Scott, 1992).

Although decision makers obviously are not completely rational, these assumptions and the generalizations that flow from them should not be rejected without careful consideration. In fact, administrative practices have been developed to enhance goal specification and goal achievement. For example, management by objectives, setting individual goals (see Chapter 10), and instructional objectives for courses are used to specify the goals and criteria to judge their achievement. Similarly, state and local boards of education and administrators attempt to enhance goal attainment by centralizing and formalizing school organizations, by mandating guidelines for core curricula, and by using assessment criteria and criterion-referenced tests. However, shortcomings of the goal concept and the goal model should be noted.

Criticisms of the Goal Approach

Cameron (1978) details the following criticisms of using goals to assess organization effectiveness:

- Too often the focus is on the administrators' goals rather than those set by teachers, students, parents, and other constituencies.
- The contradictory nature of multiple goals is frequently overlooked. For instance, educators are expected to maintain secure and orderly environments in schools, and at the same time, to develop the values of trust, group loyalty, and caring among students.
- Organizational goals are retrospective. They merely serve to justify school and educator action, not to direct it.
- Organizational goals are dynamic, while the goal model is static. Goals change as the situation and behavior vary, but the model remains the same.
- Official goals of the organization may not be its operative goals.

Given such strong criticisms, a persuasive argument can be formulated that a goal model of organizational effectiveness is inadequate. Indeed, a system-resource model has been proposed as an alternative approach to organizational effectiveness.

SYSTEM-RESOURCE MODEL OF ORGANIZATIONAL EFFECTIVENESS

Similar to the resource-dependence view of external environments (see Chapter 7), the **system-resource model** defines effectiveness as the organization's ability to secure an advantageous bargaining position in its environment and to capitalize on that position to acquire scarce and valued resources (Yuchtman and Seashore, 1967). The concept of bargaining position implies the exclusion of specific goals as ultimate effectiveness criteria. Rather, the system-resource model directs attention toward the more general capacity of the organization to procure assets. Consequently, this definition of effectiveness emphasizes the continuous, never-ending processes of exchange and competition for scarce and valued resources. This process is visible each time a state legislature meets to appropriate tax monies for schools. Educational organizations compete in an environment of state politics with transportation, social welfare, correctional, and other agencies and organizations to acquire the valued commodity of state aid. With the proposals for vouchers, charter schools, and alternative and choice schools, competition between public and private schools is likely to increase. When public school enrollments decline and the employment prospects weaken for educators, competition for students intensifies. According to the system-resource model, the most effective schools sustain growth or minimize decline by advantageous bargaining with parents, students, and legislators. Hence, the criterion for effectiveness becomes the organization's ability to acquire resources.

Assumptions and Generalizations

The system-resource model contains several implicit assumptions (Yuchtman and Seashore, 1967; Campbell, 1977; Goodman and Pennings, 1977):

- The organization is an open system that exploits its external environment.
- Harmony within the system improves performance.
- Organizations compete for scarce resources.
- An organization of any size faces such complex demands that defining a small number of meaningful goals may be impossible.

It follows that when the internal elements of bureaucratic expectations, group culture, political expectations, and individual needs work more harmoniously to exploit the environment, the organization will be more effective. Educational administrators, for instance, place great importance on maintaining harmony because conflict impedes the system's ability to garner resources. In schools, as in all organizations, the quality levels of internal processes and performance outputs are clearly connected (Cameron and Whetten, 1995).

Because of their dependence on environmental forces, organizations must concentrate on adaptive functions to compete successfully for resources. From the system-resource perspective, effective organizations are those with sensitive monitoring mechanisms that provide information about new behavior that can lead to the acquisition of more assets. Hence, the primary criteria for assessing organizational effectiveness from a system-resource perspective are the consistency of the internal processes and structures and the ability to monitor and adapt to environmental constraints.

Criticisms of the System-Resource Approach

The system-resource model of organizational effectiveness also has alleged defects, especially when applied to educational organizations (Cameron, 1978; Scott, 1977; Steers, 1977; Kirchhoff, 1977):

- Too much emphasis on acquiring resources may have damaging effects on outcomes. For example, in order to stem declining enrollments, public and private schools might engage in intense and expensive competition for students that compromises program rigor and quality.
- Too much stress on inputs masks the importance of outcomes.
- The system-resource model is actually a goal model in which the operative goal is acquiring resources. Thus, the differences between the goal and the system-resource approaches may represent an argument over goals and semantics.

In other words, the system-resource model actually verifies the operative goal concept and the two approaches are complementary (Steers, 1977). Indeed, a possible, even highly desirable approach is to combine the two perspectives.

AN INTEGRATED GOAL AND SYSTEM-RESOURCE MODEL OF EFFECTIVENESS

Both the goal and system-resource models share the crucial assumption that it is possible and desirable to develop a single set of evaluative criteria, and therefore, a single statement of organizational effectiveness (Connolly, Conlon, and Deutsch, 1980). In the goal model, effectiveness is defined in terms of the relative attainment of feasible objectives that can be exchanged for other resources. The resource model, based on the open-systems perspective, places great value on the harmonious operations of the organization's internal components; the ability to monitor and adapt to the environment; and the optimization of such administrative processes as deciding, communicating, motivating and leading people.

Several theorists (Goodman and Pennings, 1977; Steers, 1977; Campbell, 1977) have attempted to integrate the two approaches, and although their ideas differ slightly, they agree that the use of goals cannot be avoided. Behavior is explicitly or implicitly goal directed, and organizational functioning is no exception. However, from a system-resource framework, goals become more diverse and dynamic; they are not static, ultimate states, but are subject to change over relatively short periods of time. Moreover, the attainment of some short-term goals can represent new resources to achieve subsequent goals. Thus, when a systems framework is used, a cyclic nature characterizes goals.

In order to convey an understanding of the subtle nuances of organizational effectiveness, an integrated model must address three important characteristics—time, multiple constituencies, and multiple criteria.

Time

A neglected factor in the study of organizations and the assessment of their effectiveness is time. Yet issues of time are absolutely of central importance (Bluedorn and Denhardt, 1988). Martin Burlingame (1979) speaks of the rhythm of seasons; that is, clear cycles characterize the school calendar—the year begins in the fall, breaks for a holiday in the winter, and ends in the late spring. Educators know that certain times of the school year hold greater potential for crises, disruption of the system, and reduced goal attainment. The last few days of the school year, for example, provide conditions for chaos. Knowing this, educators develop coping mechanisms to handle these short-term performance problems, such as strict interpretation of discipline rules, field trips, and other special activities.

The time dimension in a model of organizational effectiveness can be conceptualized with a continuum of success ranging from the short to the long term. For schools, representative indicators of short-term effectiveness include student scores on achievement tests, faculty morale, and job satisfaction. Criteria for intermediate success encompass adaptiveness and development of the school organization and instructional programs, career advancement of educators, and success of the former students. From the system-resource framework, the ultimate long-term criterion is survival of the organization. Declining enrollments, school closings, and consolidation of small school districts represent long-term problems of survival. To illustrate this point, Emil J. Haller and David H. Monk (1988) found that between 1930 and 1988 the number of school districts in the United States declined from 128,000 to 14,000. Just during the 1960s, the number of school districts was halved.

Another influence of time is that the criteria for organizational effectiveness do not remain constant. As constituencies change their preferences, new constraints and expectations evolve to define school effectiveness. During the 1970s, for example, schools emphasized socioemotional growth of students and equity, but with the reform reports of the early 1980s, the public started to demand that efficiency, cognitive growth, and employment skills (Bacharach, 1988; Wimpelberg, Teddlie, and Stringfield, 1989). Currently, schools are emphasizing thinking and problem-solving abilities so that their graduates can advance the nation's pragmatic economic goals well into the twenty-first century.

In sum, performance that is effective today is likely to be ineffective tomorrow as preferences and constraints change (Cameron, 1984). Therefore, the goal of the effective school is, continually, to *become* effective rather than *be* effective (Zammuto, 1982). Hence, when discussing school effectiveness, the dimension of time is an essential component.

Multiple Constituencies

A **constituency** is a group of individuals within or outside who hold similar preferences or interests about the activities and outcomes of an organization (Cameron, 1978; Tsui, 1990). Effectiveness criteria always reflect the values and biases of multiple constituencies or stakeholders. For organizations like schools, with multiple constituencies, effectiveness criteria typically are drawn from many interest groups. That is, multiple stakeholders play critical roles in defining and assessing the goals (Connolly, Conlon, and Deutsch, 1980). The debate to define school effectiveness has been joined by parents, administrators, students, teachers, school board members, businesspeople, politicians, governmental officials, news media, and taxpayers. To say the least, this list depicts a diverse set of interest groups. In terms of a political model of organizations (Kanter and Brinkerhoff, 1981), schools can be viewed as battle-grounds where stakeholders compete to influence the criteria for effectiveness in ways that will advance their own interests. Consequently, effectiveness becomes less a scientific and more a political concept.

As a further complicating factor, constituent groups actively prefer different criteria (Hall, 1980; Kanter and Brinkerhoff, 1981; Scott, 1992). For example, administrators and board of education members emphasize input resources and structural indicators of effectiveness such as available facilities and their use, amount of financial resources, and personnel practices. These are important in part because they are factors under administrative control. In contrast, teachers emphasize the processes of educational effectiveness. They argue that effectiveness must be conceived in terms of the quality and appropriateness of their instructional methods. Students, taxpayers, and politicians, however, focus primarily on outcomes and efficiency measures. They evaluate schools in terms of academic achievement, the values of graduates, and cost per student.

Therefore, a combination of the goal and system-resource models requires the inclusion of multiple constituencies who define and evaluate school effectiveness using a variety of criteria. The relativistic approach (Keeley, 1984) assumes that multiple statements about organizational effectiveness are not only possible but necessary because stakeholders in and around schools require different kinds of effectiveness measures. No single effectiveness indicator, nor a simple, general list, will suffice (Kanter and Brinkerhoff, 1981) and power and politics affect both the definition and the measurement of effectiveness.

Multiple Criteria

A basic assumption throughout this discussion has been that organizational effectiveness is a many faceted concept—that is, models must include multiple criteria. No single ultimate criterion such as student achievement or overall performance can capture the complex nature of school effectiveness. Choosing the most appropriate and representative effectiveness variables can be an overwhelming task. For instance, John P. Campbell (1977) used thirty categories for a comprehensive list of organizational effectiveness indicators. Similarly, Steers (1975) found fifteen different criteria in a sample of only seventeen studies of effectiveness.

The development of a multidimensional index or composite measure of organizational effectiveness requires the selection of key concepts. The open-systems perspective developed in Chapter 2 can be employed to guide the choice of effectiveness criteria or goals in the combined goal and system-resource approach. Effectiveness indicators can be derived for each phase of the open-systems cycle—inputs (human and financial resources), transformations (internal processes and structures), and outputs (performance outcomes).[2] This point is illustrated by considering each phase of the open-systems cycle as a category of effectiveness indicators.

Performance outcomes constitute the quality and quantity of the school's services and products for students, educators, and other constituents. These are the effects of the organization. Examples of outcome indicators are academic achievement, job satisfaction, teacher and student attitudes, student dropout rates, teacher absenteeism levels, employee commitment to the organization, and society's perceptions of school effectiveness. Scott (1992) observes that outcomes are frequently considered the quintessential criteria of effectiveness.

Structure and process criteria are the quantity, quality, and harmony of the internal processes and structures. System harmony among the internal elements is a key in acquiring external resources and transforming the resources to performance outcomes. Performance outcomes reflect effects; transformation resonates effort (Scott, 1992; Cameron and Whetten, 1995). Examples of structural criteria include congruence among the organizational, individual, cultural, and political systems. Process criteria include the health of the interpersonal climate; motivation levels of students and teachers; and quality-control procedures such as the number of tests given, amount of time on task and use of instructional technology, and personnel evaluations. These criteria are one step removed from performance outcomes. Thus, schools characterized by positive internal criteria should produce high performance outcomes (Ostroff and Schmitt, 1993).

Input criteria (see Figure 2.4) are the school's beginning capacity and potential for effective performance. These include all environmental constraints, organizational features, or participant characteristics understood to influence organizational effectiveness (Scott, 1992). Examples of input criteria are wealth of the school district, abilities of students, quality of the faculty, number of volumes in the library, quality and quantity of instructional technology, and condition of the physical facilities. If the structure and process criteria are once removed from performance outcomes, then input criteria are twice removed. Input criteria do not indicate either the amount or quality of the work performed, but rather they set the limits for the transformation and outcomes of the system.

Virtually every input, transformation, or outcome variable can be and has been used as an indicator of goal or resource effectiveness. The next step is to combine the time, constituency, and effectiveness criteria into a coherent formulation.

Integrating Time, Multiple Constituencies, and Multiple Criteria: A Goal and System-Resource Model

The results of merging the general dimensions, specific criteria or indicators, and other perspectives of effectiveness are summarized in Figure 8.1. Consequently, an integrated **goal and system-resource model** uses specific indicators of the input, throughput, or output concepts as operative goals and combines them with the time frame and constituencies applicable to each indicator.

As illustrated in Figure 8.1, the result is a more comprehensive theoretical formulation for defining the quality and effectiveness of schools. To apply this model of organizational effectiveness to schools, a series of steps must be taken.

- The constituencies who would define the important operative goals must be identified.

FIGURE **8.1**

Integrated Model of Organizational Effectiveness

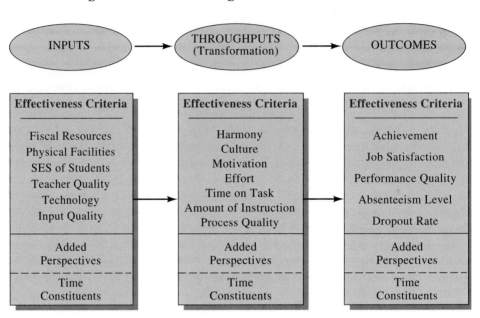

- A time dimension (short-term, medium-term, or long-term) must be specified.
- Criterion indicators must be selected.
- A comprehensive evaluation of school effectiveness must include outcomes for each of the three systems phases.

For example, an assessment of short-term and intermediate-term school effectiveness from the perspective of students might be teacher quality, strength of culture, academic achievement, and student satisfaction with instruction.

THREE OUTCOME CRITERIA

Several of the concepts that have been suggested as indicators of organizational effectiveness have been given detailed attention in earlier chapters. Others, such as productivity and efficiency in the classic, private economic sense, seem less applicable to school organizations. Three important performance outcome indicators of schools have not yet been discussed—academic achievement, job satisfaction, and overall perceptions of school effectiveness. These concepts will now be considered systematically.

ACADEMIC ACHIEVEMENT

Many parents and other citizens, government policy makers, and scholars define organizational effectiveness narrowly; they equate school effectiveness with academic achievement. While most acknowledge other criteria, they typically ignore the school's role in developing creativity, self-confidence, aspirations, and expectation—all of which are needed for future success in school and adult life.

Two apparent reasons help explain the overreliance on standardized test scores as measures of achievement. The first is political and the second practical. On the political side, a number of important educational constituencies—students, parents, and business leaders—see test scores as having intrinsic value. On the practical side, although the goals of education are numerous and vague, student achievement is the only school outcome that is readily available and widely and publicly measured (Bidwell and Kasarda, 1975; Madaus, Airasian, and Kellaghan, 1980). Even though expediency, rather than theory, has too often guided research on school effectiveness, student achievement remains one of the important performance indicators and should not be neglected. Two research approaches dominate the study of cognitive achievement.

Input-Output Research

Input-output, or production-function, research became popular in the mid-1960s. Developed by microeconomists to predict the output of a system using sets of input variables, the underlying model is forthright (Hanushek, 1989). The **production-function model** assumes that performance output of the educational process is related directly to a series of inputs. For schools, the input groups usually are classified as family resources, school resources, community characteristics, student resources, and peer group characteristics, while the outputs are scores on achievement tests (Lau, 1978). The purpose of production-function research is to predict an outcome rather than to explain how the result was produced. In terms of the open-systems model, production-function research ignores the system's internal transformational process and uses only inputs to predict outputs.

The most influential educational study reflecting this approach, *Equality of Educational Opportunity*, was conducted by James S. Coleman and his associates (1966). Popularly known as the Coleman Report, it remains the largest survey of American public education ever undertaken. Nationally, 645,000 students completed standardized ability and achievement tests as well as forms to describe their family backgrounds. Approximately 60,000 teachers responded to questionnaires about their educational experiences, teaching tenure, attitudes, and verbal ability. Finally, data on a variety of organizational input or capacity variables, including class size, school organization, libraries, and laboratory facilities, were collected from over 4,000 schools. The most surprising finding was the role the school-capacity variables had in predicting pupil achievement. When home background variables were controlled, school factors showed limited relationships to test scores. What mattered most was not the characteristics of the school but the students' home backgrounds before entering the school and their peers in school.

Since the Coleman Report, a large number of additional production function studies have been conducted and several excellent reviews of this literature are available.[3] In a recent review, Eric A. Hanushek (1989) concludes that two decades of production-function research in education has produced startlingly consistent results—variations in school expenditures are not systematically related to variations in student performance. The factors that he examined were: teacher/pupil ratio, teacher education, experience, salary, expenditures per pupil, administrative inputs, and facilities. Stated simply, production-function research finds little evidence to support the idea that the way money is allocated in schools helps student learning.

In an effort to clarify Hanushek's conclusions, Albert Shanker (1989) offers a number of cogent explanations. As a preliminary assertion, he maintains that the "facts" in this type of research do not necessarily speak for themselves. To make a reasoned interpretation of the findings, a number of questions must be addressed. For example, what is meant by student performance? In over 70 percent of the studies, it was measured by standardized tests. While test scores tell something basic about performance, the results do not tell us whether students can write a good essay, engage in good discussions, or create something. What about the finding that pupil/teacher ratio does not make a difference? Shanker offers two explanations. First, this ratio is not the same thing as class size. Large numbers of teachers do not regularly work with children. Instead, they are assigned to duties that make little difference to students. Second, small class size may not lead to better scores on standardized tests, but the condition makes it more likely that teachers will give more writing assignments and be able to comment on them. Shanker concludes that the production-function studies should not be dismissed, but that they do not make the case that money and other resources do not matter in education. Nevertheless, he further asserts that the research should give pause to those who insist that more money for doing things the same way will improve the effectiveness of schools. If most children cannot learn by sitting still all day, listening passively to lessons, following prescribed textbooks and workbooks at a set pace, doing these things in smaller classes with more experienced and educated teachers and greater administrative support will not help them learn any better. As a persistent critic, Shanker holds that to improve organizational effectiveness significantly, fundamental changes must occur in the way schools are organized and operated.

Although production-function research has been plagued by inconsistent and insignificant results (Monk, 1992), the studies still leave little doubt that learning in the home is extremely important. No matter how they are measured, differences in socioeconomic background of the family lead to significant differences in student achievement. A reasonable interpretation is that measures of socioeconomic status are proxies for the quality of the learning environment in the home—nutrition, physical surroundings, parental attitudes, education, and so forth. Nevertheless, little room for doubt exists that differences among schools and teachers also produce important changes in academic achievement. Schools are not homogeneous in their effects on students; schools differ in the effectiveness of their efforts to influence achievement test scores. As Steven T. Bossert (1988) maintains, input-output studies typically do not consider how students actually use resources that are available in the school.

Based on reasoning similar to Shanker's and Bossert's, a new line of inquiry emerged that was designed to explain how home, school, and internal-system factors influence academic achievement.

Input-Throughput-Output Research

If the findings are accepted from production-function research that home factors explain as well as predict student achievement, building a case for additional resources from the external environment to provide more teachers, better facilities, and new curricula becomes exceedingly difficult. Reacting to this realization and wanting to improve academic achievement in low-income, largely minority schools, educational researchers developed a new line of inquiry during the 1970s (Cuban, 1984). Using a system's perspective, input-throughput-output research not only considers inputs but relates such throughputs as classroom practices (instructional methods, classroom organization, time on task), school climate or culture, organizational operations, and political relationships to a variety of outputs, including student achievement on standardized tests. This general approach has been called various names, including **process-product research,** systems research, and organizational research, but the most commonly used designation is probably **effective-schools research.** A number of excellent descriptions, analyses, and reviews of this literature have been published.[4]

Scholars have deduced what they believe are the few critical school factors for enhancing scores on standardized tests. As popularized by Ronald Edmonds (1979), Lawrence C. Stedman (1987) observes that most educators are now familiar with the five-factor effective-schools formula:

- Strong leadership by the principal, especially in instructional matters
- High expectations by teachers for student achievement
- An emphasis on basic skills
- An orderly environment
- Frequent, systematic evaluations of students

Similar lists have been derived from the research by Bossert (1988), Terry A. Astuto and David L. Clark (1985b), and Wimpelberg, Teddlie, and Stringfield (1989). A larger number of school factors are suggested by S. C. Purkey and Marshall S. Smith (1983). The factors from the reviews by Edmonds, Purkey and Smith, and Stedman are summarized in Table 8.1.

Stated simply, the effective schools research has had a tremendous impact on school practice. Good and Brophy (1986) and Stedman (1987) provide summaries of a number of the change programs—for example, Project RISE in Milwaukee and School Improvement Project in New York City—that are based on this body of research. Other programs have been initiated in Atlanta, Chicago, Minneapolis, Pittsburgh, San Diego, St. Louis, Washington, D.C., and many, many other smaller school districts (Cuban, 1984). Nevertheless, the results of these efforts to apply a formula

TABLE **8.1** Three Sets of Factors in the Effective-Schools Formula		
Edmonds	**Smith and Purkey**	**Stedman**
• Principal leadership	• Instructional leadership	• Pluralism
• Emphasis on basic skills	• Planned and purposeful curriculum	• Academically rich programs
• High expectations for student achievement	• Clear goals and high expectations	• Personal attention to students
	• Time on task	• Student responsibility
• Frequent and systematic evaluation of students	• Recognition of academic success	• Supportive environment
• Orderly environment	• Orderly climate	• Skilled use and training of teachers
	• Sense of community	• Teaching to prevent academic problems
	• Staff development	• Shared governance
	• Staff stability	• Parent participation
	• Collegial and collaborative planning	
	• School site management	
	• Parental support and involvement	
	• District support	

for changing a limited number of school factors to improve academic performance has produced mixed results. According to Brophy and Good, Project RISE appears to have achieved some success. The scores on the achievement tests did improve to an extent, especially in some schools and in the area of mathematics.

Stedman takes a more critical stance on Project RISE. While acknowledging that some schools did improve their math scores, most RISE schools continued to do poorly in reading. Moreover, those schools that achieved success often did so by teaching to the test. In a similar vein, Cuban (1983, 1984) offered a cautionary note about rushing to implement the changes called for by the effective-schools advocates. He lists and describes several significant problems and unanticipated consequences that occur in the research and application of the effective-schools findings.

- No one knows how to create effective schools.
- There is little agreement on definitions of such key concepts as effectiveness, leadership, and climate.
- Effectiveness is defined too narrowly; it is more than test scores for lower order skills.
- Weak research methods have produced many of the findings.
- The changes have produced increased uniformity—e.g., standard curricula and district-wide use of the same textbooks and workbooks.

- The projects have narrowed the educational agenda; music, art, speaking and self-esteem receive less attention.
- The effectiveness innovations have heightened conflict between teachers and administrators over instructional leadership.

Four characteristics of effective-school principals have typically been identified—goals and production emphasis, power and strong decision making, effective management, and strong human relations skills (Bossert, 1988). The results are not as clear as some proponents of the effective-schools programs claim. For instance, Good and Brophy (1986) assert that nearly all studies of effective schools support the importance of principal leadership, but limited accord exists on the behaviors and practices that characterize leadership for enhanced academic achievement. In an even stronger assessment, Bossert (1988) maintains that effective-schools studies have tried to resurrect the bureaucratic ideal by stating that strong principal leadership is needed in order to structure schools for effectiveness. However, the research is silent on what processes must be structured and what structures need to be created to produce success.

From the effective-schools research, two generalizations regarding principals are supported: administrative behaviors are important to school effectiveness, and no single style of leadership appears appropriate for all schools (Bossert et al., 1982). Effectiveness depends on the appropriate matching of such situational variables as the shape of the administrative hierarchy and organization of the curricular program with the leadership style of the principal. More specifically, Valerie E. Lee, Anthony S. Bryk, and Julia B. Smith (1993) propose three functional roles principals play in effective secondary schools:

- *Administration:* Allocating resources, developing and enforcing policies and procedures, and supervising professional development
- *Mediation:* Helping communication to internal and external constituencies and buffering the teachers from environmental disturbances
- *Leadership:* Shaping school goals and guiding instructional processes

Although standardized achievement tests contain conceptual, empirical, and political traps for educators, they are an essential ingredient of school effectiveness. Moreover, the interrelationships among school inputs, transformation, and such outcomes as academic achievement are highly complex. Another performance outcome, job satisfaction, is less controversial than student achievement, though it too is little understood.

JOB SATISFACTION

The formal study of job satisfaction did not start until the Hawthorne studies in the early 1930s (see Chapter 1). However, even prior to those studies, scientific managers had implicitly recognized the concept in conjunction with worker fatigue. Since the 1930s, job satisfaction probably has been the most extensively and enthusiastically studied concept in organizational science. C. J. Cranny, Patricia Cain Smith, and Eugene F. Stone (1992) estimate that over 5,000 articles, books, and dissertations have been published on the subject.

Why does job satisfaction attract so much interest? Originally, the early proponents of a human relations approach convinced both theorists and administrators that a happy worker was a productive worker. The study of job satisfaction intensified with a general concern for the quality of working life, epitomized during the 1970s by the publication of *Work in America* (U.S. Department of Health, Education and Welfare, 1973).

Definition

The classic attempt to define job satisfaction was made in 1935 by Robert Hoppock. He cautioned about the difficulty of formulating an adequate definition because of the limited amount of knowledge then available on the subject. Nevertheless, he defined job satisfaction as any combination of psychological, physiological, and environmental circumstances that cause a person to say, "I am satisfied with my job."

Other definitions of the concept have been formulated:

- The extent to which employees like their work (Agho, Mueller, and Price, 1993)
- The affective orientations of individuals toward work roles that they are presently occupying (Vroom, 1964)
- An affective response of an individual to the job; it results when on-the-job experiences relate to the individual's values and needs (Muchinsky, 1987)
- A pleasurable or positive emotional state resulting from the appraisal of one's job or job experiences (Locke, 1976)

In contrast to many other concepts in organizational science, there appears to be general agreement that **job satisfaction** is an affective or emotional reaction to a job that results from the employee's comparing actual outcomes to desired, expected, or deserved outcomes (Cranny, Smith, and Stone, 1992).

Discrepancy Model of Job Satisfaction

The **discrepancy model** of job satisfaction postulates that job satisfaction is best explained by a discrepancy between the work motivation of jobholders and the incentives offered by the organization (Smith, Kendall, and Hulin, 1969). Similar conceptualizations are found in inducements-contributions theory (March and Simon, 1958) and cognitive-dissonance theory (Festinger, 1957). These perspectives posit that job satisfaction levels are related to the perceived difference between what is expected or desired as fair and reasonable return (individual motivation) and what is actually experienced in the job situation (organizational incentives). The discrepancy or comparison hypothesis of job satisfaction is presented pictorially in Fig-

FIGURE **8.2**

Discrepancy Model of Job Satisfaction

If the subtraction yields a positive value and motivational factors are greater than the incentives received, dissatisfaction results. Conversely, if the subtraction produces a negative value, rewards exceed motivational factors and satisfaction results.

ure 8.2. Findings by Cecil Miskel, Douglas Glasnapp, and Richard Hatley (1975) support the discrepancy hypothesis in the educational setting.

Situational Model of Job Satisfaction

The **situational model** of job satisfaction relates combinations of task, organizational, and personal variables to indicators of job satisfaction (Glisson and Durick, 1988; Quarstein, McAfee, and Glassman, 1992; Agho, Mueller, and Price, 1993). As shown in Figure 8.3, this contingency perspective generally divides the variables

FIGURE **8.3**

Situational Model of Job Satisfaction

into three groups: (1) characteristics of the job tasks (e.g., autonomy, pay and other benefits, routinization, significance, challenge, variety); (2) characteristics of the work organization (e.g., centralization, professionalism, supervision, feedback, culture); and (3) characteristics of the employees (e.g., age, gender, education, motivation, ability, age, predisposition to be happy). The general hypothesis explains job satisfaction by combining the critical variables suggested in the social-systems model (see Chapter 2). Several excellent reviews of the research testing the general situational model are available (e.g., Locke 1976; Holdaway 1978b; Rice 1978). A brief review of selected findings follows.

A Brief Overview of the Job-Satisfaction Research

After reviewing the literature, Ratsoy (1973) concluded that teacher job satisfaction, in general, is lower in schools where the teachers perceive a high degree of bureaucracy. Other evidence, however, suggests that this statement is too general. When specific bureaucratic dimensions of schools are related to job satisfaction, a complex picture emerges. Bureaucratic factors that enhance status differences among the professionals, such as the hierarchy of authority and centralization, produce low satisfaction levels. But factors that clarify the job and yield equal applications of school policy promote high levels of satisfaction (Carpenter, 1971; Gerhardt, 1971; Grassie and Carss, 1973; Miskel, Fevurly, and Stewart, 1979).

Work motivation is also consistently correlated with job satisfaction. Expectancy motivation is related to teacher job satisfaction; teachers who believe that they have the capabilities to do the job and envision positive consequences for their efforts will generally have high levels of satisfaction (Miskel, DeFrain, and Wilcox, 1980; Miskel, McDonald, and Bloom, 1983). Similarly, as the organizational climates of schools become more open or participative (see Chapter 5), the level of teacher satisfaction increases (Grassie and Carss, 1973; Miskel, Fevurly, and Stewart, 1979).

Leadership, decision making, and communication processes also influence job satisfaction. The nature of the relationships between teachers and administrators and the quality of leadership correlate highly with teacher satisfaction. Greater participation in decision making, especially concerning instructional methods, yields enhanced teacher job satisfaction (Belasco and Allutto, 1972; Mohrman, Cooke, and Mohrman, 1978). Moreover, the lack of opportunities to participate in decision making is the greatest source of teacher dissatisfaction (Holdaway, 1978b). Finally, the quality of the communication processes also relates to overall teacher job satisfaction (Nicholson, 1980). Communicating clearly to employees the scope of the job, how their contributions are related to the school's goals, and how they are being judged, for instance, are positively correlated with job satisfaction.

We conclude from this brief overview that interest in job satisfaction has been high among scholars in educational administration. Moreover, useful models and generalizable findings for job satisfaction are available to guide research and to inform administrative practice.

PERCEIVED ORGANIZATIONAL EFFECTIVENESS

To formulate a model of perceived organizational effectiveness, Paul E. Mott (1972) combined several important performance outcomes—quantity of the product, quality of the product, efficiency, adaptability, and flexibility. Mott reasoned that these five criteria define the ability of an organization to mobilize its centers of power for action to achieve goals and to adapt. Effective schools produce higher student achievement, generate more positive student attitudes, adapt better to environmental constraints, and deal more potently with internal problems. Clearly, Mott's perspective is consistent with the integrated goal and system-resource model of organizational effectiveness developed in this chapter.

Although we have cautioned against single indicators, a short global measure based strongly in a theoretical model and used with other instruments can begin to improve our understanding of organizational effectiveness. Mott developed an 8-item measure for use in a variety of organizational settings, which has been modified for studies in schools (Miskel, Fevurly, and Stewart 1979; Miskel, Bloom, and McDonald, 1980). The resultant *index of perceived organizational effectiveness* (IPOE) is shown in Table 8.2. Its careful adaptation to school situations makes it a strong candidate for use as an overall measure in future studies; in fact, Mott concludes that the subjective evaluations of employees provide a fairly valid measure of organizational effectiveness. Support for this conclusion has been provided by Wayne K. Hoy and Judith Ferguson (1985). Using the index of perceived organizational effectiveness, they found that perceived overall effectiveness of secondary schools was significantly related to four sets of school output variables.

Mott (1972) has made extensive use of the index of perceived organizational effectiveness. In highly centralized organizations, effectiveness tended to be lower. Moreover, effectiveness was greater when the leaders provided more structure for the tasks to be done and when the climate was open. Findings in the school setting by Miskel, Fevurly, and Stewart (1979) support Mott's conclusions. Formalization and complexity of the school structure and participative climates are conducive to organizational effectiveness. Similarly, Miskel, McDonald, and Bloom (1983) found that high organizational effectiveness as perceived by teachers is associated with strong linkages to the principal in the area of student discipline, support from special-education experts, time for classroom activities and high expectancy motivation. More recently and supportive of the foregoing results, Connie S. Logan, Chad D. Ellett, and Joseph Licata (1993) found that structural coupling, robustness, academic achievement, and student attendance were related to perceived organizational effectiveness as measured by the IPOE.

It is clear from what has been said thus far that many variables are needed to assess adequately the complex effects of organizational and administrative processes on school effectiveness. Although the knowledge of organizational effectiveness remains somewhat limited, it is being indirectly expanded by the tremendous attention on organizational quality.

TABLE **8.2**	The Index of Perceived Organizational Effectiveness

Every educator produces something during work. It may be a "product" or a "service." The following list of products and services are just a few of the things that result from efforts in schools:

Lesson plans	Student learning	Athletic achievements
Community projects	Instruction	Art and music programs
New curricula	Teacher-parent meetings	Classroom activities

Please indicate your responses by checking the appropriate line for each item.

1. Of the various things produced by the people you know in your school, how much are they producing?

___Low production ___Moderate
___High ___Fairly low ___Very high production

2. How good is the quality of the products or services produced by the people you know in your school?

___Poor quality ___Fair quality ___Good quality
___Low quality ___Excellent quality

3. Do the people in your school get maximum output from the available resources (money, people, equipment, etc.)? That is, how efficiently do they do their work?

___Not efficiently ___Fairly efficiently
___Not too efficiently
___Very efficiently ___Extremely efficiently

4. How good a job is done by the people in your school in anticipating problems and preventing them from occurring or minimizing their effect?

___A poor job ___A fair job ___A very good job
___An adequate job ___An excellent job

5. How informed are the people in your school about innovations that could affect the way they do their work?

___Uninformed ___Very informed ___Informed
___Somewhat informed ___Moderately informed

6. When changes are made in the methods, routines, or equipment, how quickly do the people in your school accept and adjust to the changes?

___Very slowly ___Fairly rapidly ___Rapidly
___Rather slowly ___Immediately

7. How many of the people in your school readily accept and adjust to the changes?

___Many less than half ___Nearly everyone
___The majority ___Less than half
___Many more than half

8. How good a job do the people in your school do in coping with emergencies and disruptions?

___A poor job ___A fair job ___A good job
___An adequate job ___An excellent job

QUALITY OF SCHOOLS

Discussions of quality have begun to replace those of organizational effectiveness. Like the integrated model of effectiveness proposed in this chapter, the notion of quality is not tied to products. Rather, it deals with the **quality** of the system and all its components; hence, researchers and practitioners are interested in the quality of inputs and processes as well as the quality of outputs.

The emphasis on quality in the contemporary organizational literature can also be traced to the popularity of the work of W. Edwards Deming (1983, 1986, 1993) on **total quality management (TQM).** After World War II, it was Deming and his philosophy of management that turned around Japanese industry and helped make Japan a dominant business force in the postwar world. Japan set a new standard for industry and business success, and by the 1980s, more and more American business, governmental, and service organizations were turning to Deming's teachings, philosophy, and principles of total quality management. By the 1990s, total quality management (Deming, 1986) had become an important focus in the management of both business (Scherkenbach, 1991, 1992) and educational organizations (AASA, 1991) in the United States.

DEMING ON QUALITY

The Deming approach (1986) can be summarized as a set of fourteen principles for transforming and improving organization and administration. These principles of transformation represent a complex, prescriptive set of interrelated rules stated in terms of a series of commands. Do the Deming principles apply to schools? More and more educational administrators and commentators believe so (Glaub, 1990; Rhodes, 1990; AASA, 1991; Leonard, 1991; Meany, 1991; Bonstingl, 1992), but some remain skeptical (Capper and Jamison, 1993; Pallas and Neuman, 1993). We have taken each of the principles and briefly interpreted its relevance and consequences for schools.

Deming's Principles of Management

❶   Create a constancy of purpose for improvement. The educational process starts with the student. The needs of students must be at the forefront of any program to change or reform education. Moreover, improvement of education involves not only dealing with the dilemmas of today but also seeking opportunities for improvement. Put differently, avoid tomorrow's problems by seeking opportunities to improve quality today.

Quality schools today do not assure quality tomorrow. Schools, like all organizations, must not focus narrowly on short-term issues and neglect long-term goals. It is too easy to become tangled up in the knot of immediate problems and solutions. Schools must never be content to rest on their laurels; they must constantly be studying themselves and changing in ways that improve teaching and learning.

❷   Adopt a new philosophy. This new philosophy is one of taking administrative responsibility for quality and making leadership for change central to improvement. The perspective calls for a balance between constancy of purpose and continual improvement, between the individual and the group, between short-term and long-term results, and between knowledge and action. The goal of the philosophy is to create "a joy of ownership through a joy of workmanship" (Scherkenbach, 1991: 4). Administrators must make schools places where students and teachers want to be rather than have to be, and places that value teaching and learning for their own sake rather than as merely necessary.

Today's school administrators must not only reduce waste and inefficiency but also add value to products and services. To add value they must take responsibility for the school's teaching and learning and improve them. Leadership for change means continuous research, planning, change, evaluation, and improvement. In the case of schools, the goal is continuous improvement of teaching and learning. Improvement is a process without end (Hoy and Forsyth, 1986). The process of continuous improvement is a cycle: finding opportunities for improvement, developing an improvement plan, implementing the plan, assessing the results, acting on the results, and beginning the cycle anew.

❸ Cease dependence on inspection and ratings to achieve quality. Inspection and ratings to improve quality are too late and typically ineffective and costly. Quality in schools comes not from inspection (ratings and evaluations) but actions to improve teaching and learning. Unfortunately, much of the supervision in schools is empty ritual or ratings. Ratings do not improve teaching and learning; only teachers themselves can change their teaching. It is the quality of the teaching that affects the quality of student learning. Inspection is too late; the learning has occurred.

This principle underscores the likely failure of supervisory programs in schools that rely on rating teachers. Rating, regardless of the basis (student achievement scores or specific teacher behaviors), is not the route to quality. Self-regulated professional behavior that emphasizes continuous growth and development of teaching and learning is a better aim. Engaging professionals in the process of continual improvement is the key to quality. The process is not simple. People, materials, methods, equipment, and environment are all vital ingredients of the school system (see Chapter 2).

❹ Stop awarding business on the basis of price tag alone. At first blush this principle seems most relevant for business organizations. But the lessons for educational administration are there. The lowest priced goods and services are not necessarily the best. The policy of driving down costs by always selecting the low bid is foolhardy; it drives out good vendors and quality services. New ideas and novel approaches should not be eliminated on the basis of cost alone. Cost should not be the bottom line in educational decisions; quality should be. Smaller classes, newer technology, and teacher aids are simply a few examples of issues that may have long-term positive effects on student learning. Short-term costs may be high, but long-term benefits may be great.

Schools need to develop long-term relationships with suppliers and partners based on commitment and loyalty. Of course, schools should find groups and organizations who consistently meet their needs and expectations. This is a high standard alone. But once good business and educational partners are found, the relationships should be nurtured. Schools should encourage their partners to engage in the same processes of improvement to which quality schools themselves are committed.

❺ Constantly improve every system in the organization to enhance the quality of products and services. The school district is a social organization composed of many systems and subsystems—for example, schools within the district and classes within the school (see Chapter 2). Every system needs to constantly improve. The quality of the product produced by the organization is a function of the harmony within and among its subsystems. That is, cooperation and teamwork are necessary both within and among the systems. All teams (for example, teams of administrators, teams of teachers, and teams of administrators and teachers) must work together and monitor and regulate themselves if they are to move toward continuous improvement.

Quality starts with intent, which in the case of schools is often collaboratively fixed by teachers and administrators. The intent, however, must be translated into plans, specifications, and tests in an attempt to deliver a quality education to students. The process of recognizing an opportunity to improve, testing a theory to achieve the opportunity, observing the test results, and acting on the opportunity is the prime responsibility of teachers and administrators (Deming, 1986). Although Deming stresses the importance of seeking opportunities for improvement rather than merely reacting to problems, the cyclical process he advocates is similar to the decision-making models found in Chapter 9. The process is a rational cycle of action based on theory, prediction, systematic observation, and quantitative and qualitative analyses.

6 Institute training on the job. Training and education are needed for everyone, but new employees and administrators especially need on-the-job training. Beginning teachers are often uneasy and sometimes unprepared for the rigors of teaching. Professional development programs will not only save the school administration grief but should help beginners develop the security they need to perform well in the classroom. Investment in professional development at this level should reduce the costs of turnover and absenteeism. In-service training is wasted, however, if administrative action is uninformed and insensitive. For example, a new teacher excited by a novel approach from the university is thwarted when confronted by a principal who insists that it won't work in the real world.

Administrators need to be well trained to manage people, but human relations skills alone will not suffice. According to Deming and his associates (Deming, 1986; Scherkenbach, 1992), a thorough knowledge of statistical skills as well as an understanding of theory as it applies to their jobs are essential tools, tools that can be more skillfully used if learned in the context of their job.

7 Institute leadership. The job of administration is not supervision; it is leadership, a special kind of leadership that will transform the workplace of the school (see Chapter 12) so that teachers and administrators are partners in improving education. Teachers must work in a culture (see Chapter 5) whose shared values are service to students, teamwork, quality teaching, self-evaluation, and continual improvement—a culture that balances knowledge and action, science and philosophy. Management that emphasizes numbers (e.g., test standards, MBO, and appraisal of performance) has no place in this new leadership (Deming, 1986).

A principal of school must be a leader with vision, one that stresses the development of human capital in the school. A prime responsibility of principals is to develop in their professional staffs an ethic of continual self-improvement, a pride in teaching, and a focus on quality. In the final analysis, the only people who can change the instruction in the classroom are the teachers themselves. Thus, ultimately the teacher must decide what changes are needed to improve student learning. Such change cannot be mandated; it must grow from within the professional. Principals cannot simply be managers. They must be leaders who can build a culture of openness, collegiality, confidence, and introspection among their teachers (Hoy and Forsyth, 1986).

❽ Drive out fear. Few, if any individuals, can put forth their highest level of performance in an atmosphere of constant fear. Mediocrity is the result when fear permeates the organization (Scherkenbach, 1992). People need to be secure if they are to perform well; they need to ask important questions, to challenge accepted practices, to take risks, and to be innovative. There is a reluctance, however, to embrace new knowledge and technology if insecurity pervades the workplace; in fact, change and improvement are most likely to thrive in organizations in which people are encouraged and rewarded for trying novel approaches. In such organizations, people are not afraid to try because failure is not fatal; innovation is viewed as a positive activity in which learning and improvement are the goals. Put simply, if we want teachers to grow, experiment, and continue to improve their professional practices, then we must drive out fear and create a school climate of trust and mutual respect (see Chapter 5).

❾ Break down barriers between departments. Teamwork and openness are hallmarks of quality. Teachers and administrators together need to attack the complex problem of improving teaching and learning. Teachers can ill afford to isolate themselves in the confines of traditional departments. Language skills are central to mathematics, and analytical skills are critical to language and social studies. Student problems cut across disciplines, and improvement of student learning is more often than not an interdisciplinary task. Schools must avoid artificial barriers that inhibit cooperation and teamwork. Structural features that foster isolation and extreme specialization are counterproductive to quality in schools (see Chapter 3).

❿ Eliminate slogans, exhortations, and targets for the workforce. Slogans and exhortations that urge teachers to be better are doomed to failure. Why? Because they are usually directed at the wrong people. As often as not, difficulties rest with the system—administration, procedures, structures—not with teachers per se. Slogans such as "Do it right the first time," "Be a quality teacher," and "Take pride in your teaching" all assume that teachers can do better simply by working harder. The exhortations mask administrative responsibility and organizational impediments and highlight teacher shortcomings. The slogans also generate frustration, cynicism, and resentment among teachers who see administrators as either naive about the complexity of their problems or, worse, as hiding behind a cloak of authority. When a problem exists, a slogan can always be found to mask the cause; slogans are not solutions.

⓫ Eliminate work standards and management by numbers. Work standards are numerical quotas for workers. They are typically used in industry to predict costs. But schools are also often managed by using standards and quotas. Teachers, for example, may be expected to spend a half an hour each day after school helping students or have all students in third grade reading at grade level. Such standards and virtually all numerical quotas are obstacles to improvement of quality and productivity because they tend to cap improvement. Once a teacher has reached the standard, there is little need to continue. Standards confuse an individual's understanding of the job. Effectiveness is judged by achieving some magical number. This is not a system that fosters continual improvement; it is a mechanical process that has negative consequences for quality. To use Deming's (1986:76) words, "Management by numerical goal is an attempt to manage without knowledge of what to do, and in fact is usually management by fear."

⑫ Remove barriers that rob people of pride of workmanship. If educational administrators want to meet student needs and fulfill parental expectations, they must examine their administrative practices and procedures with an eye to eliminating those that inhibit continuing improvement. Performance appraisal and merit rating are two such practices. Both focus attention on end products rather than on people and process, keys to system success.

For instance, the idea of merit pay is alluring. The rhetoric captures the imagination of school boards. "Pay higher teacher salaries only to good teachers." "Pay for what you get." "Pay teachers according to merit, not seniority." The results of merit salary programs in schools have been for the most part a disaster. Criteria for merit are ambiguous and produce claims of administrative favoritism, or they are clear, but focus on short-term goals at the expense of long-term outcomes. Merit rating rewards people who do well in the system, but it does not reward attempts to improve the system (Deming, 1983). In brief, performance-appraisal systems work against continual improvement because they destroy teamwork, reduce initiative and risk taking, and focus on the short term. The responsibility of administrators must shift from stressing numbers to producing quality. Rewards and ratings make teachers competitive; they work against each other rather than with each other. Teaching and learning become secondary. And ratings dominate and destroy motivation, morale, and pride in the craft of teaching.

⑬ Institute a program of education and self-improvement. For all organizations a program of education and self-improvement is indispensable to continued growth and development. Organizations must learn to reinvest in their members. People are an organization's most important asset. Organizations need not only good people but people who improve with education. In schools, most teachers have the promise of lifetime employment through tenure. Thus it is especially important for school administrators and teachers to continue to learn. After all, their business is learning and learning itself is a continuous process. Educators should not ask students to do anything that they are not willing to do themselves—continually learn and improve.

New techniques of teaching and managing need to be taught, learned, and tried within the context of the school. The school should be a laboratory for learning at all levels—student, teacher, and administrator. If there is one principle of total quality management that schools should excel in, it is to provide all members a sound program of training, education, and self-improvement. To be true to the Deming philosophy, such on-the-job education should be anchored in fostering teamwork and cooperation. It may be no accident that cooperative learning is one of the most widely respected and successful contemporary teaching innovations in schools today (Slavin, 1992).

⑭ Put everyone to work transforming the organization. Implementing the previous thirteen principles is no easy task. School administrators and teachers must first understand and agree with the philosophy and new responsibilities of the approach. The essence of the philosophy is that management should start stressing improvement of system processes and stop making ratings and judgments of results. Indeed, as Tveite (1991) has noted, half of Deming's management principles are directed at improving processes (principles 1, 2, 5, 6, 7, 13, 14) and the other half are directed to stopping judgments of results (principles 3, 4, 8, 9, 10, 11, 12).

Quality schools have as their purpose the continual improvement of learning and teaching. School administrators lead their schools by transforming the culture into one that emphasizes cooperation, trust, openness, and continuous improvement. Education and on-the-job training for teachers as well as administrators are essential if educators are to improve and regulate their own behavior. Not only administrators but everyone in the system, including students, teachers, and parents, must be committed to the goal of continual improvement.

Research, Theory, and Practice: Some Observations

Deming's principles of management seem applicable to schools. They are clearly consistent with the systems approach taken in this text; in fact, they reinforce many of the concepts that we have developed—for example, the importance of theory, knowledge, systems thinking, involvement, motivation, rational decision making, culture, and transformational leadership, to mention only a few. The close link between total quality management (TQM) and systems theory has been noted (Spencer, 1994). TQM does not abandon a rational systems approach in favor of a natural one, but rather, skillfully blends both in an open-systems perspective. For example, the Deming perspective describes organizations as systems embedded in a broader environment, which at the same time are concerned about making rational decisions as well as establishing a culture of participation and trust among employees.

Support for total quality management comes from success stories of managers of business corporations, first in Japan and more recently in the United States. There is little doubt that such Japanese corporations as Honda, Toyota, and Sony were highly successful in producing quality products in the 1980s. More recently, TQM has become a popular management approach in many of the *Fortune* 500 companies in America, including winners of the prestigious Malcolm Baldrige National Quality Award (Blackburn and Rosen, 1993; Lawler, 1992, 1994). Systematic research on the quality management approach has been neither as abundant nor as uncritical as its widespread acceptance might suggest (Lawler, 1994). Nevertheless, few researchers or scholars dispute the success of the approach. Total quality management is also becoming a widespread managerial technique in educational institutions.

Although some scholars (Gartner and Naughton, 1988) describe Deming's approach to management as his "theory of management," most agree that Deming's fourteen points are more aptly termed a "management philosophy" (Lawler, 1994) or a "management method" for improving administrative practice (Anderson, Rungtusanatham, and Schroeder, 1994). Nevertheless, Deming's fourteen points of total quality management (TQM) suggest an interesting set of concepts that might be developed into a theory of management. The challenge is to engage in empirical research to discover, or perhaps to invent, the underlying theory of quality management; such a theory will describe, explain, and predict the effects of adopting the Deming management method (Anderson, Rungtusanatham, and Schroeder, 1994).

Five propositions summarize some of the critical concepts undergirding the Deming approach. These propositions can be used to develop a tentative theoretical scheme to explain the success of total quality management (Anderson, Rungtusanatham, and Schroeder, 1994), as follows:

Proposition 1: Transformational leadership enables the simultaneous creation of a cooperative and a learning organization.

Proposition 2: An organization that simultaneously facilitates cooperation and learning enhances opportunities for process-management practices and limits management by results.

Proposition 3: Process-management practices simultaneously produce a press toward continuous improvement and employee fulfillment.

Proposition 4: An organization's simultaneous efforts at continuous improvement and employee fulfillment lead to higher client gratification.

Proposition 5: An organization's simultaneous efforts at continuous improvement and employee fulfillment lead to quality in processes, services, and products.

In brief, Deming's formulation of total quality management has provided renewed emphasis on a systems approach to organizations. The perspective shifts attention away from the effectiveness of results to the quality of all aspects of the system. Although systematic research on the formulation is sparse, it remains one of the most popular formulations of the 1990s. Finally, the concepts that underlie TQM provide researchers and theorists with rich conceptual capital to formulate a theory of management based on Deming's philosophy.

SUMMARY AND SUGGESTED READINGS

Organizational effectiveness and quality now play such central roles in the theory and practice of education that thorough understandings of the concepts are essential. Two general approaches, a goal perspective and a system-resource model, dominate the study of organizational effectiveness. Quality, like effectiveness, is a multidimensional construct that refers to continuous improvement in all phases of a system. Discussions on quality have begun to replace those on organizational effectiveness. This new emphasis in the organizational literature can be traced to the work of W. Edwards Deming and the success of Japanese industry during the 1980s.

Effectiveness is a more abstract and theoretical concept while quality seems to be a more pragmatic approach to the success of organizations; effectiveness and quality are two sides of the same coin.

Our review of the theory and research on quality and effectiveness leads us to conclude that simple measures of organizational outcomes are insufficient indicators of either effectiveness or quality. This should come as no surprise to those who use a systems approach to understand organizational behavior. Outcomes are only one part of the system and perhaps not the most important element. The inputs as well as the transformational process of the system are equal partners in determining both quality and effectiveness of schools.

We have proposed an integrated goal and system-resource model of school performance. The perspective addresses the importance of all aspects of a social system, including the effectiveness and quality of inputs, transformation process, and outcomes. This system sequence and the elements of environment, structure, individual, culture, and politics were first presented in Chapter 2. In Chapters 3 to 7, these system elements were elaborated. The concepts of effectiveness and quality in this chapter complete the sequence and provide the ends for which the elements of the system are the means.

School administrators can improve the quality and effectiveness of schools by using a number of other critical processes. We call these functions the big four: deciding, motivating, communicating, and leading. These are administrative processes that educators must employ effectively if they are to help develop quality schools. Thus, Chapter 9 to 12 of this book provide an in-depth examination of the theory, research, and practice in each of these areas.

Several sources are recommended to further your exploration of organizational effectiveness. Two classic treatments are Goodman and Penning's (1977) *New Perspectives on Organizational Effectiveness* and Cameron and Whetten's (1983) *Organizational Effectiveness*. They provide excellent sets of readings on the theoretical underpinning of the construct. Paul M. Mott (1972) develops a useful conceptualization and perceptual measure of effectiveness. For a contemporary review of job satisfaction, the recent work by Cranny, Smith, and Stone (1992) is a valuable resource. The roots of quality as a substitute for effectiveness can be traced to the work of W. Edwards Deming (1986). His *Out of Crisis* has become the bible for advocates of total quality management. S. C. Purkey and Marshall Smith's (1983) review of the literature remains a must reading for students interested in school effectiveness. Finally, Kim Cameron and David Whetten (1995) provide a recent comprehensive preview of the next generation of effectiveness and quality studies.

NOTES

1. Cameron and Whetten (1995) list seven common models of organization effectiveness. Our integrated model of organizational effectiveness uses four of the seven—goal, system resource, internal processes, and strategic constituencies.

2. The employment of input, transformation, and output phases of open-systems theory to identify effectiveness indicators seems to parallel Scott's (1992) use of structural capabilities, processes, and outcomes for the same purpose.

3. The following reviews of the production function literatures are recommended: Averich et al. (1972); Jamison, Suppes, and Wells (1974); Hanushek (1989); Lau (1978); Murnane (1981); MacKensie (1983); Rowen, Bossert, and Dwyer (1983); Monk (1992).

4. See, for example, the following sources: Brookover et al. (1978); Edmonds (1979); Madaus, Airasian, and Kellaghan (1980); Purkey and Smith (1983); Clark, Lotto, and Astuto (1984); Brophy and Good (1986); Good and Brophy (1986); Bossert (1988); Bryk (1993); and Lee, Bryk, and Smith (1993).

KEY CONCEPTS AND IDEAS

Constituency

Discrepancy model

Effective-schools research

Goal and system-resource model

Goal model

Input criteria

Job satisfaction

Official goals

Operative goals

Performance outcomes

Process-product research

Production-function model

Quality

Situational model

Structure and process criteria

System-resource model

Total quality management (TQM)

9 Deciding

The task of "deciding" pervades the entire administrative organization.
. . . A general theory of administration must include principles of
organization that will insure correct decision making, just as it must
include principles that will insure effective action.

—Herbert A. Simon
Administrative Behavior

PREVIEW

1. The classical decision-making model uses a strategy of optimizing to maximize the achievement of goals, but the model is an ideal rather than an actual description of practice.

2. Satisficing is a pragmatic decision-making strategy that some administrators use to solve the problems of practice.

3. Most administrators probably use an incremental model of deciding; they muddle through.

4. An adaptive strategy of deciding unites the rationalism and comprehensiveness of satisficing with the flexibility and utility of the incremental model.

5. Like most complex processes, however, there is no single best way to decide; the best approach is the one that best fits the circumstances: a contingency approach is proposed.

6. Not all organizational decisions are rational; the garbage can model helps explain nonrational decision making.

7. Irrationality in decision making is often produced by stress; the Janis-Mann conflict model describes the pitfalls of defective decision making.

8. Sometimes participation improves the quality of decisions; sometimes it does not. The Hoy-Tarter model suggests when and how to involve subordinates in decision making.

9. One of the dangers of group decision making is groupthink, shared illusions about the correctness and invulnerability of the group.

10. Groupthink can be avoided by understanding its causes and by appropriately structuring group decision making.

Decision making is a major responsibility of all administrators, but until decisions are converted into action they are only good intentions. Deciding is a sine qua non of educational administration because the school, like all formal organizations, is basically a decision-making structure. Our analysis begins with an examination of classical decision making.

THE CLASSICAL MODEL: AN OPTIMIZING STRATEGY

Classical decision theory assumes that decisions should be completely rational; it employs an **optimizing** strategy by seeking the best possible alternative to maximize the achievement of goals and objectives. According to the classical model, the decision-making process is a series of sequential steps:

1. A problem is identified.
2. Goals and objectives are established.
3. *All* the possible alternatives are generated.
4. The consequences of each alternative are considered.
5. All the alternatives are evaluated in terms of the goals and objectives.
6. The *best* alternative is selected—that is, the one that maximizes the goals and objectives.
7. Finally, the decision is implemented and evaluated.

The **classical model** is an ideal (a normative model), rather than a description of how most decision makers function (a descriptive model). Most scholars, in fact, consider the classical model an unrealistic ideal, if not naive. Decision makers virtually never have access to all the relevant information. Moreover, generating all the possible alternatives and their consequences is impossible. Unfortunately, the model assumes information-processing capacities, rationality, and knowledge that decision makers simply do not possess; consequently, it is not very useful to practicing administrators.

THE ADMINISTRATIVE MODEL: A SATISFICING STRATEGY

Given the severe limitations of the classical model, it should not be surprising that more realistic conceptual approaches to decision making in organizations have evolved. The complexity of most organizational problems and the limited capacity of the human mind make it virtually impossible to use an optimizing strategy on all but the simplest problems. Herbert Simon (1947) was first to introduce the **administrative model** of decision making to provide a more accurate description of the way administrators both do and should make organizational decisions.[1] The basic approach is **satisficing**—that is, finding a satisfactory solution rather than the best one. Before analyzing the satisficing strategy in detail, we examine the basic assumptions upon which it rests.

SOME BASIC ASSUMPTIONS[2]

Assumption 1. *The decision-making process is a cycle of events that includes the identification and diagnosis of a difficulty, the reflective development of a plan to alleviate the difficulty, the initiation of the plan, and the appraisal of its success.*

Decision making is a dynamic process that solves some problems and creates others. Specific decisions that foster the achievement of the organization's purposes frequently interfere with other conditions that are also important. Peter M. Blau and W. Richard Scott (1962: 250–251) explain that the process of decision making is dialectical:"problems appear, and while the process of solving them tends to give rise to new problems, learning has occurred which influences how the new challenges are met." Thus at best, decision making by thoughtful and skillful executives and their staffs should lead to more rational decisions, but it typically will not result in final decisions. The complex nature of organizations usually precludes that possibility.

In deciding, those with the responsibility must go through a sequence of steps:

- Recognize and define the problem or issue.
- Analyze the difficulties in the situation.
- Establish criteria for a satisfactory solution.
- Develop a strategy for action.
- Initiate a plan of action.

These steps will be developed, elaborated, and discussed in some detail later in this chapter.

Although the process is conceptualized as a sequential pattern because each step serves as a logical basis for the next, the process is also cyclical. Thus, decision making may be entered into at any stage. Moreover, the steps are taken again and again in the process of administering organizations.

Assumption 2. *Administration is the performance of the decision-making process by an individual or group in an organizational context.*

Being responsible for decision making, the administration exhibits a number of important attributes:

- It tends to perpetuate itself.
- It attempts to protect itself from disruption and destruction.
- It seeks to survive and is competitive.
- It seeks to progress and grow.

The impetus for growth is made not only on behalf of the organization but also on behalf of a specifically identifiable administration. Thus, administrators try to decide in ways that maintain internal integrity, enhance their position in relation to competing interests, and help their administration develop and expand (Litchfield, 1956).

Assumption 3. *Complete rationality in decision making is virtually impossible; therefore, administrators seek to satisfice because they do not have the ability and cognitive capacity to maximize the decision-making process.*

Effective administration requires rational decision making. Decisions are rational when they are appropriate for accomplishing specific goals. People typically try to make rational decisions (Tversky, 1969; Payne, Bettman, and Johnson, 1988). Administrative decisions, however, are often extremely complex, and their rationality is limited for a number of reasons. First, all the alternatives cannot be considered simply because there are too many options that do not come to mind. Second, all the probable consequences for each alternative cannot be anticipated because future events are exceedingly difficult to predict accurately and to evaluate realistically. Finally, rationality is limited not only by the administrators' information-processing capacities but also by their unconscious skills, habits, and reflexes as well as their values and conceptions of purpose that may deviate from the organization's goals (Simon 1947, 1991). In brief, individuals are not capable of making completely rational decisions on complex matters; hence, administrators are concerned with the selection and implementation of satisfactory alternatives rather than optimal ones. To use Simon's words, administrators "satisfice" rather than "optimize." Nonetheless, they continue to talk about finding the best solutions to problems. What is meant, of course, is the best of the satisfactory alternatives.

Administrators look for solutions that are "good enough." They recognize that their perception of the world is a drastically simplified model of the complex interacting forces that constitute the real world. They are content with this oversimplification because they believe that most real-world facts are not important to the particular problem(s) they face and that most significant chains of cause and effect are short and simple. Consequently, they are satisfied to ignore most aspects of reality because they consider them substantially irrelevant. Administrators make choices, then, using a simplified picture of reality that accounts for only a few of the factors that they consider most relevant and important (Simon, 1947).

Assumption 4. *The basic function of administration is to provide each subordinate with an internal environment of decision so that each person's behavior is rational from both individual and organizational perspectives.*

Because individuals cannot make completely rational decisions, administrators limit the scope of the decisions so that rationality can be approached. Organizations provide members with an environment of goals, objectives, and purposes. This environment narrows and defines the roles, thereby limiting the number of alternatives. According to Simon (1947), rational behavior consists of a means-ends chain. Given certain ends, appropriate means are selected, but once those ends are achieved, they in turn become means for further ends, and so on. After organizational objectives are agreed on, the administrative structure serves as a basis for the means-ends chains. To illustrate, once the ends for organizational members are defined by the directives from a superior, the subordinate's responsibility is primarily to determine the "best" means for attaining those ends. That pattern, along with procedural regulations, narrows the alternatives and establishes **bounded rationality.**

An individual's decision is rational if it is consistent with the values, alternatives, and information that were analyzed in reaching it. An organization's decision is rational if it is consistent with its goals, objectives, and information. Therefore, the organization must be constructed so that a decision that is rational for the individual remains rational for the organization when reassessed from the organizational perspective (Simon, 1957b).

Assumption 5. *Decision making is a general pattern of action found in the rational administration of all major functional and task areas.*

The specific tasks of school administration can be catalogued in a number of ways. School administrators are responsible for the following areas: curriculum and instruction; negotiations; physical facilities; finance and business; pupil personnel; evaluation and supervision; recruitment, selection, and retention of employees; and public relations.

Decision making is essential not only for these tasks but also in the broader functional areas of administration. Edward H. Litchfield (1956) has identified three broad, functional areas of administration—policy, resources, and execution. A **policy** is a general statement of objectives that guide organizational actions. The key resources of administration are people, money, authority, and materials. Execution is the integration of resources and policy necessary to achieve a purposeful organization.

The policy function is often termed "policy making" or "policy formulation," but it is substantially more.[3] Policies are not only formulated but also programmed, communicated, monitored, and evaluated. Policy making is a special instance of decision making in which issues revolve around policy matters. The rational process of deciding also is the vehicle for resource allocation. In determining the need for personnel, supplies, physical facilities, and monies, the administrator is confronted with difficulties and problems that require both deliberate and reflective choice and implementation—the use of the action cycle of the decision-making process. Finally, the cycle is repeated in performing the executive function. In order to allocate and integrate the resources consistent with policy mandates and to accommodate conflicting values and tendencies, the executive attempts to administer the system through a continuous series of the cyclical actions that constitute the decision-making process (Litchfield, 1956).

Not only is the action cycle the same regardless of functional area, but each of the functions is a requisite of the total process. Furthermore, although policy helps shape the character of the resource and executive functions, resources have an equally important impact on policies, and execution can lead to effective implementation of policy or can undermine its very existence. Hence, these three functional areas are interdependent (Litchfield, 1956).

Assumption 6. *The decision-making process occurs in substantially the same generalized form in most complex organizations.*

The cyclical evolution of rational, deliberate, purposeful action—beginning with the development of a decision strategy and moving through implementation and appraisal of results—occurs in all types of organizations (Litchfield, 1956). The structure of the process is the same in, for example, military, industrial, educational, or health services organizations. The universality of rational decision making calls attention to the fact that essentially it is the same regardless of specific context.

Educational organizations are different from industrial organizations in a great many substantive and important ways. For example, the technologies and the products are quite different. Yet the decision-making process in the areas of policy, resources, and execution are substantively the same.

DECISION-MAKING PROCESS: AN ACTION CYCLE

The specific sequence of steps in the decision-making process have already been outlined. The action cycle of that process is illustrated in Figure 9.1. Many decision-making action cycles may be occurring simultaneously. One elaborate cycle, regarding fundamental goals and objectives (strategic planning), may be proceeding at the level of the board of education, while smaller and related sequential cycles, regarding curriculum and instruction, pupil personnel services, finance and business management, and facilities planning, may be progressing at the district level.

Let us turn to a more detailed analysis of each step in the action cycle.[4]

Step I. Recognize and Define the Problem or Issue

The recognition of a difficulty or disharmony in the system is the first step in the decision-making process. Effective administrators are sensitive to organizational actions and attitudes that do not measure up to the prescribed standards. The common retort, "We don't have problems; we have answers," is symptomatic of insensitive administrators who are headed for trouble. Although it may be possible for them to maintain equilibrium in the organization over the short run, the likelihood of organizational chaos over the long run seems great.

The recognition and definition of a problem are crucial to deciding and often do not receive adequate attention. The way a problem is conceptualized is important to subsequent analysis and solution. Not only are sensitivity and perceptual acuteness in the administrator necessary, but a rich conceptual background and a thorough understanding of formal and informal organizations are desirable in framing the problem. Too often administrators define problems quickly and narrowly and, in so doing, restrict their options. They treat only the symptoms of the problems, not the problem itself. For example, the response to a request from a teacher group for more

FIGURE **9.1**

Decision-Making Action Cycle

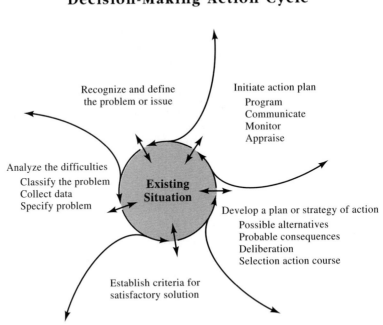

autonomy in selecting curricular materials can be seen by a principal as an attempt to undermine administrative authority. The problem so conceived yields a set of alternatives that likely will be unduly narrow and restrictive. Such a teacher request, however, can open up a host of positive, creative possibilities for long-range curriculum development. This example, coincidentally, underscores the importance of security and confidence; the secure and confident administrator is unlikely to view such a teacher request as a threat to his or her authority.

During this first stage in the process, it is important to place the problem in perspective. If the problem is complex, its definition likewise will be complicated, perhaps multidimensional. The problem may need to be broken down into subproblems, with each subproblem cycled through the decision-making process. Furthermore, the problem may require several solutions. For instance, the problem of districting in a school system, where large numbers of parents want their children in school X rather than Y, may be settled in the short run by a policy statement indicating that a child will be assigned to a school solely on the basis of geographical location. The long-run solution, however, might well involve equalizing educational opportunities and improving the program of instruction in one or more schools.[5]

In deciding, the executive does not necessarily merely react to existing problems. Effective administrators are constantly alert to issues that might become problems. In that way they can adopt a course of action that will prevent problems as well as promote organizational health and growth.

Step 2. Analyze the Difficulties in the Existing Situation

This stage of the decision-making process is directly related to the first stage; in fact, some writers prefer to combine definition and analysis. However, analysis calls for the classification of the problem. Is the problem unique? Or is it a new manifestation of a typical difficulty for which a pattern of action has already been developed?

Chester I. Barnard (1938) distinguished three kinds of decisions based on where the need for them originates. Intermediary decisions arise from authoritative communications from superiors that relate to the interpretation, application, or distribution of instruction; appellate decisions grow out of cases referred by subordinates; and creative decisions originate in the initiative of the executive concerned.

In contrast, Peter F. Drucker (1966) proposed two basic kinds of decisions—generic or unique. **Generic decisions** arise from established principles, policies, or rules. Indeed, recurring problems are routinely solved by formulaic rules and regulations. A great many of the intermediary or appellate decisions that confront school principals (indeed, all middle-level administrators) are generic. That is, the organization has established mechanisms and procedures for dealing with problems. This does not mean, however, that they are unimportant; it simply means that they belong to a general group of organizational problems that frequently occur and that the organization wants to be prepared to deal with. Such decisions are needed when a principal implements policy mandated by the board, monitors absenteeism among teachers, mediates student-teacher conflicts, and interprets disciplinary procedures. All these generic decisions can be intermediary or appellate decisions (originating from above or below the principal in the hierarchy). In all cases the principal should be able to handle the situation by applying the appropriate rule, principle, or policy to the concrete circumstances of the case.

Unique decisions, however, are probably creative decisions that require going beyond established procedures for a solution; in fact, they may require a modification of the organizational structure. Here the decision maker deals with an exceptional problem that is not adequately answered by a general principle or rule. Creative decisions quite often change the basic thrust or direction of an organization. In order to seek a creative solution, decision makers explore all ideas that are relevant to the problem.

A unique decision might arise when principal and staff work to resolve a curricular issue where there are no established guidelines. The superintendent may specifically request an innovative solution. Completely unique events are rare; nevertheless, the distinction between problems that are routine and those that are unique is an important one in terms of deciding. Two common mistakes administrators need to guard against are:

- Treating a routine situation as if it were a series of unique events
- Treating a new event as if it were just another old problem to which old procedures should be applied

Once the problem has been classified as generic or unique, the administrator is in a position to address a number of other questions. How important is the problem? Can the problem be more fully specified? What information is needed to specify the problem? The original definition of a problem is usually global and general. After classifying and determining the importance of the problem, the decision maker begins to define more precisely the problem and issues involved. This entails the need for information. The amount of information that should be collected depends on a number of factors, including the importance of the problem, time constraints, and existing procedures and structure for data collection. The more important the problem, the more information the decision maker gathers. Time, of course, is almost always a constraint. Finally, the existing procedures for data collection may facilitate or prohibit the search for relevant information.

In brief, decision makers need relevant facts. What is involved? Why is it involved? Where is it involved? When? To what extent? Answers to these questions provide information to map the parameters of the problem. Such information can be collected in formal, sophisticated ways, making use of operations research and computer facilities, as well as in informal ways, through personal contacts, by telephone, or in conversations.

Step 3. Establish Criteria for a Satisfactory Solution

After the problem has been analyzed and specified, the decision maker must decide what constitutes an acceptable solution. What are the minimum objectives that are to be achieved? What are the musts compared to the wants? It is not unusual for the perfect solution in terms of outcomes to be unfeasible. What is good enough? Answers to such questions help the decision maker establish his or her aspiration level. That is, what are the criteria for a satisfactory decision? At this point, sometimes the decision maker will rank possible outcomes along a continuum from minimally satisfying to maximally satisfying; a completely satisfactory outcome usually does not remain after compromise, adaptation, and concession.

Criteria of adequacy need to be specified early so that the decision maker knows that a "right" decision is being made and not just one that will be accepted. In general, the criteria used to judge the decision should be consistent with the organization's mission. What we have referred to as criteria of adequacy, scientists often refer to as **boundary conditions**—the limits that the decision maker must meet if the decision is to be judged satisfactory.

Step 4. Develop a Plan or Strategy for Action

This is the central step in the process. After recognizing the problem, collecting data, and specifying the problem and its boundary conditions, decision makers develop a systematic and reflective plan of action. The process involves at least the following steps:

- Specify alternatives.
- Predict the consequences of each alternative.
- Deliberate.
- Select a plan of action.

Before we proceed to analyze each of these steps, several limitations need to be reiterated. Administrators base their plans of action on simplified pictures of reality; they choose the factors that they regard as most relevant and crucial; and thus they are able to come to some general conclusions and take actions without becoming paralyzed by the facts that "could be" indirectly related to the immediate problems. In describing the art of administrative decision making, Barnard (1938) warns:

- Do not decide questions that are not pertinent.
- Do not decide prematurely.
- Do not make decisions that cannot be effective.
- Do not make decisions that others should make.

The search for alternatives to solve a particular organizational problem is called **problemistic search.** It is distinguished from random curiosity and from the search for understanding per se (Cyert and March, 1963; Bass, 1985). Problemistic search is straightforward, usually reflecting simplified notions of causality, and based on two simple rules:

- Search in the area of the problem symptom(s).
- Search in the area of the current alternative(s).

When these two rules do not produce enough reasonable alternatives, expand the search. Problemistic search probably is the dominant style of administrators; hence, most decision making is reactive.

But deciding need not be reactive. James D. Thompson (1967) has suggested that it is possible to develop behavior-monitoring procedures to search the environment for opportunities that are not activated by a problem. He calls this process **opportunistic surveillance;** it is the organizational counterpart of curiosity in the individual. Obviously, a decision-making structure that encourages opportunistic surveillance is more desirable than one that allows for only problemistic search.

SPECIFYING ALTERNATIVES A preliminary step in formulating an intention to act is to list all possible alternatives. In actuality, only some of the options are specified because, as we have noted earlier, people do not have the information-processing capacity to think of all alternatives. Nonetheless, advancing a greater number of choices increases the likelihood of finding satisfactory alternatives that meet the already specified conditions.

Creative decision makers are able to develop unique, viable alternatives, an often time-consuming task. Unfortunately, too many administrators do not take the time to develop a comprehensive set of possible options; they see the solution as a simple dichotomy—it is either this or that. Don't be overly impressed with speed in deciding; it is often a symptom of sloppy thinking. The impact of a solution is much more important than the technique. Educational organizations need sound decisions, not clever techniques.

Time is necessary to develop a comprehensive set of alternatives, yet time is limited. Consider as your first alternative doing nothing. Once in a great while, such an alternative turns out to solve the problem; things work themselves out. Unfortunately, most problems do not just work themselves out, but the decision not to decide should always be reflectively considered.

Another choice available is the use of temporary alternatives that do not really solve the problem but do provide more time for further deliberation. Temporary alternatives, once refined and more completely thought through, are often the basis for more elaborate proposals. The key in developing preliminary and temporary alternatives is that, if successful, they buy time without creating hostility. There is always the danger that options that buy time will be seen as stalling; hence, buying time should be used sparingly and adroitly.

Routine decisions often can be handled quickly and effectively. Unique decisions demand more thoughtful and creative decision making. Creative thinking is of particular value in generating options. To think creatively, individuals must be able to reduce external inhibitions on the thinking process, to make relativistic and nondogmatic distinctions, to be willing not only to consider but to express irrational impulses, and to be secure and amenable to brainstorming. Of course, the climate and culture (see Chapter 5) of the organization can either inhibit or facilitate creative thinking.

In brief, the development of effective solutions typically requires:

- A willingness to make fewer black-and-white distinctions
- The use of divergent and creative thinking patterns
- Time to develop as many reasonable alternatives as possible

PREDICTING CONSEQUENCES For each alternative that is developed, probable consequences should be proposed. Although for analytic purposes we have treated specifying alternatives and predicting consequences as separate operations, they usually occur simultaneously. The formulation of alternatives and probable consequences is a good place to use groups—pooling brainpower and experience to make predictions as accurately as possible. By and large, predicting consequences to proposed alternatives is hazardous. On some issues—for example, those involving financial costs—accurate predictions of consequences can be made; however, when trying to anticipate the reactions of individuals or groups, the results typically are much more problematic.

Predicting consequences underscores the need for a good management-information system, and those school structures that have built-in capacities to collect, codify, store, and retrieve information have a distinct advantage in the decision-making process. In addition, consulting with a number of individuals who are in a position to know improves one's predictive power. For each decision alternative, the consequences can be predicted only in terms of probable rather than certain outcomes.

DELIBERATING AND SELECTING THE COURSE OF ACTION The final phase of developing a strategy for action involves a reflective analysis of the alternatives and consequences. Sometimes it is helpful to list all the alternatives with their accompanying probable consequences in a probability-event chain (see Figure 9.2). The figure is read as follows: Alternative A has three possible consequences (C_1A, C_2A, C_3A), and the probability of each of these consequences occurring is designated $P(C_1A)$, $P(C_2A)$, $P(C_3A)$. Although this procedure may not be completed for each problem-solving issue, every option typically has a number of consequences, each with a certain probability, that should be considered.

In the deliberation, prior to selecting the appropriate alternatives, decision makers carefully weigh the probable consequences of each alternative in light of the criteria for a satisfactory solution. After such reflection, they choose the "best" alternative or select a series of alternatives that are linked in some sequential order, which

FIGURE **9.2**

Example of Probability Event Chain

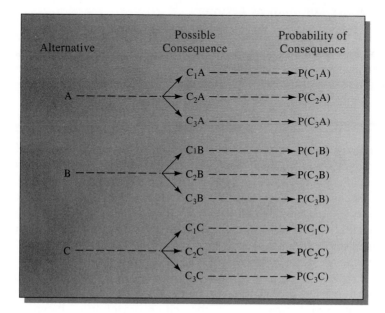

provides a strategy and plan of action; the more problematic the issue, the more likely a complex course of action.

To illustrate the planning of strategy, let us simplify the procedure. It may be possible to set up a strategy several moves in advance, just as a good chess player does. Alternative A may result in a positive and acceptable solution; however, if it does not, the decision maker goes to alternative B and, if need be, to alternative C, and so on, provided the probable consequences are still satisfactory. Of course, unanticipated consequences may require a rethinking of viable alternatives.

Occasionally decision makers cannot find an acceptable alternative. A reduction in the aspiration level may be necessary; that is, the criteria for a satisfactory solution are reconsidered (return to step 3). A new set of objectives, new alternatives, new data, and a new and more feasible strategy may have to be formulated. In the process of searching for satisfactory alternatives, decision makers seek to keep the activity manageable by using simplified decision rules called **heuristics**—simple rules of thumb that guide the decision making.[6] For example, rules about when to take a "hit" in blackjack or when to bet with the house or when to search for more information in decision making are heuristics.

Obviously, a large number of factors mediate the choice of a preferred alternative or alternatives. The values of the administrator, the cultural context in which the decision is made and implemented, the perceptions of those involved, the importance of the situation, the pressure on the decision maker, and the importance of the goal—all of these and other factors intervene in the selection of a final course of action. Nonetheless, deliberate, rational, and reflective decisions generally result from following a systematic sequence of steps.

Step 5. Initiate the Plan of Action

Once the decision has been made and a plan of action formulated, the decision needs to be implemented—the final element in the decision-making cycle. The initiation of the plan of action requires at least four steps: programming, communicating, monitoring, and appraising.

PROGRAMMING Decisions must be translated and interpreted into specific programs—that is, the mechanics and specific details for implementing the plan must be specified. For example, the plan to change the system of grading elementary school students contains a specific and detailed set of operations that require answers to a number of questions. Who has to have information about the plan? What actions need to be taken and by whom? What preparation is needed so that those who have to take action can do so? The action that is to be programmed must be appropriate to the abilities of the people involved. In brief, the program must be realistic and capable of implementation.

What we call "programming" others have called "program planning"—the activity designed to implement decisions. Program planning can be accomplished through a wide range of specific methods and techniques. Which ones are used depends on the sophistication and capabilities of the school organization. Programming may include budgeting, setting behavioral objectives, using network-based management techniques, and specifying other ways of translating a decision into specific programs for allocating authority and human resources.

COMMUNICATING Once the plan has been programmed, it is necessary that each involved individual become aware of his or her responsibilities. Channels of communication among the individuals as well as opportunities for communicating both horizontally and vertically must be given careful attention. For a program to be successful, individuals need to know clearly not only what their own roles are but also the roles of others as they relate to the total plan. Otherwise, efforts may be duplicated, counterproductive, or ineffective. The communication system developed to implement the plan in large part can and should be a crucial mechanism to initiate action and to enhance coordination of the program. Communicating is discussed in detail in Chapter 11.

MONITORING The process of overseeing the implementation of the plan of action is monitoring. Evaluation and reporting must be built into the action cycle to provide continuous assessment of actual outcomes as compared to expected ones. Monitoring is a control process using systematic feedback. Standards of performance, once they are set, need to be enforced. Enforcement does not necessarily mean coercive control. There are many techniques of control such as rewards and incentives, persuasion, and identification with organizational goals. Different modes of control and enforcement are more or less effective depending on the situation and the individuals involved. Continuous feedback is necessary to evaluate the progress of implementing the plan of action.

APPRAISING Once the decision has been programmed, communicated, and monitored, the outcomes still need to be appraised to determine how successful the decision has been. Has the decision been a satisfactory one? What new issues or problems have arisen? Decisions commonly are made in situations where probabilities, not certainties, are weighed. Even the most carefully conceived and executed decisions can fail or become obsolete. Organizational decisions are made in a context of change—facts, values, and circumstances change. Therefore, a fully articulated decision—one that has been reflectively made, programmed, communicated, and monitored—in itself brings about sufficient change to necessitate its own further reevaluation and appraisal (Litchfield, 1956). Hence, the appraisal stage is both an end and a new beginning in the action cycle of decision making. Clearly, there are no ultimate solutions—only satisfactory decisions and solutions for the moment.

THE INCREMENTAL MODEL: A STRATEGY OF SUCCESSIVE LIMITED COMPARISONS

Although the satisficing strategy that we have just described in detail is well suited to dealing with many problems in educational administration, occasionally some situations require an incremental strategy. When relevant alternatives are difficult to discern or the consequences of each alternative are so complicated as to elude prediction, even satisficing does not work well (Grandori, 1984). For example, to what new activities should a school administrator allocate more resources? The answer to this question is probably more adequately addressed by considering only alternatives that differ marginally from existing conditions. The underlying assumption of the strategy is that small incremental changes will not produce major unanticipated negative consequences for the organization.

Charles Lindblom (1959, 1965, 1968, 1980; Braybrook and Lindblom 1963; Lindblom and Cohen, 1979) first introduced and formalized the incremental strategy. He characterizes this method of deciding as the science of **muddling through** and argues that it may be the only feasible approach to systematic decision making when the issues are complex, uncertain, and riddled with conflict. The process is best described as a method of successive limited comparisons. Deciding does not require objectives, exhaustive analysis of alternatives and consequences, or *a priori* determination of either optimum or satisfactory outcomes. Instead only a small and limited set of alternatives, similar to the existing situation, is considered by successively comparing their consequences until decision makers come to some agreement on a course of action.

This incremental approach has a number of important features. First, the setting of objectives and the generation of alternatives are not separate activities. Goals and objectives are not established prior to decision analysis. Rather, a feasible course of action emerges as alternatives and consequences of action are explored. The more complex the problems, the more likely objectives will change as the decision evolves. Thus, the marginal differences in value among alternative courses of action serve as the basis for deciding rather than do any prior objectives.

The **incremental model** also greatly reduces the number of alternatives. The strategy considers only alternatives that are very similar to the existing situation, analyzes only differences between the current state and proposed outcomes, and ignores all outcomes that are outside the decision maker's narrow range of interest. With this approach, the complexity of the decision making is dramatically reduced and made manageable. Lindblom (1959) argues that this simplification of analysis, achieved by concentrating on alternatives that differ only slightly, is not capricious; simplifying by limiting the focus to small variations from existing situations merely makes the most of available knowledge. Administrators who limit themselves to a reasonable set of alternatives based on their experience can make predictions of consequences with accuracy and confidence. Moreover, by emphasizing only differences among alternatives, time and energy are conserved. The narrow focus on outcomes avoids possible paralysis caused by attempts to predict and analyze all possible outcomes of a specific course of action.

Finally, successive comparison is often an alternative to theory. In both the classical and the administrative models, theory is viewed as a useful way to bring relevant knowledge to bear on specific problems. As problems become increasingly complex, however, the inadequacies of our theories to guide deciding become more prevalent. The strategy of successive limited comparisons suggests that, in such complex situations, decision makers make more progress if they successively compare concrete practical alternatives rather than emphasize more abstract, theoretical analyses.

In brief, the incremental approach has the following distinctive features:

- Means-end analysis is inappropriate because setting objectives and generating alternatives occur simultaneously.

- Good solutions are those upon which decision makers agree regardless of objectives.

- Alternatives and outcomes are drastically reduced by considering only options similar to the current state of affairs.

- Analysis is restricted to differences between the existing situation and proposed alternatives.

- The incremental method eschews theory in favor of successive comparisons of concrete, practical alternatives.

THE MIXED-SCANNING MODEL: AN ADAPTIVE STRATEGY

Although widely used, muddling through has its limitations: it is conservative and aimless (Hoy and Tarter, 1995). Yet most administrators make decisions with only partial information and under the press of time. Amitai Etzioni (1967, 1986, 1989) offers a model of decision making that is a pragmatic approach to complexity and uncertainty. His adaptive model, or **mixed-scanning model,** is a synthesis of the administrative and incremental models that we have just described (Thomas, 1984; Wiseman, 1979a, 1979b).

Mixed scanning involves two questions:

- What is the organization's mission and policy?
- What decisions will move the organization toward its mission and policy?

Mixed scanning seeks to use partial information to make satisfactory decisions without either getting bogged down examining all the information or proceeding blindly with little or no information.[7] This **adaptive strategy** is "a mixture of shallow and deep examination of data—generalized consideration of a broad range of facts and choices followed by detailed examination of a focused subset of facts and choices" (Etzioni, 1989: 124). Higher-order, fundamental decision making (mission or policy decisions) is combined with lower-order, incremental decisions that work out the higher-order ones (Etzioni, 1986; Goldberg, 1975; Haynes, 1974). Mixed scanning unites the rationalism and comprehensiveness of the administrative model with the flexibility and utility of the incremental model.

As we have suggested, there are times when alternatives are difficult to discern and when consequences are hard to predict. In these situations, administrators often muddle through. Their incremental decisions are tentative or remedial—small steps taken in directions not far afield from the existing state. Such decision making has its downside, however; it is patently conservative and often without direction. That is, unless decision makers evaluate these incremental decisions in terms of some broad, fundamental policy, drift is likely. Broad guidelines, however, are not incrementally formulated; in fact, they have all the trappings of grand, a priori, decisions, which incrementalism seeks to avoid (Etzioni, 1989).

The mixed-scanning model has its roots in medicine. It is the way effective physicians make decisions. Unlike incrementalists, doctors know what they are trying to achieve and on which parts of the organism to focus attention. Moreover, unlike decision makers who seek to optimize, they do not engage all their resources on the basis of an initial diagnosis, nor do they wait for every conceivable bit of personal history and scientific data before beginning treatment. Doctors survey the symptoms of a patient, analyze the difficulty, initiate a tentative treatment, and, if it fails, they try something else (Etzioni, 1989).

The principles for mixed scanning are straightforward; in fact, Etzioni (1989) advances seven basic rules for a mixed-scanning strategy, which Wayne Hoy and John Tarter (1995) have summarized as follows:

1. *Use focused trial and error.* First, search for reasonable alternatives; then select, implement, and test them; and finally, adjust and modify as the outcomes become clear. Focused trial and error assumes that, despite the fact that important information is missing, the administrator must act. Thus, decisions are made with partial information and then carefully monitored and modified in light of new data.

2. *Be tentative; proceed with caution.* Be ready to modify a course of action as necessary. It is important that administrators view each decision as experimental, expecting to revise it.

3. *If uncertain, procrastinate.* Waiting is not always bad. When the situation is ambiguous, delay as long as possible so that more information can be collected and analyzed before taking action. Complexity and uncertainty frequently justify delay.

4. *Stagger your decisions.* Commit to a decision in stages, evaluating the outcomes of each phase before proceeding to the next phase.

5. *If uncertain, fractionalize decisions.* Staggered decisions can be tested in parts. Do not invest all your resources to implement a decision, but instead use partial resources until the consequences are satisfactory.

6. *Hedge your bets.* Implement several competing alternatives, provided that each has satisfactory outcomes. Then make adjustments based on results.

7. *Be prepared to reverse your decision.* Try to keep decisions tentative and experimental. Reversible decisions avoid overcommitment to a course of action when only partial information is available.

All of these adaptive techniques can be skillfully employed by educational administrators; all illustrate flexibility, caution, and a capacity to proceed with partial knowledge.

In sum, the mixed-scanning model has the following distinctive features:

- Broad, organizational policy gives direction to tentative incremental decisions.
- Good decisions have satisfactory outcomes that are consistent with organizational policy and mission.
- The search for alternatives is limited to those close to the problem.
- Analysis is based on the assumption that important information is missing but action is imperative.
- Theory, experience, and successive comparisons are used together.

The major differences in the four models of decision making—classical, administrative, incremental, and mixed scanning—are compared in Table 9.1.

TABLE **9.1**	Comparison of the Classical, Administrative, Incremental, and Mixed-Scanning Models of Decision Making		
Classical	**Administrative**	**Incremental**	**Mixed Scanning**
Objectives are set prior to generating alternatives.	Objectives are usually set prior to generating alternatives.	Setting objectives and generating alternatives are intertwined.	Broad policy guidelines are set prior to generating alternatives.
Decision making is a means-ends analysis: first, ends are determined, and then the means to obtain them are sought.	Decision making is typically means-ends analysis; however, occasionally ends change as a result of analysis.	Since means and ends are not separable, means-ends analysis is inappropriate.	Decision making is focused on broad ends and tentative means.
The test of a good decision is that it is shown to be the best means to achieve the end.	The test of a good decision is that it can be shown to result in a satisfactory means to achieve the end; it falls within the established boundary conditions.	The test of a good decision is that decision makers can agree an alternative is in the "right" direction when the existing course proves to be wrong.	The test of a good decision is that it can be shown to result in a satisfactory decision that is consistent with the organization's policy.
(Optimizing)	(Satisficing)	(Successive comparing)	(Adaptive satisficing)
Engage in comprehensive analysis; all alternatives and all consequences are considered.	Engage in "problemistic search" until a set of reasonable alternatives is identified.	Drastically limit the search and analysis; focus on alternatives similar to the existing state. Many alternatives and important outcomes are ignored.	Limit the search and analysis to alternatives close to the problem, but evaluate tentative alternatives in terms of broad policy. More comprehensive than incrementalism.
Heavy reliance on theory.	Reliance on both theory and experience.	Successive comparisons reduce or eliminate the need for theory.	Theory, experience, and successive comparisons used together.

THE RIGHT STRATEGY FOR THE SITUATION

We have proposed four decision-making models thus far. Which is the best way to decide? There is no best way to decide just as there is no best way to organize, to teach, to do research, or to do myriad other tasks. As in most complex tasks, the best approach is the one that best matches the circumstances—a contingency approach.

The decision strategies can be ordered according to their capacity to deal with complexity and conditions of increasing uncertainty and conflict (Grandori, 1984). When decisions are simple, information complete and certain, and a collective preference (no conflict) exists, then an optimizing strategy is most appropriate. As we have already noted, however, organizational problems are almost never simple, certain, and without conflict in preferences. Even in the case of the traditional application of the classical model—the economic theory of competitive decision—questions abound concerning its suitability.

When uncertainty and conflict prevail, as is typically the case in administrative decision making, a satisficing strategy becomes appropriate. The administrative model is flexible and heuristic. Decisions are based on comparisons among consequences of alternatives and the decision maker's aspiration level. Only a partial exploration of the alternatives is performed until a satisfactory course of action is discovered. If satisfactory solutions are not found, then the aspiration level is lowered.

When alternatives are difficult if not impossible to discern or consequences are so complicated as to elude prediction, even a satisficing strategy has its limits. In such situations an incremental strategy may be appropriate because it deals with both uncertainty and conflict of interest by assuming that small changes will not produce large negative consequences for the organization (Grandori, 1984). Thus, when the organization is in turmoil and without direction, the incremental approach may be the appropriate short-run strategy.

Some students of organization (Starkie, 1984; Etzioni, 1989), however, argue that even when the decisions are complex and outcomes are difficult to predict, incrementalism is too conservative and self-defeating. Small, incremental decisions made without guidelines lead to drift—to action without direction. Instead, mixed scanning or adaptive decision making is recommended to deal with exceedingly complex decisions. Mixed scanning combines the best of both the satisficing and the incremental models; a strategy of satisficing is combined with incremental decisions guided by broad policy. Full scanning is replaced by partial scanning of a set of satisfactory options, and tentative and reversible decisions are emphasized in an incremental process that calls for caution as well as a clear sense of destination.

We have suggested that the appropriate decision model depends upon the amount of information and the complexity of the situation. A summary guide for matching the appropriate decision models with situations is found in Table 9.2.

THE GARBAGE CAN MODEL: NONRATIONAL DECISION MAKING

Individuals and institutions sometimes need ways of doing things for which there are no good reasons. Not always, not even usually, but occasionally people need to

| TABLE **9.2** | Matching the Right Decision Strategy with the Appropriate Circumstance |

Strategy	Appropriate Circumstance
Optimizing ⟶	Narrow, simple problems with complete information and certain outcomes.
Satisficing ⟶	Complex problems with partial information, uncertainty, but with definable satisfactory outcomes and adequate time to deliberate.
Muddling Through ⟶	Incomplete information, complex problems, outcomes uncertain, no guiding policy, and general organizational chaos.
Adaptive Satisficing ⟶	Incomplete information, complex problems, outcomes uncertain, but a guiding policy and mission.

act before they think (March, 1982, 1994). The so-called **garbage can model** describes this tendency, which is most likely to occur in organizations that experience extremely high uncertainty. Michael Cohen, James March, and Johan Olsen (1972), the originators of the model, call such organizations organized anarchies. These organizations are characterized by *problematic preferences, unclear technology, and fluid participation.* That is, ambiguity accompanies each step of the decision process; cause-and-effect relationships within the organization are virtually impossible to determine; and there is a rapid turnover in participants and time is limited for any one problem or decision. Although no organization fits this extremely organic and loosely coupled system all the time, the model is often useful for *understanding* the pattern of decisions for situations of organized anarchy.

The basic feature of the garbage can model is that the decision process does not begin with a problem and end with a solution; rather, decisions are a product of independent streams of events in the organization (Cohen, March, and Olsen, 1972; Cohen and March, 1974; March, 1982; Estler, 1988; Daft, 1989). The following four streams are particularly relevant for organizational decision making in organized anarchies:

- *Problems* are points of dissatisfaction that need attention; however, problems are distinct from solutions and choices. A problem may or may not lead to a solution and problems may or may not be solved when a solution is adopted.
- *Solutions* are ideas proposed for adoption, but they can exist independently of problems. In fact, the attractiveness of an idea can produce a search for a problem to justify the idea. Cohen and colleagues (1972: 3) argue that "Despite the dictum that you cannot find the answer until you have formulated the question well, you often do not know what the question is in organizational problem solving until you know the answer."

- *Participants* are organizational members who come and go. Since personnel is fluid, problems and solutions can change quickly.

- *Choice opportunities* are occasions when organizations are expected to make decisions—for example, contracts must be signed, people hired and fired, money spent, and resources allocated.

Within these four streams of events, the overall pattern of organizational decision making takes on a quality of randomness. Organizational decision makers do not perceive that something is occurring about which a decision is necessary until the problem matches one with which they already have had some experience (Hall, 1987). When problems and solutions happen to match, a decision may occur. An administrator who has a good idea may suddenly find a problem to solve. When a problem, solution, and participant just happen to connect at one point, a decision may be made and the problem may be solved, but it will not be solved if the solution does not fit the problem. In the garbage can model, organizations are viewed as a set of choices looking for problems, issues and feelings looking for decision arenas in which they might be aired, solutions looking for questions to which they might be answers, and decision makers looking for work (Cohen, March, and Olsen, 1972).

The garbage can model helps explain why solutions may be proposed to problems that don't exist; why choices are made without solving problems; why problems persist without being solved; and why few problems are solved. Events may be so poorly defined and complex that problems, solutions, participants, and choice opportunities act as independent events. When they mesh, some problems are solved, but in this chaotic decision process many problems are not solved—they simply persist (Daft, 1989). Undoubtedly the garbage can metaphor contains elements of truth, and it appears to be an apt description of the way decisions are reached in some situations but not in others. The model has received support in a number of studies of different kinds of organizations (Sproull, Weiner, and Wolf, 1978; Bromiley, 1985; Levitt and Nass, 1989), but other recent research has questioned its utility as a *general* model of decision making, even in organizations of complexity, uncertainty, discontinuity, and power politics (Janis and Mann, 1977; Padgett, 1980; Hickson et al., 1986; Pinfield, 1986; Heller et al., 1988).

In brief, the garbage can model has the following distinctive features:

- Organizational objectives emerge spontaneously; they are not set before hand.

- Means and ends exist independently; chance or happenstance connects them.

- A good decision occurs when a problem matches a solution.

- The decision relies more on chance than rationality.

- Administrators scan existing solutions, problems, participants, and opportunities looking for matches.

The garbage can metaphor is a description of how decisions sometimes occur; it is not a suggestion for action.

JANIS-MANN CONFLICT THEORY: STRESS AND IRRATIONALITY IN DECISION MAKING

Regardless of which decision-making strategy is employed, the pressures of the situation and the decision-making process itself often produce stress. Irving Janis and Leon Mann (1977) have developed an insightful model of conflict that answers the following two questions: Under what conditions does stress have unfavorable effects on the quality of decision making? Under what conditions will individuals use sound decision-making procedures to avoid choices that they would quickly regret?[8]

People handle psychological stress in different ways as they make vital decisions. The main sources of such stress are the fear of suffering from the known losses that will occur once an alternative is selected, worry about unknown consequences when a critical decision is at stake, concern about making a public fool of oneself, and losing self-esteem if the decision is disastrous (Janis, 1985). Critical decisions usually involve conflicting values; therefore, decision makers face the unsettling dilemma that any choice they make will require sacrificing ideals or other valued objectives. Thus, the decision makers' anxiety, shame, and guilt rise, which increases the level of stress (Janis, 1985).

There is no question that errors in decision making are a result of many causes, including poor analysis, ignorance, bias, impulsiveness, time constraints, and organizational policies. But another major reason for many poorly conceived and implemented decisions is related to the motivational consequences of conflict—in particular, attempts to overcome stress produced by extremely difficult choices of vital decisions. As a result, a variety of defensive mechanisms are employed by people as they try to cope with the stress of the decision-making situation, most of which impede the efficiency of the process.

Janis (1985) identified five basic patterns of coping with psychological stress:

- **Unconflicted adherence:** The decision maker ignores information about risks and continues what has begun.
- **Unconflicted change:** The decision maker uncritically accepts whatever course of action is most salient or popular, without concern for costs or risks.
- **Defensive avoidance:** The decision maker evades the conflict by procrastinating, shifting the responsibility elsewhere, constructing wishful rationalizations, minimizing expected unfavorable consequences, and remaining selectively inattentive to corrective feedback.
- **Hypervigilance:** The decision maker panics and searches frantically for a solution, rapidly vacillating back and forth between alternatives, and then impulsively seizes upon a hastily contrived solution that promises immediate relief. The full range of alternatives and consequences is neglected because of emotional excitement, repetitive thinking, and cognitive schema that produce simplistic ideas and a reduction in immediate memory span.

- **Vigilance:** The decision maker searches carefully for relevant information, assimilates the information in an unbiased manner, and then evaluates the alternatives reflectively before making a choice.

The first four patterns are typically dysfunctional and lead to defective decisions. Although vigilance is no panacea, it is most likely to lead to effective decisions.

Even when decision makers are vigilant, however, they sometimes make mistakes by taking cognitive shortcuts to deal with the multiplicity of judgments that are essential. All kinds of people, including scientists and statisticians, make cognitive errors such as overestimating the likelihood that events can be easily imagined, giving too much weight to information about representativeness, relying too much on small samples, and failing to discount biased information (Tversky and Kahneman, 1973; Nisbet and Ross, 1980; Janis, 1985). Moreover, these kinds of errors probably increase when decision makers are under psychological stress.

The coping strategies of unconflicted adherence or unconflicted change promote sloppy and uncritical thinking because of a lack of motivation to engage in careful decision analysis. Defensive avoidance is used to elude the work required for vigilant decision making. If the decision maker cannot pass the buck or postpone the decision, the defensively avoidant person usually makes a quick choice to "get it over with" and then engages in wishful thinking and rationalization—playing up the positive reasons and playing down the negative ones. Hypervigilance produces a panic-like state in which the decision maker temporarily is overwhelmed by information as a result of being overly attentive to both relevant and trivial data. The informational overload and sense of imminent catastrophe contribute to the hypervigilant decision maker's tendency to use such simple-minded decision rules as "do whatever the first expert advises" (Janis, 1985).

The vigilant decision maker is most effective because he or she avoids many of the traps of the other four patterns and also because vigilance requires (Janis and Mann, 1977):

- A careful survey of a wide range of alternatives
- An analysis of the full range of objectives to be fulfilled and the values implicated by the choice
- An analysis of the risks and drawbacks of the choice
- Intensive search for new information relevant to further evaluation of alternatives
- Conscientious evaluation of new information or expert judgment, even when such information does not support the initial preferred course of action
- Reexamination of both positive and negative consequences of alternatives, including those originally regarded as unacceptable
- Detailed plans for implementing the selected course of action with special attention to contingency plans that might be required if various anticipated risks were to develop

Notice the similarity of these seven criteria for vigilant information processing and the satisficing strategy that we have already discussed.

What are the conditions that make for vigilance? When confronted with a decision, reflective decision makers either consciously or unconsciously consider four issues (Janis and Mann, 1977).

Issue 1: Once the process begins, the decision maker's first question to himself or herself is: Are the risks serious if I don't change? If it is determined that the risks of not changing anything are not serious, then the result is a state of unconflicted adherence. The decision maker simply adheres to the current situation and avoids stress and conflict.

Issue 2: If the answer to the first question is affirmative, however, then the level of stress increases slightly, and the decision maker is likely to ask a second question: Are the risks serious if I do change? Here the emphasis is on losses associated with changing. If the anticipated losses of changing are minimal, then the risks are not serious and the decision maker is predicted to accept uncritically the first reasonable alternative—that is, to opt for a state of unconflicted change. Again stress is limited.

Issue 3: If the answer to the second question is yes, then stress builds because there are serious risks in both changing and not changing. The anxiety typically produces the next question: Is it realistic to hope to find a better solution? If the decision maker believes there is no realistic hope of finding a better solution, then the result is a state of defensive avoidance. In order to escape from the conflict and reduce the stress, the individual avoids making the decision by either passing the buck or rationalizing the current situation.

Issue 4: If, however, there is some perceived hope for a better solution, then the decision maker inquires: Is there sufficient time to search and deliberate? If the decision maker perceives insufficient time, then a state of hypervigilance may occur. Panic sets in and the individual seizes upon a hastily contrived solution that promises immediate relief. If time is ample, then the decision maker is much more likely to engage in vigilant information processing, a process that enhances the effectiveness of the decision making through careful search, appraisal, and contingency planning.

Clearly, administrators should avoid unconflicted adherence, unconflicted change, defensive avoidance, and hypervigilance; however, the forces of labor, time, and stress are operating against vigilance. Nevertheless, knowing the dangers of defective decision making and when they are most likely to occur should help avoid them.

PARTICIPATION IN DECISION MAKING

In 1948, Lester Coch and John R. P. French conducted a classic study on the effects of participation in decision making, using a series of field experiments at the Harwood Manufacturing Corporation. The results were clear and conclusive: employee participation in decision making improved productivity. Other studies also have supported the desirability and influence of participation in decision making, both in business and in educational organizations.[9] The following generalizations summarize much of the research and theoretical literature on teacher participation in decision making.

- The opportunity to share in formulating policies is an important factor in the morale of teachers and in their enthusiasm for the school.
- Participation in decision making is positively related to the individual teacher's satisfaction with the profession of teaching.
- Teachers prefer principals who involve them in decision making.
- Decisions fail because of poor quality or because they are not accepted by subordinates.
- Teachers neither expect nor want to be involved in every decision; in fact, too much involvement can be as detrimental as too little.
- The roles and functions of both teachers and administrators in decision making need to be varied according to the nature of the problem.

Should teachers be involved in decision making and policy formulation? Wrong question! Sometimes they should. Other times they should not. Involvement can produce either positive or negative consequences. The appropriate questions are: Under what conditions should subordinates be involved in decision making? To what extent? How?

There are a number of models of shared decision making that are useful in answering these questions. The most well-known model is one originally developed by Victor Vroom and Phillip Yetton (1973) and refined by Vroom and Jago (1978). The Vroom-Jago model matches participation in decision making with the nature of the problem and situation. From the extant research, a set of eight rules is developed to improve the quality and acceptance of a decision. In addition, the constraints of time and development are formulated as two additional rules. In brief, these ten rules provide a complicated model of participation that requires the use of a complex set of decision trees or a computer (Vroom and Jago, 1978). The model has its limitations for practice, in that it is initially difficult to learn and then challenging to apply; nonetheless, students of administration would be well advised to examine the formulation in some depth (Vroom and Jago, 1978; Hoy and Tarter, 1995). We focus our attention on a simplified model of shared decision making developed by Hoy and Tarter (1992, 1993a, 1993b, 1995).

HOY-TARTER MODEL OF SHARED DECISION MAKING

The Propositions

Subordinates accept some decisions without question because they are indifferent to them. As Barnard (1938: 167) explains, there is a **zone of indifference** "in each individual within which orders are accepted without conscious questioning of their authority." Simon prefers the more positive term of **zone of acceptance,** but the terms are used interchangeably in the literature.

Drawing on the work of Barnard (1938), Simon (1947), and Chase (1952), Edwin M. Bridges (1967) advances two propositions about shared decision making:

1. As subordinates are involved in making decisions located within their zone of acceptance, participation will be less effective.

2. As subordinates are involved in making decisions located outside their zone of acceptance, participation will be more effective.

The problem for the administrator is to determine which decisions fall inside and which outside the zone. Bridges suggests two tests to answer this question:

* *The test of relevance:* Do the subordinates have a personal stake in the decision outcomes?

* *The test of expertise:* Do subordinates have the expertise to make a useful contribution to the decision?

The answers to these two questions define the four situations pictured in Figure 9.3. When subordinates have both expertise and a personal stake in the outcomes, then the decision is clearly outside their zone of acceptance. But if subordinates have neither expertise nor a personal stake, then the decision is inside the zone. There are, however, two marginal conditions, each with different decisional constraints. When subordinates have expertise but no personal stake, or have a personal stake but no particular expertise, the conditions are more problematic. Hoy and Tarter (1995) propose two additional theoretical propositions for guidance:

FIGURE **9.3**

The Zone of Acceptance and Involvement

		Do Subordinates Have a Personal Stake?	
		Yes	No
Do Subordinates Have Expertise?	Yes	Outside Zone of Acceptance (Probably Include)	Marginal with Expertise (Occasionally Include)
	No	Marginal with Relevance (Occasionally Include)	Inside Zone of Acceptance (Definitely Exclude)

3. As subordinates are involved in making decisions for which they have marginal expertise, their participation will be marginally effective.

4. As subordinates are involved in making decisions for which they have marginal interest, their participation will be marginally effective.

One more consideration is useful if we are to be successful in applying the model to actual problems. Commitment of subordinates should sometimes moderate their degree of involvement. When subordinates' personal goals conflict with organizational ones, it is ill-advised to delegate decisions to them because of the high risk that decisions will be made on personal bases at the expense of the overall welfare of the school.[10] Thus, subordinate commitment is important, and to gauge commitment, we propose a final test.

• *The test of commitment:* Are subordinates committed to the mission of the organization? And can they be trusted to make decisions in the best interests of the organization?

If the decision is outside the zone of acceptance and if subordinates can be trusted to make decisions in the best interest of the organization, then participation should be extensive. We call this a *democratic situation* because the only issue is whether the decision should be made by consensus or majority rule. But if the decision is outside the zone and there is little subordinate commitment, then we have a *conflictual situation* and participation should be restricted. To do otherwise invites moving in directions inconsistent with the overall welfare of the organization.

If the decision issue is not relevant to subordinates and they have no expertise, however, then the decision clearly falls within their zone of acceptance and involvement should be avoided; this is a *noncollaborative situation.* Indeed, participation in such cases will likely produce resentment because subordinates typically are not interested.

When subordinates have a personal stake in the issue but little expertise, we have a *stakeholder situation* and subordinate participation should be limited and only occasional. To do otherwise courts trouble. If subordinates have nothing substantive to contribute, the decision ultimately will be made by those with the expertise (not subordinates), and a sense of frustration and hostility may be generated. Subordinates, in fact, may perceive the experience as an empty exercise in which the decisions have "already been made." Daniel L. Duke, Beverly K. Showers, and Michael Imber (1980) conclude from their research that shared decision making is often viewed by teachers as a formality or attempt to create the illusion of teacher influence. On the other hand, occasionally it may be useful to involve teachers in a limited way. When involvement is sought under these circumstances, it must be done skillfully. Its major objectives should be to open communication with subordinates, to educate them, and to gain support for the decision.

Finally, when there is an *expert situation*—when subordinates have no personal stake in the outcomes but do have the knowledge to make a useful contribution.

Should subordinates be involved? Only occasionally! To involve them indiscriminately in decisions of this type is to increase the likelihood of alienation. Although involvement under these circumstances increases the administrator's chances of reaching a higher quality decision, subordinates too often are likely to wonder aloud "what the administrator gets paid for." These decision situations and appropriate responses are summarized in Figure 9.4.

Once the administrator has determined that subordinates should be involved in deciding, the next question becomes how the process should proceed. Hoy and Tarter (1995) suggest five decision-making structures:

1. *Group consensus:* The administrator involves participants in the decision making, then the group decides. All group members share equally as they generate and evaluate a decision, but total consensus is required before a decision can be made.

2. *Group majority:* The administrator involves participants in the decision making, then the group decides by majority rule.

FIGURE **9.4**

Decision Situation and Subordinate Involvement

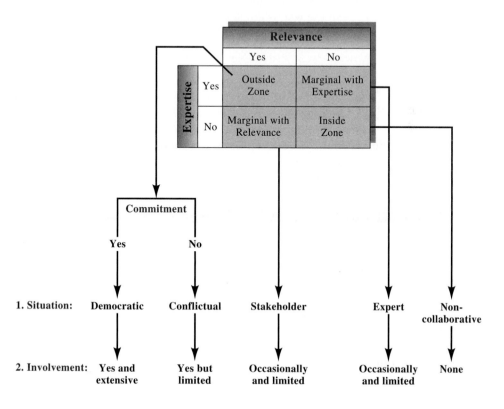

3. *Group advisory:* The administrator solicits the opinions of the entire group, discusses the implications of group suggestions, then makes a decision that may or may not reflect subordinates' desires.

4. *Individual advisory:* The administrator consults with subordinates individually who have expertise to inform the decision, then makes a decision that may or may not reflect their opinion.

5. *Unilateral decision:* The administrator makes the decision without consulting or involving subordinates in the decision.

Thus far we have focused on subordinates in shared decision making. Now we turn to the administrator and define five leadership roles: integrator, parliamentarian, educator, solicitor, and director. The *integrator* brings subordinates together for consensus decision making. Here the task is to reconcile divergent opinions and positions. The *parliamentarian* facilitates open communication by protecting the opinions of the minority and leads participants through a democratic process to a group decision. The *educator* reduces resistance to change by explaining and discussing with group members the opportunities and constraints of the decisional issues. The *solicitor* seeks advice from subordinate-experts. The quality of decisions is improved as the administrator guides the generation of relevant information. The *director* makes unilateral decisions in those instances where the subordinates have no expertise or personal stake. Here the goal is efficiency. The function and aim of each role is summarized in Table 9.3.

Putting It Together

Administrators are too often exhorted to involve teachers in all decisions. The more appropriate stance is to reflect upon the question: When should others be involved in decision making and how? We have proposed a model that answers this question.

TABLE **9.3** Administrative Roles for Shared Decision Making		
Role	**Function**	**Aim**
Integrator	Integrates divergent positions	To gain consensus
Parliamentarian	Promotes open discussion	To support reflective group deliberation
Educator	Explains and discusses issues	To seek acceptance of decisions
Solicitor	Solicits advice	To improve quality of decisions
Director	Makes unilateral decisions	To achieve efficiency

The key concept in the model, drawn from Barnard (1938) and Simon (1947), is the zone of acceptance. There are some decisions that subordinates simply accept and, therefore, in which they need not be involved. The administrator identifies those situations by asking two questions:

1. *Relevance question:* Do the subordinates have a personal stake in the outcome?
2. *Expertise question:* Can subordinates contribute expertise to the solution?

If the answer to both these questions is yes, the subordinates have both a personal stake in the outcome and the expertise to contribute, then the situation is outside the zone of acceptance. Subordinates will want to be involved, and their involvement should improve the decision. However, one must next evaluate their commitment to the organization by asking the following question:

3. *Commitment question:* Can subordinates be trusted to make a decision in the best interests of the organization?

If they are committed, their involvement should be extensive as the group tries to develop the "best" decision. In the process, the role of the administrator is to act either as an integrator (if consensus is essential) or as a parliamentarian (if a group majority is sufficient). If subordinates are not committed (conflictual situation), their involvement should be limited. In this situation the administrator acts as an educator, and the group serves to advise and identify pockets of resistance.

If, however, subordinates have only a personal stake in the decision but no expertise (stakeholder situation), their involvement should be occasional and limited. Subordinates are interested in the outcome, but they have little knowledge to bring to bear on the decision. The reason for occasional involvement in this situation is to lower resistance and educate participants. If the involvement is more than occasional, the danger is alienation as teachers feel manipulated because their wishes are not met. At the outset, all parties should know that the group is clearly advisory to the leader. The administrator's role is to decide and educate.

If subordinates have expertise but no personal stake (expert situation), their involvement should also be occasional and limited as the administrator attempts to improve the decision by tapping the expertise of significant individuals who are not normally involved in this kind of action. At first blush, one might think that expertise should always be consulted in a decision, but if workers have no personal stake in the outcomes, their enthusiasm will quickly wane. They may well grumble, "This isn't my job."

In noncollaborative situations the teachers have neither the interest nor the expertise to contribute to the decision. Yet there is such a strong norm about involving teachers in all sorts of decisions that school administrators often feel constrained to involve teachers regardless of their knowledge or interest. Such ritual is dysfunctional and illogical. Why would you involve someone in a decision when that person doesn't care and can't help? The model suggests that administrators make direct unilateral decisions when the issue is within the zone of acceptance of subordinates. The entire model is summarized in Figure 9.5.

This model for shared decision making is not a panacea. It is not a substitute for sensitive and reflective administrative thought and action; it simply provides some guidelines for determining when and how teachers and principals should be involved in joint decision making. The effectiveness of decisions is determined by both the quality of the decision and the acceptance and commitment of subordinates to implement the decision.

FIGURE **9.5**

A Normative Model for Participative Decision Making

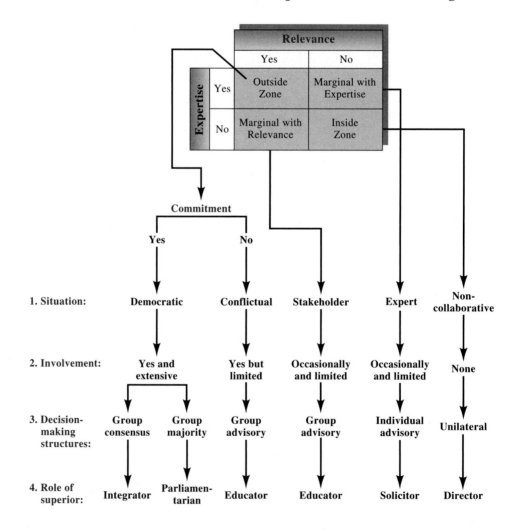

A CAUTION ON GROUP DECISION MAKING: GROUPTHINK

There is little question that group decision making can be an effective process, but there are some dangers even when the conditions call for a group decision. Time is always a potential constraint on participation in decision making, and group decisions typically require more time than individual decisions. Participation involves discussion, debate, and often conflict; in fact, as the number of actors increases in the process, coordination becomes more important and difficult. Speed and efficiency are not basic advantages of group decision making.

Although participation in decision making can produce rampant conflict in the group, success in group problem solving often produces a strong cohesiveness, especially among members of smaller "in" groups. Too much cohesiveness can be as dangerous as conflict. Conflict prevents action; strong cohesiveness promotes uniformity within the group. The problem with uniformity is that it can produce a likemindedness that is uncritical. Janis (1985) highlights this concurrence-seeking tendency among moderately or highly cohesive groups. When the tendency is dominant, the members use their collective cognitive resources to develop rationalizations consistent with the shared illusion about the invulnerability of their organization; that is, they display the **groupthink syndrome.**

The following eight main symptoms of groupthink characterize historic decision-making fiascoes (Janis and Mann, 1977; Janis, 1982):

- *Illusion of invulnerability:* Members ignore obvious danger, take extreme risks, and are overly optimistic.
- *Collective rationalization:* Members discredit and explain away warning contrary to group thinking.
- *Illusion of morality:* Members believe their decisions are morally correct, ignoring the ethical consequences of their decisions.
- *Excessive stereotyping:* The group constructs negative stereotypes of rivals outside the group.
- *Pressure for conformity:* Members pressure any in the group who express arguments against the group's stereotypes, illusions, or commitments, viewing such opposition as disloyalty.
- *Self-censorship:* Members withhold their dissenting views and counter arguments.
- *Illusion of unanimity:* Members perceive falsely that everyone agrees with the group's decision; silence is seen as consent.
- *Mindguards:* Some members appoint themselves to the role of protecting the group from adverse information that might threaten group complacency.

Conditions That Foster Groupthink

Janis (1985) provides a comprehensive analysis of the conditions that encourage groupthink. The likelihood that groupthink will occur in cohesive groups depends on a number of conditions. One of the most potent conditions is insulation from direct contact with others in the same organization who are not members of the "in" group of policy makers. As Janis (1985) explains:

> For example, an insulated group of executives is likely to receive only brief and unimpressive summaries of warning about the insurmountable difficulties of implementing a strategic reorganization or a new method of production that is under consideration. The top commanders of the organization may end up concurring on a course of action that many middle-level and lower-level personnel on the firing line could have informed them in advance would not be feasible. (p. 174)

Lack of impartial leadership also will encourage concurrence seeking, especially when the leader is strong and charismatic. Followers seek to please such leaders, and knowing a leader's initial preferences channels their thinking. Moreover, lack of norms requiring systematic analysis as well as homogeneity of members' social background and ideology contribute to likemindedness.

Similarly, the situational context may nurture groupthink. We have already discussed the negative consequences produced by stress. High stress from external threats combined with little hope that the leader will advance a better solution pushes the group toward uncritical consensus. Furthermore, low self-esteem of the group, temporarily induced by recent failures, excessive difficulties, and moral dilemmas, fosters groupthink. All these antecedent conditions promote a tendency toward concurrence seeking, which in turn produces the consequences of groupthink—overestimation of the group, closed-mindedness, and pressure of unanimity. Such behavior makes for low vigilance in decision making, which ultimately results in defective decision making with a low probability of a successful outcome.

Avoiding Groupthink

There are a number of ways to prevent groupthink. The following ten recommendations are a tentative set of prescriptions for counteracting the conditions that foster groupthink (Janis, 1985).

1. The group should be made aware of the causes and consequences of groupthink.

2. The leader should be neutral when assigning a decision-making task to a group, initially withholding all preferences and expectations. This practice will be especially effective if the leader consistently encourages an atmosphere of open inquiry.

3. The leader should give high priority to airing objections and doubts, and be accepting of criticism.

4. Groups should always consider unpopular alternatives, assigning the role of devil's advocate to several strong members of the group.

5. Sometimes it is useful to divide the group into two separate deliberative bodies as feasibilities are evaluated.

6. The group should spend a sizable amount of time surveying all warning signals from rival groups and organizations.

7. After reaching a preliminary consensus on a decision, all residual doubts should be expressed and the matter reconsidered.

8. Outside experts should be included in vital decision making.

9. Tentative decisions should be discussed with trusted colleagues, not in the decision-making group.

10. The organization should routinely follow the administrative practice of establishing several independent decision-making groups to work on the same critical issue or policy.

THE CASE OF THE ANONYMOUS LETTER

We conclude our analysis of decision making with a case study for students to ponder as they begin to apply decision theory to the problems of practice.[11]

Jack Garner is principal of Dewey Elementary School. Dewey is one of five elementary schools in Pleasantville, a community of 30,000 in a middle Atlantic state.

Pleasantville is an interesting cross section of America. It is a working-class community in transition to a different kind of workforce. The old work of farms, mills, and mines has given way to newer occupations in a small aircraft plant and in the emergence of the state college (recently renamed the State University at Pleasantville). The paper mill, a carpet factory, a chemical plant, a small steel mill, and a coal mine were formerly the major employers of the townspeople. But recently, much to the dismay of the working people in Pleasantville, most of the factories and mills were in decline. Unemployment was up to 13 percent and not getting better. The people blamed the government. In the old days, there had been no EPA and no environmentalists and no interference from the state and federal bureaucrats. In those days, people worked hard and made a decent living.

With the advent of environmental-protection regulations and changes in the marketplace, the steel mill employed only half of what it had employed fifteen years ago. So too with the paper mill and the coal mine. The chemical plant was on the verge of bankruptcy as newer dyes were imported from abroad and expensive chemical cleanup projects plagued the plant for the past three years. In fact, there seemed to be only one major industry that was thriving in Pleasantville—the state university. It was growing, from an enrollment of 2,000 ten years ago to nearly 10,000 students today. Although construction of the expanding campus had produced many jobs during the past five years, it did not offset the decline of the old industries. Moreover, many of the jobs that were produced by the state university were professional positions that required employment of outsiders rather than townspeople.

Some people resented the intrusion from the outside and harkened back to the halcyon days of the past. Others in the community, especially businesspeople, welcomed the expansion of the school and were proud of the fact that Pleasantville was becoming sophisticated.

Jack Garner was no stranger to Pleasantville. At thirty-five, his entire life had been spent in and around Pleasantville. He had gone to elementary school, junior high, and high school in town. Upon graduation, he went to the local state college and majored in education. His first job was as science teacher at Pleasantville High. During his first year of teaching, Jack Garner decided that he wanted an expanded role in education down the road. He began taking curriculum classes in the summers at the main campus of the state university, sixty-five miles from Pleasantville.

Taking courses at the main campus was Garner's first real exposure to life outside of Pleasantville. A chronic bad knee had kept him out of the service, and perhaps just as well. Thinking back, Garner judged the experience at the main campus to be an eye-opener for a country boy, as he sometimes referred to himself. Ten years later, he had completed his doctorate in educational curriculum, served as district-wide elementary science curriculum coordinator, and as a result of his success in working with people and his genuine good sense, he was promoted to principal of the new Dewey Elementary School. Some might think that Dewey was a progressive school, but the Dewey this elementary school was named after was Thomas, the former governor of New York, not the educator. Therein lay a substantial difference. Dewey Elementary School was not a place hospitable to change. Students had grown up in the system and sent their children to Dewey. They wanted the same good education they had received—no frills, no life adjustment, no multiculturalism, no debates on right to life or the nature of families, just basic learning in reading, math, science, writing, and history.

There was no question that the surrounding neighborhood of Dewey was conservative, but it was slowly changing as more and more college professors bought houses in Dewey Heights. In fact, the Dewey neighborhood was becoming a choice residential area for young professionals in the community.

As a curriculum person and skillful administrator, Garner had been able to initiate a strong elementary school curriculum. He had combined many of the elements of cooperative learning and mastery education to engage students individually and collectively in the pursuit of math, science, and reading. His whole-language approach to the teaching of English and composition was a model that was frequently observed by students from the local college. (Garner had a hard time thinking of his undergraduate school as a state university; he still thought of it as his college.) Five years as curriculum coordinator and five years as principal had produced a school of which he was proud. The elementary school students continued to do well and parents were generally supportive of his initiatives, even though some complained that he was getting away from the basics.

It was Monday morning. As Jack reviewed his mail, he was shocked at the third letter that he opened and read.

Matt Jenkins had been Garner's new elementary science supervisor for the past three years. Although Garner had not hired Jenkins directly, he was consulted by the former superintendent, who had thought highly of Jenkins. Garner had called one of

May 11, 19—

Dear Dr. Garner:

You should know that your science curriculum supervisor is a homo. He lives with another man and I have seen them fondling each other in the tavern in Greenville. I don't care what people do in their private lives, but teachers are different. I don't want my son endangered by this guy. Of course, there is always the question of AIDS, and I don't want him abusing my child. There is a rumor that Jenkins has not been well. Frankly, we're worried for the safety of our children.

   We know that you are with us on this issue. After all, you are one of us. Why don't you do something about this? Everyone is talking about it. And if you don't do something, I can't be responsible for what some hotheads might do. Jenkins is in some danger.

   I am not going to sign this letter because I don't want to be involved in this, but I think you ought to know about the situation. Someone is going to get hurt. Do something before it becomes a police matter.

Sincerely,

A Concerned Parent

his former professors in curriculum at the state university and the professor had said, "He is a little peculiar but without question he is one of the brightest and most creative students I have known. He will be an asset to your program." Without much further ado, Jenkins was hired, even though he was an outsider and a segment of the community was opposed to hiring from outside.

There was no question in Garner's mind that Jenkins had shown strong leadership in improving the science curriculum at Dewey. Other teachers liked him because he was low-key, supportive, sensitive, and nurturing. He had a few odd mannerisms, but they didn't seem to bother anyone. He stayed to himself and lived ten miles outside of the city, in a small suburb of Pleasantville called Greenville. No one seemed to know much about Jenkins or his personal life. Rumor had it that Jenkins spent a lot of his time at University Station, the main campus of the state university. Many of the townspeople took a dim view of the liberal goings-on in University Station, but it was a world away. Only one time could Garner remember any negative comments about Jenkins. One of the parents had complained that he was always touching her son. Garner had discreetly looked into this matter and found nothing substantial. Rather, he found that Jenkins had grabbed the student in question a number of times to correct his aggressive behavior with the other children. The student in question was a little on the wild side.

Garner was a bit surprised to discover that Jenkins lived with a new high school English teacher, Brad Korbus. Garner had been instrumental in the recruitment and selection of Korbus, and now they were roommates in Greenville. Garner was inclined to feel that whatever people did privately was their own business. His policy for dealing with anonymous letters was to file them in the circular file. Yet the implied threat of this letter troubled him.

He felt constrained to do something, but what? He thought about turning the matter over to the local police. Should he talk to his superintendent? Was this a crank letter from an isolated individual? Did he have a right to make inquiries—even if done discreetly? Should he talk to Jenkins? What would he say, if he did? Supposing Jenkins was gay and living with another man, would it matter? Is there a problem? A potential problem? Is this a time for preventive action? Or will any action simply exacerbate the situation? Is it time for the district to develop a policy on private behavior or alternate lifestyles?

DISCUSSING THE CASE

Assume the role of principal in this case and define the short-term and long-term problems.

- Is this a case for satisficing, muddling through, or adaptive scanning?
- What are your immediate and long-term plans?
- Who should be involved in this decision and how?

No matter what your eventual strategy, make sure it includes a plan to address the dysfunctional consequences of your actions.

SUMMARY AND SUGGESTED READINGS

An understanding of the decision-making process is vital to successful administration. Four basic strategies of managerial decision making are identified and described. The optimizing strategy of the classical model is found not to be useful to administrators because it assumes perfect information, rationality, and human capacity not found in the actual world of administration.

Although completely rational decision making is impossible, administrators need a systematic process to enhance the selection of satisfactory solutions. Thus, a strategy of satisficing is central to decision making in the administrative model. Here decision making is a cycle of activity that includes recognition and definition of the problem, analysis of difficulties, establishment of criteria for a satisfactory resolution, development of a plan of action, and initiation of the plan. Because of its cyclical nature, the decision-making action cycle may be entered at different stages and the stages are gone through again and again in the process of administration.

The satisficing strategy is well suited for dealing with many problems in educational administration; however, when the set of alternatives is undefinable or the consequences of each alternative are unpredictable, then an incremental strategy may seem more appropriate. This process is a method of successive limited comparisons; only a limited set of alternatives, similar to the existing situation, is considered by successively comparing their consequences until agreement is reached on a course of action. It is assumed that small changes are not likely to produce large negative consequences for the organization.

Incrementalism, however, can be too conservative and self-defeating. Incremental decisions made without fundamental guidelines can lead to action without direction. Thus, the mixed-scanning model of decision making is proposed for complex decisions. Mixed scanning unites the best of both the administrative and the incremental models. A strategy of satisficing is used in combination with incremental decision making guided by broad policy. Full scanning is replaced by partial scanning and tentative decisions are made incrementally in a process that is guided by a clear sense of destination.

As in most complex tasks, however, there is no single best approach to deciding; the best strategy is the one that best matches the circumstances. We have proposed a set of guidelines that matches the right strategy with the situation.

The garbage can model of organizational decision making is useful for understanding nonrational decisions. In this model, the decision does not begin with a problem and end with a solution; rather, organizations are viewed as sets of choices looking for problems, issues and feelings seeking opportunities, solutions searching for problems, and administrators looking for work. Problems, solutions, participants, and choice opportunities act as independent events. When they mesh, some problems are solved, but in this chaotic decision process many problems are not solved—they simply persist. The model explains why solutions may be proposed to problems that do not exist and why irrelevant choices are made.

Regardless of the strategy, decision making often causes stress, which produces irrationality. The conditions under which stress has unfavorable effects on the quality of decision making are discussed, and five coping mechanisms that decision makers are most likely to use in stressful situations are analyzed.

It is not always beneficial for administrators to involve subordinates in decision making. A simplified model of shared decision making is proposed to help administrators determine under what conditions subordinates should and should not participate in the decision-making process. The framework uses the tests of relevance, expertise, and commitment as guides for participation. Administrators, depending on the circumstances, use the roles of integrator, parliamentarian, educator, solicitor, and director. Finally, the conditions that foster groupthink are analyzed, and suggestions are proposed for avoiding them.

Decision making is a complex process. Ideas and theories are drawn from such diverse disciplines as cognitive science, economics, political science, psychology, and sociology. Several supplementary books are useful to beginning students. James G. March (1994) provides a primer on decision making; his book is concerned with how decisions actually happen rather they how they should; his ideas are simple and straightforward. Amitai Etzioni (1988) reminds us of the moral dimension of decision making and the centrality of moral issues in economic thought. Two edited selections are worth perusing: Mary Zey's (1992) collection pursues alternatives to the rational-choice models, while the March (1988) selections examine decision making under ambiguity. For those students who want a sophisticated treatment of participation in decision making, Victor Vroom and Arthur Jago (1988) provide an excellent and comprehensive model. Finally, Hoy and Tarter (1995) use case studies to link decision theory to problems of practice; they demonstrate the utility of good theory in solving actual administrative problems in schools.

NOTES

1. Recent research suggests that many administrators ignore normative methods prescribed by scholars for effective decision making and persist in questionable decision tactics. See Nutt (1984).

2. The basic assumptions in the following section come from Edward Litchfield (1956).

3. What has been termed policy making in the public sector is often discussed as strategic formulation in the private sector; for example, see Henry Mintzberg (1978) and Johannes Pennings (1985).

4. Iterations of this cycle occur frequently in the organizational literature. For example, see Griffiths (1959) and Daft (1989).

5. The problem is much more complex, however, if it also involves the integration of minority students into segregated schools.

6. A critical and interesting analysis of heuristics is made by a group of cognitive psychologists called the *prospect school.* Their main thesis is that individuals cope with their limited cognitive abilities by using heuristic devices to solve complex problems. Although the heuristics help, they themselves sometimes introduce systematic biases that may subvert decision making. For example, see Nisbett and Ross (1980) and Kahneman, Solvic, and Tversky (1982).

7. Etzioni (1967) reports that fifty articles and Ph.D. dissertations have been written on mixed scanning since his original article. For his synthesis, see Etzioni (1986).

8. This section draws heavily on the work of Janis (1985) and Janis and Mann (1977).

9. For studies that support the desirability of participation in decision making, see Sharma, 1955; Guest, 1960; Vroom, 1960, 1976; Belasco and Allutto, 1972; Allutto and Belasco, 1973; Conway, 1976; Hoy, Newland, and Blazovsky, 1977; Driscoll, 1978; Mohrman, Cooke, and Mohrman, 1978; Moon, 1983). For a comprehensive and somewhat critical review of participation in decision making, see Locke and Schweiger (1979). Likewise, for a review of participative decision making in education, see Conway (1984). The effects of subordinate participation in decision making, however, are neither simple nor unambiguous; for example see Imber, 1983; Conway, 1984; Imber and Duke, 1984; Vroom and Jago, 1988; Conley, Bower, and Bachrach, 1989; Bachrach et al., 1990; Conley, 1990.

10. For a useful distinction between shared decision making and delegation of decision making, see Hoy and Sousa (1984).

11. Hoy and Tarter (1995) illustrate the application of decision theory to practice with actual contemporary cases and then provide thirty new cases from educational settings for consideration. The anonymous letter was written by Hoy and Tarter for this chapter.

KEY CONCEPTS AND IDEAS

Adaptive strategy	Generic decisions
Administrative model	Groupthink syndrome
Boundary conditions	Heuristics
Bounded rationality	Hypervigilance
Classical model	Incremental model
Defensive avoidance	Mixed-scanning model
Garbage-can model	Muddling through

Opportunistic surveillance

Optimizing

Policy

Problemistic search

Satisficing

Unconflicted adherence

Unconflicted change

Unique decisions

Vigilance

Zone of acceptance

Zone of indifference

Motivating

Neither regulations nor resources, neither technical innovations nor
program reorganizations, can significantly alter school performance
if the teacher motivation system fails to energize and shape teacher
behavior in ways that link educational program requirements to student
learning needs.

—Douglas E. Mitchell, Flora Ida Ortiz, and Tedi K. Mitchell
Work Orientation and Job Performance

PREVIEW

1. Theories of individual motivation provide useful guides and programs that can alleviate school performance problems.

2. No magic formulae exist to make individuals want to learn, work hard, and be responsible. Desired motivational patterns can be facilitated, however, by applying six general motivational principles that enhance motivation in work organizations.

3. Goal-setting programs that produce specific difficult goals and provide feedback, improve work quality, clarify expectations, raise job satisfaction, and promote pride in achievement.

4. As the organizational counterpart to individual motivation, incentives motivate participants to improve their work performance by making jobs attractive, interesting, and satisfying.

5. To be effective, incentive systems in schools need to be elaborate, stable, and dependable, and offer a wide range of intrinsic and extrinsic rewards.

6. Work-redesign interventions modify specific jobs to increase both the quality of the employees' work experience and performance.

7. Motivation-hygiene theory posits that motivator factors combine to contribute more to job satisfaction than to job dissatisfaction and that hygienes combine to contribute more to job dissatisfaction than to job satisfaction.

8. Job enrichment increases motivator factors and reduces negative hygiene factors.

9. The job-characteristics model of work design unifies Maslow's need fulfillment, Herzberg's motivation-hygiene, and Vroom's expectancy theories.

10. School reform advocates argue that the quality of public education can only improve by transforming school teaching into a full-fledged profession.

11. A profession is characterized by knowledge and training; autonomy and control in decision making; a core ideology; and a colleague-oriented association.

12. Career-ladder programs redesign jobs to provide prospects for promotion, formalize status ranks, match abilities with tasks, and distribute improvement responsibilities.

13. An alternative career path open to teachers who want to remain in education is an administrator track.

14. The school-leader-as-motivator model stimulates student motivation by combining task goals and actions to build a supportive school culture.

Our public and private-sector institutions—schools, government agencies, and businesses—are the objects of intense criticism. Underlying this faultfinding is the implicit assumption that our most important societal institutions are plagued by problems of productivity. Using strong military and economic metaphors, the *Nation at Risk* report (National Commission on Excellence in Education, 1983) crystallized the issues about education for the American public. Its message is clear: unless the educational system is improved, the United States will lose the economic war with Japan, Germany, and other developed countries. Many policy makers and citizens continue to believe that the real and perceived performance problems are rooted in declining levels of work motivation and competence in our schools. In efforts designed to increase individual motivation and organizational productivity in schools, policy makers mandated an array of plans to recruit, reward, and retain the best educators (Johnson, 1986). While well intended for the most part, many of the merit pay, career-ladder, mentoring, and job-enrichment schemes were not founded in the theory or practice of motivating humans.

As shown in Chapter 4, information-processing and motivation theories help explain the causes of individual behavior in schools, predict effects of administrative actions, and direct behavior to achieve school goals. If the criticisms and assumptions about our societal institutions are reasonably valid, practitioners, policy makers, and researchers must recognize the fundamental importance of motivation and acquire a sound knowledge about the role motivational processes play in effective work. School administrators who are knowledgeable about why people behave as they do will have an advantage in meeting the challenges and solving the problems that will confront education well into the twenty-first century. However, recognizing and understanding are not enough (Ford, 1992); educators must also be able to design and implement actions that will promote positive motivational patterns.

Managers and administrators in all organizations are interested in actions or programs that can enhance the motivation of their staffs. School administrators are no different; they would like to know how their own motivation and that of teachers and students can be increased. As is the case with policy makers, scholars, and consultants, educational practitioners frequently look naively at the theories as offering relatively simple prescriptions. But the theories of information processing and motivation not only lack the precision to provide simple, mechanical, and unequivocal answers, they show that such prescriptions are impossible to derive. Individuals are simply too complex and idiosyncratic to think of motivating them by pushing a button or flipping a switch.

The theories presented in Chapter 4, when used judiciously, offer the basis for many suggestions and techniques for enhancing motivation in schools. In fact, the very large number of motivational approaches and programs that have been proposed make it impossible to consider all of them. Therefore, we will review what we think are some of the most important and frequently mentioned motivation-based formulations. In this regard, six general principles will be stated to set a foundation for reviewing goal setting, organizational incentives, several work designs, and leadership programs.

GENERAL PRINCIPLES UNDERLYING MOTIVATIONAL ENHANCEMENT PROGRAMS

Motivating individuals is a complex and rather idiosyncratic process of trying to facilitate desired motivational patterns. There are no magic formulas to make individuals want to learn, work hard, and be responsible (Ford, 1992). In designing and implementing programs to motivate individuals, facilitation should be the guiding concept. Efforts to facilitate desired motivational patterns will be more successful, Ford believes, if they are viewed as collaborations between people where individual goals, emotions, values, and expectations of individuals can be accounted for and respected. Without collaboration and respect, motivational programs may produce short-term effects, but in the longer term, they are likely to flounder or even boomerang. In other words, when individuals feel coerced or manipulated they often lose interest in the activities, even when the motivational strategies were intended to be positive and rewarding. For example, teachers' interest in a new program can be replaced by resentment and resistance when the principal implements the effort without collaboration. In addition to framing the problem of motivating individuals as one of facilitation, Ford (1992) proposed a series of general **motivational principles** that can be used to guide practices for motivating individuals:

- Attempts to increase individual motivation always involve the whole person.
- The strongest motivational patterns are anchored in multiple goals; interventions should allow people to attain as many goals as possible.
- Clear, useful feedback regarding goal attainment should be provided.
- Motivation is maximized under conditions of optimal challenge; interventions should produce high but attainable goals.

- There are many ways to motivate people; interventions should incorporate different strategies—that is, use multiple approaches and keep trying!
- People should be treated with respect.

These six general principles for motivating individuals serve as the foundation of many programs to enhance motivation in work organizations. However, schools are complex social systems that make the application of the simple principles of work motivation difficult to implement (Pinder, 1984). With this caveat in mind, we turn to specific applications.

GOAL SETTING

Goal setting is defining and stating what you are trying to accomplish in a job. Locke and Latham (1990) claim that overwhelming evidence has been found that goal setting has positive effects on motivation and performance. These positive effects generalize across tasks, settings, subjects, countries, performance criteria, different methods of goal setting, and time spans. Specific, difficult goals and feedback improve work quality, clarify expectations, raise job satisfaction, and produce pride in achievement (Locke and Latham, 1984). Given such a powerful foundation, goal-setting theory (see Chapter 4) can be applied in schools.

MANAGEMENT BY OBJECTIVES

At the organizational level, goal setting is the core of the well known technique called management by objectives, or simply MBO (Locke and Latham, 1990). MBO was given prominence by Peter Drucker (1954) during the 1950s. Since its early popularization, a large variety of MBO or MBO-like programs have been implemented and have had widespread appeal in industrial organizations. As a major proponent of the technique, George S. Odiorne (1979) maintains that MBO has been used extensively in a variety of organizational settings, including many educational organizations.

Definition and Application

Management by objectives is an administrative process that identifies and accomplishes organizational purposes by joining superiors and subordinates in the pursuit of mutually agreed goals that are specific, measurable, time bound, and joined to an action plan. Progress and goal attainment are assessed and monitored in appraisal sessions that focus on mutually determined standards of performance (McConkie, 1979). In educational settings, MBO is a system for motivating and integrating the efforts of school employees toward common objectives. The MBO process works by setting goals for the district as a whole and then cascading these goals down through each organizational level. As the goals cascade down the hierarchy, they become consistent across the hierarchical levels and more specific at each lower level. Assessment and monitoring occur at each level and the results are combined as they are passed up the hierarchy. Each level then helps attain goals at the next-highest level and ultimately for the entire school district. A typical scheme for designing and starting an MBO intervention in a school district would include the following five steps.

- Develop a set of overall educational goals for the school district.
- Establish goals for each job.
- Integrate the goals of the different positions so that every unit of the school district is working to accomplish the same overall goals.
- Establish plans for attaining the goals, methods for measuring the outcomes, evaluation, and feedback procedures.
- Implement the MBO program.

In sum, MBO applies the major postulate of goal-setting theory (that behavior is largely the result of intentional actions taken by individuals) to the work setting and adds action plans and assessment procedures to the process. Although MBO has elements of participation, it is basically a top-down administrative approach, which attempts to motivate and integrate the efforts of school participants toward common goals that are set at the highest levels of the organization.

Research and Evaluation of MBO

During the 1980s extensive reviews of the MBO research literature were made by Jack N. Kondrasuk (1981), Stephen J. Carroll (1986), and R. C. Rogers and J. E. Hunter (1989). Even after reviewing 185 studies conducted in diverse settings, Kondrasuk (1981) concludes that rigorously designed research that tests the theoretical underpinnings of MBO programs remains somewhat limited. Nonetheless, approximately 90 percent of the studies reported positive outcomes for MBO. The support, however, was found to be inversely related to the power of the research design. In other words, as the sophistication of the research approach declined, the support for MBO increased. Case studies were very supportive; true experiments were at best partially supportive. Kondrasuk further concludes that he found some evidence, but not conclusive proof, for the effectiveness of MBO. The reviews by Carroll (1986) and Rogers and Hunter (1989) found similar results—MBO does have positive effects on performance. After reviewing the reviews, Locke and Latham (1990) assert that goal setting works at the group and organizational levels as well as at the individual level. We agree with the more cautious assessments of Kondrasuk: research results on the effectiveness of MBO are generally supportive but not definitive.

Although the research evidence seems generally positive, the relative benefits may be marginal because of the costs and difficulties of introducing an MBO program in an educational setting. Until more research is available, administrators will have to make their own assessments about whether or not to experiment with formal goal-setting programs such as MBO. Before starting an MBO program, however, three of Kondrasuk's (1981) conclusions should be considered carefully:

- MBO is more likely to succeed in the private sector than in the public.
- MBO is more likely to succeed with administrative than with instructional staff.
- MBO is more likely to succeed in the short term than in the long term.

Table 10.1 concisely states the claims for and against the procedure.

The needed congruence between getting individuals to strive toward specific, relatively difficult goals and accomplishing the overall organizational goal certainly is not an assured relationship (Miner, 1980). The basic idea of goals cascading down the school district level by level until an integrated group of goals emerge is problematic. Goal setting by individuals in schools with relatively ambiguous aims and loosely coupled organizational units can produce particularly diverse and marginally relevant sets of objectives.

Finally, politics and power struggles at the implementation stage can produce failures (Pinder, 1984). School districts typically are political and exhibit struggles among individuals and coalitions for power, influence, and resources. Failure to recognize and deal with the political factors at the time of implementation is bound to limit the success of an intervention. For example, MBO, properly practiced, calls for setting goals and sharing power and participation by the public, board of education, administrators, and teachers. This is a mix of issues and participants that will surely create political conflict.

As an overall assessment, MBO-type interventions now have strong theoretical and some research support, especially in the private sector. For educational organi-

---

TABLE 10.1 Conflicting Claims Regarding MBO

Claims by MBO Proponents	Counterclaims by MBO Critics
Enhances individual motivation to work by appealing to higher-order needs	Asserts that all individuals are ready to assume increased responsibility and self-discipline
Facilitates communication between superordinates and subordinates	Fails to allow lower-level employees full participation in setting objectives
Focuses on achieving organizational goals	Increases paperwork
Evaluates results, not personalities or politics	Emphasizes only quantitative evaluations of tangible results
Provides job improvement and personal growth	Generates extra work for administrators
Yields common understandings of organizational goals	Yields ambiguous and abstract goals in education

zations, implementing and maintaining long-term MBO programs will require large investments and their success may be problematic.

INDIVIDUAL GOAL SETTING

While the applicability of MBO programs in education may be somewhat tenuous, the positive potential of goal setting for motivating both educators and students should not be lost. In other words, the effects of goal setting on motivation and performance are so well established that goal setting should not be dependent on a grand scheme such as MBO. In fact, the success of MBO as a strategy for raising productivity is less pronounced than that of just goal setting (Pinder, 1984; Guzzo, 1988). Whether a school has a formal goal-setting program or not, having individual teachers and administrators with the expertise to use goal-setting techniques constitutes a positive intervention to increase motivation and performance. Therefore, the following guidelines apply to both informal and formal programs of goal setting.

Writing goals that enhance motivation and performance is a difficult task. As an aid, Table 10.2 contains suggestions for developing goal statements. Two types of criteria are proposed—general and flexible. The **general goal-setting criteria** are applicable to all objective statements. Objectives should be clearly stated, acceptable to affected parties, realistic, and attainable. They should comprise tasks that are challenging and contribute directly or indirectly to the organization's overall goals.

Flexible goal-setting criteria improve the applicability of performance objectives. Statements of objectives should concentrate on what and when, not on why and how (Lasagna, 1971). As such, four types of objectives—innovative, problem-solving, administrative, and personal—are proposed to help individuals write differ-

TABLE 10.2 Criteria for Developing Individual Goals	
General Criteria	**Flexible Criteria**
Sufficient task	Type
	Innovative
Clarity	Problem-solving
Easily communicated	Administrative
Simple to understand	Personal
Acceptability	Time frame
Personal	Short-range
Superordinate	Long-range
Subordinate	
	Evaluation methods
Realistic parameters	Quantitative
Number	Qualitative
Time	
Related to organization's goals	

ent types of objectives according to their situations. In some schools or groups, administrators and subordinates may not be concerned with innovation or with a particular problem; they may simply want to ensure that important responsibilities are exercised most effectively. In such a situation, administrative or personal-improvement objectives take priority. Similarly, flexibility and diversity are needed in writing short-range and long-range objectives. Finally, evaluation methods should include quantitative measures of tangible outcomes, such as student achievement, as well as qualitative evaluations of less tangible results, such as satisfaction and improvement in self-concept.

Locke and Latham's (1984) guide on how to set goals can be a useful adjunct to the foregoing criteria. Seven steps are proposed:

1. Specify the general goal or tasks to be done.
2. Specify how the performance will be measured.
3. Specify the standard or target to be reached.
4. Specify the time span.
5. Prioritize the goals.
6. Rate goals on difficulty and importance.
7. Determine coordination requirements.

By combining the general and flexible criteria and these seven steps, a powerful approach to goal setting can be realized.

In sum, implementing individual or school district goal-setting programs requires a commitment of financial and personnel resources. While goal setting is no panacea, properly applied it can be an effective school and individual technique to enhance the work motivation of students, teachers, and administrators.

INCENTIVE SYSTEMS

A common theme among work-motivation theories is that work behavior can be motivated by many different rewards—for example, money, praise, social relationships, sense of accomplishment, alleviation of boredom (Guzzo, 1979). **Incentives** or **rewards,** as the organizational counterpart to individual motivation, are inducements that participants receive in return for being productive members of the organization. One purpose of organizational incentives is to motivate participants to improve their work performance by making jobs attractive, interesting, and satisfying. However, a perceived link between important rewards and effective performance must be developed (Lawler, 1987). Inherently, individuals are neither motivated nor unmotivated to perform effectively. Instead, they use their information-processing schema to select behaviors that satisfy their needs. Thus, schools get the kind of behavior that leads to the rewards that educators and students value and expect.

To initiate and maintain motivation and work behavior, organizations develop incentive systems to allocate a portion of whatever is accomplished by cooperative action to their working participants. Money, prestige, recognition, and achievement, for example, are distributed in schools to students and educators. When the incentive system is properly designed, financial and nonfinancial inducements can indeed increase performance (Pritchard et al., 1988). In other words, the incentive system largely determines the strength of teacher motivation to perform work responsibilities (Mitchell, Ortiz, and Mitchell, 1982, 1987). This fundamental role of incentives in organizations was emphasized nearly sixty years ago by Chester I. Barnard (1938) when he noted that inadequate incentives mean dissolution, change in organizational purpose, or failure of cooperation.

INTRINSIC AND EXTRINSIC INCENTIVES

Incentives are frequently thought of as being extrinsic and intrinsic. Although the distinctions are neither precise nor mutually exclusive, the two categories are useful in thinking about incentives. Generally speaking, **extrinsic incentives** are provided by the organization or other people; **intrinsic incentives** are outcomes mediated within the individual or granted to the individual himself or herself. Extrinsic outcomes include recognition, money, promotion, social interactions with colleagues, and well-behaved students. Intrinsic outcomes encompass feelings of accomplishment, achievement, competence, efficacy, self-esteem, and self-actualization (Miskel, 1982). Obviously, educators receive both types of incentives for their work, but generally find intrinsic rewards more meaningful and attractive than extrinsic ones (Mitchell, Ortiz, and Mitchell, 1987; Cohn and Kottkamp, 1993).

Intrinsic incentives are under the direct control of the individual and extrinsic incentives are not. Writers in education have tended to emphasize the importance of intrinsic motivation for teachers. For example, James L. Bess (1977) maintained that motivation to high teaching performance depends fundamentally on the strength and quality of satisfaction that can be derived from the task itself. In a study of incentives in schools, Dennis W. Spuck (1974) found that perceived levels of intrinsic rewards are more strongly associated with teacher attendance, recruitment, and retention than extrinsic inducements. Based on her investigation of reward systems, Ruth Wright (1985) concluded that intrinsic incentives hold greater potential for motivating teacher involvement in curriculum tasks than do extrinsic rewards. Moreover, intrinsic incentives that promote participation in curriculum tasks are not usually prescribed in school incentive plans. Similarly, Dan Lortie (1975) and Marilyn M. Cohn and Robert B. Kottkamp (1993) found that teachers consider intrinsic rewards as their major source of work satisfaction, especially feelings that they had reached their students.

One interpretation of this emphasis on intrinsic motivation and incentives for educators, which is rarely mentioned, is that having constrained access to extrinsic rewards, educational organizations rely on intrinsically motivated behavior of their employees (Sherman and Smith, 1984). Because this has been the prevalent condition in education for so long, policy makers have developed extensive mechanisms to convince employees to accept low extrinsic and high intrinsic rewards as being sufficient. Even in the reform movement started by the *Nation at Risk* report, teacher empowerment and job-enrichment programs focus on increasing intrinsic motivational and incentive factors in schools (Conger and Kanungo, 1988).

Although extrinsic rewards are not a primary focus of attention in today's schools, it is a big mistake to think of them as unimportant. Individuals are motivated by both extrinsic and intrinsic rewards (Malen, Murphy, and Hart, 1988). Moreover, the potential for providing nonmonetary extrinsic rewards is immense (Hajnal and Dibski, 1993). For educators and students alike, extrinsic rewards in schools are many, varied, and valued—for instance, commendations, favorable job assignments, group memberships, performance feedback, and participation in decision making.

Money

The most discussed extrinsic reward, or any reward for that matter, is probably money. In debates about money and its importance to motivation in education, strong points can be made on both sides of the issue. Based on considerable research, teachers, when asked, indicate a greater preference for intrinsic rewards than for salary (Lortie, 1975; Mitchell, Ortiz, and Mitchell, 1987; Cohn and Kottkamp, 1993). Hence, some would argue that the path to enhanced educator motivation is through intrinsic rewards.

Other findings suggest the importance of money. In allocating tax funds, a definite emphasis on increasing educator salaries is apparent. The after-inflation income of educators increased by about 10 percent during the 1980s (Bok, 1993). Research on teacher retention also indicates that salary is the first or second most important reason for leaving teaching; those who are paid more stay in teaching longer (Firestone and Bader, 1992). Susan Moore Johnson (1986) observes that to say teachers are *primarily* motivated by intrinsic incentives does not necessarily mean that they are motivated *solely* by them. Money does matter, particularly to educators whose income falls short of meeting basic needs. Clearly, even with all the discussion about intrinsic rewards, teachers are motivated by the opportunity to earn more (Firestone and Bader, 1992).

In fact, William A. Firestone (1991) calls for a reassessment of the role of money in teacher motivation. While teachers generally oppose merit pay, they are unlikely to do certain tasks unless extra pay is provided. He further observes that those who advocate increasing teacher commitment through the use of intrinsic rewards fail to note that teachers benefit from more time to do the things that are intrinsically rewarding. Frequently, the only way to get extra time is to buy it. Johnson (1986) seems to agree when she notes that financial incentives can promote specific behaviors (e.g., taking additional or difficult teaching assignments) and can direct teachers' efforts toward measurable goals (e.g., achieving higher test scores). Richard J. Murnane and David K. Cohen (1986) are even more adamant. They assert that teachers will engage in specific acts for which they are compensated. The risk in pay for tasks is that tasks not rewarded will not get done. In other words, money generates the behavior, but not the motivation to maintain the activity without the reward.

Merit Pay

The most controversial use of money in school organizations is in merit pay plans. In its pure form, **merit pay** is a compensation system in which pay is based on an individual's performance with at least a portion of a person's financial compensation being a performance bonus. High performers receive more money; low performers receive less money. The underlying principle is that some teachers or administrators earn more for doing the same work as others, only better (Firestone, 1991). As practiced in school settings, however, merit pay supplements the standard salary schedule and forms only a small part of an employee's salary (Hatry and Greiner, 1985; Hajnal and Dibski, 1993).

Since the early 1900s numerous merit pay plans for educators have been instituted in the United States. The most recent flurry of activity was generated in the mid-1980s. Derek Bok (1993) suggests two reasons for this renewed interest. One was the familiar hope of using money to motivate teachers to work harder and increase productivity. The other was an unspoken suspicion that many educators were neither talented nor effective. The idea was to find a way of raising salaries to reward better teachers and attract able recruits without spending a lot on mediocre people.

In their research, Mark A. Smylie and John C. Smart (1990) found teacher support for merit pay depends on its perceived effects on collegial relationships among teachers. Opposition is highest among teachers who believe that merit pay systems will increase competition and reduce cooperation among colleagues. Similar findings were made by Firestone (1991).

According to Betty Malen, Michael J. Murphy, and Ann W. Hart (1988), the criteria for receiving merit pay typically include being assessed as an excellent teacher (e.g., displaying prescribed teaching behaviors, increasing student test scores) and doing extra work for extra pay (e.g., serving as a mentor, leading extracurricular activities, conducting in-service workshops). Two common types of merit rewards are salary bonuses and increased status through public recognition of superior performance. They found that merit pay systems do not significantly alter either anticipated reward. As a salary benefit, merit pay is used to supplement, not supplant, the basic salary schedule. Even with a merit pay plan, the dominant portion of educator compensation is still the base salary determined by education and experience. Moreover, merit stipends are dispersed broadly to all or nearly all who apply. In such instances, merit pay becomes a general pay raise for all educators. In regard to status, procedural and peer pressures within schools combine to keep the recipients and rewards secret. In cases where public disclosure occurs, the benefit is offset by peer sanctions.

Although merit pay policies have been enacted, removed, revived, and retried for decades, few endure (Malen, Murphy, and Hart, 1988). Merit pay does not appear to be a viable approach to redistribute economic or status rewards in school settings. Even in the most favorable circumstances, true merit pay schemes are not likely to succeed (Astuto and Clark, 1985a; Johnson, 1986) and are not a promising way to strengthen incentives in schools (Bok, 1993).

In sum, while there is some dispute about the precise dividing line between intrinsic and extrinsic outcomes, a reasonable conclusion is that both intrinsic and extrinsic rewards are useful methods of motivating behavior. Therefore, the incentive system in educational organizations should be elaborate, stable, and dependable, and offer a wide range of intrinsic and extrinsic incentives to their students and employees. Unless individuals can count on rewards to meet their needs, values, and expectations, there is little reason to increase performance (Malen, Murphy, and Hart, 1988). The need and value theories of Maslow, Hodgkinson, and McClelland suggest a wide range of incentives that are either needed or valued. Similarly, Johnson (1986) calls for further research to understand the effects and possible interaction of intrinsic and extrinsic incentives for educators. For example, what type of incentive motivates teachers to work harder and longer, to teach in different ways, or to assume added responsibilities?

REDESIGN OF WORK

Work redesign modifies specific jobs to increase both the quality of the employees' work experience and the performance. **Jobs,** as a central concern in work design, are defined simply as a set of tasks grouped together under one job title (e.g., teacher, principal, student) and designed to be performed by a single individual. Moreover, jobs are bureaucratic; they are part of the organization; they exist independently of job incumbents; and they are relatively static. Jobs do change, but not on a day-to-day basis (Ilgen and Hollenbeck, 1991). As a strategy for change, then, work-redesign programs alter the content and process of jobs to match the work motivation of individuals. That is, work-redesign efforts modify the school organization to enhance educator and student motivation.

From a motivational perspective, work design makes assumptions about the needs, values, expectations, and goals of individuals and uses the assumptions as guides to develop jobs (Ilgen and Hollenbeck, 1991). This approach tries to maximize individual work motivation by increasing intrinsic aspects of the job itself. The idea is to have task motivation stem from intrinsic properties of the task or job rather than from extrinsic incentives or rewards attached to holding the job or to job performance. As a consequence of using a motivational approach, proponents claim that work-redesign programs improve the lives of individuals in at least four ways (Hackman and Suttle, 1977):

- The fit between individual motivation and job content is improved.
- Behavior is altered directly and tends to stay changed.
- Opportunities for starting other needed organizational changes arise.
- The long-term result is an organization that humanizes rather than dehumanizes the people.

Five approaches to work design will be considered. The first two—job-enrichment theory and job-characteristics model—were originally developed for private-sector organizations, but attempts have been made to generalize the ideas to schools. The next three—professionalization, career ladders, and career paths—are work design approaches to enhance motivation in schools.

HERZBERG'S APPROACH TO MOTIVATION AND JOB ENRICHMENT

Frederick Herzberg and his colleagues (Herzberg, Mausner, and Snyderman, 1959) developed the motivation-hygiene theory based on their findings from their now famous study of engineers and accountants. Motivation-hygiene theory could have been included in Chapter 4 as an example of need theory. The factors leading to positive job attitudes (motivators) do so because of their potential to satisfy the individual's need for self-actualization, or in Herzberg's terms, promote psychological growth. Conversely, hygienes can be related to physiological, safety, and social needs. Both theories emphasize the same set of relationships. Maslow focuses on general human needs of the psychological person, while Herzberg concentrates on the psychological person in terms of how the job affects basic needs. However, Herzberg (1982) tends to downplay the similarities that his model shares with Maslow's need-hierarchy theory. Motivation-hygiene theory is being considered in this chapter, however, because Herzberg (1966, 1982) used it so extensively in his own efforts to design work.

Herzberg's Theory of Motivation

The theory, variously termed the two-factor theory, dual-factor theory, and simply Herzberg's theory, has been widely accepted by administrators and policy makers. Herzberg and his colleagues found that positive events were dominated by references to achievement, recognition (for achievement), the work itself (challenging), responsibility, and advancement (promotion). Negative events were dominated by references to interpersonal relations with superiors and peers, technical supervision, company policy and administration, working conditions, salary, and personal life.

Based on these findings, they posited that the presence of certain factors act to increase an individual's job satisfaction, but absence of these factors does not necessarily produce job dissatisfaction. Theoretically, individuals start from a neutral stance; they possess neither positive nor negative attitudes toward a job (see Table 10.3). Hence, motivation-hygiene theory postulates that one set of factors (motivators) produces satisfaction, while another set (hygienes) produces dissatisfaction. Work satisfaction and dissatisfaction are not opposites; rather, they are separate and distinct dimensions of a person's attitude about work. The gratification of certain factors, called **motivators** (i.e., achievement, recognition, work itself, responsibility, and advancement), increase job satisfaction beyond the neutral point, but when the motivators are not gratified, only minimal dissatisfaction results. On the other hand, when factors called **hygienes** (i.e., interpersonal relations, supervision, policy and administration, working conditions, salary, and personal life) are not gratified, negative attitudes are created, producing job dissatisfaction. Gratification of hygienes leads only to minimal job satisfaction. Consequently, motivators combine to contribute more to job satisfaction than to job dissatisfaction. Hygienes combine to contribute more to job dissatisfaction than to job satisfaction.

TABLE **10.3**	Job Satisfaction Continuum—A Graphic Representation of the Motivation-Hygiene Theory	
Hygienes		**Motivators**
Interpersonal relations (with subordinates)		Achievement
		Recognition
Interpersonal relations (with peers)		Work itself
		Responsibility
Supervision (technical)		Advancement
Policy and administration		
Working conditions		
Personal life		
Dissatisfaction ⟵——— 0 ———⟶ *Satisfaction*		
(−) (+)		

Herzberg (1966) contrasts hygiene seekers and motivation seekers in the following ways. Hygiene seekers have chronic and heightened dissatisfaction with various aspects of the job context—for example, salary, supervision, status, and security. When these factors are improved, any alleviation of dissatisfaction is of short duration. Moreover, hygiene seekers realize little satisfaction from accomplishments and express cynicism about positive virtues of work and life in general.

On the other hand, motivation seekers are motivated by the nature of the task and have a higher tolerance for poor hygiene factors. The effect of improving hygiene factors is of short duration. Motivation seekers realize great satisfaction from job accomplishments and have positive feelings toward work and life in general.

Miner (1980) observes further that the five motivator factors are both conceptually and empirically related. When the elements are present in work, the individual's basic needs of personal growth and self-actualization will be satisfied; positive feelings and improved performance will also result. The hygiene factors, when provided appropriately, can serve to remove dissatisfaction and improve performance up to a point. But hygiene elements do not produce as positive feelings or as high performance levels as are potentially possible.

Although Herzberg's theory became quite controversial, it has had a major impact on the field of work motivation and job design. Steers and Porter (1991) argue that Herzberg deserves a great deal of credit. By calling attention to the need for improved understanding of the role played by motivation in work organizations, he filled a void in the late 1950s. His approach is systematic and his language understandable. He advanced a theory that is simple to grasp, based on empirical data, and offers specific action recommendations to administrators. Pinder (1984) offers an even stronger defense for the model. He believes that substantial evidence exists that

Herzberg's ideas concerning the design of jobs have considerable validity and practical utility.

Herzberg's Approach to Job Enrichment

Herzberg named his approach to work redesign *job enrichment*. Its purpose is to assist in motivating employees to good work performance. Herzberg (1982) forcefully distinguishes between job enrichment and job enlargement, which he judges a failure. Job enrichment provides the opportunity for the psychological growth of employees, while job enlargement merely makes the job bigger by adding snippets of various activities.

A key aspect in job enrichment is the concept of psychological growth. When Herzberg (1966) discusses psychological growth, many of the ideas are similar to those found in the more contemporary cognitive approaches to information processing and motivation presented in Chapter 4. For example, he posits that individuals who are psychologically more advanced know more (have more schema), see relationships in knowledge (schemas are linked for understanding), can use them creatively (schemas can be combined to generate new knowledge), and can be effective in ambiguous situations (apply knowledge in new situations or expertise); in a word, they have superior information-processing abilities.

For Herzberg (1982), **job enrichment** essentially consists of adding motivator factors to a job and reducing negative hygiene factors. The idea is that jobs should be designed so that motivators meet individual needs for psychological growth. For example, achievement and recognition provide opportunities to increase knowledge; responsibility produces opportunities to enhance understanding; possibility for growth promotes creativity; and advancement produces the opportunity to experience ambiguity in decision making (Herzberg, 1966). In other words, job-enrichment programs use two methods:

- Emphasize motivators to use people effectively and promote their growth
- Supplement motivators with a good hygiene program to treat people well and provide for their comfort

Hence, the basic postulate of Herzberg's job-enrichment theory is that when people are used and treated well, the result will be motivated performance.

The focus in Herzberg's approach to job enrichment is on the work itself as a means to fulfilling individual motivational needs. Jobs are redesigned to maximize the opportunities for individual growth at work. While specific job-enrichment programs may target various aspects for change, Herzberg (1982) identified at least six components of enriched jobs.

1. *Client centered:* Jobs should provide services to clients.
2. *Feedback:* Jobs should supply knowledge of results to employees.
3. *New learning:* Jobs should provide individuals with access to new and meaningful expertise.

4. *Discretionary resources:* Jobs should allow workers control over some resources to promote task accomplishment.

5. *Direct communication:* Jobs should link individuals directly to the sources of needed information.

6. *Individual accountability:* Jobs should encourage personal responsibility for results.

Starting in the late 1960s, job-enrichment programs became very popular. Herzberg (1982) worked on numerous job-enrichment programs—for example, AT&T and several units of the U.S. Air Force. He reported over 100 projects had reached maturity and claimed that they were paying off in terms of enhanced motivation and productivity.

WORK DESIGN AND THE JOB-CHARACTERISTICS MODEL

Since the late 1970s, the dominant perspective on job design has been the **job-characteristics model** (Staw, 1984; Fox and Feldman, 1988). Ricky W. Griffin (1987) speculates that the reasons for its popularity are its provision of an academically sound model, a set of easily used measures, a package of practitioner-oriented implementation guidelines, and an initial body of empirical support. J. Richard Hackman and Greg R. Oldham (1975, 1976, 1980) are its primary creators and proponents. The approach combines and unifies Maslow's need fulfillment theory, Herzberg's concern for job enrichment, and expectancy theory into a theory of job design.

The concepts and generalizations of the job-characteristics model are outlined in Figure 10.1. The theory specifies that an employee will experience internal or intrinsic motivation when the job generates three critical psychological states. First, *feeling of meaningfulness* of the work is the degree to which the individual experiences the job as being valuable and worthwhile. For work to be meaningful, three necessary characteristics are hypothesized: skill variety (work involves a number of activities using different skills and talents), task identity (job requires the completion of an entire segment of work), and task significance (job has a substantial impact on the lives of other people).

Second, *feeling of responsibility* for work outcomes is the degree to which the individual feels personally accountable for the results of the work he or she performs. Autonomy is postulated to be the primary job characteristic that creates a feeling of responsibility. Autonomy depends on the amount of freedom, independence, and discretion that an individual has to schedule the work and determine the procedures to be used. For educational settings, it is important to distinguish between autonomy and isolation (Hart, 1990b). Autonomy is control over time, decisions, important resources, and information necessary to accomplish the work. Isolation is aloneness and lack of interaction with peers.

Third, *knowledge of results* is the degree to which the individual knows and understands on a continuous basis how effectively he or she is performing the job.

FIGURE **10.1**

The Job-Characteristics Model

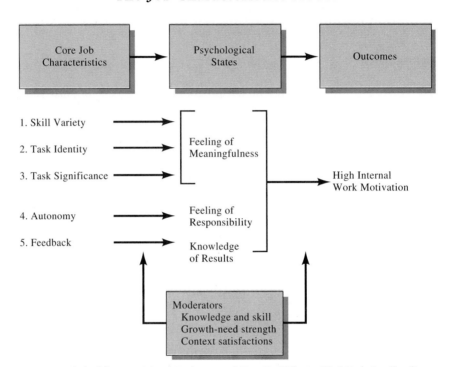

Source: Adapted from J. Richard Hackman and Greg R. Oldham, *Work Redesign* (Reading, Mass.: Addison-Wesley, 1980), p. 83

The focus is on feedback directly from the job—for example, when a teacher provides individual instruction to a student and observes the student's learning. In this case the knowledge of results comes from the work activities themselves and not from another person such as an administrator or colleague who collects data or makes a judgment about how well the job is being performed.

The three psychological states are internal to individuals and, therefore, not directly manipulable in designing work. Instead, the five job characteristics, which are reasonably objective, measurable, and changeable properties of the work, foster the psychological states and produce work motivation. Consequently, Hackman and Oldham propose the generalization that the motivating potential of a job is a result of meaningfulness, autonomy, and feedback. Meaningfulness is a function of skill variety, task identity, and task significance (see Figure 10.1).

Jobs with high motivating potential create conditions that reinforce employees who have high performance levels (Hackman and Oldham, 1980). In other words, the characteristics of a job set the stage for the internal motivation or positive psychological states of individuals. Therefore, an additional generalization from the theory is that as the motivating potential scores of employees increase, the outcomes (intrinsic work motivation, growth satisfaction, job satisfaction, and work effectiveness) also increase.

However, for the relationships among the components (job characteristics, psychological states, and outcomes) to hold, three moderating conditions must be fulfilled (Hackman and Oldham, 1980; Gardner and Cummings, 1988). First, workers must possess sufficient knowledge and skills to perform the enriched jobs. Second, individuals must be satisfied with job-context factors such as compensation, job security, and relations with colleagues. Third, the employees must have strong needs for personal accomplishment, learning, and development—that is, growth-need strength. If high levels of the moderators are present, then the positive relationships among the components should be enhanced.

Research and Evaluation of the Job-Characteristics Model

A major strength of the job-characteristics model is that the assessment of the core characteristics is relatively easy to accomplish. To measure the primary variables, Hackman and Oldham developed the job diagnostic survey (JDS) questionnaire (Hackman and Oldham, 1975, 1980). The JDS has recently been revised (Cordery and Sevastos, 1993).

The initial field research by Hackman and Oldham (1976) supports the major generalizations of the theory. Later investigations provide mixed support.[1] In a recent review of thirty-one well-designed studies, John Kelly (1992) also found limited support for the job-characteristics model. He concludes that while job redesign guided by the job-characteristics model appears to increase job satisfaction, no strong evidence was found that it motivates higher performance. Although Griffin (1991) tends to agree with this conclusion, his own research demonstrated a link between performance and job redesign using the job-characteristics model, but it took nearly four years for the performance increases to appear.

In the educational setting, a number of researchers have used many concepts of the model to assess the motivation potential of teaching positions.[2] In contrast, Larry Frase and his colleagues (Frase and Heck, 1992; Frase and Sorenson, 1992; Frase and Matheson, 1992) worked with a number of school districts to help redesign the jobs of educators based on the job-characteristics model. Their results generally support the model.

Hackman and Oldham (1980) acknowledge several shortcomings in their theory. Individual differences exist among people, and the best ways to define, measure, and include variations among individuals in the model remain open to question. Similarly, the links between job characteristics and psychological states are apparently not as strong as originally anticipated. Another problem involves the lack of independence of the job characteristics. The model treats them as though they were independent or uncorrelated, but jobs that are high on one characteristic tend to be high on the others. The concept of feedback as used in the model is not adequately defined. Determining what is and is not job-based feedback is difficult. Finally, the relationships between objective properties of jobs and people's perceptions of those properties are not clear. The model does not consider the inevitable redefinition of the tasks that employees will make to draw more consistent relationships between their jobs and their needs, values, and attitudes. In this regard, Karlene H. Roberts and William Glick (1981) strongly criticize the job-characteristics model because the approach treats perceptions as "real" data as distinct from objective descriptions of the job characteristics. They maintain that perceptions of task characteristics are just perceptions and do not represent the attributes of tasks. However, convincing arguments have been made that Roberts and Glick's assertion is not true and that perceptions are indeed a useful source of information about jobs (Griffin, 1983).

Application

While recognizing its limitations, the job-characteristics model does provide measures and guidelines that can be used in diagnosing and implementing job redesign for professional employees (Miner, 1980; Oldham and Kulik, 1984). In this model, work redesign essentially involves improving the five core characteristic of jobs, or increasing the overall motivating potential of the job. Six guidelines are typically given for directing job redesign efforts (Hackman and Suttle, 1977).

- Diagnose the work system to determine the need for systematic change in the core job characteristics.
- Focus the redesign on the work itself—that is, skill variety, task identity, task significance, autonomy, and feedback.
- Prepare contingency plans ahead of time for unanticipated problems and side effects.
- Monitor and evaluate the redesign efforts continuously to determine whether the anticipated changes are occurring or not.
- Confront the difficult problems as early in the project as possible.
- Design the change processes to fit the goals of the job-redesign program.

Hart (1990b) suggests that the job-characteristics model could provide a useful framework for examining teacher task, autonomy, and feedback structures in schools and their emerging influence on teacher motivation, attitudes, and performance. She also thinks that other applications to teacher work could include the assessment of new task structures, supervision systems, and feedback mechanisms. Overall, job redesign seems to offer high potential for producing positive results in educational organizations, but given the difficulties in implementing the changes, success will be difficult to achieve.

WORK DESIGN IN SCHOOLS

Shortly after the *Nation at Risk* report was published, the educational policy scene was inundated by critical reports. They diagnosed a variety of illnesses that appeared to afflict schools and prescribed a variety of reform remedies to cure the various afflictions (Labaree, 1992). Two of the most influential reports were *Tomorrow's Teachers* (Holmes Group, 1986) and *A Nation Prepared* (Carnegie Task Force on Teaching as a Profession, 1986). From David F. Labaree's (1992) analysis, the two reports argue that the quality of public education can improve only by transforming school teaching into a full-fledged profession. Moreover, a key element in this move to professionize teaching is to redesign the jobs and work of educators. Both reports called for the abandonment of what Dan C. Lortie (1975) had called the "unstaged" career, in which teachers occupy the same organizational level and receive compensation based on experience and education. A similar call was made in 1987 to professionalize the careers of educational administrators in the report entitled, *Leaders for America's Schools* (National Commission on Excellence in Educational Administration, 1987). The motivating advantages of professionalizing school teaching and administration include increasing task variety, status, autonomy, responsibility, opportunities for psychological growth, and compensation.

PROFESSIONALIZATION IN SCHOOLS

Since the mid-1980s, extensive efforts have been made to professionalize teaching and to redesign their jobs. Labaree (1992) offers a number of reasons to justify professionalization of teaching.

1. By the early 1980s a shift had occurred from equity to excellence in the goals for public education. A swing from political goals (e.g., equity, equality, citizenship training) to market goals (excellence, vocational training, individual accomplishment) characterized the American scene.

2. A disenchantment with bureaucratic reform efforts developed. Policy makers and reformers concluded that mandating structural changes in schools not only had weak and transitory effects on teaching and learning, but had increased the size and complexity of the school bureaucracy. Hence, decentralizing administrative control and increasing individual professionalism were logical outgrowths of their disenchantment.

3. The rise in feminism called into question teaching as a prototypical form of women's work. Not only are most teachers female, but teaching puts women in situations that mimic both the nurturing role of mother in relation to students and the subordinate role of wife in relation to male administrators. Consequently, in the increasingly feminist environment and opening of opportunities in medicine, law and business, teaching began to look less attractive to women seeking a professional career.

4. A growing recognition emerged that the status and working conditions of teaching had to be improved in ways comparable to other college graduates. For example, most elementary and secondary school teachers have limited access to an office, telephone, computer terminal, or secretary; compensation is not comparable to jobs requiring similar levels of education and activity;

and the workload is so large that it denies many, if not most teachers the right to excel in teaching without undue hardship and personal sacrifice.

5. Improvements in the knowledge of teaching made it possible to claim legitimately a professional foundation for teaching. The Holmes Group both popularized and made extensive claims about the science of teaching and how it could be transmitted to professionals.

As a reasonable hypothesis, these factors combined in an unstable policy environment to create a strong movement to professionalize the jobs and work of educators.

Characteristics of a Profession

Janet A. Weiss (1989: 2) asserts that "Teaching is professional work. The work teachers do is predominantly intellectual, requires the consistent application of judgment, cannot be standardized or routinized, and calls for prolonged preparation through education." Definitions of the term "professional," such as the one by Weiss, typically list a number of common attributes. Lists of structural attributes or traits have been heavily influenced by images of occupations that already were viewed as highly professionalized—for example, law and medicine (Hall, 1986). In a recent work, David L. Torres (1991) argues that four structural traits link much of the knowledge about professionalism together. A **profession** then is defined by four characteristics—knowledge, regulation and control, ideology, and association.

Knowledge, as a primary characteristic of a profession, deals with expertise that professionals possess (Torres, 1991). Decisions are based on formal knowledge that is acquired through extensive education and practice. Eliot Freidson (1986) believes that the pervasive use of reason, sustained where possible by measurement, to gain functional efficiency best captures the meaning of formal knowledge in the professions. In other words, a primary attribute of a profession is having and systematically using a coherent knowledge base (Bowman, 1989). Based on a codified body of knowledge, professionals are experts in specific and limited areas who do work that is characterized by complexity and adaptiveness. They diagnose and treat on a case-by-case basis; generalized step-by-step solutions either do not exist or are very complicated.

Regulation and control includes standards of practice, nature of self-regulation, and a structure responsible for enforcing professional rules and regulations—for example, a state board of professional practice (Torres, 1991). In a given field, professionals constitute a group of equals who control themselves. Professionals expect extensive autonomy in exercising their special competence because they claim that they alone are best suited to make decisions in their specialized area. An explanation of how autonomy is gained is through social contract (Sykes, 1987). The contract involves the exchange of autonomy for obligation. In other words, a profession agrees to develop and enforce standards of good practice in exchange for the right to practice free of bureaucratic supervision and outside regulation. Furthermore, the legitimacy of professional control rests on two kinds of expectations for trust—that professionals will use current expert knowledge and skill in competent ways and that professionals will demonstrate a special concern of others' interests above their own. Social control within professions may be eroding. Eliot Freidson (1984) believes that organized professional associations have flouted the public interest and the informal norms of social control among professionals have not been exercised judiciously and systematically. Numerous scholars have criticized the performance of the professions and most particularly the degree to which economic self-interest rather than common good has motivated the activities of professionals and their associations (Freidson, 1986).

Ideology holds that a core set of values guide professional behavior (Torres, 1991). An important indicator of professional ideology is that practitioners have an internalized code of ethics to guide their activities. Indeed, the service ideal is pivotal in most codes of ethics. Professionals are expected to subordinate their own interests and to act in the best interests of clients. In addition, the clients are particularly vulnerable to the actions of professionals because clients typically need assistance but do not know how to help themselves. They place themselves in the hands of professionals, confident that professionals will act in their best interests. If a professional acts primarily from self-interest, then condemnation and sanctions by colleagues and community members usually damage that self-interest. Hence, the "altruism" of professionals is maintained because failure to conform to the service norm is less rewarding than conformity.

Association refers to a professed collegiality, or unity of purpose, and to an actual organizational structure or professional association that formally represents the profession (Torres, 1991). The "significant others" for professionals are colleagues whose knowledge and competence in the field are useful in decision making. The professional's loyalty is to the integrity of the profession and to the service of clients.

In summary, a profession is characterized by knowledge acquired through long periods of training in higher education; autonomy and control in professional decision making based upon knowledge, standards, and peer review; a core ideology based on the adherence to a code of conduct and service ideals; and a colleague-oriented reference group. Rather than classifying some occupations as professions and others not, Edward Gross and Amitai Etzioni (1985) propose a continuum. At one pole of the continuum would be the occupations that have earned the right to call themselves professions. At the opposite pole, the occupations that would still be struggling for recognition. An occupation comes closer to the professional pole as it gains more traits of a profession. In other words, occupations tend to acquire, rather than inherently possess, the attributes associated with professionalism (Torres, 1991) and evolve into full professional status.

In regard to educators, our assessment is that during the past two decades both school teachers and administrators have made significant movement toward the professional end of the continuum. Both groups have growing knowledge bases and extensive preparation; several states have created professional practice commissions to control training and licensure standards; codes of conduct and shared values are reasonably common; and strong associations exist at the state and national levels. Problems are still evident, however, in compensation, status, and the design of jobs.

CAREER LADDERS FOR TEACHERS

As a redesign of educational work, career-ladder programs are seen by many policy makers as moving teaching careers closer to the professional end of the occupational continuum. Career ladders became one of the most touted and widely mandated reforms of teaching and schools during the 1980s (Bacharach, Conley, and Shedd, 1986). In 1987, for example, approximately forty states had or were developing career-ladder or other teacher-incentive programs (Hart, 1987).

Three reasons are generally offered as rationale for creating career-ladder programs. The first is based on the research finding that many of the best teachers leave their instructional careers after a brief foray in the classroom. Historically, about 50 percent of a teacher cohort will leave teaching during the first five to six years (Chapman and Hutcheson, 1982; Darling-Hammond, 1984; Mark and Anderson, 1985; Murnane, 1987). Moreover, a disproportionate percentage of those leaving teaching are the most academically talented (Vance and Schlechty, 1981, 1982). These data suggest that new teachers lack strong professional career orientations and that schools depend on new, transient college graduates to maintain the teaching force. The second reason given for redesign is based on the observation that teaching in the elementary and secondary schools has a flat career path or is "unstaged" (Lortie, 1975). Teachers have limited opportunities for advancement in their instructional work. New and experienced teachers have the same role expectations. Teachers with motivations to advance or gain new responsibilities generally have two choices—they can remain frustrated in their self-contained classrooms or they can leave. A third reason supporting the need for career ladders is that, although teaching is demanding work requiring creativity and versatility, it is repetitive. Despite the variety of classroom challenges and achievements, one year can look a lot like the next and there is little prospect to change the year to year pattern (Johnson, 1986). Hence, career-ladder programs were seen as ways to attract and retain highly talented individuals to education.

A **career-ladder program** redesigns jobs to provide individuals with prospects for promotion, formalizes status ranks for teachers, matches teacher abilities with job tasks, and distributes the responsibilities for school and faculty improvements to the professional staff (Murphy, 1985). In essence, the goal of career-ladder programs is to enrich work and enlarge teacher responsibilities (Johnson, 1986). Career ladders, as job-enrichment models, generally include promotions to higher ranks with the assumption of additional duties at each higher step—for example, mentoring and supervising new teachers, developing curriculum materials, and program evaluation. That is, the central conceptual feature is a differentiation of responsibilities among teachers (Bacharach, Conley, and Shedd, 1986).

By using job-enrichment strategies, career-ladder programs can address some of the concerns about teaching jobs. Such programs can provide teachers with opportunities and incentives to grow professionally, to develop new skills, to increase task variety and responsibility, to accept new challenges, and to promote collegiality. The innovation also increases teacher involvement in the professional aspects of schooling—that is, authority over the decision-making process for their clients. Career-ladder plans focus on recruitment, retention, and performance incentives to enhance the attractiveness of teaching. At their best this approach to work redesign reflects the belief that intelligent and creative teachers can be attracted to teaching and that the overall quality of the teaching force can be improved by a staged career with differential staffing responsibilities and reward allocations.

A general characteristic of career-ladder plans based on a job-enrichment model is a hierarchical set of job categories, usually three or four, with different role expectations. A career-ladder program could include the following steps.

Status I: Beginning or novice teachers. This is the time when individuals assume the primary responsibility for teaching various student groups, receive modest levels of supervision and mentoring, and complete the probationary period of employment and certification.

Status II: Professional classroom teachers. They are autonomous teachers who are qualified to assume full responsibility for teaching the subjects and students in their areas of professional expertise.

Status III: A simple enlargement of the regular classroom teacher's job. They would be encouraged to assume responsibility for special projects for extra compensation. For example, they might assume responsibility for designing an in-service workshop or create a new set of curriculum materials.

Status IV: The most advanced level, typically called teacher leader or master teacher. It is reserved for teachers who accept responsibilities beyond a single classroom (e.g., evaluate curriculum materials, supervise probationary teachers in their own schools and across the district, conduct research, develop and deliver in-service projects, and work as curriculum specialists). Usually they continue to serve as classroom teachers, but on a reduced teaching load.

As a type of work redesign, career-ladder programs represent complex organizational interventions. For example, Hart and Murphy (1990) assert that restructuring requires explicit decisions about redesigning tasks, responsibilities, supervision, collegial and authority relationships, and compensation patterns. More specifically, as new organizational positions and levels of hierarchy are created, the actual content, processes, length of terms, and amount of special compensation of the new roles must be defined; existing role definitions of teachers, principals, and curriculum supervisors also require new formulations. Moreover, implementing a career-ladder program will likely create confusion, conflict, and extra work for everyone in the school system. While the drawbacks are substantial, such work redesigns do have the potential to make greater use of professional expertise and provide teachers with motivating work and career experiences (Conley and Levinson, 1993). As is the case with most attempts to create and implement significant work-redesign programs, the research evidence for career-ladder programs is mixed.

Research and Evaluation
of Career-Ladder Programs

Probably the most extensive series of empirical examinations of career-ladder programs has been conducted by Malen, Murphy, and Hart (1988). In a comprehensive analysis, they conclude that job expansion and job redesign in career-ladder programs can be successfully implemented. While neither quick nor easy, they found that career-ladder interventions can be potent enough to improve teacher performance and retention. In a study of teachers with five years or less experience, Hart and Murphy (1990) found that the most talented ones hold more favorable attitudes toward career-ladder programs than their less talented colleagues. In particular, the talented group showed relatively high interest in professionalism, power, and leadership. They also felt less constrained in their future career options and the prospect of new roles raised their expectations to high levels.

Hart (1987, 1990a) also reports on two studies of career-ladder programs. She found that teachers identified collegiality as important. Teachers participating in the program held more positive attitudes toward the interventions than nonparticipants and experienced teachers tend to be less involved and more critical than less experienced teachers. Hart also found that the norms, beliefs, and values common to the teaching occupation influenced the work redesign at both schools. Expectations of equality, cordiality, and privacy affect the way the teachers interpret career-ladder intervention. When these values are violated, support for the intervention declines and where the leaders were positive, the intervention was more successfully implemented.

An assessment of career-ladder programs in three school districts was made by William A. Firestone and his colleague Beth D. Bader (Firestone, 1991; Firestone and Bader, 1992). Their findings indicate that job-enlargement programs can increase teacher motivation. Depending on the design and implementation processes, the outcomes varied substantially across the three districts. Their study and others (Rowan, 1990; Smylie, 1994) support the notion that professional changes such as job enlargement, teacher participation, and decentralization were more effective than the bureaucratic techniques of merit pay, top-down management, and a reliance on the organization to implement innovations.

Howard Ebmeir and Hart (1992) report that teachers in schools with career-ladder programs exhibit more positive attitudes than do teachers in schools without such programs. Smylie and Smart (1990) found that teacher support for career-ladder programs is highest when they perceive that the redesign promotes professional learning and collegial relationships. Using a micropolitical perspective, Smylie and Jean Brownlee-Conyers (1992) conclude that the principals and teacher leaders seek to reduce ambiguities and uncertainties, attempt to define their roles and relationships, and evoke strategies that influence the new roles. In contrast, Conley and Levinson (1993) found that participation in career-ladder programs is positively associated with satisfaction only for more experienced teachers.

Overall, the research findings indicate that career-ladder programs as examples of work redesign in schools are conceptualized and implemented with varying degrees of success. When designed and instituted appropriately, they can have positive effects on school programs, curricula, and instruction. Moreover, they can promote teacher and administrator satisfaction and motivation by making the work itself more interesting, increasing autonomy and responsibility, and raising expectations for psychological growth.

CAREER PATHS
IN EDUCATIONAL ADMINISTRATION

Even though various forms of career ladders are the object of extensive interest, an alternative career path open to teachers who want to remain in education requires that they leave classroom teaching and enter the administrative hierarchy. They must move into different organizational strata to achieve new and different work, responsibilities, and achievements. In terms of career paths, Karen N. Gaertner (1980) describes the administrative hierarchy of schools as being relatively simple. Administrative positions in schools are limited in number and job titles tend to have the same meaning across school districts and over time. Yet the structure is neither trivial nor totally regularized, as might be the case in a civil service bureaucracy.

Based on her conclusion that little effort had been made to identify and describe the career paths of school administrators and to study administrator mobility, Gaertner grouped twenty-five administrative positions into ten categories shown in Table 10.4. Two regularities in administrator careers emerged from her study. First, public school administrators are relatively immobile. Second, most moves are into or out of administrative positions, not among administrative jobs (Gaertner, 1980).

Gaertner (1980) also identified three career paths or patterns for school administrators. One leads to the superintendancy through the following linkages: teacher, secondary curriculum specialist, assistant secondary principal, secondary principal,

---

TABLE 10.4 Classification of Administrative Positions in Schools

1. Superintendent

2. Assistant, Associate, or Deputy Superintendent

3. Administrative Specialist—business, plant and facilities, personnel

4. Administrator of Instruction

5. Secondary School Principal

6. Elementary School Principal

7. Assistant Principal, Secondary

8. Assistant Principal, Elementary

9. Curriculum Specialist, Secondary—Consultant, Subject Coordinator, Supervisor

10. Curriculum Supervisor, Elementary—Consultant, Subject Coordinator, Supervisor, Special Education Director

superintendent. This path involves direct supervision of the primary work of the school. A second path to the superintendancy moves through the following pattern: teacher, secondary curriculum specialist, administrator of instruction, assistant superintendent, superintendent. This is an administrative specialist path. The third pattern is essentially isolated from the top of the hierarchy, peaking at the elementary principal level. This position is fed by the assistant elementary principal position.

In a study of Wisconsin superintendents, James C. March and James G. March (1977, 1978) found that after becoming superintendents, educators' career changes tend to be almost random events. However, movement tends to be systematic in two ways. First, localism is profound. Second, superintendents move to better districts— that is, larger and wealthier. Superintendents apparently have a rating hierarchy of districts and attempt to move up the hierarchy. In contrast, while superintendents can make distinctions among districts, superintendents are indistinguishable to the districts. The process of evaluating prospective superintendents by school districts does not provide sufficient performance sampling to allow the decisions to be made on a systematic basis. Hence, the careers are almost random sequences of moves. Nevertheless, moving to larger and wealthier districts suggests motivation patterns among superintendents of both valuing extrinsic incentives (e.g., better working conditions, higher status, better compensation) and intrinsic incentives (e.g., different job challenges, task variety and achievement, recognition).

Charol Shakeshaft (1986), Sandra Prolman (1982), and Judith A. Adkinson (1981) assert that the career paths for men and women in school administration not only are different but that women are underrepresented in administrative positions. Shakeshaft (1986) maintains that the portraits of women and men administrators are vastly different. In comparison to her male counterpart, the average female administrator is likely to be older; of a different race, religion, and political party; unmarried; from a more urban background; more liberal; and able to understand the issues of single parents and divorce more personally.

Prolman (1982) notes that career contingencies disadvantage women's careers in school administration. For example, women tend to teach longer than men; women tend to be grouped in elementary schools and promotions to the upper levels tend to be made from the secondary level; and women hold staff positions in the central office rather than line positions at the school or central-office level. For women, early sex role socialization combined with sex stereotyping of occupations contribute to the decision to teach, to the lack of mobility, and to the lack of mobility expectations. The lack of expectations in turn, relates to the longer teaching careers of women and lack of mobility. Shakeshaft (1986) concludes that women turn to administration in their thirties, almost always at the urging of someone in the district. If a woman seeks a position on her own, and does not get it, she will try only once or twice before stopping her pursuit of an administrative position.

We agree with Shakeshaft (1986) that **administrative careers** do not preclude seeing teaching as an equally valid and legitimate career path. When individuals seek administrative positions, however, their searches are likely motivated to gain additional and different kinds of incentives.

SCHOOL LEADERS AS MOTIVATORS

Martin L. Maehr and his colleagues Carol Midgley, Timothy Urdan, and Stewart Wood (Maehr, Midgley, and Urdan, 1992; Wood and Midgley, 1994) propose, develop, and test an approach to enhance motivation in schools. Their model is based on recent research on motivation and achievement involving two contrasting types of goals— task focused and ability focused. An **ability-focused goal** is concerned with being judged "able"; the goal is to outperform others or achieve success even when the task is easy. A **task-focused goal** is concerned with learning; the goal is to gain understanding, insight, or skill and to accomplish something challenging. With a task focus, achievement and mastery are seen as being dependent on one's effort. As children define the purpose of learning, profound motivational consequences arise. The goals that they accept in performing a task are likely to affect their predilection to try hard, assume or avoid challenges, or persist when faced with failure. Ability and task goals lead to broadly different approaches to learning and learning outcomes. Children with task orientations tend to use more powerful information-processing strategies (see Chapter 4). For example, they can distinguish important from unimportant information and attempt to figure out how the new information fits with existing schemas. In contrast, children with an ability focus tend to use less powerful information-processing strategies such as rereading text, memorizing, and rehearsing. Hence, goal orientation has a pervasive influence on both the nature and the quality of student motivation and learning (Maehr, Midgley, and Urdan, 1992).

The school-leader-as-motivator approach concentrates on how school leaders can affect student motivation. Maehr and his colleagues reason that as leaders inaugurate, support, and maintain certain policies and practices, a school environment or culture emerges that reflects a rationale for teaching and learning. These factors then define the meaning of school for students and affect the character and quality of student investment or motivation. They propose a number of actions that administrators, teachers, and other leaders can take to enhance the saliency of task-focused goals in the learning environment in schools (Maehr, Midgley, and Urdan, 1992). Seven types of action follow.

1. *Move the curriculum and instruction to authentic tasks and active learning.*
   For instance, students should be given tasks that are relevant to their lives and require creative thinking and problem solving rather than drill and practice exercises focused on memorization.

2. *Provide opportunities for student initiative and responsibility.*
   Maehr, Midgley, and Urdan (1992) urge that students be encouraged to participate in school decision making. They believe that this helps students understand the nature of the school's mission, its relevance to their lives, and the intrinsic worth of learning.

3. *Recognize student initiative and responsibility.*
   High grades and listings on honor rolls tend to be related more to ability than to effort. Maehr and his colleagues recommend "personal best" awards to recognize

the intrinsic worth of learning and the hard work needed to attain new levels of achievement.

4. *Eliminate homogeneous ability grouping of students.*
Ability grouping fosters ability goals and can reduce both student and teacher motivation. Instead, students should be grouped by topic, interest, and their choice. Moreover, groups and their members should be changed frequently (Wood and Midgley, 1994).

5. *Evaluate for student effort and progress.*
Assessment practices that focus on comparisons, outcomes, and performance regardless of where the learner starts can advance ability goals at the expense of task goals. Too often they define some students as perpetual losers. From this perspective school leaders should advocate evaluation practices for diagnosing problems and building improvement plans. Portfolio and other alternative assessment procedures should be encouraged.

6. *Distribute school resources to reflect the value of task goals.*
As new resources are brought into a school (e.g., a new computer laboratory), access should be based on effort rather than ability.

7. *Organize the school day for more flexibility.*
Dividing the school day into short periods of time severely limits the type of tasks that students can pursue in their classes with teachers. The traditional 40- to 50-minute period, for example, is more conducive to rote learning of large numbers of facts than to interesting, hands-on activities that are fewer in number but more likely to motivate students.

Overall, this approach employs task goals and actions to build a supportive school culture, which increases student motivation. A three-year collaborative effort was used to assess the school-leader-as-motivator model in an elementary and a middle school (Wood and Midgley, 1994). Within each school, a leadership team was formed to guide and develop the intervention. The team membership included an administrator, teachers, parents, and university representatives. During a series of weekly meetings, the leadership team discussed the motivation-based approach and ways to apply it. Lists of policies and practices were developed and examined from the perspective of goal theory. In both schools, the leadership teams planned and initiated structural changes to enhance the task focus in their respective learning environments. The research findings show mixed support for the model's implementation and effect, however. While the changes are striking for the elementary school, they are much less noticeable for the middle school. Wood and Midgley (1994) conclude that teachers can shed beliefs and practices that maintain an ability-focused school culture and replace them with beliefs and practices that support a task-focused school culture. We agree that the strong theoretical foundation and empirical support provide a framework to guide school change that is viable and generalizable. School leaders as motivators can change policies and practices that shift the emphasis from relative ability and comparative performance to accent effort, improvement, and mastery.

SUMMARY AND SUGGESTED READINGS

A basis for the intense criticism of public and private-sector institutions is the implicit assumption that they are plagued by problems of low motivation and productivity. When used judiciously, theory and research offer many insights and techniques for improving motivation in schools. In this chapter we have reviewed a number of approaches and programs that have special promise for schools. Specifically, six general principles were presented and used to review goal setting, organizational incentives, work-design models, and a leadership program.

Management by objectives and individual goal-setting programs produce specific difficult goals and provide feedback, which improve work quality, clarify expectations, increase job satisfaction, and develop pride in achievement. Similarly, organizational incentives motivate participants to improve their work performance by making jobs attractive, interesting, and satisfying. To be effective, however, incentive systems in schools need to be elaborate, stable, and dependable and offer a wide range of both intrinsic and extrinsic rewards.

Five strategies for work redesign were presented—two are general strategies and three are specific interventions for schools. Redesigning work modifies jobs to increase both the quality of the employees' work experience and the level of their performance. Based on motivation-hygiene theory, job-enrichment plans can be designed to increase motivation and decrease negative hygiene factors. The job-characteristics model of work design unifies Maslow's need-fulfillment, Herzberg's motivation-hygiene, and Vroom's expectancy theories and provides a comprehensive model for redesigning work roles. At the school level, professionalization, career ladders and career paths in educational administration are ways to apply motivation theory to schools. For example, career-ladder programs redesign jobs to provide educators with prospects for promotion, enrichment of their work, and enlargement of their responsibilities, all of which make their work motivating.

Finally, a model of motivation by school leaders, based on goal theory, provides a strategy to stimulate student motivation. Leaders must integrate goals and actions as they build a supportive school culture.

To gain a historical sense of the intense and continuing criticism of education, four early reports are essential reading: *The Nation at Risk, Tomorrow's Teachers, A Nation Prepared,* and *Leaders for America's Schools.* A book that we strongly recommend for your further reading is *Motivating Humans: Goals, Emotions, and Personal Agency Beliefs* by Martin E. Ford (1992). In this work, Ford presents a conceptual model for understanding individual motivation and applying the knowledge to work settings. Two classics are Chester Barnard's *Functions of an Executive* and Frederick Herzberg's *The Motivation to Work.* In terms of work redesign, Hart (1990b) offers an excellent review with some applications to education, and Malen, Murphy, and Hart (1988) and Firestone and Bader (1992) provide excellent reports of compensation and work-redesign issues and research in education.

NOTES

1. Studies providing support include Oldham and Miller (1979); Orpen (1979); Bhagat and Chassie (1980); Kiggundu (1980); Johns, Xie, and Fang (1992). Investigations providing partial support include Evans, Kiggundu, and House (1979) and Griffeth (1985); ones showing little or no support include Arnold and House (1980); Adler, Skov, and Salvemini (1985); and Tiegs, Tetrick, and Fried (1992).

2. See, for example, Gorsuch (1977), Pastor and Erlandson (1982), Mennuti and Kottkamp (1986), and Barnabe and Burns (1994).

KEY CONCEPTS AND IDEAS

Ability-focused goal

Administrative careers

Career-ladder program

Extrinsic incentives

Flexible goal-setting criteria

General goal-setting criteria

Goal setting

Hygienes

Incentives

Incentive system

Intrinsic incentives

Job-characteristics model

Job enrichment

Jobs

Management by objectives (MBO)

Merit pay

Motivational principles

Motivators

Profession

Rewards

Task-focused goal

Work redesign

Communicating

Humans live by communication, and many of the practices that we think define us as human are a direct outgrowth of the ways in which we communicate: our language, our reasoning, our morality, and our social organization.

—Nicholas C. Burbules
Dialogue in Teaching

PREVIEW

1. Communication pervades virtually all aspects of school life. It does not, however, provide all the answers to the problems confronting educational administrators.

2. Nearly all current conceptions of communication rely on notions that communication involves meaningful exchanges of symbols between at least two people.

3. One-way communication is unilateral, initiated by a speaker, and terminated at a listener.

4. Two-way communication is a reciprocal, interactive process with all participants in the process initiating and receiving messages. Interactive communication is transactional; it has no necessary beginning or ending.

5. Conversation, inquiry, debate, and instruction are four types of two-way communication.

6. Humans use two major symbol systems in their efforts to communicate—verbal and nonverbal.

7. As the content of communication becomes more ambiguous, richer media can improve communication performance.

8. Each new communication technology imposes its own special requirements on how messages are composed. Technology also governs the speed and convenience of sending message and influences the ways receivers reconstruct meaning.

9. Formal channels are communication networks sanctioned by the organization and directed toward organizational goals.

10. Individuals bypass formal channels of communication by using informal networks or "grapevines."

11. Centralization of decision making, shape of the hierarchy, and the level of information technology are influential to the operation of the formal communication system in schools.

12. Although the formal network is usually larger and better developed than the informal, they are closely related, can be complementary, and are critical to the organization.

Communication is complex, subtle, and ubiquitous; it permeates every aspect of school life. As individuals, teachers instruct, using oral, written, and other media such as videotapes, computers, and art forms. Students demonstrate their learning through similar media. And superintendents and principals spend the majority of their time communicating. In a real sense, teachers, students, and administrators earn their livings by communicating. Furthermore, in organizations such as schools, the translation of goals into concrete actions and accomplishments depends on successful information exchanges. Goals of schools become dynamic—that is, known and useful—only when they are communicated, which permits people to organize and coordinate their activities (Myers and Myers, 1982). Because there can be no organization without communication (Simon, 1957), establishing a communication process becomes the first task of the organizer and the continuous task of the administrator (Barnard, 1938).

An understanding of communication, therefore, is central to the study of educational administration because it offers an additional conceptual viewpoint for examining the schools. As a basic, dynamic process, communication underlies virtually all interpersonal, organizational, and administrative variables, including formal structure, informal organization and culture, motivation, leadership, and decision making. Communication skills, therefore, are essential tools for an effective administrator. However, before concluding that communication provides all the answers to the problems confronting educational administrators, four caveats must be observed.

- Communication is difficult to isolate from such other administrative processes as deciding, motivating, and leading.

- Not all school problems involve unsuccessful communication. Problems commonly attributed to poor interactions may reflect breakdowns in other fundamental components of school life.

- Communication reveals and hides as well as eliminates problems (Katz and Kahn, 1978). It can surface conflicts in values among teachers, students, and administrators that may otherwise go unnoticed, and it also may obscure existing problems by glossing over issues with empty rhetoric.

- Communication is a process that evokes action, but it is far from being the substance of good administration. It is no substitute for faulty ideas and misguided educational programs.

Even though these cautions are limitations, communication does serve several pervasive and integrative functions in schools. To claim that communication is either the universal problem or problem solver oversimplifies and limits both the analysis and the solution of educational problems. In this chapter, we will discuss a variety of conceptual approaches while attempting to keep both the important functions and the cautionary guides in proper perspective.

THEORETICAL APPROACHES TO COMMUNICATION

In everyday usage, communication is the process that people use to exchange significant messages and share meaning about their ideas and feelings with one another (Porter and Roberts, 1976; Manning, 1992). **Communication,** in other words, is sharing messages, ideas, or attitudes in ways that produce a degree of understanding between two or more people (Lewis, 1975). Practically all conceptions of communication contain explicit or implicit notions that involve meaningful interactions between at least two people. For example, educators do not communicate in a vacuum but with other educators, citizens, and students; and successful exchange does not occur unless both parties develop shared interpretations of the information.

Kathleen J. Krone, Fredric M. Jablin, and Linda L. Putnam (1987) observe that virtually all theoretical perspectives on communication recognize and use the same concepts. Although each term varies somewhat across different theoretical perspectives, we agree with the definitions summarized by Krone and her colleagues.

- **Message** is typically the verbal or nonverbal cues or symbols that each communicator conveys. It is the idea that an individual hopes to communicate.

- **Channel** is the vehicle, medium, or form in which a message travels. Form can range from light waves of nonverbal cues to sound waves of talking face-to-face, to electronic signals in telephones and e-mail.

- **Sender** is the person or a generalized source (e.g., Office of the Superintendent) sending a message, while **receiver** marks the destination of the message or the individual who deciphers it.

- **Transmission** is the actual sending and receiving of messages through designated channels or media.

- **Encoding** and **decoding** involve cognitive structures and processes to create, transform, and decipher messages. Encoding is converting the intended message to symbolic form by the sender. Decoding is retranslating the message by the receiver. Through encoding and decoding processes, individuals compose **meanings** by interpreting or making sense of the message. Interpreting a message is facilitated by using feedback.

- **Feedback** is the message sent in response to the initial message or, as defined in Chapter 2, it is information that enables corrections to be made.
- **Communication effects** are the outcomes or general results of the message exchange process—for example, new knowledge, different attitudes, culture, and satisfaction.

Hence, a more elaborate definition is that human communication is a process during which source individuals initiate messages using symbols, signs, and contextual cues to express meaning by transmitting information in ways that similar understandings are constructed by the receiving individual(s) (DeFleur, Kearney, and Plax, 1993). This definition incorporates the concepts defined above and produces the general model shown in Figure 11.1.[1]

A sender encodes a message with certain intentions and transmits it by some channel to a receiver who then decodes the message and provides feedback to original sender (see Figure 11.1). Both the source and the receivers are communicators in this process. Note the process is interactive and transactional (Adler and Rodman, 1991); it flows back and forth, often going both ways simultaneously as both talk or as one talks and the other listens and gives feedback through nonverbal cues. Hence, the process has no necessary beginning or end (Harris, 1993).

As important as communication is to the effective operation of schools and other institutions, few comprehensive theories of interpersonal or organizational communication have been developed (Jablin et al., 1987). For present purposes, we will first describe important components of a general process model (see Figure 11.1) and then use a network framework to analyze organizational communication in schools. These two approaches are amalgams of several models and perspectives.

FIGURE **11.1**

A General Model of the Communication Process

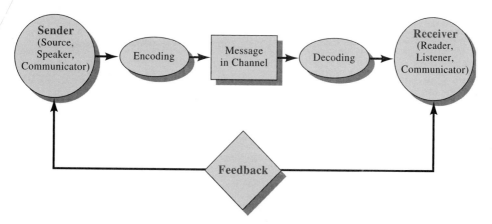

COMPONENTS OF A GENERAL MODEL OF THE COMMUNICATION PROCESS

Michele Tolela Myers and Gail E. Myers (1982) posit that communication can be viewed as a transactional process where people construct meaning and develop expectations about what is happening around them through the exchange of symbols. In constructing meanings, people use **symbols** (i.e., objects or words that stand for ideas, feelings, intentions, and other objects) to describe their experiences and develop a common symbol system or language for sharing their experiences with others. Learning symbols or a language and associating learning symbols with experiences come about by interacting with people and observing what they do when they use symbols. As a result of these interactions and observations, individuals not only learn to construct meanings that are reasonably similar to those of people around them but develop expectations or make predictions about what people will do and think. Every day individuals in schools exchange symbols using several different verbal and nonverbal forms (e.g., lecturing, exhorting, explaining, visiting, arguing, negotiating, discussing, dressing, making visual displays). These transactions to gain shared meanings can be conceptualized as a continuum from one-way to two-way communication.

One-Way Communication

As shown in Figure 11.2, **one-way communication** occurs when one person tells another person something. This type of communication is unilateral; it is initiated by a speaker and terminated at a listener (Schmuck and Runkel, 1985). Lectures in classrooms about subject matter or exhortations in the principal's office about appropriate demeanor represent widespread applications of one-way communication in schools. Other examples include announcements over the public address system in a school or during meetings. A metaphor for one-way communication as shown in Figure 11.2 is the hypodermic needle approach of injecting information into another person (Broms and Gahmberg, 1983).

The advantages of one-way communication are twofold (Clampitt, 1991). First, it emphasizes the skills of the message sender and encourages administrators and

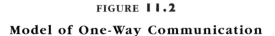

FIGURE **11.2**

Model of One-Way Communication

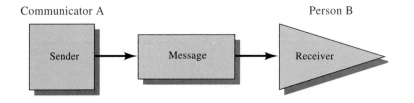

teachers to think through their ideas, accurately articulate them, and provide specificity in their instructions, explanations, and descriptions. Second, one-way strategies typically imply strong linkages between communication behavior and action. Teachers and administrators who use one-way communication discourage idle chatter, discussions of personal problems, and unnecessary information sharing. In other words, it conveys a strong emphasis on efficiency and goal achievement.

Given the need for shared understandings in schools, one-way communication many times is inadequate. For instance, Philip G. Clampitt (1991) asserts that the basic flaw in one-way communication lies in the belief that effective expression equals effective communication. Even if the message sender effectively articulates an idea, it does not necessarily guarantee that it will be understood as intended. Clampitt believes that two faulty assumptions explain the continued reliance on one-way communication. First, receivers are seen as passive information processors. Instead of being passive processing machines, however, people actively reconstruct messages and create their own meanings. Second, words are seen as containers of meaning. Language works against this assumption. For example, meaning depends on how the words are used, the context in which the statement is made, and the people involved. Words do not serve so much as containers of meaning as stimulators of meaning. Therefore, the need for understanding in schools suggests that additional or other forms of communication are required for goal achievement, change, and social purposes.

Two-Way Communication

By **two-way communication** we mean a reciprocal, interactive process; all participants in the process initiate and receive messages. In contrast to the one-way approach, two-way communication requires continuous exchanges and transactions. As shown in Figure 11.3, this means that each participant initiates messages and that each message affects the next one. Such interactive exchanges can improve the communication process by reducing the chance of major disparities between the information or idea received and the one intended.

A special case is **autocommunication,** or communicating with oneself. A number of instances of sharing symbols and images with oneself are evident. Examples include keeping a diary, writing an autobiography, engaging in a monologue, reflecting, and meditating. These are instances of a person turning to himself or herself to pacify and clarify the mind. Similarly, when an individual writes a memorandum, she or he is *both* informing the other person and building communication schema within his or her cognitive structure (Broms and Gahmberg, 1983).

We conceive of two-way communication as being very similar to the concept of dialogue as defined and discussed by Nicholas C. Burbules (1993).[2] From a perspective of dialogue, two-way communication also is an activity directed toward discovery and new understandings; it advances knowledge, insights, and sensitivity. In other words, two-way interactions help the participants learn and change. According to Burbules, the process is a continuous and developmental interchange through which the participants gain a fuller awareness of education, themselves, and each other.

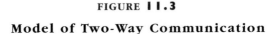

FIGURE **11.3**

Model of Two-Way Communication

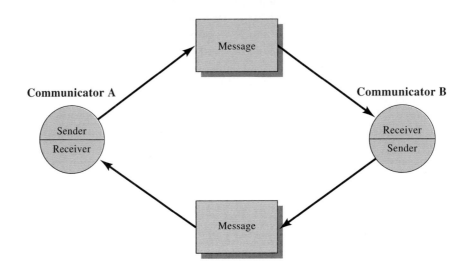

An information-processing perspective (see Chapter 4) provides an explanation of communication, learning, and understanding. Recall that schemas represent organized knowledge about given concepts or types of experience in an individual's memory. They are internal models of the outside world and arise from a variety of sources, including interpersonal communication. Hence, understanding or encoding/decoding involves creating new schemas and incorporating new information into existing schema. Moreover, schemas serve as criteria against which newly encountered messages are judged. As such, schemas are extremely powerful screens; they often cause people to misperceive messages or to misremember them. While existing schemas can be called upon to interpret or decode messages that may be unfamiliar to less experienced people, entrenched schemas may prevent people from making fresh and uncontaminated interpretations about messages they may encounter. For example, educators holding stereotypes (one type of cognitive schemas) of certain ethnic, gender, or ability groups will screen new information against their current criteria and probably distort the intent of the message.

Two-way communication is a reciprocal, interactive process directed toward discovery and new understandings through speaking and listening. It offers promise for creating similar schemas (mutual understanding, shared meanings) and for modifying stereotypical schemas. An important corollary of the information-processing model of learning is that merely presenting new information without adequate attention to current schemas virtually guarantees that the new material will be forgotten or misunderstood (Burbules, 1993). As a critical theorist, Burbules also gives the cognitive explanation an explicit political interpretation. He explains that in communication encounters, we do not change people; they change themselves. In other words, people construct their own understandings, change their own minds, decide on alternative courses of action, and define their own goals.

PRINCIPLES OF TWO-WAY COMMUNICATION Burbules (1993) elaborates his ideas for dialogue by positing three principles or normative standards.

- *The principle of participation* maintains that engagement in a dialogue relationship must be voluntary and open to active involvement by all of its participants in such activities as questioning, trying out new ideas, and hearing diverse points of view.

- *The principle of commitment* holds that engagement must allow the flow of conversation to be persistent and extensive across a range of shared concerns, even when they are difficult and divisive.

- *The principle of reciprocity* proposes that engagement in two-way exchanges must be undertaken in the spirit of mutual respect and concern, and must not take for granted the role of privilege or expertise.

These three principles, then, provide guidelines developing and using two-way communication strategies and communication with creativity, spontaneity, and understanding.

TYPES OF TWO-WAY COMMUNICATION Burbules (1993) also describes four types or patterns of two-way interaction—conversation, inquiry, debate, and instruction.

Conversation is distinguished by two traits—a generally cooperative, tolerant spirit and a direction toward mutual understanding. This form is used when individuals are interested in understanding each other's perspectives and experiences. An example would be two students talking about how they spent their summer vacations and what they learned as a result.

Inquiry seeks to answer a question, resolve a problem, or reconcile a dispute in a way that is agreeable to all. Dialogue of this nature typically investigates alternatives and examines possible answers within a structure that encourages a range of perspectives and approaches to the problem. An example would be a group of science teachers exploring why some students are thriving in classes using a new project-based curriculum while others are failing.

Debate exhibits sharp questioning, a skeptical spirit, and no necessary need for agreement among the participants. The potential benefit of debate is for the participants to see their alternative ideas and positions receive the most intense challenge possible. An example would be seeing policy makers discuss the relative merits of providing public tax support to private schools.

Instruction, as dialogue, generally uses critical questions and other statements to move a discussion to a definite conclusion. The exemplar of this type of two-way communication is the *Socratic method.* A good example of instruction as dialogue is reciprocal teaching. In reciprocal teaching, teachers and students engage in a highly interactive process in which participants take turns assuming the role of teacher (Palincsar, 1986).

In sum, the many types of one-way and two-way communication clearly show that none of the models shown in Figures 11.1, 11.2, and 11.3 is a single technique. To be a good communicator is to know the various types of communication, their particular strengths and weaknesses, and how to choose among them.

Channels of Communication: Methods of Exchanging of Symbols

In their efforts to communicate, humans use two major symbol systems—verbal and nonverbal (Dahnke and Clatterbuck, 1990). Verbal symbols include:

- Human speech—direct, face-to-face conversation or electronic exchanges via telephone, radio, or television
- Written media—memos, letters, electronic mail, and newspapers

Nonverbal symbols include:

- Body language or gestures—facial expressions, posture, and arm movements
- Physical items or artifacts with symbolic value—office furnishings, clothing, and jewelry
- Space—territoriality and personal space
- Touch—hugging
- Time
- Other nonverbal symbols—intonation, accents, pitch, intensity of the voice, and rate of speech

Hence, messages can be communicated in a variety of channels, ways, forms, or media.

VERBAL CHANNELS Richard L. Daft and Robert H. Lengel (1984, 1986) hypothesize that media determine the richness of communication, where **richness** is the medium's potential to carry information and resolve ambiguity. Four criteria define media richness: speed of feedback, variety of communication channels, personalness of source, and richness of language. Rich media combine multiple cues, rapid or timely feedback, tailoring the messages to personal circumstances, and a variety of language (Huber and Daft, 1987). Rich media are characterized by high touch and qualitative data; they are best for lessening ambiguity. Lean media are suitable for technology-based, high-volume data exchanges and are best for conveying quantitative data with precision and accuracy to large audiences (Daft, Bettenhausen, and Tyler, 1993). Using these four criteria, Daft and his colleagues place communication media and richness on the parallel continua as shown in Figure 11.4.

The face-to-face medium is the richest form because it provides immediate feedback through verbal and visual cues. Although verbal feedback is rapid, the telephone medium is less rich than face-to-face because the visual cues are absent. Writ-

FIGURE **11.4**

Continua for Communication Media and Richness

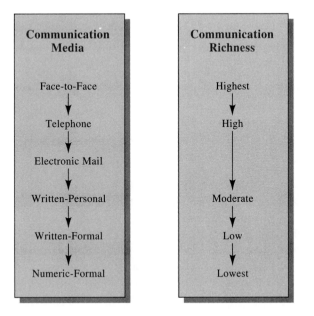

ten communication is described as being moderate or low in richness because feedback is slow and only written information is conveyed. Addressed correspondence is personal in character and somewhat richer than general memos and bulletins, which are anonymous and impersonal. Formal numeric documents—for example, computer printouts containing quantitative data such as achievement test scores—convey the least rich information because numbers do not have the information-carrying capacity of natural language. Electronic messaging can be placed between telephone and written personal media on the richness continuum (Steinfield and Fulk, 1986).

The basic hypothesis is that as the content of communication becomes more ambiguous or uncertain, richer media will be selected to improve communication performance. A growing number of studies have tested the hypothesis with the number supporting and not supporting being about equal (Schmitz and Fulk, 1991). Studies by Daft and his colleagues (Trevino, Lengel, and Daft, 1987; Russ, Daft, and Lengel, 1990) are generally supportive of the basic richness hypothesis. Other studies (Steinfield and Fulk, 1986; Rice, 1992) have found weak or mixed support. Overall, the results are more supportive of the media richness hypothesis when applied to traditional (e.g., face-to-face) rather than newer media (e.g., computers and other electronic devices) (Fulk and Boyd, 1991).

As might be expected from the discussion of richness, when the effects of written and oral media are compared, a problem faces the communicator (Porter and

Roberts, 1976). Comprehension is higher when information is presented in written form. However, opinion change or persuasiveness is greater in face-to-face interactions. The appropriate medium thus depends on the purpose—that is, understanding or persuading.

Redundancy in media increases both the richness of the information and the accuracy of message transmission (Redding, 1972). Generally, the most effective and accurate communication efforts use a combination of written and oral media; the next most effective is oral alone; and written is least powerful (Level, 1972). The combination of written and oral media is seldom inappropriate. Written communication alone can be effective in two situations—where information requires future action or where it is general. The oral medium by itself also can be effective in two situations demanding immediate feedback—for administering reprimands and settling disputes.

NONVERBAL CHANNELS OF COMMUNICATION   While redundancy in media usually leads to better understanding, vocal and written media carry only a portion of the information that administrators convey when they interact with others. At least as important as verbal signals are the less fully understood nonverbal symbols. **Nonverbal communication** is all behavior of communicative value done in the presence of another that does not use words. The raised eyebrow, the firm handshake, and the impatient tapping of the fingers are well-known actions of nonverbal media that convey meaning. Even silence and rigid inactivity may signal anger, annoyance, depression, or fear. Although this definition of nonverbal communication suggests a rather all-inclusive domain, a gray area still exists between verbal and nonverbal forms. Paralanguage is vocal but not strictly oral. It includes stress, inflection, and speed of speech, as well as nonword vocalizations such as grunts, laughter, sighs, and coughs (Knapp, 1972; Wietz, 1974).

Research on nonverbal communication often explores the meanings of paralanguage, body motion, and spatial cues. For example, a combination of five types of nonverbal behaviors consistently exert the strongest positive influence on one individual's attempts to build rapport with another person: smiling, touching, affirmative head nods, immediacy behavior (e.g., leaning forward), and eye behavior. These behaviors are essential in communicating a sense of warmth, enthusiasm, and interest (Heintzman et al., 1993).

The face is the most obvious nonverbal conveyor of feelings (McCaskey, 1979). Most feeling is communicated through facial expression. Without formal training, observers of facial expression can distinguish a variety of human emotions such as excitement, humiliation, and fear (Harris, 1993). Eye-to-eye contact is one of the most direct and powerful ways that people communicate nonverbally. In mainstream American culture, the social rules indicate that in most situations eye contact for a short period is appropriate. Direct eye contact is also seen as an indication of honesty and credibility. Prolonged eye contact is usually taken to be either threatening or, in another context, a sign of romantic interest. Speakers know that a way to enhance the impact of their presentations is to look directly at individual members of the audience and establish eye contact.

In regard to work space, Michael B. McCaskey (1979) notes that an office represents personal territory, which separates what belongs to one person from what belongs to others. Where a meeting is held may intimate the purpose of the meeting. To conduct an adversarial discussion, to emphasize hierarchy and authority, or to give directions, McCaskey advises the superordinate to hold the meeting in his or her own office. The office arrangement itself might communicate the intended nature of the interactions. For example, many administrators arrange their offices with two different areas. In one, the administrator talks across the desk to a person seated at the other side. This layout emphasizes the administrator's authority and position. In the second area, chairs are in a circle at a round table. Because the arrangement signals a willingness to downplay hierarchical differences, freer exchanges are encouraged. Hence, an office arrangement with a center for informal conversations, a display of personal memorabilia and decorations, and a relatively close distance between the chairs and desk, represent nonverbal symbols that transmit powerful messages of welcome to visitors. In one of the few studies of nonverbal meaning in educational administration, James M. Lipham and Donald C. Francke (1966) confirmed these propositions in schools.

CONGRUENCE OF VERBAL AND NONVERBAL MESSAGES Verbal and nonverbal messages must be consistent for effective understanding. An illustration of this generalization usually occurs when a new administrator meets with the staff. A typical verbal statement is, "If you have any questions or problems, please come by my office, and we'll discuss the situation. My door is always open." When a staff member interprets the words literally and does visit the principal, the nonverbal messages probably will determine the meaning of the verbal message. If the person is met at the door, ushered to a chair, and a productive conference results, the verbal message is reinforced and the meaning is understood. If, however, the administrator remains in the chair behind the desk, leaves the staff member standing or seats him or her across the room, and continues to write, the verbal message is contradicted. When verbal and nonverbal message conflict, a problem of meaning results.

NEW AND EMERGING TECHNOLOGIES A plethora of rapidly developing information technologies are coming to society and education. Information technologies include all types of computing and communications hardware and software (Harris, 1993). For example, high-speed personal computers, computer networks, E-mail, fax machines, voice mail, CD-Roms, digitized audio and video information storage and retrieval devices, and their use in combination as multimedia interactive units are already having significant impacts on communication forms in schools. The current revolution is more than just replacing traditional paper-based media with computer screens and other technological marvels. The change to new communication technologies promises to have personal, social, and pedagogical consequences. The widespread adoption of new technologies has altered the communication process itself. Each new medium imposes its own special requirements on how messages are composed, governs the speed and convenience of message transmission, and influences the ways receivers reconstruct meaning (DeFleur, Kearney, and Plax, 1993). In terms of pedagogy, the potential seems almost unlimited. Teachers and students can access vast stores of information almost instantly, interact with colleagues around the world with computer or video conferences, and create new knowledge in many different media forms. The new technologies can change the emphasis from passive to active learning.

Sources in the Communication Process: Senders and Receivers

The source of a message does not have to be a person. It can be organizations, supervisors, co-workers, or the task itself (Northcraft and Earley, 1989; Bantz, 1993). In considering the source, credibility and cognitive capacities are important factors.

CREDIBILITY The credibility or believability (Adler and Rodman, 1991) of the sender influences the effectiveness of a message. Two characteristics that influence credibility are expertness and trustworthiness (Shelby, 1986; Becker and Klimoski, 1989). Credibility consists of the trust and confidence that the receiver has in the words and actions of the sender. The level of credibility, in turn, influences the reactions of the receiver to the words and actions of the communicator (Gibson, Ivancevich, and Donnelly, 1976). In some cases the identity and reputation of the sender, far from authenticating the message, lead instead to the receiver's distorting the information or ignoring the message completely (Bowers, 1976). For example, faculty members who view the principal as less than competent, dishonest, or both probably will distort all communications from him or her.

Expertise can be shown by being prepared to speak. It starts by organizing the idea into a series of symbols such as words or pictures that will communicate the intended meaning. These symbols are arranged for rationality, coherence, and compatibility with the methods of delivery, or media. An E-mail message, for instance, usually is worded differently from a formal letter of reprimand, and both are different from face-to-face conversation. In other words, a message that is well researched, organized, written, or presented will greatly increase the receiver's assessment of the sender's competence and hence credibility.

COGNITIVE CAPACITIES Psychological characteristics limit an individual's ability to communicate. Information-processing capacity (e.g., schemas for communication skills and knowledge of the subject) and personality and motivation factors (e.g., attitudes, values, interests, and expectations) combine to limit and filter the content and the quality of the message (Berlo, 1970). Cognitive schema significantly influence not only what information is attended to, conveyed, and interpreted but also how the information is processed (Krone, Jablin, and Putnam, 1987; see Chapter 4). For example, the assistant superintendent for instruction when communicating with principals screens out information that he or she thinks is not pertinent to building administrators; principals filter information to the assistant superintendent that might reflect negatively on their performance.

Cognitive structures and processes also influence the recipient's ability to understand or decode the message. If the listener is effective, cooperative, and knowledgeable, he or she attempts to interpret the message as intended by the sender. However, as is the case with the sender, the receiver has communication capacities, knowledge of the subject, interests, values, and motivational characteristics that combine to limit qualitatively what is decoded. Consequently, the meaning the receiver applies is not exactly what the sender intended. Meanings may, of course, be relatively comparable, but they are never identical. The receiver's cognitive schemas and processes limit the range of response alternatives. Based on experience as represented by cognitive structures and processes, the receiver selects how to act or respond to the message. The actions serve as feedback to the sender.

Feedback

In all types of communication environments, there is a significant probability that what we say will be ambiguous and misinterpreted. For example, "I'll be there in a minute" and "Call me later and we'll talk about it" make vague references to time. How long a "minute" or "later" varies greatly across individuals and cultures. Through the use of feedback, however, even unclear statements can become part of specific effective communications (Alessandra and Hunsaker, 1993).

Feedback is a response from a person who has received a message. It provides knowledge about the meaning and impact of the message for the receiver and an opportunity for the sender to correct any problems. Hence, if a dialogue is to continue for any length of time and still have meaning, feedback is important. This process provides at least two benefits. First, it supplies clues about the success of the communication and improves the accuracy and clarity of a message. Asking questions and paraphrasing what the speaker has said are forms of verbal feedback (Adler and Rodman, 1991). Statements such as "What do you mean by . . . ?" or "Let me review what you have said . . . ." check for mutual understanding (Alessandra and Hunsaker, 1993). Second, the knowledge of results forms a basis for correcting or modifying future communications (Ashford, 1986). The point is, feedback increases the accuracy and clarity of communication.

Communicating in Context

Communication among people also depends on a combination of contextual, cultural, or environmental factors. The process is clouded by contextual factors that are typically called *noise* or *barriers*. **Noise** is any distraction that interferes with the communication process. Noise can be so intense that it becomes more important than the content of the message itself (Reilly and DiAngelo, 1990).

In schools, noise resulting from social and personal factors can produce more troublesome problems than physical interference. For example, closed organizational climates, punishment-centered bureaucratic structures, cultural and gender differences, and authoritarian leaders create distortions in the communication processes.

In such cases, group membership becomes important. Militant teachers cannot hear arbitrary administrators and vice versa; bureaucratic educators do not pay attention to demanding parents.

Prejudices toward age, gender, race, social class, and ethnic group differences constitute barriers in the communication process that distort messages. In a multicultural society, demographic attributes such as race, occupation, and gender provide surrogate indicators for the common experiences and background attributes that shape language development and communication abilities (Zenger and Lawrence, 1989). For example, a man who believes that his particular work can be done effectively only by a man is predisposed to deny facts, information, and messages that suggest that a woman can do the work equally well or better. Every message is filtered through barriers, predispositions, or in the term developed in Chapter 4, cognitive schemas (Reilly and DiAngello, 1990).

Similarly, both the written and spoken language used by American women and men has traditionally been somewhat different.[3] Women tend to adopt upper-class speech patterns, certain words (e.g., "darling" as an adjective) and expressive language (e.g., "adorable," "lovely"). Men tend to be more comfortable with slang expressions. In comparison to men, women tend to hedge or use qualified constructions (e.g., "perhaps," "seem," "could"), shy away from universal pronouncements, and employ language that encourages community building, politeness, cheerfulness, and concern (Shakeshaft, 1986). In taking turns in speaking, women in social settings and professional meetings talk less, are interrupted more, and are challenged more than are men. However, gender differences in taking turns appear to be related more to women's concern for permitting others to speak than in expressing their own opinions. Thus, language characteristics such as expressiveness, hedging, and taking turns make women appear more affiliative, collegial, or interpersonally oriented than men (Baker, 1991).

Brenda M. Wilkins and Peter A. Andersen (1991) note that research seeking to identify gender differences in communication styles of managers has become very popular. Using a meta-analysis technique, they found women and men managers do differ in their communication behaviors, but that the amount of variance was so small that the statistical differences appear to have little social value. In her review, Charol Shakeshaft (1986) concludes that the traditional and stereotypic styles of women are more like those of good administrators than are the styles of traditional and stereotypic men. She observes that the communication styles of women respond to needs for less autocratic downward communication, noncoercive motivational and persuasive skills, humanized feedback, and threat-reducing strategies. To become effective school administrators, she believes, men would be well advised to watch how women speak and listen and try to make those styles their own rather than pushing women to modify their language to mimic men.

Within education, male and female educators and students frequently have very different socioeconomic, ethnic, educational, and work backgrounds. These differences can be expected to produce contextual noise as women and men administrators, teachers, and students communicate in schools. However, where females achieve a more equal status with males, the differences in language usage may diminish. Young men and women today are much more likely to have similar vocabularies and speech patterns than was the case fifty years ago (McNall and McNall, 1992).

Hence, context noise of all types—for example, physical, social, and personal—may produce language disparities that constrain communication within schools even further. Given the growing diversity and other changes of school contexts (e.g., in economic wealth, ethnicity, gender in administrative positions, and at-risk children), the challenge of communicating accurately and clearly will surely increase. As shown in Figure 11.1, creating shared meaning through the communication process depends on the individuals involved, content of the message, methods used, and context. Succinctly stated, the relationship is shown with the following formula:

Meaning = Information + Communicators + Media + Context

The essence of the formula and approach can be understood by considering the following questions.

- Who is speaking to whom and what roles do they occupy? Administrators? Administrator and teacher? Teachers? Men and women? Teacher and student? Administrator and parent?

- Is the language or set of symbols able to convey the information and be understood by both the sender and receiver?

- What is the content and affect of the communication? Positive or negative? Relevant or irrelevant?

- What methods or media are being used?

- What is the context in which the communication is taking place? What factors are creating noise that might block or distort the message?

As a general conclusion, the lack of two-way communication, the use of conflicting media and messages, and the existence of situational noise constitute the most serious problems for understanding in educational organizations.

ORGANIZATIONAL PERSPECTIVES OF COMMUNICATION

Organizations are information-processing systems. Information flows through organizations and influences virtually all structures and processes. Moreover, organizations are processing an increasing volume of data and the preferred media are becoming face-to-face discussion and group participation (Daft, Bettenhausen, and Tyler, 1993). Consequently, the escalating volume and change to richer media make understanding organizational communication in schools even more important than previously thought.

ORGANIZATIONAL COMMUNICATION AND NETWORKS

The earlier general definition can be adapted to define **organizational communication** as the sending of messages through both formal and informal networks of a deliberately designed group that results in the construction of meaning and influences both individuals and groups (DeFleur, Kearney, and Plax, 1993). Thomas E. Harris (1993) observes that **networks** are formal or informal patterns or channels of communication that have become regularized. **Formal channels** are methods sanctioned by the organization and are related to such organizational goals as regulation and innovation. When individuals communicate through **informal channels** and networks, they are using **grapevines.** These forms of communication are part of the organizational structure of schools, even though they are not shown on the hierarchical chart (Lewis, 1975). The direction of formal and informal channels can be vertical (up and down) and horizontal as well as one- or two-way. Hence, networks and channels are simply methods, vehicles, or forms a message travels in organizations such as schools; they are lines of communication.

The general notions of a network and channels are familiar because we all have had extensive experience with physical networks and channels, such as rivers, streets and highways, telephone lines, and sewer pipes (Monge, 1987). In contrast, communication networks in organizations are more difficult to identify because they comprise abstract human behaviors over time rather than physical materials such as pavement, streams, and pipes. Nevertheless, communication networks are regular patterns of person-to-person contacts that can be identified as people exchange information in schools. By observing the communication behavior over time, inferences can be made about which individuals are informationally connected to other individuals.

As shown in Figure 11.5, a variety of roles are assumed by the members within communication networks. The communication role that a person serves within a communication network is important because it can influence the person's attitudes and behaviors. A **star role** is where a large number of people communicate with an individual. The star is a nexus within the network. Having a central role, the star is potentially powerful because he or she has greater access to and possible control over group resources (McElroy and Shrader, 1986; Yamagishi, Gillmore, and Cook, 1988). Hence, a star can be thought of as a leader in the network. In contrast, an **isolate role** is one where individuals are involved in communication with others only infrequently (see Figure 11.5). Isolates are loosely coupled or even decoupled from the network—that is, removed from the regular flow of communication and out of touch with the rest of the network. Isolates are a concern because their lack of communication activity is often accompanied by feelings of alienation, low job satisfaction, little commitment to the work organization, and low performance. Active participation in communication networks seems to produce positive outcomes, while isolation is associated with disaffection (Harris, 1993).

Exchanges occur across networks through individuals who fill special roles as bridges and liaisons. For example, people who belong to more than one group are called **bridges.** By belonging to a district curriculum committee and the department

FIGURE **11.5**

Examples of Star, Isolate, Bridge, and Liaison Roles
in Communication Networks

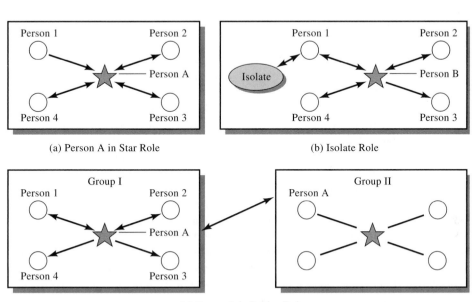

(a) Person A in Star Role

(b) Isolate Role

(c) Person A in Bridge Role

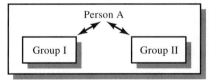

(d) Person A in Liaison Role

within a school, an English teacher serves in a bridging role for the two groups and will likely pass information between them (see Figure 11.5). If individuals link groups to which they do not belong, they are called **liaisons,** who serve as intermediaries among various groups within schools. In other words, liaisons perform the vital function of keeping groups informed about each other's activities. Interactions among liaisons and group members do not occur with great frequency or formality, but when communication occurs regularly, the members usually know what the others are doing. As described in Chapter 3, these important linkages are weak ties or loose couplings. Liaisons many times are formally assigned by the organization to link different departments or committees and ensure accurate communication among them. By supervising the English curriculum committees in two schools, for example, the assistant superintendent for curriculum and instruction is a liaison for the two groups. There are formal as well as informal liaisons.

PURPOSES OF COMMUNICATION IN SCHOOL ORGANIZATIONS

Communication in organizations such as schools serves a number of key purposes—for example, production and regulation, innovation, and individual socialization and maintenance (Myers and Myers, 1982). Production and regulation purposes include activities aimed at doing the primary work of the organization—for example, teaching and learning in schools. They include setting goals and standards, transmitting facts and information, making decisions, leading and influencing others, and assessing outcomes. Innovation purposes include messages about generating new ideas and changing programs, structures, and procedures in the school. Finally, socialization and maintenance purposes of communication affect the participants' self-esteem, interpersonal relationships, and motivation to integrate their individual goals with the school's objectives. The capacity of a school to maintain such complex, highly interdependent patterns of activity is limited by its ability to handle communication for these purposes.

To serve the multiple purposes of production, regulation, innovation, socialization, and maintenance in schools, communication must promote high levels of shared understandings. Human action is needed to accomplish goals in schools. Goal-directed behavior is elicited through communication; hence, the greater clarity and understanding of the message, the more likely administrator, teacher, and student actions will proceed in fruitful, goal-oriented directions. Within an effectively operating school, for example, administrators, teachers, and students want to understand and accept each other's ideas and to act on them. School goals and guidelines for their accomplishment are developed through extensive dialogue. One innovative goal might be to implement a project-based approach of instruction. The accompanying guidelines to accomplish the goal would include the development of new curricula, new interactive instructional strategies, socializing and training teachers, portfolio-assessment procedures, and plans for maintaining the programs. As group leaders, the principal, teachers, parents, and students emphasize the validity of the goal, stress the usefulness of the new procedures, promote shared understandings, encourage collective actions to implement the program, and assist in implementation and continuation. The extent and success of the actions depend in large measure on how effectively communication about the goal and accompanying procedures are initiated and maintained by the school organization.

FORMAL COMMUNICATION NETWORKS IN SCHOOLS

Communication is embedded in all school structures. In the traditional bureaucratic model (see Chapter 3), formal communication channels, or networks, traverse the organization through the hierarchy of authority. Barnard (1938) calls these formal networks "the communication system." According to Barnard, several factors must be considered when developing and using the formal communication system:

- The channels of communication must be known.
- The channels must link every member of the organization.
- Lines of communication must be as direct and as short as possible.
- The complete network of communication typically is used.
- Every communication is authenticated as being from the correct person occupying the position and within his or her authority to issue the message.

Figure 11.6 illustrates a school district's formal communication network using Barnard's descriptive statements. Note that the chart delineates the formal communication channels and that every member reports to someone. The directors report to the assistant superintendent for instruction, who, with the assistant superintendent for finance, report to the superintendent. The line of communication from the superintendent to the teachers goes through five hierarchical levels. This is reasonably short and direct for a large school district. Adding specific names and the bureaucratic rules and regulations that define the jobs places this system in compliance with Barnard's suggestions.

Within all organizations, formal restrictions on the communication process are apparent. "Making certain to go through proper channels" and "following the chain of command" are two common expressions that reflect a demand for control and structure of communication in organizations (Harris, 1993). Three characteristics of school bureaucracies seem particularly critical to the formal system of communication. They are centralization in the hierarchy, the organization's shape or configuration, and the level of information technology.

Centralization—the degree that authority is not delegated but concentrated in a single source in the organization—is important to the effectiveness of communication systems (Porter and Roberts, 1976). In centralized schools, a few positions in the structure have most of the information-obtaining ability. For example, the superintendent and two assistant superintendents pictured in Figure 11.6 would gather most of the information for the formal system of communication. If the district is decentralized or loosely coupled (see Chapter 3), however, the information-obtaining potential is more or less spread across all of the positions. Research examining the different information-obtaining abilities supports the finding that centralized structures are more efficient communicators when the problems and tasks are relatively simple and straightforward. When the problems and tasks become more complex, however, decentralized hierarchies appear to be more efficient (Argote, Turner, and Fichman, 1989).

Shape—the number of hierarchical levels or tallness versus flatness of the school organization—also affects the communication processes. Hierarchical levels and size are structural characteristics that are commonly associated with shape. A school district with five levels, such as the one depicted in Figure 11.6, differs from systems with more or fewer levels in its ability to communicate across levels and from top to bottom. The number of levels can be seen as the distance a message must travel. As the distance increases, the chance for message distortion increases and the satisfaction with the quality and quantity of communication decreases (Clampitt, 1991;

FIGURE **11.6**

Formal Communication Channels for Program Implementation in a School District

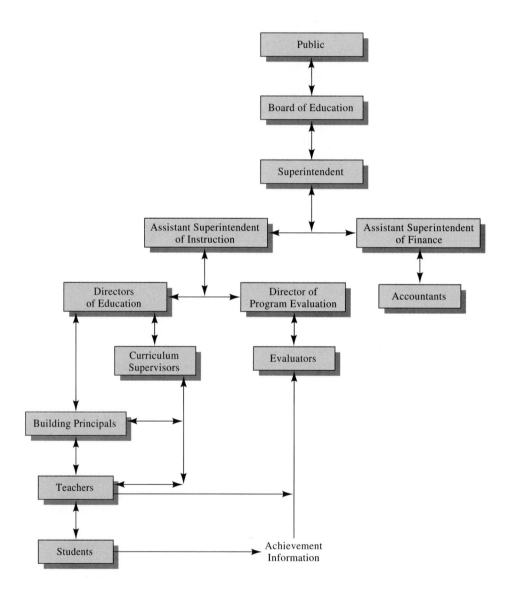

Zahn, 1991). Teachers will generally express less satisfaction with messages from superintendents than from principals. In addition, organizational size is negatively related to communication quality; as the district becomes larger, communication becomes more impersonal or formal and quality declines (Jablin, 1987).

Technology also appears to have a significant effect on organizational communication, though that effect remains somewhat speculative. As we noted in Chapter 3, writers subscribing to the position that schools are loosely coupled systems argue that educational organizations have a relatively low level of technology. However, as communication technology becomes more sophisticated in schools, its use will dramatically alter the communication that takes place in both the formal and informal networks (Huseman and Miles, 1988).

We are living in a creative and dynamic era that is producing fundamental changes, as is apparent in such advances as computer networks, electronic mail, computer conferences, communication satellites, and data-handling devices. Until recently, electronic information exchange has largely been adapted to convey voice, vision, text, and graphics as distinct and separate types of communication. During the next few years, simultaneous and instantaneous transmission of voice, vision, text, and graphics to many locations will be common. Even while imagining these tremendous changes, the usual descriptions of the forthcoming power of electronic technologies together with the geographic distribution of participants do not adequately capture the differences between these and traditional media (Culhan and Markus, 1987). Consequently, the potential influence of such technologies on all aspects of communication in schools—administrative, instructional, and social—is probably underestimated.

INFORMAL COMMUNICATION NETWORKS IN SCHOOLS

Informal networks or grapevines exist in all organizations regardless of how elaborate the formal communication system happens to be. One generalization that has been observed repeatedly by researchers and by participants in organizations is that people who are in groups, cliques, or gangs tend to reach an understanding on things or issues very quickly. They communicate easily and well among themselves. Facts, opinions, attitudes, suspicions, gossip, rumors, and even directives flow freely and rapidly through the grapevine. Built around social relationships among the school members, informal channels develop for such simple reasons as common office areas, similar duties, shared coffee breaks, carpools, and friendships. Social relationships and communication channels arise at all organizational levels of the school. Returning to Figure 11.6, informal communication patterns exist at the central office. One central office group might include some of the directors, an assistant superintendent, some supervisors, an evaluator, and an accountant. Certainly, informal communication channels thrive among building principals and within teacher groups and the student body.

While a major disadvantage of grapevines is the spread of rumors, informal networks serve a number of purposes in formal school organization. First, they reflect the quality of activities in a school. Communication through informal sources provides vital feedback to administrators and other school leaders. Moreover, active informal networks are indicative of a school's culture and leaders can learn a great deal by listening to them. Second, informal channels may satisfy social or affiliation needs not met by formal channels. Third, grapevines fill an information void by carrying a great deal of information. No matter how elaborate, formal communication networks simply cannot carry all of the information required in contemporary schools. Informal networks provide outlets when formal channels are clogged. Informal channels are particularly helpful during periods of change, when the information is new, and when face-to-face or electronic communication is relatively easy. Fourth, informal networks provide meaning for activities within the school. As messages travel through informal networks, the messages are translated with surprising accuracy into terms that make sense to the participants. The accuracy is 75 to 90 percent for noncontroversial information. When distortions occur, they generally reflect an incorrect emphasis based on incomplete information. A problem is that even a small distortion or error can have dramatic consequences (Clampitt, 1991; Harris, 1993).

COMPLEMENTARY NETWORKS: FORMAL AND INFORMAL COMMUNICATION

As we have noted, formal and informal communication networks exist in all educational organizations. The results from research studying networks across a variety of settings indicate that communication patterns in organizations are extraordinarily complex. Within schools, there is not a single unitary network, but rather a series of overlapping and interrelated networks (Jablin, 1980). A large majority of all participants interact consistently with many other individuals and in far greater numbers than is suggested by formal organizational charts. Generally, communication groups form along task-focused lines rather than around formal authority. Moreover, if the authority network is taken as the formal organization and the social network represents the informal one, the amount of overlap between the two is not great. While the task network is larger and better developed than the social network, both are closely related to each other and critical to the organization (O'Reilly and Pondy, 1979). Both the substance and the direction of communication can make the two systems complementary.

Substance

In terms of content, communication can be thought of as instrumental or expressive (Etzioni, 1961). Instrumental communication distributes information and knowledge that affect cognitive structures and processes. Administrative directives, policies, curricular objectives and materials, and attendance data are typical examples. The purpose of instrumental communication is to develop consensus about methods and procedures. Expressive communication, on the other hand, attempts to change or reinforce attitudes, norms, and values. Appropriate affective orientations toward students, militancy, discipline, and organizational rewards are typical examples of the substance of expressive communication.

Formal communication channels carry both instrumental and expressive content. The informal network can enhance both. For example, the grapevine serves as a barometer of opinion and sentiment. School administrators can often tap the informal flow for information about morale of students, teachers, and other administrators. They also can float trial balloons to test the receptivity of a new procedure or program. For instance, an administrator may want to introduce a new in-service program for teacher preparation. Before making a final decision, the hypothetical possibilities are discussed informally with some staff members. As the information flows through the grapevine, the sentiment can be monitored. Depending on the reaction, the administrator uses the formal communication system to announce plans for the new program, allows the program to remain hypothetical, or formally quashes the rumor. Barnard (1938) suggests that this type of communication flows without interruption in the informal networks, but would be either inconvenient or raise issues calling for premature decisions in the formal channels. Hence, informal can complement formal instrumental communication by serving as a testing ground for possible courses of action. In terms of expressive communication, the informal network can be a positive vehicle for personal expression by allowing participants to communicate and interact socially. Informal networks then provide gratification of the social needs of many school members at little financial cost to the district.

Direction

Messages do not sit around waiting to be discovered, nor do they float around randomly to be picked up by some lucky accident (Myers and Myers, 1982). Communication in organizations flows directionally through the formal and informal networks. The direction of information flow also demonstrates the possible complementary nature of formal and informal communication networks. Information flows vertically and horizontally in both networks.

Vertical flow refers to the upward and downward direction of communication through the different levels of the school's hierarchy. Information is passed down or up the line of authority through memos, directions, policies, and programs of action. An important point about the vertical flow of organizational communication is that messages moving in the formal network are extremely important to the people who send them and those who receive them. The jobs of individuals can depend on the messages they receive about such matters as directives, assessments, requests, and instructions (DeFleur, Kearney, and Plax, 1993).

In formal downward communication, information passes through the chain of command—that is, through the superordinate-subordinate status structure. The majority of these messages reaffirm the hierarchical structure and reinforce control (Harris, 1993). Five types of communications from superior to subordinate include (Katz and Kahn, 1978):

- Instructions about specific tasks
- Rationale about why the task needs to be done and how it relates to other tasks
- Information about organizational procedures and practices
- Feedback about the performance levels of individuals
- Information regarding the organization's goals

Downward vertical communication is relatively easy to send, but subordinates often may misunderstand the message. To ensure that the intended meanings are understood, administrators must develop two-way communication channels and use extensive feedback processes up and down the hierarchy.

Communication from the lower levels of the hierarchy to the upper levels is upward communication. Upward communication provides four types of messages (Katz and Kahn, 1978; DeFleur, Kearney, and Plax, 1993):

- Routine operational messages
- Reports on problems
- Suggestions for improvement
- Information on how subordinates feel about each other and the job

Upward communication is one means by which subordinates are made accountable to superiors. Such communication is often viewed as an instrument of administrative control. Consequently, subordinates have a tendency to emphasize positive information, withhold negative data, and communicate what they think the "boss wants to hear." Because many decisions are made at the top of the hierarchy, the quality of the decisions will depend on the accuracy and timeliness of the communication that moves through the formal system. In general, the more tangible and the more objective the information, the more likely that subordinates will communicate accurately with their superiors. Frequent two-way exchanges also improves accuracy (Porter and Roberts, 1976). In addition, a well-developed informal network can help administrators gain timely information and assess the accuracy of formal upward communication.

Horizontal flow indicates that communication moves across organizational members at the same hierarchical level. A principal, for instance, may provide information to another principal, who in turn, passes it to still other principals. Such communication is the strongest and most easily understood (Lewis, 1975). Horizontal communication can be either formal or informal. In Figure 11.6, the lateral communication link between the two assistant superintendents would be formal when they are working on ways to finance the introduction of a new curriculum. Another common example is teachers talking with each other in a lounge or planning room during class periods when they are not teaching. The major purposes of horizontal communication are coordinating tasks, problem solving, sharing information with colleagues, resolving conflicts, and building rapport (Harris, 1993). For example, principals communicate so that their activities or curriculum emphases will be similar in different schools, share information about content, avoid potential conflicts, and build friendly relationships with peers. The direction affects the ease, content, and accuracy of organizational communication.

EXTERNAL ENVIRONMENT AND ORGANIZATIONAL COMMUNICATION

In Chapter 7, the effects of uncertainty and complexity on school structures and processes were considered. Organizations with greater environmental turbulence and complexity face two problems with respect to internal information processing: a larger volume and greater ambiguity (i.e., multiple meanings) of information. Schools must deal with this heightened volume and ambiguity through their internal communication networks and media (Daft, Bettenhausen, and Tyler, 1993).

As ambiguity and volume increase, two factors emerge that require heightened information processing. First, in situations of high ambiguity, strategies must be developed to obtain some degree of clarity of meaning. When information from the environment is messy, people in the organization can reach very different, but defensible conclusions after observing the same objective information. Probably the most powerful way to resolve ambiguity is through debate, clarification, and discussion. In this way, educators can construct meanings on which they can agree. Hence, in ambiguous situations, the appropriate response is characterized by low technology and high touch. People need to use rich media—that is, face-to-face interactions—to build shared understandings based on previously shared assumptions and experiences.

Second, in conditions of high volume, the communication capacity must be enhanced to meet increasing demands. Fast-changing and complex environments can generate huge amounts of information for organizations. To stay informed, school organizations develop specialized monitoring and boundary-spanning units, special teams to integrate the incoming information, and computer technologies to store and retrieve information quickly (Daft, Bettenhausen, and Tyler, 1993).

RESEARCH ON ORGANIZATION COMMUNICATION

Charles A. O'Reilly III and Karlene H. Roberts (1977) argue that task structures of work groups act to improve or detract from the accuracy and openness of the transmitted message. Group cohesion and two-way communication produce greater accuracy. Groups with specialized skills and high status are more open in information exchanges than other groups. Further, accuracy and openness have a positive impact on performance, but the frequency of communication among educators may not be high (Miskel, McDonald, and Bloom, 1983).

In a study of communication isolates, Patrick Forsyth and Wayne Hoy (1978) found that, without exception, being isolated in one instance carries over to other instances. The results of a subsequent study were similar, except that isolation from friends was not related to isolation from formal authority (Zielinski and Hoy, 1983).

In other words, communication isolates in schools tend to be separated from perceived control, respected co-workers, the school's control structure, and sometimes friends. The potentially destructive aspect of this isolation is alienation. To counteract this negative effect, administrators must devise alternative communication processes because the isolates are not reachable by existing channels.

Administrators are likely to be dependent on teachers who have access to certain resources, especially information. In exchange for these resources, teachers can influence administrator behavior. Some teachers gain influence and power because they have information about how to get things accomplished or who can resolve specific problems. Similarly, department chairs, committee members, and teachers with specialized skills possess valued information. As a result of their knowledge and positions in the communication network, they can exert considerable power in decision making (Barnett, 1984).

The communication patterns among principals in elementary and secondary schools are quite different (Licata and Hack, 1980). Secondary school principals form informal groups that are guildlike. That is, the communication patterns are based on common professional interests and the need for mutual aid and protection. In contrast, elementary principals cluster into clanlike groups in which their communications revolve around social ties with mentors, friends, neighbors, and relatives. In brief, secondary principals structure the grapevine around professional survival and development while elementary principals communicate informally about social matters.

An excellent study executed by Charters (1967) found a gross difference in the amount of communication in elementary schools and in high schools. Elementary schools exhibited a much larger volume, with most teachers in direct contact with one another. In contrast, only 15 percent of the high school staff interacted regularly. This difference in communication volume is partially explained by staff size. The average number of contacts per staff member declined with increasing faculty size. Larger facilities and physical dispersion along with specialized personnel (guidance counselors or special teachers) who are not in the main flow of classroom instruction, help explain the impact of size on communication volume. Charters did note, however, that size alone does not account for the entire difference. Elementary school staffs communicate more than high school staffs. Finally, Charters found that stability in the communication patterns is related to the division of labor and physical proximity. Teachers in the same subject speciality and, to a lesser extent, those in closer physical proximity form enduring communication networks. Thus, three factors—level and size of school, specialization, and proximity—affect the horizontal communication patterns in schools.

IMPROVING COMMUNICATION PROCESSES

Communication does not have an opposite. There is no way for people not to behave and all behaviors have communication value (Myers and Myers, 1982). Similarly, totally planned and accurate communication is impossible. Accuracy in sending messages, however, is significantly associated with leader and organization performance (Penley et al., 1991). Using knowledge from communication theory can improve the efficiency and effectiveness of individual and organizational communication. For example, improvement guidelines can be drawn from the steps of the general process described in Figure 11.1. General guides suggested by Sayles and Strauss (1966) are still applicable:

- Determine the objective of the planned communication.
- Identify the intended receivers and characteristics that might facilitate or complicate constructing a shared understanding.
- Encode the message to fit the relationship between the sender and receiver.
- Determine ways to establish a mutual interest with the receiver and design the media for sending the message.
- Assess the results with feedback.

Improving school communication requires a planned program of organizational development. Suggestions for this approach to improving school communication include the following:

- Assess the organizational design of the communication system against criteria suggested earlier in this chapter by Barnard.
- Develop mechanisms to facilitate the process—e.g., close proximity of personnel, convenient sites for formal and informal interaction, mechanical links such as telephones and computers, and a committee system to accomplish tasks and make decisions.
- Establish information storage and retrieval systems.
- Select personnel with good communication skills.
- Develop a training program to improve communication skills.

Despite the many barriers to effective communication, these general guidelines can be incorporated with a number of techniques to minimize inaccuracies, add clarity, and enhance richness in the process. Three sets of skills stand out: sending, listening, and feedback.

Sending skills are abilities of a person to make oneself understood. As a key to effective communication, sending skills of educators can be enhanced through the following five methods. First, appropriate and direct language should be used. Educational jargon and complex concepts should be avoided when simpler words will do. However, to establish credibility, the language must demonstrate that the sender is knowledgeable about educational issues. Second, clear and complete information should be provided to the listener. Information is needed to build or reorganize the listener's cognitive schemas. Third, noise from the physical and psychological environments should be minimized. During parent conferences, for example, steps need to be taken to eliminate telephone interruptions and to reduce stereotypes held by either the professional educator or parent. Fourth, multiple and appropriate channels of media should be employed. Being skillful in matching richness of media to situational and communication needs may be a key factor in administrator performance (Alexander, Penley, and Jernigan, 1991). Fifth, face-to-face communication and redundancy should be used when communicating complex or equivocal messages. Richness, repetition, and feedback enhance the likelihood that the intended effect of gaining a shared meaning for the message will occur.

Listening skills are the abilities of individuals to understand others. Listening is a form of behavior in which individuals attempt to comprehend what is being communicated to them through the use of words, actions, and things by others (DeFleur, Kearney, and Plax, 1993). In active listening, a listener reflects back to the speaker what he or she has heard—content, feeling, and meaning—from the speaker's perspective (Elmes and Costello, 1992). Listening skills are required for relatively accurate, two-way exchanges.

Burbules (1993) observes that listening exhibits respect, interest, and concern for one's fellow communicator. It enables another's voice to be heard. When it is an active effort, it can encourage others to develop and express their own points of view. Active listening requires both a willingness and an ability to listen to a complete message, and to respond appropriately to the message's content and intent—that is, feelings, values, and emotions. Accepting another individual's feelings and trying to understand his or her message in the context of those feelings can improve the accuracy of exchanges. An important component of administrator behavior, therefore, is to create conditions that allow people to say what they really mean and to be heard.

Giving and **seeking feedback** is a special case of two-way communication. In work settings, we usually think of feedback as involving information about task performance or how others perceive and evaluate an individual's behavior (Ashford, 1986; Cusella, 1987). Two types of feedback are possible. When feedback reinforces, accentuates, or adds to the direction being taken by the person or school, it is positive. Feedback is negative when it corrects a deviation (Harris, 1993). It can be communicated either verbally or nonverbally, consciously or unconsciously. For example, a student who falls asleep during a class lecture may provide as much feedback to the teacher as the student who responds to examination questions.

Susan J. Ashford (1986) defines the concept of feedback-seeking behavior as the conscious devotion of effort to determining the correctness and adequacy of behaviors for attaining goals. Individuals should develop feedback-seeking behaviors because such actions will help them adapt and be successful employees. Two strategies for seeking feedback are suggested. The first is monitoring the environment by observing naturally occurring informational cues, other individuals, and how others respond. In other words, monitoring involves receiving feedback vicariously through watching how others are responded to and reinforced. The second strategy is to inquire directly about how others perceive and evaluate your behavior. As a caution, feedback-seeking can be hard on an individual's self-esteem because it potentially increases the chances of hearing information that one would rather not know or confront. In fact, individuals who suspect that they are performing poorly tend to use feedback-seeking strategies to minimize the amount of negative information they receive (Larson, 1989).

A number of criteria or guidelines have been proposed for developing **feedback skills** (Anderson, 1976; Harris, 1993).

- Feedback should be *intended* to be helpful to the recipient.
- Feedback should be specific rather than general and recent rather than old.
- Feedback should be directed toward behavior that the person can change.
- Feedback should be timely; the more immediate, the better.

While circumstances always exist that make the acceptance of negative feedback difficult, Anderson (1976) argues that acceptance is dependent on trust within the group, expression of wanting to help, use of descriptive rather than evaluative information, and appropriate timing of the meeting. When these criteria for giving and receiving feedback are met, the likelihood of successful communication increases substantially.

Unfortunately, feedback is not always useful. Three points are important in this regard. First, feedback must be pursued vigorously because people do not always give it voluntarily. In many situations, administrators, teachers, or students would rather risk doing the task incorrectly than ask for clarification. Second, feedback consists of nonverbal as well as verbal messages; people sometimes speak loudest with their feet (i.e., they walk away to avoid contact). Third, bogus feedback is common (Downs, 1977). People are reluctant to give negative feedback (Becker and Klimoski, 1989; Larson, 1989). Neutral or positive feedback is easier to give than negative assessments, even when holding negative reactions. Most of us are fairly adept at sending back messages that do not really represent our true reactions. Some people rationalize such behavior as tact, human relations, or survival. Consequently, both personal skill and preparation are critical to give and receive helpful feedback (Anderson, 1976; Rockey, 1984).

Because communication plays such a central role in schools, the key issue is not whether administrators, teachers, and students engage in communication but whether they communicate effectively. People must exchange information in schools, but to develop shared meanings requires the effective use of sending, listening, and feedback skills in a situation with minimal noise or barriers.

SUMMARY AND SUGGESTED READINGS

Communication is so pervasive in schools that it is a fundamental and integrative process in educational administration. Communication means sharing messages, ideas, or attitudes to produce understanding or shared meanings among people. Four conclusions seem clear. First, to be a good communicator is to know the various types of communication, their particular characteristics, how to choose among them, and to apply them skillfully. Second, individuals exchange symbols with other persons when interacting in social situations; the meanings of those symbols are constructed by the people who interpret them in a given situation. This means that direct transmission of an intended meaning is not always straightforward. Third, messages traverse formal and informal channels, using a variety of verbal and nonverbal media. Although the formal network is usually larger and better developed than the informal, they are closely related, can be complementary, and are critical to the organization. Fourth, to ensure a high level of shared understanding, feedback is essential. Although perfection is impossible, several techniques are available to measure and improve the communication process at both the individual and the organizational levels.

An early and still important set of ideas about individual and organizational communication was proposed by Chester Barnard (1938). This is an excellent source to consult on communication and other concepts. Two excellent general sources dealing with the communication literature are the textbooks by DeFleur, Kearney, and Plax (1993) and Harris (1993). They provide relatively comprehensive and in-depth coverage of the various theories and applications in the communication field. Clampitt's (1991) book *Communicating for Managerial Effectiveness* is useful. He presents the models of communication in a context of administrative applications, myths, and tactics. For an excellent review of the literature and suggestions for further research on gender and communication, we suggest the article by Baker (1991).

NOTES

1. Excellent discussions and elaboration of models similar to the one portrayed in Figure 11.1 can be found in Lysaught (1984) and Hoy and Miskel (1991).

2. Probably the most intense form of two-way communication is what Nicholas C. Burbules (1993) designates as dialogue. Burbules develops an extensive and excellent scholarly treatise on the concept of dialogue in schools, particularly as it relates to teaching. Although the narrative dealing with two-way and interpersonal communication in this section relies heavily on the ideas advanced by Burbules regarding dialogue, we primarily employ the term "two-way communication." Although "two-way communication" and "dialogue" are not exactly the same, we think that the two terms share enough common characteristics for the theoretical foundations of dialogue (as advanced by Burbules) to be applied to our usage of two-way communication. Moreover, "two-way communication" is a more commonly used term in organization analysis than dialogue.

3. Evidence of language differences between women and men also appears in the popular press. Two recent examples are *You Just Don't Understand: Women and Men in Conversation* by Deborah Tannen (1990), and *Men are from Mars, Women are from Venus* by John Gray (1992).

KEY CONCEPTS AND IDEAS

Autocommunication

Bridges

Channel

Communication

Communication effects

Conversation

Debate

Decoding

Encoding

Feedback

Feedback skills

Formal channels

Grapevines

Informal channels

Inquiry

Instruction

Isolate role

Liaisons

Listening skills

Meanings

Message

Networks

Noise

Nonverbal communication

One-way communication

Organizational communication

Receiver

Richness

Sender

Sending skills

Star role

Symbols

Transmission

Two-way communication

Leading

The effective functioning of social systems from the local PTA to the
United States of America is assumed to be dependent on the quality of
their leadership.

—Victor H. Vroom
"Leadership"

PREVIEW

1. Leaders are important because they serve as anchors, provide guidance in times of change, and are responsible for the effectiveness of organizations.

2. Leadership is a social influence process.

3. Leader and administrator refer to individuals who occupy positions in which they are expected to exert leadership.

4. The work of leaders exhibits similar patterns across different countries and organizational settings.

5. The most influential theories of leadership are contingency models, which explain the interrelationships among traits, situations, behaviors, and effectiveness.

6. Personality, motivation, and skill traits appear to be systematically related to leadership in schools.

7. Critical situational factors in educational leadership are environment, leader roles, nature of subordinates, and characteristics of the organization.

8. Four basic categories of leader behavior are building personal relationships, motivating, deciding, and communicating.

9. Leader effectiveness can be conceptualized as having three dimensions—personal, organizational, and individual.

10. Fiedler postulates that leadership effectiveness is contingent upon matching leadership style with an appropriate situation.

11. Four characteristics of transformational leadership are idealized influence, inspirational motivation, intellectual stimulation, and individualized consideration.

12. Educating potential leaders, selecting new administrators, changing administrators (succession), engineering the situation, and transforming organizational culture are ways to improve schools.

eadership continues to be an elusive but fascinating topic to students of administration. During the past several decades the sheer volume of writing devoted to leadership attests to its prominence in our collective efforts to understand and improve organizations. Romanticized, heroic images of leaders—what they do, what they are able to accomplish, and the general effects they have on individuals and organizations—have developed among both scholars and lay people (Meindl, Ehrich, and Dukerich, 1985). When we think of specific leaders, names such as Gandhi, Churchill, King, Mao Zedong, Napoleon, Roosevelt, and Thatcher come to mind. The term itself projects images of powerful, dynamic individuals who command victorious armies, build wealthy and influential empires, or alter the course of nations (Yukl, 1994). Stated succinctly, people commonly believe that leaders make a difference and want to understand why.

Nevertheless, a number of scholars, especially during the 1970s, questioned the usefulness of the leadership concept (e.g., Lieberson and O'Connor, 1972; Salancik and Pfeffer, 1977; McCall and Lombardo, 1978; Kerr and Jermier, 1978). Radical humanists (e.g., Gemmil and Oakley, 1992) also voice strong reservations about leadership and call it an alienating social myth. From their perspective, deeply ingrained cultural assumptions produce conceptions of leadership that assume leaders are unquestionably necessary to the functioning of organizations. In sharp contrast, others (e.g., Roberts, 1985; Day and Lord, 1988; Thomas, 1988; Bass, 1990) see leadership as a key in understanding and improving organizations such as schools. They argue that the earlier critical investigations were flawed, and present compelling evidence that individual leaders do make a difference in organizational effectiveness. Indeed, leadership is often regarded as the single most important factor in the success or failure of institutions (Bass, 1990). With a primary focus on administrative leadership in schools, we will build on the premise that leaders are important to educational organizations, and we will select and develop useful theoretical perspectives.

DEFINITIONS OF LEADERSHIP

"Leadership" is a word from the common language that has been incorporated into the technical vocabulary of organizational studies without being precisely redefined (Yukl, 1994). Therefore, it is not surprising that definitions of the concept are almost as numerous as the scholars engaged in its study. Bennis (1989) opined that leadership is like beauty: it is hard to define, but you know it when you see it. Typical definitions of leadership include the following.

- "Leadership is the initiation of a new structure or procedure for accomplishing an organization's goals and objectives or for changing an organization's goals and objectives."—*James Lipham* (1964: 122)

- "The leader is the individual in the group given the task of directing and coordinating task-relevant group activities."—*Fred E. Fiedler* (1967: 8)

- "The essence of organizational leadership is the influential increment over and above mechanical compliance with the routine directives of the organization."—*Daniel Katz* and *Robert L. Kahn* (1978: 528)

- "Leadership takes place in groups of two or more people and most frequently involves influencing group member behavior as it relates to the pursuit of group goals."—*Robert J. House* and *Mary L. Baetz* (1979: 345)
- "Leadership is the process of persuasion or example by which an individual (or leadership team) induces a group to pursue objectives held by the leader and shared by the leader and his or her followers."—*John W. Gardner* (1990: 1)

The only assumption shared by these and most other definitions is that **leadership** involves a social influence process in which intentional influence is exerted by one individual over others to structure activities and relationships in a group or organization (Yukl, 1994). Other than these, definitions of leadership have little in common.

In addition to these varying definitions of leadership, two continuing definitional controversies need to be noted. The first issue is whether leadership should be viewed as a property of particular individuals or a property of a social system (Yukl, 1994). One view is that all groups have a specialized leadership role that includes some responsibilities and functions that cannot be shared without jeopardizing the effectiveness of the group. The individual who has the most influence and who is expected to carry out the leadership role is the leader; other members are followers. An alternative view is that leadership is a social process that occurs naturally within a social system and is shared among its members. Leadership, then, is a process of the organization rather than a property of the individual. Katz and Kahn (1978) clarified the controversy when they identified three major components of leadership: (1) an attribute of an office or position, (2) a characteristic of a person, and (3) a category of actual behavior. Hence, both views are partially accurate—leadership can profitably be examined as a property of individuals and as a process of the social system.

The second issue involves distinctions between leaders and administrators and what and how they try to influence (Yukl, 1994).[1] Obviously, individuals can be leaders without being administrators (e.g., an informal leader); conversely, individuals can be administrators without being leaders. Some argue that leadership and administration are fundamentally different concepts. The basis of the dispute appears to be that **administrators** emphasize stability and efficiency, while **leaders** stress adaptive change and getting people to agree about what needs to be accomplished. For example, administrators plan and budget, organize and staff, and control and solve problems; leaders establish direction, align people, and motivate and inspire (Kotter, 1990). While no one suggests that administering and leading schools are equivalent, the degree of overlap is disputed. Rather than argue about the specific amount of overlap, we will use both terms to refer to individuals (e.g., administrators, teachers, school board members, students) who occupy positions in which they are expected to exert leadership, but without the assumption that they actually do so.

Thus, the definition of leadership remains elusive and controversial because it depends not only on the position, behavior, and personal characteristics of the leader but also on the character of the situation. We agree with Gary A. Yukl (1994), however, that research on leadership should be designed to provide information across the entire range of definitions, so that it will eventually be possible to compare the utility of different conceptualizations and arrive at some consensus. Nevertheless, an abundance of useful conceptual and empirical capital is available for both practitioners and scholars of school administration and leadership.

THE NATURE OF LEADERS' WORK

Given the intense and long-standing interest in leaders and leadership, what is it that leaders do that is so intriguing? Can describing the nature of leaders' work advance our understanding of leadership? Certainly, partial responses to these questions can be gained by observing them as they administer and lead their organizations. A number of studies have used a structured observation approach to describe what managers, administrators, and leaders do in their everyday jobs.[2] These studies provide detailed and vivid pictures of what business managers and school administrators do in their jobs, and with whom and where they spend their time. Given the regularities in the research, Kyung Ae Chung and Cecil Miskel (1989) summarize the major findings.

- In both business and educational organizations, managerial work is feverish and consuming; school administrators work long hours at an unrelenting, physically exhausting pace.
- School leaders rely on verbal media; they spend a great deal of time walking around the building and talking to individuals and groups.
- Administrator activities vary widely; hence, administrators constantly change gears and tasks.
- The work of school administrators is fragmented; the pace is rapid, discontinuity prevalent, and the span of concentration short.

Overall, the descriptions of administrators' and leaders' work are similar across different countries and organizational settings. Administrators work primarily in their offices or school buildings. Their jobs are characterized by long hours and brief verbal encounters across a wide range of issues with diverse individuals and groups. Structured observation studies are useful because they respond descriptively and clearly to the question: What do school administrators and leaders do in their jobs? Nevertheless, it is not clear how individuals engaged in work characterized as consuming and fragmented can actually provide leadership to their organizations. While the results from these studies are important and interesting, the key question for present purposes—How do we understand the nature of this work in terms of leading organizations?—remains largely unanswered. To respond to this question, we will present a schema and the dominant theoretical approaches to understanding leadership.

A CONTINGENCY SCHEMA FOR UNDERSTANDING LEADERSHIP

Since the 1970s, the most influential models guiding leadership research use contingency approaches. At best, a **contingency approach** involves at least four sets of concepts—traits of leaders, characteristics of the situation, behaviors of the leader, and effectiveness of the leader (see Figure 12.1). Hence, the contemporary question in understanding leadership is: What traits under what situations are important to leader behavior and effectiveness? The basic hypothesis shown in Figure 12.1 is that traits of the leaders and characteristics of the situation combine to produce leader behavior and effectiveness.

Contingency approaches specify the conditions or situational variables that moderate the relationship between leader traits, behaviors, and performance criteria. The evidence indicates that under one set of circumstances, one type of leader is effective; under another set of circumstances, a different type of leader is effective. In the useful words of Robert K. Merton (1969: 2015), "Leadership does not, indeed cannot, result merely from the individual traits of leaders; it must also involve attributes of the transactions between those who lead and those who follow. . . . Leadership is, then, some sort of social transaction." To advance our understanding of contingency approaches, each component—that is, leader traits, situations, behavior, and performance—will be considered separately and then examples of contingency theories will be discussed.

TRAITS AND LEADERSHIP

Many individuals still believe, as Aristotle did centuries ago, that from the hour of birth, some are marked for subjection, others for rule. Aristotle thought that individuals are born with characteristics that would make them leaders. The conception

FIGURE **12.1**

A Contingency Schema for Understanding Leadership

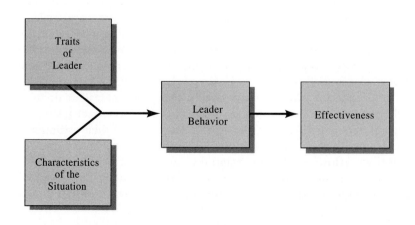

that the key factors in determining leadership are inherited produced the so-called trait approach of leadership. Bass (1990) observes that early in this century, leaders were generally regarded as superior individuals who, because of fortunate inheritance or social circumstance, possessed qualities and abilities that differentiated them from people in general. Until the 1950s investigations to find the traits that determine who will be leaders dominated the study of leadership. Researchers attempted to isolate unique traits or characteristics of leaders that differentiated them from their followers. Frequently studied traits included physical characteristics (height, weight), a host of personality factors, needs, values, energy and activity levels, task and interpersonal competence, intelligence, and charisma. Over time, recognition grew that traits can generally be affected by inheritance, learning, and environmental factors.

Early Trait Research

Pure trait approaches—that is, the view that only traits determine leadership capacity—were all but put to rest with the publication of literature reviews during the 1940s and 1950s. In particular, Ralph M. Stogdill (1948) reviewed 124 trait studies of leadership that were completed between 1904 and 1947. He classified the personal factors associated with leadership into the following five general categories:

- Capacity—intelligence, alertness, verbal facility, originality, judgment
- Achievement—scholarship, knowledge, athletic accomplishments
- Responsibility—dependability, initiative, persistence, aggressiveness, self-confidence, desire to excel
- Participation—activity, sociability, cooperation, adaptability, humor
- Status—socioeconomic position, popularity

Although Stogdill found a number of traits (e.g., above-average intelligence, dependability, participation, and status) that consistently differentiated leaders from nonleaders, he concluded that the trait approach *by itself* had yielded negligible and confusing results. He asserted that a person does not become a leader by virtue of the possession of some combination of traits because the impact of traits varies widely from situation to situation. As consequence, Stogdill added a sixth factor associated with leadership—situational components (e.g., characteristics of followers and goals to be achieved). R. D. Mann's (1959) later review produced similar conclusions.

Current Perspectives on Leadership Traits

Not withstanding the lack of success in identifying general leadership traits, research persisted. More recent trait studies, however, use improved and a wider variety of measurement procedures, including projective tests and assessment centers; and they focus on managers and administrators rather than other kinds of leaders. Yukl

(1981) explains that while the 1948 literature review by Stogdill greatly discouraged many leadership researchers from studying leader traits, industrial psychologists interested in improving managerial selection continued to conduct trait research. Their emphasis on selection focused trait research on the relationship between leader traits and leader effectiveness, rather than on the comparison of leaders and nonleaders. This distinction is a significant one. Predicting who will become leaders and predicting who will be more effective are quite different tasks. Hence, the so-called trait studies continue, but they now tend to explore the relationship between traits and leadership effectiveness of administrators in particular types of organizations and settings.

This second generation of studies has produced a more consistent set of findings; in fact, in 1970, after reviewing another 163 new trait studies, Stogdill (1981) concluded that a leader is characterized by the following traits: a strong drive for responsibility and task completion, vigor and persistence in pursuit of goals, venturesomeness and originality in problem solving, drive to exercise initiative in social situations, self-confidence and sense of personal identity, willingness to accept consequences of decision and action, readiness to absorb interpersonal stress, willingness to tolerate frustration and delay, ability to influence other persons' behavior, and capacity to structure interaction systems to the purpose at hand. Similarly, Glenn L. Immegart (1988) concluded that the traits of intelligence, dominance, self-confidence, and high energy or activity level are commonly associated with leaders. Nevertheless, the evidence that traits are an important factor in leadership does not represent a return to the original trait assumption that "leaders are born, not made." Rather, it is a more sensible and balanced view, one that acknowledges the influence of both traits and situations.

Given the plethora of concepts and for ease of discussion, we will classify the trait variables that currently are associated with effective leadership into one of three groups. The categories are: personality, motivation, and skills (see Table 12.1). We will discuss selected traits within each group.[3]

PERSONALITY TRAITS According to Yukl (1994), **personality traits** are relatively stable dispositions to behave in a particular way. The list of personality factors associated with effective leadership is quite long. Four seem particularly important.

TABLE **12.1** Example Traits Associated with Effective Leadership		
Personality	**Work Motivation**	**Skills**
Self-confidence	Task	Technical
Stress tolerance	Interpersonal needs	Interpersonal
Emotional maturity	Values	Conceptual
Integrity	Expectations	Administrative

- Self-confident leaders are more likely to set high goals for themselves and their followers, to attempt difficult tasks, and to persist in the face of problems and defeats.

- Stress-tolerant leaders are likely to make good decisions, to stay calm, and to provide decisive direction to subordinates in difficult situations. As shown by the structured observation studies, the pace, long hours, fragmentation, and demands for decisions place leaders under intense pressure that can best be addressed by stress-tolerant individuals.

- Emotionally mature leaders tend to have an accurate awareness of their strengths and weaknesses, to be oriented toward self-improvement; they do not deny their shortcomings or fantasize about success. Consequently, emotionally mature administrators can maintain cooperative relationships with subordinates, peers, and supervisors.

- Integrity means that the behaviors of leaders are consistent with their stated values and that they are honest, ethical, responsible, and trustworthy. Yukl believes that integrity is an essential element in building and retaining loyalty and obtaining cooperation and support of others.

Hence, self-confidence, stress confidence, emotional maturity, and integrity are personality traits associated with leader effectiveness.

MOTIVATION TRAITS As discussed in Chapter 4, work motivation is a set of energetic forces that originate both within as well as beyond an individual to initiate work-related behavior and to determine its form, direction, intensity, and duration. The process can be understood as a motivation sequence: needs, values, expectancy-choice, and goal-setting. A basic postulate is that motivation factors play key roles in explaining both the choice of action and its degree of success. Generally, highly motivated leaders are likely to be more effective than individuals with low need, value, expectation, and goal levels. Three sets of **motivational traits** are especially critical for leaders.

- Task and interpersonal needs are two underlying dispositions that motivate effective leaders. Effective leaders are characterized by their drive for the task and their concern for people.

- Power and achievement values refer to motives of individuals to seek positions of authority, to exercise power over others, and to achieve.

- High expectations for success of school administrators refers to their belief that they can do the job and will receive valued outcomes for their efforts.

Hence, strong task and interpersonal needs, power and achievement values, and high expectations to succeed are important traits associated with effectiveness (Fiedler, 1967; McClelland, 1985; Yukl, 1994). In addition to these motivation traits, the physical traits of energy and activity levels allow individuals to exhibit competence through active engagement with others.

SKILL TRAITS Other important components, which are often neglected in the leadership literature, are skills and experience. Competence, or having a mastery of task-relevant knowledge and skills, is mandatory for a leader. Yukl (1994) discusses four types of administrative **skill traits.**

- Technical skills deal with specialized knowledge, procedures, and techniques to accomplish the task.
- Interpersonal skills focus on the ability to understand feelings and attitudes of others and to establish cooperative work relationships.
- Conceptual skills involve developing and using ideas and concepts to solve complex problems.
- Administrative skills combine technical, interpersonal, and conceptual skills to help perform managerial functions.

These four skills must be developed in the context of practice. Experience represents an opportunity to learn the job and apply the skills; experience has been found to be central in determining job performance of professional and managerial employees (Schmidt and Hunter, 1992). We have identified three sets of traits that are related to leadership. Our summary of the most important of these traits is shown in Table 12.1.

SITUATIONS AND LEADERSHIP

Reaction, or perhaps more appropriately overreaction, to the trait approach was so intense during the late 1940s and 1950s that for a time it seemed that scholars had substituted a strictly situational analysis for the then-questionable trait approach. The view that leaders are born was rejected (Bass, 1990). Researchers sought to identify distinctive characteristics of the setting to which the leader's success could be attributed; they attempted to isolate specific properties of the **leadership situation** that had relevance for leader behavior and performance (Campbell et al., 1970; Lawler, 1985; Vecchio, 1993). As shown throughout this book and summarized in Table 12.2, a number of variables have been postulated to influence behavior in schools and, hence, can be viewed as situational determinants of leadership. A few general examples follow:

TABLE **12.2** Situational Factors in Educational Leadership				
Subordinate	**Organizational**	**Leader Role**	**Internal Environment**	**External Environment**
Personality	Size	Position power	Climate/Culture	Social
Motivation	Hierarchy	Task situation	Status	Economic
Abilities	Formalization	Procedural rules		

- Structural properties of the organization—size, hierarchical structure, formalization, technology
- Role characteristics—position power, type and difficulty of task, procedural rules, content and performance expectations
- Subordinate characteristics—education, age, knowledge and experience, tolerance for ambiguity, responsibility, power
- Internal environment—climate, culture, openness, participativeness, group atmosphere, values, and norms
- External environment—complexity, stability, uncertainty, resource dependency, institutionalization

Some scholars even go so far as to suggest that situational components can act as substitutes for leadership (Kerr and Jermier, 1978; Pitner, 1982). Steven Kerr and John M. Jermier (1978) assert that data from numerous studies collectively demonstrate that in many situations some leadership behaviors are irrelevant, and hierarchical leadership per se does not seem to matter. For example, when the subordinates have high ability, are experienced and knowledgeable, or the task is unambiguous and routine, task-oriented leadership is not needed. Similarly, when the task is intrinsically satisfying or the work group is closely knit and cohesive, relationship or supportive leadership is of limited usefulness. Taken to its logical conclusion, knowledge of these substitutes would enable the design of a situation that permits free information flow, effective decision making, and exercise of authority without a designated leader (Fiedler and Garcia, 1987). In other words, the **substitutes-for-leaders model** sees performance as dependent on subordinate, task, and organizational characteristics rather than on those of the leader. This approach has generated substantial interest among leadership researchers, but results from recent attempts to test the model have not been particularly supportive (Podsakoff et al., 1993).

John P. Campbell and his colleagues (1970) came to an interesting conclusion about the situational phase of leadership study. Everyone believed that the need for research was great, but actual empirical activity was scarce. Consequently, the jump from "leaders are born, not made" to "leaders are made by the situation, not born," was short-lived. Bass (1990) maintains that the situational view overemphasized the situational and underemphasized the personal nature of leadership. To restrict the study of leadership to either traits or situations is unduly narrow and counterproductive.

Two fundamental generalizations emerge. First, the properties of the situation combine with the traits of the leader to produce a behavior on the part of the leader that is related to leadership effectiveness. Second, characteristics of the situation have a direct impact on effectiveness. For example, the motivation and ability levels of teachers and students are related to the goal attainment of schools. Moreover, the socioeconomic status of individuals attending a school is strongly related to student achievement on standardized tests. From a short-range perspective, at least, the situational characteristics of the school may have a greater influence on leader effectiveness than the leader's own behavior. These two generalizations represent tentative hypotheses that should be tested in educational settings.

BEHAVIORS AND LEADERSHIP

Early conceptualizations of leadership typically relied on two distinct categories of **leader behavior**—one concerned with people and interpersonal relations and the other with production and task achievement. For example, Dorwin Cartwright and Alvin Zander (1953) describe leadership in terms of two sets of group functions. They conclude that most group objectives can be subsumed under one of two headings: goal achievement—the achievement of some specific group goal; and group maintenance—the maintenance or strengthening of the group itself. Similar finding were reflected in other early studies of leadership. We now turn to a description of an early program of research and a more recent perspective on leader behavior.

The Ohio State Leadership Studies

To students of educational administration, probably the most well-known leader research inquiries are the **leader behavior description questionnaire (LBDQ)** studies started at Ohio State University in the 1940s. Originally developed there by John K. Hemphill and Alvin Coons (1950), the LBDQ was later refined by Andrew Halpin and B. J. Winer (1952). It measures two basic dimensions of leader behavior— initiating structure and consideration.

Initiating structure includes any leader behavior that delineates the relationship between the leader and subordinates and, at the same time, establishes defined patterns of organization, channels of communication, and methods of procedure. **Consideration** includes leader behavior that indicates friendship, trust, warmth, interest, and respect in the relationship between the leader and members of the work group (Halpin, 1966). Using the LBDQ, subordinates, superiors, or the individual himself or herself can describe the leader behavior. For example, the LBDQ has been used by students to describe teachers, by teachers to describe principals and superintendents, by principals and superintendents to describe each other, and by board of education members to describe superintendents.

Early studies using the LBDQ indicated that consideration and initiating structure were separate and distinct, not opposite ends of the same continuum. Therefore, four quadrants, or leadership styles, can be formed by cross-partitioning the consideration and initiating scores of the LBDQ. Each dimension is divided into high and low groups and then combined with one another to yield four groups, or quadrants (see Figure 12.2).

Figure 12.2 is interpreted as follows. Given a set of people who occupy leader positions and their respective LBDQ scores on initiating structure and consideration, those who score high on both dimensions are in quadrant I and are labeled dynamic leaders; those low on both dimensions are in quadrant III and are called passive leaders; those who score low in consideration but high in initiating structure are in quadrant II and are designated structured leaders; while those in quadrant IV are named considerate leaders. Consequently, using these two dimensions, four leadership styles are possible.

Four major findings emerged from the Ohio State University LBDQ studies (Halpin, 1966).

FIGURE **12.2**

Quadrants Formed by Using the LBDQ Dimensions

		Consideration	
		Low	High
Initiating Structure	High	**Quadrant II** Low consideration High initiating structure	**Quadrant I** High consideration High initiating structure
	Low	**Quadrant III** Low consideration Low initiating structure	**Quadrant IV** High consideration Low initiating structure

- Initiating structure and consideration are fundamental dimensions of leader behavior.

- Effective leader behavior tends most often to be associated with frequent behaviors on both dimensions.

- Superiors and subordinates tend to evaluate the contributions of the leader behavior dimensions oppositely in assessing effectiveness. Superiors tend to emphasize initiating structure; subordinates are more concerned with consideration.

- Only a slight relationship exists between how leaders say they should behave and how subordinates describe that they do behave.

In brief, school administrators were generally found to be most effective when they score high on both dimensions of leader behavior (quadrant I). After an extensive LBDQ study, however, Alan F. Brown (1967) suggests that, although strength on both dimensions is highly desirable, principals committed to developing effective organizational dynamics may make up for weakness on one dimension with unusual strength in the other. Leaders weak on both dimensions (quadrant III), tend to be ineffective; indeed, they tend to suffer from a lack of leadership, and general chaos can imbue the work situation. Early studies of superintendents by Halpin (1966) suggest that public school norms supported considerate behavior. He speculates that the lack of emphasis on initiating structure may reflect the fact that human relations and group dynamics are stressed in education. Apparently, many educators tend to equate initiating structure with an authoritarian leadership style, although this is not the case.

Related LBDQ Research

Hoy and his colleagues (Kunz and Hoy, 1976; Leverette, 1984; Hoy and Brown, 1988) investigated the relationship between the leadership styles of principals and the "zone of indifference or acceptance" (Barnard, 1938; Simon, 1957a) of teachers—that is, the range of behavior within which subordinates are ready to accept the decisions made by their leaders. The LBDQ findings suggests that principals who exhibit frequent behaviors on both initiating structure and consideration (quadrant I) produce situations that are conducive to relatively broad zones of acceptance by teachers. The results indicate that the relationships between the leadership behaviors of elementary and secondary principals and the zone of acceptance of teachers differ slightly. Similar to the secondary schools, both initiating structure and consideration were positively related to the zone of acceptance. But *both* dimensions had significant independent effects on the professional zone of acceptance of teachers. Unlike the secondary schools, the consideration of the elementary principals had a significant independent relationship with the zone of acceptance of teachers.

The findings of Kunz, Hoy, and Leverette support the conclusions made by other scholars (Vroom, 1976; House and Baetz, 1979; Mitchell, 1979). Consideration is typically related to subordinate satisfaction with work and with the leader. While the evidence is somewhat mixed, initiating structure has been identified as a source of subordinate performance. However, situational variables apparently affect the relationship between consideration and initiating structure and affect the criteria of organizational effectiveness as well. Consideration has its most positive effect on the satisfaction of subordinates who work in structured situations or who work on stressful, frustrating, or dissatisfying tasks. In contrast, initiating structure has the greatest impact on group performance when subordinates' tasks are ill-defined.

The implications of these findings are fairly clear to us. To neglect initiation of structure limits the leader's impact on the school; to ignore consideration reduces the satisfaction of the subordinates. Certainly, leader behavior that integrates strength on both initiating structure and consideration into a consistent pattern is desirable. Nevertheless, the converse also seems likely; there are situations especially favorable to considerate leadership style that is characterized by strong consideration and limited initiating structure. The matching of leadership style with the appropriate situation in order to maximize effectiveness is a knotty problem to which we will return throughout this chapter.

A Recent Perspective on Leader Behavior

Yukl (1994) also cautions not to interpret the results of these early studies as universal theories of effective leader behavior. In other words, concluding that the same style of leader behavior is optimal across all situations is not warranted. Blake and Mouton's (1985) managerial grid is a well-known universal theory. Its basic hypothesis is that the most effective leaders are high on both production and people concerns. Production and people concerns are similar to the earlier models using terms such as "task" or "initiating structure" and "relationship" or "consideration." Yukl notes that Blake and Mouton suggest a situational aspect with the idea that the behaviors must be relevant to the situation to be effective. However, they never actually state specific generalizations linking appropriate behaviors to different situations. As we have shown in our discussion of the earlier studies, situational factors do affect the effectiveness of leader behavior, even when an individual is high on both people and task dimensions.

TABLE **12.3** Leader Behavior of Educational Administrators			
Building Personal Relationships	**Deciding**	**Motivating**	**Communicating**
Mentoring	Planning	Recognizing	Informing
Team Building	Problem Solving	Rewarding	Listening

While concern for tasks and concern for relationships are important aspects of administrative behavior, they are not sufficient. Additional specific functional content of leader behavior should be considered. Based on Yukl's work, four basic behavior categories and eight administrative practices are shown in Table 12.3.

In sum, current views of leader behavior employ more specific types of administrative practices than the general person and task categories of the early studies. Nonetheless, each administrative practice includes some behavioral aspects of task and people (Yukl, 1994). The appropriate applications of these behaviors in varying situations can result in enhanced leader performance.

LEADERSHIP EFFECTIVENESS

The final set of concepts in a contingency model are the criteria used to judge leadership effectiveness. To both practicing administrators and scholars, effectiveness is a complicated, multifaceted, and subtle topic. Three types of effectiveness outcomes are suggested in Table 12.4.

- Personal—other perceptions of reputation and self-assessments
- Individual member satisfaction
- Organizational goal attainment

Perceived evaluations of performance are important: subjective judgments of the leader by himself or herself, subordinates, peers, and superiors within the school and by members of the public outside the school yield measures of effectiveness. In schools, the opinions held by students, teachers, administrators, and patrons are highly significant. However, these groups may view the performance levels quite differently. A second indicator of leadership effectiveness is the satisfaction of organizational participants. Finally, the relative levels of school goal achievement also

TABLE **12.4** Dimensions of Effectiveness of Educational Leaders		
Personal	**Organizational**	**Individual**
Perceived reputation	Goal attainment	Group member satisfaction
Self-assessment		

define the effectiveness of educational leaders (see Chapter 8). **Leadership effectiveness,** then, can be defined as having a more objective dimension—accomplishment of organizational goals—and two subjective dimensions—perceptual evaluations of significant reference groups and overall job satisfaction of subordinates.

AN ELABORATED CONTINGENCY SCHEMA FOR UNDERSTANDING LEADERSHIP

We started this discussion of contingency theory of leadership by presenting a general schema in Figure 12.1. Each component—traits, situation, behavior, effectiveness—was considered in some detail. Conclusions were drawn about which concepts exhibit either an empirical or a theoretical linkage to leader behavior or effectiveness. As shown in Figure 12.3, adding these concepts to the original formulation produces a specific and elaborated contingency schema for leadership. The

FIGURE **12.3**

An Elaborated Contingency Schema for Understanding Leadership in Schools

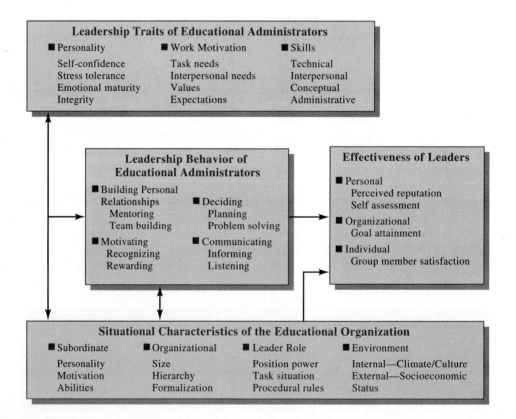

components can be summarized as follows: *traits* of leaders associated with effectiveness include personality, work motivation, and skills; important *situational factors* influencing outcomes include subordinate, organizational, role, and internal and external environmental attributes; key leader *behaviors* include building personal relationships, motivating, deciding, and communicating; and *effectiveness indicators* include personal, organizational, and individual outcomes. The fundamental hypothesis of the elaborated contingency model, therefore, becomes: leadership effectiveness depends upon the fit between the characteristics and behavior of the leader and situational variables. While the general hypothesis can be stated succinctly, the multitude of specific factors associated with leadership produce immense complexity and room for contradictory directions for both research and practice. Hence, the most popular contingency theories typically focus on a reduced set of concepts.

FIEDLER'S CONTINGENCY MODEL OF LEADERSHIP

Fiedler (1967) constructed the first major theory to propose specific contingency relationships in the study of leadership. The basic postulates of Fiedler's model are:[5]

- Leadership style is determined by the motivational system of the leader.
- Situational control is determined by group atmosphere, task structure, and position power.
- Group effectiveness is contingent on the leader's style and control of the situation.

The theory departed from previous thinking because it viewed the leadership situation as an arena in which the leader seeks both to satisfy personal needs and to accomplish organizational goals.

LEADERSHIP STYLE

Fiedler carefully and clearly distinguishes between the terms "leadership behavior" and "leadership style." Leadership behavior denotes the specific acts of a leader in directing and coordinating the work of group members. For instance, the leader can direct, commend, make helpful suggestions, and show consideration for the well-being of group members. In contrast, **leadership style** refers to the underlying need structure of the leader that motivates behavior in various interpersonal situations. In essence, leadership style is a personality characteristic; it does not describe a consistent type of leader behavior. Fiedler (1967) underscores this critical distinction when he observes that important leadership behaviors of the same individual differ from situation to situation, while the need structure that motivates these behaviors remains constant.

To identify leadership styles, Fiedler developed a simple personality measure called the **least preferred co-worker (LPC) scale**. The LPC scale is a semantic differential consisting of bipolar items—for example, pleasant/unpleasant, back-biting/loyal, cold/warm, and kind/unkind. The respondent selects the person with whom he or she works least well (least preferred co-worker) and then describes that individual on the scale. The least preferred co-worker need not be someone who is personally disliked, but it must be the one person with whom it was most difficult to work. A person scoring high on the LPC describes the least preferred co-worker positively, as being pleasant, loyal, warm, kind, efficient, and so forth. Thus, even a person with whom it is difficult to work might be seen as an individual who otherwise has some acceptable, if not admirable, traits. In contrast, the individual scoring low on the LPC describes the least preferred co-worker negatively, as being unpleasant, backbiting, cold, unkind, inefficient, and so forth. The person who rates a least preferred co-worker negatively states a strong rejection of people with whom he or she cannot work (Fiedler, 1967). In effect, this person says, "If I cannot work with you, then there is something wrong with you."

The LPC score is now interpreted as measuring a motivational hierarchy (Fiedler and Garcia, 1987). It indicates the extent to which the individual sets a higher priority or value on task accomplishment (task-motivated) or on maintaining good interpersonal relations (relationship-motivated). The LPC is thought to identify two styles of leadership. Task-oriented leaders score low on the LPC and are motivated by (i.e., derive satisfaction from) successful task accomplishment. Conversely, relationship-oriented leaders score high on the LPC and receive satisfaction from successful interpersonal interactions. In short, leadership style as measured by the LPC represents a cognitive goal process that appears to indicate the degree to which an individual is primarily motivated by accomplishing assigned tasks or by developing or maintaining close working relationships with others. If the current interpretation of the LPC is correct, then it becomes clear why individuals respond differently on the LPC scale. Those with a low LPC score have negative reactions toward their least preferred co-worker because a co-worker with whom it is difficult to "get the job done" threatens the central motivational orientation of the leader—succeeding at a task. But those with a high LPC score can have neutral or even positive attitudes toward their least preferred co-worker because an ineffective co-worker does not necessarily threaten the leader's orientation of interpersonal success (Rice, 1978).

SITUATIONAL CONTROL

As a contingency approach, the second major component of the theory is the situation. The power and influence of leaders determine the degree to which leaders can implement plans, decisions, and action strategies. Clearly, power, influence, and control come from the leadership situation (Fiedler and Garcia, 1987). Which factors in the situation enable leaders to exert influence? Within Fiedler's model, three major factors determine situational control: position power of the leader, task structure, and leader-member relations.

Position power is the power that the organization confers on the leader for the purpose of getting the job done. In other words, it is the degree to which the position itself enables the leader to get subordinates to comply with directives. Examples of position power include the extent to which a leader can reward and punish members and whether the group can depose the leader. The *actual* position power of a leader can be rather limited. Many jobs simply do not grant the leader high position power. The leaders' own bosses, however, play important parts in determining the level of position power. Bosses who support their subordinates' decisions provide them with a number of options in dealing with their groups; hence, their control of the situation increases. Despite a number of formal constraints, most leaders do gain high position power (Fiedler and Garcia, 1987). The ability to use position power effectively is difficult to do unless the leader understands how the task is to be done and when it has been done correctly.

Task structure is the extent to which the task has clearly specified goals, methods, and standards of performance. In particular, four dimensions constitute task structure—goal clarity, number of methods, solution specificity, and decision verifiability. With highly structured tasks—that is, clearly defined assignment, a single method, one acceptable solution, and periodic checks of decisions—the leader and group know exactly what to do and how to do it. Unstructured tasks—that is, ambiguous goals, a multiplicity of approaches, no clear-cut solutions, and no feedback on progress—create uncertainty and make definitive action by the leader and group difficult. Thus, the more structured the task, the more control the leader has in directing the group.

Leader-member relations is the extent to which the leader is accepted and respected by group members. Two factors are important with respect to leader-member relations: the quality of interpersonal relations between the leader and subordinates, and the level of informal authority granted to the leader. In contrast to position power and task structure, which are determined in large part by the organization, the quality of leader-member relations is determined primarily by the leader's personality and behavior.

The quality of leader-member relations is the most important factor in determining the leader's influence over group members, followed by task structure and position power. The relative importance of the three components has been shown to be a 4:2:1 ratio (Fiedler and Garcia, 1987). Therefore, the leader has more control and influence when the group is supportive, the leader knows exactly what to do and how to do it, and the organization gives the leader means to reward and punish the group members.

Fiedler uses these three factors to form eight situations ordered in terms of leader control. The three factors are each dichotomized—that is, good or bad leader-member relations, structured or unstructured tasks, and high or low position power. The eight combinations or octants map the range of situations from high control to low control. Table 12.5 portrays the eight situations. Octant 1 suggests very high situational control with good relations, structured task, and high position power. Octants 2 and 3 also indicate high leader control. Octants 4 to 6 are moderate-control situations. Good group relations, the most important component, combines with two negative factors to form octant 4 and poor-good relations combines with two positive factors to form octant 5. Finally, octants 7 and 8 are low-control situations with two of the most important factors or all three components being negative (Fiedler and Garcia, 1987).

TABLE **12.5**	Classification of Situations in Fiedler's Contingency Theory			
Octant	Level of Control	Leader- Member Relations	Task Structure	Position Power
1	Very high	Good	Structured	High
2	High	Good	Structured	Low
3	High	Good	Unstructured	High
4	Moderate	Good	Unstructured	Low
5	Moderate	Poor	Structured	High
6	Moderate	Poor	Structured	Low
7	Low	Poor	Unstructured	High
8	Low	Poor	Unstructured	Low

LEADER EFFECTIVENESS

Fiedler uses a straightforward criterion of effectiveness—namely, the extent to which the group accomplishes its primary task. Even though the group's output is not entirely a function of the leader's skills, the leader's effectiveness is judged on how well the group achieves its task. According to Fiedler (1967), turnover rate, job satisfaction, morale, and personal adjustment may contribute to group performance, but they are not in themselves criteria of performance. In many of Fiedler's studies, objective measures of group effectiveness are used—net profit, cost per unit, percentage of wins, number of problems solved. If a reliable objective measure of group performance is not available, then the boss's rating of the leader's or group's performance must be used. But in all cases, leader effectiveness is determined by the degree to which the task is or judged to be achieved.

THE MATCH: STYLE AND SITUATION

The question still remains: Which style of leadership is most effective in which type of situation? Using data that he collected from a wide variety of group situations (more than eight hundred groups) over more than ten years, Fiedler categorized the type of situation (one of eight octants), determined the style of the leader, and determined which groups performed their tasks successfully or unsuccessfully. From the data, Fiedler developed three major propositions of his contingency theory.

- In high-control situations, task-oriented leaders are more effective than relationship-oriented leaders.
- In moderate-control situations, relationship-oriented leaders are more effective than task-oriented leaders.

- In low-control situations, task-oriented leaders are more effective than relationship-oriented leaders.

The basic explanation for effectiveness emerging from Fiedler's research is that situational control elicits leader behavior that is consistent with the motivational system of the leader (House and Baetz, 1979). The primary motivational pattern of leaders appears in situations in which the individual is threatened, while leaders pursue their secondary goals in situations in which primary goals are either satisfied or appear secure. Therefore, high LPC leaders will concern themselves with relationships in low-control situations but with the task in high-control situations. Conversely, low LPC leaders will concern themselves with the task in low-control situations, but in high-control situations, they will be concerned with having good interpersonal relations (Fiedler, 1971).

In situations with low control, leaders with low LPC scores who concentrate on task accomplishment are more effective because the situation triggers directing and controlling behavior that is most likely to get the job done. In contrast, anxious concern with interpersonal relations by leaders with high LPC scores does not produce effectiveness in low-control situations.

In situations of medium control, relations-oriented leaders (with high LPC scores) are more effective, though it is not clear why. One possible explanation is that the two kinds of leaders respond to stress differently. Relationship-oriented leaders experience less stress than task-oriented leaders (with low LPC scores) in response to the same levels of low situational control. For example, low LPC scorers in stressful conditions become more assertive, task oriented, directive and controlling. Such behaviors suggest that they become more rigid and exhibit less variability in behavior than high-scoring leaders, given the same low levels of control. It is possible that under moderate-control situations behavioral flexibility on the part of leaders is required. If low-scoring leaders experience stress in this type of situation, then it is doubtful that they would be able to exhibit the flexibility needed for group effectiveness. In contrast, leaders with high LPC scores experiencing less stress would be more flexible and adapt as the situation demands. Thus, the differential perception and response to stress provides an explanation for the high performance of leaders with high LPC scores under conditions of medium situational control.

In situations with high control, leaders can focus on secondary goals because their primary goal is being met. Consequently, the task-oriented leader (with a low LPC score) displays considerate behavior while the relations-oriented leader (with a high LPC score) exhibits task-relevant behaviors. Since task-relevant behaviors are redundant in high-control situations (structured tasks, high position power, and good leader-member relations), the leader with a low LPC score is more effective than the high LPC score in high-control situations (House and Baetz, 1979).

RESEARCH AND EVALUATION OF FIEDLER'S THEORY

The contingency model was inductively developed on the basis of data collected before 1962. Since then, the model has been used to predict group performance in a large variety of social settings (Fiedler, 1967, 1973; Fiedler and Garcia, 1987). To date only two studies provide rigorous and complete tests of the model—that is, investigations that meet the criteria set by Fiedler and include leaders from all eight situations. One study was supportive (Chemers and Skrzypek, 1972); one was not (Vecchio, 1977). However, three meta-analyses of research testing the contingency model have been performed, and all provide some support. Michael Strube and Garcia's (1981) analysis provides strong statistical support for the model. Similarly, the meta-analysis of Lawrence Peters and his associates (1985) is generally supportive, and Ellen Crehan (1985) concludes that results of studies that adhered to Fiedler's methodology were typically supportive of his model.

Fiedler's model also has been used to predict the leadership effectiveness of principals in the school context. The results of studies by Vincent McNamara and Frederick Enns (1966), Leonard B. Williams and Hoy (1973), and Yvonne M. Martin and her associates (1976) support Fiedler's contingency theory. In schools with principals who are well supported by their teachers (high-control situation), a task-oriented style is significantly associated with group effectiveness. In schools with principals who are less well supported (moderate-control situation), there is some tendency for a relationship-oriented style to be associated with school effectiveness.

The LPC theory has been subject to several criticisms. A frequent complaint is that the definition of what the LPC measures has varied over the years. At first, it was seen simply as a measure of an emotional reaction to individuals with whom the leader found it difficult to work; then it was thought to differentiate between individuals who had a task orientation as opposed to an interpersonal one. Now the LPC score is interpreted as an indicator of a leader's motivational hierarchy. The most parsimonious interpretation is as a value-attitude indicator. Low LPC leaders value task success and high LPC leaders value interpersonal success (Rice, 1978). Moreover, the model essentially ignores the medium LPC leaders, who probably outnumber both the high and low LPC leaders. Medium LPC leaders may even be more effective than either high or low LPC leaders in a majority of situations because they balance interpersonal and task concerns more successfully (Yukl, 1994).

Overall, Fiedler's theory represents an ambitious and laudable effort to build a powerful contingency theory of leadership. While interest has waned, the model demonstrates that a combination of situational and individual characteristics partly explains the leadership phenomenon. Like most pioneering efforts, it undoubtedly is incorrect in detail if not in substance. Yet Fiedler's contingency model was the first and, to date, the longest-lasting attempt to answer the question: What particular style in what special situation?

TRANSFORMATIONAL LEADERSHIP

During the last two decades, new approaches have emerged that invoke inspirational, visionary, and symbolic or less rationalistic aspects of leader behavior (House, Spangler, and Woycke, 1991). Called by various names and based on similar ideas—transformational, charismatic, visionary, or inspirational leadership—this new genre of theory is evoking high levels of interest among scholars and practitioners (Carey, 1992; House and Howell, 1992; Howell and Avolio, 1993).

Transformational leadership theory is stated most explicitly by Bernard M. Bass (1985a) and is based on James MacGregor Burns's (1978) ideas of transactional and transformational political leaders. For Burns, transactional political leaders motivate followers by exchanging with them rewards for services rendered—for example, jobs for votes and influence for campaign contributions. In organizations such as schools, transactional leaders recognize what employees want from work and try to provide them with what they want, if their performance warrants it; exchange rewards and promises of reward for effort; and respond to employees' immediate self-interests if they can be done by getting the work done. Transactional leaders pursue a cost-benefit, economic exchange to meet followers' current material and psychic needs in return for contracted services rendered by the subordinate (Bass, 1985a). Stated simply, transactional leaders give followers things they want in exchange for things leaders want (Kuhnert and Lewis, 1987).

In sharp contrast, **transformational leadership** (Bennis and Nanus, 1985; Tichy and Devanna, 1986; Howell and Frost, 1989; Howell and Avolio, 1993) goes well beyond exchanging inducements for desired performance. Transformational leaders are expected to:

- Define the need for change.
- Create new visions and muster commitment to the visions.
- Concentrate on long-term goals.
- Inspire followers to transcend their own interests for higher-order goals.
- Change the organization to accommodate their vision rather than work within the existing one.
- Mentor followers to take greater responsibility for their own development and that of others. Followers become leaders and leaders become change agents, and ultimately transform the organization.

The basis of transformational leadership is in the personal values and beliefs of leaders. By expressing their personal standards, transformational leaders are able to both unite followers and change their goals and beliefs in ways that produce higher levels of performance than previously thought possible (Kuhnert and Lewis, 1987). The concept of charismatic leadership comes close to capturing the ideas of transformational leadership—that is, leaders who by the force of their personal abilities are capable of making a profound and extraordinary impact on followers (House, 1977; Shamir, House, and Arthur, 1993).

House and Howell (1992) conclude that charismatic leaders are differentiated from noncharismatic leaders by several personality traits:

- Achievement orientation
- Strong tendencies to be creative, innovative, and inspirational
- High levels of energy and involvement

- Self-confidence
- High need for social influence coupled with a strong concern for the moral and nonexploitive use of power

House (1988) further maintains that transformational leadership depends on leaders effectively expressing their need for power by using metaphors and other imagery to represent socially desirable examples of change and outcomes.

Similarly, Bass (1985a) observes that transformational leadership is seen when leaders stimulate others to view their work from new perspectives, generate an awareness of the mission or vision of the organization, develop colleagues and followers to higher levels of ability and potential, and motivate them to look beyond their own interests toward those that will benefit the group. Transformational leaders set more challenging goals and typically achieve higher performances than transactional leaders. Bass views transformational leadership as an expansion of transactional leadership that goes beyond simple exchanges and agreements by employing one or more of the four I's—*i*dealized influence, *i*nspirational motivation, *i*ntellectual stimulation, and *i*ndividualized consideration.

Idealized influence represents the building of trust and respect in followers and provides the basis for accepting radical and fundamental changes in the ways individuals and organizations do their work. The leaders are admired, respected, and trusted. Followers identify with their leaders and want to emulate them. Without such trust and commitment to the leaders, attempts to change and redirect the organization's mission are likely to be met with extreme resistance (Avolio, 1994). Idealized influence results from transformational leaders behaving as role models to their followers. Among the behaviors that transformational leaders exhibit in exerting idealized influence include (Bass and Avolio, 1994):

- Demonstrating high standards of ethical and moral conduct
- Sharing risks with followers in setting and attaining goals
- Considering the needs of others over their own
- Using power only when necessary and never for personal gain

In the earlier formulations and measures, idealized influence was referred to as charismatic leadership (see Bass, 1990).

Inspirational motivation changes the expectations of group members to believe that the organization's problems can be solved (Atwater and Bass, 1994). It also plays a central role in developing the vision to guide the organization goals and how it will operate (Avolio, 1994). Inspirational motivation comes primarily from leader behaviors that provide meaning and challenge to work for followers. Transformational leaders get people involved in creating visions and attractive futures for the organization and clearly communicate expectations that followers want to meet. Hence, team spirit, enthusiasm, optimism, goal commitment, and a shared vision arise and coalesce within the work group or organization (Bass and Avolio, 1994).

Intellectual stimulation addresses the problem of creativity (Atwater and Bass, 1994). Transformational leaders stimulate followers to be innovative and creative by questioning assumptions, reframing problems, and approaching old situations in new ways. Transformational leaders encourage creativity in new procedures, programs, and problem solving; foster unlearning and eliminate the fixation on old ways of doing things; and do not publicly criticize individual members for mistakes (Bass and Avolio, 1994). Leaders insist on constant open examination of everything and total receptivity to change (Avolio, 1994).

Individualized consideration means that transformational leaders pay particular attention to each individual's needs for achievement and growth. The purpose of individualized consideration is to determine the needs and strengths of others (Atwater and Bass, 1994). Using this knowledge and acting as a mentor, transformational leaders help followers and colleagues develop to successively higher levels of potential and to take responsibility for their own development (Avolio, 1994). This is accomplished by creating new learning opportunities in a supportive climate, recognizing and accepting individual differences in needs and values, using two-way communication, and interacting with others in a personalized fashion. The individually considerate leader listens actively and effectively.

Overall, transformational leadership is close to what people have in mind when they describe their ideal leader. Practically, it means that leaders develop in their followers an expectation of high performance rather than merely spending time in transactional activities. In other words, the leader must be a developer of people and a builder of teams (Bass, 1990).

MULTIFACTOR LEADERSHIP QUESTIONNAIRE

Empirical research to date has predominantly dealt with models of transactional leadership, but there is a growing body of research dealing with transformational leadership (Bass, 1990). Most research studies testing transformational leadership theory have used the **multifactor leadership questionnaire (MLQ)** to measure various aspects of transformational and transactional leadership. The MLQ has been refined and now includes more items describing observable leader behaviors than earlier versions (Yukl, 1994). Nonetheless, criticism continues that the MLQ does not adequately incorporate key theoretical elements of transformational leadership, especially power and its use (Saskin and Burke, 1990).

Bass (1990) reports relatively high relationships between initiating structure and consideration on the LBDQ and the transformational and transactional indicators on the MLQ. He concludes that active leadership is common to initiating structure, consideration, transformational, and transactional leadership behavior, and that there are particularly strong associations between transformational leadership and consideration. Adding transformational leadership measures to the transactional indicators of initiating structure and consideration significantly enhances the prediction of perceived leader effectiveness and satisfaction with the leadership. In comparison to transactional leaders, transformational leaders receive higher ratings, are perceived as leading more effective organizations, and have subordinates who exert greater effort.

RESEARCH AND EVALUATION

In a four-year study of schools making a variety of structural changes, Keith Leith-wood (1994) assessed the effects of transformational leadership. His conceptual framework is based on two assertions. First, transformational leadership in schools directly affects such school outcomes as teacher perceptions of student goal achievement and student grades. Second, transformational leadership indirectly affects these outcomes by influencing three critical psychological characteristics of staff—perceptions of school characteristics, teacher commitment to change, and organizational learning—which in turn affect the outcomes. From his research, Leithwood draws the following generalizations:

- Transformational leadership depends on attending to all aspects of leadership—for example, in the terms of Bass, idealized influence, inspirational motivation, intellectual stimulation, and individualized consideration.

- School organizations may require unique formulations of transformational leadership with its base being individualized consideration.

- Except for the expert thinking, transformational leadership represents a contingency approach.

- Distinctions between management and leadership cannot be made in terms of observed behavior.

Hence, Leithwood concludes that reasonably robust support exists for the claim that transformational forms of leadership are of significant value in restructuring schools.

Bass's approach to theory development and testing has been criticized on three bases by James G. Hunt (1991). First, he believes that questionnaires were used before sufficient knowledge of transformational leadership was available. Early reliance on descriptive interviews and observational methods would have advanced the theory's development more powerfully than immediate use of questionnaires such as the MLQ. Second, leadership outcomes were confused with leader behavior. For example, inspirational behavior on the part of the leader might be used as a criterion variable instead of followers' emotional attachment to the leader. And third, insufficient attention is given to the two-way aspects of leader-follower interactions that were very important to Burns's original approach.

As an overall assessment, Yukl (1994) concludes that transformational, charismatic, visionary, or inspirational leadership seem to be making important contributions to the explanation of leadership processes and outcomes. In particular, the approach recognizes the importance of the symbolic aspects of leadership, the importance of shared leadership, and recognition that leadership processes are embedded within the culture of the organization, shaping it and being shaped by it. As such, leadership is more than the technical and interpersonal aspects of efficient management. Leadership occurs in a cultural context and has a symbolic side. It rests upon meanings as well as actions. Leaders make meanings. Indeed Thomas J. Sergiovanni (Sergiovanni and Corbally, 1984) argues that what a leader stands for is more important than what he or she does. Yukl cautions, however, that the distinction between transactional and transformational leadership should not become another oversimplified two-factor theory. Leadership is much too complex to be reduced to two things.

In sum, leadership in schools is a complex process. It involves more than mastering a set of skills, finding the right situation, exhibiting a certain style of behavior, combining these factors in a contingency approach, or even deciding to become a transformational leader. Matching the appropriate leader traits and behaviors with a specific situation is important, but so too is the symbolic and cultural side of leadership. The issue is not one of choosing between leadership as an instrumental and behavioral activity and leadership as a symbolic and cultural one; it is clearly both. Hence, many models of leadership call for diverse sets of applications for enhancing the leadership capacity in schools.

IMPROVING LEADERSHIP IN SCHOOLS

Theory and research suggest several ways to advance leadership in schools. Steps can be taken to enhance the trait and situational factors related to effectiveness. Examples include selecting individuals with the desired personality, motivational, and skill traits and placing them in situations that will benefit from their talents. Education and experience can improve the skill levels of potential and practicing administrators. Although the application possibilities are numerous, we will discuss five general applications—education, selection, succession, situational engineering, and transformations.

EDUCATING FUTURE LEADERS

As shown by the elaborated leadership schema in Figure 12.3 and as elaborated throughout this chapter, school administrators must deal with a wide array of problems, situations, and people. To lead effectively, they must have a range of abilities and skills. To enhance their abilities and learn the needed skills, prospective leaders typically complete administrator preparation or training programs. Griffiths, Stout, and Forsyth (1988) believe that such preparation programs should emphasize theoretical and clinical knowledge, applied research, and supervised practice. To include these ideas, they propose that administrator education programs should include the following five strands for **educating leaders.**

Strand 1: Study theoretical models. Administration and leadership actions have an intellectual and value basis found in administrative theory, the behavioral sciences, philosophy, and experience.

Strand 2: Learn the technical core of school administration. Every profession, including school leadership, has a core of technical knowledge that practitioners must possess or at least be familiar with. Typical core areas include finance, law, personnel, information systems, curriculum theory and design, and teaching pedagogy.

Strand 3: Develop problem-solving skills through the use of applied and active methods. This strand can best be taught through the collaboration of universities and schools. By working on authentic problems in schools (e.g., low student achievement, organizational change), essential problem-solving skills can be developed (e.g., creating visions, effective speaking, conducting meetings, research design, negotiating).

Strand 4: Practice leadership under supervised conditions. Prospective leaders need their clinical experiences to begin early in their preparation and gradually increase in responsibility throughout the training.

Strand 5: Demonstrate competence. This could take such forms as creating computer simulations, building portfolios, conducting a field test of a new program, or handling a difficult case study.

Exactly how these strands are blended together will vary from program to program because the goals of each strand can be achieved in a variety of ways. Combining these five strands to produce a comprehensive program of preparation can help develop school administrators as effective leaders.

SELECTING NEW ADMINISTRATORS THROUGH ASSESSMENT CENTERS

Our knowledge about leader traits and skills holds a high potential for use in **selecting leaders** (Yukl, 1994). However, impressionistic measurements such as simple interviews and application forms lack the power and accuracy to assess the desired characteristics of prospective leaders. Rather intensive, systematic measurement procedures such as those used in assessment centers provide relatively accurate information about motivation, communication skills, cognitive skills, and personality factors.

An **assessment center** is a standardized set of procedures and activities that are designed to evaluate individuals for selection, placement, development, or promotion, usually in administrative positions. A fundamental task in constructing an assessment center is to identify trait and skill dimensions that are related to the job (Wendel et al., 1983). Based on trait and situational theories of leadership, the key is to choose personal factors that are job related—that is, defined by the situation. To evaluate the traits and skills, a variety of activities can be included in an assessment center that evoke samples of behavior. Examples include such assessment center activities as in-baskets, leaderless group discussions, case studies, negotiations, and management games. While not all types of activities are employed in a given assessment center, multiple exercises are used.

In the United States, the National Association of Secondary School Principals (NASSP) has made an extensive effort to develop a reliable and valid assessment center program. According to Hersey (1982), the NASSP Assessment Center process requires participants who are candidates for administrative selection, promotion, or development to complete simulated activities commonly expected of principals. The simulations include leaderless group activities, fact-finding and stress exercises, and in-basket tasks dealing with typical school problems. While completing the assessment exercises, each participant is observed by trained assessors who record behavior relating to twelve dimensions. Example categories are problem analysis, judgment, leadership, stress tolerance, and oral communication. Each participant's observed behavior and skills are discussed by the team of assessors and a comprehensive assessment report is prepared describing strengths, improvement needs, and development suggestions for each candidate.

Overall ratings made in the assessment centers were reliable, relevant to the principal's job, and related to subsequent measures of performance and school climate (Hersey, 1982). Hence, assessment centers offer some promise in identifying and selecting potential school administrators who have and display the desired personality, motivation, and ability traits associated with future leadership effectiveness.

ASSUMING A NEW POSITION: SUCCESSION

Leader succession is the process of replacing key officials in organizations (Grusky, 1961). This generic phenomenon of changing leaders produces naturally occurring instabilities in the organization and offers challenging opportunities for individuals. The replacement of principals or superintendents is disruptive because it changes the lines of communication, realigns relationships of power, affects decision making, and generally disturbs the equilibrium of normal activities. Administrative succession substantially raises the level of consciousness among organizational participants about the importance of school leaders (Hart, 1993). Those who appoint new leaders, individuals who work with them, and those who may be affected by their actions watch for signs that change will occur. In other words, new leaders face high performance expectations to maintain or improve existing levels of organizational effectiveness (Miskel and Cosgrove, 1985). A number of factors in the succession process are important in affecting the probability of being hired and one's success after being appointed as an administrator. Three situational factors seem particularly important in school settings—selection process, reason for the succession, and source of the new leader.

Selection Process

Understanding who participates and the methods of recruitment used in the selection process is important for aspiring administrators. In school districts, participants in the selection process for principals typically include the superintendent, senior administrators, personnel directors, long-term principals, and school board members. Superintendents play a primary role in choosing future principals because the management of their school systems depends on principals' carrying out their districts' decisions and plans. Teacher candidates for principalships usually come to the attention of their superintendents through the support of their principals. As teachers volunteer for committees, handle discipline problems, and spend extra time in schools, the principal becomes a mentor, encouraging the teacher to pursue administrative certification and providing opportunities to become visible at the district level (Griffiths, Goldman, and McFarland, 1965). Having obtained a broad reputation, the career path to a principalship is often through being a vice-principal or curriculum coordinator. Then as vacancies occur for school principals, the candidate can apply and, if patient enough, will eventually obtain an appointment. Assessment centers or outside agencies may be used in the recruitment of potential candidates. Their purpose is to provide rigor, structure, and standardization to the evaluation of the candidate's potential as an administrator (Baltzell and Dentler, 1983).

Reason for the Succession

A number of reasons account for changing administrators. Succession can be environmentally controlled, as in death, illness, or movement to a better position; or succession can be directly controlled by the organization, as in promotion, demotion, or dismissal (Grusky, 1960). The successor confronts a different set of circumstances depending on the reason for the vacancy. For instance, death prevents the transfer of accumulated knowledge of the predecessor to the new leader, and consequently, discontinuity may result, accompanied by rapid policy changes. In contrast, if the predecessor remains in the organization, his or her presence acts as a stabilizing influence. In the case of the predecessor's advancing to a superior position, the outside recognition of administrator performance is an indicator of successful policies. The successor may feel a reluctance to initiate immediate changes, and because of the apparent inheritance of a well-managed school, may not receive due credit for improvements that are made.

Source of the New Leader

The source of leaders can be divided into two categories—insiders and outsiders. Depending on situational factors, either an insider or an outsider can be the best choice for an administrative position. When conflict within the organization is high, a candidate from within may better understand and be able to cope than an outsider. An outsider joining a school at a difficult time may unintentionally "step on toes" or be unable to discern the source of problems because he or she lacks the appropriate historical perspective. Inside succession can lead to problems as well. When an educational organization trains several people to fill future vacancies, a surplus often results. The qualified but unchosen individuals often either leave the organization or remain as frustrated and unsupportive employees. To reduce this type of conflict, the selection process might avoid vertical promotions from within the organization in an attempt to prevent unproductive competition among prospective candidates and their supporters. Instead, candidates can be selected from similar institutions whose characteristics would result in comparable socializing experiences for potential leaders and thus facilitate the smooth assimilation of the new leader in the organization (Birnbaum, 1971).

Mandate for Action

During the selection process, new administrators often are given, or perceive that they are given, a mandate either to maintain the existing stability or to initiate change and innovation (Grusky, 1960; Gordon and Rosen, 1981). They may be told to get rid of "dead wood," "clean house," reorganize the administrative staff, or essentially maintain the status quo. The type of mandate may depend on whether the successor is an insider or an outsider. Superintendents, and to a lesser degree principals, recruited from the outside often receive a mandate to break established patterns and make structural or personnel changes. For insiders the mandate typically is to continue present operations with only minor changes. In a study of principal succession by Dorothy Cosgrove (1985), little evidence was found that the principals in her study received a mandate from the superintendent or other district officials. However, Rodney T. Ogawa (1991) also found a general expectation among teachers that the succession would bring changes to the school.

In sum, truly critical phenomena occur for prospective leaders before they arrive on the scene and shortly after arrival. Knowing the workings of the selection process and being aware that instability arising during the succession period makes the new leader particularly visible and can be used to enhance the success in getting and keeping an administrative position.

ENGINEERING THE SITUATION

Another approach for applying knowledge to improve leadership in schools is **situational engineering.** Instead of trying to select or train leaders to fit an existing condition, the situation is changed to be more congruent with the traits of the leader. For example, the upper-level administrators of a school district could modify the conditions within the school building by changing the responsibilities and scope of authority of the principal, by transferring certain personnel, or by creating an inservice training program to improve the interpersonal climate among the professional staff members. Taking this idea further, Fiedler, Chemers, and Mahar (1976) proposed that administrators such as principals can be trained to modify certain aspects of their situation. They have developed a programmed textbook to teach leaders how to analyze their situation in terms of leader-member relations, task structure, and position power of the leader, and based on the analysis, to change the conditions that will improve group performance. A major limitation of the studies supporting situational engineering is their failure to determine how much change actually occurred during the experiments (Yukl, 1994). Nevertheless, the approach can be of some value in designing situations to enhance the level of leadership in schools.

TRANSFORMING SCHOOLS AND STRENGTHENING THEIR CULTURES

Yukl (1994) concludes that the knowledge base is good enough to suggest a number of guidelines for leaders who seek to transform their organizations and the cultures within them. An essential first step in **transforming schools** is to create a clear and appealing vision of what the school can achieve or become. Before educators and the public will make a commitment to fundamental change, they need an image of a better future that is attractive enough to justify changing their routine ways of doing tasks. The vision should be simple and idealistic. For instance, the vision might call for becoming the best school in the district. A next step is to develop a strategy for accomplishing the vision. Clear links must be made between the vision and the strategies to attain the vision. Yukl (1994) believes that these links are easier to establish if the strategy uses three or four lucid themes that epitomize the shared values of the participants. For example, a theme might be to "improve the academic achievement of all the school's students." Then the vision must be communicated to others.

Jay A. Conger (1991) agrees and elaborates Yukl's ideas when he proposes that two distinct skills are required to effectively communicate strategic visions for organizations. The first is a "framing skill," or simply stating the vision clearly and logically. The second is "rhetorical crafting," or the leader's ability to use symbolic language to give emotional power to the vision. In other words, rhetorical crafting of the vision laces the message with metaphors, stories, symbols, and other forms of colorful and emotional language. The leader must act confident, lead by example, and express confidence in the followers as they work together to implement the strategy and attain the vision of transforming the organization. Early successes should be used to build confidence and the successes should be celebrated in ways that emphasize key values of the school.

Based on the work of Trice and Beyer (1993), Yukl (1994) also developed several guidelines for strengthening the existing culture of schools. The key first step is to identify aspects of the culture that are essential and worthy of preservation—that is, the ideologies that inspire commitment and persist as conditions change. Another way to strengthen school culture is to eliminate components of the culture that are inconsistent with the core values of the ideology. For instance, most schools have old rules and policies that are no longer useful and are inconsistent with core values. These can be identified and eliminated. Leaders can then articulate the ideology lucidly and persistently through a variety of media. In other words, school culture can be strengthened by repeatedly publicizing the core ideology in speeches at meetings and ceremonies, statements in newsletters, and distribution or display of physical symbols. Leaders must then keep decisions and actions consistent with the ideology and emphasize the ideology through rituals, ceremonies, and rites of passage.

SUMMARY AND SUGGESTED READINGS

Leadership remains an important topic for students of educational administration. Given the fact that leadership is an extremely complex and elusive concept, some conceptual confusion and empirical shortcomings are to be expected. Nevertheless, substantial progress has been made in building a solid body of knowledge about leadership. General agreement exists that leadership involves a social influence process in which intentional influence is exerted by an individual over others to structure activities and relationships in a group or organization. To explain the influence process, a number of leadership models have been proposed and tested. We have developed a schema to categorize and link together four sets of concepts:

traits of the leader, situational factors, leader behaviors, and effectiveness criteria. Contingency theory has been illustrated by expanding Fiedler's postulate that leadership effectiveness is contingent upon matching leadership style with the appropriate situation. Transformational leadership is an exciting approach that currently is receiving extensive attention from scholars and practitioners. It has four critical elements—idealized influence, inspirational motivation, intellectual stimulation, and individualized consideration. From these conceptual frameworks, useful practical applications for selecting and educating leaders, assuming new leadership positions, and transforming schools have been created. It is our conclusion that all of these developments attest to an enhanced understanding of the leadership phenomenon.

The leadership literature is huge with over 5,000 published studies and the number continues to increase by hundreds each year (Yukl, 1994). Within this expansive body of knowledge, rich sources of theories, empirical studies, and practical applications of leadership can be found in the three editions of Yukl's (1981, 1989, 1994) book, *Leadership in Organizations.* The editions take moderately different approaches to the leadership concept and each contains some unique insights not found in the other editions or in other works. Probably the most complete review of the leadership literature is found in *Bass and Stogdill's Handbook of Leadership* (Bass, 1990). For an extensive and interesting discussion of specific measures of leadership, the book by Clark and Clark (1990) should be consulted. If you want to explore leadership preparation, the work by Griffiths, Stout, and Forsyth (1988) contains some very good chapters. A new journal has been started, *Leadership Quarterly,* that publishes only papers focusing on leadership. For those interested in transformational leadership, two recently published sources are recommended—Bass and Avolio (1994) and Leithwood (1994). Many other worthy publications could have been given as examples, but our recommendation to individuals interested in exploring leadership in detail is to review this chapter, consult the references we cited, and then plunge yourself into a very deep pool of literature.

NOTES

1. John P. Kotter (1990) provides a detailed analysis of the distinction between management and leadership. We consider the term "administration," as commonly used in educational settings, to be essentially synonymous with "management."

2. Structured observation techniques typically observe and question leaders intensively as they perform their work. Two of the best-known investigations were completed in business organizations by Mintzberg (1973) and Kotter (1982). A number of investigations using structured observation procedures also have been conducted in school settings across a number of countries on superintendents (O'Dempsey, 1976; Friesen and Duignan, 1980; Duignan, 1980; Pitner and Ogawa, 1981); on principals (Peterson, 1977-78; Willis, 1980; Martin and Willower, 1981; Morris and his associates, 1981; Kmetz and Willower, 1982; Phillips and Thomas, 1982; Chung, 1987; Chung and Miskel, 1989); and on educational innovators (Sproull, 1981). In addition to providing a fascinating glimpse of their work, the findings are important because the behaviors of school administrators have been described systematically and found to be consistent across organizational types—businesses and schools—across organizational roles—superintendents, supervisors, and principals—and across countries—Australia, Canada, and the United States.

3. For readers interested in a detailed consideration of the traits associated with effective leadership, a comprehensive treatment can be found in Bass (1990). While less extensive, Yukl (1994) provides an insightful discussion of traits and leader effectiveness.

4. Over the past three decades, a number of promising contingency theories have been developed. Path-goal theory (House, 1971, 1973; House and Mitchell, 1974) and cognitive-resource theory (Fiedler, 1984; Fiedler and Garcia, 1987) are relatively well-known perspectives. Although each of these models attempted to explain the contingencies of leadership, neither has received strong support nor continuing interest by a critical mass of scholars.

5. Descriptions of Fiedler's model and the related research can be found in a number of sources by Fiedler and his colleagues (e.g., Fiedler, 1967, 1971; Fiedler and Chemers, 1974; Fiedler, Chemers, and Mahar, 1976; Fiedler and Garcia, 1987).

KEY CONCEPTS AND IDEAS

Administrators	Leadership situation
Assessment center	Leadership style
Consideration	Leader succession
Contingency approach	LPC (least preferred
Educating leaders	co-worker)
Idealized influence	MLQ (multi-factor leadership
Individualized consideration	questionnaire)
Initiating structure	Motivation traits
Inspirational motivation	Personality traits
Intellectual stimulation	Selecting leaders
LBDQ (leader behavior	Situational engineering
description questionnaire)	Skill traits
Leader behavior	Substitutes-for-leaders model
Leader effectiveness	Traits
Leaders	Transforming schools
Leadership	Transformational leadership

A Final Look at the School as a Social System

Systems thinking is the fifth discipline. It is the discipline that integrates the disciplines, fusing them into a coherent body of theory and practice . . . it continually reminds us that the whole can exceed the sum of its parts.

—Peter M. Senge
The Fifth Discipline

T he preceding chapters present a substantial body of knowledge that constitutes a strong argument for the value of an open social-systems approach to educational administration. In this chapter, we review the social-systems model that serves as a theoretical guide to the ideas developed in our work. Intrinsic dilemmas of the model will then be considered.

A MODEL OF SYNTHESIS

Open-systems theory (see Chapter 2) is organic rather than mechanical. As a conceptual language, it is useful in describing the recurring structures and dynamic processes in educational organizations. According to the social-systems model for schools, organizational performance is determined by at least four sets of key elements—structure, the individual, culture and climate, and power and politics. These elements take inputs from the environment and transform them. The elements and their interactions form the transformation system, which is constrained by the opportunities and demands from the environment. In addition, internal and external feedback mechanisms enable the system to evaluate the quality of all its systems and inputs. As discrepancies between actual and expected performance are detected, feedback enables the system to adjust.

In brief, the model in Figure 13.1 (first developed in Chapter 2) summarizes the major external and internal features of organizations conceived as open social systems. Of course, the figure cannot capture the dynamic movement of a system as it responds to its environment through internal processes and as it produces such products as student learning or employee satisfaction. Although we examine the

parts of the system, do not lose sight of the fact that the system is a working whole.

FIGURE **13.1**

Social System Model for Schools

Environment

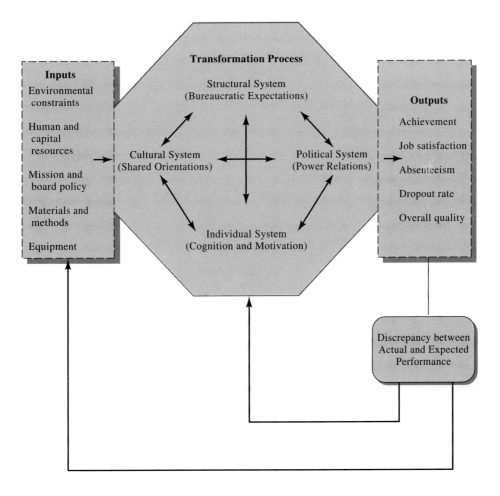

Transformation Process

Inputs

Environmental constraints

Human and capital resources

Mission and board policy

Materials and methods

Equipment

Structural System
(Bureaucratic Expectations)

Cultural System
(Shared Orientations)

Political System
(Power Relations)

Individual System
(Cognition and Motivation)

Outputs

Achievement

Job satisfaction

Absenteeism

Dropout rate

Overall quality

Discrepancy between
Actual and Expected
Performance

STRUCTURE IN SCHOOLS

Bureaucratic structure (see Chapter 3) is the formal organization specifically established to achieve explicit goals and carry out administrative tasks. Whatever the organizational goals, such structural properties as rules, regulations, hierarchy, and division of labor are consciously designed to attain those goals. In Weber's analysis of ideal types, bureaucracy employs authority through these means to achieve rational decision making and maximize efficiency. Division of labor and specialization produce impersonal experts who make technically correct, rational decisions based on   407 fact. Once these decisions have been made, the hierarchy of authority implements a disciplined, coordinated compliance to directives through rules and regulations. Career-oriented employees have an incentive to be loyal and productive.

Although probably the best known, Weber's is not the only theory of organizational structure. Henry Mintzberg provides still another framework for examining bureaucratic structure. He describes structure simply as the ways in which an organization divides its labor into tasks and then achieves coordination among them. Mutual adjustment, direct supervision, and standardization are basic coordinating mechanisms—the glue that holds the organization together. His analysis yields five ideal types. Mintzberg describes organizations as structures that are influenced by their environments—that is, open systems. Bolman and Deal underscore the importance of structure in organizations, but also point to the critical issues and dilemmas that all organizations struggle with as they try to find the right structure.

A recent body of theory and research challenges some of the traditional notions of the school as a bureaucratic structure. Critical theory, postmodernist theory, and feminist theory provide major challenges to assumptions of mainline theory of organizations (see Chapter 1). The concept of loose coupling in schools calls attention to ambiguity in goals, unclear educational technologies, fluid participation, coordination problems, and a structure disconnected from educational outcomes. The distinctive combination of bureaucracy and structural looseness has important consequences for organizational performance and quality (see Chapter 3).

INDIVIDUAL IN THE SCHOOL

The fact that an organization has been formally established does not mean that all its activities and interactions conform to structural requirements. Regardless of the official positions and bureaucratic expectations, members have their own individual motivations and cognitive understanding of their roles. Cognitive theories of information processing and of motivation provide useful insights about managing and working with individuals in schools. Such cognitive structures and mechanisms as schemas and metacognition provide the cognitive architecture that the individual uses to process information, leads to action, and organizes and applies knowledge.

Work motivation is a set of energetic forces that originate both within as well as beyond an individual's being. These forces initiate work-related behavior and determine the form, direction, intensity, and duration of motivation. Three organizing perspectives are useful to our understanding of motivation: need and value theories, cognitive-choice theories, and metacognition theories.

Need and value theories view the motivating force as coming from some type of internal tension or arousal. Values are enduring beliefs about preferable outcomes; they give expression to human needs and guide actions. Maslow's need-hierarchy model and McClelland's theory of achievement are useful examples of this perspective.

Cognitive-choice theories focus on processes involved in individual decision making and selection. Expectancy-choice theory is supported empirically; individuals work hard when they think that working hard is likely to result in valued rewards.

When individuals make causal attributions, they are essentially seeking and creating knowledge, which they use to better manage themselves and their environments. Helpful models are Vroom's expectancy theory and Weiner's attribution theory.

Metacognition theories center on self-regulation and motivational processes that govern the effect of goals on behaviors. Self-efficacy contributes to motivation by determining what goals individuals set for themselves, how much effort they expend, how long they persevere in the face of difficulties, and their resilience to failures. Within organizational science, goal-setting theory is widely supported. Goal-setting effects generalize across tasks, settings, subjects, countries, performance criteria, time spans, individuals, groups, and different methods of goal setting. Bandura's conception of self-efficacy and Locke's formulations of goal theory are valuable tools for understanding work motivation.

Because it is difficult to understand these theories as a unified whole, we employ Locke's idea of a motivation sequence composed of needs, values, expectancy-choice, and goal-setting, which integrates the diverse motivational models. The sequence shows the complementary linkages among the various models.

CULTURE AND CLIMATE OF SCHOOLS

Our analysis of the internal atmosphere of schools focused on two related concepts—culture and climate (see Chapter 5). Each of these notions goes beyond the formal and individual aspects of organizational life. Each suggests a natural, spontaneous, and human side to organization; each suggests that the whole is greater than the sum of its parts; and each deals with shared meanings and unwritten rules that guide organizational behavior.

Organizational culture is the set of shared orientations that holds a unit together and gives it a distinctive identity. Although climate tends to focus on shared perceptions, culture is defined in terms of shared assumptions, values, and norms. These three levels of culture—assumptions, values, and norms—are explored as alternative ways of describing and analyzing schools. Recent research on business organizations suggests that effective systems have strong corporate cultures: cultures characterized by intimacy, trust, cooperation, egalitarianism, a bias for action, and orientations that stress quality, innovation, and people. Ouchi's formulation of Theory Z cultures, Peters and Waterman's description of strong corporate cultures, and Schein's analysis of the elements of organizational culture are especially useful vantage points for understanding the importance and dynamic aspects of organizations.

Organizational climate is a relatively enduring quality of the school environment that is experienced by teachers, affects their behavior, and is based on their collective perceptions of behavior in schools. A climate emerges through the interaction of members and exchange of sentiments among them. The climate of a school is its "personality." Three different conceptualizations of climate were described and analyzed.

When schools have an open climate, we find that principals and faculty are acting authentically, but when the climate is closed, everyone simply goes through the motions of education without dedication and commitment. As might be expected, research has shown that such affective characteristics as positive student and faculty attitudes are related to openness of climate.

The climate of schools can also be examined in terms of organizational health. A healthy school is one that is meeting both its instrumental and its expressive needs, while successfully coping with disruptive outside forces as it directs its energies toward its mission. The healthier the organizational dynamics of a school, the greater are the trust and openness in member relations and the greater the student achievement.

Finally, social climate of schools was conceived along a continuum of pupil-control orientation ranging from custodial to humanistic. This formulation is based on the dominant expectations teachers and principals have of how their methods will control student behavior. Schools with custodial expectations are rigidly controlled settings in which the primary concern is order. In contrast, humanistic schools are characterized by an emphasis on student self-discipline and cooperative student-teacher actions and experiences. A humanistic climate is associated with less student alienation and goal displacement than a custodial climate.

POWER AND POLITICS IN SCHOOLS

Even before joining an organization, individuals grant the use of formal authority to the system when they voluntarily agree to comply with legitimate commands. Once in the organization, however, power relations expand; in fact, power becomes a central aspect of relations within the system.

Power is a broad construct that includes both legitimate and illegitimate and formal and informal methods of ensuring compliance. Hence, four basic kinds of organizational power exist: two forms are legitimate—formal and informal authority— and two kinds are illegitimate—coercive and political power.

The legitimate system of authority promotes coordination and compliance, and contributes to attainment of the formal goals. Legitimate power comes from the formal organization by virtue of position, from informal norms and values of the culture, and from the expertise of individuals in the system. These three systems of control typically contribute to the needs of the organization; that is, they are legitimate. But those with power also have personal needs. In the process of striving to accomplish the broader organizational needs, individuals find they have discretion, and discretion opens the way to political power. Thus a system of political power emerges that is not sanctioned by the formal authority, culture, or certified expertise; in fact, it is typically divisive, parochial, and illegitimate. Politics is illegitimate because it is a means to serve personal ends at the expense of the overall organization.

Politics, however, is a fact of organizational life. Although there are powerful individuals, the political arenas of organizations are composed of coalitions of individuals and groups, which bargain among themselves to determine the distribution of resources. External as well as internal coalitions influence organizational politics. Political tactics are the bases of a system of political games played to resist authority, to counter resistance, to build power bases, to defeat opponents, and to change the organization. The system of politics typically coexists with the more legitimate systems of influence without dominating them, but power and politics generate conflict. Thus, conflict management is a useful administrative tool.

EXTERNAL ENVIRONMENTS OF SCHOOLS

Schools are open systems, which must adapt to changing environmental conditions to be effective and, in the long term, to survive. The environments of schools (see Chapter 7) affect their internal structures and processes. Social, economic, political, and technological trends influence the internal operations of schools as do more specific aspects such as unions, taxpayer associations, and state legislatures.

Environments are complex and difficult to analyze, but two general perspectives are useful—task and institutional. The task perspective includes both information and resource-dependency theories, which define the task environment as all aspects of the external setting that are potentially relevant for goal setting, goal achievement, effectiveness, and survival.

The information model treats the external environment as a source of information for decision makers. Three general dimensions of this framework are complexity, stability, and uncertainty. The more complex and unstable the environment, the greater the uncertainty for the organization. Perceived organizational uncertainty in turn affects the flexibility and bureaucratic configuration of organizations. Like all organizations, schools strive for certainty because they are under pressure to demonstrate rationality.

The resource-dependency approach assumes that organizations cannot generate internally the needed resources; resources must come from the environment. Thus, schools must enter into exchanges and competition with environmental units to obtain the requisite products and services. Scarcity produces competition with other organizations for resources.

Since environmental uncertainty and scarcity of resources threaten organizational autonomy and effectiveness, administrators often attempt to develop strategies to gain more control over the environment. Internal coping strategies include buffering the technical core, planning or forecasting, adjusting internal operations based on contingency theory, and spanning organizational boundaries. Interorganizational coping strategies include establishing favorable linkages with important external constituencies and shaping environmental elements through political actions.

In contrast to the task perspectives, institutional theory assumes that the environment encourages schools to conform to powerful sets of rules and requirements that are imposed by the legal, social, professional, and political institutions. The theory asserts that school structures and processes mirror the norms, values, and ideologies institutionalized in society. The essence of the theory is that the environment of schools presses more for form than for substance.

Nevertheless, technical and institutional environments do coexist; schools function in relatively strong institutional but weak technical environments. Current drives for systemic reform and competitive markets suggest that worried businesspeople and policy makers may be seeking to place heightened emphasis on task environments. A shift from primarily institutional to technical environments would shatter the rationalized myths and lead to fundamental changes in schools, a shift that will be bitterly fought by current institutional forces.

EFFECTIVENESS AND QUALITY

Outputs of schools are a function of the interaction of structure, individual, culture, and politics as constrained by environment forces. Issues of organizational effectiveness and quality represent fundamental challenges to practice in school administration. In our open-systems model, school outputs are the performances of students, teachers, and administrators. All can be used as indicators of organizational effectiveness and can be assessed for their quality. Although effectiveness and quality are not synonyms, they both are terms used to assess all aspects of the system.

Simple measures of organizational outcomes are insufficient indicators of either effectiveness or quality. This should come as no surprise to those who use a systems approach to understand organizational behavior. Outcomes are only one part of the system and perhaps not the most important element. The inputs as well as the transformational process of the system are equal partners in determining both quality and effectiveness of schools.

We have proposed an integrated goal and system-resource model of school performance. The perspective underscores the importance of all the aspects of a social system, especially the quality of inputs, transformation process, and outcomes. Each of these system phases needs to be assessed over the short term as well as the long, using a variety of such constituencies as students, teachers, and administrators. Teacher quality, internal harmony, effort, student achievement, job satisfaction, and overall performance quality are examples of indicators of organizational effectiveness and quality.

Feedback Loops

The knowledge of the outcomes enters two different types of feedback loops. Internally, the relative level of goal achievement serves as an indicator of the need to adjust one or more of the elements of the transformation process. Externally, the school's products are evaluated by different constituencies in the community. This assessment provides information that also influences the structural, cultural, individual, and political subsystems.

Put bluntly, administrators are responsible for school effectiveness and quality. On the one hand, they must respond to the expectations and information carried in the feedback loops; on the other hand, they must maintain or increase goal-directed behavior of teachers, students, and other employees. One of the major administrative problems—control of performance—requires not only the allocation of resources but also the integration of the basic organizational dimensions (structure, culture, individual, and politics). Fulfillment of administrative functions requires deciding, motivating, communicating, and leading.

DECIDING

Deciding means selecting and implementing a course of action from among alternatives (see Chapter 9). This behavior affects the total organization, including the system phases of inputs, throughputs, and outputs.

Although completely rational decision making is impossible, administrators need systematic ways to enhance the selection of satisfactory solutions; hence, a strategy of satisficing is central to administrative decision making. The process is conceptualized as being cyclical with distinct phases: recognition and definition of a problem, analysis of difficulties, establishment of criteria of success, development of an action plan, and initiation and appraisal of the plan. Owing to its cyclical nature, administrators go through the stages repeatedly.

This administrative strategy is well suited for dealing with most problems. Occasionally, however, the set of alternatives is undefinable or the consequences of each alternative are unpredictable with respect to a given aspiration level; here an incremental strategy is more appropriate. This process is a method of successive limited comparisons; only a limited set of alternatives, similar to the existing situation, is considered by successively comparing their consequences until agreement is reached on a course of action. Incrementalism, however, can be too conservative and self-defeating. Incremental decisions made without fundamental guidelines can lead to action without direction. Thus, the mixed-scanning model of decision making is proposed for complex decisions. Mixed scanning unites the best of both the administrative and the incremental models. A strategy of satisficing is used in combination with incremental decision making guided by broad policy.

Research suggests that the quality of administrative action can be judged by the amount of preparation for implementing a course of action and by the amount of work done in making the decision. Effective decision makers engage in substantial preliminary work; they seek more information, differentiate between fact and opinion, and frequently encourage subordinate participation in the process. Sometimes participation improves the quality of decisions; sometimes it does not. We have proposed a model that suggests when and how to involve subordinates in decision making. In complex organizations, motivation, communication, and leadership are necessary to translate the decisions into concrete action.

MOTIVATING

No magic formulae exist to make individuals want to learn, work hard, and be responsible. Desired motivational patterns can be facilitated, however, by using a variety of motivational principles and theories.

Goal-setting programs that produce specific, difficult goals and provide feedback can improve work quality, clarify expectations, increase job satisfaction, and develop pride in achievement. Similarly, organizational incentives can be used to motivate participants to improve their work performance by making jobs attractive, interesting, and satisfying. To be effective, however, incentive systems in schools need to be elaborate, stable, and dependable, and offer a wide range of both intrinsic and extrinsic rewards.

Work design is another strategy to stimulate individual actions. Redesigning work modifies jobs to increase both the quality of the employees' work experience and the level of their performance. Based on motivation-hygiene theory, job-enrichment plans can be designed to increase motivation and decrease negative hygiene factors. The job-characteristics model of work design unifies Maslow's need fulfillment, Herzberg's motivation-hygiene, and Vroom's expectancy theories and provides a comprehensive model for redesigning work roles.

At the school level, professionalization, career ladders, and career paths in educational administration are specific ways to apply motivation theory to schools. For example, career-ladder programs redesign jobs to provide educators with prospects for promotion, enrichment of their work, and enlargement of their responsibilities, all of which make their work motivating.

COMMUNICATING

Verbal and nonverbal interactions pervade virtually all aspects of school life. Good communication does not, however, provide all the answers to the problems confronting educational administrators. Nearly all current conceptions of information exchange rely on the notion that communication involves meaningful exchanges of symbols between at least two people (see Chapter 11). The process is dynamic because it continually influences the transformation and environmental elements of the social system.

One-way communication is unilateral, initiated by a speaker and terminated at a listener. In contrast, two-way communication is reciprocal and interactive with all participants initiating and receiving messages. It has no necessary beginning or ending. Messages flow through formal and informal channels of the school. Although the formal network is usually larger and better developed than the informal, they are closely related, can be complementary, and are critical to the organization.

LEADING

Leaders are important because they serve as anchors, provide guidance in times of change, and are responsible for the effectiveness of organizations (see Chapter 12). General agreement exists that leadership involves a social influence process. Intentional influence is exerted by the leader over others to structure activities and relationships in a group or organization. The most influential theories of leadership are contingency models, which explain the interrelationships among traits, situations, behaviors, and effectiveness. We developed a schema to categorize and link together these four sets of concepts. Contingency theory was further illustrated by expanding Fiedler's postulate that leadership effectiveness is contingent upon matching leadership styles with the appropriate situation.

Transformational leadership is an approach that currently is receiving extensive attention from scholars and practitioners. It has four critical elements—idealized influence, inspirational motivation, intellectual stimulation, and individualized consideration.

Leadership in schools is a complex process. It involves more than the mastering of a set of leadership skills or the matching of the appropriate leader behavior with a specific situation. Useful methods to improve school leadership are selecting and educating leaders, assuming new leadership positions, engineering the situation, and transforming schools. Leadership is not only an instrumental and behavioral activity but also a symbolic and cultural one.

ADMINISTRATOR BEHAVIOR, INTERDEPENDENT ELEMENTS, AND EQUIFINALITY

We have been arguing that administrative behavior must be considered in relation to the primary dimensions or elements of a social system. Structure, individual, culture, and politics represent "leverage points" that can be used to influence the performance of organizational members. Two observations are important and bear repeating. First, deciding, motivating, communicating, and leading are key processes that modify school performance. If one dimension of the system is consciously manipulated by a leader, a ripple effect is created; the other dimensions are affected, and a new combination of expectations and behaviors results. Second, a variety of means are available to reach desired goals (the principle of equifinality).

Table 13.1 contains four examples of the first generalization. Deciding to decentralize the decision-making process delegates formal authority to individuals lower in the organization's structure. This represents a change in the system's bureaucratic structure. The decrease in the hierarchy of authority results in modified role expectations and perhaps a change in goal. Consequently, more people will be interacting, and the climate and culture should become more open and participative. Decentralization also alters the individual element by increasing the emphasis on responsibility and risk. However, the change may bring instability and conflict into the political network. Clearly, changing one element modifies the others. The anticipated overall outcome is an increase in group work activity.

Similarly, if one were to implement a new goal-setting program to motivate teachers, effects would ripple throughout all elements in the system. For instance, the structure would likely become more formalized; the culture with its norms for personal autonomy would be reinforced; the individual would experience increased motivational force; and there would be a decrease in game playing in the political arena.

In considering communicating, if the levels of informal communication between the principal and teachers were increased, the elements of the transformation process might be influenced as follows (see Table 13.1). The formal structure of the school would become less impersonal; the individual expectations for personal integrity, self-respect, and independent choice would increase; as the climate and culture change, information exchange and behavior that is mutually supportive might increase; and finally these changes would increase political activity within the informal organization. The anticipated overall effect is an increase in teacher and principal interaction, which should result in better decisions, higher loyalty, and greater individual satisfaction.

TABLE **13.1**	Effects of Administrative Behavior on the Social System and Observed Behavior		
	Administrative Behavior	**Anticipated Effects on Social System Elements**	**Anticipated Behavioral Effects**
Leading	Recognize and reward excellent performance	Structure—more differentiated role expectations Individual—more emphasis on higher levels of motivation Culture—raised normative standards Politics—Increased personal conflict	Increased outcome quality—higher job satisfaction and effectiveness, some divisiveness
Deciding	Place the decision-making authority close to the problem's origin (decentralization)	Structure—decreased hierarchy of authority Individual—increased responsibility Culture—more open and trusting Politics—formation of coalitions	Increased group work activity
Communicating	Maintain informal information exchanges	Structure—decreased impersonalization Individual—increased emphasis on social needs Culture—increased normative support Politics—increased interaction	Increased superordinate-subordinate interaction
Motivating	Implement a goal-setting program	Structure—more formalization Culture—support for norms for personal autonomy Individual—increased motivation Politics—decreased game playing	Increased performance levels of individuals

As a final example, assume leadership behavior is changed (through training or replacement) so that the principal recognizes and rewards outstanding teacher performance. As a result, such higher levels of motivation as recognition and achievement are emphasized. But when this input occurs, bureaucratic expectations and incentives must also be raised; the group may increase the normative expectations regarding what constitutes appropriate standards, but politics may produce increased personal conflict. Therefore, all of the dimensions are modified, thus increasing effectiveness and quality.

Thus, the administrative processes of deciding, motivating, communicating, and leading affect not one but all elements of the social system, which in turn influence the school outcomes. A given administrator may rely primarily on a single leverage point (e.g., improving school culture), but the resulting interaction will influence the structural, individual, and political dimensions as well.

The preceding conclusion leads to the second major generalization regarding the concept of equifinality: If a particular outcome is desired, a number of different administrative actions can be used on different leverage points to attain similar results. In other words, different patterns of administrative behavior and organizational expectations can lead to the same outcome. The implication from this statement is that a variety of alternatives exist to improve the effectiveness and quality of educational organizations; there is no one best way. The challenge is to match the strengths of the leaders with appropriate leverage points.

CONTINUING DILEMMAS

Both change and dilemmas will always be with us, but dilemmas, unlike change, need not accelerate. Peter M. Blau and W. Richard Scott (1962) maintain that the concept of dilemma contributes to our understanding of internal pressures for change. A dilemma arises when one is confronted by decision alternatives in which any choice sacrifices some valued objectives in the interest of others. Daniel Katz and Robert L. Kahn (1978) have elaborated on this definition by distinguishing between problems and dilemmas. Problems are difficulties that can be solved by past precedents or by the application of existing policy. Dilemmas are unsolvable within the existing framework. Solutions and perfect adjustments are impossible. Because dilemmas are endemic to organizations, they serve as perpetual sources of change.

The fundamental dilemma facing formal organizations is order versus freedom. Both order and freedom are desirable and necessary conditions for high levels of effectiveness and quality, but increasing one decreases the other. The tension between order and freedom is manifest in three operational dilemmas: coordination and communication, bureaucratic discipline and professional expertise, and administrative planning and individual initiative. These elements or dimensions have been discussed throughout the book.

COORDINATION AND COMMUNICATION

Based on the work of Blau and Scott (1962), two-way communication with unrestricted exchange of ideas, criticism, and advice contributes to effective problem solving in at least three ways: it furnishes social support to individual participants; it provides an error-correcting mechanism; and it fosters a healthy competition for respect.

Problem-solving situations often produce stress and anxiety for individual participants and lead to mental blocks that interfere with effective development of their thinking. However, when individuals communicate openly, good ideas are likely to receive the approval of others (thus reducing anxiety) and to promote further participation, development, and refinement of ideas; hence, the social support derived from an unrestricted exchange of ideas aids in problem solving.

It is not easy for a person to detect mistakes in his or her own thinking. An individual takes a set framework to the problem-solving situation that makes it difficult to see the problem from a different perspective. Open and free-flowing communication brings a variety of perspectives, experiences, and information to bear on the common task; hence, the chances of identifying an error in thinking are increased. Other members of the group are more prone to spot inconsistencies and blind spots than the individual; therefore, two-way communication facilitates error correction. Finally, open, two-way communication motivates members of a group to make expert suggestions in order to win the respect and esteem of fellow participants.

While the free flow of information improves problem solving, it also impedes coordination. Unrestricted communication may drown effective action in a sea of conflicting ideas. True, information helps in selecting good ideas, but too many ideas hinder agreement, and coordination requires agreeing on a single master plan.

Coordination in organizations is accomplished primarily through hierarchical differentiation, but such structure impedes decision making because it interferes with the free flow of information (see Chapter 3). In fact, differentiation, centralized direction, and restricted communication appear essential for effective coordination. In brief, those very things that enhance the coordination process also hinder the free flow of communication. Organizations require both effective coordination and effective problem solving. But the hierarchical structure in organizations that facilitates efficient coordination also impedes communication and problem solving. The dilemma seems inherent in the conflicting requirements of coordination and problem solving because there is the simultaneous need for restricted and unrestricted communication. The conflict, which causes adaptation and change, cannot be readily resolved and needs continuing attention.

BUREAUCRATIC DISCIPLINE AND PROFESSIONAL EXPERTISE

The similarities and differences in the characteristics of professional and bureaucratic orientations (see Chapters 3 and 10) lead to a second dilemma. While both orientations stress technical competence, objectivity, impersonality, and service, the unique structure of the professions is a basic source of conflict. Professionals attempt to control themselves through self-imposed standards and group surveillance. In contrast, bureaucratic employees are expected to adhere to rules and regulations and to subordinate themselves to the hierarchy. The ultimate basis for a professional act is the professional's knowledge; the ultimate justification of a bureaucratic act is its consistency with organizational rules and regulations and approval by a superior. The conflict is between professional expertise and autonomy, and bureaucratic discipline and control. The significance of the discord is brought into sharp focus when we examine employees who are subject to both forms of social control: professionals working in bureaucracies.

There are different ways to resolve the strain created by the merger of these two institutional means of control. In some organizations, major structural changes have been instituted through the development of two separate authority lines—one professional and one administrative. Nonetheless, when professional considerations conflict with bureaucratic ones, dividing authority seems to be a partial solution at best. Without organizational change some individuals attempt to accommodate themselves to the conflict by developing role orientations that are compatible with the bureaucracy or the profession, and some adopt orientations that are compatible with both. Although accommodation is made, the conflict remains a continuing dilemma and thus a fundamental issue.

Professional expertise and bureaucratic discipline are alternative modes of coping with uncertainty. Discipline restricts its scope, while expertise provides knowledge and social support to cope with uncertainty. Blau and Scott held that the struggle will remain as long as professionals are employed in bureaucratic organizations. It seems likely that the professional-bureaucratic dilemma will become an even more significant internal one in schools as teachers and administrators become more professionalized and continue to function in school organizations that are essentially bureaucratic in nature.

ADMINISTRATIVE PLANNING AND INDIVIDUAL INITIATIVE

A third manifestation of the tension between order and freedom is the need for both administrative planning and individual initiative. The disharmony between them poses a major difficulty in the administrative process, which includes not only the development of plans to solve problems but their subsequent implementation and appraisal. The setting of organizational decision making is the organization as a collectivity. The exercise of any independent judgment must be compatible with the thrust of the formal organization. There is continuous pressure from the formal organization through its elaborate bureaucratic machinery to subordinate individual initiative to organizational directives. The organization is, of course, interested in creative, individual efforts, but only when they do not conflict with formal plans.

How can the organization encourage individual initiative without confounding administrative planning? We have suggested a number of organizational responses. A model for shared decision making has been introduced that delineates under what conditions the individual should be involved in the decision-making process (see Chapter 9). The arrangement calls for harnessing the creative initiative of individuals in a constructive way that is beneficial to both the organization and the person. We have sketched the characteristics of a professional organizational structure in which emphasis is placed on shared decision making rather than on autocratic bureaucracy (see Chapter 3). Further, we described a number of organizational climates—the open climate, the healthy school climate, and the humanistic school—that would tend to lessen the conflict between compliance and initiative (see Chapter 5).

In brief, organizations can be structured and organizational climates and cultures can be developed to minimize the conflict between administrative planning and individual initiative. This is not to suggest that the dilemma can be resolved. The best that we can probably hope for is a healthy balance between compliance and initiative, a balance continually disrupted by the conflicting needs for order and freedom.

CONCLUSION

The position that we have held throughout this book embodies what Peter F. Drucker (1968) calls *reality.* Knowledge has become a central resource. The systematic acquisition of knowledge—that is, organized formal education—must supplement experience as the foundation for increasing productive capacity and improving performance. Increasingly, performance will depend on the ability to use concepts, ideas, and theories as well as skills acquired through experience.

The dilemmas we have explored demand basic changes in administrators. They require new training, knowledge, and policies and a sloughing off of deeply entrenched practices of today's society. The practice of administration can become one of deepened dilemmas or of heightened achievements. We hold that a path to the latter is through further theory and research in educational organizations.

Bibliography

AASA (1991). *An Introduction to Total Quality Management: A Collection of Articles on the Concepts of Total Quality Management and W. Edwards Deming.* Arlington, VA: American Association of School Administrators.

Abbott, M. (1965a). Hierarchical Impediments to Innovation in Educational Organizations. In M. Abbott and J. Lovell (Eds.), *Change Perspectives in Educational Administration* (pp. 40-53). Auburn, AL: Auburn University.

Abbott, M. (1965b). Intervening Variables in Organizational Behavior. *Educational Administration Quarterly, 1,* 1-14.

Abbott, M., and Caracheo, F. (1988). Power, Authority, and Bureaucracy. In N. J. Boyan (Ed.), *Handbook of Research on Educational Administration* (pp. 239-257). New York: Longman.

Abramowitz, S., and Tenenbaum, E. (1978). *High School '77.* Washington, DC: National Institute for Education.

Adkinson, J. A. (1981). Women in School Administration: A Review of the Research. *Review of Educational Research, 51,* 311-343.

Adler, R. B., and Rodman, G. (1991). *Understanding Human Communication.* Fort Worth, TX: Holt, Rinehart and Winston.

Adler, S., Skov, R. B., and Salvemini, N. J. (1985). Job Characteristics and Job Satisfaction: When Cause Becomes Consequence. *Organizational Behavior and Human Decision Processes, 35,* 266-278.

Agho, A. O., Mueller, C. W., and Price, J. L. (1993). Determinants of Employee Job Satisfaction: An Empirical Test of a Causal Model. *Human Relations, 46,* (8), 1007-1027.

Aiken, M., and Hage, J. (1968). Organizational Interdependence and Intra-Organizational Structure. *American Sociological Review, 33,* 912-930.

Aldrich, H. E. (1972). An Organization-Environment Perspective on Cooperation and Conflict between Organizations in the Manpower Training System. In A. R. Negandi (Ed.), *Conflict and Power in Complex Organizations* (pp. 11–37). Kent, OH: Center for Business and Economic Research, Kent State University.

Aldrich, H. E. (1979). *Organizations and Environment.* Englewood Cliffs, NJ: Prentice Hall.

Aldrich, H. E., and Herker, D. (1977). Boundary Spanning Roles and Organization Structure. *Academy of Management Review, 2,* 217–230.

Aldrich, H. E., and Mindlin, S. (1978). Uncertainty and Dependence: Two Perspectives on Environment. In L. Karpik (Ed.), *Organization and Environment: Theory, Issues and Reality* (pp. 149–170). Beverly Hills, CA: Sage.

Aldrich, H. E., and Pfeffer, J. (1976). Environments of Organizations. *Annual Review of Sociology, 2,* 79–105.

Alessandra, T., and Hunsaker, P. (1993). *Communicating at Work.* New York: Simon and Schuster.

Alexander, E. R., Penley, L. E., and Jernigan, I. E. (1991). The Effect of Individual Differences on Managerial Media Choice. *Management Communication Quarterly, 5,* (2), 155–173.

Alinsky, S. (1971). *Rules for Radicals.* New York: Random House.

Allen, R. F., and Kraft, C. (1982). *The Organizational Unconscious: How to Create the Corporate Culture You Want and Need.* Englewood Cliffs, NJ: Prentice-Hall.

Allison, G. T. (1971). *Essence of Decision: Explaining the Cuban Missile Crisis.* Boston: Little Brown.

Allutto, J. A., and Belasco, J. A. (1973). Patterns of Teacher Participation in School System Decision Making. *Educational Administration Quarterly, 9,* 27–41.

Anderson, B. (1971). Socioeconomic Status of Students and Schools Bureaucratization. *Educational Administration Quarterly, 7,* 12–24.

Anderson, C. S. (1982). The Search for School Climate: A Review of the Research. *Review of Educational Research, 52,* 368–420.

Anderson, D. P. (1964). *Organizational Climate of Elementary Schools.* Minneapolis: Educational Research and Development Council.

Anderson, J. (1976). Giving and Receiving Feedback. In P. R. Lawrence, L. B. Barnes, and J. W. Lorsch (Eds.), *Organizational Behavior and Administration* (pp. 103–111). Homewood, IL: Irwin.

Anderson, J. C., Rungtusanatham, M., and Schroeder, R. G. (1994). A Theory of Quality Management Underlying the Deming Management. *Academy of Management Review, 19,* (3), 472–450.

Anderson, J. R. (1990). *Cognitive Psychology and Its Implications* (3rd ed.). New York: Freeman.

Anderson, M. B. G., and Iwanicki, E. F. (1984). Teacher Motivation and Its Relationship to Burnout. *Educational Administration Quarterly, 20,* 109–132.

Andrews, J. H. M. (1965). School Organizational Climate: Some Validity Studies. *Canadian Education and Research Digest, 5,* 317–334.

Appleberry, J. B., and Hoy, W. K. (1969). The Pupil Control Ideology of Professional Personnel in 'Open' and 'Closed' Elementary Schools. *Educational Administration Quarterly, 5,* 74–85.

Argot, L., Turner, M. E., and Fichman, M. (1989). To Centralize or Not to Centralize: The Effects of Uncertainty and Threat on Group Structure and Performance. *Organizational Behavior and Human Performance, 43,* 58–74.

Aristotle (1883). *Politics.* Book I, Chapter 5. London: MacMillan.

Armor, D., Conry-Oseguera, P., Cox, M., King, N., McDonnell, L., Pascal, A., Pauly, E., and Zellman, G. (1976). *Analysis of the School Preferred Reading Program in Selected Los Angeles Minority Schools* (No. R-2007-LAUSD). Santa Monica, CA: Rand.

Arnold, H. J., and House, R. J. (1980). Methodological and Substantive Extensions to the Job Characteristics Model of Motivation. *Organizational Behavior and Human Performances, 25,* 161–183.

Ashford, S. J. (1986). Feedback-Seeking in Individual Adaptation: A Resource Perspective. *Academy of Management Journal, 29,* 465–487.

Ashforth, B. E. (1985). Climate Formations: Issues and Extensions. *Academy of Management Review, 10,* 837–847.

Ashton, P. T., and Webb, R. B. (1986). *Making a Difference: Teachers' Sense of Efficacy.* New York: Longman.

Astley, W. G. (1985). Administration Science as Socially Constructed Truth. *Administrative Science Quarterly, 30,* 497–513.

Astuto, T. A., and Clark, D. L. (1985a). *Merit Pay for Teachers.* Bloomington: School of Education, University of Indiana.

Astuto, T. A., and Clark, D. L. (1985b). Strength of Organizational Coupling in the Instructionally Effective School. *Urban Education, 19,* 331–356.

At-Twaijri, M. I. A., and Montanari, J. R. (1987). The Impact of Context and Choice on the Boundary-Spanning Process: An Empirical Study. *Human Relations, 40,* 783–798.

Atwater, D. C., and Bass, B. M. (1994). Transformational Leadership in Teams. In B. M. Bass and B. J. Avolio (Eds.), *Improving Organizational Effectiveness Through Transformational Leadership* (pp. 48–83). Thousand Oaks, CA: Sage.

Aupperle, K. E., Acar, W., and Booth, D. E. (1986). An Empirical Critique of *In Search of Excellence:* How Excellent Are the Excellent Companies? *Journal of Management, 12,* 499–512.

Averich, H. A., Carroll, S. J., Donaldson, T. S., Kiesling, H. J., and Pincus, J. (1972). *How Effective Is Schooling: A Critical Review and Synthesis of Research Findings.* Santa Monica, CA: Rand.

Avolio, B. J. (1994). The Alliance of Total Quality and the Full Range of Leadership. In B. M. Bass and B. J. Avolio (Eds.), *Improving Organizational Effectiveness Through Transformational Leadership* (pp. 121–145). Thousand Oaks, CA: Sage.

Babbie, E. R. (1990). *Survey Research Methods* (2nd ed.). Belmont, CA: Wadsworth Publishing.

Bacharach, S. B. (1988). Four Themes of Reform: An Editorial Essay. *Educational Administration Quarterly, 24,* 484–496.

Bacharach, S. B. (1989). Organizational Theories: Some Criteria for Evaluation. *Academy of Management Review, 14,* 496–515.

Bacharach, S. B., Bamberger, P., Conley, S. C., and Bauer, S. (1990). The Dimensionality of Decision Participation in Educational Organizations: The Value of Multi-Domain Educative Approach. *Educational Administration Quarterly, 26,* 126–167.

Bacharach, S. B., Conley, S., and Shedd, J. (1986). Beyond Career Ladders: Structuring Teacher Career Development Systems. *Teachers College Record, 87,* 565–574.

Bacharach, S. B., and Mundell, B. L. (1993). Organizational Politics in Schools: Micro, Macro, and Logics of Action. *Educational Administration Quarterly, 29,* (4), 423–452.

Baker, M. A. (1991). Gender and Verbal Communication in Professional Settings: A Review of Research. *Management Communication Quarterly, 5,* (1), 36–63.

Baltzell, D. C., and Dentler, R. A. (1983). *Selecting American School Principals: A Sourcebook for Educators.* Cambridge, MA: Abt Associates.

Bandura, A. (1986). *Social Foundations of Thought and Action.* Englewood Cliffs, NJ: Prentice-Hall.

Bandura, A. (1990). Forword. In E. A. Locke and G. P. Latham (Eds.), *A Theory of Goal Setting and Task Performance* (pp. xi–xii). Englewood Cliffs, NJ: Prentice-Hall.

Bandura, A. (1991). Social Cognitive Theory of Self-Regulation. *Organizational Behavior and Human Decision Processes, 50,* 248–287.

Bandura, A. (1993). Perceived Self-Efficacy in Cognitive Development and Functioning. *Educational Psychologist, 28,* 117–148.

Bantz, C. R. (1993). *Understanding Organizations: Interpreting Organizational Communication Cultures.* Columbia, SC: University of South Carolina Press.

Barnabe, C., and Burns, M. L. (1994). Teachers' Job Characteristics and Motivation. *Educational Research, 36,* (2), 171–185.

Barnard, C. I. (1938). *Functions of an Executive.* Cambridge, MA: Harvard University Press.

Barnard, C. I. (1940). Comments on the Job of the Executive. *Harvard Business Review, 18,* 295–308.

Barnes, R. M. (1949). *Motion and Time Study.* New York: Wiley.

Barnes, K. M. (1994). The organizational health of middle schools, trust and decision participation. Doctoral diss., Rutgers University, New Brunswick.

Barnett, B. G. (1984). Subordinate Teacher Power in School Organizations. *Sociology of Education, 57,* 43–55.

Bass, B. M. (1985a). *Leadership and Performance Beyond Expectation.* New York: Free Press.

Bass, B. M. (1985b). *Organizational Decision Making.* Homewood, IL: Irwin.

Bass, B. M. (1990). *Bass and Stogdill's Handbook of Leadership* (3rd ed.). New York: Free Press.

Bass, B. M., and Avolio, B. J. (1994). Introduction. In B. M. Bass and B. J. Avolio (Eds.), *Improving Organizational Effectiveness Through Transformational Leadership* (pp. 1–10). Thousand Oaks, CA: Sage.

Bates, R. (1987). Conceptions of School Culture: An Overview. *Educational Administration Quarterly, 23,* 79-116.

Becker, T. E., and Klimoski, R. J. (1989). A Field Study of the Relationship Between the Organizational Feedback Environment and Performance. *Personnel Psychology, 42,* 343-358.

Belasco, J. A., and Allutto, J. A. (1972). Decisional Participation and Teacher Satisfaction. *Educational Administration Quarterly, 8,* 44-58.

Bennis, W. G. (1959). Leadership Theory and Administrative Behavior. *Administrative Science Quarterly, 4,* 259-301.

Bennis, W. G. (1989). *On Becoming a Leader.* Reading, MA: Addison-Wesley.

Bennis, W., and Nanus, B. (1985). *Leaders: The Strategies for Taking Charge.* New York: Harper & Row.

Benson, J. K. (1975). The Interorganizational Network as a Political Economy. *Administration Science Quarterly, 20,* 229-249.

Berlo, D. K. (1970). *The Process of Communication.* New York: Holt, Rinehart & Winston.

Berman, P., McLaughlin, M., Bass, G., Pauly, E., and Zellerman, G. (1977). *Federal Programs Supporting Educational Change: Factors Affecting Implementation and Continuation,* Volume 7 (No. R-1589/7-HEW). Santa Monica, CA: Rand.

Bess, J. L. (1977). The Motivation to Teach. *Journal of Higher Education, 48,* 243-258.

Betz, E. L. (1984). Two Tests of Maslow's Theory of Need Fulfillment. *Journal of Vocational Behavior, 24,* 204-220.

Beyer, J. M., and Trice, H. M. (1987). How an Organization's Rites Reveal Its Culture. *Organizational Dynamics, 15,* 4-24.

Bhagat, R. S., and Chassie, M. B. (1980). Effects of Changes in Job Characteristics on Some Theory-Specific Attitudinal Outcomes: Results from a Naturally Occurring Quasi-Experiment. *Human Relations, 33,* 297-313.

Bidwell, C. E. (1965). The School as a Formal Organization. In J. G. March (Ed.), *Handbook of Organization* (pp. 972-1022). Chicago: Rand McNally.

Bidwell, C. E., and Kasarda, J. D. (1975). School District Organization and Student Achievement. *American Sociological Review, 40,* 55-70.

Bimber, B. (1993). *School Decentralization: Lessons from the Study of Bureaucracy.* Santa Monica, CA: Rand.

Birnbaum, R. (1971). Presidential Succession: An Interinstitutional Analysis. *Educational Record, 52,* 133-145.

Blackburn, R., and Rosen, B. (1993). Total Quality and Human Resources Management: Lessons Learned from Baldrige Award-Winning Companies. *Academy of Management Executive, 2,* (3), 49-66.

Blake, R. R., and Mouton, J. S. (1985). *The Managerial Grid III.* Houston, TX: Gulf.

Blau, P. M. (1955). *The Dynamics of Bureaucracy.* Chicago: University of Chicago Press.

Blau, P. M. (1956). *Bureaucracy in Modern Society.* New York: Random House.

Blau, P. M., and Scott, W. R. (1962). *Formal Organizations: A Comparative Approach.* San Francisco: Chandler.

Bluedorn, A. C., and Denhardt, R. B. (1988). Time and Organizations. *Journal of Management, 4,* 299–320.

Blumberg, A. (1984). The Craft of School Administration and Some Other Rambling Thoughts. *Educational Administration Quarterly, 20,* 24–40.

Blumberg, A. (1989). *School Administration as a Craft: Foundations of Practice.* Needham Heights, MA: Allyn & Bacon.

Bobbit, F. (1913). Some General Principles of Management Applied to the Problems of City School Systems. *The Supervision of City Schools, Twelfth Yearbook of the National Society for the Study of Education, Part I* (pp. 137–196). Chicago: University of Chicago Press.

Boje, D. M., and Whetten, D. A. (1981). Effects of Organizational Strategies and Contextual Constraints on Centrality and Attributions of Influence in Interorganizational Networks. *Administrative Science Quarterly, 26,* 378–395.

Bok, D. (1993). *The Cost of Talent.* New York: Free Press.

Bolman, L. G., and Deal, T. E. (1984). *Modern Approaches to Understanding and Managing Organizations.* San Francisco: Jossey-Bass.

Bolman, L. G., and Deal, T. E. (1991). *Reframing Organizations: Artistry, Choice, and Leadership.* San Francisco: Jossey-Bass.

Bonstingl, J. J. (1994). The Quality Revolution in Education. *Educational Leadership, 50,* 4–9.

Bose, C., Feldberg, R., and Sokoloff, N. (1987). *Hidden Aspects of Women's Work.* New York: Praeger.

Bossert, S. T. (1988). School Effects. In N. J. Boyan (Ed.), *Handbook of Research on Educational Administration* (pp. 341–352). New York: Longman.

Bossert, S. T., Dwyer, D. C., Rowan, B., and Lee, G. V. (1982). The Instructional Management Role of the Principal. *Educational Administration Quarterly, 18,* 34–64.

Bowditch, J. L., and Buono, A. F. (1985). *A Primer on Organizational Behavior.* New York: Wiley.

Bowers, D. G. (1976). *Systems of Organizations: Management of the Human Resource.* Ann Arbor: University of Michigan Press.

Bowman, B. T. (1989). Self-Reflection as an Element of Professionalism. *Teachers College Record, 90,* 444–451.

Boyan, N. J. (1951). A study of the formal and informal organization of a school faculty: the identification of the systems of interactions and relationships among the staff members of a school and an analysis of the interplay between these systems. Doctoral diss. Harvard University, Cambridge.

Boyd, W. L. (1976). The Public, the Professional, and Educational Policy Making: Who Governs? *Teachers College Record, 77,* 539–577.

Boyd, W. L., and Walberg, H. J. (1990). Introduction and Overview. In W. L. Boyd and H. J. Walberg (Eds.), *Choice in Education: Potential and Problems* (pp. ix–xiii). Berkeley, CA: McCutchan.

Brady, L. (1985). The 'Australian' OCDQ: A Decade Later. *Journal of Educational Administration, 23,* 53–58.

Braybrook, D., and Lindblom, C. E. (1963). *The Strategy of Decision.* New York: Free Press.

Bridges, E. M. (1967). A Model for Shared Decision Making in the School Principalship. *Educational Administration Quarterly, 3,* 49–61.

Bromily, P. (1985). Planning Systems in Large Organizations: Garbage Can Approach with Applications to Defense PPBS. In J. G. March and R. Weissinger-Baylon (Eds.), *Ambiguity and Command: Organization Perspectives on Military Decision Making* (pp. 120–139). Marshfield, MA: Pitman.

Broms, H., and Gahmberg, H. (1983). Communication to Self in Organizational Cultures. *Administrative Science Quarterly, 28,* (3), 482–495.

Brookover, W. B., Schweitzer, J. H., Schneider, J. M., Beady, C. H., Flood, P. K., and Wisenbaker, J. M. (1978). Elementary School Social Climate and School Achievement. *American Educational Research Journal, 15,* 301–318.

Brophy, J. E., and Good, T. L. (1986). Teacher Behavior and Student Achievement. In M. C. Wittrock (Ed.), *Handbook of Research on Teaching* (pp. 328–375). New York: Macmillan.

Brown, A. F. (1965). Two Strategies for Changing Climate. *CAS Bulletin, 4,* 64–80.

Brown, A. F. (1967). Reactions to Leadership. *Educational Administration Quarterly, 3,* 62–73.

Brown, D. (1990). *Decentralization and School-Based Management.* New York: Falmer Press.

Bryk, A. S. (1993). Educational Indicator Systems: Observations on their Structure Interpretation, and Use. *Review of Research in Education, 19,* 451–484.

Bryk, A. S., Lee, V. E., and Holland, P. (1993). *Catholic Schools and the Common Good.* Cambridge, MA: Harvard University Press.

Burbules, N. C. (1993). *Dialogue in Teaching: Theory and Practice.* New York: Teachers College Press.

Burlingame, M. (1979). Some Neglected Dimensions in the Study of Educational Administration. *Educational Administration Quarterly, 15,* 1–18.

Burns, J. M. (1978). *Leadership.* New York: Harper & Row.

Burns, T., and Stalker, G. M. (1961). *The Management of Innovation.* London: Travistock.

Burrell, G., and Morgan, G. (1980). *Sociological Paradigms and Organizational Analysis.* London: Heinemann.

Calas, M. B., and Smircich, L. (1992). Using the 'F' Word: Feminist Theorists and the Social Consequences of Organizational Research. In A. J. Mill and P. Tancred (Eds.), *Gendering Organizational Analysis.* Newbury Park, CA: Sage.

Callahan, R. E. (1962). *Education and the Cult of Efficiency.* Chicago: University of Chicago Press.

Cameron, K. S. (1978). Measuring Organizational Effectiveness in Institutions of Higher Education. *Administrative Science Quarterly, 23,* 604–632.

Cameron, K. S. (1984). The Effectiveness of Ineffectiveness. *Research in Organizational Behavior, 6,* 235–285.

Cameron, K. S., and Whetten, D. A. (1983). *Organizational Effectiveness: A Comparison of Multiple Models.* New York: Academic.

Cameron, K. S., and Whetten, D. A. (1995). Organizational Effectiveness and Quality: The Second Generation. *Higher Education: Handbook of Theory and Research, XI.* Forthcoming.

Campbell, J. P. (1977). On the Nature of Organizational Effectiveness. In P. S. Goodman and J. M. Pennings (Eds.), *New Perspectives on Organizational Effectiveness* (pp. 13–55). San Francisco: Jossey-Bass.

Campbell, J. P., Dunnette, M. D., Lawler, E. E. III., and Karl E. Weick, J. (1970). *Managerial Behavior, Performance, and Effectiveness.* New York: McGraw-Hill.

Campbell, J. P., and Pritchard, R. D. (1976). Motivation Theory in Industrial and Organizational Psychology. In M. D. Dunnette (Ed.), *Handbook of Industrial and Organizational Psychology* (pp. 63–130). Chicago: Rand McNally.

Campbell, R. (1971). NCPEA—Then and Now. National Conference of Professors of Educational Administration Meeting, University of Utah, Salt Lake City.

Campbell, R., Fleming, T., Newell, L. J., and Bennion, J. W. (1987). *A History of Thought and Practice in Educational Administration.* New York: Teachers College Press.

Capper, C. A., and Jamison, M. T. (1993). Let the Buyer Beware: Total Quality Management and Educational Research and Practice. *Educational Researcher, 22,* (8), 25–30.

Carey, M. R. (1992). Transformational Leadership and the Fundamental Option for Self-Transcendence. *Leadership Quarterly, 3,* (3), 217–236.

Carey, S., and Smith, C. (1993). On Understanding the Nature of Scientific Inquiry. *Educational Psychologist, 28,* 235–252.

Carlson, R. O. (1962). *Executive Succession and Organizational Change.* Chicago: University of Chicago, Midwest Administration Center.

Carlson, R. O. (1964). Environmental Constraints and Organizational Consequences: The Public School and Its Clients. In D. E. Griffiths (Ed.), *Behavioral Science and Educational Administration* (pp. 262–276). Chicago: University of Chicago Press.

Carnegie Task Force on Teaching as a Profession (1986). *A Nation Prepared: Teachers for the 21st Century.* New York: Carnegie Corporation, Carnegie Forum on Education and the Economy.

Carpenter, H. H. (1971). Formal Organizational Structural Factors and Perceived Job Satisfaction of Classroom Teachers. *Administrative Science Quarterly, 16,* 460–465.

Carroll, S. J. (1986). Management by Objectives: Three Decades of Research and Experience. In S. L. Rynes and G. T. Milkovich (Eds.), *Current Issues in Human Resource Management.* Plano, TX: Business Publications.

Cartwright, D., and Zander, A. (1953). *Group Dynamics: Research and Theory.* Evanston, IL: Row, Peterson.

Carver, F. D., and Sergiovanni, T. J. (1969). Notes on the OCDQ. *Journal of Educational Administration, 7,* 71–81.

Casner-Lotto, J. (1988). Expanding the Teacher's Role: Hammond's School Improvement Process. *Phi Delta Kappan, 69,* 349–353.

Castrogiovanni, G. J. (1991). Environmental Munificence: A Theoretical Assessment. *Academy of Management Review, 16,* (3), 542–565.

Chapman, D. W., and Hutcheson, S. M. (1982). Attrition from Teaching Careers: A Discriminant Analysis. *American Educational Research Journal, 19,* 93–105.

Charters, W. W., Jr. (1967). Stability and Change in the Communication Structure of School Faculties. *Educational Administration Quarterly, 3,* 15–38.

Chase, F. S. (1951). Factors for Satisfaction in Teaching. *Phi Delta Kappan, 33,* 127–132.

Chatman, J. A., and Jehn, K. A. (1994). Assessing the Relationship Between Industry Characteristics and Organizational Culture: How Different Can You Be? *Academy of Management Journal, 37,* (3), 522–553.

Chemers, M. M., and Skrzypek, G. J. (1972). Experimental Test of Contingency Model of Leadership Effectiveness. *Journal of Personality and Social Psychology, 24,* 172–177.

Cherrington, D. J. (1991). Need Theories of Motivation. In R. M. Steers and L. W. Porter (Eds.), *Motivation and Work Behavior* (pp. 31–44). New York: McGraw-Hill.

Chisolm, G. B., Washington, R., and Thibodeaux, M. (1980). Job Motivation and the Need Fulfillment Deficiencies of Educators. Annual Meeting of the American Educational Research Association, Boston.

Chubb, J. E., and Moe, T. M. (1990). *Politics, Markets, and America's Schools.* Washington, DC: Brookings Institution.

Chung, K. A. (1987). A comparative study of principals' work behavior. Doctoral diss., University of Utah, Salt Lake City.

Chung, K. A., and Miskel, C. (1989). A Comparative Study of Principals' Administrative Behavior. *Journal of Educational Administration, 27,* 45–57.

Clampitt, P. G. (1991). *Communicating for Managerial Effectiveness.* Newbury Park, CA: Sage.

Clark, D. L., Astuto, T. A., Foster, W. P., Gaynor, A. K., and Hart, A. W. (1994). Organizational Studies: Taxonomy and Overview. In W. K. Hoy, T. A. Astuto, and P. B. Forsyth (Eds.), *Educational Administration: The UCEA Document Base.* New York: McGraw-Hill Primus.

Clark, D. L., Lotto, L. S., and Astuto, T. A. (1984). Effective Schools and School Improvement: A Comparative Analysis of Two Lines of Inquiry. *Educational Administration Quarterly, 20,* 41–68.

Clark, K. E., and Clark, M. B. (Eds.) (1990). *Measures of Leadership.* West Orange, NJ: Leadership Library of America.

Clune, W. H., and White, J. F. (Eds.) (1990). *Choice and Control in American Education. Volume 2: The Practice of Choice, Decentralization and School Restructuring.* New York: Falmer Press.

Coch, L., and French, J. R. P., Jr. (1948). Overcoming Resistance to Change. *Human Relations, 1,* 512–532.

Cohen, D. K. (1987). Schooling More and Liking It Less: Puzzles of Educational Improvement. *Harvard Educational Review, 57,* 174–177.

Cohen, M. D., and March, J. G. (1974). *Leadership and Ambiguity.* New York: McGraw-Hill.

Cohen, M. D., March, J. G., and Olsen, J. P. (1972). A Garbage Can Model of Organizational Choice. *Administrative Science Quarterly, 17,* 1-25.

Cohn, M. M., and Kottkamp, R. B. (1993). *Teachers: The Missing Voice in Education.* Albany, NY: State University of New York Press.

Coleman, J. (1990). *Foundations of Social Theory.* Cambridge, MA: Belknap.

Coleman, J. S. (1961). *The Adolescent Society.* New York: Free Press.

Coleman, J. S., Campbell, E. Q., Hobson, C. J., McPartland, J., Mood, A. M., Weinfeld, F. D., and York, R. L. (1966). *Equality of Educational Opportunity.* Washington, DC: U. S. Government Printing Office.

Commons, J. R. (1924). *Legal Foundations of Capitalism.* New York: Macmillan.

Conant, J. B. (1951). *Science and Common Sense.* New Haven: Yale University Press.

Conger, J. A. (1991). Inspiring Others: The Language of Leadership. *Academy of Management Executive, 5,* (1), 31-45.

Conger, J. A., and Kanungo, R. N. (1988). The Empowerment Process: Integrating Theory and Practice. *Academy of Management Journal, 13,* 471-482.

Conley, S. C. (1990). A Metaphor for Teaching: Beyond the Bureaucratic-Professional Dichotomy. In S. B. Bacharach (Ed.), *Educational Reform: Making Sense of It All* (pp. 313-324). Boston: Allyn and Bacon.

Conley, S. C., and Bacharach, S. B. (1990). From School Site-Management to Participatory Site-Management. *Phi Delta Kappan, 72,* 539-544.

Conley, S. C., Bower, S., and Bacharach, S. B. (1989). The School Work Environment and Teacher Career Satisfaction. *Educational Administration Quarterly, 25,* 58-81.

Conley, S., and Levinson, R. (1993). Teacher Work Redesign and Job Satisfaction. *Educational Administration Quarterly, 29,* (4), 453-478.

Connolly, T., Conlon, E. J., and Deutsch, S. J. (1980). Organizational Effectiveness: A Multiple-Constituency Approach. *Academy of Management Review, 5,* 211-217.

Constas, H. (1958). Max Weber's Two Conceptions of Bureaucracy. *American Journal of Sociology, 63,* 400-409.

Conway, J. A. (1976). Test of Linearity Between Teachers' Participation in Decision Making and Their Perceptions of Schools as Organizations. *Administrative Science Quarterly, 21,* 130-139.

Conway, J. A. (1984). The Myth, Mystery, and Mastery of Participative Decision Making in Education. *Educational Administration Quarterly, 3,* 11-40.

Cordery, J. L., and Sevastos, P. P. (1993). Responses to the Original and Revised Job Diagnostic Survey: Is Education a Factor in Responses to Negatively Worded Items? *Journal of Applied Psychology, 78,* (1), 141-143.

Cornwall, J. R., and Grimes, A. J. (1987). Cosmopolitan-Local: A Cross-Lagged Correlation Analysis of the Relationship Between Professional Role Orientations and Behaviors in an Academic Organization. *Human Relations, 40,* 281-298.

Corwin, R. G. (1961). The Professional Employee: A Study of Conflict in Nursing Roles. *American Journal of Sociology, 66,* 604–615.

Corwin, R. G. (1965). Professional Persons in Public Organizations. *Educational Administration Quarterly, 1,* 1–22.

Corwin, R. G., and Borman, K. M. (1988). School as Workplace: Structural Constraints on Administration. In N. J. Boyan (Ed.), *Handbook of Research on Educational Administration* (pp. 209–237). New York: Longman.

Corwin, R. G., and Herriott, R. E. (1988). Occupational Disputes in Mechanical and Organic Social Systems: An Empirical Study of Elementary and Secondary Schools. *American Sociological Review, 53,* 528–543.

Cosgrove, D. (1985). The effects of principal succession on elementary schools. Doctoral diss., University of Utah, Salt Lake City.

Cox, A. (1982). *The Cox Report on the American Corporation.* New York: Delacorte.

Cranny, C. J., Smith, P. C., and Stone, E. F. (1992). *Job Satisfaction.* New York: Lexington.

Crehan, E. P. (1985). A meta-analysis of Fiedler's contingency model of leadership effectiveness. Doctoral diss., University of British Columbia, Vancouver.

Cropanzano, R., James, K., and Citera, M. (1992). A Goal Hierarchy Model of Personality, Motivation, and Leadership. *Research in Organizational Behavior, 15,* 267–322.

Crozier, M. (1964). *The Bureaucratic Phenomenon.* Chicago: University of Chicago Press.

Cuban, L. (1983). Effective Schools: A Friendly but Cautionary Note. *Phi Delta Kappan, 64,* 695–696.

Cuban, L. (1984). Transforming the Frog into a Prince: Effective Schools Research, Policy, and Practice at the District Level. *Harvard Educational Review, 54,* 129–151.

Culbertson, J. A. (1981). Three Epistemologies and the Study of Educational Administration. *UCEA Review, 22,* 5.

Culbertson, J. A. (1988). A Century's Quest for a Knowledge Base. In N. J. Boyan (Ed.), *Handbook of Research on Educational Administration* (pp. 3–26). New York: Longman.

Culhan, M. J., and Markus, M. L. (1987). Information Technologies. In F. M. Jablin, L. L. Putnam, and L. W. Porter (Eds.), *Handbook of Organizational Communication: An Interdisciplinary Perspective* (pp. 130–164). Newbury Park, CA: Sage.

Cunningham, W. G., and Gresso, D. W. (1993). *Cultural Leadership.* Boston: Allyn & Bacon.

Cusella, L. P. (1987). Feedback, Motivation, and Performance. In F. M. Jablin, L. L. Putnam, K. Roberts, and L. W. Porter (Eds.), *Handbook of Organizational Communication: An Interdisciplinary Perspective* (pp. 624–678). Newbury Park, CA: Sage.

Cusick, P. A. (1981). A Study of Networks Among Professional Staffs in Secondary Schools. *Educational Administration Quarterly, 17,* 114–138.

Cusick, P. A. (1987). Organizational Culture and Schools. *Educational Administration Quarterly, 23,* 3–117.

Cyert, R. M., and March, J. G. (1963). *A Behavioral Theory of the Firm.* Englewood Cliffs, NJ: Prentice-Hall.

D'Aunno, T., Sutton, R. L., and Price, R. H. (1991). Isomorphism and External Support in Conflicting Institutional Environments: A Study of Drug Abuse Treatment Units. *Academy of Management Journal, 34,* (3), 636-661.

Daft, R. L. (1989). *Organization Theory and Design* (3rd ed.). St. Paul, MN: West.

Daft, R. L. (1994). *Organizational Theory and Design.* St. Paul, MN: West.

Daft, R. L., Bettenhausen, K. R., and Tyler, B. B. (1993). Implications of Top Managers' Communication Choices for Strategic Decisions. In G. P. Huber and W. H. Glick (Eds.), *Organizational Change and Redesign.* New York: Oxford University Press.

Daft, R. L., and Lengel, R. H. (1984). Information Richness: A New Approach to Managerial Behavior and Organizational Design. *Research in Organizational Behavior, 6,* 191-233.

Daft, R. L., and H. Lengel, R. (1986). Organizational Information Requirements, Media Richness, and Structural Design. *Management Science, 32,* 554-571.

Dahl, R. A. C. (1961). *Who Governs?* New Haven, CT: Yale University Press.

Dahnke, G. L., and Clatterbuck, G. W. (Eds.) (1990). *Human Communication: Theory and Research.* Belmont, CA: Wadsworth.

Darling-Hammond, L. (1984). *Beyond the Commission Reports: The Coming Crisis in Teaching.* Santa Monica, CA: Rand.

Darling-Hammond, L. (1985). Valuing Teachers: The Making of a Profession. *Teachers College Record, 87,* 205-218.

Darling-Hammond, L., and Wise, A. (1985). Beyond Standardization: State Standards and School Improvement. *Elementary School Journal, 85,* 315-336.

David, J. L., Purkey, S., and White, P. (1989). *Restructuring in Progress: Lessons from Pioneering Districts.* Washington, DC: Center for Policy Research, National Governor's Association.

Day, D. V., and Lord, R. G. (1988). Executive Leadership and Organizational Performance: Suggestions for a New Theory and Methodology. *Journal of Management, 14,* 453-464.

Deal, T. E. (1985). The Symbolism of Effective Schools. *Elementary School Journal, 85,* 601-620.

Deal, T. E., and Celotti, L. D. (1980). How Much Influence Do (and Can) Educational Administrators Have on Classrooms? *Phi Delta Kappan, 61,* 471-473.

Deal, T. E., and Kennedy, A. A. (1982). *Corporate Cultures: The Rites and Rituals of Corporate Life.* Reading, MA: Addison-Wesley.

Deal, T. E., and Peterson, K. D. (1990). *The Principal's Role in Shaping School Culture.* Washington DC: U. S. Printing Office.

Deal, T., and Wise, M. (1983). Planning, Plotting, and Playing in Education's Era of Decline. In V. Baldridge and T. Deal (Eds.), *The Dynamics of Educational Change.* San Francisco: McCutchan.

DeFleur, M. L., Kearney, P., and Plax, T. G. (1993). *Mastering Communication in Contemporary America.* Mountain View, CA: Mayfield.

Deming, W. E. (1983). *Quality, Productivity, and Competitive Advantage.* Cambridge: Massachusetts Institute of Technology, Center for Advanced Engineering.

Deming, W. E. (1986). *Out of Crisis.* Cambridge: Massachusetts Institute of Technology, Center for Advanced Engineering.

Deming, W. E. (1993). *The New Economics for Economics, Government, Education.* Cambridge: Massachusetts Institute of Technology, Center for Advanced Engineering.

Denhardt, R. B., and Perkins, J. (1976). The Coming Death of Administrative Man. *Women in Public Administration, 36,* 379-384.

Dennison, D. R. (1990). *Corporate Culture and Organizational Effectiveness.* New York: Wiley.

Derrida, J. (1978). *Writing and Difference.* London: Routledge and Kegan Paul.

Derrida, J. (1981). *Positions.* Chicago: University of Chicago Press.

Dewey, J. (1929). *The Sources of a Science of Education.* New York: Horace Liveright.

Dewey, J. (1933). *How We Think.* Boston: Heath.

Diebert, J. P., and Hoy, W. K. (1977). Custodial High Schools and Self-Actualization of Students. *Educational Research Quarterly, 2,* 24-31.

Dill, R. W. (1958). Environment as an Influence on Managerial Autonomy. *Administrative Science Quarterly, 2,* 409-443.

DiMaggio, P. J. (1988). Interest and Agency in Institutional Theory. In L. G. Zucker (Ed.), *Institutional Patterns in Organizations: Culture and Environments* (pp. 3-21). Cambridge, MA: Ballinger.

DiMaggio, P. J., and Powell, W. (1983). The Iron Cage Revisited: Institutional Isomorphism and Collective Rationality in Organizational Fields. *American Sociological Review, 48,* 147-160.

DiMaggio, P. J., and Powell, W. W. (1991). The Iron Cage Revisited: Institutional Isomorphism and Collective Rationality. In W. W. Powell and P. J. DiMaggio (Eds.), *The New Institutionalism in Organizational Analysis* (pp. 41-62). Chicago: University of Chicago Press.

DiPaola, M. F., and Hoy, W. K. (1994). Teacher Militancy: A Professional Check on Bureaucracy. *The Journal of Research and Development in Education, 27,* 78-82.

Donmoyer, R. B., Schurich, J., and Imber, M. L. (Eds.) (1994). *The Knowledge Base in Educational Administration: Multiple Perspectives.* Albany: SUNY Press.

Downs, C. W. (1977). *Organizational Communicator.* New York: Harper & Row.

Driscoll, J. W. (1978). Trust and Participation in Decision Making as Predictors of Satisfaction. *Academy of Management Journal, 1,* 44-56.

Drucker, P. F. (1954). *The Practice of Management.* New York: Harper & Row.

Drucker, P. F. (1966). *The Effective Executive.* New York: Harper & Row.

Drucker, P. F. (1968). *The Age of Discontinuity.* New York: Harper & Row.

Drucker, P. F. (1980). *Managing in Turbulent Times.* New York: Harper & Row.

Dubin, R. (1969). *Theory Building.* New York: Free Press.

Duignan, P. (1980). Administrative Behavior of School Superintendents: A Descriptive Study. *Journal of Educational Administration, 18,* 5-26.

Duke, D. L., Showers, B. K., and Imber, M. (1980). Teachers and Shared Decision Making: The Costs and Benefits of Involvement. *Educational Administration Quarterly, 16,* 93-106.

Duncan, R. B. (1972). Characteristics of Organizational Environments and Perceived Environmental Uncertainty. *Administrative Science Quarterly, 17,* 313–327.

Duncan, R. B. (1979). What Is the Right Organizational Structure? Decision Free Analysis Provides the Answer. *Organizational Dynamics, 7,* 59–80.

Ebmeier, H., and Hart, A. W. (1992). The Effects of a Career-Ladder Program on School Organizational Process. *Educational Evaluation and Policy Analysis, 14,* (3), 261–281.

Edmonds, R. (1979). Some Schools Work and More Can. *Social Policy, 9,* 28–32.

Einstein, A., and Infeld, L. (1938). *The Evolution of Physics.* New York: Simon & Schuster.

Ellis, J. (1989). *Against Deconstruction.* Princeton: Princeton University Press.

Elmes, M. B., and Costello, M. (1992). Mystification and Social Drama: The Hidden Side of Communication Skills Training. *Human Relations, 45,* (5), 427–445.

Elmore, R. F. (1988). *Early Experiences in Restructuring Schools: Voices from the Field.* Washington, DC: Center for Policy Research, National Governor's Association.

Elsbach, K. D., and Sutton, R. I. (1992). Acquiring Organizational Legitimacy Through Illegitimate Actions: A Marriage of Institutional and Impression Management Theories. *Academy of Management Journal, 35,* (4), 699–738.

Emerson, R. (1962). Power-Dependence Relations. *American Sociological Review, 27,* 31–41.

Emery, F. E., and Trist, E. L. (1965). The Causal Texture of Organization Environments. *Human Relations, 18,* 21–32.

English, F. W. (1994). *Theory in Educational Administration.* New York: HarperCollins.

Enoch, Y. (1989). Change of Values During Socialization for a Profession: An Application of the Marginal Man Theory. *Human Relations, 42,* 219–239.

Erez, M., and Earley, P. C. (1993). *Culture, Self-Identity, and Work.* New York: Oxford University Press.

Estler, S. E. (1988). Decision Making. In N. J. Boyan (Ed.), *Handbook of Research on Educational Administration* (pp. 304–320). New York: Longman.

Etzioni, A. (1960). Two Approaches to Organizational Analysis: A Critique and Suggestion. *Administrative Science Quarterly, 5,* 257–278.

Etzioni, A. (1964). *Modern Organizations.* Englewood Cliffs, NJ: Prentice-Hall.

Etzioni, A. (1967). Mixed Scanning: A Third Approach to Decision Making. *Public Administration Review, 27,* 385–392.

Etzioni, A. (1975). *A Comparative Analysis of Complex Organizations.* New York: Free Press.

Etzioni, A. (1986). Mixed Scanning Revisited. *Public Administration Review, 46,* 8–14.

Etzioni, A. (1988). *The Moral Dimension: Toward a New Economics.* New York: Free Press.

Etzioni, A. (1989). Humble Decision Making. *Harvard Business Review, 67,* 122–126.

Evans, M. G., Kiggundu, M. N., and House, R. J. (1979). A Partial Test and Extension of the Job Characteristics Model of Motivation. *Organizational Behavior and Human Performance, 24,* 354–381.

Feigl, H. (1951). Principles and Problems of Theory Construction in Psychology. In W. Dennis (Ed.), *Current Trends in Psychological Theory* (pp. 179-213). Pittsburgh: University of Pittsburgh Press.

Fennell, M. L., and Alexander, J. A. (1987). Organizational Boundary Spanning in Institutionalized Environments. *Academy of Management Journal, 30,* (3), 456-476.

Ferguson, K. E. (1984). *The Feminist Case Against Bureaucracy.* Philadelphia: Temple University Press.

Festinger, L. (1957). *A Theory of Cognitive Dissonance.* Evanston, IL: Row, Peterson.

Fiedler, F. E. (1967). *A Theory of Leadership Effectiveness.* New York: McGraw-Hill.

Fiedler, F. E. (1971). Validation and Extension of the Contingency Model of Leadership Effectiveness: A Review of Empirical Findings. *Psychological Bulletin, 76,* 128-148.

Fiedler, F. E. (1973). The Contingency Model and the Dynamics of the Leadership Process. *Advances in Experimental Social Psychology, 11,* 60-112.

Fiedler, F. E. (1984). *The Contribution of Cognitive Resources and Leader Behavior to Organizational Performance.* Organization Research Technical Report No. 84-4. Seattle: University of Washington.

Fiedler, F. E., and Chemers, M. M. (1974). *Leadership and Effective Management.* Glenview, IL: Scott, Foresman.

Fiedler, F. E., Chemers, M. M., and Mahar, L. (1976). *Improving Leadership Effectiveness: The Leader Match Concept.* New York: Wiley.

Fiedler, F. E., and Garcia, J. E. (1987). *New Approaches to Effective Leadership: Cognitive Resources and Organizational Performance.* New York: Wiley.

Firestone, W. A. (1991). Merit Pay and Job Enlargement as Reforms: Incentives, Implementation, and Teacher Response. *Educational Evaluation and Policy Analysis, 13,* (3), 269-288.

Firestone, W. A., and Bader, B. D. (1992). *Redesigning Teaching: Professionalism or Bureaucracy.* Albany, NY: State University of New York Press.

Firestone, W. A., and Herriott, R. E. (1981). Images of Organization and the Promotion of Change. *Research in the Sociology of Education and Socialization, 2,* 221-260.

Firestone, W. A., and Herriott, R. E. (1982). Two Images of Schools as Organizations: An Explication and Illustrative Empirical Test. *Educational Administration Quarterly, 18,* 39-60.

Firestone, W. A., and Wilson, B. L. (1985). Using Bureaucratic and Cultural Linkages to Improve Instruction: The Principal's Contribution. *Educational Administration Quarterly, 21,* 7-31.

Fish, S. (1989). *Doing What Comes Naturally.* Durham, NC: Duke University Press.

Follett, M. P. (1924). *Creative Experience.* London: Longmans and Green.

Follett, M. P. (1941). In H. C. Metcalf and L. Urwick (Eds.), *Dynamic Administration: The Collected Papers of Mary Parker Follett.* New York: Harper.

Ford, M. E. (1992). *Motivating Humans: Goals, Emotions, and Social Agency Beliefs.* Newbury Park, CA: Sage.

Forsyth, P. B., and Hoy, W. K. (1978). Isolation and Alienation in Educational Organizations. *Educational Administration Quarterly, 14,* 80-96.

Foster, W. (1986). *Paradigms and Promises.* Buffalo, NY: Prometheus.

Foucault, M. (1983). The Subject and Power. In H. Dreyfus and P. Rabinow (Eds.), *Michel Foucault, Beyond Structuralism and Hermeneutic.* Chicago: Chicago University Press.

Foucault, M. (1984). *The Foucault Reader.* New York: Pantheon.

Fox, S., and Feldman, G. (1988). Attention State and Critical Psychological States as Mediators Between Job Dimensions and Job Outcomes. *Human Relations, 41,* 229–245.

Frase, L. E., and Heck, G. (1992). Restructuring in the Fort McMurray Catholic Schools: A Research-Based Approach. *The Canadian School Executive, 11,* (8), 3–9.

Frase, L. E., and Matheson, R. R. (1992). Restructuring: Fine-Tuning the System in Fort McMurray Catholic Schools. *Challenge, 29,* (1), 16–22.

Frase, L. E., and Sorenson, L. (1992). Teacher Motivation and Satisfaction: Impact on Participatory Management. *NASSP Bulletin, 76,* 37–43.

Freeman, J. H. (1979). Going to the Well: School District Administrative Intensity and Environmental Constraint. *Administrative Science Quarterly, 24,* 119–133.

Freidson, E. (1984). The Changing Nature of Professional Control. *Annual Review of Sociology, 10,* 1–20.

Freidson, E. (1986). *Professional Powers: A Study of the Institutionalization of Formal Knowledge.* Chicago: University of Chicago Press.

French, J. R. P., and Raven, B. H. (1968). Bases of Social Power. In D. Cartwright and A. Zander (Eds.), *Group Dynamics: Research and Theory* (pp. 259–270). New York: Harper & Row.

Friedman, R. A., and Podolny, J. (1992). Differentiation of Boundary Spanning Roles: Labor Negotiations and Implications for Role Conflict. *Administrative Science Quarterly, 37,* 28–47.

Friesen, D., and Duignan, P. (1980). How Superintendents Spend Their Working Time. *Canadian Administrator, 19,* 1–5.

Fromm, E. (1948). *Man for Himself.* New York: Farrar & Rinehart.

Frost, P. J., Moore, L. F., Louis, M. R., Lundberg, C. C., and Martin, J. (Eds.) (1991). *Reframing Organizational Culture.* Newbury Park, CA: Sage.

Fulk, J., and Boyd, B. (1991). Emerging Theories of Communication in Organizations. *Journal of Management, 17,* (2), 407–446.

Furhman, S. H., Elmore, R. F., and Massell, D. (1993). School Reform in the United States: Putting It into Context. In S. L. Jacobson and R. Berne (Eds.), *Reforming Education: The Emerging Systemic Approach* (pp. 3–27). Thousand Oaks, CA: Corwin.

Gaertner, K. N. (1980). The Structure of Organizational Careers. *Sociology of Education, 53,* 7–20.

Galbraith, J. (1977a). *Designing Complex Organizations.* Reading, MA: Addison-Wesley.

Galbraith, J. (1977b). *Organizational Design.* Reading, MA: Addison-Wesley.

Galbraith, J., and Cummings, L. L. (1967). An Empirical Investigation of the Motivational Determinants of Task Performance: Interactive Effects Between Instrumentality-Valence and Motivation-Ability. *Organization Behavior and Human Performance, 2,* 237–257.

Ganz, H. J., and Hoy, W. K. (1977). Patterns of Succession of Elementary Principals and Organizational Change. *Planning and Changing, 8,* 185–196.

Gardner, D. G., and Cummings, L. L. (1988). Activation Theory and Job Design: Review and Reconceptualization. *Research in Organizational Behavior, 10,* 81–122.

Gardner, H. (1987). *The Mind's New Science: A History of the Cognitive Revolution.* New York: Basic Books.

Gardner, H. (1991). *The Unschooled Mind: How Children Think and How Schools Should Teach.* New York: Basic Books.

Gardner, J. W. (1990). *On Leadership.* New York: Free Press.

Gartner, W. B., and Naughton, M. J. (1988). The Deming Theory of Management. *Academy of Management Review, 17,* 138–142.

Geertz, C. (1973). *The Interpretation of Cultures.* New York: Basic.

Gemmill, G., and Oakley, J. (1992). Leadership: An Alienating Social Myth. *Human Relations, 45,* (2), 113–129.

Gerhardt, E. (1971). Staff conflict, organizational bureaucracy, and individual satisfaction in selected Kansas school districts. Doctoral diss., University of Kansas, Lawrence.

Gerth, H. H., and Mills, C. W. (Eds.) (1946). *From Max Weber: Essays in Sociology.* New York: Oxford University Press.

Getzels, J. W., and Guba, E. G. (1957). Social Behavior and the Administrative Process. *School Review, 65,* 423–441.

Getzels, J. W., Lipham, J. M., and Campbell, R. F. (1968). *Educational Administration as a Social Process: Theory, Research, and Practice.* New York: Harper & Row.

Gibson, J. L., Ivancevich, J. M., and James H. Donnelly, J. (1976). *Organizations: Behavior, Structure, and Processes* (rev. ed.). Dallas, TX: Business Publications.

Gilligan, C. (1982). *In a Different Voice: Psychological Theory and Women's Development.* Cambridge, MA: Harvard University Press.

Gilmer, B. H. (1966). *Industrial Psychology* (2nd ed.). New York: McGraw-Hill.

Gist, M. E. (1987). Self-Efficacy: Implications for Organizational Behavior and Human Resource Management. *Academy of Management Review, 12,* (3), 472–485.

Gist, M. E., and Mitchell, T. R. (1992). Self-Efficacy: A Theoretical Analysis of Its Determinants and Malleability. *Academy of Management Review, 17,* (2), 183–211.

Glaser, B. (1965). The Local-Cosmopolitan Scientist. *American Journal of Sociology, 69,* 249–259.

Glaser, R., and Chi, M. T. H. (1989). Overview. In M. T. H. Chi, R. Glaser, and M. J. Farr (Eds.), *The Nature of Expertise* (pp. xv–xxviii). Hillsdale, NJ: Erlbaum.

Glaub, J. (1990). Made in Japan. *Illinois School Board Journal, 58,* 5–7.

Glauser, M. J. (1984). Upward Information Flow in Organizations: Review and Conceptual Analysis. *Human Relations, 8,* 613–643.

Glisson, C., and Durick, M. (1988). Predictors of Job Satisfaction and Organizational Commitment in Human Service Organizations. *Administrative Science Quarterly, 33,* 61–81.

Goffman, E. (1957). The Characteristics of Total Institutions. *Symposium on Prevention and Social Psychiatry* (pp. 43-84). Washington, DC: Walter Reed Army Institute of Research.

Goldberg, M. A. (1975). On the Efficiency of Being Efficient. *Environment and Planning, 7,* 921-939.

Goldring, E. B., and Chen, M. (1992). Preparing Empowered Teachers for Leadership. *Planning and Changing, 23,* 3-15.

Good, T. L., and Brophy, J. E. (1986). School Effects. In M. C. Wittrock (Ed.), *Handbook of Research on Teaching* (pp. 570-602). New York: Macmillan.

Goodman, P. S., and Pennings, J. M. (1977). Toward a Workable Framework. In P. S. Goodman and J. M. Pennings (Eds.), *New Perspectives on Organizational Effectiveness* (pp. 147-184). San Francisco: Jossey-Bass.

Goodstein, J. D. (1994). Institutional Pressures and Strategic Responsiveness: Employer Involvement in Work-Family Issues. *Academy of Management Journal, 37,* (2), 350-382.

Gordon, C. W. (1957). *The Social System of the High School.* New York: Free Press.

Gordon, G. E., and Rosen, N. (1981). Critical Factors in Leadership Succession. *Organizational Behavior and Human Performance, 27,* 227-254.

Gorsuch, R. A. (1977). An Investigation of the Relationships Between Core Job Dimensions, Psychological States, and Personal Work Outcomes Among Public School Teachers (Doctoral diss. University of Maryland, 1976). *Dissertation Abstracts International, 38,* 1779A.

Gouldner, A. (1950). *Studies in Leadership.* New York: Harper.

Gouldner, A. (1954). *Patterns of Industrial Bureaucracy.* New York: Free Press.

Gouldner, A. (1958). Cosmopolitans and Locals: Toward an Analysis of Latent Social Roles—II. *Administrative Science Quarterly, 3,* 444-479.

Gouldner, A. (1959). Organizational Analysis. In R. K. Merton, L. Broom, J. Leonard, and S. Cottrell (Eds.), *Sociology Today* (pp. 400-428). New York: Basic Books.

Govindarajan, V. (1988). A Contingency Approach to Strategy Implementation at the Business-Unit Level: Integrating Administrative Mechanisms with Strategy. *Academy of Management Journal, 31,* 828-853.

Graen, G. (1963). Instrumentality Theory of Work Motivation: Some Experimental Results and Suggested Modifications. *Journal of Applied Psychology Monograph, 53,* 1-25.

Graham, L. L. (1980). Expectancy theory as a predictor of college student grade point average, satisfaction, and participation. Doctoral diss., University of Kansas, Lawrence.

Graham, S. (1991). A Review of Attribution Theory in Achievement Contexts. *Educational Psychology Review, 3,* (1), 5-39.

Grandori, A. (1984). A Prescriptive Contingency View of Organizational Decision Making. *Administrative Science Quarterly, 29,* 192-208.

Grassie, M. C., and Carss, B. W. (1973). School Structure, Leadership Quality, Teacher Satisfaction. *Educational Administration Quarterly, 9,* 15-26.

Gray, J. (1992). *Men Are from Mars, Women Are from Venus.* New York: HarperCollins.

Greene, C. N., and Podsakoff, P. M. (1981). Effects of Withdrawal of a Performance Contingent Reward of Supervisory Influence and Power. *Academy of Management Journal, 24,* 527–542.

Greenfield, T. B. (1975). Theory About Organizations: A New Perspective and Its Implications for Schools. In M. Hughes (Ed.), *Administering Education: International Challenge* (pp. 77–79) London: Athlone.

Greenfield, T. B., and Ribbins, P. (Eds.). (1993). *Greenfield on Educational Administration: Towards a Human Science.* London: Routledge.

Griffeth, R. W. (1985). Moderation of the Effects of Job Enrichment by Participation: A Longitudinal Field Experiment. *Organizational Behavior and Human Decision Processes, 35,* 73–93.

Griffin, R. W. (1983). Objective and Social Sources of Information in Task Redesign: A Field Experiment. *Administrative Science Quarterly, 28,* 184–200.

Griffin, R. W. (1987). Toward an Integrated Theory of Task Design. *Research in Organizational Behavior, 9,* 79–120.

Griffin, R. W. (1991). Effects of Work Redesign on Employee Perceptions, Attitudes, and Behaviors: A Long-Term Investigation. *Academy of Management Journal, 34,*(2), 425–435.

Griffiths, D. E. (1959). *Administrative Theory.* New York: Appleton-Century-Crofts.

Griffiths, D. E. (1988). Administrative Theory. In N. Boyan (Ed.), *Handbook of Research on Educational Administration* (pp. 27–51). New York: Longman.

Griffiths, D. E. (1994). Theoretical Pluralism in Educational Administration. In R. B. Donmoyer, J. Schurich, and M. L. Imber (Eds.), *The Knowledge Base in Educational Administration: Multiple Perspectives.* Albany: SUNY Press.

Griffiths, D. E., Goldman, S., and McFarland, W. J. (1965). Teacher Mobility in New York City. *Educational Administration Quarterly, 1,* 15–31.

Griffiths, D. E., Stout, R. T., and Forsyth, P. B. (1988). The Preparation of Educational Administrators. In D. E. Griffiths, R. T. Stout, and P. B. Forsyth (Eds.), *Leaders for America's Schools* (pp. 284–304). Berkeley, CA: McCutchan.

Gross, E., and Etzioni, A. (1985). *Organizations in Society.* Englewood Cliffs, NJ: Prentice-Hall.

Grusky, O. (1960). Administrative Succession in Formal Organizations. *Social Forces, 39,* 105–115.

Grusky, O. (1961). Corporate Size, Bureaucratization, and Managerial Succession. *American Journal of Sociology, 67,* 261–269.

Guest, R. H. (1960). *Organizational Change: The Effect of Successful Leadership.* Homewood, IL: Dorsey.

Guidette, M. R. M. (1982). The relationship between bureaucracy and staff sense of powerlessness in secondary schools. Doctoral diss., Rutgers University, New Brunswick.

Guzzo, J. R. (1979). Types of Rewards, Cognitions, and Work Motivation. *Academy of Management Review, 4,* 75–86.

Guzzo, R. A. (1988). Productivity Research: Reviewing Psychological and Economic Perspectives. In J. P. Campbell and R. J. Campbell (Eds.), *Productivity in Organizations* (pp. 63–81). San Francisco: Jossey-Bass.

Hackman, J. R., and Oldham, G. R. (1975). Development of the Job Diagnostic Survey. *Journal of Applied Psychology, 60,* 159–170.

Hackman, J. R., and Oldham, G. R. (1976). Motivation Through the Design of Work: A Test of a Theory. *Organizational Behavior and Human Performance, 16,* 250–279.

Hackman, J. R., and Oldham, G. R. (1980). *Work Redesign.* Reading, MA: Addison-Wesley.

Hackman, J. R., and Suttle, J. L. (1977). *Improving Life at Work.* Santa Monica, CA: Goodyear.

Hage, J. (1980). *Theories of Organizations.* New York: Wiley.

Hajnal, V. J., and Dibski, D. J. (1993). Compensation Management: Coherence Between Organization Directions and Teacher Needs. *Journal of Educational Administration, 31,* (1), 53–69.

Hall, O. (1954). Some Problems in the Provision of Medical Services. *Canadian Journal of Economics and Political Science, 20,* 456–466.

Hall, R. H. (1962). The Concept of Bureaucracy: An Empirical Assessment. *American Sociological Review, 27,* 295–308.

Hall, R. H. (1980). Effectiveness Theory and Organizational Effectiveness. *Journal of Applied Behavioral Science, 16,* 536–545.

Hall, R. H. (1986). *Dimensions of Work.* Beverly Hills, CA: Sage.

Hall, R. H. (1987). *Organizations: Structures, Processes, and Outcomes* (4th ed.). Englewood Cliffs, NJ: Prentice-Hall.

Hall, R. H. (1991). *Organizations: Structures, Processes, and Outcomes* (5th ed.). Englewood Cliffs, NJ: Prentice-Hall.

Hall, R. H., Haas, J. E., and Johnson, N. (1967). An Examination of the Blau-Scott and Etzioni Typologies. *Administrative Science Quarterly, 12,* 118–139.

Haller, E. J., and Monk, D. H. (1988). New Reforms, Old Reforms, and the Consolidation of Small Rural Schools. *Educational Administration Quarterly, 24,* 470–483.

Halpin, A. W. (Ed.), (1958). *Administrative Theory in Education.* Chicago: Midwest Administration Center, University of Chicago.

Halpin, A. W. (1966). *Theory and Research in Administration.* New York: Macmillan.

Halpin, A. W., and Croft, D. B. (1963). *The Organization Climate of Schools.* Chicago: Midwest Administration Center of the University of Chicago.

Halpin, A. W., and Croft, D. B. (1962). *The Organization Climate of Schools.* Contract #SAE 543-8639. U. S. Office of Education, Research Project.

Halpin, A. W., and Winer, B. J. (1952). *The Leadership Behavior of the Airplane Commander.* Washington, DC: Human Resources Research Laboratories, Department of the Air Force.

Hannum, J. (1994). The organizational climate of middle schools, teacher efficacy, and student achievement. Doctoral diss., Rutgers University, New Brunswick.

Hanson, E. M. (1991). *Educational Administration and Organizational Behavior.* Boston: Allyn & Bacon.

Hanushek, E. A. (1989). The Impact of Differential Expenditures on School Performance. *Educational Researcher, 18,* 45–51, 62.

Hardy, Charles B. (1993). *Understanding Organizations.* New York: Oxford University Press.

Harris, T. E. (1993). *Applied Organizational Communication.* Hillsdale, NJ: Erlbaum.

Harrison, M. I. (1987). *Diagnosing Organizations: Methods, Models, and Processes.* Newbury Park, CA: Sage.

Hart, A. W. (1987). A Career Ladder's Effect on Teacher Career and Work Attitudes. *American Educational Research Journal, 24,* (4), 479–503.

Hart, A. W. (1990a). Impacts of the School Social Unit on Teacher Authority During Work Redesign. *American Education Research Journal, 27,* (3), 503–532.

Hart, A. W. (1990b). Work Redesign: A Review of Literature for Education Reform. *Advances in Research and Theories of School Management, 1,* 31–69.

Hart, A. W. (1993). *Principal Succession: Establishing Leadership in Schools.* Albany, NY: State University of New York Press.

Hart, A. W. and Murphy, M. J. (1990). New Teachers React to Redesigned Teacher Work. *American Journal of Education, 93,* (3), 224–250.

Hartley, M., and Hoy, W. K. (1972). Openness of School Climate and Alienation of High School Students. *California Journal of Educational Research, 23,* 17–24.

Hatry, H. P., and Greiner, J. M. (1985). *Issues and Case Studies in Teacher Incentive Plans.* Washington, DC: Urban Institute Press.

Hayes, A. E. (1973). A Reappraisal of the Halpin-Croft Model of the Organizational Climate of Schools. Annual Meeting of the American Educational Research Association, New Orleans.

Haymond, J. E. (1982). Bureaucracy, climate, and loyalty: an Aston study in education. Doctoral diss., Rutgers University, New Brunswick.

Haynes, P. A. (1974). Towards a Concept of Monitoring. *Town Planning Review, 45,* 6–29.

Heath, D. H. (1970). Student Alienation and Schools. *School Review, 78,* 515–528.

Heintzman, M., Leathers, D. G., Parrot, R. L., and Adrian Bennett Cairns, I. (1993). Nonverbal Rapport-Building Behaviors' Effects on Perceptions of a Supervisor. *Management Communication Quarterly, 7,* (2), 181–208.

Heller, F., Drenth, P., Koopman, P., and Rus, V. (1988). *Decisions in Organizations.* Beverly Hills, CA: Sage.

Hellriegel, D., Slocum, J. W., and Woodman, R. W. (1992). *Organizational Behavior* (6th ed.). St. Paul, MN: West.

Hemphill, J. K., and Coons, A. E. (1950). *Leader Behavior Description Questionnaire.* Columbus: Personnel Research Board, Ohio State University.

Henderson, J. E., and Hoy, W. K. (1983). Leader Authenticity: The Development and Test of an Operational Measure. *Educational and Psychological Research, 2,* 123–130.

Heneman, H. G. I., and Schwab, D. P. (1972). An Evaluation of Research on Expectancy Theory Predictions of Employee Performance. *Psychological Bulletin, 78,* 1–9.

Herrick, H. S. (1973). *The Relationship of Organizational Structure to Teacher Motivation in Multiunit and Non-multiunit Elementary Schools No. 322.* Madison: Wisconsin Research and Development Center for Cognitive Learning, University of Wisconsin.

Herriott, R. F., and Firestone, W. A. (1984). Two Images of Schools as Organizations: A Refinement and Elaboration. *Educational Administration Quarterly, 20,* 41–58.

Hersey, P. W. (1982). *The NASSP Assessment Center: Validation and New Development.* Reston, VA: National Association of Secondary School Principals.

Herzberg, F. (1966). *Work and the Nature of Man.* Cleveland: World.

Herzberg, F. (1982). *The Managerial Choice: To be Efficient and to be Human* (Rev. ed.). Salt Lake City, UT: Olympus.

Herzberg, F., Mausner, B., and Snyderman, B. (1959). *The Motivation to Work.* New York: Wiley.

Heydebrand, W. (1977). Organizational Contradictions in Public Bureaucracies: Toward a Marxian Theory of Organization. In J. K. Benson (Ed.), *Organizational Analysis* (pp. 85–109). Beverly Hills, CA: Sage.

Hickson, D., Butler, R., Gray, D., Mallory, G., and Wilson, D. (1986). *Top Decisions: Strategic Decision Making in Organizations.* Oxford: Basil Blackwell.

Hill, P. T., and Bonan, J. (1991). *Decentralization and Accountability in Public Education.* Santa Monica, CA: Rand.

Hirchman, A. O. (1970). *Exit, Voice, and Loyalty: Responses to the Decline in Firms, Organizations, and States.* Cambridge, MA: Harvard University Press.

Hitt, M. A., and Ireland, R. D. (1987). Peters and Waterman Revisited: The Unended Quest for Excellence. *Academy of Management Executive, 1,* 91–98.

Hodgkinson, C. (1978). *Towards a Philosophy of Administration.* Oxford: Blackwell.

Hodgkinson, C. (1991). *Educational Leadership: The Moral Art.* Albany, NY: State University of New York Press.

Hoffman, J. D. (1993). The organizational climate of middle schools and dimensions of authenticity and trust. Doctoral diss., Rutgers University, New Brunswick.

Hoffman, J. D., Sabo, D., Bliss, J., and Hoy, W. K. (1994). Building a Culture of Trust. *Journal of School Leadership, 3,* x.

Holdaway, E. A. (1978a). Facet and Overall Satisfaction of Teachers. *Educational Administration Quarterly, 14,* 30–47.

Holdaway, E. A. (1978b). *Job Satisfaction: An Alberta Report.* Edmonton: University of Alberta.

Holdaway, E. A., Newberry, J. F., Hickson, D. J., and Heron, R. P. (1975). Dimensions of Organizations in Complex Societies: The Educational Sector. *Administrative Science Quarterly, 20,* 37–58.

Holmes Group. (1986). *Tomorrow's Teachers.* East Lansing, MI: Holmes Group.

Homans, G. C. (1950). *The Human Group.* New York: Harcourt, Brace and World.

Hoppock, R. (1935). *Job Satisfaction.* New York: Harper.

House, R. J. (1971). A Path-Goal Theory of Leadership Effectiveness. *Administrative Science Quarterly, 16,* 321–338.

House, R. J. (1973). A Path-Goal Theory of Leader Effectiveness. In E. A. Fleishman and J. G. Hunt (Eds.), *Current Developments in the Study of Leadership* (pp. 141–177). Carbondale, IL: Southern Illinois University Press.

House, R. J. (1977). A 1976 Theory of Charismatic Leadership. In J. G. Hunt and L. L. Larson (Eds.), *Leadership: The Cutting Edge* (pp. 189–207). Carbondale, IL: Southern Illinois University Press.

House, R. J. (1988). Leadership Research: Some Forgotten, Ignored, or Overlooked Findings. In J. G. Hunt, B. R. Baliga, H. P. Dachler, and C. A. Schriesheim (Eds.), *Emerging Leadership Vistas* (pp. 245–260). Lexington, MA: Lexington.

House, R. J., and Baetz, M. L. (1979). Leadership: Some Empirical Generalizations and New Research Directions. *Research in Organizational Behavior, 1,* 341–423.

House, R. J., and Howell, J. M. (1992). Personality and Charismatic Leadership. *Leadership Quarterly, 3,* (2), 81–108.

House, R. J., and Mitchell, T. R. (1974). Path-Goal Theory and Leadership. *Journal of Contemporary Business, 3,* 81–97.

House, R. J., Spangler, W. D., and Woycke, J. (1991). Personality and Charisma in the U.S. Presidency: A Psychological Theory of Leader Effectiveness. *Administrative Science Quarterly, 36,* 364–396.

Howell, J. M., and Avolio, B. J. (1993). Transformational Leadership, Transactional Leadership, Locus of Control, and Support of Innovation: Key Predictors of Consolidated Business-Unit Performance. *Journal of Applied Psychology, 78,* (6), 891–902.

Howell, J. M., and Frost, P. J. (1989). A Laboratory Study of Charismatic Leadership. *Organizational Behavior and Human Decision Processes, 43,* 243–269.

Hoy, W. K. (1967). Organizational Socialization: The Student Teacher and Pupil Control Ideology. *Journal of Educational Research, 61,* 153–155.

Hoy, W. K. (1968). Pupil Control and Organizational Socialization: The Influence of Experience on the Beginning Teacher. *School Review, 76,* 312–323.

Hoy, W. K. (1969). Pupil Control Ideology and Organizational Socialization: A Further Examination of the Influence of Experience on the Beginning Teacher. *School Review, 77,* 257–265.

Hoy, W. K. (1972). Dimensions of Student Alienation and Characteristics of Public High Schools. *Interchange, 3,* 38–51.

Hoy, W. K. (1978). Scientific Research in Educational Administration. *Educational Administration Quarterly, 14,* 1–12.

Hoy, W. K. (1990). Organizational Climate and Culture: A Conceptual Analysis of the School Workplace. *Journal of Educational and Psychological Consultation, 1,* 149–168.

Hoy, W. K., and Aho, F. (1973). Patterns of Succession of High School Principals and Organizational Change. *Planning and Changing, 2,* 82–88.

Hoy, W. K., and Appleberry, J. B. (1970). Teacher Principal Relationships in "Humanistic" and "Custodial" Elementary Schools. *Journal of Experimental Education, 39,* 27–31.

Hoy, W. K., Astuto, T. A., and Forsyth, P. B. (Eds.) (1994). *Educational Administration: The UCEA Document Base.* New York: McGraw-Hill Primus.

Hoy, W. K., Blazovsky, R., and Newland, W. (1983). Bureaucracy and Alienation: A Comparative Analysis. *The Journal of Educational Administration, 21,* 109–121.

Hoy, W. K., Blazovsky, R., and Newland, W. (1980). Organizational Structure and Alienation from Work. Annual Meeting of the American Educational Research Association, Boston.

Hoy, W. K., and Brown, B. L. (1988). Leadership Behavior of Principals and the Zone of Acceptance of Elementary Teachers. *Journal of Educational Administration, 26,* 23–39.

Hoy, W. K., and Clover, S. I. R. (1986). Elementary School Climate: A Revision of the OCDQ. *Educational Administration Quarterly, 22,* 93–110.

Hoy, W. K., and Feldman, J. (1987). Organizational Health. The Concept and Its Measure. *Journal of Research and Development in Education, 20,* 30–38.

Hoy, W. K., and Ferguson, J. (1985). A Theoretical Framework and Exploration of Organizational Effectiveness in Schools. *Educational Administration Quarterly, 21,* 117–134.

Hoy, W. K., and Forsyth, P. B. (1987). Beyond Clinical Supervision: A Classroom Performance Model. *Planning and Changing, 18,* 210–223.

Hoy, W. K., and Forsyth, P. B. (1986). *Effective Supervision: Theory into Practice.* New York: Random House.

Hoy, W. K., and Henderson, J. E. (1983). Principal Authenticity, School Climate, and Pupil-Control Orientation. *Alberta Journal of Educational Research, 2,* 123–130.

Hoy, W. K., Hoffman, J., Sabo, D., and Bliss, J. (1994). *The Organizational Climate of Middle Schools: The Development and Test of the OCDQ-RM.* Forthcoming.

Hoy, W. K., and Miskel, C. G. (1991). *Educational Administration: Theory, Research, and Practice* (4th ed.). New York: McGraw-Hill.

Hoy, W. K., Newland, W., and Blazovsky, R. (1977). Subordinate Loyalty to Superior, Esprit, and Aspects of Bureaucratic Structure. *Educational Administration Quarterly, 13,* 71–85.

Hoy, W. K., and Sousa, D. (1984). Delegation: The Neglected Aspect of Participation in Decision Making. *Alberta Journal of Educational Research, 30,* 320–331.

Hoy, W. K., and Rees, R. (1977). The Bureaucratic Socialization of Student Teachers. *Journal of Teacher Education, 28,* 23–26.

Hoy, W. K., and Rees, R. (1974). Subordinate Loyalty to Immediate Superior: A Neglected Concept in the Study of Educational Administration. *Sociology of Education, 47,* 268–286.

Hoy, W. K., and Tarter, C. J. (1990). Organizational climate school health and student achievement: a comparative analysis. Unpublished paper.

Hoy, W. K., and Tarter, C. J. (1992). Collaborative Decision Making: Empowering Teachers. *Canadian Administration, 32,* 1–9.

Hoy, W. K., and Tarter, C. J. (1993a). A Normative Model of Shared Decision Making. *Journal of Educational Administration, 31,* 4–19.

Hoy, W. K., and Tarter, C. J. (1993b). Crafting Strategies, Not Contriving Solutions: A Response to Downey and Knight's Observations on Shared Decision Making. *Canadian Administration, 32,* 1–6.

Hoy, W. K., and Tarter, C. J. (1995). *Administrator Solving the Problems of Practice: Decision-Making Concepts, Cases, and Consequences.* Boston: Allyn & Bacon.

Hoy, W. K., Tarter, C. J., and Kottkamp, R. (1991). *Open Schools/Healthy Schools: Measuring Organizational Climate.* Beverly Hills, CA: Sage.

Hoy, W. K., Tarter, C. J., and Wiskowskie, L. (1992). Faculty Trust in Colleagues: Linking the Principal with School Effectiveness. *Journal of Research and Development in Education, 26,* (1), 38-58.

Hoy, W. K., and Williams, L. B. (1971). Loyalty to Immediate Superior at Alternate Levels in Public Schools. *Educational Administration Quarterly, 7,* 1-11.

Hoy, W. K., and Woolfolk, A. E. (1989). Socialization of Student Teachers. Annual Meeting of the American Educational Research Association, San Francisco.

Hoy, W. K., and Woolfolk, A. E. (1990). Socialization of Student Teachers. *American Educational Research Journal, 27,* (2), 279-300.

Hoy, W. K., and Woolfolk, A. E. (1993). Teachers' Sense of Efficacy and the Organizational Health of Schools. *Elementary School Journal, 93,* (4), 355-372.

Huber, G. P., and Daft, R. L. (1987). The Information Environments of Organizations. In F. M. Jablin, L. L. Putnam, K. Roberts, and L. W. Porter (Eds.), *Handbook of Organizational Communication: An Interdisciplinary Perspective* (pp. 130-164). Newbury Park, CA: Sage.

Huber, V. L. (1981). The Sources, Uses, and Conservation of Managerial Power. *Personnel, 51,* 66-67.

Hunt, J. G. (1991). *Leadership: A New Synthesis.* Newbury Park, CA: Sage.

Hunter, F. (1953). *Community Power Structure.* Chapel Hill, NC: University of North Carolina Press.

Huseman, R. C., and Miles, E. W. (1988). Organizational Communication in the Information Age: Implications of Computer-Based Systems. *Journal of Management, 14,* 181-204.

Huyssen, A. (1984). Mapping the Postmodern. *The New German Critique, 33,* 22-52.

Iannaccone, L. (1962). Informal Organization of School Systems. In D. Griffiths, D. L. Clark, R. Wynn, and L. Iannacone (Eds.), *Organizing Schools for Effective Education* (pp. 227-293). Danville, IL: Interstate.

Ilgen, D. R., and Hollenbeck, J. R. (1991). The Structure of Work: Job Design and Roles. In M. D. Dunnette and L. M. Hough (Eds.), *Handbook of Industrial and Organizational Psychology.* Palo Alto, CA: Consulting Psychologists Press.

Imber, M. (1983). Increased Decision Making Involvement for Teachers: Ethical and Practical Considerations. *Journal of Educational Thought, 17,* 36-42.

Imber, M., and Duke, D. L. (1984). Teacher Participation in School Decision Making: A Framework for Research. *Journal of Educational Administration, 22,* 24-34.

Immegart, G. L. (1988). Leadership and Leader Behavior. In N. J. Boyan (Ed.), *Handbook of Research on Educational Administration* (pp. 259-277). New York: Longman.

Ingersoll, R. M. (1993). Loosely Coupled Organizations Revisited. *Research in the Sociology of Organizations, 11,* 81-112.

Isaacson, G. (1983). Leadership behavior and loyalty. Doctoral diss., Rutgers University, New Brunswick.

Isherwood, G., and Hoy, W. K. (1973). Bureaucracy, Powerlessness, and Teacher Work Values. *Journal of Educational Administration, 9,* 124-138.

Jablin, F. M. (1987). Formal Organization Structure. In F. M. Jablin, L. L. Putman, K. Roberts, and L. W. Porter (Eds.), *Handbook of Organizational Communication: An Interdisciplinary Perspective* (pp. 389-419). Newbury Park, CA: Sage.

Jablin, F. M. (1980). Organizational Communication Theory and Research: An Overview of Communication Climate and Network Research. *Communication Yearbook, 4,* 327-347.

Jablin, F. M., Putnam, L. L., Roberts, K., and Porter, L. W. (Eds.), (1987). *Handbook of Organizational Communication: An Interdisciplinary Perspective.* Newbury Park, CA: Sage.

Jamison, D., Suppes, P., and Wells, S. (1974). The Effectiveness of Alternative Instructional Media: A Survey. *Review of Educational Research, 44,* 1-67.

Janis, I. L. (1982). *Groupthink: Psychological Studies of Policy Decisions and Fiascoes.* Boston: Houghton Mifflin.

Janis, I. L. (1985). Sources of Error in Strategic Decision Making. In J. M. Pennings (Ed.), *Organizational Strategy and Change* (pp. 157-197). San Francisco: Jossey-Bass.

Janis, I. L., and Mann, L. (1977). *Decision Making: A Psychological Analysis of Conflict, Choice, and Commitment.* New York: Free Press.

Jepperson, R. L. (1991). Institutions, Institutional Effects, and Institutionalism. In W. W. Powell and P. J. DiMaggio (Eds.), *The New Institutionalism in Organizational Analysis* (pp. 164-182). Chicago: University of Chicago Press.

Johns, G., Xie, J. L., and Fang, Y. (1992). Mediating and Moderating Effects in Job Design. *Journal of Management, 18,* (4), 657-676.

Johnson, S. M. (1986). Incentives for Teachers: What Motivates, What Matters. *Educational Administration Quarterly, 22,* 54-79.

Jurkovich, R. (1974). A Core Typology of Organizational Environments. *Administrative Science Quarterly, 19,* 380-394.

Kahneman, D., Solvic, P., and Tversky, A. (1982). *Judgment Under Uncertainty: Heuristics and Biases.* Cambridge, England: Cambridge University Press.

Kanfer, R. (1990). Motivation theory and industrial organizational psychology. In M. D. Dunnette and L. M. Hough (Eds.), *Handbook of Industrial and Organizational Psychology* (pp. 75-170). Palo Alto, CA: Consulting Psychologists Press.

Kanner, L. (1974). Machiavellianism and the secondary schools: teacher-principal relations. Doctoral diss., Rutgers University, New Brunswick.

Kanter, R. (1977). *Men and Women of the Corporation.* New York: Basic Books.

Kanter, R., and Brinkerhoff, D. (1981). Organizational Performance: Recent Developments in Measurement. *Annual Review of Sociology, 7,* 321-349.

Karper, J. H., and Boyd, W. L. (1988). Interest Groups and the Changing Environment of State Educational Policymaking: Developments in Pennsylvania. *Educational Administration Quarterly, 24,* 21-54.

Katz, D., and Kahn, R. L. (1966). *The Social Psychology of Organizations.* New York: Wiley.

Katz, D., and Kahn, R. L. (1978). *The Social Psychology of Organizations* (2nd ed.). New York: Wiley.

Katz, D., Maccoby, N., and Morse, N. (1950). *Productivity, Supervision, and Morale in an Office Situation.* Detroit: Darel.

Katzell, R. A., and Thompson, D. E. (1990). Work Motivation: Theory and Practice. *American Psychologist, 45,* (2), 144-153.

Keeley, M. (1984). Impartiality and Participant-Interest Theories of Organizational Effectiveness. *Administrative Science Quarterly, 29,* 1-25.

Kelly, J. (1992). Does Job Re-Design Theory Explain Job Re-Design Outcomes? *Human Relations, 45,* (8), 753-774.

Kelsey, J. G. T. (1973). Conceptualization and instrumentation for the comparative study of secondary school structure and operation. Doctoral. diss., University of Alberta, Edmonton.

Kerlinger, F. N. (1986). *Foundations of Behavioral Research* (3rd ed.). New York: Holt Rinehart & Winston.

Kerr, S., and Jermier, J. M. (1978). Substitutes for Leadership: Their Meaning and Measurement. *Organizational Behavior and Human Performance, 22,* 375-403.

Kiggundu, M. N. (1980). An Empirical Test of the Theory of Job Design Using Multiple Job Ratings. *Human Relations, 33,* 339-351.

Kilmann, R. H. (1984). *Beyond the Quick Fix.* San Francisco: Jossey-Bass.

Kilmann, R. H., and Saxton, M. J. (1983). *The Kilmann-Saxton Culture Gap Survey.* Pittsburgh, PA: Organizational Design Consultant.

Kilmann, R. H., Saxton, M. J., and Serpa, R. (1985). *Gaining Control of the Corporate Culture.* San Francisco: Jossey-Bass.

Kim, J. S. (1984). Effect of Behavior Plus Outcome Goal Setting and Feedback on Employee Satisfaction and Performance. *Academy of Management Journal, 27,* 139-149.

Kimbrough, R. (1964). *Political Power and Educational Decision Making.* Chicago: Rand McNally.

King, N. (1970). Clarification and Evaluation of the Two-Factor Theory of Job Satisfaction. *Psychological Bulletin, 74,* 18-31.

Kirchhoff, B. A. (1977). Organization Effectiveness Measurement and Policy Research. *Academy of Management Review, 2,* 347-355.

Kmetz, J. T., and Willower, D. J. (1982). Elementary School Principals' Work Behavior. *Educational Administration Quarterly, 18,* 62-78.

Knapp, M. L. (1972). *Nonverbal Communication in Human Interaction.* New York: Holt, Rinehart, & Winston.

Koberg, C. S., and Ungson, G. R. (1987). The Effects of Environmental Uncertainty and Dependence on Organizational Structure and Performance: A Comparative Study. *Journal of Management, 13,* 725-737.

Kolesar, H. (1967). An empirical study of client alienation in the bureaucratic organization. Doctoral diss., University of Alberta, Edmonton.

Kondrasuk, J. N. (1981). Studies in MBO Effectiveness. *Academy of Management Review, 6,* 419–430.

Kornhauser, W. (1962). *Scientists in Industry.* Berkeley: University of California Press.

Kotter, J. P. (1978). Power, Success, and Organizational Effectiveness. *Organizational Dynamics, 6,* 27–40.

Kotter, J. P. (1982). *The General Managers.* New York: Free Press.

Kotter, J. P. (1985). *Power and Influences: Beyond Formal Authority.* New York: Free Press.

Kotter, J. P. (1990). *A Force for Change: How Leadership Differs from Management.* New York: Free Press.

Kottkamp, R. B., and Mulhern, J. A. (1987). Teacher Expectance Motivation, Open to Closed Climate and Pupil Control Ideology in High Schools. *Journal of Research and Development in Education, 20,* 9–18.

Kottkamp, R. B., Mulhern, J., and Hoy, W. K. (1987). Secondary School Climate: A Revision of the OCDQ. *Educational Administration Quarterly, 23,* 31–48.

Kraiger, K. J., Ford, J. K., and Salas, E. (1993). Application of Cognitive, Skill-based, and Affective Theories of Learning Outcomes to New Methods of Training Evaluation. *Journal of Applied Psychology, 78,* (2), 311–328.

Krone, K. J., Jablin, F. M., and Putnam, L. L. (1987). Communication Theory and Organizational Communication: Multiple Perspectives. In F. M. Jablin, L. L. Putnam, K. Roberts, and L. W. Porter (Eds.), *Handbook of Organizational Communication: An Interdisciplinary Perspective* (pp. 18–40). Newbury Park, CA: Sage.

Kuhlman, E., and Hoy, W. K. (1974). The Socialization of Professionals into Bureaucracies: The Beginning Teacher in the School. *Journal of Educational Administration, 8,* 18–27.

Kuhnert, K. W., and Lewis, P. (1987). Transactional and Transformational Leadership: A Constructive/Developmental Analysis. *Academy of Management Review, 12,* (4), 648–657.

Kunz, D., and Hoy, W. K. (1976). Leader Behavior of Principals and the Professional Zone of Acceptance of Teachers. *Educational Administration Quarterly, 12,* 49–64.

Labaree, D. F. (1992). Power, Knowledge, and the Rationalization of Teaching: A Genealogy of the Movement to Professionalize Teaching. *Harvard Educational Review, 62,* (2), 123–154.

Landy, F. J., and Becker, W. S. (1987). Motivation Theory Reconsidered. *Research in Organizational Behavior, 9,* 1–38.

Larson, J. R. J. (1989). The Dynamic Interplay Between Employee's Feedback-Seeking Strategies and Supervisors' Delivery of Performance Feedback. *Academy of Management Review, 14,* 408–422.

Lasagna, J. B. (1971). Make Your MBO Pragmatic. *Harvard Business Review, 49,* 64–69.

Latham, G. P., and Locke, E. A. (1991). Self-Regulation Through Goal Setting. *Organizational Behavior and Human Decision Processes, 50,* 212–247.

Latham, G. P., and Yukl, G. A. (1975). A Review of Research on the Application of Goal Setting in Organizations. *Academy of Management Journal, 18,* 824–845.

Lau, L. J. (1978). Education Production Functions. Conference on School Organization and Effects, National Institute of Education, Washington, DC.

Lawler, E. E., III. (1973). *Motivation in Work Organizations.* Monterey, CA: Brooks/Cole.

Lawler, E. E., III. (1985). Education, Management Style, and Organizational Effectiveness. *Personnel Psychology, 38,* 1–26.

Lawler, E. E., III. (1987). The Design of Effective Reward Systems. In J. W. Lorsch (Ed.), *Handbook of Organizational Behavior* (pp. 225–271). Englewood Cliffs, NJ: Prentice-Hall.

Lawler, E. E., III. (1992). *The Ultimate Advantage.* San Francisco, CA: Jossey-Bass.

Lawler, E. E., III. (1994). Total Quality Management and Employee Involvement: Are They Compatible? *Academy of Management Executive, 8,* (1), 68–76.

Lawrence, P. R. (1992). The Challenge of Problem-Oriented Research. *Journal of Management Inquiry, 1,* 139–142.

Lawrence, P. R., and Lorsch, J. W. (1967). *Organization and Environment: Managing Differentiation and Integration.* Boston: Graduate School of Business Administration, Harvard University.

Leavitt, H. J., Dill, W. R., and Eyring, H. B. (1973). *The Organizational World.* New York: Harcourt Brace Jovanovich.

Lee, V. E., Bryk, A. S., and Smith, J. B. (1993). The Organization of Effective Secondary Schools. *Review of Research in Education, 19,* 171–267.

Lefkowitz, J., Somers, M. J., and Weinberg, K. (1984). The Role of Need Level and/or Need Salience as Moderators of the Relationship between Need Satisfaction and Work Alienation-Involvement. *Journal of Vocational Behavior, 24,* 142–158.

Leithwood, K. (1994). Leadership for School Restructuring. *Educational Administration Quarterly, 30,* (4), 498–518.

Lensky, H. W. (1959). *Intellectuals in Labor Unions.* New York: Free Press.

Leonard, J. F. (1991). Applying Deming's Principles to Our Schools. *South Carolina Business, 11,* 82–87.

Level, D. A., Jr. (1972). Communication Effectiveness: Method and Situation. *Journal of Business Communication, 9,* 19–25.

Leverette, B. B. (1984). Professional zone of acceptance: its relation to the leader behavior of principals and socio-psychological characteristics of teaching. Doctoral diss., Rutgers University, New Brunswick.

Levitt, B., and Nass, C. (1989). The Lid on the Garbage Can: Institutional Constraints on Decision Making in The Technical Core of College-Text Publishers. *Administrative Science Quarterly, 34,* 190–207.

Lewin, K. (1938). *The Conceptual Representation and the Measurement of Psychological Forces.* Durham, NC: Duke University Press.

Lewis, P. V. (1975). *Organizational Communications: The Essence of Effective Management.* Columbus, OH: Grid.

Liao, Y. M. (1994). School climate and effectiveness in Taiwan's secondary schools. Doctoral diss., St. John's University, Queens.

Licata, J. W., and Hack, W. G. (1980). School Administrator Grapevine Structure. *Educational Administration Quarterly, 16,* 82–99.

Lieberson, S., and O'Connor, J. F. (1972). Leadership and Organizational Performance: A Study of Large Corporations. *American Sociological Review, 37,* 117–130.

Lindblom, C. E. (1959). The Science of Muddling Through. *Public Administrative Review, 19,* 79–99.

Lindblom, C. E. (1965). *The Intelligence of Democracy: Decision Making Through Mutual Adjustment.* New York: Free Press.

Lindblom, C. E. (1968). *The Policy-Making Process.* Englewood Cliffs, NJ: Prentice-Hall.

Lindblom, C. E. (1980). *The Policy-Making Process* (2nd ed.). Englewood Cliffs: Prentice-Hall.

Lindblom, C. E., and Cohen, D. K. (1979). *Usable Knowledge: Social Science and Social Problem Solving.* New Haven, CT: Yale University Press.

Lipham, J. A. (1964). Leadership and Administration. In D. Griffiths (Ed.), *Behavioral Science and Educational Administration, Sixty-Third Yearbook of the National Society for the Study of Education* (pp. 119–141). Chicago: University of Chicago Press.

Lipham, J. A. (1988). Getzel's Model in Educational Administration. In N. J. Boyan (Ed.), *Handbook of Research on Educational Administration* (pp. 171–184). New York: Longman.

Lipham, J. A., and Francke, D. C. (1966). Nonverbal Behavior of Administrators. *Educational Administration Quarterly, 2,* 101–109.

Litchfield, E. H. (1956). Notes on a General Theory of Administration. *Administrative Science Quarterly, 1,* 3–29.

Litwin, G. H., and Stringer, R. A., Jr. (1968). *Motivation and Organizational Climate.* Boston: Harvard University Press.

Locke, E. A. (1968). Toward a Theory of Task Motivation and Incentives. *Organizational Behavior and Human Performance, 3,* 157–189.

Locke, E. A. (1976). The Nature and Causes of Job Satisfaction. In M. D. Dunnette (Ed.), *Handbook of Industrial and Organizational Psychology* (pp. 1297–1349). Chicago: Rand McNally.

Locke, E. A. (1991a). Introduction to Special Issue. *Organizational Behavior and Human Decision Processes, 50,* 151–153.

Locke, E. A. (1991b). The Motivation Sequence, the Motivation Hub, and the Motivation Core. *Organizational Behavior and Human Decision Processes, 50,* 288–299.

Locke, E. A., and Latham, G. P. (1984). *Goal Setting: A Motivational Technique That Works.* Englewood Cliffs, NJ: Prentice-Hall.

Locke, E. A., and Latham, G. P. (1990). *A Theory of Goal Setting and Task Performance.* Englewood Cliffs, NJ: Prentice-Hall.

Locke, E. A., Latham, G. P., and Erez, M. (1988). The Determinants of Goal Commitment. *Academy of Management Review, 13,* 23–39.

Locke, E. A., and Schweiger, D. M. (1979). Participation in Decision Making: One More Look. *Research in Organizational Behavior, 1,* 265-339.

Locke, E. A., Shaw, K. N., Saari, L. M., and Latham, G. P. (1981). Goal Setting and Task Performance. *Psychological Review, 90,* 125-152.

Logan, C. S., Ellet, C. D., and Licata, J. W. (1993). Structural Coupling, Robustness, and Effectiveness of Schools. *Journal of Educational Administration, 31,* (1), 19-32.

Lord, R. G., and Hall, R. J. (1992). Contemporary Views of Leadership and Individual Differences. *Leadership Quarterly, 3,* (3), 137-157.

Lord, R. G., and Maher, K. J. (1990). Alternative Information Processing Models and Their Implications for Theory, Research and Practice. *Academy of Management Review, 15,* (1), 9-28.

Lord, R. G., and Maher, K. J. (1991a). Cognitive Theory in Industrial and Organizational Psychology. In M. D. Dunnette and L. M. Hough (Eds.), *Handbook of Industrial and Organizational Psychology* (pp. 1-62). Palo Alto, CA: Consulting Psychologists Press.

Lord, R. G., and Maher, K. J. (1991b). *Leadership and Information Processing.* Boston: Unwin Hyman.

Lorsch, J. W. (1979). Making Behavioral Science More Useful. *Harvard Business Review, 57,* 171-180.

Lorsch, J. W. (1985). Strategic Myopia: Culture as an Invisible Barrier to Change. In R. H. Kilmann, M. J. Saxton, and R. Serpa (Eds.), *Gaining Control of the Corporate Culture* (pp. 84-102). San Francisco: Jossey-Bass.

Lortie, D. C. (1969). The Balance of Control and Autonomy in Elementary School Teaching. In A. Etzioni (Ed.), *The Semiprofessions and Their Organization* (pp. 1-53). New York: Free Press.

Lortie, D. C. (1975). *Schoolteacher: A Sociological Study.* Chicago: University of Chicago Press.

Louis, M. R. (1985). Perspectives on Organizational Cultures. In P. J. Frost, L. F. Moore, M. R. Lousi, C. C. Lundberg, and J. Martin (Eds.), *Organizational Culture* (pp. 27-29). Beverly Hills, CA: Sage.

Louis, M. R., and Sutton, R. I. (1991). Switching Cognitive Gears: From Habits of Mind to Active Thinking. *Human Relations, 44,* (1), 55-76.

Lugg, C. A., and Boyd, W. L. (1993). Leadership for Collaboration: Reducing Risk and Fostering Resilience. *Phi Delta Kappan, 75,* 252-258.

Lunenburg, F. C. (1983). Pupil Control Ideology and Self-Concept as a Learner. *Educational Research Quarterly, 8,* 33-39.

Lunenburg, F. C., and Schmidt, L. J. (1989). Pupil Control Ideology, Pupil Control Behavior, and Quality of School Life. *Journal of Research and Development in Education, 22,* 35-44.

Lysaught, J. P. (1984). Toward a Comprehensive Theory of Communications: A Review of Selected Contributions. *Educational Administration Quarterly, 20,* (3), 101-128.

Machiavelli, N. (1974). *The Prince.* New York: Dutton.

MacKay, D. (1964). An empirical study of bureaucratic dimensions and their relations to other characteristics of school organization. Doctoral diss., University of Alberta, Edmonton.

MacKensie, D. E. (1983). Research for School Improvement: An Appraisal and Some Recent Trends. *Educational Research, 12,* 5-17.

MacKinnon, J. D., and Brown, M. E. (1994). Inclusion in Secondary Schools: An Analysis of School Structure Based on Teachers' Images of Change. *Educational Administration Quarterly, 30,* 126-152.

Madaus, G. F., Airasian, P. W., and Kellaghan, T. (1980). *School Effectiveness: A Reassessment of the Evidence.* New York: McGraw-Hill.

Maehr, M. L., Midgley, C., and Urdan, T. (1992). School Leader as Motivator. *Educational Administration Quarterly, 28,* (3), 410-429.

Maeroff, G. I. (1988). *The Empowerment of Teachers: Overcoming the Crisis of Confidence.* New York: Teachers College Press.

Malen, B. (1993). Enacting site based management: a political utilities analysis. Unpublished paper, College of Education, University of Washington.

Malen, B., Murphy, M. J., and Hart, A. W. (1988). Restructuring Teacher Compensation Systems: An Analysis of Three Incentive Strategies. In K. Alexander and D. H. Monk (Eds.), *Eighth Annual Yearbook of the American Educational Finance Association* (pp. 91-142). Cambridge, MA: Ballinger.

Malen, B., Ogawa, R. T., and Kranz, J. (1990). What Do We Know About School-Based Management? A Case Study of the Literature—A Call for Research. In W. H. Clune and J. F. White (Eds.), *Choice and Control in American Education Volume 2: The Practice of Choice, Decentralization and School Restructuring* (pp. 289-342). New York: Falmer Press.

Malen, B., and Ogawa, R. T. (1992). Site-Based Management: Disconcerting Policy Issues, Critical Policy, and Choices. In J. J. Lane and E. G. Epps (Eds.), *Restructuring the Schools: Problems and Prospects* (pp. 185-206). Berkeley, CA: McCutchan.

Mann, R. D. (1959). A Review of the Relationships Between Personality and Performance. *Psychological Bulletin, 56,* 241-270.

Manning, P. K. (1992). *Organizational Communication.* New York: Aldine De Gruyer.

March, J. C., and March, J. G. (1977). Almost Random Careers: The Wisconsin School Superintendency, 1940-1974. *Administrative Science Quarterly, 22,* 377-409.

March, J. C., and March, J. G. (1978). Performance Sampling in School Matches. *Administrative Science Quarterly, 23,* 434-453.

March, J. G. (1981). Footnotes to Organizational Change. *Administrative Science Quarterly, 26,* 563-577.

March, J. G. (1982). Emerging Developments in the Study of Higher Education. *Review of Higher Education, 6,* 1-18.

March, J. G. (1988). *Decisions and Organizations.* Oxford: Blackwell.

March, J. G. (1994). *A Primer of Decision Making.* New York: Free Press.

March, J. G., and Olsen, J. P. (1976). *Ambiguity and Choice in Organization.* Bergen, Norway: Universitetsforlaget.

March, J. G., and Simon, H. (1958). *Organizations.* New York: Wiley.

March, J. G., and Simon, H. (1993). *Organizations* (2nd ed.). Cambridge, MA: Blackwell.

Marjoribanks, K. (1977). Bureaucratic Orientation, Autonomy and Professional Attitudes of Teachers. *Journal of Educational Administration, 15,* 104–113.

Mark, J. H., and Anderson, B. D. (1985). Teacher Survival Rates in St. Louis, 1969–1982. *American Educational Research Journal, 22,* 413–421.

Martin, J. (1985). Can Organizational Culture Be Managed? In P. J. Frost, L. F. Moore, M. R. Lousi, C. C. Lundberg, and J. Martin (Eds.), *Organizational Culture* (pp. 95–98). Beverly Hills, CA: Sage.

Martin, J. (1990a). Deconstructing Organizational Taboos: Suppression of Gender Conflict in Organizations. *Organizational Science, 1,* 339–359.

Martin, J. (1990b). Rereading Weber: Searching for Feminist Alternatives to Bureaucracy. Annual Meeting of the Academy of Management, San Francisco.

Martin, W. J., and Willower, D. J. (1981). The Managerial Behavior of High School Principals. *Educational Administration Quarterly, 17,* 69–90.

Martin, Y. M., Isherwood, G. B., and Lavery, R. G. (1976). Leadership Effectiveness in Teacher Probation Committees. *Educational Administration Quarterly, 12,* 87–99.

Maslow, A. H. (1965). *Eupsychian Management.* Homewood, IL: Irwin.

Maslow, A. H. (1970). *Motivation and Personality* (2nd ed.). New York: Harper & Row.

Mayo, E. (1945). *The Social Problems of an Industrial Civilization.* Boston: Graduate School of Business Administration, Harvard University.

Mazzoni, T. L., and Malen, B. (1985). Mobilizing Constituency Pressure to Influence State Education Policy Making. *Educational Administration Quarterly, 21,* 91–116.

McCabe, D. L., and Dutton, J. E. (1993). Making Sense of the Environment: The Role of Perceived Effectiveness. *Human Relations, 46,* (5), 623–643.

McCall, M. W., Jr., and Lombardo, M. M. (Eds.) (1978). *Leadership: Where Else Can We Go?* Durham, NC: Duke University Press.

McCaskey, M. B. (1979). The Hidden Messages Managers Send. *Harvard Business Review, 57,* 135–148.

McClelland, D. C. (1961). *The Achieving Society.* Princeton, NJ: Van Nostrand.

McClelland, D. C. (1965). Toward a Theory of Motive Acquisition. *American Psychologist, 20,* (5), 321–333.

McClelland, D. C. (1985). *Human Motivation.* Glenview, IL: Scott, Foresman.

McConkie, M. L. (1979). A Clarification of the Goal Setting and Appraisal Process in MBO. *Academy of Management Review, 4,* 29–40.

McElroy, J. C., and Schrader, C. B. (1986). Attribution Theories of Leadership and Network Analysis. *Journal of Management, 12,* 351–362.

McNall, S. G., and McNall, S. A. (1992). *Sociology.* Englewood Cliffs, NJ: Prentice-Hall.

McNamara, V., and Enns, F. (1966). Directive Leadership and Staff Acceptance of the Principal. *Canadian Administrator, 6,* 5–8.

McNeil, L. M. (1986). *Contradictions of Control: School Structure and School Knowledge.* New York: Routledge & Kegan Paul.

McNeil, L. M. (1988a). Contradictions of Control, Part 1: Administrators and Teachers. *Phi Delta Kappan, 69,* 333-339.

McNeil, L. M. (1988b). Contradictions of Control, Part 2: Administrators and Teachers. *Phi Delta Kappan, 69,* 432-438.

Meany, D. P. (1991). Quest for Quality. *California Technology Project Quarterly, 2,* 8-15.

Mechanic, D. (1962). Sources of Power of Lower Participants in Complex Organizations. *Administrative Science Quarterly, 6,* 349-364.

Meidl, J. R., Ehrlich, S. B., and Dukerich, J. M. (1985). The Romance of Leadership. *Administrative Science Quarterly, 30,* 78-102.

Mennuti, N., and Kottkamp, R. B. (1986). Motivation Through the Design of Work: A Synthesis of the Job Characteristics Model and Expectancy Motivation Tested in Middle and Junior High Schools. Annual Meeting of the American Educational Research Association, San Francisco.

Merton, R. (1957). *Social Theory and Social Structure.* New York: Free Press.

Merton, R. (1969). The Social Nature of Leadership. *American Journal of Nursing, 69,* 2614-2618.

Metz, M. H. (1986). *Different by Design: The Context and Character of Three Magnet Schools.* New York: Routledge and Kegan Paul.

Meyer, J. W. (1992). Centralization of Funding and Control in Educational Governance. In J. W. Meyer and W. R. Scott (Eds.), *Organization Environments: Ritual and Rationality* (pp. 179-197). Newbury Park, CA: Sage.

Meyer, J. W., and Rowan, B. (1977). Institutionalized Organizations: Formal Structure as Myth and Ceremony. *American Journal of Sociology, 83,* 440-463.

Meyer, J. W., and Rowan, B. (1978). The Structure of Educational Organizations. In M. W. Meyer (Ed.), *Environments and Organizations* (pp. 78-109). San Francisco: Jossey-Bass.

Meyer, J. W., and Scott, W. R. (1983). *Organizational Environments: Ritual and Rationality.* Beverly Hills, CA: Sage.

Meyer, J. W., Scott, W. R., Cole, S., and Intilli, J. K. (1978). Instructional Dissensus and Institutional Consensus in Schools. In M. W. Meyer (Ed.), *Environments and Organizations* (pp. 233-263). San Francisco: Jossey-Bass.

Meyer, J. W., Scott, W. R., and Deal, T. E. (1992). Institutional and Technical Sources of Organizational Structure: Explaining the Structure of Educational Organizations. In J. W. Meyer and W. R. Scott (Eds.), *Organization Environments: Ritual and Rationality* (pp. 45-67). Newbury Park, CA: Sage.

Meyer, J. W., Scott, W. R., and Strang, D. (1987). Centralization, Fragmentation, and School District Complexity. *Administrative Science Quarterly, 32,* 186-201.

Meyer, M. W. (1978). Introduction: Recent Developments in Organizational Research and Theory. In M. W. Meyer (Ed.), *Environments and Organizations* (pp. 1-19). San Francisco: Jossey-Bass.

Midgley, C., Feldlaufer, H., and Eccles, J. S. (1989). Change in Teacher Efficacy and Student Self- and Task-Related Beliefs in Mathematics During the Transition to Junior High School. *Journal of Educational Psychology, 81,* (2), 247-258.

Midgley, C., and Wood, S. (1993). Beyond Site-Based Management: Empowering Teachers to Reform Schools. *Phi Delta Kappan, 75,* 245-252.

Miles, M. B. (1965). Education and Innovation: The Organization in Context. In M. Abbott and J. Lovell (Eds.), *Changing Perspectives in Educational Administration* (pp. 54-72). Auburn, AL: Auburn University.

Miles, M. B. (1969). Planned Change and Organizational Health: Figure and Ground. In F. D. Carver and T. J. Sergiovanni (Eds.), *Organizations and Human Behavior* (pp. 375-391). New York: McGraw-Hill.

Miller, D. (1992). Environmental Fit versus Internal Fit. *Organization Science, 3,* (2), 159-178.

Miller, L. E., and Grush, J. E. (1988). Improving Predictions in Expectancy Theory Research: Effects of Personality, Expectancies, and Norms. *Academy of Management Journal, 31,* 107-122.

Milliken, F. J. (1987). Three Types of Perceived Uncertainty About the Environment: State, Effect, and Response Uncertainty. *Academy of Management Review, 12,* 133-143.

Milliken, F. J. (1990). Perceiving and Interpreting Environmental Change: An Examination of College Administrators' Interpretation of Changing Demographics. *Academy of Management Journal, 33,* (1), 42-63.

Mindlin, S. E., and Aldrich, H. (1975). Interorganizational Dependence: A Review of the Concept and a Reexamination of the Findings of the Aston Group. *Administrative Science Quarterly, 20,* 382-392.

Miner, J. B. (1980). *Theories of Organizational Behavior.* Hinsdale, IL: Dryden.

Miner, J. B. (1988). *Organizational Behavior.* New York: Random House.

Miner, A. S., Amburgey, T. L., and Stearns, T. M. (1990). Interorganizational Linkages and Population Dynamics: Buffering and Transformational Shields. *Administrative Science Quarterly, 35,* 689-713.

Mintzberg, H. (1973). *The Nature of Managerial Work.* New York: Harper & Row.

Mintzberg, H. (1978). Patterns in Strategy Formulation. *Management Science, 24,* 934-948.

Mintzberg, H. (1979). *The Structuring of Organizations.* Englewood Cliffs, NJ: Prentice-Hall.

Mintzberg, H. (1980). Organizational Structure and Alienation from Work. Annual Meeting of the American Educational Research Association, Boston.

Mintzberg, H. (1981). The Manager's Job: Folklore and Fact. *Harvard Business Review, 53,* (4), 49-61.

Mintzberg, H. (1983a). *Power In and Around Organizations.* Englewood Cliffs, NJ: Prentice-Hall.

Mintzberg, H. (1983b). *Structure in Fives.* Englewood Cliffs, NJ: Prentice-Hall.

Mintzberg, H. (1989). *Mintzberg on Management.* New York: Free Press.

Mintzberg, H., Raisinghani, D., and Theoret, A. (1976). The Structure of "Unstructured" Decision Processes. *Administrative Science Quarterly, 23,* 246-275.

Miskel, C. (1982). Motivation in Educational Organizations. *Educational Administration Quarterly, 18,* 65–88.

Miskel, C., and Cosgrove, D. (1985). Leader Succession in School Settings. *Review of Educational Research, 55,* 87–105.

Miskel, C., DeFrain, J., and Wilcox, K. (1980). A Test of Expectancy Work Motivation Theory in Educational Organizations. *Educational Administration Quarterly, 16,* 70–92.

Miskel, C., Fevurly, R., and Stewart, J. (1979). Organizational Structures and Processes, Perceived School Effectiveness, Loyalty, and Job Satisfaction. *Educational Administration Quarterly, 15,* 97–118.

Miskel, C., Glasnapp, D., and Hatley, R. (1975). A Test of the Inequity Theory for Job Satisfaction Using Educators' Attitudes toward Work Motivation and Work Incentives. *Educational Administration Quarterly, 11,* 38–54.

Miskel, C., McDonald, D., and Bloom, S. (1983). Structural and Expectancy Linkages Within Schools and Organizational Effectiveness. *Educational Administration Quarterly, 19,* 49–82.

Miskel, C., and Ogawa, R. (1988). Work Motivation, Job Satisfaction, and Climate. In N. J. Boyan (Ed.), *Handbook of Research on Educational Administration* (pp. 279–304). New York: Longman.

Mitchell, D. E., Ortiz, F. I., and Mitchell, T. K. (1982). Executive Summary. *Controlling the Impact of Rewards and Incentives on Teacher Task Performance.* Washington, DC: National Institute of Education, U. S. Department of Education.

Mitchell, D. E., Ortiz, F. I., and Mitchell, T. K. (1987). *Work Orientation and Job Performance: The Cultural Basis of Teaching Rewards and Incentives.* Albany: State University of New York Press.

Mitchell, T. R. (1974). Expectancy Models of Job Satisfaction, Occupational Preference, and Effort: A Theoretical, Methodological and Empirical Appraisal. *Psychological Bulletin, 81,* 1053–1077.

Mitchell, T. R. (1979). Organization Behavior. *Annual Review of Psychology, 30,* 243–281.

Moeller, G. H., and Charters, W. W. Jr. (1966). Relation of Bureaucratization to Sense of Power Among Teachers. *Administrative Science Quarterly, 10,* 444–465.

Mohan, M. L. (1993). *Organizational Communication and Cultural Vision.* Albany, NY: State University of New York Press.

Mohrman, A. M., Jr., Cooke, R. A., and Mohrman, S. A. (1978). Participation in Decision Making: A Multidimensional Perspective. *Educational Administration Quarterly, 14,* 13–29.

Monge, P. R. (1987). The Network Level of Analysis. In C. R. Berger and S. H. Chaffee (Eds.), *Handbook of Communication Science* (pp. 239–270). Newbury Park, CA: Sage.

Monk, D. H. (1992). Education Productivity Research: An Update and Assessment of Its Role in Education Finance Reform. *Educational Evaluation and Policy Analysis, 14,* (4), 307–332.

Moon, N. J. (1983). The construction of a conceptual framework for teacher participation in school decision making. Doctoral diss., University of Kentucky, Lexington.

Moran, E. T., and Volkwein, J. F. (1992). The Cultural Approach to the Formation of Organizational Climate. *Human Relations, 45,* (1), 19–47.

Morgan, G. (1986). *Images of Organizations.* Beverly Hills, CA: Sage.

Morris, V. C., Crowson, R. L., Hurwitz, E. Jr., and Porter-Gehrie, C. (1981). *The Urban Principal.* Chicago: College of Education, University of Illinois at Chicago.

Mott, P. E. (1972). *The Characteristics of Effective Organizations.* New York: Harper & Row.

Mowday, R. T. (1978). The Exercise of Upward Influence in Organizations. *Administrative Science Quarterly, 23,* 137–156.

Mowday, R. T., Porter, L. W., and Steers, R. M. (1982). *Employee-Organizational Linkages: The Psychology of Commitment, Absenteeism, and Turnover.* New York: Academic Press.

Muchinsky, P. M. (1987). *Psychology Applied to Work* (2nd ed.). Chicago: Dorsey.

Mullins, T. (1983). Relationships among teachers' perception of the principal's style, teachers' loyalty to the principal, and teachers' zone of acceptance. Doctoral diss., Rutgers University, New Brunswick.

Murnane, R. J. (1981). Interpreting the Evidence on School Effectiveness. *Teachers College Record, 83,* 19–35.

Murnane, R. J. (1987). Understanding Teacher Attrition. *Harvard Educational Review, 57,* 177–182.

Murnane, R. J., and Cohen, D. K. (1986). Merit Pay and the Evaluation Problem: Why Most Merit Pay Plans Fail and Few Survive. *Harvard Educational Review, 56,* (1), 1–17.

Murphy, M. J. (1985). Testimony before the California Commission on the Teaching Profession. Sacramento.

Myers, M. T., and Myers, G. E. (1982). *Managing by Communication: An Organizational Approach.* New York: McGraw-Hill.

Nadler, D. A. (1979). The Effects of Feedback on Task Group Behavior: A Review of the Experimental Research. *Organizational Behavior and Human Performance, 23,* 309–338.

Nadler, D. A., and Lawler, E. E., III. (1977). Motivation: A Diagnostic Approach. In J. R. Hackman, E. E. Lawler III, and L. W. Porter (Eds.), *Perspectives on Behavior in Organizations* (pp. 26–38). New York: McGraw-Hill.

Nadler, D. A., and Tushman, M. L. (1983). A General Diagnostic Model for Organizational Behavior Applying a Congruence Perspective. In J. R. Hackman, E. E. Lawler III, and L. W. Porter (Eds.), *Perspectives on Behavior in Organizations* (pp. 112–124). New York: McGraw-Hill.

Nadler, D. A., and Tushman, M. L. (1989). Organizational Frame Bending: Principles for Managing Reorientation. *Academy of Management Executive, 3,* 194–203.

National Commission on Excellence in Education (1983). *A Nation at Risk.* Washington, DC: Government Printing Office.

National Commission on Excellence in Educational Administration (1987). *Leaders for America's Schools.* Tempe, AZ: University Council for Educational Administration.

Newberry, J. F. (1971). A comparative analysis of the organizational structures of selected post-secondary educational institutions. Doctoral diss., University of Alberta, Edmonton.

Nicholson, J. H. (1980). Analysis of communication satisfaction in an urban school system. Doctoral diss., George Peabody College for Teachers of Vanderbilt University, Nashville, TN.

Nisbett, R. E., and Ross, L. (1980). *Human Interferences: Strategies and Shortcomings in Social Judgments.* Englewood Cliffs, NJ: Prentice-Hall.

Northcraft, G. B., and Earley, P. C. (1989). Technology, Credibility, and Feedback Use. *Organizational Behavior and Human Performance, 44,* 83-96.

Nutt, P. C. (1984). Types of Organizational Decision Processes. *Administrative Science Quarterly, 29,* 414-450.

O'Dempsey, K. (1976). Time Analysis of Activities, Work Patterns and Roles of High School Principals. *Administrator's Bulletin, 7,* 1-4.

Odiorne, G. S. (1965). *Management by Objectives: A System of Managerial Leadership.* New York: Pitman.

Odiorne, G. S. (1969). *Management Decisions by Objectives.* Englewood Cliffs, NJ: Prentice-Hall.

Odiorne, G. S. (1979). *MBO II: A System of Managerial Leadership for the 80s.* Belmont, CA: Pitman.

Ogawa, R. T. (1991). Enchantment, Disenchantment, and Accommodation: How a Faculty Made Sense of the Succession of a Principal. *Educational Administration Quarterly, 27,* (1), 30-60.

Ogawa, R. T. (1992). Institutional Theory and Examining Leadership in School. *International Journal of Educational Management, 6,* (3), 14-21.

Ogawa, R. T. (1994). The Institutional Sources of Educational Reform: The Case of School-Based Management. *American Educational Research Journal, 31,* (3), 519-548.

Okeafor, K. R., and Teddlie, C. (1989). Organizational Factors Related to Administrator's Confidence in Teachers. *Journal of Research and Development in Education, 22,* 28-36.

Oldham, G. R., and Kulik, C. T. (1984). Motivation Enhancement Through Work Redesign. In J. L. Bess (Ed.), *College and University Organization* (pp. 85-104). New York: New York University Press.

Oldham, G. R., and Miller, H. E. (1979). The Effect of Significant Other's Job Complexity and Employee Reactions to Work. *Human Relations, 32,* 247-260.

Olsen, M. E. (1965). *The Logic of Collective Action: Public Goods and the Theory of Groups.* Cambridge, MA: Harvard University Press.

Olsen, M. E. (1968a). *The Process of Social Organization.* New York: Holt, Rinehart, & Winston.

Olsen, M. E. (1968b). A Theory of Groups and Organizations. In B. M. Russett (Ed.), *Economic Theory of International Politics.* Chicago: Markham.

O'Reilly, C. A. I., Chatman, J. A., and Caldwell, D. (1991). People and Organizational Culture: A Q-sort Approach to Assessing Person-Organization Fit. *Academy of Management Journal, 34,* (3), 487-516.

O'Reilly, C. A. I., and Pondy, L. R. (1979). Organizational Communication. In S. Kerr (Ed.), *Organizational Behavior* (pp. 119-150). Columbus, OH: Grid.

O'Reilly, C. A. I., and Roberts, K. H. (1977). Task Group Structure, Communication, and Effectiveness in Three Organizations. *Journal of Applied Psychology, 62,* 674-681.

Orpen, C. (1979). The Effects of Job Enrichment on Employee Satisfaction, Motivation, Involvement, and Performance: A Field Experiment. *Human Relations, 32,* 189-217.

Ortiz, F. I., and Marshall, C. (1988). Women in Educational Administration. In N. J. Boyan (Ed.), *Handbook of Research on Educational Administration* (pp. 123-141). New York: Longman.

Ostroff, C., and Schmitt, N. (1993). Configurations of Organizational Effectiveness and Efficiency. *Academy of Management Journal, 36,* (6), 1345-1361.

Ouchi, W. (1981). *Theory Z.* Reading, MA: Addison-Wesley.

Ouchi, W., and Wilkins, A. L. (1985). Organizational Culture. *Annual Review of Sociology, 11,* 457-483.

Pace, C. R., and Stern, G. C. (1958). An Approach to the Measure of Psychological Characteristics of College Environments. *Journal of Educational Psychology, 49,* 269-277.

Packard, J. S. (1988). The Pupil Control Studies. In N. J. Boyan (Ed.), *Handbook of Research on Educational Administration* (pp. 185-207). New York: Longman.

Packard, J. S., and Willower, D. J. (1972). Pluralistic Ignorance and Pupil Control Ideology. *Journal of Educational Administration, 10,* 78-87.

Padgett, J. F. (1980). Managing Garbage Can Hierarchies. *Administrative Science Quarterly, 25,* 583-604.

Page, C. H. (1946). Bureaucracy's Other Face. *Social Forces, 25,* 88-94.

Palincsar, A. S. (1986). The Role of Dialogue in Providing Scaffolding Instruction. *Educational Psychologist, 21,* 73-98.

Pallas, A. M., and Neumann, A. (1993). Blinded by the Light: The Applicability of Total Management to Educational Organizations. Annual Meeting of the American Educational Research Association, Atlanta, GA.

Pallas, A. M., Natriello, G., and McDill, E. L. (1989). The Changing Nature of the Disadvantaged Population: Current Dimension and Future Trends. *Educational Researcher, 18,* 16-22.

Parsons, T. (1947). Introduction. In Max Weber, *The Theory of Social and Economic Organization* (pp. 3-86). A. M. Henderson and T. Parsons (Trans.). New York: Free Press.

Parsons, T. (1960). *Structure and Process in Modern Societies.* Glencoe, IL: Free Press.

Parsons, T. (1967). *Sociological Theory and Modern Society.* New York: Free Press.

Parsons, T., Bales, R. F., and Shils., E. A. (1953). *Working Papers in the Theory of Action.* New York: Free Press.

Parsons, T., and Shils, E. A. (Eds.), (1951). *Toward a General Theory of Action.* Cambridge, MA: Harvard University Press.

Pastor, M. C., and Erlandson, D. A. (1982). A Study of Higher Order Need Strength and Job Satisfaction in Secondary Public School Teachers. *Journal of Educational Administration, 20,* 172-183.

Payne, J. W., Bettman, J. R., and Johnson, E. J. (1988). Adaptive Strategy Selection in Decision Making. *Journal of Experimental Psychology: Learning, Memory, and Cognition, 14,* 534–552.

Peabody, R. L. (1962). Perceptions of Organizational Authority: A Comparative Analysis. *Administrative Science Quarterly, 6,* 463–482.

Pelz, D. C., and Andrews, F. M. (1966). *Scientists in Organizations.* New York: Wiley.

Penley, L. E., Alexander, E. R., Jernigan, I. E., and Henwood, C. I. (1991). Communication Abilities of Managers: The Relationship to Performance. *Journal of Management, 17,* (1), 57–76.

Pennings, J. M. (1985). *Organizational Strategy and Change.* San Francisco: Jossey-Bass.

Pennings, J. M. (1992). Structural Contingency Theory: A Reappraisal. *Research in Organizational Behavior, 14,* 267–309.

Perrow, C. (1978). Demystifying Organization. In R. Saari & Y. Hasenfeld (Eds.), *The Management of Human Services* (pp. 105–120). New York: Columbia University Press.

Perrow, C. (1986). *Complex Organizations: A Critical Essay* (3rd ed.). Glencoe, IL: Scott, Foresman.

Peters, T. J., and Waterman, R. H. Jr. (1982). *In Search of Excellence.* New York: Harper & Row.

Peters, L. H., Hartke, D. D., and Pohlmann, J. T. (1985). Fiedler's Contingency Theory of Effectiveness: An Application of the Meta-Analysis Procedures of Schmidt and Hunter. *Psychological Bulletin, 97,* 274–285.

Peterson, K. D. (1977–78). The Principal's Tasks. *Administrator's Notebook, 26,* 1–4.

Peterson, P. E. (1989). The Public Schools: Monopoly or Choice? Conference on Choice and Control in American Education. Robert M LaFollette Institute of Public Affairs, University of Wisconsin, Madison.

Pfeffer, J. (1972). Size and Composition of Corporate Boards of Directors: The Organization and Its Environment. *Administrative Science Quarterly, 17,* 218–228.

Pfeffer, J. (1976). Beyond Management and the Worker: The Institutional Function of Management. *Academy of Management Review, 1,* 36–46.

Pfeffer, J. (1981). *Power in Organizations.* Boston: Pitman.

Pfeffer, J. (1982). *Organizations and Organization Theory.* Boston: Pitman.

Pfeffer, J., and Leblebici, H. (1973). The Effect of Competition on Some Dimensions of Organizational Structure. *Social Forces, 52,* 268–279.

Pfeffer, J., and Salancik, G. (1978). *The External Control of Organizations: A Resource Dependence Perspective.* New York: Harper & Row.

Pfeffer, J., and Salancik, G. R. (1982). *The Organizational Control of Organizations: A Resource Dependence Perspective.* Englewood Cliffs, NJ: Prentice-Hall.

Phillips, D., and Thomas, A. R. (1982). Principals' Decision Making: Some Observations. In W. S. Simpkins, A. R. Thomas, and E. B. Thomas (Eds.), *Principal and Task: An Australian Perspective* (pp. 74–83). Armidale, NSW, Australia: University of New England.

Pinder, C. C. (1984). *Work Motivation: Theory, Issues, and Applications.* Dallas: Scott, Foresman.

Pinfield, L.T. (1986). A Field Evaluation of Perspectives on Organizational Decision Making. *Administrative Science Quarterly, 31,* 365–388.

Pintrich, P. R. (1988). A Process-Oriented View of Student Motivation and Cognition. In J. S. Stark and L.A. Mets (Eds.), *Improving Teaching and Learning Through Research* (pp. 65–79). San Francisco: Jossey-Bass.

Pintrich, P. R., and Garcia, T. (1991). Student Goal Orientation and Self-Regulation in the College Classroom. In M. Maehr and P. R. Pintrich (Eds.), *Advances in Motivation and Achievement* (pp. 371–402). Greenwich, CT: JAI.

Pintrich, P. R., Marx, R.W., and Boyle, R. A. (1993). Beyond Cold Conceptual Change: The Role of Motivational Beliefs and Classroom Contextual Factors in the Process of Conceptual Change. *Review of Educational Research, 63,* (2), 167–199.

Pitner, N. (1982). Principal Influence of Teacher Behavior: Substitutes for Leadership. Annual Meeting of the American Educational Research Association, New York.

Pitner, N., and Ogawa, R.T. (1981). Organizational Leadership: The Case of the Superintendent. *Educational Administration Quarterly, 17,* 45–65.

Podgurski, T. P. (1990). School effectiveness as it relates to group consensus and organizational health of middle schools. Doctoral diss., Rutgers University, New Brunswick.

Podsakoff, P. M., Niehoff, B. P., MacKenzie, S. B., and Williams, M. L. (1993). Do Substitutes for Leadership Really Substitute for Leadership? An Empirical Examination of Kerr and Jermier's Situational Leadership Model. *Organizational Behavior and Human Decision Processes, 54,* 1–44.

Poole, M. S. (1985). Communication and Organizational Climates: Review, Critique, and a New Perspective. In R. D. McPhee and P. K. Tompkins (Eds.), *Organizational Communications: Traditional Themes and New Directions* (pp. 79–108). Beverly Hills, CA: Sage.

Porter, L. W. (1963). Job Attitudes in Management: II. Perceived Importance of Needs as a Function of Job Level. *Journal of Applied Psychology, 47,* 141–148.

Porter, L. W., and Lawler, E. E., III. (1968). *Managerial Attitudes and Performance.* Homewood, IL: Dorsey.

Porter, L. W., and Roberts, K. H. (1976). Communication in Organizations. In M. D. Dunnette (Ed.), *Handbook of Industrial and Organizational Psychology* (pp. 1533–1589). Chicago: Rand McNally.

Powell, W. W. (1991). Expanding the Scope of Institutional Analysis. In W. W. Powell and P. J. DiMaggio (Eds.), *The New Institutionalism in Organizational Analysis* (pp. 183–203). Chicago: University of Chicago Press.

Powell, W. W., and DiMaggio, P. J. (1991). Introduction. In W. W. Powell and P. J. DiMaggio (Eds.), *The New Institutionalism in Organizational Analysis* (pp. 1–38). Chicago: University of Chicago Press.

Presthus, R. V. (1958). Toward a Theory of Organizational Behavior. *Administrative Science Quarterly, 3,* 48–72.

Presthus, R. V. (1962). *The Organizational Society.* New York: Random House.

Presthus, R. V. (1978). *The Organizational Society* (Rev. ed.). New York: St. Martin's Press.

Prestine, N. A. (1991). Shared Decision Making in Restructuring Essential Schools: The Role of the Principal. *Planning and Changing, 22,* 160–178.

Pritchard, R. D., Jones, S. D., Roth, P. L., Stuebing, K. K., and Ekeberg, S. E. (1988). Effects of Group Feedback, Goal Setting, and Incentives on Organizational Productivity. *Journal of Applied Psychology Monograph, 73,* 337–358.

Prolman, S. (1982). Gender, Career Paths, and Administrative Perceptions. *Administrator's Notebook, 30,* 1–4.

Pugh, D. S., and Hickson, D. J. (1976). *Organizational Structure in its Context.* Westmead, Farnborough, Hants., England: Saxon House, D. C. Heath.

Pugh, D. S., Hickson, D. J., and Hinnings, C. R. (1968). Dimensions of Organizational Structure. *Administrative Science Quarterly, 13,* 56–105.

Pugh, D. S., Hickson, D. J., Hinings, C. R., and Turner, C. (1969). The Context of Organizational Structure. *Administration Science Quarterly, 14,* 91–114.

Purkey, S. C., and Smith, M. S. (1983). Effective Schools: A Review. *Elementary School Journal, 83,* 427–452.

Quarstein, V. A., McAfee, R. B., and Glassman, M. (1992). The Situational Occurrences Theory of Job Satisfaction. *Human Relations, 45,* (8), 859–872.

Ratsoy, E. W. (1973). Participative and Hierarchical Management of Schools: Some Emerging Generalizations. *Journal of Educational Administration, 11,* 161–170.

Rauschenberger, J., Schmitt, N., and Hunter, J. E. (1980). A Test of the Need Hierarchy Concept by a Markov Model of Change in Need Strength. *Administrative Science Quarterly, 25,* 654–670.

Redding, W. C. (1972). *Communication Within the Organization.* West Lafayette, IN: Purdue Research Council.

Reder, L. M., and Anderson, J. R. (1980). A Comparison of Texts and Their Summaries: Memorial Consequences. *Journal of Verbal Learning and Verbal Behavior, 19,* (2), 121–134.

Reilly, B. J., and Joseph A. DiAngelo, J. (1990). Communication: A Cultural System of Meaning and Value. *Human Relations, 43,* (2), 129–140.

Reiss, F. (1994). Faculty loyalty in and around the urban elementary school. Doctoral diss., Rutgers University, New Brunswick.

Reynolds, P. D. (1971). *A Primer in Theory Construction.* Indianapolis, IN: Bobbs-Merrill.

Rhodes, L. A. (1990). Why Quality is Within our Grasp . . . If We Reach. *The School Administrator, 47,* (10), 31–34.

Rice, A. W. (1978). Individual and work variables associated with principal job satisfaction. Doctoral diss., University of Alberta, Edmonton.

Rice, R. E. (1992). Task Analyzability, Use of New Media, and Effectiveness: A Multi-Site Exploration of Media Richness. *Organization Science, 3,* (4), 475–500.

Rice, R. W. (1978). Psychometric Properties of the Esteem for Least Preferred Co-Worker (LPC Scale). *Academy of Management Review, 3,* 106–118.

Robbins, S. P. (1983). *The Structure and Design of Organizations.* Englewood Cliffs, NJ: Prentice-Hall.

Robbins, S. P. (1991). *Organizational Behavior: Concepts, Controversies, and Applications* (5th ed.). Englewood Cliffs, NJ: Prentice-Hall.

Roberts, K. H., and Glick, W. (1981). The Job Characteristics Approach to Task Design: A Critical Review. *Journal of Applied Psychology, 66,* 193-217.

Roberts, K. H., Hulin, C. L., and Rousseau, D. M. (1978). *Developing an Interdisciplinary Science of Organizations.* San Francisco: Jossey-Bass.

Roberts, N. C. (1985). Transforming Leadership: A Process of Collective Action. *Human Relations, 38,* 1023-1046.

Rockey, E. H. (1984). *Communication in Organizations.* Lanham, MD: University Press of America.

Roethlisberger, F. J., and Dickson, W. J. (1939). *Management and the Worker.* Cambridge: Harvard University Press.

Rogers, R. C., and Hunter, J. E. (1989). The impact of management by objectives on organizational productivity. Unpublished paper, School of Public Administration, University of Kentucky, Lexington.

Rokeach, M. (1973). *The Nature of Human Values.* New York: Free Press.

Rosenau, P. M. (1992). *Post-Modernism and the Social Sciences: Insights, Inroads, and Intrusions.* Princeton: Princeton University Press.

Rossman, G. B., Corbett, H. D., and Firestone, W. A. (1988). *Change and Effectiveness in Schools: A Cultural Perspective.* Albany, NY: State University of New York Press.

Rousseau, D. (1990). Quantitative Assessment of Organizational Culture: The Case for Multiple Measures. In B. Schneider (Ed.), *Frontiers in Industrial and Organizational Psychology* (pp. 153-192). San Francisco: Jossey-Bass.

Rowan, B. (1981). The Effects of Institutionalized Rules on Administrators. In S. B. Bacharach (Ed.), *Organizational Behavior in Schools and School Districts* (pp. 47-75). New York: Praeger.

Rowan, B. (1982). Organizational Structure and the Institutional Environment: The Case of Public Schools. *Administrative Science Quarterly, 27,* 259-279.

Rowan, B. (1990). Commitment and Control: Alternative Strategies for the Organizational Design of School. *Review of Research in Education, 16,* 353-389.

Rowan, B. (1993). Institutional Studies of Organization: Lines of Analysis and Data Requirements. Annual Meeting of the American Educational Research Association, Atlanta, GA.

Rowan, B., Bossert, S. T., and Dwyer, D. C. (1983). Research on Effective Schools: A Cautionary Note. *Educational Researcher, 12,* 24-31.

Russ, G. S., Daft, R. L., and Lengel, R. H. (1990). Media Selection and Managerial Characteristics in Organizational Communication. *Management Communication Quarterly, 4,* 151-175.

Russell, R. D., and Russell, C. J. (1992). An Examination of the Effects of Organizational Norms, Organizational Structure, and Environmental Uncertainty on Entrepreneurial Strategy. *Journal of Management, 18,* (4), 639-656.

Rutter, M., Maugham, B., Mortimore, P., Ousten, J., and Smith, A. (1979). *Fifteen Thousand Hours: Secondary Schools and Their Effects on Children.* London: Open Books.

Sackney, L. E. (1976). The relationship between organizational structure and behavior in secondary schools. Doctoral diss., University of Alberta, Edmonton.

Salancik, G. R., and Pfeffer, J. (1977). Constraints on Administrative Discretion: The Limited Influence of Mayors on City Budgets. *Urban Affairs Quarterly, 12,* 475-498.

Sarup, M. (1989). *An Introductory Guide to Post-Structuralism and Postmodernism.* Athens: University of Georgia Press.

Sashkin, M., and Burke, W. W. (1990). Understanding and Assessing Organizational Leadership. In K. E. Clark and M. B. Clark (Eds.), *Measures of Leadership* (pp. 297-325). West Orange, NJ: Leadership Library of America.

Sayles, L. R., and Strauss, G. (1966). *Human Behavior in Organizations.* Englewood Cliffs, NJ: Prentice-Hall.

Schein, E. H. (1985). *Organizational Culture and Leadership.* San Francisco: Jossey-Bass.

Schein, E. H. (1990). Organizational Culture. *American Psychologist, 45,* (2), 109-119.

Scherkenbach, W. (1991). *Deming's Road to Continual Improvement.* Knoxville, TN: SPC Press.

Scherkenbach, W. (1992). *The Deming Route to Quality and Production.* Washington, DC: CEEPress.

Schermerhorn, J. R., Hunt, J. G., and Osborn, R. N. (1994). *Managing Organizational Behavior.* New York: Wiley.

Schmidt, F. L., and Hunter, J. E. (1992). Development of a Causal Model of Processes Determining Job Performance. *Current Directions in Psychological Science, 1,* (3), 89-92.

Schmidt, G. L. (1976). Job Satisfaction Among Secondary Administrators. *Educational Administration Quarterly, 12,* 68-86.

Schmitz, J., and Fulk, J. (1991). Organizational Colleagues, Media Richness, and Electronic Mail. *Communication Research, 18,* (4), 487-523.

Schmuck, R. A., and Runkel, P. J. (1985). *The Handbook of Organization Development in Schools* (3rd ed.). Prospect Heights, IL: Waveland Press.

Schneider, S. C., and Angelmar, R. (1993). Cognition in Organizational Analysis. *Organization Studies, 14,* (3), 347-374.

Schunk, D. (1991). Self-Efficacy and Academic Motivation. *Educational Psychologist, 26,* 207-231.

Schwartz, H. M., and Davis, S. M. (1981). Matching Corporate Culture and Business Strategy. *Organizational Dynamics, 10,* 30-48.

Scott, W. R. (1977). Effectiveness of Organizational Effectiveness Studies. In P. S. Goodman and J. M. Pennings (Eds.), *New Perspectives on Organizational Effectiveness* (pp. 63-95). San Francisco: Jossey-Bass.

Scott, W. R. (1981). *Organizations: Rational, Natural, and Open System.* Englewood Cliffs, NJ: Prentice-Hall.

Scott, W. R. (1983). Introduction: From Technology to Environment. In J. W. Meyer and W. R. Scott (Eds.), *Organizational Environments: Ritual and Rationality* (pp. 13–17). Beverly Hills, CA: Sage.

Scott, W. R. (1987). *Organizations: Rational, Natural, and Open System* (2nd. ed.). Englewood Cliffs, NJ: Prentice-Hall.

Scott, W. R. (1987). The Adolescence of Institutional Theory. *Administrative Science Quarterly, 32,* 493–511.

Scott, W. R. (1991). Unpacking Institutional Arguments. In W. W. Powell and P. J. DiMaggio (Eds.), *The New Institutionalism in Organizational Analysis* (pp. 164–182). Chicago: University of Chicago Press.

Scott, W. R. (1992). *Organizations: Rational, Natural, and Open Systems* (3rd. ed.). Englewood Cliffs, NJ: Prentice-Hall.

Scott, W. R., and Meyer, J. W. (1991). The Organization of Societal Sectors: Propositions and Early Evidence. In W. W. Powell and P. J. DiMaggio (Eds.), *The New Institutionalism in Organizational Analysis* (pp. 108–140). Chicago: University of Chicago Press.

Selznick, P. (1949). *TVA and the Grass Roots.* Berkeley: University of California Press.

Selznick, P. (1957). *Leadership in Administration.* New York: Harper & Row.

Senge, P. M. (1990). *The Fifth Dimension: The Art and Practice of the Learning Organization.* New York: Doubleday.

Sergiovanni, T., and Corbally, J. E. (Eds.) (1984). *Leadership and Organizational Culture.* Urbana: University of Illinois Press.

Sergiovanni, T. J. (1992). *Moral Leadership: Getting to the Heart of School Improvement.* San Francisco: Jossey-Bass.

Shakeshaft, C. (1986). *Women in Educational Administration.* Newbury Park, CA: Sage.

Shamir, B., House, R. J., and Arthur, M. B. (1993). The Motivational Effects of Charismatic Leadership: A Self-Concept Based Theory. *Organization Science, 4,* (4), 577–594.

Shanker, A. (1989, May 14). Does Money Make a Difference? A Difference Over Answers. *New York Times.*

Sharma, C. L. (1955). Who Should Make What Decisions? *Administrator's Notebook, 3,* 1–4.

Shelby, A. N. (1986). The Theoretical Bases of Persuasion: A Critical Introduction. *Journal of Business Communication, 23,* 5–29.

Sherman, J. D., and Smith, H. L. (1984). The Influences of Organizational Structure on Intrinsic Versus Extrinsic Motivation. *Academy of Management Journal, 27,* 877–885.

Sickler, J. L. (1988). Teachers in Charge: Empowering the Professionals. *Phi Delta Kappan, 69,* 354–356.

Sievers, B. (1986). Beyond the Surrogate of Motivation. *Organization Studies, 7,* (4), 335–351.

Silver, P. (1983). *Educational Administration: Theoretical Perspectives in Practice and Research.* New York: Harper & Row.

Simon, H. A. (1947). *Administrative Behavior.* New York: Macmillan.

Simon, H. A. (1957a). *Administrative Behavior* (2nd ed.). New York: Macmillan.

Simon, H. A. (1957b). *Models of Man.* New York: Wiley.

Simon, H. A. (1968). Administrative Behavior. In D. Suls (Ed.), *International Encyclopedia of the Social Sciences* (pp. 74–79). New York: Macmillan.

Simon, H. A. (1991). Keynote Address. UCEA Conference, Baltimore, MD.

Simon, H. A. (1987). Making Management Decisions: The Role of Intuition and Emotion. *Academy of Management Executive, 1,* 57–64.

Simon, H. A. (1993). Decision-Making: Rational, Nonrational, and Irrational. *Educational Administration Quarterly, 29,* (3), 392–411.

Sirotnik, K. A., and Clark, R. (1988). School-Centered Decision Making and Renewal. *Phi Delta Kappan, 69,* 660–664.

Slavin, R. E. (1992). Synthesis on Research on Cooperative Learning. *Educational Leadership, 48,* (5), 71–82.

Smith, P. C., Kendall, L. M., and Hulin, C. L. (1969). *The Measurement of Satisfaction in Work and Retirement.* Chicago: Rand McNally.

Smylie, M. A. (1988). The Enhancement Function of Staff Development: Organization and Psychological Antecedents to Individual Teacher Change. *American Educational Research Journal, 25,* 1–30.

Smylie, M. A. (1994). Redesigning Teachers' Work: Connections to the Classroom. *Review of Research in Education, 20,* 129–177.

Smylie, M. A., and Brownlee-Conyers, J. (1992). Teacher Leaders and Their Principals: Exploring the Development of New Working Relationships. *Educational Administration Quarterly, 28,* (2), 150–184.

Smylie, M. A., and Smart, J. C. (1990). Teacher Support for Career Enhancement Initiatives: Program Characteristics and Effects on Work. *Educational Evaluation and Policy Analysis, 12,* (2), 139–155.

Sousa, D. A., and Hoy, W. K. (1981). Bureaucratic Structure in Schools: A Refinement and Synthesis in Measurement. *Educational Administration Quarterly, 17,* 21–40.

Spencer, B. A. (1994). Models of Organization and Total Quality Management. *Academy of Management Review, 19,* (3), 446–471.

Sproull, L. (1981). Managing Educational Programs: A Microbehavioral Analysis. *Human Organization, 40,* 113–122.

Sproull, L., Weiner, S., and Wolf, D. (1978). *Organizing an Anarchy: Beliefs, Bureaucracy, and Politics in the National Institute of Education.* Chicago: University of Illinois.

Spuck, D. W. (1974). Reward Structures in the Public High School. *Educational Administration Quarterly, 10,* 18–34.

Starkie, D. (1984). Policy Changes, Configurations, and Catastrophes. *Policy and Politics, 12,* 71–84.

Staw, B. M. (1984). Organizational Behavior: A Review and Reformulation of the Field's Outcome Variables. *Annual Review of Psychology, 35,* 627–666.

Stearns, T. M., Hoffman, A. N., and Heide, J. B. (1987). Performance of Commercial Television

Stations as an Outcome of Interorganizational Linkages and Environmental Conditions. *Academy of Management Journal, 30,* 71-90.

Stedman, L. C. (1987). It's Time We Changed the Effective Schools Formula. *Phi Delta Kappan, 69,* 214-224.

Steers, R. M. (1975). Problems in the Measurement of Organizational Effectiveness. *Administrative Science Quarterly, 20,* 546-558.

Steers, R. M. (1977). *Organizational Effectiveness: A Behavioral View.* Santa Monica, CA: Goodyear.

Steers, R. M., and Porter, L. W. (Eds). (1983). *Motivation and Work Behavior* (3rd ed.). New York: McGraw-Hill.

Steers, R. M., and Porter, L. W. (Eds.) (1991). *Motivation and Work Behavior* (5th ed.). New York: McGraw-Hill.

Steinfield, C. W., and Fulk, J. (1986). Task Demands and Managers' Use of Communication Media: An Information Processing View. Meeting of the Academy of Management, Chicago.

Steinhoff, C. R., and Owens, R. G. (1989). The Organizational Culture and Assessment Inventory: A Metaphorical Analysis in Educational Settings. *Journal of Educational Administration, 27,* (3), 17-23.

Stevenson, H., and Stigler, J. W. (1992). *The Learning Gap.* New York: Summit Books.

Stinchcombe, A. L. (1959). Bureaucratic and Craft Administration of Production. *Administrative Science Quarterly, 4,* 168-187.

Stipek, D. J. (1993). *Motivation to Learn* (2nd ed.). Boston: Allyn & Bacon.

Stogdill, R. M. (1948). Personal Factors Associated with Leadership: A Survey of the Literature. *Journal of Psychology, 25,* 35-71.

Stogdill, R. M. (1981). Traits of Leadership: A Follow-Up to 1970. In B. M. Bass (Ed.), *Stogdill's Handbook of Leadership* (pp. 73-97). New York: Free Press.

Strang, D. (1987). The Administrative Transformation of American Education: School District Consolidation. *Administrative Science Quarterly, 32,* 352-366.

Strauss, G. (1964). Workflow Frictions, Interfunctional Rivalry, and Professionalism. *Human Organization, 23,* 137-149.

Strube, M. J., and Garcia, J. E. (1981). A Meta-Analytic Investigation of Fiedler's Contingency Model of Leadership Effectiveness. *Psychological Bulletin, 90,* 307-321.

Sutcliffe, K. M. (1994). What Executives Notice: Accurate Perceptions in Top Management Teams. *Academy of Management Journal, 37,* (5), 1360-1378.

Sykes, G. (1987). Reckoning with the Spectre. *Educational Researcher, 16,* 19-21.

Tagiuri, R. The Concept of Organizational Climate. In R. Tagiuri and G. H. Litwin (Eds.), *Organizational Climate* (pp. 11-32). Boston: Harvard Graduate School of Business Administration.

Tannen, D. (1990). *You Just Don't Understand: Women and Men in Conversation.* New York: Ballantine.

Tarter, C. J., and Hoy, W. K. (1988). The Context of Trust: Teachers and the Principal. *High School Journal, 72,* 17–24.

Tarter, C. J., Hoy, W. K., and Bliss, J. R. (1989). Principal Leadership and Organizational Commitment: The Principal Must Deliver. *Planning and Changing, 20,* 139–140.

Tarter, C. J., Hoy, W. K., and Kottkamp, R. (1990). School Health and Organizational Commitment. *Journal of Research and Development in Education, 23,* 236–243.

Taylor, F. W. (1947). *Scientific Management.* New York: Harper.

Terreberry, S. (1968). The Evolution of Organizational Environments. *Administrative Science Quarterly, 12,* 590–613.

Thomas, A. B. (1988). Does Leadership Make a Difference to Organizational Performance. *Administrative Science Quarterly, 33,* 388–400.

Thomas, A. R., and Slater, R. C. (1972). The OCDQ: A Four Factor Solution for Australian Schools? *Journal of Educational Administration, 12,* 197–208.

Thomas, H. (1984). Mapping Strategic Management Research. *Journal of General Management, 9,* 55–72.

Thomas, K. (1976). Conflict and Conflict Management. In M. D. Dunnette (Ed.), *Handbook of Industrial and Organizational Psychology* (pp. 889–936). Chicago: Rand McNally.

Thomas, K. (1977). Toward Multi-Dimensional Values in Teaching: The Example of Conflict Behaviors. *Academy of Management Review, 20,* 486–490.

Thompson, J. D. (1967). *Organizations in Action.* New York: McGraw-Hill.

Thornton, R. (1970). Organizational Involvement and Commitment to Organization and Profession. *Administrative Science Quarterly, 15,* 417–426.

Tichy, N. M., and Devanna, M. A. (1986). *The Transformational Leader.* New York: Wiley.

Tiegs, R. B., Tetrick, L. E., and Fried, Y. (1992). Growth Need Strength and Context Satisfactions as Moderators of the Relations of the Job Characteristics Model. *Journal of Management, 18,* (3), 575–593.

Tolman, E. C. (1932). *Purposive Behavior in Animals and Men.* New York: Appleton-Century-Crofts.

Torres, D. L. (1991). What, If Anything, Is Professionalism?: Institutions and the Problem of Change. *Research in the Sociology of Organizations, 8,* 43–68.

Trentham, L., Silvern, S., and Brogdon, R. (1985). Teacher Efficacy and Teacher Competency Ratings. *Psychology in Schools, 22,* 343–352.

Trevino, L. K., Lengel, R. H., and Daft, R. L. (1987). Media Symbolism, Media Richness, and Media Choice in Organizations: A Symbolic Interactionist Perspective. *Communication Research, 14,* 553–574.

Trice, H. M., and Beyer, J. M. (1993). *The Culture of Work Organizations.* Englewood Cliffs, NJ: Prentice-Hall.

Trusty, F. M., and Sergiovanni, T. J. (1966). Perceived Need Deficiencies of Teachers and Administrators: A Proposal for Restructuring Teacher Roles. *Educational Administration Quarterly, 2,* 168–180.

Tsui, A. S. (1990). A Multiple-Constituency Model of Effectiveness: An Empirical Examination at the Human Resource Subunit Level. *Administrative Science Quarterly, 35,* 458-483.

Turban, D. B., and Keon, T. L. (1993). Organizational Attractiveness. An Interactionist Perspective. *Journal of Applied Psychology, 78,* (2), 184-193.

Tveite, Michael D. (1991). The Theory Behind the Fourteen Points: Management Focused on Improvement Instead of on Judgment. In AASA, *An Introduction to Total Quality Management: A Collection of Articles on the Concepts of Total Quality Management and W. Edwards Deming.* Arlington, VA: American Association of School Administrators.

Tversky, A. (1969). Intransitivity of Preferences. *Psychological Review, 76,* 31-84.

Tversky, A., and Kahneman, D. (1973). Availability: Heuristic for Judging Frequency and Probability. *Cognitive Psychology, 5,* 207-232.

U. S. Department of Health, Education and Welfare (1973). *Work in America, Report of a Special Task Force.* Cambridge: MIT Press.

Udy, S. H. (1959). "Bureaucracy" and "Rationality" in Weber's Organization Theory. *American Sociological Review, 24,* 791-795.

Urwick, L. F. (1937). Organization as a Technical Problem. In L. Gulick and L. F. Urwick (Eds.), *Papers on the Science of Administration* (pp. 47-88). New York: Institute of Public Administration, Columbia University.

Vaillancourt, P. M. (1986). *When Marxists Do Research.* Westport, CT: Greenwood Press.

Van De Ven, A. H., and Ferry, D. L. (1980). *Measuring and Assessing Organization.* New York: Wiley.

Van De Ven, A. H. (1989). Nothing is Quite so Practical as a Good Theory. *Academy of Management Review, 14,* 486-489.

Vance, V. S., and Schlechty, P. C. (1981). Do Academically Able Teachers Leave Education: The North Carolina Case. *Phi Delta Kappan, 63,* 106-112.

Vance, V. S., and Schlechty, P. C. (1982). The Distribution of Academic Ability in the Teaching Force: Policy Implications. *Phi Delta Kappan, 64,* 22-27.

Vecchio, R. P. (1977). An Empirical Examination of the Validity of Fiedler's Model of Leadership Effectiveness. *Organizational Behavior and Human Performance, 19,* 180-206.

Vecchio, R. P. (1988). *Organizational Behavior.* Chicago: Dryden Press.

Vecchio, R. P. (1993). The Impact of Differences in Subordinate and Supervisor Age on Attitudes and Performance. *Psychology and Aging, 8,* (1), 112-119.

Vroom, V. H. (1960). *Some Personality Determinants of the Effects of Participation.* Englewood Cliffs, NJ: Prentice-Hall.

Vroom, V. H. (1964). *Work and Motivation.* New York: Wiley.

Vroom, V. H. (1976). Leadership. In M. D. Dunnette (Ed.), *Handbook of Industrial and Organizational Psychology* (pp. 1527-1551). Chicago: Rand McNally.

Vroom, V. H., and Jago, A. G. (1978). On the Validity of the Vroom-Yetton Model. *Journal of Applied Psychology, 63,* 151-162.

Vroom, V. H., and Yetton, P. W. (1973). *Leadership and Decision Making.* Pittsburgh: University of Pittsburgh Press.

Wahba, M. A., and Bridwell, L. G. (1976). Maslow Reconsidered: A Review of Research on Need Hierarchy Theory. *Organizational Behavior and Human Performance, 15,* 211–240.

Waller, W. (1932). *The Sociology of Teaching.* New York: Wiley.

Walsh, J. P., and Ungson, G. R. (1991). Organizational memory. *Academy of Management Review, 16,* (1), 57–91.

Weber, J. (1993). Exploring the Relationship Between Personal Values and Moral Reasoning. *Human Relations, 46,* (4), 435–463.

Weber, M. (1947). *The Theory of Social and Economic Organizations.* In T. Parsons (Ed.), A. M. Henderson and T. Parsons (Trans.)., New York: Free Press.

Weick, K. E. (1976). Educational Organizations as Loosely Coupled Systems. *Administrative Science Quarterly, 21,* 1–19.

Weick, K. E. (1979). Cognitive Processes in Organizations. *Research in Organizational Behavior, 1,* 41–74.

Weick, K. E. (1989). Theory Construction as Disciplined Imagination. *Academy of Management Review, 14,* 516–531.

Weick, K. E. (1992). Agenda Setting in Organizational Behavior: A Theory-focused Approach. *Journal of Management Inquiry, 1,* 171–183.

Weiner, B. (1972). *Theories of Motivation: From Mechanism to Cognition.* Chicago: Academic Press.

Weiner, B. (1985). An Attributional Theory of Achievement Motivation and Emotion. *Psychological Review, 92,* 548–573.

Weiner, B. (1986). *An Attributional Theory of Motivation and Emotion.* New York: Springer-Verlag.

Weiss, J. A. (1989). Theories of Control in Organization: Lessons for Schools. Conference on Choice and Control in American Education, University of Wisconsin at Madison.

Wellberg, D. (1985). Appendix 1: Postmodernism in Europe: On Recent German Writing. In S. Trachtenberg (Ed.), *The Postmodern Moment.* Westport, CT: Greenwood Press.

Wendel, F. C., Kelley, E. A., Kluender, M., and Palmere, M. (1983). *Use of Assessment Center Processes: A Literature Review.* Lincoln, NB: Teachers College, University of Nebraska.

Whetten, D. A. (1989). What Constitutes a Theoretical Contribution? *Academy of Management Review, 14,* 490–495.

Whitehead, A. N. (1925). *Science and the Modern World.* New York: Macmillan.

Wietz, S. (1974). *Non-Verbal Communication.* New York: Oxford.

Wiggins, T. (1970). Why Our Urban Schools Are Leaderless. *Education and Urban Society, 2,* 169–177.

Wilensky, H. (1964). Professionalization of Everyone? *American Journal of Sociology, 70,* 137–158.

Wilkins, A., and Patterson, K. (1985). You Can't Get There From Here: What Will Make Culture-Change Projects Fail. In R. H. Kilmann, M. J. Saxton, and R. Serpa (Eds.), *Gaining Control of the Corporate Culture* (pp. 262–291). San Francisco: Jossey-Bass.

Wilkins, B. M., and Andersen, P. A. (1991). Gender Differences and Similarities in Management Communication: A Meta-Analysis. *Management Communication Quarterly, 5,* (1), 6–35.

Williams, L. B., and Hoy, W. K. (1973). Principal-Staff Relations: Situational Mediator of Effectiveness. *Journal of Educational Administration, 9,* 66–73.

Willis, Q. (1980). The Work Activity of School Principals: An Observational Study. *Journal of Educational Administration, 18,* 27–54.

Willower, D. J. (1963). The Form of Knowledge and the Theory-Practice Relationship. *Educational Theory, 13,* 47–52.

Willower, D. J. (1975). Theory in Educational Administration. *Journal of Educational Administration, 13,* 77–91.

Willower, D. J. (1979). Some Issues in Research on School Organization. In G. L. Immegart and W. Boyd (Eds.), *Currents in Administrative Research: Problem Finding in Education* (pp. 63–86). Lexington, MA: Heath.

Willower, D. J. (1987). Inquiry into Educational Administration: The Last Twenty-Five Years and the Next. *Journal of Educational Administration, 24,* 12–29.

Willower, D. J. (1994). Values, Valuation, and Explanation in School Organizations. *Journal of School Leadership, 4,* (5), 466–483.

Willower, D. J., Eidell, T. L., and Hoy, W. K. (1967). *The School and Pupil Control Ideology.* Monograph No. 24. University Park: Pennsylvania State University.

Willower, D. J., and Jones, R. G. (1967). Control in an Educational Organization. In J. D. Raths, J. R. Pancella, and J. S. V. Ness (Eds.), *Studying Teaching* (pp. 424–428). Englewood Cliffs, NJ: Prentice-Hall.

Wimpelberg, R. K., Teddlie, C., and Stringfield, S. (1989). Sensitivity to Context: The Past and Future of Effective Schools Research. *Educational Administration Quarterly, 25,* 82–107.

Wise, A. (1988). The Two Conflicting Trends in School Reform: Legislated Learning Revisited. *Phi Delta Kappan, 69,* 328–332.

Wiseman, C. (1979a). Selection of Major Planning Issues. *Policy Sciences, 12,* 71–86.

Wiseman, C. (1979b). Strategic Planning in the Scottish Health Service—A Mixed Scanning Approach. *Long Range Planning, 12,* 103–113.

Wofford, J. C. (1994). An Examination of the Cognitive Processes Used to Handle Employee Job Problems. *Academy of Management Journal, 37,* (1), 180–192.

Wolin, S. S. (1960). *Politics and Vision: Continuity and Innovation in Western Political Thought.* Boston: Little, Brown.

Wood, R., and Bandura, A. (1989). Social Cognitive Theory of Organizational Management. *Academy of Management Review, 14,* 361–384.

Wood, D. J., and Gray, B. (1991). Toward a Comprehensive Theory of Collaboration. *Journal of Applied Behavioral Science, 27,* (2), 139–162.

Wood, S., and Midgley, C. (1994). Collaborating to change school goals: effects on teachers. Unpublished paper, University of Michigan, Ann Arbor.

Woolfolk, A. E., and Hoy, W. K. (1990). Prospective Teachers' Sense of Efficacy and Beliefs About Control. *Journal of Educational Psychology, 82,* 81-91.

Woolfolk, A. E., Rosoff, B., and Hoy, W. K. (1990). Teachers' Sense of Efficacy and Their Beliefs about Managing Students. *Teaching and Teacher Education, 6,* (2), 137-148.

Worthy, J. C. (1950). Factors Influencing Employee Morale. *Harvard Business Review, 28,* 61-73.

Wright, R. (1985). Motivating Teacher Involvement in Professional Growth Activities. *Canadian Administrator, 24,* 1-6.

Yamagishi, T., Gillmore, M. R., and Cook, K. S. (1988). Network Connections and the Distribution of Power in Exchange Networks. *American Journal of Sociology, 93,* 833-851.

Yekovich, F. R. (1993). A Theoretical View of the Development of Expertise in Credit Administration. In P. Hallinger, K. Leithwood, and J. Murphy (Eds.), *Cognitive Perspectives on Educational Leadership* (pp. 146-166). New York: Teachers College.

Yuchtman, E., and Seashore, S. E. (1967). A System Resource Approach to Organizational Effectiveness. *American Sociological Review, 32,* 891-903.

Yukl, G. A. (1981). *Leadership in Organizations.* Englewood Cliffs, NJ: Prentice-Hall.

Yukl, G. A. (1989). *Leadership in Organizations* (2nd ed.). Englewood Cliffs, NJ: Prentice-Hall.

Yukl, G. A. (1994). *Leadership in Organizations* (3rd ed.). Englewood Cliffs, NJ: Prentice-Hall.

Zahn, C. L. (1991). Face-to-Face Communication in an Office Setting. *Communication Research, 18,* (6), 737-754.

Zald, M. M., and Berger, M. A. (1978). Social Movements in Organizations: Coup d'Etat, Insurgency, and Mass Movements. *American Journal of Sociology, 42,* 823-861.

Zaltman, G., Duncan, R., and Holbek, J. (1973). *Innovations and Organizations.* New York: Wiley.

Zammuto, R. F. (1982). *Assessing Organizational Effectiveness.* Albany: State University of New York Press.

Zeichner, K. M., and Tabachnick, B. R. (1981). Are the Effects of University Teacher Education "Washed Out" by School Experience? *Journal of Teacher Education, 32,* 7-11.

Zenger, T. R., and Lawrence, B. S. (1989). Organizational Demography: The Differential Effects of Age and Tenure Distributions on Technical Communication. *Academy of Management Journal, 32,* 353-376.

Zey, M. (1992). *Decision Making: Alternatives to Rational Choice.* Newbury Park, CA: Sage.

Zielinski, A. E., and Hoy, W. K. (1983). Isolation and Alienation in Elementary Schools. *Educational Administration Quarterly, 19,* 27-45.

Zucker, L. (1987). Institutional Theories of Organization. *Annual Review of Sociology, 13,* 443-464.

Name Index

◆◆◆

AASA, 257
Abbott, M., 42, 44, 59, 60, 63
Abramowitz, S., 77
Acar, W., 132
Adkinson, J. A., 334
Adler, R. B., 343, 352, 353
Adler, S., 338
Adrian Bennett Cairns, I., 350
Agho, A. O., 252, 253
Aho, F., 87
Aiken, M., 211
Airasian, P. W., 247, 265
Aldrich, H. E., 76, 206, 209–215, 217, 233
Alessandra, T., 353
Alexander, E. R., 367, 368
Alexander, J. A., 213, 221
Alinsky, S., 170
Allen, R. F., 129
Allison, G. T., 39, 191, 193
Alutto, J. A., 254, 305
Amburgey, T. L., 213
Andersen, P. A., 354
Anderson, B. D., 62, 330
Anderson, C. S., 141, 161
Anderson, D. P., 150
Anderson, J. C., 262, 263
Anderson, J. R., 24, 25, 369
Anderson, M. B. G., 104
Andrews, F. M., 82
Andrews, J. H. M., 150
Angelmar, R., 97
Appleberry, J. B., 158, 159
Argot, L., 359
Aristotle, 376
Armor, D., 116
Arnold, H. J., 338
Arthur, M. B., 393

Ashford, S. J., 353, 368
Ashforth, B. E., 141
Ashton, P. T., 116
Astley, W. G., 22
Astuto, T. A., 15, 17, 19, 24, 59, 136, 249, 265, 318
At-Twaijri, M. I. A., 215
Atwater, D. C., 394, 395
Aupperle, K. E., 132
Averich, H. A., 265
Avolio, B. J., 393–395, 403

Babbie, E. R., 1
Bacharach, S. B., 23, 180, 223, 225, 243, 305, 330
Bader, B. D., 317, 330, 337
Baetz, M. L., 374, 384, 391
Baker, M. A., 354, 370
Bales, R. F., 151
Baltzell, D. C., 400
Bamberger, P., 305
Bandura, A., 94, 95, 98, 113–115
Bantz, C. R., 138, 352
Barnabe, C., 338
Barnard, C. I., 16, 39, 56, 57, 127, 173, 174, 273, 275, 291, 295, 316, 341, 358, 362, 370, 383
Barnes, K. M., 150, 155
Barnes, R. M., 9
Barnett, B. G., 366
Bass, B. M., 4, 275, 373, 377, 380, 381, 393–395, 403, 404
Bass, G., 116
Bates, R., 139
Bauer, S., 305
Beady, C. H., 136, 265
Becker, T. E., 352, 369
Becker, W. S., 103, 104, 108
Belasco, J. A., 254, 305

Bennis, W. G., 30, 373, 393
Benson, J. K., 210
Berger, M. A., 197
Berlo, D. K., 352
Berman, P., 116
Bess, J. L., 316
Bettenhausen, K. R., 348, 355, 365
Bettman, J. R., 269
Betz, E. L., 104
Beyer, J. M., 137, 402
Bhagat, R. S., 338
Bidwell, C. E., 34, 71, 76, 81, 247
Bimber, B., 63
Birnbaum, R., 400
Blackburn, R., 262
Blake, R. R., 384
Blau, P. M., 47, 50, 54, 57, 58, 79, 82, 172–176, 268, 417
Blazovsky, R., 63, 74, 77, 78, 305
Bliss, J. R., 143, 149, 156, 175
Bloom, S., 110, 254, 255, 365
Bluedorn, A. C., 242
Blumberg, A., 8
Bobbit, F., 20
Boje, D. M., 218
Bok, D., 317, 318
Bolman, L. G., 47, 60, 64, 65, 139, 171, 187, 191, 200, 203
Bonan, J., 63
Bonstingl, J. J., 257
Booth, D. E., 132
Borman, K. M., 59, 78
Bose, C., 58
Bossert, S. T., 248, 249, 251, 265
Bowditch, J. L., 203, 213
Bower, S., 305
Bowers, D. G., 352
Bowman, B. T., 328
Boyan, N. J., 57
Boyd, B., 349
Boyd, W. L., 180, 208, 217, 219, 231
Boyle, R. A., 98
Brady, L., 145
Braybrook, D., 280
Bridges, E. M., 291
Bridwell, L. G., 103
Brinkerhoff, D., 244
Brogdon, R., 116
Bromily, P., 286
Broms, H., 344, 345
Brookover, W. B., 136, 265
Brophy, J. E., 249, 251, 265
Brown, A. F., 162, 383
Brown, B. L., 383
Brown, D., 63

Brown, M. E., 62
Brownlee-Conyers, J., 332
Bryk, A. S., 86, 224, 231, 251, 265
Buono, A. F., 203, 213
Burbules, N. C., 340, 345–347, 368, 370
Burke, W. W., 395
Burlingame, M., 242
Burns, J. M., 393
Burns, M. L., 338
Burns, T., 215
Burrell, G., 19, 24
Butler, R., 286

Calas, M. B., 20
Caldwell, D., 134
Callahan, R. E., 20
Cameron, K., 236, 238, 240, 241, 243, 245, 264
Campbell, E. Q., 160, 247
Campbell, J. P., 99, 101, 110, 124, 240–242, 244, 380, 381
Campbell, R. F., 20, 34
Capper, C. A., 257
Caracheo, F., 59, 60, 63
Carey, M. R., 393
Carey, S., 2
Carlson, R. O., 87, 157
Carnegie Task Force on Teaching as a Profession, 327
Carpenter, H. H., 254
Carroll, S. J., 265, 312
Carss, B. W., 254
Cartwright, D., 382
Carver, F. D., 143
Casner-Lotto, J., 63
Castrogiovanni, G. J., 210
Celotti, L. D., 76, 77
Chapman, D. W., 330
Charters, W. W., Jr., 62, 366
Chase, F. S., 291
Chassie, M. B., 338
Chatman, J. A., 134
Chemers, M. M., 392, 401, 404
Chen, M., 63
Cherrington, D. J., 101, 103, 105, 106
Chi, M. T. H., 96
Chisolm, G. B., 104
Chubb, J. E., 231
Chung, K. A., 375, 403
Citera, M., 105
Clampitt, P. G., 344, 345, 359, 362, 370
Clark, D. L., 15, 17, 19, 24, 59, 136, 249, 265, 318
Clark, K. E., 403
Clark, M. B., 403
Clark, R., 63

Clatterbuck, G. W., 348
Clover, S. I. R., 143
Clune, W. H., 63
Cohen, D. K., 63, 280, 317
Cohen, M. D., 285, 286
Cohn, M. M., 316, 317
Cole, S., 76
Coleman, J. S., 86, 157, 160, 247
Commons, J. R., 173
Conant, J. B., 1
Conger, J. A., 317, 402
Conley, S. C., 180, 305, 330–332
Conlon, E. J., 242, 243
Connolly, T., 242, 243
Conry-Oseguera, P., 116
Constas, H., 58
Conway, J. A., 305
Cook, K. S., 356
Cooke, R. A., 254, 305
Coons, A. E., 382
Corbally, J. E., 396
Corbett, H. D., 139
Cordery, J. L., 325
Cornwall, J. R., 82
Corwin, R. G., 59, 62, 78, 82, 84
Cosgrove, D., 399, 401
Costello, M., 368
Cox, A., 193
Cox, M., 116
Cranny, C. J., 252, 264
Crehan, E. P., 571
Croft, D. B., 140–143, 150, 167
Cropanzano, R., 105
Crowson, R. L., 403
Crozier, M., 46
Cuban, L., 249, 250
Culbertston, J. A., 19, 21
Culhan, M. J., 361
Cummings, L. L., 107, 325
Cunningham, W. G., 139
Cusella, L. P., 368
Cusick, P. A., 136, 176
Cyert, M., 187, 275

Daft, R. L., 38, 39, 204, 206, 214, 215, 217, 285, 286,
    304, 348, 349, 355, 365
Dahl, R. A., 189
Dahnke, G. L., 348
Darling-Hammond, L., 76, 330
D'Aunno, T., 221
David, J. L., 63
Davis, S. M., 129
Day, D. V., 373

Deal, T. E., 47, 60, 64, 65, 76, 77, 132, 136, 138, 139,
    171, 187, 191, 200, 203, 205, 221, 223, 228
DeFleur, M. L., 343, 351, 356, 363, 364, 368, 370
DeFrain, J., 110, 254
Deming, W. E., 238, 256, 257, 259, 261, 264
Denhardt, R. B., 59, 242
Dennison, D. R., 135, 167
Dentler, R. A., 400
Derrida, J., 18
Deutsch, S. J., 242, 243
Devanna, M. A., 393
Dewey, J., 8, 23
DiAngelo, J. A., Jr., 353, 354
Dibski, D. J., 317, 318
Dickson, W. J., 12
Diebert, J. P., 160
Dill, R. W., 204, 209
Dill, W. R., 44
DiMaggio, P. J., 221, 222, 232, 233
DiPaola, M. F., 84
Donaldson, T. S., 265
Donmoyer, R. B., 24
Donnelly, J. H., Jr., 352
Downs, C. W., 369
Drenth, P., 286
Driscoll, J. W., 305
Drucker, P. F., 10, 273, 311, 420
Dubin, R., 4
Duignan, P., 403
Duke, D. L., 292, 305
Dukerich, J. M., 373
Duncan, R. B., 204, 206, 208, 209, 215
Dunnette, M. D., 124, 380, 381
Durick, M., 253
Dutton, J. E., 207, 208
Dwyer, D. C., 251, 265

Earley, P. C., 105, 122, 352
Ebmeier, H., 332
Eccles, J. S., 116
Edmonds, R., 249, 265
Ehrlich, S. B., 373
Eidell, T. L., 157, 158, 167, 183,
Einstein, A., 2
Ekeberg, S. E., 316
Ellet, C. D., 255
Ellis, J., 18
Elmes, M. B., 368
Elmore, R. F., 63, 76, 230
Elsbach, K. D., 227, 228
Emery, F. E., 206, 233
English, F. W., 24
Enns, F., 392

Enoch, Y., 85
Erez, M., 105, 118, 122
Erlandson, D. A., 338
Estler, S. E., 285
Etzioni, A., 15, 24, 29, 30, 44, 80, 171, 179, 180, 182,
    183, 201, 213, 281, 282, 284, 304, 305, 329, 362
Evans, M. G., 338
Eyring, H. B., 44

Fang, Y., 338
Fayol, H., 10
Feigl, H., 2
Feldberg, R., 58
Feldlaufer, H., 116
Feldman, G., 323
Feldman, J., 6, 150, 152
Fennell, M. L., 213, 221
Ferguson, J., 255
Ferguson, K. E., 19, 20, 58, 59
Ferry, D. L., 210
Festinger, L., 252
Fevurly, R., 254, 255
Fichman, M., 359
Fiedler, F. E., 373, 379, 381, 387–392, 401, 404
Firestone, W. A., 59, 63, 73, 74, 78, 137, 139, 317, 318,
    330, 337
Fish, S., 18
Flood, P. K., 136, 265
Follett, M. P., 12
Ford, J. K., 96
Ford, M. E., 98, 118, 119, 123, 309, 310, 337
Forsyth, P. B., 24, 56, 57, 150, 258, 260, 365, 397, 403
Foster, W. P., 15, 17, 19, 24, 59
Foucault, M., 18
Fox, S., 323
Francke, D. C., 351
Frase, L. E., 325
Freeman, J. H., 212
Freidson, E., 328, 329
French, J. R. P., 176, 180
Fried, Y., 338
Friedman, R. A., 215
Friesen, D., 403
Fromm, E., 158
Frost, P. J., 167, 393
Fuhrman, S. H., 230
Fulk, J., 349

Gaertner, K. N., 333
Gahmberg, H., 344, 345
Galbraith, J., 4, 65, 107
Ganz, H. J., 87
Garcia, J. E., 381, 388, 389, 392, 404

Garcia, T., 116
Gardner, D. G., 325
Gardner, H., 91, 92, 94, 96, 123
Gardner, J. W., 373
Gartner, W. B., 262
Gaynor, A. K., 15, 17, 19, 24, 59
Geertz, C., 137
Gemmill, G., 373
Gerhardt, E., 254
Gerth, H. H., 47, 58
Getzels, J. W., 26, 27, 34, 44
Gibson, J. L., 352
Gilligan, C., 59
Gillmore, M. R., 356
Gilmer, B. H., 140
Gist, M. E., 114–116
Glaser, B., 83
Glaser, R., 96
Glasnapp, D., 253
Glassman, M., 253
Glaub, J., 257
Glick, W., 326
Glisson, C., 253
Goffman, E., 157
Goldberg, M. A., 281
Goldman, S., 192, 400
Goldring, E. B., 63
Good, T. L., 249, 251, 265
Goodman, P. S., 241, 242, 264
Goodstein, J. D., 227
Gordon, C. W., 157
Gordon, G. E., 401
Gorsuch, R. A., 338
Gouldner, A., 29, 49–53, 57, 58, 61, 82
Govindarajan, V., 299
Graen, G., 107
Graham, L. L., 111
Graham, S., 112
Grandori, A., 280, 284
Grassie, M. C., 254
Gray, B., 213
Gray, D., 286
Gray, J., 370
Greene, C. N., 178
Greenfield, T. B., 21, 24, 44
Greiner, J. M., 318
Gresso, D. W., 139
Griffin, R. W., 323, 325, 326, 338
Griffiths, D. E., 2, 3, 21, 22, 192, 304, 397, 400, 403
Grimes, A. J., 82
Gross, E., 24, 80, 171, 213, 329
Grush, J. E., 107
Grusky, O., 399–401
Guba, E. G., 27, 34, 44

Guest, R. H., 305
Guidette, M. R. M., 87
Gulick, L., 10, 11
Guzzo, R.A., 314, 315

Haas, J. E., 182
Hack, W. G., 366
Hackman, J. R., 319, 323-326
Hage, J., 62, 211
Hajnal, V. J., 318
Hall, O., 81
Hall, R. H., 47, 60, 62, 182, 212
Hall, R. J., 95, 96
Haller, E. J., 243
Halpin, A. W., 2, 140-143, 150, 167, 382, 383
Handy, C. B., 24
Hannum, J., 150, 156
Hanson, E. M., 44, 132
Hanushek, E. A., 247, 248, 265
Harris, T. E., 343, 350, 351, 356, 358, 359, 362-364, 368-370
Harrison, M. I., 44
Hart, A. W., 15, 17, 19, 24, 59, 317-319, 323, 326, 330, 332, 337, 399
Hartke, D. D., 392
Hartley, M., 150
Hatley, R., 253
Hatry, H. P., 318
Hayes, A. E., 143
Haymond, J. E., 87
Haynes, P.A., 281
Heath, D. H., 161
Heck, G., 325
Heide, J. B., 218
Heintzman, M., 350
Heller, F., 286
Hellriegel, D., 38
Hemphill, J. K., 382
Henderson, J. E., 175
Heneman, H. G. I., 110
Henwood, C. I., 367
Herker, D., 214, 215
Heron, R. P., 87
Herrick, H. S., 110
Herriott, R. E., 59, 62, 63, 73, 74, 78
Hersey, P.W., 398, 399
Herzberg, F., 320-323, 337
Heydebrand, W., 21
Hickson, D., 286
Hickson, D. J., 86, 87
Hill, P.T., 63
Hinnings, C. R., 86
Hirchman, A. O., 190

Hitt, M.A., 132
Hobson, C. J., 160, 247
Hodgkinson, C., 100, 104, 124
Hoffman, A. N., 218
Hoffman, J. D., 143, 149, 175, 176
Holbeck, J., 204
Holdaway, E.A., 87, 254
Holland, P., 86, 224, 231
Hollenbeck, 319
Holmes Group, 327
Homans, G. C., 27
Hoppock, R., 252
House, R. J., 338, 373, 384, 391-394, 404
Howell, J. M., 393
Hoy, W. K., 6, 24, 56, 57, 60, 62, 63, 74, 77, 78, 84, 85, 87, 116, 139, 143, 148-150, 152, 155-160, 162, 163, 167, 174, 175, 183, 255, 258, 260, 281, 282, 290, 291, 293, 304-305, 365, 370, 383, 384, 392
Huber, G. P., 348
Huber, V. L., 178
Hulin, C. L., 1, 22, 252
Hunsaker, P., 353
Hunt, J. G., 92, 93, 180, 396
Hunter, F., 189
Hunter, J. E., 104, 312, 380
Hurwitz, E., Jr., 403
Huseman, R. C., 361
Hutcheson, S. M., 330
Huyssen, A., 18

Iannaccone, L., 56
Ilgen, D. R., 319
Imber, M. L., 24, 292, 305
Immegart, G. L., 378
Infeld, L., 2
Ingersoll, R. M., 78, 225, 228
Intilli, J. K., 76
Ireland, R. D., 132
Isaacson, G., 175
Isherwood, G. B., 60, 62, 63, 392
Ivancevich, J. M., 352
Iwanicki, E. F., 104

Jablin, F. M., 342, 343, 352, 361, 362
Jago, A. G., 290, 304, 305
James, K., 105
Jamison, D., 265
Jamison, M.T., 257
Janis, I. L., 286-289, 297, 298, 305
Jehn, K.A., 134
Jepperson, R. L., 220
Jermier, J. M., 373, 381

Jernigan, I. E., 367, 368
Johns, G., 338
Johnson, E. J., 269
Johnson, N., 182
Johnson, S. M., 309, 317–319, 330
Jones, R. G., 157
Jones, S. D., 316
Jurkovich, R., 206, 207

Kahn, R. L., 44, 218, 341, 363, 364, 373, 374, 404
Kahneman, D., 288, 305
Kanfer, R., 99, 101, 104, 106, 107, 110, 112, 113, 123
Kanner, L., 150
Kanter, R., 194, 195, 197, 201, 244
Kanungo, R. N., 317
Karper, J. H., 208, 219
Kasarda, J. D., 247
Katz, D., 44, 218, 341, 363, 364, 373, 374, 404
Katzell, R. A., 106
Kearney, P., 343, 351, 356, 363, 364, 368, 370
Keeley, M., 244
Kellaghan, T., 247, 265
Kelley, E. A., 398
Kelly, J., 325
Kelsey, J. G. T., 87
Kendall, L. M., 252
Kennedy, A. A., 132, 136, 138
Keon, T. L., 105
Kerlinger, F. N., 2, 5
Kerr, S., 373, 381
Kiesling, H. J., 265
Kiggundu, M. N., 338
Kilmann, R. H., 135, 162, 164–166
Kimbrough, R., 189
King, N., 116
Kirchoff, B. A., 241
Klimoski, R. J., 352, 369
Kluender, M., 398
Kmetz, J. T., 403
Knapp, M. L., 350
Koberg, C. S., 206, 211, 212
Kolesar, H., 60, 62
Kondrasuk, J. N., 312, 313
Koopman, P., 286
Kornhauser, W., 83
Kotter, J. P., 171, 173, 178, 374, 403
Kottkamp, R. B., 110, 143, 148, 150, 152, 155, 156, 167, 316, 317, 338
Kraft, C., 129
Kraiger, K. J., 96
Kranz, J., 63
Krone, K. J., 342, 352
Kuhlman, E., 85

Kuhnert, K. W., 393
Kulik, C. T., 326
Kunz, D., 383, 384

Labaree, D. D., 327
Landy, F. J., 103, 104, 108
Larson, J. R. J., 368, 369
Lasagna, J. B., 314
Latham, G. P., 99, 116–120, 123, 311, 312, 315
Lau, L. J., 247, 265
Lavery, R. G., 392
Lawler, E. E., III., 101, 107, 108, 124, 262, 315, 380, 381
Lawrence, B. S., 354
Lawrence, P. R., 22, 30, 206, 208, 233
Leathers, D. G., 350
Leavitt, H. J., 44
Leblebici, H., 233
Lee, G. V., 251
Lee, V. E., 86, 224, 231, 251, 265
Lefkowitz, J., 104
Leithwood, K., 396, 403
Lengel, R. H., 348, 349
Lensky, H. W., 82
Leonard, J. F., 257
Level, D. A., Jr., 350
Leverette, B. B., 383, 384
Levinson, R., 331, 332
Levitt, B., 286
Lewin, K., 107
Lewis, P., 393
Lewis, P. V., 342, 356, 364
Liao, Y. M., 156
Licata, J. W., 255, 366
Lieberson, S., 373
Lindblom, C. E., 280
Lipham, J. A., 44, 351, 373
Lipham, J. M., 26, 34
Litchfield, E. H., 269–271, 279, 304
Litwin, G. H., 140
Locke, E. A., 90, 99, 100, 103–105, 116–123, 252, 254, 305, 311, 312, 315
Logan, C. S., 255
Lombardo, M. M., 373
Lord, R. G., 92, 93, 95–98, 123, 124, 373
Lorsch, J. W., 22, 30, 128, 206, 208, 233
Lortie, D. C., 87, 316, 317, 327, 330
Lotto, L. S., 136, 265
Louis, M. R., 93, 128, 167
Lugg, C. A., 180
Lundberg, C. C., 167
Lunenburg, F. C., 160
Lysaught, J. P., 370

Machiavelli, N., 200
MacKay, D., 60, 62
MacKensie, D. E., 265
MacKenzie, S. B., 381
MacKinnon, J. D., 62
Madaus, G. F., 247, 265
Maehr, M. L., 335
Maeroff, G. I., 63
Maher, K. J., 92, 93, 95-98, 123, 124
Mahar, L., 401, 404
Malen, B., 63, 219, 223, 233, 317-319, 332, 337
Mallory, G., 286
Mann, L., 286-289, 297, 305
Mann, R. D., 377
Manning, P. K., 342
March, J. C., 334
March, J. G., 11, 76, 86, 173, 187, 218, 252, 275, 285, 286, 304, 334
Marjoribanks, K., 84
Mark, J. H., 330
Markus, M. L., 361
Marshall, C., 21
Martin, J., 58, 128, 167
Martin, W. J., 403
Martin, Y. M., 392
Marx, R. W., 98
Maslow, A. H., 100, 103, 123
Massell, D., 230
Matheson, R. R., 325
Maugham, B., 136
Mausner, B., 320
Mayo, E., 127
Mazzoni, T. L., 219
McAfee, R. B., 253
McCabe, D. L., 207, 208
McCall, M. W., Jr., 323
McCaskey, M. B., 350, 351
McClelland, D. C., 100, 105, 106, 379
McConkie, M. L., 311
McDill, E. L., 204
McDonald, D., 110, 254, 255, 365
McDonnell, L., 116
McElroy, J. C., 356
McFarland, W. J., 192, 400
McLaughlin, M., 116
McNall, S. A., 355
McNall, S. G., 355
McNamara, V., 392
McNeil, L. M., 76
McPartland, J., 160, 247
Meany, D. P., 257
Mechanic, D., 193
Meidl, J. R., 373
Mennuti, N., 338

Merton, R., 28, 50, 173, 376
Metz, M. H., 139
Meyer, J. W., 76, 77, 203, 205, 220-225, 227-230, 233
Meyer, M. W., 27
Midgley, C., 116, 180, 335, 336
Miles, E. W., 361
Miles, M. B., 59, 151
Miller, D., 208, 215
Miller, H. E., 338
Miller, L. E., 107
Milliken, F. J., 208, 212
Mills, C. W., 47, 58
Mindlin, S., 206, 210-213, 215
Miner, A. S., 213
Miner, J. B., 103-106, 113, 118, 165, 166, 313, 321, 326
Mintzberg, H., 3, 39, 44, 60, 66, 70-72, 74, 81, 87, 126, 128, 183, 187-189, 193, 194, 196, 197, 215, 216, 304, 403
Miskel, C., 110, 141, 161, 220, 253-255, 316, 365, 370, 375, 399, 403
Mitchell, D. E., 308, 316, 317
Mitchell, T. K., 308, 316, 317
Mitchell, T. R., 110, 114-116, 384, 404
Moe, T. M., 231
Moeller, G. H., 62
Mohan, M. L., 138
Mohrman, A. M., Jr., 254, 305
Mohrman, S. A., 254, 305
Monge, P. R., 356
Monk, D. H., 243, 248, 265
Montanari, J. R., 215
Mood, A. M., 160, 247
Moon, N. J., 305
Moore, L. F., 167
Moran, E. T., 162
Morgan, G., 19, 24
Morris, V. C., 403
Mortimore, P., 136
Mott, P. E., 255, 264
Mouton, J. S., 384
Mowday, R. T., 110, 135
Muchinsky, P. M., 252
Mueller, C. W., 252, 253
Mulhern, J. A., 110, 143, 148
Mullins, T., 175
Mundell, B. L., 223, 225
Murnane, R. J., 265, 317, 330
Murphy, M. J., 317-319, 330-332, 337
Myers, G. E., 341, 344, 358, 363, 366
Myers, M. T., 341, 344, 358, 363, 366

Nadler, D. A., 44, 108
Nanus, B., 393

Nass, C., 286
National Commission on Excellence in Education, 208, 309
National Commission on Excellence in Educational Administration, 327
Natriello, G., 204
Naughton, M. J., 262
Neumann, A., 257
Newberry, J. F., 87
Newland, W., 63, 74, 77, 78, 305
Nicholson, J. H., 254
Niehoff, B. P., 381
Nisbett, R. E., 288, 305
Northcraft, G. B., 352
Nutt, P. C., 304

Oakley, J., 373
O'Connor, J. F., 373
O'Dempsey, K., 403
Odiorne, G. S., 311
Ogawa, R. T., 63, 141, 161, 223, 226, 229, 231, 233, 401, 403
Okeafor, K. R., 77
Oldham, G. R., 323–326, 338
Olsen, J. P., 76, 285, 286
Olsen, M. E., 188
O'Reilly, C. A. I., 134, 362, 365
Orpen, C., 338
Ortiz, F. I., 21, 308, 316, 317
Osborn, R. N., 180
Ostroff, C., 245
Ouchi, W., 128, 131, 136, 161, 167, 238
Ousten, J., 136
Owens, R. G., 138

Pace, C. R., 140
Packard, J. S., 158, 159, 163
Padgett, J. F., 286
Page, C. H., 57
Palincsar, A. S., 347
Pallas, A. M., 204, 257
Palmere, M., 398
Parrot, R. L., 350
Parsons, T., 16, 36, 57, 87, 151
Pascal, A., 116
Pastor, M. C., 338
Patterson, K., 128
Pauly, E., 116
Payne, J. W., 269
Peabody, R. L., 173, 175
Pelz, D. C., 82
Penley, L. E., 38, 367

Pennings, J. M., 208, 213, 215, 241, 242, 264, 304
Perkins, J., 59
Perrow, C., 29, 47
Peters, L. H., 392
Peters, T. J., 56, 57, 128, 132, 136, 167, 238
Peterson, K. D., 139, 403
Peterson, P. E., 231
Pfeffer, J., 206, 211, 217, 218, 233, 373
Phillips, D., 403
Pincus, J., 265
Pinder, C. C., 99, 102, 103, 105, 106, 108, 111, 311, 313, 314, 321
Pinfield, L. T., 286
Pintrich, P. R., 93, 98, 116
Pitner, N., 381, 403
Plax, T. G., 343, 351, 356, 363, 364, 368, 370
Podgurski, T. P., 155
Podolny, J., 215
Podsakoff, P. M., 178, 381
Pohlmann, J. T., 392
Pondy, L. R., 362
Poole, M. S., 140
Porter, L. W., 99–101, 103, 104, 107, 123, 135, 321, 342, 343, 349, 359, 364
Porter-Gehrie, C., 403
Powell, W. W., 221, 222, 228, 233
Presthus, R. V., 82
Prestine, N. A., 76
Price, J. L., 252, 253
Price, R. H., 221
Pritchard, R. D., 99, 101, 110, 316
Prolman, S., 334
Pugh, D. S., 86
Purkey, S. C., 63, 249, 264, 265
Putnam, L. L., 342, 343, 352

Quarstein, V. A., 253

Raisinghani, D., 196
Ratsoy, E. W., 254
Rauschenberger, J., 103
Raven, B. H., 176, 180
Redding, W. C., 350
Reder, L. M., 24
Rees, R., 85, 174, 175
Reilly, B. J., 353, 354
Reiss, F., 150, 175, 176
Reynolds, P. D., 3
Rhodes, L. A., 257
Ribbins, P., 24, 44
Rice, A. W., 254
Rice, R. E., 349
Rice, R. W., 388, 392

Robbins, S. P., 56, 57, 128, 135, 214
Roberts, K., 343
Roberts, K. H., 1, 22, 326, 342, 350, 359, 364, 365
Roberts, N. C., 373
Rockey, E., 369
Rodman, G., 343, 352, 353
Roethlisberger, F. J., 12
Rogers, R. C., 312
Rokeach, M., 104
Rosen, B. 262
Rosen, N., 401
Rosenau, P. M., 17, 18
Rosoff, B., 116
Ross, L., 288, 305
Rossman, G. B., 139
Roth, P. L., 316
Rousseau, D. M., 1, 22, 134
Rowan, B., 76, 77, 202, 205, 220-222, 224, 226-230,
    233, 251, 265, 332
Rungtusanatham, M., 262-263
Runkel, P. J., 344
Rus, V., 286
Russ, G. S., 349
Russell, C. J., 209
Russell, R. D., 209
Rutter, M., 136

Sabo, D., 143, 149, 175
Sackney, L. E., 87
Salancik, G. R., 233, 373
Salas, E., 96
Salvemini, N. J., 338
Sarup, M., 18
Sashkin, M., 395
Saxton, M. J., 135, 164, 165
Sayles, L. R., 367
Schein, E. H., 129, 133, 134, 139, 162, 166, 167
Scherkenbach, W., 257, 259, 260
Schermerhorn, J. R., 180
Schlechty, P. C., 330
Schmidt, F. L., 380
Schmidt, L. J., 160
Schmitt, N., 103, 245
Schmitz, J., 349
Schmuck, R. A., 344
Schneider, J. M., 136, 265
Schneider, S. C., 97
Schrader, C. B., 356
Schroeder, R. G., 263
Schunk, D., 116
Schurich, J., 24
Schwab, D. P., 110
Schwartz, H. M., 129

Schweiger, D. M., 305
Schweitzer, J. H., 136, 265
Scott, W. R., 5, 24, 27-29, 31, 32, 34, 44, 47, 50, 53, 54,
    58, 76, 79, 80, 82, 172-174, 176, 203-205, 212,
    221-225, 227-230, 233, 240, 241, 245, 264, 268,
    417
Seashore, S. E., 240, 241
Selznick, P., 127, 220
Senge, P. M., 44, 406
Sergiovanni, T. J., 104, 143, 189, 396
Serpa, R., 135, 164
Sevastos, P. P., 325
Shakeshaft, C., 21, 106, 334, 354
Shamir, B., 393
Shanker, A., 248
Sharma, C. L., 305
Shedd, J. B., 330
Shelby, A. N., 352
Sherman, J. D., 316
Shils, E. A., 36, 151
Showers, B. K., 292
Sickler, J. L., 63
Sievers, B., 123
Silver, P., 143
Silvern, S., 116
Simon, H. A., 11, 16, 28, 86, 94, 96, 172, 173, 252, 266,
    267, 269, 270, 291, 295, 341, 383
Sirotnek, K. A., 63
Skov, R. B., 338
Skrzypek, G. J., 392
Slater, R. C., 145
Slavin, R. E., 261
Slocum, J. W., 38
Smart, J. C., 318, 332
Smircich, L., 20
Smith, A., 136
Smith, C., 2
Smith, H. L., 316
Smith, J. B., 251, 265
Smith, M. S., 249, 264, 265
Smith, P. C., 252, 264
Smylie, M. A., 116, 318, 330, 332
Snyderman, B., 320
Sokoloff, N., 58
Solvic, P., 305
Somers, M. J., 104
Sorenson, L., 325
Sousa, D. A., 87, 305
Spangler, W. D., 392
Spencer, B. A., 262
Sproull, L., 286, 403
Spuck, D. W., 316
Stalker, G. M., 215
Starkie, D., 284

Staw, B. M., 323
Stearns, T. M., 213, 218
Stedman, L. C., 249
Steers, R. M., 99–101, 103, 104, 123, 135, 239, 241, 242, 244, 321
Steinfield, C. W., 349
Steinhoff, C. R., 138
Stern, G. C., 140
Stevenson, H., 231
Stewart, J., 254, 255
Stigler, J. W., 231
Stinchcombe, A. L., 58
Stipek, D. J., 111, 114
Stogdill, R. M., 377, 378
Stone, E. F., 252, 264
Stout, R. T., 397, 403
Strang, D., 224–226
Strauss, G., 39, 191, 367
Stringer, R. A., Jr., 140
Stringfield, S., 243, 249
Strube, M. J., 392
Stuebing, K. K., 316
Suppes, P., 265
Sutcliffe, K. M., 210
Suttle, J. L., 319, 326
Sutton, R. I., 93, 227, 228
Sutton, R. L., 221
Sykes, G., 328

Tagiuri, R., 140
Tannen, D., 370
Tarter, C. J., 143, 148, 150, 152, 155, 156, 167, 281, 282, 290, 291, 293, 304, 305
Taylor, F. W., 9
Teddlie, C., 77, 243, 249
Tenenbaum, E., 77
Terreberry, S., 233
Tetrick, L. E., 338
Theoret, A., 196
Thibodeaux, M., 104
Thomas, A. B., 373
Thomas, A. R., 145, 403
Thomas, H., 281
Thomas, K., 198, 199
Thompson, D. E., 106
Thompson, J. D., 11, 206, 208, 233, 275
Thornton, R., 83
Tichy, N., 393
Tiegs, R. B., 338
Tolman, E. C., 107
Torres, D. L., 328, 329
Trentham, L., 116
Trevino, L. K., 349

Trice, H. M., 137, 402
Trist, E. L., 206, 233
Trusty, F. M., 104
Tsui, A. S., 243
Turban, D. B., 105
Turner, C., 86
Turner, M. E., 359
Tushman, M. L., 44
Tveite, M. D., 262
Tversky, A., 269, 288, 305
Tyler, B. B., 348, 355, 365

Udy, S. H., 58
Ungson, G. R., 98, 206, 211, 212
U.S. Department of Health, Education and Welfare, 252
Urdan, T., 335
Urwick, L. F., 10, 11

Vaillancourt, P. M., 18
Van De Ven, A. H., 23, 210
Vance, V. S., 330
Vecchio, R. P., 192, 193, 380, 392
Volkwein, J. F., 162
Vroom, V. H., 99, 107, 252, 290, 304, 305, 372, 384

Wahba, M. A., 103
Walberg, H. J., 231
Waller, W., 34, 157
Walsh, J. P., 98
Washington, R., 104
Waterman, R. H., Jr., 56, 57, 128, 132, 136, 167, 238
Webb, R. B., 116
Weber, J., 104
Weber, M., 16, 47–50, 58, 86, 171, 172
Weick, K. E., 22, 23, 76, 77, 93, 98, 124, 380, 381
Weinberg, K., 104
Weiner, B., 107, 111–113
Weiner, S., 286
Weinfeld, F. D., 160, 247
Weiss, J. A., 328
Wellberg, D., 18
Wells, S., 265
Wendel, F. C., 398
Whetten, D. A., 24, 218, 236, 238, 245, 264
White, J. F., 63
White, P., 63
Whitehead, A. N., 27
Wietz, S., 350
Wilcox, K., 110, 254
Wilensky, H., 85

Wilkins, A. L., 128, 161
Wilkins, B. M., 354
Williams, L. B., 174, 175, 392
Williams, M. L., 381
Willis, Q., 403
Willower, D. J., 1, 2, 4, 7, 21, 22, 157, 158, 163, 167, 183, 403
Wilson, B. L., 78, 137, 139
Wilson, D., 286
Wimpelberg, R. K., 243, 249
Winer, B. J., 382
Wise, A., 76
Wise, M., 138
Wiseman, C., 281
Wisenbaker, J. M., 136, 265
Wiskowskie, L., 156
Wofford, J. C., 93
Wolf, D., 286
Wolin, S. S., 28
Wood, D. J., 213
Wood, R., 114, 115
Wood, S., 180, 335, 336
Woodman, R. W., 38
Woolfolk, A. E., 116, 156, 158, 159, 163
Worthy, J. C., 11
Woycke, J., 392

Wright, R., 316

Xie, J. L., 338

Yamagishi, T., 356
Yekovich, F. R., 97
Yetton, P. W., 290
York, R. L., 160, 247
Yuchtman, E., 240, 241
Yukl, G. A., 120, 178–180, 373–375, 377–380, 384, 385, 392, 395, 396, 398, 401–404

Zahn, C. L., 361
Zald, M. M., 197
Zaltman, G., 204
Zammuto, R. F., 243
Zander, A., 382
Zellerman, G., 116
Zellman, G., 116
Zenger, T. R., 354
Zey, M., 304
Zielinski, A. E., 365
Zucker, L., 1

Subject Index

◆◆◆

Ability-focused goals, 335
Acceptance of decisions, rules for, 296
Achievement, 247-251, 412, 413, 416
    goal (*see* Goal achievement)
    leadership and, 337
    McClelland's theory of, 104-106, 108, 408
Action cycle, decision making and, 268, 271-279,
    303
Adaptability culture, 136
Adaptation, 35
    open systems and, 31
    in social systems, 151
Adaptive decision making strategy, 281
Adhocracy, 68
Administration, 174-176, 178-180
    communication and, 341-342
    decision making in, 268-269
    rational, 58, 270
    (*See also* Administrators; Educational
        administration; Schools)
Administrative behavior, 10, 173-176, 200, 415-417
Administrative Behavior (Simon), 16
Administrative hierarchy of schools, 333-334
Administrative management theory, 10, 23
Administrative model of decision making, 267-279,
    283, 284, 303, 413
Administrative succession, 399-401
Administrators, 8, 269, 374, 375
    authority and, 173-178
    career paths for, 333-334, 337
    decision making and, 291-296
    effective, 271-272
    leader traits of, 378
    selecting, through assessment centers, 398-399
    system of ideology of, 184, 185
    (*See also* Leaders; Principals)
Alienation, 179, 181, 185, 410
    self-actualization and, 160
Alternatives in decision making, 275-276

Ambivalents, 83
Antibureaucratic structure, 59
Appraising in decision making, 279
Assessment centers, 398-400
Association, 329
Assumptions, 4-5, 23, 60, 64-65, 319, 409
    of expectancy theory, 107
    of goal model, 239-240
    of social systems model, 33-35
    of system-resource model, 241
    tacit, culture as, 132-135, 166
Attribution theory, 111-113, 409
Authenticity, 175
Authoritarian behavior as administrative style,
    174-175
Authoritarian structures, 61-64
Authority, 39, 51, 61, 171-201
    and administrative behavior in schools, 173-176,
        200
    functional, 173, 200
    hierarchy of, 37, 48, 50, 60, 408, 415
    informal, 173-175, 186, 200, 410
    legal, 172-173, 200
    sources of, 171-176
    system of, 184, 185
    traditional, 172, 200
    zone of acceptance and, 291-292, 295, 296, 384
    zone of indifference and, 173, 177, 290
    (*See also* Power)
Autocommunication, 345
Autocratic organizations, 70, 419
Autonomy, 175, 184-185, 213, 232, 323, 411, 415, 418

Behavior, 35, 37, 38
    administrative, 10, 173-176, 200, 415-417
    authoritarian, 174-175
    expectancy theory of, 107-108
    feedback loops and, 42-43

Behavior *(Cont.)*:
group norms and, 14-15
of leaders, 382-385, 387, 416
nonverbal, 350
of organizations (*see* Organizational behavior)
teacher-principal, 141-150
of teachers, 36
Body language, 348
Boundaries of social systems, 32
Boundary conditions, 274
Boundary-spanning strategies, 214-215, 229-230, 233, 411
Bounded rationality, 270
Bridges, 357
Buffering strategies, 213-214, 228-229, 233, 411
Bureaucracies, 46-87
loosely coupled systems as, 78
machine, 68, 70-71, 74
professional, 68, 69, 71-72
punishment-centered, 61
semiprofessional, 73, 74
simple, 72-74
simple professional, 73
Weberian model of, 47-59, 71
Bureaucratic control, 184
Bureaucratic expectations, 35-38, 41, 43, 79, 408, 416
Bureaucratic impersonality, 48, 50, 60
Bureaucratic internal coalitions, 188-190, 200
Bureaucratic model, 358
Bureaucratic rules, 48, 50, 52-53

Calculation, 181
Career-ladder programs, 330-333, 337, 414
Career orientation, promotion and, 48, 50
Career paths, 333-334, 337, 414
Careers of teachers and administrators, 330-334
Casual attributions, 111, 409
Categorical conformity, 229
Centralization, 62, 63
in bureaucracies, 72-73
communication and, 359
fragmented, 225
Change games, 196-197
Channels in communication, 342, 348-351, 356
Chaotic structures, 62-64
Charismatic authority, 172, 200
Charismatic organizations, 70
Chunking approach (*see* Expert model)
Classical model of decision making, 267, 283, 303
Climate, 161-162, 415, 419
closed, 142-143, 147-148
disengaged, 147
engaged, 146-147

Climate *(Cont.)*:
open, 142, 146, 419
organizational, 140-150, 166
of schools, 141, 409-410
changing, 162-166
Clinical strategy for change, 162-163
Cliques, 54, 55
Closed climate, 142-143, 147-148
Closed-systems perspective of organizations, 21, 27
Coalitions, 187, 200
external, 187-190, 200, 410
internal, 188-190, 200, 410
Coercive conformity, 222
Coercive organizations, 182, 183
Coercive power, 177-181, 200, 410
Cognition, 37, 91, 97-98, 122, 123
Cognitive architecture, 92-95, 408
Cognitive capacities, 352-353
Cognitive-choice theories, 100, 106-113, 408
Commitment, 181, 292, 414-418
Communication, 254, 340-370
administration and, 341-342
channels in, 342, 348-351, 356
feedback in, 343, 353, 368-369
formal, 56, 70-71, 358-365, 414
hierarchy of authority and, 50
informal, 70, 138, 361-365, 414
media in, 348-350, 365, 370
messages in, 342-346, 351, 356
networks in, 356, 358-365
nonverbal channels of, 350-351, 414
one-way, 344-345, 414
organizational perspectives of, 355-366
of plan of action, 279
in political organization, 74
process of, 366-369
receivers in, 342, 352, 353
in schools, 358-362
senders in, 342-345, 352, 353
theoretical approaches to, 342-355
two-way, 345-348, 368, 414, 417, 418
verbal channels of, 348-350
(*See also* Formal communication; Informal communication)
Communication effects, 343
Competitive market, 231, 232, 411
Compliance, 180-182, 200
Concepts, 3-4, 7
Conflict, 191
administrative succession and, 400
in political organization, 74
professional-bureaucratic, 71-72, 418
Conflict management, 198-200, 411
Conformity, 222-223, 229-230, 233

Congruence postulate, 41
Consequences, predicting, in plan for action, 276-277
Consideration, 382
  individualized, 395
Consistency culture, 136
Constituency, 243
  multiple, 243-244
Constituency mobilization, 219
Content analysis in communication, 362-363
Contingency approaches to leadership, 5, 376-392, 414
Control, 10, 11, 183-184, 328-329, 389
  environment and, 65
  formal authority and, 173-174
  of situation, 388-390
Controllability, 112
Conversation, 347
Cooptation, 218
Coordinating mechanisms, 66-67
Coping strategies:
  internal, 213-217, 233, 411
  interorganizational, 217-219, 233, 411
Cosmopolitans, 82, 84
Credibility in communication, 352
Critical theory, 19, 23, 408
Culture, 35, 38-39, 43, 161-162, 415
  organizational (*see* Organizational culture)
  of school, 136-140
    changing, 162-166, 409
  Theory Z, 131, 409
Custodial schools, 157-161, 410
Cybernetic model, 97, 123

Debate, 347
Decision making, 7, 266-304, 413, 416, 419
  action cycle and, 268, 271-279, 303
  job satisfaction and, 254
  kinds of, 273-274
  limiting scope of, 269
  perceived information and, 206-209
  rational, 49
Decoding, 342, 343, 346
Deconstruction, 18, 19
Decoupling, 228
Defensive avoidance, 287
Democratic practices, 20-21
Dependence, resources and, 210-212
Diagnosis in changing school workplace, 162-163
Direct supervision, 66
Direction of communication, 363-365
Discrepancy model of job satisfaction, 252-253
Disengaged climate, 147

Divided external coalitions, 188
Division of labor, 10, 11, 47-48, 50, 407
Divisionalized form, 68
Dominated external coalitions, 187-188
Dual-factor theory, 320-322
Dual orientation, 83

Economic incentives, 15
Educational administration:
  career paths in, 333-334, 414
  human relations approach to, 12-15
  nontraditional perspectives to, 17-20
  social science approach to, 15-17, 20-21, 23, 27-33
  theoretical developments in, 20-23
  (*See also* Administration)
Effective-schools research, 249-251
  criteria for, 242, 245-256
Effectiveness:
  administrative succession and, 399
  of administrators, 271-272
  criteria for, 243-246
  of leaders, 385-386, 390, 414
  organizational (*see* Organizational effectiveness)
  of schools, environment and, 63
Efficiency, 49
Elementary schools, 78, 81, 141
  OCDQ-RE and, 143-148, 166
Empire-builder cosmopolitans, 82
Empowerment, 180
Encoding, 342, 343, 346
Engaged climate, 146-147
Entropy, 33
Environment(s), 32-33, 35
  closed systems and, 21
  control of, by organizations, 65
  external, of schools, 202-233, 365, 411-412
  institutional (*see* Institutional environments)
  open systems and, 30-33, 40
  organizational, 203-204
  resource-dependency perspective of, 205, 209-219, 232
  school effectiveness and, 63
  stability of, 206-209, 216
  task, 204-205, 232
  typologies of, 206-207, 209
  uncertainty in, 207-209, 411
  unstable, 206-208, 215-217
Environmental resources, 210
Equality of Educational Opportunity study, 247
Equifinality, 33, 415, 417
Equilibrium of systems, 33
Evaluation, process of, 163

Exit, Voice, and Loyalty (Hirschman), 190
Expectancy, 107-109, 122
Expectancy theory, 107-111, 122, 409, 414
    valence concept in, 108, 110, 111, 122
Expectations (*see* Bureaucratic expectations)
Expert model, 96-97, 123
Expert power, 178, 179, 200
Expertise, 178, 179, 195, 292, 295, 328, 352, 410,
        418-419
    system of, 184-185
Expressive communication, 362-363
External coalitions, 187-190, 200, 410
External environments of schools, 202-233, 365,
        411-412
External feedback loops, 43, 412
Extrinsic incentives, 316-319
Eye contact in communication, 350

Factions, 194
Factor analysis, 142
    of OCDQ-RE, 145
    of OHI, 152
Feedback, 42-43, 119, 324, 413
    in communication, 343, 353, 368-369
    in open systems, 32
Feedback loops, 412
    internal and external, 42-43, 412
Feedback skills, 369
Feminist critique, 19-20, 23, 408
    of bureaucracy, 58-59
Flexible goal-setting criteria, 314-315
Focused trial and error, 282
Force of motivation (FM), 109-110
Formal authority, 173-175, 186, 195, 200, 410
Formal channels, 356
Formal communication, 56, 414
    informal communication and, 362-365
    in machine bureaucracy, 68, 70-71
    in schools, 358-361
Formal organizations, 11, 26, 407, 419
    impact of informal organizations on, 56
    as social system, 35-43
    (*See also* Informal organizations; Organizations)
Formal structure in schools, 59-76
Formalization, 28, 73
Fragmented centralization, 225
Functional authority, 173, 200
Functions of the Executive (Barnard), 16

Games, power, 190-200
Garbage can model in decision making, 284-286,
        303

General goal-setting criteria, 314-315
Generalizations, 5, 7, 240, 415, 417
Generic decisions, 273
Goal achievement, 205, 411
    organizational effectiveness and, 240
    in social systems, 35, 151
Goal content, 118
Goal displacement, 50, 52, 410
Goal intensity, 18
Goal mechanisms, 118-119
Goal model:
    of organizational effectiveness, 239-240, 263
    system-resource model and, 242-246, 264, 412
Goal setting, 311-315, 337, 413
    management by objectives and, 311-314
    performance and, 119
Goal-setting theory, 116-121, 409
Goal specificity, 27-28
Goals, 27-28, 117-123, 184
    in decision making, 280
    of natural systems, 29
    official, 239
    operative, 239
    organizations and, 35
    task-focused, 335
Grapevines, 56, 57, 356, 361, 362
Group norms, 14-15, 43, 49
Groups, 54
Groupthink, 297-299, 304
Groupthink syndrome, 297
Growth-centered strategy, 163-164

Hawthorne studies, 12-15, 20, 23, 42, 50
Health of organizations, 150-157
Healthy schools, 154, 419
Heuristics, 2, 278
Hierarchy of authority, 37, 48, 60, 408, 415
    communication and, 50
Hierarchy of needs, 100-105, 408
Homogeneity, principle of, 11
Homostasis, 33
Horizontal flow in communication, 364
How We Think (Dewey), 8
Hoy-Tarter model, 290-296
Human relations approach, 12-15
Humanistic schools, 157-161, 410, 419
Hygienes, 320
Hypervigilance, 287, 288
Hypotheses, 5-7

Icons, 137
Ideal types, 49, 50, 60, 408

Idealized influence, 394
Ideologic internal coalitions, 189, 190
Ideology, 329
    system of, 184, 185
Imitative conformity, 223
Impersonality, bureaucratic, 48, 50, 60
Impression management, 192-193
In Search of Excellence (Peters and Waterman), 238
Incentive systems, 315-319, 413
Incentives, 15, 108, 315-319, 337, 416
Incremental model in decision making, 279-281,
    283, 303, 413
Index of perceived organizational effectiveness
    (IPOE), 255, 256
Indifferents, 82-83
Individual element of a social system, 35-43
Individual goals, 117-118
Individual needs, 37-38, 41, 43
Individualized consideration, 395
Individuals:
    communication skills of, 367-369
    formal organization and, 35, 37-38
    intrinsic incentives and, 316-317
    in schools, 90-123, 408-409
Influence, 394
Informal authority, 173-175, 186, 200, 410
Informal channels, 356
Informal communication, 70, 138, 414
    formal communication and, 362-365
    in schools, 361-362
Informal norms, 14-15
Informal objectives, 184
Informal organizations, 14
    character of work group and, 184
    communication and, 361
    and feedback loops, 42
    functions of, 57
    impact of, on formal organizations, 56
    neglect of, 53-57
    in schools, 185
Information, 206
Information perspective of environments, 205-209,
    212, 232, 411
Information processing, 92-98, 122-123, 346, 355,
    408
    models of, 95-97
Ingratiation, 192
Initiating structure, 382-383
Input criteria, 245
Inputs, 31, 244, 412, 413
Inquiry, 347
Inspirational motivation, 394
Institutional environments, 205, 220-225
    administering, 227-230

Institutional environments *(Cont.):*
    changing, for education, 230-232
Institutional perspective of environments, 205,
    220-232, 411
Institutionalization, 220
Institutions, 220-221
Instruction, 347
Instrumental communication, 362-363
Instrumentality, 108-111
Insurgency games, 193-194
Integration:
    organizational effectiveness and, 242-246
    in social systems, 35, 151
Intellectual stimulation, 394-395
Interacting approach (*see* Cybernetic model)
Interactions in organizational behavior, 14-15, 34, 41
Internal coalitions, 188-190, 200, 410
Internal coping strategies, 213-217, 233, 411
Internal feedback loops, 42-43, 412
Internal operations, adjusting, 215-217, 233, 411
Internal power systems, 184-185
Interorganizational coping strategies, 217-219, 233,
    411
Intrinsic incentives, 316-319
Involvement culture, 136
IPOE (index of perceived organizational
    effectiveness), 255, 256
Isolate role, 356

Janis-Mann model of decision making, 287-289
Job-characteristics model in motivation, 323-326,
    414
Job diagnostic survey (JDS), 325
Job enrichment, 322-323, 337, 414
Job satisfaction, 251-254, 412
    goal setting and, 119
Jobs, 319
Joint ventures, 218

Kilman-Saxton Culture-Gap Survey, 165
Knowledge, 7, 328, 418
    of organization in change strategies, 162
    (*See also* Expertise)

Latency in social systems, 35, 151
Laws, 5, 7
LBDQ (*see* Leader behavior description
    questionnaire)
Leader behavior, 382-385, 387, 416
Leader behavior description questionnaire (LBDQ),
    382-384, 395

Leader-member relations, 389
Leaders, 374
  control and, 389
  educating, 397-398
  effectiveness of, 381, 385-386, 390
  school, as motivators, 335-337
  selecting, 398-399
  succession of, 399-401
  traits of, 376-380, 386
  (*See also* Administrators; Principals)
Leadership, 372-403, 414-416
  achievement and, 337
  contingency approach to, 376-392, 414
  identified by LPC scale, 387-388
  improving, in schools, 397-402
  job satisfaction and, 254
  participation and, 337
  situational determinants and, 380-381, 386
  studies of, 382-385
  transformational, 392-397
  (*See also* Leader behavior; Leaders)
Leadership style, 387-388, 414
  situation and, 390-391
Least preferred co-worker (LPC) scale, 387-388, 391
Legal authority, 172-173, 200
Legal prerogatives, 184
Legalism, 52
Legends, 137
Legitimate power, 171-179, 186-187, 200, 410
Liaisons, 357
Limited-capacity model, 95-96, 123
Linkages, 218
Listening skills in communication, 368
Locals, 82-84
Locus, 112
Logic of confidence, 77
Loose coupling perspective, 76-78, 408
Loyalty, 174-176, 179
LPC (least preferred co-worker) scale, 387-388, 391

Machine bureaucracy, 68, 70-71, 74
Management by objectives (MBO), 28, 311-314
Mechanistic organizations, 11, 215
Mechanistic structures, 63
Media in communication, 348-350, 365, 370
Merit pay, 318-319
Messages in communication, 342-346, 351, 356, 414
Metacognition theories, 100, 113-121, 408, 409
Metacognitive processes, 94-95, 408
Middle line, 67
Mission culture, 136
Mixed-scanning model, 281-283, 303, 413
MLQ (multifactor leadership questionnaire), 4, 395

Monitoring, 279
Motivation, 98-123, 308-337, 413-414, 416
  cognitive-choice theories of, 100, 106-113, 408
  dual-factor theory of, 320-322
  goal-setting theory of, 116-121, 409
  Herzberg's theory of, 320-323, 337
  inspirational, 394
  job-characteristics model in, 323-326
  job satisfaction and, 254
  metacognition theories of, 100, 113-121, 408, 409
  need hierarchy theory of, 100-105, 408
  self-efficacy theory of, 113-116
  values theory of, 104-106
  work, 37, 99, 100, 116, 254, 308-337, 408, 409
Motivation core, 122
Motivation hub, 122
Motivation-hygiene theory, 320-323, 337, 414
Motivation sequence, 121-123
Motivation traits, 379
Motivational principles, 310-311
Motivators, 320
Muddling through, 280
Multifactor leadership questionnaire (MLQ), 4, 395
Multiple constituencies, 243-244
Multiple criteria, 244-245
Munificence of resources, 210
Mutual adjustment, 66
Myths, 137
  rationalized, 221, 232, 412

Nation at Risk, 208, 237, 309, 317, 326
Natural systems, 27, 29-30
Need hierarchy theory, 100-105, 408
  motivation-hygiene theory and, 320
Needs, 100-104, 121, 123
  hierarchy of, 100-105, 408
  individual, 37-38, 41, 43
  work, 37-38
Networking, 192
Networks in communication, 356, 358-365
Noise in communication, 353-355
Nonverbal channels of communication, 350-351
Norm-changing strategy, 165
Normative conformity, 223
Normative model in decision making, 267
Normative organizations, 183
Normative power, 181, 183, 200
Norms, 38-39, 41, 409-411
  changing, in the organization, 164-166
  group, 14-15, 39, 43
  shared, 129-130, 166

Objectives, informal, 184
OCDQ (Organizational Climate Description Questionnaire), 142, 143, 149-150, 159
OCDQ-RE (Revised Organizational Climate Descriptive Questionnaire for Elementary Schools (OCDQ-RE), 143-148, 166
OCDQ-RM (Revised Organizational Climate Descriptive Questionnaire for Middle Schools (OCDQ-RM), 149, 166
OCDQ-RS (Revised Organizational Climate Descriptive Questionnaire for Secondary Schools (OCDQ-RS), 148-149, 166
Official goals, 239
OHI (Organizational Health Inventory), 152, 154-157, 159, 166
Ohio State University leadership studies, 382-383
One-way communication, 344-345, 414
Open climate, 142, 146, 419
Open systems, 17, 27, 30, 203, 232, 237, 262, 406
    boundaries and, 32
    environment and, 30-33, 40
    properties of, 30-33
Openness:
    in faculty relations, 145
    in principal behavior, 145
Operating core, 67
Operational definition, 4
Operative goals, 239
Opportunistic surveillance, 275
Optimizing approach (*see* Rational model)
Optimizing strategy, 27, 284, 303
Organic structures, 215
Organizational behavior, 412
    interactions in, 14-15, 34, 41
Organizational climate, 140-150, 166, 409
Organizational Climate Description Questionnaire (OCDQ), 142, 143, 149-150, 159
Organizational cognition, 98
Organizational communication, 355-366
Organizational culture, 38-39, 127-140, 166, 409
    definition of, 128-129
    levels of, 129-135
    types of, 135-136
Organizational dynamics and organizational health, 150-157
Organizational effectiveness, 41, 412, 414
    achievement and, 247-251
    goal model of, 239-240, 263
    job satisfaction and, 251-254
    perceived, 255-256
    of schools, 237-256, 263
    system-resource model of, 240-242, 263
    theoretical approaches to, 238-246
Organizational environment, 203-204

Organizational Health Inventory (OHI), 152, 154-157, 159, 166
Organizational inventory, 60-64
Organizational politics, 187-190
Organizational power, 187-190
Organizational science, 1
Organizational structure:
    mechanistic and authoritarian, 61-63
    types, 60-61
Organizational thought, classical, 9-12
Organizations, 16, 21-23, 27, 60-62, 70, 182, 183
    closed-systems perspective of, 21, 27
    coordination in, 418
    functions of rules in, 50-51
    goals and, 35
    health of, 150-157, 410
    knowledge of, 162
    mechanistic, 11
    political, in schools, 73-76
    technostructure of, 67, 69-71, 74
    (*See also* Formal organizations; Informal organizations)
Organized anarchies, 285
Out of Crisis (Deming), 238
Outputs, 31, 67, 244, 412, 413

Paralanguage, 350
Participation:
    in decision making, 290
    leadership and, 337
Partnerships, 218
Passive external coalitions, 188
PCI (Pupil-Control Ideology) form, 158-161, 166
Performance:
    administrative succession and, 399
    goal setting and, 119
Performance evaluation and review techniques (PERT), 28
Performance outcomes, 41, 244-245
Personal control, 184
Personality traits, 378-379
Personalized internal coalitions, 188, 190
PERT (performance evaluation and review techniques), 28
Plan for action in decision making, 274-279
Planning and forecasting strategies, 214, 233, 411
Planning, programming, and budgeting systems (PPBS), 28
Policy, 270
Political games, 193-198, 200
Political organization in schools, 73-76
Political tactics, 191-193, 200, 410
Politicized internal coalitions, 189, 190

Politicking, 218
Politics, 35, 39–40, 190, 191, 200, 410–411, 416
 organizational, 187–190
 systems of, 184, 185
Position power, 388–389
Post-modernism, 18, 23, 408
Power, 171, 190, 191, 410
 administrative uses of, 178–180
 authority and, 171–201
 coercive, 177–181, 200, 410
 expert, 178, 179, 200
 legitimate, 171–179, 186–187, 200, 410
 in machine bureaucracy, 74
 normative, 181, 183, 200
 norms in, changing, 164–166
 organizational, 187–190
 in political organization, 73–74
 position, 388–389
 referent, 177–179, 200
 remunerative, 181, 182
 reward, 176–180, 200
 sources of, 176–178
 teachers and, 185
 technical skill and, 60, 183
 typologies of, 180–186
Power games, 190–200
Power relations, 39, 410
Power systems, internal, 184–185
PPBS (planning, programming, and budgeting systems), 28
Practice, theory and, 7–9
Practitioners, 8
Principals, 110, 154, 174–176
 effectiveness of, 392
 openness in behavior of, 145
 secondary schools and, 251
 system of ideology of, 185
 teachers as candidates for, 399–400
 (*See also* Administrators; Leaders)
Principle of homogeneity, 100–105
Principles, 5, 7
Principles of Scientific Management (Taylor), 9
Problem solving, 417–418
Problemistic search, 275
Procedural conformity, 229–230
Process-product research, 249
Production-function research, 247–249
Profession, characteristics of, 328–330
Professional bureaucracy, 68, 69, 71–72
Professional-bureaucratic conflict, 79–86, 418–419
Professional internal coalitions, 189, 190
Professional structures, 62–64
Professionalization in schools, 327–330, 337

Professionals, 184–185, 418–419
Program planning, 278
Programming in decision making, 278–279
Project RISE program (Milwaukee), 249–250
Promotion, 48, 50
Punishment, 51–53, 177
Punishment-centered bureaucracy, 61
Punishment-centered rules, 53
Pupil-Control Ideology (PCI) form, 158–161, 166
Pupil-control orientation, 157–161, 410

Quality of schools, 237, 256–264, 412

Rational administration, 58, 270
Rational bureaucracies, 78
Rational decision making, 49, 413
Rational model, 95, 123
Rational organizations, patterns of, 60–62
Rational systems, 27–29
Rationality, 27, 111, 221–222, 269–270, 411
Rationalized myths, 221, 232, 412
Receivers in communication, 342, 352, 353
Referent power, 177–179, 200
Regulations, 36, 37, 48, 50, 328, 407, 418
Relativistic multiple-contingency approach to organizational effectiveness, 244
Remunerative power, 181, 182
Representative rules, 53
Research, theory and, 5–7
Researchers, 8
Resource-dependency perspective of environments, 205, 209–219, 232, 411
Resources, 411
 availability of, in environments, 210
 dependence and, 210–212
 power and control of, 183
 scarcity of, 210, 411
Responsibility:
 feeling of, 323
 leadership and, 377
Revised Organizational Climate Descriptive Questionnaire for Elementary Schools (OCDQ-RE), 143–148, 166
Revised Organizational Climate Descriptive Questionnaire for Middle Schools (OCDQ-RM), 149, 166
Revised Organizational Climate Descriptive Questionnaire for Secondary Schools (OCDQ-RS), 148–149, 166
Reward power, 176–180, 200
Rewards, 108, 176, 315, 413
Richness of communication, 348–350

Rituals, 137
Rival games, 195–196
Rules, 36, 37, 50–53, 60, 407, 411, 418
   bureaucratic, 48, 50, 52–53

Satisficing, 95–96, 123, 267–279, 284, 303, 413
Scarcity of resources, 210, 411
Schemas, 93–94, 322, 346, 352, 408
School climate, 141, 162–166, 409–410
School culture, 136–140, 162–166, 409
School organizational inventory (SOI), 60
School structures, 62–64
   loosely coupled theory of, 76–78, 408
   simple, 68, 70
Schools:
   administrative hierarchy of, 333–334
   authority and administrative behavior in, 173–176, 200
   communication in, 358–362
   custodial, 157–161, 410
   external environments of, 202–233, 365, 411–412
   formal structure in, 59–76
   healthy, 154, 419
   humanistic, 157–161, 410, 419
   individuals in, 90–123, 408–409
   informal organization in, 185
   leadership in, 397–402
   organizational effectiveness of, 237–256, 263
   organizational structure in, 46–86
   political organizations in, 73–76
   professionalization in, 327–330, 337
   quality of, 237, 256–264
   as social systems, 26–44
   structure in, 46–86
   transforming, 401–402
   unhealthy, 154–155
   work motivation in, 308–337
   (*See also* Elementary schools; Secondary schools)
Science and theory, 1–3
Scientific approach, theory and, 8
Scientific management approach, 9
Secondary school teachers, 110
Secondary schools, 78, 251
   OCDQ-RS, 148–149, 166
Self-actualization, 100–102, 104, 160
Self-efficacy, 113–116, 122, 123, 409
   development of, 114–115
Self-efficacy theory, 113–116
Semiprofessional bureaucracy, 73, 74
Senders in communication, 342–345, 352, 353
Sending skills in communication, 367
Shared decision making, 290–296
Shared norms, culture as, 129–130, 166

Shared orientations, 38, 409
Shared values, culture as, 130–132, 166
Simple bureaucracy, 72–74
Simple professional bureaucracy, 73
Simple structure, 68, 70
Situation, 284
   control of, leadership behavior and, 388–390
   and leadership style, 390–391
Situational determinants in leadership, 380–381, 386
Situational engineering, 401
Situational factors, 386–387
Situational model of job satisfaction, 253–254
Skill traits, 380
Social science approach, 15–17, 20–21, 23
Social systems, 26, 32–44, 151, 406, 415, 416
   elements of, 35–43
   model of, 33–35, 42–44, 406–407
   school as, 26–44
Socratic method, 347
SOI (school organizational inventory), 60
Span of control, 10, 11
Specialization, 10, 11, 15, 36, 47–48, 50, 60, 62, 63, 407
Stability:
   in attribution theory, 112
   of environments, 206–209, 216
Standardization, 11, 408
   of output, 67
   of skills, 67, 71
   of work, 68, 70
Star role, 356
Stories, 137
Strategic apex, 67, 71
Strategy:
   for action in decision making, 274–275
   for changing school workplace, 162–166
Stress, decision making and, 287–289, 304
Strong cultures in effective organizations, 132, 409
Structural conformity, 229
Structure and process criteria, 245
Structures:
   administrative, rational, 58
   authoritarian, 61, 63, 64
   Bolman and Deal on, 64–66
   dual, of bureaucratic model, 57–58
   formal, in schools, 59–76
   formal organizations and, 35–37
   Hall on, 60–64
   mechanistic, 63
   Mintzberg on, 66–76
   organic, 215
   organizational (*see* Organizational structure)
   school (*see* School structures)

Students:
    alienation of, and school climate, 160
    normative power and, 183
    performance of, in healthy schools, 154
Subordinates, 381, 389
Substance of communication, 362–363
Substitutes-for-leaders model, 381
Superintendents, 333–334, 399, 401
Supervision, direct, 66
Support staff, 68
Symbols, 344, 348, 369
System-resource model, 240–242, 263, 412
    goal model and, 242–246, 264, 412
Systemic reform, 230, 232, 411
Systems, 27
    natural, 27, 29–30
    rational, 27–29
    social (see Social systems)
Systems view of social science approach, 27–33

Tacit assumptions, culture as, 132–135, 166
Task behavior of leaders, 382
Task environment, 204–205, 232, 412
Task-environment theories, 205–219, 411
Task-focused goals, 335
Tasks, 389
Teacher-principal behavior, 141–150
Teachers, 154–155, 174–176
    behavior of, 36
    as candidates for principalships, 399–400
    careers of, 330–333, 337
    decision making and, 290
    expectancy theory and, 110
    job satisfaction and, 254
    power and, 62, 185
    professional and bureaucratic orientations and, 83–85
Technical skill, power and, 60, 183
Technology, 351–352, 361
Technostructure of organization, 67, 69–71, 74
Theoretical developments in educational administration, 20–23
Theories, 1–5
    cognitive-choice, 100, 106–113, 406
    contingency, of leadership, 376–392
    dual-factor (two-factor), 320–322
    expectancy, 107–111, 122, 409, 414
    goal-setting, 116–121, 409
    loose-coupling, 76–78
    metacognition, 100, 113–121, 408, 409
    motivation-hygiene (Herzburg), 320–323, 337, 414
    need hierarchy, 100–105, 408
    practice and, 7–9

Theories (Cont.):
    research and, 5–7
    self-efficacy, 113–116
    task-environment, 205–219
    two-factor (dual-factor), 320–322
Theorists, 8
Theory Z (Ouchi), 238
Theory Z cultures, 131, 409
Time, 242–243
Time and motion studies, 9–11
Total quality management (TQM), 256, 262, 263
Traditional authority, 172, 200
Traits of leaders, 376–380, 386
Transformational leadership, 392–397
Transformational process, 31, 412
Transmission in communication, 342, 343
Two-factor theory of motivation, 320–322
Two-way communication, 345–348, 368, 414, 417, 418
Typology:
    of compliance, 181–182
    for conflict management, 198–200
    of cosmopolitans and locals, 82–83
    of environments, 206–207, 209
    of interpersonal power, 176–178
    of nonverbal behavior, 350
    of power, 180–186
    of school organization, 60–62
    of school structure, 62–64

Uncertainty, environmental, 207–209, 411
Unconflicted adherence, 287, 288
Unconflicted change, 287, 288
Unhealthy schools, 154–155
Unique decisions, 273–274
Uniqueness of function, 11
Unity of command, 11
Unstable environments, 206–208, 215–217
Upward mobiles, 82–83
Utilitarian organizations, 182

Valence concept in expectancy theory, 108, 110, 111, 122
Values, 100, 104–106, 117, 122, 123, 409–411
    shared, 130–132, 166
Values theory, 104–106
Variables, 4
Verbal channels of communication, 348–350
Vertical flow in communication, 363–364
Vigilant decision making, 288
Vroom-Yetton model of decision making, 290

Weberian model of bureaucracy, 47-59, 71
  criticisms of, 49-59
Weberian structure, 61, 63, 64
Western Electric Company studies (Hawthorne
  studies), 12-15, 20, 23, 42, 50
Women, career paths for, 334
Work group, character of, 127-167, 184
Work in America, 252
Work motivation, 37, 99, 100, 116, 254, 308-337, 408,
  409

Work needs, 37-38
Work redesign, 319-326, 414
Workplace, 161-162
  changing, 162-166
  organizational climate and, 166

Zone of acceptance, 291-292, 295, 296, 384
Zone of indifference, 173, 177, 290